PASSIONATE INQUIRY

PASSIONATE INQUIRY:
Psychotherapy as a Life's Work

Jesse D. Geller, PhD

IPBOOKS.net
International Psychoanalytic Books

International Psychoanalytic Books (IPBooks)
New York • http://www.IPBooks.net

Passionate Inquiry: Psychotherapy as a Life's Work

Published by IPBooks, Queens, NY
Online at: www.IPBooks.net

Cover painting by Steve Brennan

Author's Note: All papers in this volume are reproduced with the permission of the original publishers of each.

ISBN: 978-1-956864-34-2

Table of Contents

Acknowledgments

I wish to say thank you to all those who shared a role in helping me publish this book. It was 60 years in the making, and, therefore, hundreds of people have offered me the invaluable support, guidance, knowledge, and inspiration I needed to keep writing. There are countless teachers, patients, students, friends, editors, colleagues, and publishers whose intellectual energy and serious interest in my ideas fueled and directed my thinking and writing. I am extremely grateful that my wife, Ruth, and our daughters, Elizabeth and Jennifer, offered me solitude and nurturance when I needed them most. This book would never have been written if it were not for my parents, Thelma and William. I and my brothers, Norman and Mark, with whom I share a love of playing with words, are the very fortunate beneficiaries of our parents' intelligence, decency, and fortitude. Finally, I am profoundly grateful that my pleasure in having produced this book has not been diminished by the particular ways in which it is inadequate.

Introduction

Imaginary Reader: What is your book about, Jesse? Jesse: This book documents how psychotherapy has served me well as an instrument of healing, as a laboratory in which to scientifically study the mysteries of memory and feelings, as a playground in which to be creative, and as a viable and virtuous means of earning a living.

MY WORK HISTORY

My high school–educated father and his brothers had jobs. I sought a PhD in clinical psychology from the University of Connecticut, thinking that I would have an academic career (1960–1966). Fortunately, after I spent a year as a postdoctoral fellow at Clark University, I was hired by Yale University.

From 1967–1985 I was paid an upper-middle–class salary doing the work I love as a member of Yale University's Departments of Psychiatry and Psychology within the context of a pioneering community mental health center. The Connecticut Mental Health Center's mission gratified my youthful idealist's need to fashion a career that was consistent with the values of the war on poverty (Pope et al., 1975), the Civil Rights Movement (Chapter 5), and the goals of antiwar activists (Geller & Howard, 1972). My primary responsibilities included developing new ways of providing individual and group therapy to economically disadvantaged individuals, with attention given to their race, ethnicity, social class, and educational level (Zegans et al., 1973; Geller & Feirstein, 1974; Geller et al., 1976; Wexler et al., 1984; Johnson et al., 1986).

In 1984, I was invited to create an outpatient psychotherapy clinic within the offices of the Yale Department of Psychology. During the 10 years I served as its director, my primary responsibilities included teaching academically gifted and scientifically minded pre- and postdoctoral clinical psychology students the listening, observational, and relational skills required to differentiate suitable and unsuitable candidates for various forms of inpatient and outpatient psychotherapy and to conduct conversations that are meant to serve therapeutic functions.

My tenure as the director of the Yale Psychological Services Clinic regrettably came to an end in 1995. Rather than take another university position, I chose to open my first private practice of psychotherapy. My wife and I furnished my attic office with matching Eames chairs, an antique desk, rugs from Afghanistan, plants, and evocative paintings in the belief that the aesthetic properties of the physical environment in which therapies are conducted make a semi-independent contribution to their effectiveness (see Chapter 15). For the first time in my career, I began doing psychotherapy as a primary means of being my family's breadwinner. Now, as then, I have complicated feelings about the business aspects of psychotherapy and the economics of the mental health industry. I disapprove of the exorbitant fees many of my peers charge for having conversations with their "customers." To my surprise, I began writing more rather than fewer scholarly texts about psychotherapy when I was no longer living under the threat of "publish or perish."[1]

---

1 Since the COVID pandemic made it too dangerous to meet with patients in my office, I have been conducting psychotherapy over the telephone and by Zoom. As I have recently

To capture the multifaceted nature of my relationship to psychotherapy, I selected for inclusion in this book the script of a film, memoirs, and a representative sample of the research-informed clinical-theoretical essays that explicate my uniquely derivative "Gellerian" perspective on therapy. They were all inspired by the conviction that psychotherapy is an "applied science" (Chapter 8) that promotes the self-acceptance, self-understanding, and self-determination that enable individuals to find relief from unnecessary suffering and to make viable and suitable decisions about their relationships to love, work, and play at different stages of the life cycle. I arrived at this conviction by writing in a vocabulary that blends a set of interrelated ideas originally used by artists, theologians, existential philosophers, cognitive-developmental psychologists, and psychoanalysts into a nondenominational theoretical perspective that transcends the political rivalries and limitations of exclusively identifying with a single school or brand of psychotherapy.

The texts I have gathered together are presented in the order in which they were written. Another editor might have grouped them together on the basis of their shared thematic concerns and formal properties. In my mind's eye, the chapters are woven together into a tapestry that juxtaposes and intermingles shifting perspectives on my having made psychotherapy the epicenter of my life's work. I believe you would come away with a different answer to the question, What is this book about? if you began by reading the chapters that were written in the form of autobiographical narratives rather than the chapters that present my ideas about the science and technology of psychotherapy or the chapters that focus on what artists have to teach therapists about the transformative powers of aesthetic experiences.

---

written (Geller, 2021), I anticipate that this shift will contribute new and usable knowledge about what is healing about psychotherapy.

If you are like me, you will probably first read the chapters that are the most personal. I have also wondered whether a reader's judgments about the quality of my contributions to the literatures on psychotherapy would be influenced by what I revealed about myself in the memoir-like essays. Whatever your verdict, I now feel a mix of pride and humility when I evaluate what I accomplished by devoting a major portion of my career to writing projects that were arduous but ultimately rewarding.

LESSONS LEARNED FROM BOTH SIDES OF THE COUCH

Like teaching, writing challenges me to bring into verbalizable and communicable awareness my ideas about what forms of learning promote the acquisition of the concepts, values, and decision-making capacities that enable therapists to arrive at highly individualized ways of offering help to their patients.

My ideal is to write intellectual autobiographies in a style that blends the artistry and subjectivity of well-told stories and the objectivity and rigor of scientific texts. "Thank You for Jenny"—written reluctantly in 1996—ironically comes closest, in my mind, to realizing this goal. Chapter 7 tells the story of how the continuing process of learning how to coparent our profoundly deaf daughter influenced my views about the barriers to contact, communication, and mutual understanding that are encountered in the psychotherapy of patients who can hear. I believe that learning how to be a therapist prepared me for parenthood and that fathering my daughters had a maturing influence on my capacity to serve as a caregiver and authority figure for my patients.

CONVERSATIONS OR DIALOGUES ARE AT THE HEART OF ALL THERAPIES

Trying to learn American Sign Language in order to communicate with Jenny reinforced my lifelong interest in the languages of movement. As a postdoctoral fellow, I had already studied nonverbal communication by developing a method of differentiating between communicative gestures and information-bearing movements (Wiener et al., 1972). When I came to Yale, I continued my education by studying with dance therapists (e.g., Susan Sandel), yogis (e.g., Paul Spector), choreographers (e.g., Allison Chace), and practitioners of the Feldenkrais method of promoting neuromuscular awareness (e.g., Donna Blank) and by joining an Authentic Movement collective led by the movement's founder, Janet Adler. Chapter 1 summarizes what I learned about embodying consciousness by gaining firsthand knowledge of their ideas and methods. They led me to the view that the body has a mind of its own and that the mind has a body of its own. I take quiet pride in having been an early champion of the view that practitioners of these body- and movement-based disciplines have a lot to teach therapists who practice the "talking cure" about sensory and perceptual experiences that are very difficult to describe in words. I still feel that Chapter 1 is worthy of being read, but I find it pedantic and turgid. I think it resembles the term papers that overly cerebral and overly ambitious graduate students write when they are trying to impress their teachers with their seriousness and erudition.

I am willing to "try again, fail again, fail better" (Samuel Beckett, 1966) each time I attempt to make an original contribution to the literatures on psychotherapy. If Chapter 1 were written today, I would have revealed that my ideal morning begins with practicing a blend of these disciplines in my living room after a light breakfast. My practice is to pay softly focused and sympathetic attention to the fleeting body sensations, images, and verbal thoughts that accompany my attempts to free-associate in movement. I especially welcome the times when my attempts to exert as little conscious control as possible over how I move through space slightly disorganize my gestural and postural repertoire, the micromovements that give shape to my facial expressions, and the depth and rhythmicity of my breath. I am inclined to think that this ritual has enabled me to reenact and constructively modify my muscle memories of having suffered from severe and inconsolable colic during the first 18 months of my life.

Similarly, I wish I had the literary skills to have written at length about the crisis in my career that was set in motion when a patient of mine, who was a psychotherapist, accused me of committing a "boundary violation" when she pressured me into revealing to her that "X is my patient, not my supervisee." Nevertheless, I feel I gained greater distance from its painful legacy by systematically studying the boundary concept with Dr. Kenneth Pope and by writing Chapter 12, which utilizes the metaphorical boundary concept to analyze the similarities and differences between the therapies offered to psychotherapists and those who are not mental health professionals.

Chapters 11 and 15 offer complementary perspectives on how receiving psychotherapy first as a college student, then as a clinical psychology graduate student, then again as an assistant professor in the Yale Department of Psychiatry, and then again as the Director of the Yale Department of Psychology's Psychological Services Clinic have influenced who I've become and who I am becoming.

I believe it is impossible to understand the special nature of what actually goes on in psychotherapy unless one has had firsthand knowledge of this experience. I remain suspicious of psychotherapists who have never sought personal therapy. As anyone who has been a psychotherapy patient knows, it is impossible to be perfectly honest about oneself. Not surprisingly, much of the hardest work of therapy is devoted to helping patients face and deal with the painful and difficult fears and inhibitions that stifle honest and feeling-ful self-exploration and self-revelation. As Chapter 16 reveals, it can take months of painstaking work before some patients who voluntarily chose to be psychotherapy patients can actually ask for and receive help from their therapists or reveal the intimate details of their inner lives.

I was initiated into living an "examined life" in college by teachers who interested me in learning how the mind works and by a therapist who encouraged me to become intimately familiar with the felt internality of my anxiety-ridden adolescent mind. From college onward, one of my primary aims has been to practice disciplines that extend the reach of what is knowable about the sensuous fullness and kaleidoscopic complexity of the experiences that flow through the "stream of consciousness" (James, 1890).

I learned many things about myself during my five psychoanalytically informed psychotherapies. I learned how my representations of my physical and psychological characteristics were shaped by my life history. I discovered that my inner life was heavily populated with representations of others (caretakers, authority figures, heroes, teachers, friends, relatives, etc.) and learned how relationships with them proceed. (I believe that all we know of others is based on our representations of them, whether or not they are physically present.) Some of my most productive conversations with my therapists transformed generalizations about my past into more or less detailed memories of specific past events. In the vocabulary of cognitive scientists, I gained access to the episodic memories that led to my semantic memories about the past (Anderson, 1983). This shift led to a concomitant discovery of the differentiated fears that I had previously experienced as diffuse bouts of wordless anxiety (Chapter 11).

Perhaps more importantly, I learned how to listen to and speak with myself with growing acceptance of my flaws, my disavowed aggressive tendencies, my lustful sexual desires, my limited capacity for pain-filled renunciations of my addictive tendencies, my impatience with bodily suffering, my unrelenting and vain need for applause, and my impersonations of real men of feeling and conscience. Today, I believe that much of this learning took place outside of focused awareness when I was "imitating" how I had been heard, seen, and spoken to by the therapists I trusted and respected.

Much of this book is devoted to my take on the experiential learning that takes place when patients and/or students imitate their representations of the skills, personal qualities, values, and attitudes they attribute to their valued and respected therapists or teachers, both in their presence and when they are separated from one another.

During my 2½-year psychoanalysis, I developed the representational capacities that enable me to examine *how* I use words, pictures, and body sensations to bring into focal awareness the ideational and affective content of my subjective experiences. The benefits I derived from examining the complex interplay between *how* I experience and *what* I experience encouraged me to begin providing patients and student therapists with the questions and vocabulary with which to think about the extent to which their memories and feelings were composed, in varying proportions, of verbal thoughts, perceptual images, and somatosensory experiences. The importance I ascribe to encouraging individuals to forge connections between the sensory, perceptual, and linguistic aspects of their subjective experiences makes many appearances in this volume.

I sought a PhD in clinical psychology in order to study how the mind works, not to earn a living by doing psychotherapy, but I fell in love with the then-radical form of therapy championed by all of the faculty who taught at the University of Connecticut during the years I was a graduate student. They did not privilege "insight" as the goal of therapy, nor did they adopt the prototypical conversational style favored by classically trained psychoanalytic therapists. They placed the hypothesis that there is something inherently healing about courageously engaging in "truth-telling" within the context of a relationship in which one feels safe, respected, and empathically understood at the center of their theorizing about the transformative powers of psychotherapy. Their emphasis on embodying such elusive qualities as authenticity and spontaneity and the importance of taking responsibility for one's choices and their consequences deeply appealed to the aspiring existentialist in me. These ideas and values remain at the epicenter of my ever-evolving "Gellerian" theory of therapy. Moreover, they encouraged me to adopt a relational stance vis-à-vis patients that blended the careful craftsmanship of old-world artisans and the improvisational looseness of a jazz musician. At this stage of my career, I liken the moment-to-moment decisions I make about listening and speaking when I'm with my patients to the skillfulness with which I ride my bicycle in heavy traffic en route to work. In the language of cognitive scientists, my knowing how to do psychotherapy is mediated by deeply embodied procedural memories (Anderson, 1983).

I believe I live with greater humility and integrity and less narcissistically than I would have if I hadn't learned how to become a particular kind of psychotherapist in my youth. Now more than ever I feel grateful that I took my first steps toward becoming a therapist by studying with teachers who were inspired by the conviction that there is something inherently healing about participating in collaborative and intimate conversation within the context of a safe therapeutic relationship. Elders, like myself, are at risk of feeling isolated, stagnant, self-absorbed, and despairing if deprived of the opportunity to participate in relationships that are grounded in collaboration and emotional closeness. I am persuaded that the continued opportunity to give the fullness of my attention to my patients and students in my ninth decade mitigates these painful sources of suffering. As long as my listening, observational, and communication skills are not diminished in ways that adversely affect my work, I cannot imagine ever wanting to retire.

Chapter 17, which was written when I was 75, explores how providing, teaching, theorizing, and doing research about psychotherapy during early, middle, and late adulthood influenced the psychological, moral, aesthetic, and collegial domains of my existence. I brought to this task what my cowriter, Richard Howenstine, and I learned studying with Daniel Levinson when he was formulating his psychobiographical approach to analyzing men's adult development. This framework receives its most detailed exposition in Chapter 2. It was inspired by the question, What do we mean when we speak of romantic love? I do not think of romantic love as a discrete experiential state that has universally and unequivocally identifiable properties of its own. Rather, I believe that our answers to the question, Is this love that I am feeling? are based on interpretations of our bodily experiences and not the bodily experiences themselves.

WHAT ARE YOU FEELING?

Feelings, good and bad, are the "meat and potatoes" of the conversations that take place in therapy. Therefore, I believe that the well-educated therapist's knowledge base should include an empirically grounded understanding of the extraordinarily diverse forms in which individuals experience and express their pleasurable and unpleasurable "feelings."

Mine draws heavily upon my phenomenological investigations of the interplay between transient emotions and enduring moods (Chapter 3), the primacy of the emotion we call interest and its opposite, boredom (Chapter 6), the differences between fear and anxiety (Chapter 11), the subjective experience of feeling upset (Chapter 3), the meanings we ascribe to romantic love (Chapter 2), the intensity and duration of the feelings induced by the loss or threatened loss of a relationship and/or by disappointments in others (Chapter 4), the therapist's and patient's attitudes toward suffering, pity, self-pity, and compassion (Chapter 14), the feelings that are stimulated by aesthetic reactions to the beauty or ugliness of people, places, and things (Chapter 19), and the intelligibility, controllability, and communicability of emotional states that are beyond the reach of ordinary language (Chapter 3).

The results of these inquiries have strengthened my conviction that much of what people think they are feeling is based upon how they interpret their bodily experiences and not upon the immutable qualities of these bodily experiences. What patients discover with me is that the meanings they ascribe to the somatosensory experiences that flow through their bodies are a product of their personal histories and are heavily influenced by the forms of representation that bring these experiences into awareness.

THE TECHNOLOGY OF PSYCHOTHERAPY

Throughout my career, I have used the discipline of writing to arrive at personally satisfying answers to the questions I am most frequently asked by neophyte therapists. Woven throughout the chapters are decision-making frameworks that offer guidance about how to creatively grapple with the ambiguities posed by the following questions: What distinguishes listening for therapeutic purposes from other types of listening (Chapter 6)? How do you initiate conversations about matters patients would prefer to not think or talk about without frightening, hurting, or disappointing them (Chapter 13)? When is it timely and helpful to tell a patient something personal about oneself (Chapter 9)? How can I reclaim my caring concern for patients I find boring (Chapter 6)? What are therapeutic responses to a patient's negative emotional reactions to one's mistakes and empathic failures and one's power to control, where, when, and for how long therapy takes place (Chapter 4)? What clinical strategies are required to be of help to patients who cannot recognize and receive what is new and useful about their therapist's nonverbal contributions to the therapeutic dialogue (Chapter 6)? And how do you bring an ambitious psychotherapy to a natural conclusion (Chapter 4)?

There are many schemes for categorizing the methods therapists use to address these questions. Mine distinguishes therapeutic techniques on the basis of the psychological functions they are intended to serve and the styles in which they are implemented. The diagram presented in Chapter 9 summarizes the range of psychological functions I am prepared to serve on behalf of my patients.

In proportions that vary from patient to patient, I have served as a teacher, coach, mentor, historian, healer, translator, interpreter, provocateur, moral arbiter, playmate, trusted companion, confessor, and shaman. My overarching goal is to serve life-affirming and adaptation-enhancing psychological functions on behalf of my patients. I am interested in discovering what they find useful, helpful, disappointing, and hurtful.

One of my goals as an educator has been to help student therapists develop the improvisational skills required to make effective decisions about those aspects of doing therapy that are not explicitly or systematically addressed by evidence-based prescriptive therapy manuals. To this end, I provide them with the questions and concepts with which to think about the organizational contexts in which they meet with patients (Chapter 5): their clothing; how they greet patients in the waiting room; how they exchange the roles of listener and speaker; their facial expressions, gestures, and postures; the styles in which they perform therapeutic tasks; the making and breaking of eye contact; the placement of the clocks in the consulting room; the optimal duration of silences; their vocal qualities; how they bring therapy sessions to an end; the uses of humor; and touching and being touched (Chapter 13).

My basic operating premise is that in order to identify the psychological functions that require my immediate attention, I will need to arrive at highly individualized answers to the following questions: How does this patient understand the origins, nature, and consequences of his/her suffering? What psychological functions do I need to perform on behalf of this patient at this moment in time? What communicative means and stylistic choices will maximize the therapeutic impact of my efforts to be useful and helpful? To what extent is the patient capable of receiving with pleasure and making constructive use of my efforts to serve benignly influential psychological functions on his/her behalf? How does this patient remember the emotional and motivational states and actions taken during naturally occurring conversations? Do these memories influence his/her current functioning?

THE THERAPIST'S SOURCES OF KNOWLEDGE

I believe therapists would make better choices about how to serve life-changing functions on behalf of their patients if they deeply understood what is known about the following domains of human functioning:

1. The developmental tasks that are in ascendency during the successive stages of the life cycle (Chapter 2)
2. The self-maintaining and habitual cognitive styles in which individuals perceive and interpret the information presented to the senses (Chapter 6)
3. The taking and giving of pleasure (Chapter 2)
4. Leadership and followership dynamics (Chapters 4 and 16)
5. The specialized modes of knowing that expand and refine one's ability to introspectively bring into awareness the sensuous fullness and kaleidoscopic complexity of the stream of consciousness (Chapter 6)
6. The ability to visualize past and future events (Chapter 19)
7. The somatic sensations that flow through the alive human body when individuals gesture, posture, and compose their facial expression (Chapter 1)
8. The extraordinarily diverse ways in which bodily sensations, images, and words—singly and in combination— bring into awareness the experiences we catalog as feelings, thoughts, memories, and fantasies (Chapter 1)
9. The dispositional tendencies that exert a restrictive and/ or biasing influence on what is knowable about external reality (Chapters 5 and 6)
10. The representational capacities that regulate how people make the all-important distinctions between "inside" of

me and "out there," self and nonself, perceiving, remembering, and imagining, past, present, and future (Chapter 12)

11. The distinction between the content (what) of subjective experiences and the *forms* of representation (how) that bring these experiential states into awareness (Chapter 13)
12. The dyadic and dialogic structure and content of inner speech (Chapter 4)
13. The obstacles that stand in the way of accepting disagreeable truths about oneself and that undermine efforts to be honest and authentic with others (Chapter 9)
14. The psychological consequences of choosing the safety of silence rather than the dangers of truth-telling (Chapter 9)
15. What it feels like to suffer the consequences of tragedies and traumas (Chapter 14)
16. The ways in which the decision-making processes that go into arriving at an understanding of the appropriateness of a particular type of therapy, therapist, and setting for a particular patient are influenced by historical, sociopolitical, and organizational forces (Chapter 5)
17. The transformative powers of the deeply felt and memorable aesthetic experiences awakened by people, places, and works of art (Chapters 19 and 20)
18. The meanings and functions of the "facilitating human qualities" that are universally regarded as core components of the capacity to serve as an agent of therapeutic change (Chapter 4)
19. The deeply ingrained human tendency to conceive of the mind as an enclosed space that contains our subjective experiences (Chapter 10)

Passion and perseverance are required to acquire this daunting list of highly sophisticated sources of knowledge. I believe that unless this work has been done, therapists are ill-prepared to respond creatively to the novel, ambiguous, and conflict-laden aspects of doing therapy with fragile and difficult patients whose suffering is exacerbated by perfectionism, rigidity, dualistic thinking, distrust, the deeply held conviction that a better life is inconceivable or unattainable, and an absence of memories of having felt safe, respected, and empathically understood when interacting with a caretaker or authority figure.

The therapists I admire most listen with their muscles and eyes as well as with their ears, know how to gracefully exchange the roles of listener and speaker, and can communicate the fruits of their listening in the languages of words, images, and expressive movements. They do not judge others. They view what happens in psychotherapy from multiple perspectives drawn from the sciences, arts, and humanities. They have let go of certainties. They use words with care but can speak without hesitation. Their artistry lies in knowing how to accommodate their stylistic choices to meet the unique needs and communicative resources of each patient. They have freed themselves from the self-consciousness, defensiveness, and selfish desires that distract us from focusing all of our attention on others. Accordingly, much of my teaching is devoted to helping aspiring therapists develop to their highest levels the listening, observational, improvisational, and communication skills I ascribe to highly competent therapists.

THE SCIENCE OF PSYCHOTHERAPY

I belong to the Society for Psychotherapy Research, an international organization whose members are dedicated to empirically studying the reasons why therapies succeed or fail. The majority opinion in this scientific community is that there is abundant evidence to support two conclusions. The first is that the establishment and maintenance of a "therapeutic alliance" is a necessary, if not sufficient, agent of therapeutic change. The second is that therapists who consistently adopt a relational stance vis-à-vis patients that is deeply infused with specifiable facilitating human qualities are more likely to promote positive therapeutic outcomes. My inventory of the facilitating human qualities possessed by gifted therapists includes those first identified by Carl Rogers (1975)—empathy, genuineness, and unconditional positive regard—as well as patience, kindness, calmness, integrity, vitality, generosity, boldness, fortitude, and humility.

I believe that therapists who consistently embody a presence that vibrates with these personal qualities establish alliances with their patients that pave the way for arriving at life-changing insights and that activate the imitative learning that takes place when patients take their therapists as role models of what it means to participate efficaciously in task-oriented, intimate, collaborative relationships.

Because therapy is a low-technology enterprise, even the most expert therapists make mistakes. I therefore encourage patients to give voice to their negative reactions to my mistakes, empathic failures, and lapses of attention. I believe that doing so goes a long way toward fostering the sense that we are doing the hard work of therapy together. In other words, I believe that therapists who help patients to courageously overcome the fears and inhibitions that prevent them from becoming eloquent critics of the therapeutic enterprise are the same ones who promote the development of positive and durable therapeutic alliances (Chapter 4).

INTERNALIZATION AND THE TRANSFORMATIVE POWERS OF PSYCHOTHERAPY

Major portions of this book advocate the view that a comprehensive and empirically grounded understanding of the reasons why therapies succeed or fail should include hypotheses about the transformative powers of the processes of internalization that lend themselves to scientific scrutiny. "Internalization" is the shorthand term I use to collectively refer to the psychophysiological processes whereby individuals transform perceptions of their experiences interacting with personally significant others into enduring and emotionally charged memory traces that, when activated, give rise to affectively valent and functionally significant representations of the self in relation to others. I believe that emotional and cognitive development throughout the life cycle is heavily influenced by the store of (internalized) representations of the self in relation to the caretakers and authority figures encountered in childhood and adolescence that were laid down in long-term memory. They are, in important respects, the "blueprints" for all subsequent personally significant relationships.

I further believe that during adulthood, within the context of psychotherapy, the processes of internalization can bring into existence the representational capacities that enable patients to recall and use for reparative and adaptive purposes the life-changing "corrective emotional experiences" they shared with their therapists. In other words, I believe that psychotherapy becomes and remains an adaptive resource in patients' lives after termination if patients are able to constructively use representations of the therapeutic dialogue in the physical absence of their therapists. This view is based on my efforts to personalize and blend Bandura's (1977) take on the biologic bases of imitative learning, Vygotsky's (1962) studies of the acquisition of language and inner speech, Piaget's (1954) concepts of "interiorization" and "deferred imitation," and Schafer's (1968) reformulations of the psychoanalytic concepts of introjection and identification.

For more than 45 years, my American and European colleagues have been submitting this and related hypotheses to scientific scrutiny by conducting phenomenological investigations of when, how, with what feelings, and to what ends individuals recall the conversations that took place within the contexts of psychotherapy and psychotherapy supervision.

We take as evidence that the processes of internalization have been activated during the course of therapy if a patient tells us

- "When I am having a problem, I try to work it out with my therapist in mind."
- "When I am faced with a difficult situation, I sometimes ask myself, What would my therapist want me to do?"
- "I now find myself talking to other people the way I talk to my therapist."
- "I try to solve my problems in the way my therapist and I worked on them in therapy."
- "In a sense, I feel as though my therapist has become a part of me."

Statistical analyses have consistently revealed that current and former patients who rate their therapies as highly effective are the same ones who strongly endorse these statements on our research instruments. Conversely, time and again, patients who have judged their therapies to be ineffective have tended to be the same ones who have reported that they do not have access to or use memory-based, benignly influential representations of the verbal and nonverbal aspects of the therapeutic dialogue for reparative and adaptive purposes. The accumulating findings have strengthened my conviction that during the course of benignly influential therapies, patients acquire the capacity and felt readiness to engage in remembered and imagined conversations with representations of dialogic partners with whom they feel safe, respected, and emotionally understood. These representations are the raw materials that enable them to constructively imitate and/or identify with the skillfulness with which these dialogic partners deal with matters of survival, safety, pleasure, and goodness.

AN AESTHETIC PERSPECTIVE ON PSYCHOTHERAPY

What do you like? What do you dislike? What do you find pleasurable and beautiful? What do you find unpleasurable and ugly? What do you find interesting? What do you find boring?

Our answers to these questions are shaped by inborn individual differences in our aesthetic preferences and sensibilities. I identify with those who from infancy onward have intensely desired and ardently pursued aesthetic experiences. My own aesthetic sensibility has expressed itself in a career-long interest in forging connections between the "arts" and my academic responsibilities (e.g., Geller, 1971, 1987; Geller & Spector, 1987; Eicher & Geller, 1990; Clarkson & Geller, 1996).

In a tradition that dates back to Aristotle, I believe that deeply felt and memorable aesthetic experiences, which I define as sensory-based pleasurable and unpleasurable feelings, can serve therapeutic functions. In order to advocate on behalf of this view, I wrote the last three chapters of this book as I approached my ninth decade.

I am a cinephile and what is known as a "cinema therapist." In 1971, Ruth Backes and I organized the first conference devoted to films about mental health (Backes & Geller, 1971).

It therefore pleases me that I made room in this book for the film script presented in Chapter 18. In everyday language, the film's characters clarify for one another what actually happens in psychotherapy and reveal to one another why they find therapy helpful or unhelpful while waiting for their therapists to greet them in the waiting room of an outpatient clinic.

The film *Ready When You Are: Answering Your Questions About Psychotherapy* (an updated version of Geller & Schwartz, 1971) was produced to educate prospective patients about how to use therapy for personal benefit and to educate culturally competent therapists about the expectations and attitudes toward therapy held by patients who are at risk of prematurely and unilaterally dropping out of therapy. Both versions of the film can be seen for free on the internet. The conversational content of both films is based on what the scientific research has to say about the roles gender, class, and race play in shaping prospective patients' expectations about how psychotherapy should or will proceed.

Chapters 19 and 20 were written as introductions to complementary volumes of the *Journal of Clinical Psychology* that I guest-edited. Chapter 19 is devoted to an exploration of what can be learned about harnessing the transformative powers of psychotherapy by studying the aesthetic experiences awakened by dance, painting, music, novels, literature, and architecture. Chapter 20 focuses on what cinematographers, film editors, and directors can teach therapists about provoking undivided attention and powerful emotions or how to evoke reflective thought and contemplation of abstract ideas that are difficult to put into words. It begins with a narrative account of the films and film characters that were important to me personally in childhood and adolescence. I believe my values, sense of self, attitudes toward courage and romantic love, and earliest ideas about therapy were heavily influenced by the heroes and villains I saw on the silver screen when "going to the movies" in my youth.

The last paragraph of Chapter 20 is a list of the comedic movies and TV shows that provided me with a needed vacation from the hard work of bringing this introduction to a conclusion and offered a respite from my worries. There is so much to worry about these days. I don't know a person who has recently had a worry-free day. The world that we are embedded in is relentlessly frightening, tumultuous, complicated, confusing, and combative. If you are in need of some worry-free time, you might find watching the films and shows I enjoyed a source of playfulness and laughter.

CONCLUSION

Dear Imaginary Readers, I made thousands of decisions en route to finding a way to tell you what this book is about. During the seemingly endless months when the COVID pandemic was ravaging America, I found temporary respite from worry by choosing the texts included in this volume, by arranging and rearranging them, and by deciding what to name this book. That I felt playful and vibrantly alive when pursuing these tasks reassured me that more than vanity motivated my desire to create and publish this book.

Rereading myself provided me with yet another opportunity to lead an "examined life." Doing so brought back long-forgotten memories of the developmental tasks I was grappling with when each of the chapters was written. Reminiscing strengthened my sense of having a living past. Discovering the themes that run through the separate chapters strengthened my sense of personal continuity and cohesiveness. And anticipating how this book will be read projected me into the future. I gifted myself with hope that my great-grandchildren will say, "Jesse was a serious man and a cool dude" when they look at the portrait of me that I chose for the cover of this book, whether or not they think the book is worthy of being read.

Saying goodbye to writing this book means saying goodbye to writing texts whose intended audience is a group of academically gifted and scientifically minded colleagues and students. This is the last text I will write in the voice of a professor. I will not miss the extended periods of self-doubt, obsessionality, and annihilation anxieties that I inevitably experience when I attempt to bring an ambitious writing project to a natural conclusion. Midway through the seventh version of this introduction, I thought I would die before finishing it.

I live in close proximity to my own death as I am *old* old. I am a survivor who believes that creating something is one of the most efficacious means of temporarily finding relief from suffering caused by the fear of dying. I am reassured that my need to write creatively will be directed elsewhere, but I will miss the ways in which the process of writing scholarly papers about psychotherapy takes me to new and useful ways of thinking about the big questions of life.

REFERENCES

Anderson, J.R. (1983). *The Architecture of Cognition*. Cambridge, MA: Harvard University Press.

Backes, R., & Geller, J.D. (1971). A selected bibliography and review of 120 mental health films. Washington, DC: National Institutes of Health.

Bandura, A. (1977). *Social Learning Theory*. New York, NY: General Learning Press.

Beckett, S. (1966). *Stories and Texts for Nothing*. New York, NY: Grove Press.

Clarkson, G., & Geller, J.D. (1996). The Bonny method from a psychoanalytic perspective: Insights from working with a psychoanalytic psychotherapist in a guided imagery and music series. *Arts in Psychotherapy* 23(4):311–319.

Eicher, T., & Geller, J.D. (Eds.). (1990). *Fathers and Daughters: Portraits in Fiction*. New York, NY: New American Library.

Geller, J.D. (1971). A mental health film festival: Special report. *Professional Psychology* 2(2):211–213. [Also in (1971). *Psychological Aspects of Disability* 18:10–13.]

———— (1987). *Reunion: An Introduction to Group Therapy*. (Written, produced, and directed by J.D. Geller. Written in collaboration with the graduate students of the Yale Clinical Psychology PhD Program.)

———— (2021). Marshall McLuhan and the therapeutic importance of the telephone. *Counseling Psychology Quarterly* 34:319–320.

————, Astrachan, B., & Flynn, H. (1976). The development and validation of a measure of the psychiatrist's authoritative domain. *Journal of Nervous and Mental Diseases* 162:410–422.

———— & Feirstein, A.R. (1974). Professional training in community mental-health centers. In G.F. Farwell, N.R. Gamsky, & P. Mathieu-Coughlan (Eds.), *The Counselor's Handbook* (pp. 449–471). New York, NY: Intext.

———— & Howard, G. (1972). Some sociopsychological characteristics of student political activists. *Journal of Applied Social Psychology* 2:114–137.

———— & Schwartz, M. (1971). *An Introduction to Psychotherapy: A Manual for the Training of Clinicians*. New Haven, CT: Videographics Inc.

———— & Spector, P. (Eds.). (1987). *Psychotherapy: Portraits in Fiction.* Hillsdale, NJ: Jason Aronson.

James, W. (1890). *The Principles of Psychology.* New York, NY: Henry Holt.

Johnson, D., Geller, J.D., Gordon, J., & Wexler, B.E. (1986). Group psychotherapy with schizophrenic patients: The pairing group. *International Journal of Group Psychotherapy* 36(1):75–96.

Piaget, J. (1954). *The Construction of Reality in the Child.* New York, NY: Basic Books.

Pope, K.S., Geller, J.D., & Wilkinson, L. (1975). Fee assessment and outpatient psychotherapy. *Journal of Consulting and Clinical Psychology* 43(6):835–841.

Rogers, C. (1975). Empathic: An unappreciated way of being. *The Counseling Psychologist* 5:2–10.

Schafer, R. (1968). *Aspects of Internalization.* New York, NY: International Universities Press.

Vygotsky, L.S. (1962). *Thought and Language.* Cambridge, MA: MIT Press.

Wexler, B.E. Johnson, D., Geller, J.D., & Gordon, J. (1984). Group psychotherapy with schizophrenic patients: An example of the oneness assumption group. *International Journal of Group Psychotherapy* 34:451–471.

Wiener, M., Devoe, S., Rubinow, S., & Geller, J.D. (1972). Nonverbal behavior and nonverbal communication. *Psychological Review* 3:185–214.

Zegans, L., Flynn, H., Geller, J.D., Goldblatt, P., Schowalter, J., Sullivan, M., & Schwartzburg, M. (1973). Progress reports, adolescent panel. *Psychiatric Utilization and Review Project National Institute of Mental Health* (pp.125–134).

CHAPTER 1

The Body, Expressive Movement, and Physical Contact in Psychotherapy

[J.D. Geller (1978). In J.L. Singer & K.S. Pope (Eds.), The Power of Human Imagination: New Methods in Psychotherapy (pp. 347–378). New York, NY: Plenum Press.]

And blest are those
Whose blood and judgment are so well commingled,
That they are not a pipe for fortune's finger
To sound what stop she please.
—*Shakespeare, Hamlet*

INTRODUCTION

An overview of the current "therapeutic marketplace" (Frank, 1972) reveals the proliferation and increasing popularity of a wide range of body- or movement-oriented therapies, for example, orgone therapy (Reich, 1949), bioenergetic analysis (Lowen, 1967), postural relearning (Feldenkrais, 1949), Rolf Structural Integration (Rolf, 1963), psychomotor training (Pesso, 1969), the Alexander technique (Alexander, 1974), and the various forms of dance-movement therapy (e.g., Chace, 1953; Schoop, 1971; Bartenieff, 1972; Siegel, 1973). These approaches do not share a common vocabulary or a standardized repertoire of techniques, nor are they unified by a comprehensive theory of psychopathology and behavior change. They evolved to meet the needs of different types of patient populations. They are practiced in a wide variety of institutional contexts, and their practitioners come from diverse disciplinary backgrounds. Feldenkrais was originally a physicist, Rolf a biochemist, Alexander an actor. The pioneers in the scientific rediscovery of the "art" of movement as a mode of therapy were dancers.

What unifies these divergent approaches is a fundamental belief in the functional identity of personality and the physical appearance of the body at rest and in movement. They all share the belief that our capacity for growth, feeling, and change is limited by our capacity for body awareness and that our capacity for body awareness is limited by our capacity for movement. Body-movement therapists make no clear dichotomy, whether psychodynamically or experientially, between mental and bodily events. Moreover, in contrast to those who practice the so-called "talking cure,"[2] body-movement therapists all primarily deal with psychopathology as manifested in movement and body structure and attempt to effect therapeutic changes by working exclusively or primarily on this level.

The basic operational premise guiding the work of body-movement therapists is that changes in personality can be brought about directly by modifying the body structure and its functional motility. This work may or may not involve an ongoing discussion of "therapeutic" material. Ida Rolf (1963) claims that systematic realignment of the body structure at the neuromuscular level ("Rolfing") alone is sufficient to produce greater self-awareness, new suppleness and flexibility, greater ease in handling interpersonal relations, a decrease in the physical tension found in chronically contracted muscles, and an increased reservoir of energy. Borrowing ideas from sources as

---

2 Gestalt (Perls, 1971) and primal therapy (Janov, 1970) prominently include body-oriented practices, but for our purposes they are more appropriately regarded as occupying an intermediate position between the so-called verbal and body therapies. As Brown (1973) notes, Gestalt techniques are far more awareness centered than body centered. Janov's highly channelized objective is premised on the assumption that the essence of neurosis consists in the encapsulation of pain within both the psyche and body. Techniques that rely on electronic sensing devices to gain control over internal states (e.g., biofeedback) will not be considered in this paper.

disparate as the martial arts, yoga, and the twirling dances of the Sufis, Feldenkrais (1949) has developed a regimen of delicate body exercises to alter patterns of thinking and feeling. Orgone therapists (Reich, 1949) blend characterological and biophysical techniques in proportions that vary from patient to patient and, with a particular patient, from time to time. Bioenergetic therapists (Lowen, 1967) similarly supplement analytic procedures with expressive movement exercises, physical manipulation of the skeletal musculature, and deep-breathing exercises. Dance therapy originated as an adjunctive therapy for hospitalized psychiatric patients. The American Dance Therapy Association (1972) defines it as "the psychotherapeutic use of movement as a process which furthers the emotional and physical integration of the individual" (p. 1). In dance therapy, patients are given the opportunity to move freely in space, to discover or rediscover what it means to play, to discover what it feels like to have sensations in different body parts, to risk abandoning themselves to compelling musical rhythms, to become a member of a cohesive group, to participate in rituals, to spontaneously express or dramatize emotions, to shout or attach concrete images and metaphors to their actions, to touch and be touched by others, and so forth. Trudi Schoop (1971), a pioneer dance therapist, summarized this orientation when she wrote:

> If I am correct in assuming that mind and body are interactive, I feel a problem of mental disturbance can be influenced from either side. When psychoanalysis brings about change in the mental attitude, there should be a corresponding physical change. And when dance therapy brings about a change in the body behavior, there should be a corresponding change in the mind. The approach of dance therapy is through body-mind. Both methods want to change the total being, mind and body (p. 5).

From antiquity, the two dimensions of human existence, the body and the mind, have been the focus of controversy between competing approaches to education and therapeutics. In this paper we shall examine some of the contemporary manifestations of this controversy, especially as it is reflected in psychotherapists' attitudes toward the body, expressive movement, and physical contact with patients. Our aim is not to enter the debate as to whether "acting it out" is therapeutically more efficacious than "talking it out." With respect to the question of outcome in psychotherapy, we believe that it is most heuristic, following Bergin (1971), to ask the question, What treatment in the hands of which therapist is most effective for this individual with that problem and under which set of circumstances? We are, moreover, in agreement with Frank's (1972) hypothesis that the relative popularity of any mode of therapy grows not out of its demonstrable superiority but rather out of its congruence with prevailing values and lifestyles. We are also more impressed with the common denominators that unify all forms of psychotherapy. The approaches discussed here all share the common features that Frank regards as the universal components of any healing relationship:

> a confiding, emotionally charged relationship between the patient and a help-giving individual or group; a special setting containing symbols of healing; a rationale; and a set of activities prescribed by the rationale involving both patient and therapist. The fact that rationales and procedures differ so widely does not negate the necessity of both. No form of psychotherapy can exist without them (p. 31).

As Lévi-Strauss (1967) has argued, this is no less true for shamanistic practices than it is for the academically trained psychotherapist.

Within this framework we shall discuss the biases and assumptions underlying the body-movement therapies and the implications that follow from attempts to translate the kaleidoscopic multiplicity of human experience into verbal and nonverbal channels of communication. This paper focuses on the changing status of the body in the quest for self-realization, the habitual distinction between style and content, the concept of unconscious mental representation, and the roles of insight, interpretation, and physical contact in promoting a genuinely communicative relationship. In pursuing these goals, we shall contrast body-movement therapies and psychoanalytically oriented therapy. All therapies must come to terms with their relationship to psychoanalytic therapy, just as all therapists must come to terms with their "transference" to Freud. As Auden (1957) observed in his memorial poem to Freud, "To us he is no more a person now but a whole climate of opinion, under whom we conduct our differing lives" (p. 57).

THE DEMOCRATIZATION OF THE RELATIONSHIP OF THE MIND AND THE BODY

Movement and body therapies are challenging views that are deeply embedded in our philosophical and cultural heritage: the tendency to value the intangible, spiritual, and metaphysical more than the tangible and the seen; and the Cartesian view of the body as a machine directed by the soul. From classical antiquity, the body has been conceptualized as either antithetical to the objectives of the soul, the primary obstacle in man's pursuit of self-realization, or merely "inferior" to the soul. In the West as in the East, bodily needs have traditionally been subordinated to mental, moral, and spiritual development. The emphasis has been on subordinating and controlling the body as a prerequisite for spiritual advancement. Even the classical Greek educational ideal of a "sound mind in a sound body" emanates from a belief (Friedlander, 1964) in the soul's superiority over the body. In the teachings of hatha yoga, the body is similarly important as a means, not as an end. Although in modern times the concept of self has gradually replaced the concept of soul, the former is still haunted by its philosophical heritage. Thus, many use the concept of self as if it referred to an invisible, intangible something that "animates" the body without physical agency and "inhabits" it without being in any place (Langer, 1942).

It is only gradually that modern psychotherapeutic practices have been liberated from these values and implications. In this regard, the psychoanalytic tradition represents a historical link and critical point of departure for the new body-movement therapies.

Freud (1923) regarded the body as the source of all consciousness and the body image as the nucleus of the ego. Although he viewed personality as "a democracy of opposing predispositions," he clearly advocated "the primacy of the intellect." For Freud (1913/1959b), the secondary processes represented "a higher level of mental representation." He viewed primary-process thought as tied to archaic levels of the development of language and methods of representation that dominated the conscious thought of children and "primitive" people (1923). There have always been advocates of a "poetic" approach to psychoanalysis (e.g., Reik, 1949), but the ideal image of the analyst has been that of a "detached scientist." Loewald (1960) believes that Freud considered "scientific man as the most advanced form of human development" (p. 10). As Sontag (1966) notes, Freud is also heir to the Platonic tradition in two paramount and related ways: his acceptance of the view that sexuality is "lower" and the sublimations in art, science, and culture "higher," and his acceptance of the self-evident value (both practical and theoretical) of self-awareness. The so-called Freudian "analytic attitude" encourages a lack of piety toward the "higher" things, a respectful interest in the "lower," and, as Rieff (1963) claims, a detachment from both.

Freud was not a champion of libidinal expressiveness. According to Tillich (1962), the concept of sublimation is Freud's most puritanical belief. Although psychoanalytic therapies are premised on the value that we must accept our bodily needs, Freud was convinced of the fundamental antagonism between the individual's need for instinctual gratification and the oppressive but inevitable demands of civilization. The ascetic ideals of self-reliance and personal achievement are discernible in the Freudian outlook. Rieff (1963) states that Freudian pedagogy teaches the patient-student "to develop an informed (i.e., healthy) respect for the sovereign and unresolvable basic contradictions that galvanize him into the singularly complicated human being that he is" (p. 17). Psychoanalytic therapeutic re-education thus encourages a stance of reasoned disillusionment, a tolerance of ambiguities, a deeply searching yet impartial responsiveness to the paradoxes and absurdities of existence. Ever mindful of the inescapable conflict between passion and duty, psychoanalytic therapists have renounced the concept of cure. Psychological rebirth from the analytic perspective is an illusion, and for Freud the permanence of analytic gains depends crucially on whether the patient after analysis is spared "too searching a fate." Thus, despite its melioristic orientation and positive attitude toward worldly gratification, the Freudian perspective is deeply shaped by what Schafer (1970) has called the tragic and ironic visions of reality.

THE ROMANTIC VISION OF THE BODY–MOVEMENT THERAPIES

A romantic vision seems to be a particularly distinctive feature of the body-movement therapies. They are romantic to the extent that they view therapy as an archetypal quest for "naturalness," a lost golden age, "a second innocence," or as an attempt to achieve the elusive goal of self-actualization. The goals of body-movement therapists vary in accordance with the restraints imposed by time, severity of pathology, finances, and so forth. Yet, they also entertain the utopian possibility of reconciling seamlessly the split between the mind and the body. The new body-movement therapies are repudiating rationalistic biases, the dichotomy between objective reality and subjective fantasy, and the assumption that the scientific approach to the self is the highest and most mature evolutionary stage of development. They do not see adult, objective, impersonal cognition as the baseline and implicit model for all thought processes, nor do they regard an impersonal, scientific construction of reality as the absolute, fixed standard of "objectivity." External reality is not portrayed as a constraining, frustrating power in eternal opposition to the individual seeking unlimited expression of his drives. The emphasis is upon such values as expressiveness, direct immediate experience, and spontaneity.

Whereas some body-movement therapists eschew the hierarchical structuring of the personality into pejoratively toned "higher" and "lower" categories, others are in the tradition of Nietzsche (1954), who proclaimed: "But the awakened and knowing say body am I entirely and nothing else, and soul is only a word for something about the body. There is more reason in your body than in your best wisdom" (p. 146). According to Brown (1973), the new body therapies are "id affirmative" rather than "ego affirmative."

From a moral point of view, this shift is potentially revolutionary. For Rieff (1961), "health at the expense of morality" (p. 25) is a potentially dangerous by-product of this new freedom for natural biological urges. Other intellectuals deplore the lifestyle and values underlying the so-called consciousness movement. Marin (1976) dismisses it as "the new narcissism" that encourages "deification of the isolated self." The body-movement therapies do not necessarily repudiate the value of consciousness or reflectiveness. Their work is not unmindful of Gendlin's (1962) assertion that "feeling without symbolization is blind, symbolization without feeling is empty" (p. 5). Nevertheless, the new body and movement therapies would seem to believe, along with Norman O. Brown (1959), that what is needed is not Apollonian (or sublimation) consciousness, but Dionysian (or body) consciousness. For example, Perls's (1971) invitation to "lose your mind so that you can come to your senses" (p. 25) contrasts starkly with Freud's description of psychoanalysis as the instrument that would progressively conquer the id. Despite the emphasis on expressiveness, body-movement therapists recognize that the implementation of their values requires the cultivation of a very special kind of perceptual awareness.

OBSTACLES TO THE DEVELOPMENT OF BODY-AWARENESS

Listening to and attending to the wisdom of one's body is a highly refined and sophisticated act of consciousness. It should not be confused with maintaining physical fitness and sound health. Brown (1973) has aptly noted that energetic, physically fit, action-oriented people (e.g., dancers, athletes) "may be emotionally crippled because they perceive their bodies as objects-of-use to be coerced into submission" (p. 100).

A respectful attitude toward one's body, an accurate body image, and a pleasurable sense of being "a body" appear to be heroic achievements in our culture. Difficulty in accurately reading and using adaptively the messages of the body is not limited to the psychiatrically disabled. There are many reasons why people, in general, have formidable blind spots in their knowledge of their bodies. Visual inspection of important body sectors (e.g., the vagina, the anus) is extremely limited, and it is impossible to examine visually the interior of the body. Careful and extended inspection of the body geography is discouraged by those religious and moralistic systems that view the body as a source of sin. This theme still flourishes, according to Fisher (1973), in doctrines that emphasize rationality and intellectuality. Socialization practices that emphasize that action must be based on rational "reasons" rather than body feelings and the tendency to regard body arousal (e.g., emotionality) as misleading or as introducing irrationality into decision-making blunt our skill in interpreting body experiences. Because we lack publicly stated norms against which we can match our own body experiences, it is difficult for the average individual to judge what the body should "feel" like. Careful analysis of the body and body sensations is intimately enmeshed with the diagnosis of disease and associated with internalized prohibitions against being dirty or unattractive. The image of the body-as-commodity has replaced the image of the body-as-tool in our technology-dominated society. In the wake of this shift, the cosmetics and fashion industries, unrealistic standards of beauty and physique, and the denigration of aging ensure that few individuals will develop and sustain a loving and respectful attitude toward the physicality of the body.

Becker (1973) maintains that the essence of man resides in his efforts to reconcile "the existential contradiction between a symbolic self, that seems to give man infinite worth in a timeless scheme of things, and a body that is worth about 98¢" (p. 28). He has termed this paradox the "tragedy of man's dualism."[3] For Becker, we are "gods with anuses." This dilemma underscores the most powerful and ubiquitous resistances to knowing the body. According to Fisher (1973), looking directly and naively at the body is resisted because in so doing "its properties as a concrete object becomes too painfully obvious" (p. 7). Fisher goes on to say,

There is comfort in thinking of your body not as a mere physical object, which, as such, would be subject to all of the vicissitudes and happenings that befall ordinary objects in the universe. But if an individual inspects his body without reservation he must necessarily perceive that it is basically a biological phenomenon like all other biological organisms. Ultimately, it is a collection of matter, regardless of how complex the values and meanings ascribed to it. To become aware of this fact is to open the door to intimations of mortality and other forms of vulnerability. It is probably important defensively to most people to conceptualize their bodies within an elaborate framework of psychological meaning that functions almost like a halo or protective armoring—denying that the body is, after all, an aggregate of molecules not much different from those occurring widely in nature. It is difficult for man to accept that his body is not "above it all" (p. 8).

---

3 The reflected appraisals that constitute the body image include the information conveyed by mirrors. Lacan (1968) has emphasized that this source of knowledge of our physical and physiologic self—"external," "disembodied"—contributes an "otherness" to the experience of one's body. Lacan would therefore agree with Becker that the split between the symbolic self and the body can never be reconciled seamlessly.

COMMUNICATION IN PSYCHOTHERAPY

In seeking to implement their goals, psychotherapists of whatever persuasion must deal with several interrelated and inescapable problems of communication. Communication, irrespective of the medium through which it is accomplished, requires the translation of internal psychologic reality into external, social reality. Since human experience in any one moment of conscious time is both plural and voluminous, any attempt to communicate this variegated experience entails simplifications and distortions. Paraphrasing McLuhan (1964), the capacity of any given medium to reproduce the full variety of the original experience depends on the number of sensory channels that it calls into action when working properly. The larger the number of senses involved, the better the chance of transmitting a reliable copy of the sender's emotional state.

McLuhan (1964) believes that the spoken word answers these requirements more faithfully than any other medium or sense modality because spoken language arouses collateral experiences, accommodates a more fully representative range of sensory experiences than any other type of human communication, and is typically modulated by acoustic, visual, tactile, and olfactory cues.

But is spoken language the best medium for "embodying" the sources of gain in psychotherapy? Spoken language may provide us with our most faithful and indispensable picture of human experience, but the "primacy of language" as a therapeutic medium of exchange must be considered in the light of other critical issues. Preverbal and psychotic experiences do not lend themselves to the linear arrangement of ideas. The primary medium through which information is exchanged in a relationship shapes the form of the relationship that evolves. Any mode of communication imposes characteristic features upon the messages passing through them. McLuhan (1964) contrasts the hesitant creativity of speech with the dull regimentation of written language. Moreover, therapeutic skill requires a refined receptiveness and sensitivity toward "nongenuine" communication. One of the most firmly rooted psychotherapeutic assumptions is that psychopathology, to a large extent, results from and is perpetuated by distorted and inadequate communication. Despite conscious willingness, patients in psychotherapy flee from spontaneous and candid self-disclosure.

Contemporary reexaminations of the concept of insight (Schafer, 1973) have emphasized that it is not expanding awareness or the cathartic effect of becoming conscious per se that facilitates change but rather the experience of discovering oneself in the medium of communicating with another person. Schafer concludes that

> it is precisely this discovery in a medium of relationship that every patient, each in his own way and for his own reasons, has grown to feel helpless about. He anticipates that the discovery will be unbearable and the disclosure of it either intolerable in itself or intolerable as the certain cause of a forthcoming traumatic response by the other person, the therapist (p. 144).

In the wake of such fears and resistances, there are apt to emerge discrepancies between self-reports and expressive behavior observable to the therapist. The activity of speaking, moreover, during the early stages of therapy, is used primarily to appeal to the therapist to do something or to respond in some way, for example, imploring, commanding, forbidding, seducing (Loewenstein, 1956). Paraphrasing Paul (1973), free association is the goal rather than the method of psychoanalytic psychotherapy. Rarely are patients capable of establishing a "genuinely communicative relationship" from the outset of treatment.

FORM AND CONTENT IN PSYCHOTHERAPY

In general, psychopathological modes of communication are characterized by disjunctions between that which we have learned to call "content" and that which we have learned to call "form." The idea of content typically refers to the subject matter of a therapeutic dialogue (e.g., What X is saying is; What X is trying to say is, etc.). The formal aspects of a patient's self-presentation primarily comprise those expressive activities that are observable to the therapist, for example, individual variations in speech, gait, posture, gestures, dress, manner, and so forth. Despite theoretical affirmations of the indissolubility of form and content in producing an individual's unique style, in the practice of all contemporary psychotherapies reductionistic biases persist. Neither the psychoanalytic approach nor the new body-movement therapies have integrated fully these conceptually distinguishable components of a person's style, character, or mode of relating into their working clinical models.

Wilhelm Reich (1949) was the first psychoanalyst to draw systematic attention to the possibility that an overemphasis on the idea of content as essential and of form as decorative or accessory was responsible for many therapeutic failures. He observed that the "subject matter" of a therapy hour per se did not define the experience of growth-inspiring self-disclosure. He argued that what had been talked about during the course of therapy did not necessarily provide an accurate barometer of the depth of intimacy or productivity of the relationship, and he concluded that, especially during the early stages of treatment, the form of expression was far more important than ideational content in defining the unique nature of a patient's resistances and transference. This aspect of Reich's work led to a growing appreciation among traditional therapists of the formal aspects of a patient's mode of relating. Nevertheless, according to Horowitz (1972), in the psychoanalytic situation the emphasis is on thought content and control rather than on thought form. Expressive behaviors, although regarded as integral aspects of communication, are usually viewed as ancillary or alternative conveyors of content. Whereas in psychoanalytic practice content comes first, for the body-movement therapists the formal aspects of communication are primary. The innovative practices of the new body-movement therapies have tended to be experiments with form at the expense of content. Like systems analysts, they prefer to neglect the significance of what is said in favor of a study of the structures through which it is transmitted.

To discuss this and other issues, it is necessary to introduce the concept of *representation*. Horowitz (1972) defines representation as "an organization of information in a form that can be part of conscious experience" (p. 797). In discussing the course of cognitive growth, Bruner (1964) has written:

If we are to benefit from contact with recurrent regularities in the environment, we must represent them in some manner. To dismiss this problem as "mere memory" is to misunderstand it. For the most important thing about memory is not storage of past experience, but rather the retrieval of what is relevant in some usable form. This depends upon how past experience is coded and processed so that it may indeed be relevant and usable in the present when needed. The end product of such a system of coding and processing is what we may speak of as "representation" (p. 2).

Both Bruner and Horowitz distinguish three systems of process-ing information by which human beings construct models of their world: through action, through imagery, and through lan-guage. Following Horowitz, we shall refer to these three catego-ries as the enactive, image, and lexical modes of representation.

THE ROLE OF LANGUAGE IN PSYCHOANALYTIC THERAPY

The preeminence of language in traditional psychotherapy is obvious. With verbally accessible adults, private experiences are transformed and externalized primarily through the medium of syntactically articulated speech. For Merleau-Ponty (1962), "speech in the speaker does not translate ready-made thought, but accomplishes it" (p. 178). Thus, the patient's task is to trans-form simultaneously occurring emotional, sensory, and cognitive events into language capable of being made comprehensible to the therapist. In psychoanalytic therapy, patients promise "ab-solute honesty" (Freud, 1913/1959b), and the psychoanalytic method seeks to eliminate resistances to "talking about" issues that are being communicated or revealed through actions. More-over, psychoanalytically oriented therapists tend to share the belief that little in a patient changes or grows effectively that has not come within the range of competence of language and discourse.

Psychoanalytic psychotherapy, however, has never been an-chored exclusively in language. This misconception underlies many of the pseudoclashes between the body-movement ther-apies and traditional therapy. Speech is not merely a substitute for action in traditional therapy. Thus, Loewenstein (1956) has written, "Indeed speaking involves motor discharge by means of the vocal organs and in this respect plays a role in the therapeutic action of psychoanalysis" (p. 462). Despite the primacy that Freud accorded to language, he early recognized that crucial therapeutic material was inaccessible to imagistic or lexical modes of representation. The hypothesis that patients express in action what they are reluctant to discuss or cannot remember is a fundamental canon of psychoanalytic practice.

To begin with, Freud believed that nonverbal behavior, being under less conscious control than speech and therefore more likely to escape efforts at concealment, could provide information that patients were hesitant or unable to discuss verbally. Thus, in 1905 he wrote: "He that has eyes to see and ears to hear may convince himself that no mortal can keep a secret. If his lips are silent, he chatters with his fingertips; betrayal oozes out of him at every pore" (p. 94). Subsequent psychoanalysts have been primarily concerned with decoding the meaning or symbolism of nonverbal behaviors (e.g., Deutsch, 1952; Feldman, 1959).

Second, Freud designed the psychoanalytic situation so that during their sessions patients would relive and reenact rather than "just talk about" their lives. He noted (1940) that in the transference

the patient produces before us with plastic clarity an important part of his life history, of which he could otherwise have given us only an unsatisfactory account. It is as though he were acting it in front of us instead of reporting it to us (p. 194).

Anna Freud (1968) has similarly written:

This "forgotten past," so far as it refers to the preverbal period, has never entered the ego organization in the strict sense of the term, i.e., is under primary not secondary repression and, therefore, is not recoverable in memory, only apt to be relived (repeated, acted out, in behavior) (p. 167).

Third, *motility* or enactive modes of representation have never been prohibited in the psychoanalytic situation. Khan (1974) has argued that often growth-promoting experiences "in the analytic situation can have no means of symbolic and/or concrete actualization if motility is rigidly tabooed. Self-experience is intimately related to body-ego" (p. 297). Balint (1968) reported the following event, which occurred during the 2nd year of an "arduous analysis" with a young woman whose presenting complaint was an inability to achieve anything:

Apparently the most important thing for her was to keep her head safely up, with both feet firmly planted on the ground. In response, she mentioned that ever since her earliest childhood she could never do a somersault, although at various periods, she tried desperately to do one. I then said: "What about it now?"—whereupon she got up from the couch and, to her great amazement, did a perfect somersault without any difficulty. This proved to be a real breakthrough. Many changes followed, in her emotional, social and professional life, all towards greater freedom and elasticity (p. 50).

Such anecdotes appear rarely in the case reports of psychoanalytic therapists. By contrast, "acting out" with the therapist as witness and accomplice is a commonplace occurrence in the body-movement therapies. Concomitantly, although there is widespread agreement that therapeutic progress is facilitated, nurtured, and rendered possible by therapist contributions that significantly transcend verbal utterances, the therapists' nonlexical contributions to the psychotherapeutic relationship have been given scant attention in the traditional psychotherapy literature. This issue, particularly as it is reflected in the concept of countertransference and in the role of physical contact between patient and therapist, will be focused upon in a subsequent section of the paper. At this point, we will examine what Sontag (1966) has termed "the never consummated project of interpretation" (p. 17).

In pursuing this goal, we have relied on the conceptual distinction between the "experiential" and "meaning" aspects of therapeutic interaction. Following Gendlin (1962), we believe that the "creation of meaning" and "experiencing" are intimately associated and required of all psychotherapeutic work. Schachter's (1964) research compellingly demonstrates that a state of physiological arousal alone is not sufficient to induce an emotion and that cognitions exert a strong steering function in helping a person "decide" what he is feeling. In a series of experiments to determine which cues permit a person to identify his own emotional state, Schachter discovered that it was possible to lead subjects who were "experiencing" precisely the same chemically induced state of physiological arousal to believe that they were feeling angry, or euphoric, or merely showing the physical side effects of the chemical agent. These findings indicate that patients must be given the opportunity to correctly label, discuss, and differentiate the ambiguous and often unfamiliar sensations (i.e., "feelings") that are aroused in therapy. Otherwise, they are likely to confuse, distort, or find it impossible to "get in touch with" feelings that for them may be uninterpretable in terms of past experience. For example, according to Lowen (1958), patients who fear being punished for "good feelings" tend to react to genital excitation with exaggerated alarm. Thus, although pleasure demands a loosening of restraints, the mere realigning of these patients' body structures might result in increased anxiety rather than greater emotional freedom.

THE SEARCH FOR MEANING

Every therapist seeks to understand or "make sense of" his patients' communications, be they verbal or nonverbal. Freud's original clinical investigations, as Rosen (1969) points out, "were an attempt to find meaning in the meaningless" (p. 197). Indeed, psychoanalytic therapy is premised fundamentally upon the view that emotionally intensified understanding of covert or unconscious cognitive processes is antecedent to and causative of changes in overt behavior. To understand, in this tradition, is to seek indices of content and experiences that are not being verbalized. To this end, the analytically oriented therapist listens to the content of the patient's associations and/or observes the manner in which a patient speaks. As previously noted, the formal aspects of a patient's communications are primarily regarded as ancillary conveyors of content. Moreover, all observable phenomena are bracketed, in Freud's terminology, as manifest content. This manifest content must be interpreted in order to find the true meaning—the latent content—beneath. Neurotic symptoms, slips of the tongue, dreams, nonverbal gestures are all treated as occasions for interpretation. Sontag (1966) has concluded that for Freud, "these events only seem to be intelligible. Actually, they have no meaning without interpretation. To understand is to interpret. And to interpret is to restate the phenomenon, in effect to find an equivalent for it" (p. 7).

From the psychoanalytic perspective, everything that is available to consciousness should be communicable through consensually shared verbal forms, and anything that is not available to consciousness (i.e., anything being defended against) will be evident only in a form in which the patient himself could not recognize the content; that is, the material is in symbolic form. The clinical basis of these assumptions is directly related to the view of neurotic symptoms as substitutes (i.e., symbolic equivalents) for repressed memories of past traumatic events. The Freudian style of interpretation, therefore, digs "behind" the patient's utterances and nonverbal behavior to find a subtext that is the "true" one. In other words, the ultimate hope, as Rosen (1961) has written, of the psychoanalytically oriented therapist "is to understand those aspects of the patient's unconscious mental contents which produce his symptoms" (p. 450).

Because we do not know in what form unconscious memories or processes, as such, exist within our patients, we must describe them by analogy. The unconscious is first and foremost a hypothetical construct. Freud (1940) states it this way:

> We have discovered technical methods of filling up the gaps in the phenomena of our consciousness, and we make use of those methods just as a physicist makes use of experiment. In this manner we infer a number of processes which are in themselves "unknowable" and interpolate them in those that are conscious to us. And if, for instance, we say: "At this point an unconscious memory intervened," what that means is: "At this point something occurred of which we are totally unable to form a conception, but which, if it had entered our consciousness, could only have been described in such and such a way" (pp. 196–197).

At a theoretical level, Freud stated that the unconscious was much broader than the repressed. However, according to Schimek (1975), Freud's working clinical model of the unconscious was that "the primary and original form of the unconscious is an ideational one, namely contents of memories or fantasies which by acquiring drive cathexis become causal agents of behavior" (p. 182). Freud's model of cognitive growth, additionally, presumes the existence of "mental" representations from the beginning of development. From the psychoanalytic perspective, ideation invariably precedes action. Taken together, these views led Freud to describe unconscious memories, within the clinical psychoanalytic situation, in terms of the content they would have if they were conscious and verbalized.

THE UNCONSCIOUS IN THE BODY–MOVEMENT THERAPIES

The new body-movement therapies are premised, either explicitly or implicitly, on an alternative view of the relationship between cognition and action. The assumption that the attitude of activity interferes with or is an incompatible alternative to remembering is deeply rooted in the psychoanalytic tradition (Schachtel, 1959). In the body-movement therapies, movement presumably facilitates rather than endangers the evocation of unconscious memories, fantasies, and primitive ways of coping with traumatic experiences. The emphasis on direct body work, moreover, necessitates an expanded or modified view of unconscious mental representation. It is generally accepted that as individual psychomotor patterns are learned, they become so internalized with repetition that their specifics recede below consciousness, usually never to emerge again. What adult can explain or even be aware of the precise series of habitual actions employed in walking, dressing, eating? Body-movement therapists further assume that specific gaps, avoidances, and tensions in our movement patterns are rendered unconscious. Siegel (1975) writes: "The instinctive withdrawal or tightening by which we once protected ourselves from some specific threat becomes fixed in our body's repertoire and continues to govern the way we move long after the initial reason for it is gone" (p. 8). This view is consistent with Sharpe's (1938) hypothesis that the body is a carrier of explicit memories localized in its various parts and with Deutsch's (1952) assumption that certain body parts become invested with unconscious symbolic meaning according to their structure and function.

Most importantly, body-movement therapies presume the "existence" of what Piaget (1951) has called a "pre-representational level of concrete action-schemes." Piaget maintains that during the "sensorimotor" period of development (i.e., approximately the first 18 months of life), the infant does not have representations or mental images by which he can evoke persons or objects in their absence. But in the process of accommodating his innate behavioral repertoire and spontaneous movements to the demands of reality, the child presumably develops "cognitive substructures" or a complex system of "action-schemes." For Piaget and Inhelder (1969), "a scheme is a structure or organization of actions as they are transferred or generalized by repetition in similar or analogous circumstances" (p. 13). By means of a sensorimotor coordination of these action-schemes, without the intervention of symbolic representation or thought, the child, according to Piaget, begins to construct and organize his reality. That is, well before the formation of the first mental images, the child gradually discovers means to achieve different ends. He develops a logic of action. Although prerepresentational, these broad categories of action (e.g., intentional grasping) and affective reactions (e.g., smiling) imply the attribution of meaning.

It will be recalled that Freud's model of cognitive development presumes the "existence" of "mental representations" from the beginning of development and that he hypothesized that the primary and original form of the unconscious is ideational (i.e., contents of memories or fantasies). The change from random motor movements to adaptive action requires, for Freud, a cognitive representation of the goal prior to the action. For Freud, action is originally the enactment of a wishful fantasy. According to Schimek (1975), the data and concepts of contemporary developmental psychology, and of Piaget in particular, indicate that "the view of the unconscious as a storage container of specific images and memories may no longer be tenable or even necessary" and that it is legitimate to infer "unconscious sensorimotor organizers of action at a preideational as well as a preverbal level without postulating that behind the various observable manifestations of an inferred unconscious motive lies an unconscious image or fantasy" (p. 182).

From another perspective, Schachtel (1959) has pointed to the fact that even the most profound and prolonged psychoanalysis does not lead to an extensive recovery of childhood memory. For Schachtel, the progressive repression of infantile sexuality and the censorship of objectionable material is insufficient to account for gaps in and the impoverishment of autobiographical memory. For Schachtel, the quality of memory and the conditions of forgetting are closely related to the mode of prior learning and attention. He believes that the categories (or schemata) of adult memory are not suitable receptacles for early childhood experiences and therefore are not fit to preserve these experiences and enable their recall. According to Schachtel, "our minds are not capable of accommodating childhood experiences. More often than not, adults are not even capable of imagining what the child experiences" (p. 314). Schachtel further argues that although the memory of one's more recent personal past is fairly continuous, this formal continuity in time is offset by barrenness in content. During the course of development, experience becomes increasingly cliché-ridden and conventionalized. Experiences are replaced by pseudoexperiences. We see and hear what we are taught to expect, and we tend to rationalize our memories, rendering them acceptable and comfortable.

These findings and speculations are likely to have a profound effect on the theory and practice of all therapies. They argue for the value of educative or growth-oriented therapeutic opportunities to overcome "normal amnesia" (Schachtel, 1959). They lend credence to those approaches that seek to realign the body so that movement and the postural organization of the body are restructured at a neuromuscular level (i.e., Alexander technique, Rolfing). They suggest that dance therapy, with its emphasis on enactive modes of representation, may be ideally suited to those forms of psychopathology that may be caused by vicissitudes occurring at a precognitive level of organization. They support the hypothesis that the past is continually presented to the world in the form of the individual's personal style of moving.

MOVEMENTS ARE EXPRESSIVE

A review of the literature on expressive movements indicates that any given movement has been considered by different investigators, or by one investigator at different times, as an indicator of momentary affective states, enduring personality characteristics, "role" or group membership, or "unconsciously" motivated communication. The only unifying concept in the literature on body movement is the tenet, often explicitly stated, that "movements are expressive." The early investigators of this hypothesis (e.g., Allport & Vernon, 1933; Wolff, 1943) were concerned with intraindividual consistencies in psychomotor behavior patterns. Their research was designed to show that many different behaviors of an individual (e.g., his gait, his posture, the tonal quality of his voice, his handwriting) are "manifestations" of underlying personality characteristics. As used by these investigators, the hypothesis that "movements are expressive" seemed to be derived from the more general belief that, in principle, under specified conditions, everything a person does, every action or movement he makes, can be used by a knowledgeable and sensitive observer as a basis (either from the behaviors themselves or from inferences based on these behaviors) for understanding the individual. Nevertheless, there is a lack of clarity in their use of hypothesis; it is unclear whether they believed that the behaviors in question were derived from the underlying personality characteristics (i.e., genotypes) or were behaviors consistent with the posited genotype.

Another source of confusion in the literature on so-called body language is the widespread failure to distinguish between movements that are informative to an observer and those that are communicative in motivation. As Scheflen (1964) has aptly noted,

> all too often research into the meaning of "nonverbal" elements of communication has consisted merely of isolating a fragment, counting its frequency, and then free associating or asking subjects to free associate about its meaning, as if elements of behavior carried meaning in and of themselves (p. 319).

With few exceptions (Mahl, 1968; Birdwhistell, 1970), efforts to decode the meaning of nonverbal behaviors have blurred the distinction between movements as "signs" and movements as "communications." Although signs and communications may be equally valid data sources, particularly when trying to understand an individual, they differ in several important respects. Any behavior may be taken as a "sign" of something else. The concept of a sign implies only an observer making an inference or assigning significance to an event or behavior. It does not suggest an act of transmission of information from one person to another; that is, the concept does not imply a subject who is actively making his experience public to another person. The concept of "communication," on the other hand, implies a so-cially shared signal system, that is, a code, an encoder who makes something public via that code, and a decoder who re-sponds systematically to that code (Wiener et al., 1972).

A collapsing of the sign-communication distinction may be inherent in any approach that is primarily concerned with decoding the meaning of nonverbal behavior. Even if a ther-apist distinguishes theoretically between movements as signs and movements as communications, within the context of a therapy hour it is difficult, if not impossible, to know whether one is decoding a communication encoded by an individual or drawing an inference from his behavior. This issue is a matter of relative indifference to the therapist, for whom nonverbal behavior is an ancillary mode of communication, especially when trying to understand a particular individual. However, the failure to distinguish between movements as signs and move-ments as communications has retarded the development of a comprehensive notational system to study nonverbal behavior as an independent channel of communication. Moreover, be-cause movement events, within the psychoanalytic situation, acquire full significance only in the context of the verbal ut-terances that they either precede or follow, the sensorium of the psychoanalytic therapist is likely to be biased in favor of audition. For example, although Sullivan (1954) emphasized the importance of gestural and behavioral cues in communi-cating empathy, he asserted that "the psychiatric interview is primarily a matter of vocal communication, and it would be quite a serious error to presume that communication is primar-ily verbal. The sound accompaniment suggests what is to be made of the verbal propositions stated" (p. 32).

Body-movement therapists do not share this auditory bias. Expressive movements are viewed as an alternative mode of communication rather than as accessory to or preliminary to spoken language. There are a variety of implications that follow from the contrasting observational bases of the psychoanalytic and body-movement–oriented therapies.

Horowitz (1972) maintains that the focus on thought content and control rather than on thought form in the psychoanalytic situation encouraged the tendency to blur the distinction between qualities of thought form and qualities of thought organization. The frequent concurrence of visual images, for example, with regressive content during psychoanalytic hours led, according to Horowitz, to such assumptions as "(1) primary process thought is represented in images and secondary process thought is represented in words; (2) thought in images is more primitive than thought in words; or (3) thought in images is concretistic, and thought in words is abstract" (p. 794). These assumptions are clearly unwarranted. Although the enactive, imagistic, and lexical modes of representations sequentially emerge during the course of development, they each can vary in their degree of complexity, subtlety, and articulation.

Psychotherapeutic modes of representing experience are different, not hierarchically ordered. A nonutilitarian view of symbolism represents yet another challenge to the tendency to hierarchically order human functions. Theorists such as Langer (1942) have reasoned that the need or propensity to symbolically transform experience is a biological "given," i.e., an intrinsic characteristic of the human animal. Langer writes:

Despite the fact that his need gives rise to almost everything we commonly assign to the "higher" life, it is not itself a "higher" form of some "lower" need; it is quite essential, imperious, and general, and may be called "high" only in the sense that it belongs exclusively (I think) to a very complex and perhaps recent genus (p. 40).

If the process of symbolic transformation of experience is as basic an activity as, for example, eating, suppression of the symbol-making function may have a disruptive effect on the integrity of the personality. If it is further assumed that full realization of the brain's capacity for symbolization is realized to the extent that the enactive, imagistic, and lexical modes of representation are called into play, then underutilization, for whatever reason, of any of these modes should be given therapeutic attention.

AGAINST INTERPRETATION

The emphasis on insight as the crucial therapeutic ingredient in psychoanalytically oriented therapy follows from the assumption that changes in overt behavior are dependent upon and follow changes in the structure and content of covert cognitive processes. It is this broader assumption and the correlated emphasis on interpreting hidden meanings that are being questioned by body-movement therapists.

This anti-interpretive trend derives, in part, from the concern with what Sontag (1966) has identified as "the hypertrophy of the intellect at the expense of energy and sensuality in our culture" (p. 17). Critiques of the psychoanalytic method authored by body-movement therapists do not emphasize that any individual's life can accommodate a multiplicity of equally plausible interpretations. Rather, they are guided by the view, expressed most cogently by Sontag, that interpretation must itself be evaluated within a historical view of human consciousness. In some cultural contexts, interpretation is a liberating act. It is a means of revising, of transvaluing, of escaping the dead past. In other cultural contexts, it is reactionary, impertinent, cowardly, stifling (p. 17).

The body-movement therapists believe we are living in such a time. Interpretations typically take the sensory experience of an event for granted and proceed from there. Sharpness of sensory experience cannot be taken for granted in our culture. All of the conditions of modern life conspire to dull the senses. Overproduction of material goods, media bombardment, overcrowding, noise pollution, the accelerating rate of social change, bureaucratization, and so forth are all believed to be contributing to a massive sensory anesthesia. Moreover, as society has become more "psychologized," man, according to several theorists, has become increasingly disembodied. Rieff (1963) claims that the Freudian "analytic attitude" predisposes contemporary man to focus more on the determinants of action than on the action itself. May (1969) has asserted that the schizoid condition is a general tendency in our culture. This trend is reflected in the changing ecology of psychopathology. The experience of inner emptiness, boredom, inauthenticity, apathy, dread of intimacy, protective shallowness, pseudoinsightfulness, hypochondriasis, and an unappeasable hunger for exciting experiences to fill the sense of inner void have become increasingly common manifestations of psychopathology in our time (Kernberg, 1975). Psychotherapists are being confronted, in increasing numbers, with patients who "act out" their conflicts instead of sublimating or repressing them and/or with patients who are suffering from characterological problems highlighted by schizoid or narcissistic detachment (Guntrip, 1969; Kernberg, 1975). The chief block to therapy presented by such patients is emotional inaccessibility. Purportedly, the search for hidden meanings with such patients further depletes or reinforces their already impoverished ability to participate in the pure, untranslatable, sensuous immediacy of concrete experiences. The Polsters (1974) claim that the emphasis placed on the transferential or "as-if" aspects of the Freudian therapeutic relationship clouded the basic issue of direct experience. Shapiro (1975) similarly argues that a preoccupation with listening for interpretable derivatives or clues to unconscious neurotic conflicts can give rise to a discrediting of the process of conscious self-direction.

In contemporary psychoanalytic thinking, consciousness is no longer assigned a passive and innocuous role in guiding behavior (Schafer, 1976). Moreover, in the practice of psychoanalytic therapy, "what we do" does not count less than "why we do it." Interpretations are often essential to removing those resistances that interfere with "authentic experiencing" or "being." With schizoid and obsessional patients, in particular, psychoanalytic therapists make use of interpretations in order to delimit and curtail mentation in the lexical mode so as to make available simple, direct bodily experiences. In other words, interpretations are not merely "explanations"; they can be used to widen the range of sensory channels that are excited by experience. Self-knowledge has never been regarded, by traditional therapists, as an end in itself.[4]

In any case, the emphasis in the body-movement therapies is upon helping patients become aware of how they behave the way they do rather than why. Each approach, states Brown (1973), has developed its own techniques to help the patient "reclaim in immediate awareness his largely desensitized sensorimotor-af-

---

4 Psychoanalysts (e.g., Schimek, 1975) have recently acknowledged the possibility that insight might follow rather than precede personality change.

fective modalities by making the patient actively attend to them"
(p. 99). Implicit in this view is the hypothesis that the emotional
experience of overcoming a resistance is necessary and sufficient
to bring about changes in personality.

Emphasis on the immediacy of concrete experience rather
than upon the interpretation of experience does not necessarily
reflect a new species of anti-intellectualism (as has often been
charged). Contemporary art, as well, is concerned primarily with
the analysis and extension of sensations. McLuhan (1964) calls
contemporary artists "experts in sensory awareness." For Sontag
(1966),

> transparence is the highest, most liberating value in art—
> and in criticism—today. Transparence means experienc-
> ing the luminousness of the thing itself, of things being
> what they are. The function of criticism should be to show
> how it is what it is, even that it is what it is rather than to
> show what it means. In place of hermeneutics we need an
> erotics of art (p. 14).

It would appear as if art, psychological forms, and social
forms all reflect each other and change with each other. From
this perspective, the innovative practices of the body-movement
therapies can be seen as an evolutionary phase in the history of
psychoanalytically enlightened therapy.

OVERCOMING RESISTANCES: THE REICHIAN INFLUENCE

As previously noted, the divergent forms of body-movement
therapy do not question the need to make inferences about unconscious mental processes and/or repressed memories of past

traumatic events. Body-movement therapies additionally share with traditional practitioners the view that the making conscious of the unconscious does not take place directly but rather by the gradual elimination of resistance to consciousness. Loewald (1960) has written, "In sculpturing, the figure to be created comes into being by taking away from the material; in painting, by adding something to the canvas" (p. 12). He maintains that in analysis, as in sculpting, the "true form" (of the patient) comes into being by chiseling away the transference distortions and resistances and that, as in sculpture,

> we must have, if only in rudiments, an image of that which needs to be brought into its own. The patient, by revealing himself to the analyst, provides rudiments of such an image through all the distortions—an image which the analyst has to focus in his mind, thus holding it in safe keeping for the patient to whom it is mainly lost (p. 12).

Body-movement therapists emphasize such images as thawing out, softening, dissolving, and loosening muscular rigidity to describe the process of overcoming resistances. Using the elbow as well as the hands, the Rolfer digs deeply into the patient's muscles, moving them to unlock supporting tissue. The Rolfer stretches, tones, and repositions the body musculature to establish natural alignment with the forces of gravity.

In general, the body-movement therapists would appear to be resurrecting and selectively emphasizing the more ill-fated psychoanalytically inspired writings of Wilhelm Reich (1949). For Freud, the somatic correlate of a psychic disorder manifested itself in a specific fashion (e.g., paralysis or loss of feeling in the extremities). The overall impairment of an individual's predominant action patterns in everyday life remained rather peripheral in comparison to the search for the repressed, unconscious determinants of symptomatic acts and their ideational manifestations. Reich extended and somaticized the insights of Freud. In his practice, he worked at dissolving muscular rigidity as well as psychic resistances. From this work Reich (1961) states:

> The loosening of the rigid muscular attitudes resulted in peculiar somatic sensations, involuntary trembling, jerking of muscles ... and the somatic perception of anxiety, anger, and pleasure.... These manifestations were not the "result," the "causes," or the "accompaniment" of "psychic" processes; they were simply these processes in themselves in the somatic sphere (p. 242).

Reich further maintained that if the psyche and the body express themselves concurrently and identically, then "character attitudes may be dissolved by the dissolution of the muscular armor; and conversely, muscular attitudes by the dissolution of character peculiarities" (1961, p. 293). Within the mainstream of psychoanalytic tradition, the second half of Reich's conclusion has not been given extensive attention. By contrast, body-movement therapies are premised fundamentally on the assumption that changes in personality can be brought about directly by modifying the body structure and its functional motility.

Whereas psychoanalytic therapists (e.g., Mahl, 1968) are apt to view autistic gestures (i.e., movements that are not substitutable for verbal utterances) as a sign that something important but not yet present is forthcoming, dance-movement therapists fully exploit the communicative (rather than informative) function of idiosyncratic expressive movements. By reinforcing partial manifestations of a movement, dance therapists can guide their patients, via successive approximation, toward the full realization of that movement with its accompanying emotional and attitudinal equivalents. Moreover, whereas bioenergetic exercises emphasize the repetitive performance of single acts (e.g., hitting, kicking, breathing) and ritualized stress positions to invoke release, patients in dance therapy are invited to move freely. The term "dance therapy," unfortunately, implies the highly specialized, patterned activity that is dance. In dance therapy, movement is a "free" use of the body, free in the sense that many choices are possible but not in the sense of indiscriminate, undiscriminating action (Siegel, 1975). Movement should also not be confused with the misleading term "body language." "Body language" implies that there is a universal set of gestures by which, if we "read" them properly, we can ferret out the hidden meanings in people's behavior.[5]

In response to their need for a vocabulary of movement, body-movement therapists have explored more highly conscious and organized uses of systems being developed to describe aspects of nonverbal behavior, for example, Ekman and Friesen (1969); Birdwhistell (1970); Davis (1972); Mehrabian (1972); Wiener et al. (1972); Spiegel and Machotka (1974). Many dance therapists believe that the effort-shape system originally developed by Laban (1960) represents the most promising model for describing systematically the richness and variation in quality of the ongoing stream of human movement. Just as a play's script is an impoverished version of the actual "performance," a description of movement, no matter how detailed, when limited to the action itself, yields little information about how the mover

---

5 The symbolization involved in gestures is not the same as that which obtains between verbal symbols and their referents. Whereas words bear a logical or purely arbitrary relation to the subjective experiences they "mean," the movements of the body present the existence of subjective experiences. They do not consist of a system of distinctive signs corresponding to distinct ideas. The movements of the body are, moreover, not systematically coordinated by rules governing their organization and combination (i.e., grammar, syntax). Therefore, we may speak of communication by bodily signs, but there can be no such thing as "body language."

really moved. You know what he did, but you don't know how he did it. Effort-shape analysis describes the variations in how people move in any part of the body regardless of what they are doing; it does not deal directly with the semantic or symbolic meaning of gestures. The effort-shape analyst looks at the flow of movement—at tension and relaxation, strength and lightness, suddenness and sustainment, directness and indirectness, and at the forms the body makes in space. The system describes both how a person relates to the outside world (space) and how he or she discharges and modifies energy (effort). Because it focuses on quality apart from "content" or what is done, it can be used to describe, measure, and classify all human movement (Bartenieff & Davis, 1965).

STYLES OF EXERCISING AUTHORITY

Ever since Freud abandoned his efforts to stimulate reverie by putting his hands on the patient's forehead, the emphasis in the psychoanalytic literature has been upon the hazards associated with physical contact between patient and therapist.

A few scattered references indicate that psychoanalytic therapists believe that the "laying on of hands" can have potential benefits in the treatment of children and severely regressed adults. Marmor (1972) suggests that

in an anaclitic therapeutic approach to seriously ill psychosomatic patients, such as those with ulcerative colitis, or status asthmaticus, a "maternal" holding or stroking of hands may be both helpful and justified. Similar behavior may be indicated with regressed psychotic patients. Non-erotic holding or hugging of pre-adolescent children, especially autistic and withdrawn ones, may even be essential to their therapy (p. 8).

Fromm-Reichman (1950) similarly acknowledges that "at times it may be wise and indicated to shake hands with a patient, or, in the case of a very disturbed person, to touch him reassuringly or not to refuse his gesture of seeking affection or closeness" (p. 69). Both Marmor and Fromm-Reichman, nevertheless, have urged therapists to be extremely thrifty in their physical contacts with patients with neurotic and personality disorders, especially if there is the slightest possibility that they might be interpreted or responded to as erotic.

Psychoanalytic conservatism regarding physical contact between patient and therapist derives fundamentally from Freud's (1919/1959c) belief that structural (i.e., permanent) changes in the personality could only be brought about by conducting therapy "as far as is possible, under privation—in a state of abstinence; and that as far as his relations with the physician are concerned, the patient must have unfulfilled wishes in abundance" (p. 396). Thus, depending on the clinical needs of the moment and the long-term goals of the treatment effort, psychoanalytically oriented therapists strive, through an examination of the patient's problems in the therapeutic relationship, to promote self-understanding rather than to gratify, spurn, or manipulate their patients' love, demands, insults, or misperceptions. By transforming intrapsychic problems into an interpersonal struggle, the psychoanalytic therapist seeks to demonstrate compellingly to their patients, in the here and now, the ways in which they unwarrantedly, stereotypically, and habitually structure relationships in a self-defeating manner. In so doing, the patient is forced to come forth, to move toward the therapist. The psychoanalytic situation thus stimulates yet frustrates the development of an intense, intimate, "real" relationship. Concomitantly, by bringing the patient's authority conflicts into the therapy, the psychoanalytic therapist gradually democratizes the relationship. By judiciously withholding gratifications and by generally refraining from exercising various leadership functions that inhere in their authority positions (e.g., recommending courses of action and vouching for the rightness or success of actions taken), psychoanalytic therapists provoke dilemmas for their patients, the resolution of which strengthens capacities for autonomous self-direction as well as for mutuality. A patient's readiness to participate fully in an egalitarian relationship has come to be seen as an important index of readiness to terminate psychoanalytic therapy (Hurn, 1971).

Many of the innovative practices of the new body-movement therapies can be understood as value-based modifications of the psychoanalytic style of exercising authority. The term "authority" is used here in Etzioni's (1968) sense of "legitimate power," i.e., power that is used in accordance with the subject's values and under conditions that he views as proper. Because they have not been fully sanctioned or legitimized by the medical and academic communities, the new body-movement therapies are often practiced in "alternative institutions," the so-called growth centers.[6] The ecumenical pragmatic atmosphere of these "antiestablishment" settings encourages participation in a variety of modern Western therapies and the ancient disciplines of the East. Body-movement therapists themselves tend to be pluralis-

---

6 Recent evidence (Lieberman & Gardner, 1976) suggests that growth centers may not be an alternative to traditional psychotherapy but rather an addition. Eighty percent of the individuals using the facilities of growth centers, in Lieberman and Gardner's sample, had previous or current psychotherapeutic experience. In so doing, body-movement therapists can provide schizophrenic patients with direct evidence that their body boundaries are firm and definite rather than brittle and easily violated. On the other hand, the immediacy and intensity of touch can break through the emotional inaccessibility of patients whose bodily limits are excessively defined. Therapeutic discussion of the disclaimers and qualifying signals that typically accompany physical contact can also help patients identify when a communication is not to be taken literally, e.g., as a seduction or as a hostile attack.

tic in approach. The combined use of Gestalt, bioenergetic, and Rolfing techniques is not atypical. Moreover, in their efforts to direct and/or influence their patients, body-movement therapists assume either an egalitarian or a benignly authoritarian stance. The division of labor, in Rolfing, is such that the patient is a passive recipient of the procedures that are done to him. Other body-movement therapists attenuate the inherently asymmetrical structure of the "doctor-patient" relationship by expanding their expressive options. Therapist self-disclosure is central to the practice of many of the body-movement therapies. Moreover, they have repudiated taboos against physical expressions of intimacy between therapist and patient.

As yet, the countertransference implications of this permissive orientation have not been subjected to careful scrutiny by the body-movement therapists. By contrast, traditional psychotherapists have emphasized the dangers and ethical responsibilities posed by erotic transference. Undoubtedly, there are therapists who rationalize various forms of erotic interplay with their patients on the grounds of offering restitutive emotional experiences. McCartney (1966) used Reich's ideas to justify sexual intercourse with his female patients. No theory, however, is immune to distorted exploitation. Freud's fearful expectation of this possibility is revealed in his warning to Ferenczi, who sought to combat parental unkindness by acting the part of a loving parent, including the showing of physical affection. In a letter dated December 13, 1931, Freud wrote:

You have not made a secret of the fact that you kiss your patients and let them kiss you. Now picture what will be the result of publishing your technique. There is no revolutionary who is not driven out of the field by a still more radical one. A number of independent thinkers in matters of technique will say to themselves: Why stop at a kiss?

Certainly one gets further when one adopts "pawing" as well, which after all doesn't make a baby. And then bolder ones will come along who will go further, to peeping and showing—and soon we shall have accepted in the technique of analysis the whole repertoire of demi-viergerie and petting parties, resulting in an enormous increase of interest in psychoanalysis among both analysts and patients. The new adherent, however, will easily claim too much of this interest for himself; the younger of our colleagues will find it hard to stop at the point they originally intended, and God the Father Ferenczi, gazing at the lively scene he has created, will perhaps say to himself: Maybe after all I should have halted in my technique of motherly affection before the kiss (Jones, 1957, pp. 163–4).

CHANGING CONCEPTIONS OF COUNTERTRANSFERENCE

The psychotherapist's ethical responsibilities are "sacred." Yet, Freud's concerns about protecting the integrity of psychoanalysis, taken together with the "rule of abstinence," may have promoted a restrictive attitude toward the psychoanalytic therapist's expressive options and emotional reactivity. This trend is reflected in what Tower (1956) has termed the psychoanalyst's "countertransference anxieties." The classical definition of countertransference is, according to Kernberg (1975), "the unconscious reaction of the psychoanalyst to the patient's transference" (p. 50). Kernberg believes that this orientation carries with it the implication that neurotic conflicts of the analyst are the main source of the countertransference and follows from Freud's recommendation that the analyst "overcome" his countertransference. Although this conception of the therapist's role does not necessarily imply loss of spontaneity or detached coolness, its implementation does require disciplined motoric inhibition. Szasz (1957) has suggested that it is much easier to work in this mode if one is of an ascetic temperament. This point of view poses for the therapist, as a theoretical ideal, achieving a state of "desirelessness" vis-à-vis patients. Annie Reich (1950), a proponent of the "classical" conception of countertransference, maintained that any reluctance on the part of the analyst to give up the relationship with the patient indicated unresolved countertransference problems. Searles (1965) emphasized the courage it required for him to publish the hypothesis that genital excitation during analytic hours as well as erotic and romantic dreams about patients might signal the imminent successful termination of the treatment. In general, the antilibidinal pressures exerted by this professional climate may have inhibited the systematic investigation of the therapist's bodily experiences. Havens (1974) has similarly concluded that "psychoanalysis directs attention to misuses of the therapist's self, through the discovery and management of countertransference phenomena. It has not made comparable contributions to the uses of the self" (p. 1).

To counteract this imbalance, growing numbers of psychoanalytically oriented therapists have advocated the use of what Kernberg (1975) has deemed the "totalistic" conception of countertransference. From this perspective, countertransference is defined by Kernberg as "the total emotional reaction of the psychoanalyst to the patient in the treatment situation" (p. 76). Exponents of this point of view have not necessarily relaxed taboos against touching, nor do they agree on the circumstances under which "emotional reactions" might be verbally communicated to a patient. However, they have all fostered a more open exploration of the ways in which psychotherapists emotionally experience and acquire knowledge about their patients. Consequently, the image of the therapist as a "blank screen" or mirror onto which the patient projects his transference is being replaced by the notion of the therapist as a "resonating chamber." Modell (1976), for example, hypothesizes that the diagnosis of narcissistic character disorder is aided by a particular form of the countertransference response, that is, boredom and sleepiness as a result of the patient's state of nonrelatedness. Grossman (1965) suggests that the absence of sexual feelings and impulses in the therapist toward an attractive patient after they have been working together for a sufficiently long period of time can be a noteworthy signal for deeper investigation of a patient's fears about appearing attractive. Heimann (1956) maintains that, whatever our feelings and reactions, however neurotic, in a patient's presence, they are in part, at least, a response to some need of the patient. These revisions, growing out of cautious self-scrutiny, argue for "disciplined subjectivity" rather than "objectivity" on the part of the therapist. As Khan (1974) has argued, experiencing another person can never be a neutralized stance of relating. Moreover, although a therapist might never touch or hold a patient in actuality, all intimacy, even when it is purely verbal, retains its original sense of involving body closeness. This notion is contained in Winnicott's (1965) metaphorical concept of the "holding environment." The term derives from the parental function of holding the infant but more broadly implies the provision of safety and protection from dangers. It is only by providing such a background of safety that the therapist can help his patient come to the liberating recognition that the "body has a mind of its own, and the mind has a body of its own."

REFERENCES

Alexander, F.M. (1974). *The Resurrection of the Body*. New York, NY: Delta.

Allport, G.W., & Vernon, P. (1933). *Studies in Expressive Behavior*. New York, NY: Macmillan.

American Dance Therapy Association (1972). What is dance therapy really? *Proceedings of the 1972 American Dance Therapy Association*.

Auden, W.H. (1957). *Selected Poetry of W.H. Auden*. New York, NY: The Modern Library.

Balint, M. (1968). *The Basic Fault: Therapeutic Aspects of Regression*. London, UK: Tavistock.

Bartenieff, I. (1972). Dance therapy: A new profession or a rediscovery of an ancient role of the dance? *Dance Scope* 7:6–19.

———— & Davis, M. (1965). *Effort-Shape Analysis of Movement: The Unity of Function and Expression*. New York, NY: Albert Einstein College of Medicine.

Becker, E. (1973). *The Denial of Death*. New York, NY: Free Press.

Bergin, A. (1971). Some implications of psychotherapy research for psychotherapeutic practice. *Journal of Abnormal Psychology* 71:235–246.

Birdwhistell, R.L. (1970). *Kinesics and Context*. New York, NY: Ballantine Books.

Brown, M. (1973). The new body psychotherapies. *Psychotherapy: Theory, Research, and Practice* 10:98–116.

Brown, N.O. (1959). *Life Against Death*. Middletown, CT: Wesleyan University Press.

Bruner, J.S. (1964). The course of cognitive growth. *American Psychologist* 19:1–15.

Chace, M. (1953). Dance as an adjunctive therapy with hospitalized mental patients. *Bulletin of the Menninger Clinic* 17:14–19.

Davis, M. (1972). *Understanding Body Movements: An Annotated Bibliography*. New York, NY: Arno Press.

Deutsch, F. (1952). Analytic posturology. *Psychoanalytic Quarterly* 21:196–214.

Ekman, P., & Friesen, W.V. (1969). Nonverbal leakage and clues to deception. *Psychiatry* 32:88–106.

Etzioni, A. (1968). *The Active Society*. New York, NY: The Free Press of Glencoe.

Feldenkrais, M. (1949). *Body and Mature Behavior*. New York, NY: International Universities Press.

Feldman, S.S. (1959). *Mannerisms of Speech and Gesture in Everyday Life*. New York, NY: International Universities Press.

Fisher, S. (1973). *Body Consciousness*. Englewood Cliffs, NJ: Prentice Hall.

Frank, J.D. (1972). The bewildering world of psychotherapy. *The Journal of Social Issues* 28:27–43.

Freud, A. (1968). Acting out. *International Journal of Psychoanalysis* 49:165–170.

Freud, S. (1913). Totem and taboo. *Standard Edition* 13.

——— (1923). The ego and the id. *Standard Edition* 19.

——— (1940). An outline of psycho-analysis. *Standard Edition* 23:139–208.

——— (1959a). Fragment of an analysis of a case of hysteria. *Collected Papers* (Vol. 2). New York, NY: Basic Books. (Original work published 1905.)

——— (1959b). Further recommendations in the technique of psychoanalysis. *Collected Papers* (Vol. 2). New York, NY: Basic Books. (Original work published 1913.)

———— (1959c). Turnings in the ways of psychoanalytic therapy. *Collected Papers* (Vol. 2). New York, NY: Basic Books. (Original work published 1919.)

Friedlander, P. (1964). *Plato*. New York, NY: Pantheon Books.

Fromm-Reichmann, F. (1950). *Principles of Intensive Psychotherapy*. Chicago, IL: University of Chicago Press.

Gendlin, E.T. (1962). *Experiencing and the Creation of Meaning*. New York, NY: The Free Press of Glencoe.

Grossman, C.M. (1965). Transference, countertransference, and being in love. *Psychoanalytic Quarterly* 34:249–256.

Guntrip, H. (1969). *Schizoid Phenomena, Object Relations and the Self*. New York, NY: International Universities Press.

Havens, L.L. (1974). The existential use of self. *The American Journal of Psychiatry* 131:1–10.

Heimann, P. (1956). On counter-transference. *International Journal of Psychoanalysis* 31:81–84.

Horowitz, M.J. (1972). Modes of representation of thought. *Journal of the American Psychoanalytic Association* 20:793–819.

Hurn, H.T. (1971). Toward a paradigm of the terminal phase. *Journal of the American Psychoanalytic Association* 19:332–348.

Janov, A. (1970). *The Primal Scream*. New York, NY: Dell.

Jones, E. (1957). *Life and Work of Sigmund Freud* (Vol. 3). New York, NY: Basic Books.

Kernberg, O. (1975). *Borderline Conditions and Pathological Narcissism*. New York, NY: Jacob Aronson.

Khan, M.M.R. (1974). *The Privacy of the Self*. New York, NY: International Universities Press.

Laban, R. (1960). *The Mastery of Movement*. London, UK: MacDonald and Evans.

Lacan, J. (1968). The mirror phase. *New Left Review* 51:71–78.

Langer, S.K. (1942). *Philosophy in a New Key*. Cambridge, MA: Harvard University Press.

Lévi-Strauss, C. (1967). *Structural Anthropology*. New York, NY: Anchor.

Lieberman, M.A., & Gardner, J.R. (1976). Institutional alternatives to psychotherapy. *Archives of General Psychiatry* 33:157–162.

Loewald, H. (1960). On the therapeutic action of psychoanalysis. *International Journal of Psychoanalysis* 41:1–18.

Loewenstein, R.M. (1956). Some remarks on the role of speech in psychoanalytic technique. *International Journal of Psychoanalysis* 37:460–468.

Lowen, A. (1958). *Physical Dynamics of Character Structure*. New York, NY: Grune & Stratton.

——— (1967). *The Betrayal of the Body*. London, UK: Collier.

Mahl, G.F. (1968). Gestures and body movements in interviews. In J. Shlien (Ed.), *Research in Psychotherapy* (Vol. 3). Washington, DC: American Psychological Association.

Marin, P. (1976). The new narcissism. *Reflections* 11:1–16.

Marmor, J. (1972). Sexual acting-out in psychotherapy. *The American Journal of Psychoanalysis* 32:3–8.

May, R. (1969). *Love and Will*. New York, NY: Norton.

McCartney, J. (1966). Overt transference. *Journal of Sex Research* 2:227–237.

McLuhan, M. (1964). *Understanding Media: The Extensions of Man*. New York, NY: Signet Books.

Mehrabian, A. (1972). *Nonverbal Communications*. Chicago, IL: Aldine-Atherton.

Merleau-Ponty, M. (1962). *Phenomenology of Perception*. New York, NY: Humanities Press.

Modell, A. (1976). "The holding environment" and the therapeutic action of psychoanalysis. *Journal of the American Psychoanalytic Association* 24:285–309.

Nietzsche, F. (1954). Thus spoke Zarathustra. In W. Kaufmann (Ed.), *The Portable Nietzsche*. New York, NY: Viking Press.

Paul, I.H. (1973). *Letters to Simon*. New York, NY: International Universities Press.

Perls, F. (1971). *Gestalt Therapy Verbatim*. New York, NY: Bantam Books.

Pesso, A. (1969). *Movement in Psychotherapy: Psychomotor Techniques and Training*. New York, NY: New York University Press.

Piaget, J. (1951). *The Origins of Intelligence in Children*. New York, NY: International Universities Press.

———— & Inhelder, B. (1969). *The Psychology of the Child*. New York, NY: Basic Books.

Polster, E., & Polster, M. (1974). *Gestalt Therapy Integrated*. New York, NY: Vintage Books.

Reich, A. (1950). On the termination of analysis. *International Journal of Psychoanalysis* 31:179–183.

Reich, W. (1949). *Character Analysis*. New York, NY: Orgone Institute Press.

———— (1961). *Function of the Orgasm*. New York, NY: Farrar, Straus, and Giroux.

Reik, T. (1949). *Fragment of a Great Confession*. New York, NY: Farrar and Strauss.

Rieff, P. (1961). *Freud: The Mind of the Moralist*. New York, NY: Doubleday.

———— (1963). *Freud: Therapy and Technique*. New York, NY: Collier Books.

Rolf, I.P. (1963). Structural integration. *Systematics* 1:66–83.

Rosen, V. (1961). The relevance of "style" to certain aspects of defense and the synthetic function of the ego. *International Journal of Psychoanalysis* 42:447–457.

——— (1969). Sign phenomena and their relationship to unconscious meaning. *International Journal of Psychoanalysis* 50:197–207.

Schachtel, E.G. (1959). *Metamorphosis: On the Development of Affect, Perception, Attention, and Memory*. New York, NY: Basic Books.

Schachter, S. (1964). The interaction of cognitive and physiological determinants of emotional state. In L. Berkowitz (Ed.), *Advances in Experimental Social Psychology*. New York, NY: Academic Press.

Schafer, R. (1970). The psychoanalytic vision of reality. *International Journal of Psychoanalysis* 51(3):279–297.

——— (1973). The termination of brief psychoanalytic psychotherapy. *International Journal of Psychoanalytic Psychotherapy* 2:135–148.

——— (1976). *A New Language for Psychoanalysis*. New Haven, CT: Yale University Press.

Scheflen, A.E. (1964). The significance of posture in communication systems. *Psychiatry* 27:316–331.

Schimek, J.G. (1975). A critical re-examination of Freud's concept of unconscious mental representation. *International Review of Psychoanalysis* 2:171–187.

Schoop, T. (1971). Philosophy and practice. *American Dance Therapy Newsletter* 5:3–5.

Searles, H.F. (1965). Oedipal love in the countertransference. In *Collected Papers on Schizophrenia and Related Subjects*. New York, NY: International Universities Press.

Siegel, E.V. (1973). Movement therapy as a psychotherapeutic tool. *Journal of the American Psychoanalytic Association* 21:333–343.

Siegel, M.B. (1975). *Please Run on the Playground*. Hartford: Connecticut Commission on the Arts.

Shapiro, D. (1975). Dynamic and holistic ideas of neurosis and psychotherapy. *Psychiatry* 33:218–226.

Sharpe, E.F. (1938). *Dream Analysis: A Practical Handbook for Psychoanalysis*. New York, NY: Norton.

Sontag, S. (1966). *Against Interpretation*. New York, NY: Delta.

Spiegel, J., & Machotka, P. (1974). *Messages of the Body*. New York, NY: Free Press.

Sullivan, H.S. (1954). *The Psychiatric Interview*. New York, NY: Norton.

Szasz, T. (1957). On the experiences of the analyst in the psychoanalytic situation. *Journal of the American Psychoanalytic Association* 4:197–223.

Tillich, P. (1962, February). *Psychoanalysis and Existentialism*. Conference of the American Association of Existential Psychology and Psychiatry.

Tower, L.E. (1956). Countertransference. *Journal of the American Psychoanalytic Association* 4:224–255.

Wiener, M., Devoe, S., Rubinow, S., & Geller, J.D. (1972). Nonverbal behavior and nonverbal communication. *Psychological Review* 3:185–214.

Winnicott, D. (1965). *The Maturational Processes and the Facilitating Environment*. New York, NY: International Universities Press.

Wolff, W. (1943). *The Expression of Personality: Experimental Depth Psychology*. New York, NY: Harper & Brothers.

CHAPTER 2

Adult Men as Romantic Lovers

[J.D. Geller & R.A. Howenstine (1980). In K.S. Pope (Ed.), *On Love and Loving* (61–89). San Francisco, CA: Jossey-Bass.]

This chapter concerns the unfolding of romantic love in the lives of adult men. Many sources of inspiration have guided our approach to this majestic theme. We bring to this work our experiences as men, friends, lovers, husbands, and fathers. In our efforts to struggle with romantic love as psychotherapists and scholars, we are particularly indebted to Barzun (1961), Levinson et al. (1978), Loewald (1978), and Schafer (1976). They have convinced us that a comprehensive investigation of romantic love would include and specify the interrelations among the bodily changes that men label romantic love, the subjective experience and meanings, both conscious and unconscious, of these bodily changes, the expressive and instrumental ways in which men love romantically, the interpersonal modes (heterosexual, homosexual) within which men love romantically, and the situational, historical, and developmental contexts in which these events take place. To realize such a goal would require the study of romantic love, conjointly, from the multiple vantage points of biology, history, psychology, and sociology. Existing theories and research on romantic love have rarely integrated these now disparate perspectives. There is in fact a lack of information and research about the genesis, development, and vicissitudes of romantic love in the adult male. To seek clarity about these complex issues is worthy of a lifetime's commitment. We regard the discussion that follows as a "work in progress." Our hope is to encourage clear and systematic thinking about the evolving experiences, meanings, and functions of romantic love during adulthood.

MEN AS ROMANTIC LOVERS

Romantic love is an elusive concept that defies singular definition. Traditionally, romantic love has been viewed as an abstract noun, that is, as an entity with a name of its own and adjectivally designated properties of its own. Because the concept synthesizes into one commanding image complex and paradoxical themes, a wide variety of different and sometimes antithetical properties have been attributed to romantic love. A partial listing of these characteristics includes passion, tenderness, joy, anger, envy, hate, security, excitement, novelty, anxiety, intrigue, power, frustration, danger, elation, disorganization, and ecstasy (Walster & Walster, 1978). In other words, men are used to thinking of the characteristics of romantic love and not of themselves as romantic lovers. Schafer (1976) has concluded that this mode of thinking predisposes men to concretize and personify the concept of love. Thus men "speak of what it is, what it does, of its properties, and its tendencies, of its source and its influence" (p. 271). Such a view encourages a belief in the existence of a fundamental category of consciousness that can unequivocally be called romantic love, despite evidence to the contrary. There is research to suggest that the same visceral and autonomic changes (e.g., a flushed face, a pounding heart) occur in various emotional and nonemotional states (Woodworth & Schlosberg, 1954) and that the same state of physiological arousal can be labeled in terms of a great variety of emotions (Schachter, 1964). Such findings indicate that the subjective experience of romantic love is always mediated by a personal interpretation. Or to paraphrase Ortega y Gasset (1957), love, in its very essence, is choice. Anthropomorphizing romantic love, however, permits men to disavow responsibility for their choices. It is commonplace to hear men claim that romantic love "caused" their behavior. For these reasons, we advocate the implementation of Schafer's (1976) recommendation that only verbs and adverbs be used when discussing romantic love. When presenting our own views, we shall try to speak of loving romantically as a *how* or as a *thus* rather than as a reified metaphor.

The Facts and Fictions of Romantic Love

Social scientists, however, have relied heavily on the use of reified metaphors when speaking of romantic love. For example, in his writings, Freud used the term "libido" to denote the sexual energy that is directed toward the mental representation of a loved person. Schafer (1976, p. 280) has recently acknowledged that at its root libido is a "pseudoscientific poetic metaphor which enables psychoanalysts to endow discussions of sex, pleasure, and love with the (presumed) dignity of mechanics, hydraulics or electrostatics."

Social scientists have also been vulnerable to collapsing the distinction between the social facts and fictions of romantic love. In 1962, Albert Ellis offered the following composite portrait of the romantic lover. We believe his rendering illustrates this trend.

The romantic lover is unrealistic, he over-evaluates and fictionalizes his beloved. He is verbal and aesthetic about his love. He is aggressively individualistic. He insists utterly on his own romantic love choice, and on all but absolute lack of restraint in that choice. He is ... demanding perfectionistic... antisexual. He acknowledges the value of sexuality only when it is linked to love. He is... changeable, frequently going from one violent passion to another. He is jealous, often intensely so, of his beloved. He tends to emphasize physical attractiveness above all else. He is sentimental, passionate and intense. He is supposed to love madly and to be violently in love, rather than affectionately loving. Finally, in today's world, the romantic lover invariably stresses marrying only for love, and is likely to believe that one should never remain married when love dies. For him, too, the death of love from his marriage tends to become sufficient license for every sort of adultery (p. 32).

Ellis calls these "the facts of love." Psychoanalysts might recognize in this portrait the purportedly universal tendency among men to design situations that reawaken the oedipal theme and its corresponding affects. Yet Ellis's rendering does not grow out of an exact empirical representation of the ways in which today's men love romantically. In its essential features, this summary description owes more to the love literature, particularly that of the Middle Ages, than to empirically replicable observations about contemporary men. The justification for such an approach follows presumably from the generally accepted assumption that romantic love represents the historical persistence of courtly love. Yet the historical significance of courtly love itself is enmeshed in controversy.

The Art of Courtly Love, written by Andreas Capellanus early in the 13th century, represents the first effort to record a "system of courtly love." The basic idea of courtly love, as described by Capellanus, is that the lady is to be worshipped, that she is to be intensely desired and ardently pursued, not only because of her intrinsic beauty and nobility, but because of her capacity to endow the man with virtue through her acceptance of him. The lady, in turn, is to judge her pursuer, not on the basis of incidental qualities, but on the basis of his character, the latter being defined and demonstrated through the performance of acts of gentleness and courtesy (13th century/1969, p. 40).

Social scientists have tended to read Capellanus's book as an accurate description of a way of life found in the so-called "courts of love." From the text, they have inferred that medieval romanticism was an exceptionally class-limited form of love, invariably adulterous, and conducted in a ritual-like fashion. Scholars tend to agree that courtly love, as an idea, originated as a revolt against the sexual repressiveness of early Christianity and its doctrine of marriage. There are eminent medievalists, however, who doubt whether courtly love as a social institution ever existed. For some, Capellanus's book exemplifies a rather vague complex of literary conventions (Halverson, 1970). Still others argue that Capellanus's treatise should be read as a "spoof" and/or that the "rules" of courtly love were instructions for a court "game" (Donaldson, 1965). Thus, in its very origins, romantic love challenges our notions of "reality" by threatening the distinction between fact and fiction. Consequently, at the center of many perennial debates about romantic love can be found a delicate and reciprocal relation between the social reality of romantic love and the unique imaginative metaphors that influential men have used to convey the idea of romantic love. Throughout history, there have been "fictional" representations of romantic love that have been experienced by their audiences as accurate sociological descriptions. Such works of art are "exemplary" (Sontag, 1966); they invite us to imitate them. Their creators are likely to become our romantic heroes. For many of our peers, this privileged status is currently occupied by such men as Woody Allen, Jackson Browne, Bob Dylan, Dustin Hoffman, Mick Jagger, Paul McCartney, Paul Mazursky, Eric Rohmer, Philip Roth, Paul Simon, François Truffaut, John Updike, John Voight, Neil Young, and so on. Perhaps it is during adolescence that we are most vulnerable to imitating such artists' eloquent images of romantic love.

As Ortega y Gasset (1957, p. 24) realized, romantic love has been so extensively eulogized that "before experiencing it we all know about it, place high value on it, and are resolved to practice it, like an art or profession."

Empirical Study of Adult Development

The longitudinal and/or biographical study of adult development, like the study of romantic love, is just beginning. Whatever data are available suggest that we have been guided by fundamental misconceptions in our thinking about adult men. The pioneering studies of R.L. Gould (1972), Levinson et al. (1978), and Vaillant (1977) indicate that the process of entry into adulthood is far more lengthy and complex than has usually been imagined. Their work further suggests that the capacity to love romantically evolves during adulthood in accordance with developmental principles and timetables. By contrast, it has been traditionally assumed that romantic love is "a young man's sentimental passion" (Freud, 1921) and that adolescence is the last developmentally given period in the evolution of the personality. With few exceptions (Erikson, 1968; Jung, 1971), theorists have represented adulthood as a plateau, with personality changes taking place only under the impact of massive stress due to environmental trauma or the reactivation of childhood conflicts.

The psychoanalytic concept of transference is indispensable to understanding the historical dimension of a man's love life. Yet it too has carried with it the erroneous implication that each new romance is a "mere repetition" of early familial attachments, including their inherent frustrations and disruptions. Freud (1915/1953e, p. 387) maintained that "there is no love that does not reproduce infantile prototypes." In the essay "The dynamics of transference" (1912/1953d, p. 313), he wrote that the childhood capacity to love "forms a cliché" or stereotype in the person that perpetually repeats and reproduces itself as life goes on. Although emotions originally felt toward one or the other parent are undoubtedly revived when we "fall in love," we are not condemned to mindless reenactment of our early love relations throughout the life cycle. Even if a man's loving relationships are burdened with conflicts enduring since childhood, the quality and substance of these conflicts will undergo decisive changes in response to the unique challenges of each developmental era. This conclusion is supported by the theory and findings of Levinson et al. (1978) as well as Loewald's (1978) reformulation of the psychoanalytic concepts of transference and narcissism.

The integration of these complementary frameworks would permit research that locates a man and his efforts to love romantically within his ongoing biographic context. We have relied heavily on these works to develop the hypothesis that men manage the complexities of loving romantically in ways that are influenced profoundly by the ever-changing sociocultural conditions and developmental tasks that confront us as we age. Our primary aim in the next section will be to present the framework of Levinson et al. (1978) for the analysis of adult development. Once this is presented, we shall turn our attention to the following questions: Does our culture support or undermine men's efforts to love romantically? How do men reconcile the dualities of love: the tensions between longing and consummation, sexuality and tenderness, being loved and loving, passion and harmony, and so on? How does loving romantically contribute to psychological growth and development? What psychological functions does loving romantically serve at different stages of the life cycle?

A MODEL OF ADULT DEVELOPMENT

The concept of "life structure" is fundamental to the biographical approach of Levinson et al. (1978) to understanding adult development. Levinson (p. 41) defines life structure as "the basic pattern or design of a person's life at a given time" and suggests that it is composed of three integrated components: one's sociocultural world, one's self, and one's mode of participation in society. He visualizes the life structure as a "tapestry" which inherently interconnects the sociocultural world in which a person is embedded, the person's relationship with the external world, and his personality as it is reflected in these relationships. In other words, for Levinson the self or personality is an intrinsic element of the life structure and not a separate entity. The self in Levinson's theory is comparable to the psychoanalytic concept of character. Such concepts account for the stability, consistency, and predictability of our reactions to internal and external events. The sociocultural world, however, "provides a landscape, a cast of characters, a variety of resources and constraints out of which a man fashions his own life" (p. 42). The theory thus deals with the evolving process of mutual interpenetration between these components rather than with personality development per se. When Levinson speaks of adult development, he is referring to the evolution of the life structure.

According to this theory, a life structure is viable "if it works in the world," and it is suitable to the extent that it allows a man to "live out crucially important aspects of his self" (p. 54). A life structure may be both viable and suitable (a dream come true), viable but not suitable (externally viewed as successful but experienced as corrupt or empty), suitable but not viable (experienced as meaningful but economically and socially un-rewarded or scorned), or none of these (disastrous from societal and self perspectives). Since the "self" contains more wishes, talents, fantasies, values, modes of action, ideals, and potentiali-ties than can be expressed within any single life structure, flaws and contraindications can be found in all men's lives.

To understand a particular man's evolving life structure, it is necessary to clarify the key choices he has made and how he has dealt with their resulting consequences. The most important choices in adult life have to do with work, family, friendships, and love relationships. From Levinson's perspective, to choose something means to form a relationship with it: "The relation-ship becomes a vehicle for living out certain aspects of the self and for participating in the world" (p. 18). The major compo-nents of a life structure thus include the person's relationships with self, with other individuals, with groups, symbols, orga-nizations—with any aspect of the social or physical world that has significance for the person.

Although lives differ widely in the nature and patterning of these components, the biographical analyses of Levinson et al. (1978) revealed two consistent themes: Most men make their occupation and their marriage-family relationships the central components of their life structure, and the life structure evolves through a relatively orderly sequence during the adult years. The essential nature of the sequence consists of an alternating series of stable and transitional periods. The stable periods ordinarily last some 6 to 8 years, the transitional periods 4 to 5 years. The primary developmental task of a stable period is to build a life structure. To do so, a man must make crucial life choices, form a structure about them, and pursue his goals and values within that framework. The primary developmental task of a transitional period

> is to terminate the existing structure and to work toward the initiation of a new structure. This requires a man to reappraise the existing life structure, to explore various possibilities for change in the world and in the self, and to move toward the crucial choices that will form the basis for a new life structure in the ensuing stable period (p. 100).

The findings of Levinson et al. (1978) further indicate that each new transitional and stable period is rendered unique because of the changing constellation of developmental tasks that confront us as we age.[7] As an example, the transition into early adulthood (roughly ages 17 to 22) carries with it the special task of separating from one's family of origin. The distinctive character of the period extending from 22 to 28 follows from the overriding task of balancing exploration of the possibilities for adult living with the antithetical task of making a commitment to a stable life structure. By contrast, the shift from early adulthood to middle adulthood (roughly ages 40 to 45) revolves around men's efforts to integrate life's key polarities: young/old, male/female, destruction/creation, separation/attachment, and so on.

---

7 Levinson et al. (1978) acknowledge that the age linkages of the adult stages represent a preliminary picture of the timetable of the periods and that they are suggestive rather than conclusive. Nevertheless, Gould (1972) has independently arrived at a similar sequence of periods in adult personality development.

At mid-life, moreover, the reality and inevitability of one's personal death and the finitude of time force themselves, painfully, on the attention of men. Neugarten (1968, p. 97), in a study concerning the changing time perspective in middle age, reported that "life is restructured in terms of time-left-to-live rather than time-since-birth." Jaques (1965) maintains that these changes are primarily responsible for the essential features of the "mid-life crisis."

Loving romantically can serve enduring and changing, diverse, and contradictory functions during these successive transformations of the life structure. In our culture, "romantic solutions" (Becker, 1973) to problems in living appear to be a particularly conspicuous feature of transitional periods, irrespective of the era in which they occur. For many young men, romantic love is synonymous with sexual love. For these men, romantic love can serve as a rhetorical device to obtain the pleasures of sexual gratification with a variety of women. During the transition into adulthood, men are also seeking an affirmation of their autonomy and competence. Loving romantically is frequently the pathway for realizing these goals and the catalyst that precipitates the creation of a first, provisional life structure. In our culture, for example, when this chapter was written, men tended to marry during the early adult transition. Divorce and marital problems, however, have tended to peak during the developmental period that Levinson refers to as the "age thirty transition." During the mid-life transition, a man may seek in romantic love a reaffirmation of his youthfulness and potency or the opportunity to "break out" of an existing life structure. Extramarital affairs that serve this latter function can either help a man correct the imbalances of early adulthood or further contribute to the disharmonies inherent in a life structure. If they are experienced as taking place "outside" of the life structure, such romantic relationships, in our experience as psychotherapists, are not likely to be enduring. They appear to be in their very essence transitional or preparatory relationships. In our clinical work, we have also found that whereas the emphasis in young adulthood is upon being loved romantically, men at mid-life seem to be more preoccupied with their capacity to love the other romantically. Men at mid-life and beyond also appear to be more comfortable with loving romantically. R.L. Gould's (1972, p. 526) findings similarly indicate that in the 50s there is a "mellowing and warming up." He reports that men come to value their own spouses more as a source of companionship and are less likely to regard them as a parent or as a source of supplies during this era. Loewald's (1978) theorizing lends further support to the view that loving romantically holds the promise of healing the structural flaws in our personalities. He has demonstrated how transference, in its nonpathological meaning, can be understood as "the dynamic of psychological growth and development" (p. 47). Loewald's reasoning, based upon Kierkegaard's notion of the "dialectic of repetition," is that repetitions of transference paradigms during adulthood contain aspects of novelty as well as an active and imaginative reorganization and elaboration of early love relations and that, consequently, our love relations do not remain determined by the unmodified power of infantile prototypes.

It is generally assumed that it is in their romantic choices that men reveal their essential natures. In the following sections of this chapter, we shall examine how romantic choices, as a component of the life structure, are saturated with self and by the conditions of, and opportunities provided by, our sociocultural world. This presentation will focus on three trends that may change decisively the ways in which men love romantically: our culture's reevaluation of romanticism, the impact of the "new feminism" on work and sexual relationships, and our culture's growing preoccupation with narcissism.

THE ROMANTIC VISION OF REALITY

In 1880, Thomas Hardy wrote: "Romanticism will exist in human nature as long as human nature itself exists. The point is (in imaginative literature) to adopt that form of romanticism which is the mood of the age" (cited in Orel, 1969, p. 189). Hardy's statement recognizes two distinct but related meanings of the word "romantic." Following Barzun (1961), we shall refer to these meanings as "intrinsic romanticism" and "historic romanticism."

Intrinsic Romanticism

As a result of the works of Barzun (1961) and Schafer (1970), we have come to view "intrinsic romanticism" not merely as a product of literary ingenuity but rather as an archetypal perspective on "reality testing." At the core of intrinsic romanticism, Barzun has identified "the effort to create order out of experience individually required" (p. 94). The romantic emphasizes action and involvement in the world, admires energy, and idealizes individuality, self-expression, and authenticity. Extending the work of Frye (1957), Schafer has revealed that the terms "comic," "tragic," and "ironic" similarly refer to the "visions of reality" that emerge whenever the imaginative mind confronts the world. According to Schafer, these four organizing or structural principles shape each man's mode of comprehending the form and content of human situations and the changes they may undergo. Each represents a broad outlook, a theory of life, and a style of understanding and representing everyday ideas and judgments. In complex combinations, they define each man's overall "vision of reality." Clashes between such visions cannot be settled by simple appeals to the "evidence." As these visions influence the determination of facts and their interrelations and implications, men who are generally considered to be realistic and objective can therefore be expected to disagree in all sorts of ways about romantic love. Similarly, the loving relationships of those men whose life structures are saturated with the romantic vision can be expected to be quite different from those for whom it occupies a peripheral position.

In the romantic vision as formulated by Schafer (1970),

> life is a quest or a series of quests. The quest is a perilous, heroic, individualistic journey. Its destination or goal combines some or all of the qualities of mystery, grandeur, sacredness, love, and possession by or fusion with some higher power or principle (Nature, Virtue, Beauty, etc.). The seeker is an innocent, adventurous hero, and the quest ends, after crucial struggles, with exaltation (p. 31).

The reward of the quest usually is or includes a wife. In mythic literature, "this bride-figure is ambiguous, her psychological connection with the mother in the Oedipus fantasy is insistent, and she is often found in a perilous, forbidden, or tabooed place" (Frye, 1957, p. 193).

The study by Levinson et al. (1978) of male adult development indicates that the archetype of the quest embraces essential aspects of men's lives. This study suggests that romantic dreams are not confined to adolescence, nor is the failure to relinquish adolescent dreams a sign of immaturity. Apparently, most men have a dream about how their lives should be as adults. This dream, according to Levinson, has its roots in childhood but fundamentally changes over time and involves an image, or sense, of one's self in the world. Levinson's findings suggest that throughout early adulthood a man's preoccupation tends to be with himself and the creation of his dream. Other people tend to be valued for what they contribute to his quest. In their attempts to translate this dream into a social reality, many men depend on a "special woman." Levinson suggests that the special woman

> helps to animate the part of the self that contains the Dream.... She shares it, believes in him as its hero, gives it her blessing, joins him on the journey and creates a "boundary space" within which his aspirations can be imagined and his hopes nourished.... The special woman can foster his adult aspirations while accepting his dependency, his incompleteness and his need to make her into something more than (and less than) she actually is (p. 109).

It is with such women that men often fall in love.

A prevailing assumption in the literature is that romantic lovers are unmindful of reality because they idealize their special women (Walster & Walster, 1978). In their structure, romantic quests are analogous to dreams and wish-fulfillment daydreams (Frye, 1957). It does not necessarily follow, however, that romantic lovers are unrealistic or oblivious to complicating details, especially when considering romantic love as a basis for marriage. In his pioneering empirical studies, Rubin (1973) has demonstrated that men undisputedly recognize love as a prerequisite to marriage—not unreasoning love of the "head-over-heels" variety and not love that transcends all obstacles and barriers, but love nonetheless. In the terms of this discussion, Rubin's findings indicate that unqualified romanticism, as reflected in the belief that love can transcend barriers of race, religion, and social class, rarely describes the totality of a man's relationship to romantic love.

Historically, the romantic vision has been most often paired with comic and tragic perspectives on love (Frye, 1957). The unqualified hopefulness of many young lovers represents the commingling of comic and romantic perspectives on romantic love. The comic vision—with its emphasis on optimism, ultimate reconciliations, and sexual gratification unburdened by pain—promises endings that are simply happy. But, as Kafka asserted, "the decisive moment in human development is a continuous one" (1946, p. 279). Adult development, like marriage, is about the "morning after" and brings with it a growing appreciation of the difficulties of loving romantically. Thus, a sense of the tragic begins to temper naive romanticism as we age. The tragic vision confronts us with the realization that the essential conditions of love include the loss of opportunities entailed by every choice, the inevitable clashes between passion and duty, inescapable ambivalence, and the insidious influence of unresolved unconscious processes on loving romantically.

When asked why he had waited till his eighties to divorce his wife, an octogenarian replied, "We were waiting for the children to die." Whatever humor one finds in this joke derives, perhaps, from the tension between its romantic and ironic undercurrents. The ironic vision shares with the tragic vision a readiness to seek out paradoxes, contradictions, and the absurdities of human existence. However, whereas the emotionally overcharged and grandiose inclinations of romantic lovers are supported by the tragic vision, the detachment and self-deprecatory thrust of the ironic vision undermines the very terms of romantic thinking. The heroics, enchantment, idealizations, and blissful joy of loving romantically contrast starkly with the ironic effort not to take any aspect of oneself or others too seriously. We believe that today the struggle to integrate the seemingly incompatible modes of romance and irony is endemic in our culture.

Of the lovers of his day, Tolstoy remarked, "Many people's love would be instantly annihilated if they could not speak of it in French" (Morton, 1899, p. 23). Romantic loving requires a comfort with expressiveness and a capacity to yield to the concrete immediate presence of the other. However, as society has become "psychologized" and infused with a sense of irony, many men have increasingly become "spectators" of themselves. Consequently, many modern men are usually too self-conscious to engage in the rhetoric and aesthetic refinements of romantic love. Such predicaments are exemplified in the films of Woody Allen. In *Annie Hall* and *Manhattan*, Allen's romantic lovers are trying self-consciously to offset genuineness and mockery, commitment and withdrawal, earnestness and absurdity, satire and sentiment. Tension between romance and irony can also give rise to disjunctions between subjective experience and expressivity. Apparently, this trend is widespread among men. In *Family Circle* magazine, Balswick (1979, p. 110) advises troubled readers that many men who love their wives are "unable" to tell them. Rubin's (1973) findings similarly indicate that men are more reluctant than women to express the euphoric feelings that accompany "falling in love." Although they will admit to fewer of the "symptoms" of love, men appear to fall in love more quickly and to cling more tenaciously to a dying affair than women. Durkheim (1951) found that three times as many men as women commit suicide after a disastrous love affair. Hill et al. (1976), in their study of unmarried couples, found that usually the women decided whether and when an affair should end; the men seemed to stick it out to the bitter end. It was also the man who suffered most (felt more depressed, more lonely, less happy, and less free) after the breakup. Women were far more resigned and thus were better able to pick up the pieces of their lives and move on. Rubin's studies, in part, have addressed the question, Are men or women more romantic? His results led him to conclude that the answer depends on which criteria are used to define the essential features of romantic love.

Historic Romanticism

Whereas romanticism as a characteristic of human beings, or certain human beings, is perennial, romanticism as a historical movement may become cultivated, dominant, or devalued in any given period. Extraordinary events appear to stimulate and justify historic romanticism. Barzun (1961) has discerned that romantic periods in history are those that support the creation of a new society different from, and on the ruins of, its immediate forerunner. In the past, cultures were regarded as romantic to the extent that they were characterized by

> a return to the Middle Ages, a love of the exotic, an exaggeration of individualism, a liberation of the unconscious, a reaction against the scientific method, a revival of pantheism, idealism, and Catholicism, a rejection of artistic conventions, a preference for emotions, a movement back to nature or a glorification of force (p. 13).

Such cultural conditions not only lent weight and color to our ancestors' experiences of romantic love but also perhaps, in the last analysis, determined their particular form.

In recent history, these values have been held, either explicitly or implicitly, as "the enemy of reason, science, and democracy" (Barzun, 1961, p. 15). In politics, romanticism has been seen as resulting in the excessive authority that leads to totalitarianism and/or the excessive individualism that leads to anarchy. Literary critics have equated romanticism with easy sentimentality, self-indulgence, utopian aspirations, irrationalism, escapism, indolence, and insanity. In the psychoanalytic community, the romantic vision has been viewed as regressive and childlike, naive and simplistic. "Spurious" is often used as a synonym for "romantic" in academic journals. It is therefore not surprising to find that scholars, as well, have recently emphasized the perils and illusions of romantic love. Pessimism regarding the possibilities of integrating romantic love into an enduring relationship is commonplace. The most eloquent and frequently quoted spokesman for this point of view has been de Rougement (1963):

Romance is by its very nature incompatible with marriage even if the one has led to the other, for it is the very essence of romance to thrive on obstacles, delays, separations, and dreams, whereas it is the basic function of marriage daily to reduce and obliterate these obstacles. Marriage succeeds only in constant physical proximity to the monotonous present. Romance is... incapable of establishing a durable marriage, and it is not an act of courage but one of absurdity to marry someone forever because of a fever that endures for two months (p. 80).

Although the conditions we now live in are different from those of any prior civilization, we are once again living in extraordinary times. During the writing of this chapter, a test-tube baby celebrated her first birthday. The elderly are experimenting with eroticized relationships and living arrangements for which we have no previous models. In a highly publicized trial, a wife sued her husband for rape and then sought a reconciliation. As we enter the 1980s, fundamental changes are occurring in our culture's conceptions of masculinity. It is becoming increasingly difficult to define, in the abstract, sex-role characteristics as either male or female. American films are increasingly portraying men as vulnerable, sensitive, and trusting and not as "macho." Freud's (1905) assumption that the sexual inclinations of all men evolve from "polymorphous perversity" and "bisexuality" embodies today a program of reform for gay activists. In their inquiries regarding fantasy patterning during sexual stimulation for both homosexual and heterosexual couples, Masters and Johnson (1979) reported a high incidence of cross-preference fantasy. Homosexual men and women imagined heterosexual interactions, and, conversely, heterosexual men and women had homosexual fantasies. Sexologists rarely talk about romantic love but instead focus on the behavior of the human sexual apparatus. Nevertheless, their work has sensitized men to the problems that have followed their insistence on dividing lovemaking into foreplay and sexual intercourse. A recent survey of the readership of *Psychology Today* indicates that an androgynous ideal is gaining popularity in our culture (Tavris, 1977).

Concomitantly, there are suggestions that men are questioning the suitability of achievement-dominated life structures. American men today, in unprecedented numbers, are investing their personal relations, especially those with women, with greater emotional importance. A *Playboy*-financed Louis Harris survey of American male values found that men rank love second only to health as their most important need (Brozan, 1979). Many men are active participants in the culturally diffuse yet pervasive "consciousness movement." The emphasis here is upon such values as expressiveness, direct immediate experience, and spontaneity. In parallel, antiromantic opposition to these trends is also growing. Lasch (1978, p. 30), for example, argues that "the current preoccupation with self-discovery, psychic growth, and intimate personal encounters represents unseemly self-absorption, romanticism run rampant." Taken together, these trends suggest that our culture is going through a painful reevaluation of the values associated with historic romanticism.

WORK, SEX, AND THE NEW FEMINISM

Of all the reform movements that began in the 1960s, none appears as enduring as women's efforts to achieve equality with men. There is less support today for men's claim of superiority than during any other historical era. We fundamentally agree with Farber's (1976) conclusion:

In its efforts to redress sexual, social, political, economic, artistic, historical, and religious inequalities, the new feminism has thrown into question all those institutions under whose auspices men and women have sought to combine their lots and join their fates (p. 163).

The division of labor between the sexes is being irreversibly changed. Half of the women in this country are in the paid labor force, including 46% of those with children (Kahne, 1975). Whereas the working wife was a "deviant" role a half century ago, it may soon be the unpaid housewife who feels social pressure to justify her role. A recent survey of upper-middle–class professional husbands suggests that coping with the stresses of dual-career marriages, role differentiation, and the relentless chores of daily life enhances personal growth and leads to a more rewarding marital relationship (Nadelson & Eisenberg, 1977). The privileges of the upper middle class include the possibility of doing work that inspires and gratifies romantic strivings. Finding work that is both suitable to the self and viable in the world is far more problematic for the poor and uneducated. Nevertheless, working-class men pride themselves on the hard work and personal sacrifice they are making as "breadwinners." Many in the past made a "gift" of these sacrifices to their wives and children. Today, according to Goode, "they are told that it was not a gift at all. In fact their wives earned what they received. If work was a sacrifice, they are told, so were all the services, comforts, and self deprivations that women provided" (cited in Friedan, 1979, p. 5). The change that Goode believes most disturbs man

> is a loss of centrality, a decline in the extent to which they are the center of attention. Boys and grown men have always taken for granted that what they were doing was more important than what the other sex was doing. Women's attention was focused on them. Nowadays, the center of attention has shifted more to women (p. 6).

Male reactions to these shifts often include a sense of being unlovable, demeaned, and betrayed. Some men claim that the women's movement is destroying the very cornerstone of men's sexual identity, that it is responsible for unleashing anxiety, envy of women, dread, hostility, and exhaustion, and that it is the main cause of the increase in divorce, separation, and wife battering everywhere in the United States. Whether such claims exaggerate the negative impact of the women's movement has yet to be comprehensively investigated.

When such studies are conducted, we anticipate that they will reveal that men express changing attitudes toward the democratization of male-female relationships at different stages of their lives. For example, the values that Freud expressed in his scientific critiques of romantic love (published in 1910, 1912, and 1918) were "more advanced" than the attitudes that can be discerned in his love letters to his fiancée, Martha Bernays (E.L. Freud, 1961). Freud wrote approximately 900 letters to his fiancée during their 4-year engagement. In these letters, he expressed the belief that equality between the sexes would mean "the disappearance of the most lovely thing the world has to offer us: our ideal of womanhood" (p. 76). Freud's ideal young woman was possessed of "charm, beauty, goodness" and aroused erotic passions in men while remaining passive herself. In his own engagement, Freud conveyed the idea that courtship consisted of masculine initiative overcoming girlish passivity and reticence. Yet, in his later scientific studies, Freud concluded that sexuality must be freed from inclinations toward domination and submission if we are truly to love persons as persons rather than as surrogates for our lost parental love. Rieff (1961, p. 184) puts it this way: "Freud advanced an ideal of love purged of parental influences, an exchange of equals."

The sexual aspects of romantic relationships as well as the division of labor between the sexes are being altered profoundly by women's efforts to achieve equality with men. Males in our culture have traditionally been socialized to offer some degree of commitment to get sex, whereas women have been socialized to bargain with sex to get commitment (Maddock, 1973). This dilemma found expression during the 1950s in the dialectical caricatures of the "sexpot" and the "nice girl." Up until recently, this splitting tendency was paralleled by and also encoded in the paralyzing edict that no man would marry a woman who was not a virgin. This age-old virgin/whore dichotomy is being fundamentally assaulted today by the collapse of chivalry, the modern woman's increasingly insistent demand for sexual fulfillment, the scientific demystification of female sexuality, and strenuous propaganda on behalf of "open marriage" and "creative divorce," as well as the ever-present possibility that any given marriage will end in divorce.

Divorced people used to be considered failures, misfits, neurotics, selfish immoralists. Today, divorces, although still invariably traumatic, can be obtained without stigma and without jeopardizing careers—even in such sensitive fields as politics or the ministry. A century ago, there was only one divorce per 32 marriages in a given year. Nowadays, there is one divorce for every two marriages. Moreover, divorce no longer means the end to married life. Today, four out of five divorced people remarry. And, although many more young people are delaying marriage, 90% of young men and approximately 95% of young women will marry (U.S. Bureau of the Census, 1975).

Census Bureau figures show that, since 1970, the number of unmarried people of the opposite sex sharing a household has doubled from 654,000 to 1.3 million. With such shifts in mind, Farber (1976, p. 165) concluded:

> Courtship at best represented a rather stylized manner in which two people could come to know each other before sex and/or marriage. A young man and young woman today are more apt to begin with sex, and for the kinds of knowing which follows, we have no ready word.

Owing to a growing climate of permissiveness, the availability of efficient contraceptives, legalized abortions, and the promotion of sex as a "healthy" bodily function, young adults today have more sexual freedom than any previous generation. Their music and modes of dancing emphasize consummation rather than longing. Few of the colleges they attend retain parietal rules, and many have coed dormitories. Such trends both reflect and legitimize the pursuit of sexual pleasure as an end in itself. Taboos against adultery also appear to be weakening. The latest Kinsey report indicates that growing numbers of married women are participating in extramarital sexual relationships (Weinberg, 1976). It seems reasonable to conclude that men no longer treat women as "ladies" and that modern sexual imagination supports a preoccupation with variety and multiplicity. These and other "facts" represent symbolic shifts that have great significance for the ways in which men love romantically.

THE FAILURES OF LOVE

The conflict-laden dialectic between the thinking man and his penis has not been reconciled by the growing range of sexual possibilities in the modern world. Sontag (1966) has discerned that a prevailing theme of serious literature is the failure of love. She maintains that the modern cult of love "is the main way in which we test ourselves for strength of feeling, and find ourselves deficient" (p. 47). Lasch (1978) claims that as women have become more accessible as sexual partners, they have also become more threatening. He has observed that "formerly men complained about women's lack of sexual response; now they find this response intimidating and agonize about their capacity to satisfy it" and that "the famous Masters and Johnson report on female sexuality added to these anxieties by depicting women as sexually insatiable, inexhaustible in their capacity to experience orgasm after orgasm" (p. 193).

Taken together, these observations suggest that men today simultaneously overvalue yet are pessimistic about the healing possibilities of sexual love. The changing role of religion and/or spirituality in our culture is deeply implicated in this predicament. For 2000 years, among Christians and Jews, suffering has been a hallmark of a man's "seriousness" (Sontag, 1966). Resisting the temptations of premarital sex or an extramarital affair provided evidence of one's character or seriousness. The allure of unrequited romantic love was particularly appealing to those who were seeking confirmation of their ability "unselfishly" to renounce private desires. Americans no longer believe, with certainty, that "God is on our side." The growing popularity of Eastern philosophy and meditational practices suggests that many young men in our culture are measuring their seriousness today by their ability to evade or transcend suffering and achieve tranquility (Farber & Geller, 1977).

Traditionally, the emphasis has been on subordinating and controlling the body as a prerequisite for spiritual advancement. As our culture increasingly aspires to a life of the body, the relinquishment of "earthly love" for "divine love" has become more problematic, even for Catholic priests. In the wake of our culture's repudiation of the ascetic traditions of Judaism and Christianity, there has appeared a growing readiness to acknowledge that "every man can be subject, if he so chooses, to undifferentiated sexual arousal" (Farber, 1976, p. 170). (The popularity of Erica Jong's [1973] "zipless fuck" suggests that many women too are given to "undifferentiated lust.") Yet, because they are still confined by the generalized prohibitions that their religious traditions bequeathed them, many young men today share with Alexander Portnoy the complaint that they are "sex maniacs" (Roth, 1969). At 33, Portnoy tells his analyst:

And, Doctor, your Honor, whatever your name is—it seems to make no difference how much the poor bastard actually gets, for he is dreaming about tomorrow's pussy even while pounding away at today's. . . . Please, let us not bullshit one another around about "love" and its duration. Which is why I ask: How can I marry someone I "love" knowing full well that five, six, seven years hence I am going to be out on the streets hunting down fresh new pussy—all the while my devoted wife, who has made me such a lovely home, et cetera, bravely suffers her loneliness and rejection? How could I face her terrible tears? I couldn't. How could I face my adoring children? And then the divorce, right. The *child* support, the *alimony*, the *visitation* rights. Wonderful prospect, just wonderful (p. 123).

As a result of hormonal changes, men experience their lust with less urgency as they grow older. Over age 50, psychic erections become rarer, direct friction is often required to stimulate an erection, and orgasm may not be reached with every act of intercourse. This physiologically mediated change may be variously interpreted. As Masters and Johnson (1970, p. 69) discovered, "The susceptibility of the human male to the power of suggestion with regard to his sexual prowess is almost unbelievable." Many men become more passionate and sensual lovers as they age. Intimacy does not flourish if one fears "premature ejaculation." Prolonged lovemaking deepens the possibilities of intimacy. Many men, however, interpret the same bodily changes as evidence of their waning masculinity. Such men are particularly vulnerable to a variety of sexual dysfunctions. For example, although impotence is never due to "age" alone, one fourth of the men surveyed by Weinberg (1976) were impotent by the age of 65 and one half by 75.

A profound loss of self-esteem invariably accompanies the fear that one is incapable of "successful lovemaking" or of making a permanent commitment to a woman. Men in general are reluctant to explore candidly the intimate details of their romances, be they successful or unsuccessful. Even in our sexually permissive culture, romantic lovemaking, on the whole, is still conducted in private. Psychotherapists have privileged access to this private realm. A "therapeutic" outlook and sensibility pervades our contemporary views on romantic love. It is not surprising therefore that psychotherapists, including Erich Fromm (1956), Rollo May (1969), and Otto Kernberg (1976), have become the dominant theoreticians of love in our time. They report that psychotherapists are being consulted, in increasing numbers, by individuals who are suffering from characterological problems highlighted by schizoid or narcissistic detachment. The presenting complaints of such individuals prominently include feelings of emptiness and inauthenticity, the inability to mourn, an unappeasable hunger for exciting experiences to fill a sense of inner void, promiscuous pansexuality, avoidance of dependence, and a simultaneous yearning for yet dread of intimacy (Guntrip, 1969; Kernberg, 1976). Such individuals, on the one hand, appear to be able to gratify, impulsively, their sexual impulses; on the other hand, on closer inspection they are found to be profoundly alienated from their bodies. Their emotional inaccessibility precludes receptivity to the internal and external cues of romantic love. For these reasons, "many patients with a narcissistic personality structure have never fallen or been in love" (Kernberg, 1976, p. 186). The inability to "fall in love," in other words, is coming to be regarded as a sign of significant psychopathology.

If two people truly are to join together and not just place their bodies at each other's disposal, both must render themselves vulnerable, and each must be able to receive the gift of the other. In order to realize this goal, a man must be able to manage the continuous interplay and mutual shaping of the "active-rational" and "sensuous-receptive" modes of experiencing (Deikman, 1976). Models of consciousness invariably include such a bimodal conception of two opposite but complementary modes of experiencing (Ornstein, 1971). Each mode is typically associated with a distinctive constellation of physiological and psychological characteristics, and each is deeply implicated in men's capacity to experience and sustain romantic love. In the "rational-active" mode, a person functions to manipulate or act upon the environment. Sympathetic nervous activity and striate muscle activity predominate. Attention is maintained on external events, and the goal-oriented behavior of normal waking consciousness prevails. By contrast, in the "sensuous-receptive" mode, a person functions to let in sensory aspects of the environment. Parasympathetic nervous activity and sensory-perceptual activity predominate. Attention is focused inward on internal events, muscle tension is decreased, and paralogical thought characterized by intuition and sensation assume prominence (Dosamentes-Alperson, 1979).

In his efforts to blend these divergent modes of experiencing, a man may become one-sided and have only one mode available to him, he may vacillate in an unintegrated fashion between them, or ideally, he may balance harmoniously the continuous interplay between these modes. Historically, the active-rational and sensuous-receptive modes have been erroneously equated with activity and passivity. Activity and passivity in turn have been designated as masculine and feminine inclinations. Such sex-role stereotyping has unfortunately fostered a skewed distribution of these modes of functioning in men and women. Sociological authorities such as Parsons and Bales (1956) maintain that the self-esteem of females has traditionally been more dependent upon interpersonal social factors and expressiveness than is the self-esteem of males, who are believed to be more dependent on individualistic and instrumental criteria (e.g., achievement) of relative worth. In fact, dominant social stereotypes view competence, independence, competition, and intellectual achievement as qualities inconsistent with femininity but as positively related to masculinity and psychological health (Broverman et al., 1970).

Don Juans are apt to be viewed as "antisocial" because they are in rebellion against these cultural stereotypes. Don Juans violate the "truism" that women live for love and men live for work. Don Juans are lovers of love; they devote their greatest energy to being uninterruptedly in love with women. Ortega y Gasset (1957, p. 27) further suggests that they "are not the men who make love to women but the men whom women make love." According to psychiatric theorists, this trend suggests that their heterosexual seductions are in the service of camouflaging passive, feminine, homosexual trends (Reich, 1949). Don Juans may be capable of inspiring romantic love in women, but they may also be incapable of truly loving romantically. Along with the narcissistically disabled, they may perform "it" rather than live "it." Such interpretations may in part express the ambivalence with which Don Juanism has been regarded by men. As Fowles (1964, p. 281) asserted: "For every Don Juan, a hundred would like to be Don Juan." Ortega y Gasset (1957) agrees with this estimate. He maintains that, with few exceptions, men can be divided into three classes:

> those who think they are Don Juan, those who think they have been Don Juan, and those who think they could have been but did not want to be. The last are the ones who propose, with worthy intention, to attack Don Juan and perhaps decree his dismissal (p. 170).

THE HEALING POTENTIAL OF ROMANTIC LOVE

Paradoxically, fulfillment of many romantic strivings, including "infantile" wishes, is possible only when an individual has "grown up." The findings of Levinson et al. (1978) indicate that young men are novice lovers, husbands, and fathers. They are in general not capable of highly loving, sexually free, and emotionally intimate relationships because the guiding energy during early adulthood tends to be narcissistic. As previously noted, the love a man experiences for his special woman during early adulthood largely derives from her dedicated support of his dream and not from an appreciation of her in her own right. The endogenous efforts of the self to right itself after such imbalances and one-sided emphases of early adulthood crucially define the experience of mid-life. The gradual emergence of the flaws and inevitable contradictions inherent in a narcissistic life structure consequently provoke, with heightened urgency, efforts at reconciliation as middle adulthood approaches. For example, the man at mid-life who has been "married to his career" may seek in romantic love opportunities to heal the disharmonies in his life structure. For such men, the capacity to love romantically may begin to express itself, perhaps for the first time. Many men rediscover or discover romantic love with their wives and/or seek romantic love in extramarital relationships during the transition into middle adulthood. As this occurs, neglected aspects of self are reexperienced and reappropriated. Risks are taken. New sources of energy are unleashed. As Farber (1976, p. 165) has recognized, real man/woman talk and sexuality promises "the exciting possibility of receiving and offering a range of perceptions and sensibility whose otherness can be uniquely and surprisingly illuminating." In other words, we are affirmed and come to know ourselves in the process of disclosing ourselves to our lovers.

A major appeal of new love during transitional periods may be the opportunity to rewrite one's narrative history. Unencumbered by a shared past and the wounds inflicted by the sheer dailiness of existence, new lovers listen effortlessly and speak candidly. During this process, the past may be reenacted, mourned, reappraised, and integrated. To further explore the ways in which romantic love can contribute to growth and individuation, we must first clarify the distinction between object love and narcissistic love.

Psychoanalysts maintain that throughout life the opposing claims of narcissism and object love, striving for reconciliation, characterize all erotic relationships. Narcissism is our first erotic disposition in the sense that before we know that other bodies exist and/or what it is to like other bodies, we direct our libido toward our own bodies. Narcissism so conceptualized does not refer primarily to love of self in contrast to love of others but rather to a "primordial love-mentation" that, according to Loewald (1978, p. 39), "does not structure or divide reality into the poles of inner and outer, subject and object, self and others." Following Loewald, we shall refer to this process as "identificatory love." Object love, by contrast, refers to a mode of relatedness in which oneself as subject and the other as object are established at least to the extent that there is some awareness that there are differences between the other's needs, desires, and feelings and one's own.

Most developmental theorists now agree that in the early stages of life such boundaries are not yet established (Mahler et al., 1975). The prototype for identificatory love is the infant-mother unity or bond. Identificatory love enables children to enrich themselves, to take into themselves aspects or traits of their parents. Thus, in early childhood, this process plays a prominent role in the formation and consolidation of the self. However, this process continues in far more complex ways in later developmental stages as well. In adulthood, the suspension or blurring of the boundaries between self and other can be seen in psychosis, in some drug-related and ecstatic stages, and in situations of deep intimacy between people. In her work "Parenthood as a developmental phase," Benedek (1959) reported that there is also a "normative symbiosis" on the part of the adult parent to the developing child that similarly makes possible a blurring of self-definition.

Approach-avoidance motifs dominate the literature on romantic love. At their root can be found the joys and perils of identificatory love. From the perspective of self/other differentiation, romantic loving can be experienced as deeply enriching and/or as terrifying. A man may "fall in love," but he "makes love."[8] Romantically inspired lovemaking requires the capacity to tolerate "the manifold, simultaneous and/or shifting hetero-sexual and homosexual, pregenital and genital identifications activated in that context" (Kernberg, 1976, p. 222). Identifi-catory love promises the romantic lover, as George Bernard Shaw recognized, "a celestial flood of emotion and exaltation of existence" (cited in Barzun, 1961, p. 127), not merely orgasms.

Many schizophrenic "first breaks" during early adulthood are precipitated by the dissolving sense of self brought about by the experience of merging or fusing with a lover. Such individuals are still uncertain about their identity as separate beings and consequently experience "re-engulfment" (Mahler et al., 1975) with a caring other as a threat to their individuality, cohesion, and stability.

Consciousness and choice imply a commitment to rather than an identification with the external other. To the extent that a man acknowledges that he can be sexually aroused by and love more than one woman at a time, he will be burdened by the arbitrariness of his romantic and marital choices. Identificatory love lends authority, reassurance, even a sense of inevitability to one's choices. The push toward commitment is strengthened if a man can experience at crucial and delicate moments a merged identity with his lover. He can, moreover, temporarily overcome his loneliness to the extent that he can achieve a sense of one-ness with his lover. According to Bertrand Russell (1930), it is the fear of loneliness that prompts most men to marry.

It is through the medium of identificatory love that a man can also achieve transcendence of his narcissistic self-absorption or a cancellation of the self. For men who are confronting the real-

---

8 A prototype may be defined as an event, actual or symbolic, that is prefigurative, prior in time, and causally related to later behavior (Rieff, 1961). Transference, as Rieff has recog-nized, is but one instance of the power of prototypes.

ity and inevitability of their own personal death, this "spiritual" aspect of romantic loving can assume problematic importance. Near the end of his life, Rilke (1978, p. 28) wrote, "Is it easier for lovers? Ah, they only manage, by being together, to conceal each other's fate!" In their efforts to come to terms with growing old and dying, men, especially those who are alienated from the collective visions that guide their culture, seek to reinvent for themselves "the project of spirituality" (Sontag, 1969). They may come to rediscover with Pavese (Sontag, 1966, p. 46) that "love is the cheapest of religions" and that loving romantically can provide them with relief from worldly concerns or with a way of getting out of themselves and onto a higher plane of existence. In *The Denial of Death*, Becker (1973, p. 28) concludes that the failure of romantic love, in its guise as a "personal religion," to reconcile the existential contradiction "between a symbolic self, that seems to give man infinite worth in a timeless scheme of things, and a body that is worth about 98¢" is a defining feature of our time.

Although romantic loving can only anesthetize pain temporarily, identificatory love can also promote growth and change. Loving romantically promises men the possibility of developing attributes or modes of functioning that are not adequately represented in their own personalities. For example, obsessional men often fall in love with hysterical women and vice versa because they see each other as complementary to their own style, and indeed they are (see Chapter 13). The hysteric style is vivacious, emotional, empathic, and spontaneous. The obsessional style, by contrast, is more contained, intellectualized, logical, and controlled. As Barnett (1971) has documented,

> These factors of outward style aid in the initial idealization each makes of the other. The hysteric sees the obsessional as the strong silent man, profound, organized and

successful, while the obsessional views the hysteric as being warm, vital, loving and fun. Both see in the other's outward style evidence of precisely those characteristics they would like to see in themselves. They see in the other an opportunity for change and growth, a complementary relationship which may be therapeutic for their own inadequacies and liabilities or, at the very least, might enhance their own experience (p. 75).

The fate of these initial idealizations is often problematic, as Barnett has detailed. The literature on marriage has in fact emphasized the pathological aspects of forsaking an individual identity for merged identity (Wexler & Steidl, 1978). We shall, however, conclude this essay by citing one further example of how the identificatory components of loving can serve as a "force or power that not only brings people together, but equally brings oneself together into that one individuality which we become through our identifications" (Loewald, 1978, p. 40).

The desire to fuse with a lover, according to Ortega y Gasset (1957, p. 37), usually "culminates in a more or less clear desire to leave, as testimony of the union, a child in whom the perfections of the beloved are perpetuated and affirmed." A child is neither the father's nor the mother's but a "personified union" of the two. Today's young adults, especially those who are pursuing dual-career marriages, are often in severe conflict about their urge to have children. Having children has become burdened by the weightiness of decisions that are premised disproportionately on the "rational-active" mode. Erikson (Adams, 1979) has recently urged psychoanalysts to be alert to the possibility that, just as sexual repression characterized the Victorian era, repression of the urge to have children may characterize the future.

The implications of choosing not to have children are profound. Childless couples can devote their full energies to each other. They have the freedom to cultivate desire and experiment with a relationship that approximates perpetual courtship. In their work, they can also express their "procreative" urges and concern for future generations. However, the decision not to have children can weaken the idea of a permanent commitment to each other. Children may also help to reconcile the opposing claims of narcissism and object love. It is in their relationship with their children that men most closely approximate the ideal of loving unselfishly and unconditionally. Vicarious participation in a child's crushes and romances provides men with opportunities to reexperience, perhaps with greater clarity, the unfinished business of their own youth. Erikson's (1968) work suggests that mature concern for one's children encourages a decisive turn toward intimacy, generativity, and integrity rather than toward isolation, stagnation, self-absorption, and despair in later adulthood. The identificatory components of a man's love for his children can therefore facilitate the heroic quest for personal integration, which may not be achievable, according to Jung (1971), until the fifth decade of life.

In our time, the creative and constructive role that romantic love can play in fostering personal integration needs to be reaffirmed. A renewal of this belief will require continued and arduous revision of the dualities of love that this "work in progress" has briefly discussed.

REFERENCES

Adams, V. (1979, August 4). Erikson sees psychological danger in trend of having fewer children. *New York Times*, p. 17.
Allen, W. (Director). (1977). *Annie Hall* [Film]. United Artists.
———— (Director). (1979). *Manhattan* [Film]. Jack Rollins & Charles H. Joffe Productions.

Balswick, J. (1979). How to get your husband to say I love you. *Family Circle* 2:110–111.

Barnett, J. (1971). Narcissism and dependency in the obsessional-hysteric marriage. *Family Process* 10(1):75–84.

Barzun, J. (1961). *Classic, Romantic, and Modern*. Chicago, IL: University of Chicago Press.

Becker, E. (1973). *The Denial of Death*. New York, NY: Free Press.

Benedek, T. (1959). Parenthood as a developmental phase. *Journal of the American Psychoanalytic Association* 7:417–423.

Broverman, I.K., Broverman, D.M., Clarkson, F.E., Rosenkrantz, P.S., & Vogel, S.R. (1970). Sex-role stereotypes and clinical judgments of mental health. *Journal of Consulting and Clinical Psychology* 34:469–474.

Brozan, N. (1979, January 19). A study of the American man. *New York Times*, p. A14.

Capellanus, A. (1969). *The Art of Courtly Love* (J. Perry, Trans.). New York, NY: Norton. (Original work written early 13th century.)

de Rougement, D. (1963). *Love Declared*. Boston, MA: Beacon Press.

——— (1969). *Love in the Western World*. New York, NY: Fawcett World Library.

Deikman, A.J. (1976). Bimodal consciousness. In R.E. Ornstein (Ed.), *The Nature of Human Consciousness*. New York, NY: Viking Press.

Donaldson, E.T. (1965). The myth of courtly love. *Ventures* 5:16–23.

Dosamentes-Alperson, E. (1979). The intrapsychic and the interpersonal in psychotherapy. *American Journal of Dance Therapy* 3:20–31.

Durkheim, E. 1951. *Suicide: A Study in Sociology* (J.A. Spaulding & G. Simpson, Trans.). New York, NY: Free Press. (Original work published 1897.)

Ellis, A. (1962). *The American Sexual Tragedy*. New York, NY: Lyle Stuart.

Erikson, E.H. (1956). The problem of ego identity. *Journal of the American Psychoanalytic Association* 4:56–121.

———— (1963). *Childhood and Society* (2nd ed.). New York, NY: Norton.

———— (1965). Youth and the life cycle. In D.E. Hamachek (Ed.), *The Self in Growth, Teaching and Learning*. Englewood Cliffs, NJ: Prentice-Hall.

———— (1968). The life cycle. In *International Encyclopedia of the Social Sciences* (Vol. 9, pp. 286–292). New York, NY: Macmillan and Free Press.

Farber, B.A., & Geller, J.D. (1977). Student attitudes toward psychotherapy. *Journal of the American College Health Association* 25:301–307.

Farber, L.H. (1976). *Lying, Despair, Jealousy, Envy, Sex, Suicide, Drugs, and the Good Life*. New York, NY: Harper & Row.

Fowles, J. (1964). *The Aristos: A Self-Portrait in Ideas*. Boston, MA: Little, Brown.

Freud, E.L. (Ed.). (1961). *Letters of Sigmund Freud*. New York, NY: Basic Books.

Freud, S. (1905). Three essays on the theory of sexuality: III. The transformations of puberty. *Standard Edition* 7.

———— (1921). Group psychology and the analysis of the ego. *Standard Edition* 18.

———— (1953a). Contributions to the psychology of love: The most prevalent form of degradation in erotic life. In E. Jones (Ed.), *Collected Papers* (Vol. 4). London, UK: Hogarth Press. (Original work published 1912.)

———— (1953b). Contributions to the psychology of love: A special type of choice of objects made by men. In E. Jones (Ed.), *Collected Papers* (Vol. 4). London, UK: Hogarth Press. (Original work published 1910.)

———— (1953c). Contributions to the psychology of love: The taboo of virginity. In E. Jones (Ed.), *Collected Papers* (Vol. 4). London, UK: Hogarth Press. (Original work published 1918.)

———— (1953d). The dynamics of transference. In E. Jones (Ed.), *Collected Papers* (Vol. 8). London, UK: Hogarth Press. (Original work published 1912.)

———— (1953e). Observations on transference love. In E. Jones (Ed.), *Collected Papers* (Vol. 2). London, UK: Hogarth Press. (Original work published 1915.)

Friedan, B. (1979). Does equality for women have to threaten men? *Family Circle* 2:1–6.

Fromm, E. (1956). *The Art of Loving*. New York, NY: Harper & Brothers.

Frye, N. (1957). *Anatomy of Criticism*. Princeton: Princeton University Press.

Gould, R.L. (1972). The phases of adult life: A study in developmental psychology. *American Journal of Psychiatry* 129:521–531.

Guntrip, H. (1969). *Schizoid Phenomena, Object Relations and the Self*. New York, NY: International Universities Press.

Halverson, J. (1970). Amour and eros in the Middle Ages. *Psychoanalytic Review* 57:245–258.

Hill, C.T., Rubin, Z., & Peplau, L.A. (1976). Breakups before marriage: The end of 103 affairs. *Journal of Social Issues* 32(1):147–168.

Jaques, E. (1965). Death and the mid-life crisis. *International Journal of Psychoanalysis* 46:502–514.

Jong, E. (1973). *Fear of Flying*. New York, NY: Holt, Rinehart & Winston.

Jung, C.G. (1971). The stages of life. In J. Campbell (Ed.), *The Portable Jung*. New York, NY: Viking Press.

Kafka, F. (1946). *The Great Wall of China*. New York, NY: Schocken Books.

Kahne, H. (1975). Economic perspectives on roles of women in the American economy. *Journal of Economic Literature* 13:1249–1292.

Kernberg, O.F. (1976). *Object Relations Theory and Clinical Psychoanalysis*. New York, NY: Jason Aronson.

Lasch, C. (1978). *The Culture of Narcissism*. New York, NY: Norton.

Levinson, D.J., Darrow, C.N., Klein, E.B., Levinson, M.H., & McKee, B. (1978). *The Seasons of a Man's Life*. New York, NY: Knopf.

Loewald, H.W. (1978). *Psychoanalysis and the History of the Individual*. New Haven, CT: Yale University Press.

Maddock, J.W. (1973). Sex in adolescence: Its meanings and future. *Adolescence* 31:327–333.

Mahler, M.S., Pine, F., & Bergman, A. (1975). *The Psychological Birth of the Human Infant: Symbiosis and Individuation*. New York, NY: Basic Books.

Masters, W.H., & Johnson, V.E. (1970). *Human Sexual Inadequacy*. Boston, MA: Little, Brown.

——— & ——— (1979). *Homosexuality in Perspective*. Boston, MA: Little, Brown.

May, R. (1969). *Love and Will*. New York, NY: Norton.

Morton, W. (1899). *Love in Epigram*. Chicago, IL: McClurg.

Nadelson, T., & Eisenberg, L. (1977). The successful professional woman: On being married to one. *American Journal of Psychiatry* 134:1071–1076.

Neugarten, B. (Ed.). (1968). *Middle Age and Aging*. Chicago, IL: University of Chicago Press.

Orel, H. (Ed.). (1969). *Thomas Hardy's Personal Writings: Prefaces, Literary Opinions, Reminiscences*. Lawrence, KS: Regents Press.

Ornstein, R.E. (1971). *The Psychology of Consciousness*. New York, NY: Viking Press.

Ortega y Gasset, J. (1957). *On Love*. New York, NY: New American Library.

Parsons, T., & Bales, R.F. (1956). *Family: Socialization and Interaction Process*. Oxfordshire, UK: Routledge & Kegan Paul.

Reich, W. (1949). *Character Analysis*. New York, NY: Orgone Institute Press.

Rieff, P. (1961). *Freud: The Mind of the Moralist*. New York, NY: Doubleday.

Rilke, R.M. (1978). *Duino Elegies*. New York, NY: Norton.

Roth, P. (1969). *Portnoy's Complaint*. New York, NY: Random House.

Rubin, Z. (1973). *Liking and Loving: An Introduction to Social Psychology*. New York, NY: Holt, Rinehart & Winston.

Russell, B. (1930). *The Conquest of Happiness*. New York, NY: Liveright.

Schachter, S. (1964). The interaction of cognitive and physiological determinants of emotional state. In L. Berkowitz (Ed.), *Advances in Experimental Social Psychology*. New York, NY: Academic Press.

Schafer, R. (1970). The psychoanalytic vision of reality. *International Journal of Psychoanalysis* 51(3):279–297.

——— (1976). *A New Language for Psychoanalysis*. New Haven, CT: Yale University Press.

Sontag, S. (1966). *Against Interpretation*. New York, NY: Delta.

———— (1969). *Styles of Radical Will*. New York, NY: Farrar, Straus and Giroux.

Tavris, C. (1977). Men and women report their views on masculinity. *Psychology Today* 10:35–38, 42, 82.

Vaillant, G.E. (1977). *Adaptation to Life*. Boston, MA: Little, Brown.

Walster, E., & Walster, G.W. (1978). *A New Look at Love*. Reading, MA: Addison-Wesley.

Weinberg, M.S. (1976). *Sex Research: Studies from the Kinsey Institute*. New York, NY: Oxford University Press.

Wexler, J., & Steidl, J. (1978). Marriage and the capacity to be alone. *Psychiatry* 41:72–81.

Woodworth, R., & Schlosberg, H. (1954). *Experimental Psychology*. New York, NY: Holt, Rinehart & Winston.

CHAPTER 3

Moods, Feelings, and the Process of Affect Formation

[J.D. Geller (1984). In L. Temoshok, C. Van Dyke, & L.S. Zegans (Eds.), *Emotions in Health and Illness: Applications to Clinical Practice* (pp. 171–186). Orlando, FL: Grune & Stratton.]

This chapter is primarily concerned with the representational forms in which moods and feelings emerge into consciousness. It begins with an overview of the works that have guided me to a view of feelings as representations of biological processes and not as the biological processes themselves. Next, an evolving, phenomenologically based model of the forms that present to awareness and give meaning to and organize feelings at various levels of symbolic functioning is described. This is followed by a discussion of the processes of affect formation and their relevance for a psychotherapy that takes as a primary task the reembodiment and structural differentiation of feelings as experienced qualities. Throughout, the term "feelings" is used rather than the concepts of emotion or affect whenever the focus is specifically on the subjective awareness of current or remembered emotional states.

DEFINITIONS AND A THEORETICAL OVERVIEW

In our culture, the verb "to feel" serves multiple and overlapping functions. A representative list would include the following uses:

to feel some emotional state (thrilled or despondent), to feel some interpersonal situation (rejected or intimate), to feel something is so (true or about to happen), to feel like doing something (playing tennis or keeping quiet), to feel as if something is happening (as if one is being pried into or the world is crumbling), and to feel some emotionally toned bodily state (tired or hungry) (Schafer, 1976, p. 286).

These various uses indicate that in its broadest, most palpable meaning, to feel is to grasp with the senses. Feelings are embodied phenomena. They are experienced in and through a person's body. A purely disembodied emotion is, as James argued, a "non-entity" (1890, p. 452).

Theorists working in James's tradition believe that the arousal of felt emotions cannot occur without the perception of bodily changes. Whether feelings, as subjective experiences, are associated with unique arousal states or with physiological reactions that are nonspecific, however, remains a question of lively controversy. The viscera have failed to display emotion-specific activity patterns with any reliability (Schachter, 1964). Still other research data suggest that changes in the musculature and in particular the facial muscles provide the unique arousal states and feedback associated with particular feeling states (Ekman & Levenson, 1983).

Because the information provided by physiological reactions is not as precise or refined as James asserted, theories that view emotional experience and/or emotional behavior as a joint function of cognitive and excitatory processes have become increasingly influential. This trend can be observed in academic psychology, sociology, and that branch of psychoanalysis known as object relations theory. Each uses a different vocabulary in an attempt to overcome the perennial antithesis of reason and emotion. Historically, reason and emotion have been conceived of as polar principles having a point of perfect balance between them. Pure feeling from this point of view is associated with the absence of cognition, whereas at the extremes of the intellect there is presumed to be an absence of feeling. By comparison, Schachter and Singer's (1962) two-factor theory is premised on the assumption that a state of physiological arousal alone is not sufficient to induce a felt emotion and that cognitions exert a strong steering function in helping people "decide" what they are feeling.

Central to such a view is the often replicated finding that the perception and labeling of the bodily changes relevant to an emotional experience and their actual occurrence are sufficiently independent to warrant separate conceptualizations and investigations. The work of Mandler et al. (1958) further suggests that the perception of bodily changes may not even be highly dependent on their actual occurrence. Research in cultural anthropology has similarly shown that there are "styles" of emotional expression and understanding that cannot be reduced to biological processes of adaptation (Ekman, 1972).

In their critiques of reductionistic theories of emotion, sociologists of a symbolic interactions orientation (e.g., Denzin, 1981; Gordon, 1981) have emphasized that the direct and intense arousal of bodily sensations is an intermittent phase of those complex and differentiated feelings, which they refer to as sentiments. Gordon (1981) has reasoned that in order to serve as themes that organize and integrate extended actions toward others, such socially emergent emotions as love and hate must persist beyond mere bodily excitement. He conceives of sentiments as "socially constructed patterns of sensations, expressive gestures, and cultural meanings organized around a relationship to a social object, usually another person" (Gordon, 1981 p. 566).

In parallel, psychoanalytically oriented theorists have begun to develop new models to discover and reveal the developmental lines that affects traverse en route to becoming sentiments, or as they shall be called here, differentiated feelings (Loewald, 1962; Mahler, 1966; Guntrip, 1969; Blatt, 1974; Krystal, 1974; Kernberg, 1976).[9] According to the traditional Freudian "economic point of view," emotional experiences are "ultimately" to be explained in terms of the vicissitudes of impersonal, quasiphysiological drives that mechanistically press to discharge "their" accumulating energies (Rapaport, 1954). By contrast, psychoanalytic object relations theorists do not believe that the ultimate causes of emotions are to be found at the nonexperiential level of hypothetical energies, forces, and structures that are presumed to actually "exist." Instead, they are exploring the possibility of developing a general theory of affects based on the view that recurrent, relatively stable configurations of self-representations, object representations, and their accompanying affects serve as the basic building blocks or elements of personality or character style. (See Meissner, 1981, for a review of this shift.) In the analytic literature, the term "object" refers to the diverse persons, things, and events toward which feelings are directed. Although differing in important respects, the emerging view among object relations theorists is that each affect implies a particular form of relatedness. Kernberg (1976) speaks of affects as the elements for self- and object representations. Krystal (1974, p. 124) has emphasized that "primitive cognitive contents may be part of every affect." Novey (1961, p. 23) has hypothesized that "internal representations of objects are affective experiences which

---

9 Psychoanalytic object relations theorists question fundamental axioms of Freud's individualistic instinct theory as well as the value of a metapsychological conception of emotion. For example, object relations theorists believe that such empirically observed states in infancy as "attachment," "stranger anxiety," and "separation anxiety" support the view that human beings are cultural or social animals by biological origin (Lewis, 1981).

are only secondarily perceived as having ideational content." According to Klein (1976), feelings are to be conceived of as cognitive-affective structures. In other words, object relations theorists view affects as intrinsic to relationship paradigms or schemas and the readiness for certain affects rather than others in terms of "internalized object relations."

Taken together, these complementary lines of inquiry encourage a view of feelings as modes of interpreting situations that blend and blur with that form of thinking and action known as reason in the ongoing stream of consciousness. It is this orientation that constitutes the conceptual starting point of my efforts to understand the complex interplay between moods, regressed feelings, and differentiated feelings.

Following Krystal (1974), the present author distinguishes between regression in regard to the handling of affects and regression in the nature of affects themselves. As defined herein, infantile levels of affectivity are almost totally somatic. Like the infant's contentment and distress at the extremes of affect regression, feelings are represented in consciousness without significant psychic elaboration, symbolization, or ideation. During adulthood, affect regression does not generally manifest itself as a total and/or unchangeable phenomenon but as ever-changing in severity and clinical picture (Arlow & Brenner, 1964). According to Krystal (1974), such regression may, however, proceed to any point in the development of affects, such as to their resomatization and deverbalization, as in psychosomatic diseases. Affects that are located in close proximity to the primitive trunk of emotion have "import" that is directly felt or "known" but are difficult to translate into emotion words. Regressed affects thus lack specific meanings. They are experienced as "unstructured" or as unmodulated and unbridled "attacks" whose determinants are obscure and remote. At this level of affect representation may be observed the persistence of the somatic (expressive) aspects of an emotion without realization of its precise nature. Still further along this developmental line can be located affects that are experienced as differentiated, verbalizable, subtle, refined, and thoughtlike and that function as signals to oneself. When functioning in this manner, feelings serve essentially as instruments of rationality rather than as means to control others.

Although it is obvious that feelings of these varying types and levels mutually influence each other, little is specifically known about their complex interplay. In 1970, Arnold concluded that, as a topic, mood had been "investigated haphazardly" and that "there has been no attempt to provide a systematic framework that would connect moods and feelings and emotions, except for casual references" (Arnold, 1970, p. 259). This conclusion still holds true today.

MOODS AND FEELINGS: A PHENOMENOLOGICAL COMPARISON

With varying degrees of awareness and accuracy, individuals experience their feelings as responses to stimuli. The site of the stimuli that arouse differentiated feelings may be perceived of as primarily internal or external. Their effects, however, are essentially experienced as taking place within the confines of the reacting organism. By contrast, the effects of affects in their regressed forms are represented at the interface between the body and extrapersonal space. For example, such diffusely formulated feelings as "upset" are experienced as happening to us or around us but not necessarily within us (Gaylin, 1982). Moods permeate and envelop our existence. It is as if we were embedded in our moods. It is therefore often difficult to determine whether the source of a mood is internal or external. This phenomenological property is revealed in the inclination to rely on nature metaphors (e.g., the weather) or inanimate and environmental referents (e.g., colors) when speaking of moods. To convey the nonspecific experience of a bad mood, individuals will say they are "in a black cloud," "surrounded by a fog," "down in the dumps," or having a "blue Monday." As these metaphors imply, moods blur the differentiation between experienced self and the experienced world.

Discursive explicitness about feelings inevitably requires the use of metaphors. A stylistic analysis of language reveals that the metaphors that are used to group and explain moods are drawn from different models and domains than those that are used to identify differentiated feelings. When the subject matter of introspection pertains to feelings rather than moods, body-centered and anthropomorphic metaphors are dominant. For example, we speak of "a broken heart," "a lump in the throat," or "a pain in the neck."

People are generally aware of their differentiated feelings as being directed toward objects and activities. The object of such feelings may be the ongoing stream of consciousness, and the activity may be thinking about our feelings at that moment. When people talk about feelings that are clearly differentiated, they usually do so in terms of their attitudes, ideals, wishes, or fantasies toward someone or something. Remembrances of differentiated feelings typically include associations to the people by whom and toward whom they have been felt. Love and hate are recognizably organized around a relationship to special, selected persons, groups, or nonhuman objects personified with human qualities, such as pets, deities, and governments. Shame is felt toward oneself as a social object. By comparison, self-loathing or pride are experienced as emanating from internalized objects, according to Schafer (1964), whereas other affects, such as the apprehensiveness associated with suspiciousness, are *directed at* the internalized objects; and some, such as remorse concerning seductiveness, spitefulness, or withdrawal, are *reactions to* impulses ascribed to the self and directed toward, against, or away from these objects (p. 283).

As will be discussed later, the tendency to populate the "inscape" (Hopkins, 1953) with relatively autonomous internal figures manifests itself most clearly in the representational configurations that structure the experience of conflict.

As they are experienced, moods span a narrower range than feelings. The feeling aspects of moods are invariably described as vague and indefinite. Consequently, their "objects" are also more difficult to specify. Moods exert a generalized influence that contributes to the emotional coloring of all conscious contents. They provide a background against which other contents of consciousness, more or less, stand out. Whether experienced for longer or shorter periods of time, moods lend a uniform quality to all feelings, thoughts, and actions. Jacobson (1957, p. 76) has observed: "Once a mood has established itself, it affects all patterns of responses to stimuli or objects of the most different kind." Moods that assert themselves indiscriminately can bring about qualitative changes in representations of the self and external world in toto. When experiencing a depressed mood, the entire self is felt to be bad and inferior, and the entire object world appears unpleasantly transformed (Jacobson, 1957). On the other hand, an elated mood brings about a totally "different" sense of the self and relation to the external world.

FEELINGS AS INTERPRETIVE RESOURCES

As interpretive resources, moods and feelings vary in their in-formativeness and in the response guidance that they provide. Affects in their regressed forms do not relate to specific content, nor are they invested in a definite ideational representation. Nearly every patient has complained at one time or another about feeling upset. Yet only Gaylin (1982) has attempted to define the nature and meanings of this emotion word. He observes with respect to the diffusely organized experience of "feeling upset" that "we feel it in such diverse contexts that we deny its specificity as a feeling" (Gaylin, 1982, p. 88). Feelings such as surprise and jealousy have an immediate meaning and significance for the experiencing individual. The subtle distinctions conveyed by love and guilt can direct us to specific courses of action. Differentiated feelings, themselves, thus suggest specific kinds of choices and adaptive maneuvers that will enable people to avoid, prevent, or change their situation. Moods, in comparison, are wide-ranging predispositions to behave in a particular way. They broadly influence our preferences and dislikes. A bad mood can alert us to the sense that something is wrong. However, cognitive appraisal of a bad mood does not indicate the specific nature of an impending threat, danger, or malfunction. It is difficult to tell whether one is depressed, tired, hungry, or ill under the influence of an all-encompassing bad mood.

The biophysiological state that contributes to a person's prevailing mood prominently includes the diffuse and poorly localized sensations having to do with muscle tension, posture, equilibrium, temperature, vibration, pitch, and depth and rate of breathing. These sensory inputs are also fundamental constituents of a person's body image and sense of selfsameness. Because of their very familiarity, these pervasive dimensions of human experience are less likely to activate "evaluative needs"

(Schachter, 1964) than the specific occasions and bodily changes that induce feelings. Because the embodied phenomena associated with moods are rarely subjected to focal attention, they are also apt to be experienced without awareness. Consciousness is not an all-or-nothing phenomenon. Feelings that are fragmentary, of minimal intensity, fleeting, or that have not been subjected to focal attention may be experienced without awareness. As experienced qualities, moreover, people often treat their moods as if they were uninterpretable or as not requiring an explanation. In this later sense, moods are relatively unconscious.

Although individuals tend to be more self-reflective about regressed affects than about moods, such feelings do not support the sense of "self-as-agent" (Schafer, 1976). They have less of the "feel" of intentionality than differentiated feelings. This characteristic can be discerned in the synonyms that are used to describe feeling upset—"mixed up," "disturbed," "shaken up," "agitated," or "stressed out." A vulnerability to loss of control is conveyed by these concrete and physicalized images. Although it is a signal that our threshold for losing control has been lowered, the cognitive appraisal of feeling upset does not indicate the specific nature of the emerging emotional response. An element of surprise thus usually accompanies the anger, tearful distress, or anguish that erupts when the vulnerable, unstable condition we call "upset" culminates in losing control.

Gaylin (1982) hypothesized that feeling upset is a secondary response to and a means of obscuring guilt, fears, unexpressed anger, and hurt. Jacobson (1957) similarly described how denial can transform a feeling that is directed toward a specific object into a generalized mood. Denial, she maintains, harnesses the processes of "dedifferentiation" in order to camouflage the original object of one's feelings. What these authors are suggesting is that on occasion, so-called mixed (rather than differentiated) feelings are a derivative of other primary emotions and that their phenomenological properties can be exploited for defensive purposes.

THE TEMPORAL DIMENSION OF EMOTIONAL EXPERIENCE

At any given moment, affective experience, as observed clinically, is composed of complex blends or aggregates of both transient and enduring feelings. Some feelings, such as surprise, are confined to the duration of intense arousal and rarely persist beyond a single situation. Love and hate can be sustained over prolonged periods of time. Intermittently, when an individual, for example, foresees a discrepancy between what is sought and what "exists," conflictual feelings arise. By comparison, "activity-affects" (Schachtel, 1959) such as interest, zest, and intentness constitute an essential background of every coordinated and goal-directed activity. The prototype of activity-affects is perhaps first encountered in the eagerly nursing baby. As Schachtel (1959, p. 24) has keenly observed, "The torso and limbs are held quite still and the whole energy is concentrated on the sucking activity. The activity itself is the eagerly pursued and gratifying goal of the infant." In other words, activity-affects do not serve to discharge rising need tensions but are tension directed. On the other hand, the restlessness of the hungry infant in the frustrating absence of the mother's breast can be taken as the prototype of the expression of conflictually inspired feelings.

From a characterological point of view, there is no action, public or private, that is totally devoid of affect. Rapaport (1954, p. 277) has observed how, in contrast to momentary affects, anxiety, guilt, depression, and elation "may take pathological chronic forms; even more importantly they may take characterological chronic forms, as in anxious people, gay people, gloomy people, bashful people, etc." Such "frozen affects" (Reich, 1949) find expression in the chronic persistence of stereotyped postures, facial expressions, tones of voice, and movement styles without conscious affect experience. A characterological perspective recognizes that affective states can acquire the stability, properties, and functions of personality traits or character defenses. When functioning analogously to neurotic symptoms, emotions can serve to rigidly and unconsciously maintain an affectively charged mode of relatedness, for instance, the "emotional way of life" pursued by patients diagnosed as having an hysterical personality disorder (Easser & Lesser, 1965).

Behavioral theorists (Nowlis, 1968) have restricted their investigations to moods as temporary, reversible dispositions. It is a fundamental axiom of Mahler's (1966) theory that after the separation-individuation phase of development, mood represents an outstanding and conspicuous feature of the total personality. Mahler's investigations have led her to conclude that the characteristic "baseline" of a child's emotional responsiveness, what she calls "the development of a basic mood," has its beginnings as early as the last half of the 2nd year of life and derives substantially from the child's "confident expectation" or "basic mistrust." From this perspective, it is an illusion to speak of a mood-neutral self. Insofar as the dominant emotional tone or prevailing emotional climate in which individuals are embedded is a central manifestation of their character, persons are never free of continuing moods. In this sense, moods are prior to differentiated feelings. Enduring moods represent the contexts that modify the manner in which emotions are experienced and expressed.

Moods are a pervasive dimension of human functioning that, throughout life, constitute the active base and source of more differentiated and cognitively organized modes of representing feelings. They are not merely the primitive forerunners of feelings, however. In addition, moods provide a framework of meaning that plays a central role in determining subjective and behavioral responses to "emotional stimuli." Most of the feelings occurring within a person or a relationship are assimilated into a prevailing emotional atmosphere that anticipates and reflects on the meaning of the emergent feelings. Recent experiments have demonstrated that moods can create biases in the ways in which information is encoded, perceived, classified, and stored and that they can selectively influence the retrieval of information that has otherwise been processed. Bower (1981) found that depressed mood states influence the stability of pleasant memories relative to unpleasant memories and the strategies used to organize perceptual information. Moods are thus comparable to "visions of reality" (Schafer, 1970) that broadly structure each person's style of comprehending the form and content of emotions and the changes they may undergo.

Certain individuals appear to be truly "affectless." Sifneos (1975) has expressed the opinion that psychoanalytic psychotherapy with alexithymic patients is likely to eventuate in failure because such patients are "devoid of affect" rather than denying of affect. It has been argued here, however, that because of the ubiquitous presence of activity-affects and the existence of characterologically based moods, the total absence of affect is theoretically impossible. Consequently, in assessing feelings that are operative in a person at a given time, it is much more accurate and helpful, therapeutically, to think in terms of the reduction of affect rather than the total absence of feelings. The failure on the part of therapists to speak in such relative terms derives from several sources. In part, it follows from the tendency to focus attention on feelings that are self-limited in duration and intensity. Clinical work, in general, tends to concentrate attention on the urgent, dramatic, inherently distressing feelings arising from conflict, frustration, and blocking. Novey (1958) has acknowledged that, in psychoanalytic practice as well, prime attention has been given to affect crises (e.g., the anxiety attacks observed in phobic disorders) and acute emotional states (e.g., the emotions accompanying sexual excitement and orgasm), while the influence of continuing moods has been neglected.

To clarify and extend the implications of the distinctions made here, let us next consider the subjective experience of the intensity of feelings.

THE SUBJECTIVE EXPERIENCE OF INTENSITY

Viewed from one perspective, the maturation of affects "involves their separation and differentiation from a common matrix as well as their verbalization and desomatization" (Krystal, 1974, p. 123). These developmental modifications make possible the use of feelings as signals to oneself. This does not mean, however, that people whose affects are overly refined are more emotionally well-developed than people who are capable of experiencing intense and primitive feelings. It is erroneous to locate individuals who can only experience refined and thought-like affects at the "highest" levels of affective development.[10] Successful adaptation in the sphere of emotionality also requires the capacity to tolerate and enjoy affects of formidable intensity (e.g., shame, grief, anxiety, love). The unfolding of these representational capacities can profitably be conceptualized as a concurrent developmental line (Zetzel, 1964).

Individuals seek psychotherapy in order to deal with the corruptibility, truthfulness, justifiability, and appropriateness of their feelings as well as the propriety and interpersonal con-

---

10 An unfortunate byproduct of the analytic tradition of using anxiety as a model for all affects has been that affects not functioning as affect signals tend to be viewed as regressive.

sequences of their expression. In addition, many enter psychotherapy complaining of deficiencies in regard to the strength of their feelings. It is primarily in the realm of romantic love that individuals test the strength of their feelings; some discover they cannot "fall in love" (Geller & Howenstine, 1980). Affects must be experienced at "optimal strength" if they are to serve effectively in the struggle for individual and group survival, safety, pleasure, and goodness. The optimal intensity of any particular affect depends on its functions and implications. If affects are not intense enough, they lack a conviction of reality or authenticity. Affects must be of a sufficient intensity to ensure what Schafer (1964, p. 280) refers to as "the much sought after inner sense of sincere involvement in experience." On the other hand, if feelings are too intense, they may become overwhelming. Viewed solely from the perspective of intensity, the statement "I cannot stand feeling" reads as "I am suffering from an excess or too much of this feeling." The position advanced here is that it is the level of organization of an affect and not simply its intensity that clinically differentiates feelings that are overwhelming from those that can be tolerated. By analogy, when the dial of a radio is located on the boundary between two stations, the static produced is noxious; however, when the dial is located on a differentiated frequency at the same volume, the sound quality may be experienced as pleasurable. Gaylin (1982, p. 13) has noted that it is especially within the realm of negative feelings that "quantity transforms quality." For example, when fear becomes too intense, it is transformed into terror.

So far, the functions associated with intensity and the other affects that it qualifies or modifies have been discussed here. However, intensity itself can be conceptualized as a distinguishable affect. Intensity has not been studied systematically either as a subjective experience or as a mode of allocating attention and performing actions.

As a mode of relatedness, intensity is characterized by the tendency to actively and energetically seek aims, objects, and gratification from the environment (Weiss, 1959); and as a subjective experience, intensity is characterized by the qualities of eager absorption, excitability, and the sense of being keyed up for action. Like other affects, intensity may be experienced with varying degrees of awareness or pleasure and may function as an incentive that either attracts or repels. Furthermore, like many other affective states, intensity can also range from an intermittently felt category of experience to an unconscious and rigid mode of relating. We usually think of intensity as being sought episodically and in relation to specific aims and objects. Interest undergoes a change in quality when it is intense. Without the support of intensity, it is difficult to sustain exploration and attentiveness to complex stimuli or projects. As Tomkins (1962, p. 343) recognized, "There is no human competence which can be achieved in the absence of a sustaining interest." When focused, intensity lends vitality to and highlights the decisive and memorable moments of life.

Just as there are characterologically depressed, anxious, and moody people, there are also individuals who are characterologically intense. At the pathological extremes of this continuum can be found "intensity junkies," individuals who willfully or addictively attempt to sustain intensity as an essential element of all actions and relations, whether preparatory or consummatory. These individuals cannot loosen their perceptual relationship to reality, nor can they fully relinquish the diffuse and unstructured feeling of being keyed up. They appear to become eagerly absorbed in whatever stimuli the environment provides, and they are slavishly dependent on external referents as a guide to behavior. They are hypervigilantly attentive to the intensity of involvement of others. When not intensely involved with an activity or person, they may complain of feeling aimless, bored, lonely, futile, empty, or dead.

Paradoxically, many such individuals accept or tolerate but do not enjoy the relationships or "pleasurable feelings" they so eagerly pursue. Because their intensity of interest does not culminate in motor discharge, they are unable to yield in a sensuously receptive manner to sleep, tenderness, orgasm, or sustained stillness. Like hysterical emotionality, intensity can serve to deny a fear of future satisfactions. Weiss (1959) hypothesized that

the intense individual unconsciously avoids gratification but his intensity denies this avoidance. His dammed-up drive energy is partially discharged in activities of preparation but his constant frustration due to avoidance of satisfaction results, in spite of this motor discharge, in a high level of tension (p. 118).

On the other hand, intensity can serve to reassure individuals who are in doubt that they are capable of affective relatedness.

In order to compensate for and obscure a diminished capacity for pleasure as well as to avoid the feeling of being "keyed down," pathologically intense individuals may persistently and willfully sustain the intoxication that can be induced, according to Selye (1956), by the production of adrenalines and corticoids. It is as if such individuals were addicted to their stress hormones. Research indicates that an excess production of stress hormones not only causes an initial excitement but is followed inevitably by a secondary phase of depression (Pelletier, 1979). Pathologically intense individuals interpret depression as an enemy from within.

For a variety of reasons, chronic "disregulation" (Schwartz, 1983) of intensity renders reflective awareness of affects unreliable. Pathologically intense individuals often confuse fatigue and depression. Moreover, because of their need to avoid the feeling of being keyed down, they rarely are truly rested. When functioning adaptively, individuals can become aware of just noticeable differences in their level of physiological arousal. A chronically elevated state of diffuse excitation can render an individual insensitive to significant alterations. When the non-specific amplification that intensity provides exceeds a critical value, the threshold for irritability, agitation, upset, affect storms, and outbursts is significantly lowered. Similarly, the diffuse and pervasive sense of being keyed up for action tends to interfere with the ability to gauge accurately the alarm signals indicating that one's stress quota has been reached.[11]

Characterologically intense individuals tend to interpret their feelings on the basis of the actions and responses of other people rather than on the basis of internally generated cues, sensations, and thoughts. This externalizing orientation, if overgeneralized, can interfere with the differentiation of one feeling from another and limits the capacity to spontaneously express feelings or fantasies in words. When dysregulation of intensity chronically persists, other affects may appear in awareness only in their regressed forms or contribute nonspecifically to the maintenance of the desired level of intensity. At the pathological extremes, a still more widespread inability to describe, localize, and distinguish between feelings can be discerned. At this level of representation, intensity may be experienced as an "objectless" mood. By contemporary diagnostic standards, such cognitive-affective

---

11 The physiological correlates of an individual's response to stressors are thought to include increased blood pressure, heightened cholesterol levels, and an increased flow of the hormones adrenalin and noradrenaline (Temoshok, 1983). With this diffuse and undifferentiated state of physiological "arousal" in mind, the question arises as to how stress, as an experienced quality, is distinguished from intensity or other structurally similar and diffusely formulated feelings.

disturbances tend to be correlated with a reduced sense of inner conflict and difficulties in maintaining personally significant distinctions (i.e., boundaries) between self and others in fantasy and reality. Such disturbances interfere with the process of self-attention and affective relatedness, and they render object constancy tenuous. These disturbances, in turn, impair a person's capacity to participate in a psychotherapy that is specifically devoted to promoting "insight." There is general agreement that the therapeutic action of insight presumes the ability to bring to awareness information in the form of differentiated feelings, the ability to appreciate these feelings sensuously, and the capacity to sustain a particular level of emotional relatedness with the therapist both during and in between sessions.

The dysfunctional consequences of characterologically based dysregulation of intensity thus include the chronic overactivity of an affect-related function, the disruption of key regulatory processes, and the simultaneous impairment of the ability to verbalize and/or consciously distinguish subtle and informative affects. It is widely assumed that the co-occurrence of these disturbances is implicated in the development, course, and treatment of psychosomatic disorders (Krystal, 1974; Sifneos, 1975; Nemiah, 1978). Consistent with the doctrine of the multicausality of all disease (Lipowski, 1977), it is assumed here that the contribution of the unconscious conflicts embodied in characterologically sustained and amplified (or attenuated) levels of intensity varies from one psychosomatic disorder to another, from one person to another, and from one episode of the same disorder in the same person to another.

THERAPEUTIC IMPLICATIONS: THE FORMATION OF AFFECTS

As the preceding discussion implies, it may be of theoretical and clinical value to consider the relationship between the pathological dysregulation of intensity and alexithymia. The concept of alexithymia is still in the process of being refined. Essentially, it is defined with reference to two salient and general features: the inability to find words for feelings and the striking absence of fantasies referable to inner drives and affects (Sifneos, 1974). It is widely assumed that this behavioral syndrome is a basic mechanism underlying the psychosomatic process. In general, previous investigators have emphasized the relationship between severe inarticulateness with respect to feelings and fantasies and the discharge of stress. Nemiah (1978) summarized this model of psychosomatic symptom formation as follows:

> It is this condition (alexithymia) that leads secondarily to somatic arousal in psychosomatic disease. Environmental stress, in other words, sets in motion an aroused internal state in the individual subjected to stress, that arousal, instead of finding an outlet via channels leading to affect and fantasy, is discharged into channels affecting somatic function (p. 35).

According to this paradigmatic conceptualization, psychosomatic symptoms are not symbolic in either nature or origin, but are merely the result of chronically heightened autonomic activity in individuals deprived of the "safety valve" functions that emotional expression and fantasy can provide.

A wide variety of therapies have been developed to provoke the "spontaneous" and "authentic" expression of feelings. Many of these expressive therapies are premised on a discharge model of affect expression and therefore implicitly share with many patients an "excretory" view of affects as substances to be eliminated. Consequently, the therapeutic action of expressive therapies is often unnecessarily restricted to the cathartic discharge of pent-up and unexpressed emotions. Clearly, given the limits of our knowledge, there is room for other models. Gaylin (1982, p. 80), for example, has alternatively hypothesized that "the problem with people who have pent-up emotions is usually not their inability to express them but their incredible capacity to generate them."

The approach advanced here is primarily concerned with the needs of patients who are unable to bring to awareness information in the form of differentiated feelings. This emphasis argues for the efficacy of a psychotherapy that takes as a primary task the forming of feelings to the point where they are recognizable as being one kind of feeling and not another. Psychotherapy provides a variety of perspectives from which to observe and nurture the formation of differentiated affects. When required to be self-reflexive, individuals who do not experience their thoughts and feelings as differentiated must effortfully, sometimes by acts of power and cunning, manufacture substitutes for "nonfelt" feelings. When describing a feeling, they may only be relating what they have learned should be experienced in a particular situation, what they have inferred from external cues or what they have "figured out" by reason. Consequently, their public and observable emotional performances are apt to be perceived as empty, distorted, or fabricated. Such patients are often painfully aware of being "phony." They do not need to be reminded of their inauthenticity. Moreover, the transformation of their compliantly feigned or pseudoaffects into genuine affects involves far more than "affect taming" (Fenichel, 1941/1954) or increasing the strength and clarity of affective expressions. Rather, they require a psychotherapy that takes as a primary task the reembodiment and structural differentiation of feelings as experienced qualities. These processes can be discovered during the slow, faltering, and uncertain stages during which patients come to recognize and describe "preverbal" affects that presumably have never been fully conscious or capable of relatively organized expression (Schafer, 1964). They can also be observed during the crystallization of feelings to the point where they can be differentiated from prevailing moods. A dualistic tendency can be discerned in the popular classification of moods as either "good" or "bad." Because feelings arise out of and within the context of continuing moods, in much the same way as gestures are shaped by postures, this tendency, if overgeneralized, can limit the distinctiveness and variety of feelings available to an individual. Promotion of the formation of differentiated affects is therefore also essential to the psychotherapy of patients who are embedded in fixed or static negative mood states. What is assumed here is that the distinction between affective disorders and thought disorders represents a failure to conceptualize emotions as cognitive-affective structures.

In a comparable manner, the psychotherapy of bereaved individuals offers repeated opportunities to promote the formation of cognitive-affective structures and to follow the vicissitudes of their formation. The enormity of the emotional fact of death cannot be encompassed by a single experience or meaning. To successfully complete the task of mourning, in which all aspects of the loss are worked through, consists of experiencing "many small deaths" (Moffat, 1982, p. xxvii). Like a spiral, grief work is a highly individualized process that loops back and forth in ever-widening circles. The remainder of this chapter is devoted to the ways in which the intimately related concepts of representation and internalization can be harnessed to deal with the therapeutic tasks posed by these various processes of affect formation.

THE LANGUAGE OF FORM

James (1890, p. 450) concluded with respect to the range of human affective potential that "there is no limit to the number of possible different emotions which may exist and the emotions of different individuals may vary indefinitely." In my attempts to honor the uniqueness of each person's affective life, I am limited by the capacity for empathy and the representability or translatability of feelings into words. The English language provides a rich vocabulary to describe differentiated emotions as recognition patterns, that is, as actually or potentially felt by the subject or perceived by the other. Our common vocabulary provides far fewer categories for describing the representational and synthetic work required in the formation of feelings. As Hartocollis and Lester recently stressed, "for the intermediate steps, for the biological and psychological processes by which emotions are formed, we have an impoverishment of language" (1982, p. 207). We are accustomed to regarding feelings as abstract nouns, that is, as entities with names and adjectively designated properties of their own. This mode of thinking encourages a focus on the "what" rather than the "how" of feelings. In general, clinical investigations of emotion have focused primarily on their control and content rather than on process variables. For example, except for Laban-trained therapists, examinations of the non-verbal expressions of emotion have dealt primarily with static events rather than with the flow of movement (Geller, 1978).

To correct this imbalance, subtle, particularizing, and concrete vocabularies are required to discover and reveal the representational forms in which feelings of varying types and levels emerge into consciousness. Such a process-oriented phenomenological approach to emotional experience would take as point of departure feelings that are present and felt. When psychoanalytically informed, such a perspective would also include assumptions about the existence of feelings that are present but disavowed and thus remain unconscious and feelings that exist only in the form of an unconscious potential. In the language of object relations theory, the work of affect formation implies that

> fragmentation (dissociation, isolation) of the ideational content of the affect is diminished, pertinent self-representations and object representations attain consciousness more readily and vividly, potential dangers are identified and possibly modified, and effectively communicative forms of expression are reemployed or created (Schafer, 1964, p. 279).

Due to the traditional therapeutic emphasis on the undoing of repression and isolation of affect, the literature on the structuralization of unconscious feelings that exist only in the form of an unconscious potential is scant.

The approach that is developed here to the processes of information transformation (Temoshok, 1983) that culminate in feelings as mental contents and that precede speech derives from an effort to integrate object relations theory, an ego-psychological approach to style (Rosen, 1961; Shapiro, 1965; Horowitz, 1972), and the developmental psychologies of Bruner (1964), Piaget (1954), and Werner (1961).

In psychology, form is commonly identified with the how as compared to the what (content) of behavior. As ego psychology has become more articulated, form has come to be recognized as a characteristic of all that we experience as well as a characteristic of all that expresses experience. In other words, form is the "appearance" in which experiences present themselves in consciousness as well as in communicative exchanges. According to the hybrid perspective that guides this work, action, imagery, and language are the end products of three independent forms or systems of processing new experiences, constructing inner models of experiences, and representing to awareness past experiences. An extended discussion of this evolving point of view can be found in Geller et al. (1981). For the purposes of the present chapter, what I wish to emphasize is that action, imagery, and language each codify the "reality" of a feeling differently. For example, each of these forms of representation vary in their "concreteness" (Bruner, 1964) and, therefore, focus attention on a different feature of the internal experience of a remembered feeling.

Resumption of the postures, gestures, and facial expressions (enactive [Bruner, 1964] or sensorimotor [Piaget, 1954] representations) appropriate to an emotion brings one closest to the physicality of the immediate experience. Imaginings of the auditory, visual, gustatory, and so on (i.e., imagistic) events that originally aroused the emotion also highlight the quality of immediate experience. Just as music has import that is directly felt and known, representations having a sensory quality (e.g., the voice of the conscience) express feelings directly without the intervention of "intellectual" processes. Words also vary in their felt proximity to physical experience. The experiential referents of metaphors, for example, bear a closer relationship to the internal sensuous experience of a feeling than do abstract nouns. Perhaps, as Langer (1953) has concluded, the structure of nondiscursive modes of knowing (images and movement) bears a closer similarity to the "forms of feeling" than do words and their grammatical organization.

As the preceding discussion implies, promoting access to vivid imagery can serve far more than aesthetic and rhetorical purposes. Under various circumstances, such efforts can make a substantial contribution to the forming of feelings to the point where they are recognizable as being one kind of feeling and not another. Helping alexithymic patients, for example, to "allow themselves" to form concrete auditory, visual, and kinesthetic representations out of vaguely apprehended regressed feelings and pains may be an important first step toward the formation of differentiated affects. There is growing evidence to suggest that it is in the imagistic mode that preverbal memories, unresolved traumatic episodes, disavowed self-appraisals, and conflicted interpersonal fantasies may enter awareness after a prolonged period of repression (Singer, 1974).

Central to my working clinical model is the assumption that the elements of feelings may be named by separate words, but feelings themselves (as experienced qualities) and their meanings are constituted by the sensuous relations between the modes of representation. Bruner's (1964) investigations of cognitive growth indicate that during the course of development, the processes of differentiation result in the articulation of functional boundaries between each of these modes of representation. In addition to acquiring their own unique properties, therefore, their relations may eventually come to be either mutually facilitating and congruent or disjunctive. When they are disjunctive, inhibitions to awareness can occur at the boundaries between representational systems (Horowitz, 1972). One may stubbornly resist demands, that is, be angry but not feel angry, if one has dissociatively assigned the discrete or incompatible components of a conflict to the various forms of representation. Longstanding cleavages and imbalances in their relations may be an essential characteristic of "neurotic styles" (Shapiro, 1965). Like Horowitz (1983), I believe that the capacities to explore, coordinate, and integrate the forms of representation are central to each individual's unique and generalized style of information processing and that conscious efforts to attend to external reality or the state of the body itself are mediated autonomously by such styles. Rigid characterological styles may fill the field of attention with one mode of representation at the expense of others; word-ridden obsessionals have constricted access to enactive or imagistic representations of the concrete phenomena to which their words refer.

Other styles of information processing, such as the hysterical, inhibit the translation of imagistic representations into specific words describing their meanings. More broadly stated, the forms in which emotions present themselves to awareness bear a variable relationship to the forms in which they are communicated. For example, one cannot determine from the manifest content of a reported conflict alone how the opposing tendencies are represented in the privacy of consciousness.

I take it as an experiential and theoretical given that individuals with varying degrees of skill and anxiety can detach their attention from the so-called content of their private experiences and scan or distinguish their form. I have also found that the ability to empathize with others' momentary psychophysiological states can be enlarged by attending to the ways in which they translate between modes of representation. Such inquiries reveal the particular principles of arrangement that disorganize and give rise to discontinuities in subjective experience. Moreover, sustained attentiveness to this task can help to reintegrate or coordinate the continuous interplay between the modes of representation. For example, obsessives, in a sense, need to learn or relearn how to listen to the face and look at the voice of their therapists. Such therapeutic work promotes insights that are experienced synaesthetically. The ancient Greeks coined the term "synaesthesia" to refer to the sensorial effort of harmonizing different or opposing impulses (Youngblood, 1970).

THE REPRESENTATION OF CONFLICT

Viewed developmentally, the distinctive configurations of self and object representations that thematically structure the experience of conflict can be arranged in a hierarchic order. In other words, both the form and content of the inner experience of conflict are organized at different levels of emotional maturity. Patients tend to concentrate on one element at a time when describing conflicts. Conflicts tend to be expressed in terms of either/or choices. Therefore, a good deal of therapeutic work is designed to move patients in the direction of a logic that expresses conflicts in terms of both-and rather than binary yes-no formulas. The consistent representation of conflict in terms of fully integrated and divergent aspects of the self is also an advanced developmental achievement. Conflicts that are represented in what object relations theorists call "the introjective mode," by contrast, generally manifest themselves as imaged action fantasies in which the strivings and wishes of the self are confronted with the antithetical values, prohibitions, and injunctions of "internalized others" (Dorpat, 1981). Essentially, introjects are schematic representations of an individual's current and past experiences, real and fantasized, of the self in relation to others. Although this discussion emphasizes their phenomenological properties, they are seldom in conscious awareness. Their existence may not necessarily be consciously perceived, and they can be used or reacted to with or without conscious awareness of their significance (Schafer, 1968). When brought to awareness, these fantasized others tend to be experienced as "felt presences" existing within the confines of the body or mind or both. They are not, however, experienced as an expression of the subjective self. They are experienced somehow as separate from the self. On the one hand, such introjects are capable of "making" an individual feel unable to do various actions. On the other hand, they can serve as the vehicle for the discharge of unacceptable impulses. Still again, and not infrequently, individuals consult their representations of approving and/or forbidding authority figures, who in turn instruct them to control their feelings in general or to curtail the expression of certain feelings in particular.

Psychosomatic patients whom I have treated often conceive of conflicts in terms of the model of tensions between unassimilated and impersonal "forces." In contrast to psychologically symptomatic patients, they do not seem to rely primarily on anthropomorphic metaphors to interpret the experience of conflict or the "otherness" of introjects. At the most regressed levels of representation, pain may not be capable of being differentiated from the painful affects that conflicts inspire within and between people. When individuals lack the representational capacities to articulate simultaneously opposing tendencies—yes-no, good-bad, in-out—it is more appropriate to speak of emotional turmoil or upheaval than of emotional conflict.

INTROJECTION AND THE FORMATION OF AFFECT

The psychoanalytic literature, until recently, has emphasized the study of "pathological" introjects. What is being suggested here is that the psychotherapeutic role of introjection in furthering the structuralization and embodiment of feelings deserves increased attention. The introjective mode of internalization is generally described as a kind of "taking in" of external others that enables individuals to refer to and to think about them without their being physically present (Meissner, 1981). Introjection enables a patient to preserve and replicate within self-experience the new modes of looking, listening, talking, and being with that are made available in psychotherapy. The creation of such action fantasies, particularly when they serve to continue the therapeutic dialogue in the physical absence of the therapist, can humanize the "inscape" and promote the capacity to maintain affective relatedness.

Our research (Geller et al., 1981) indicates that the therapist introjects that patients create range in the extent to which they are embodied and personified. At one extreme, the felt presence of the therapist is experienced as an inert, static, two-dimensional, or aggregate of part properties rather than as a whole human being. At the other extreme, representation of therapists as human bodies in their environmental context is highly elaborated. The representation is saturated with a sense of mobility and vitality, and in evoking the representation the person has a distinctive and varied experience. Access to such representations makes remembrances of sensory experiences possible (Stanislavski, 1948) and evokes a "feeling of life." They also appear to be correlated with self-perceived growth and the relief of pain.

To summarize, from the perspective of introjection, psychotherapies promote the structuralization of the self and the acquisition of the capacities required for autonomous self-regulation to the extent that they maximize the conditions allowing for the creation of "benignly influential," recurring, relatively stable cognitive-affective representations of the functional aspects of the therapeutic relationship that develop in the direction of becoming more verbalizable, differentiated, complex, and hierarchically organized.

In subsequent publications, I hope to further explore the therapeutic implications of the many questions raised by this "work in progress," for instance:

1. What are the representational configurations that embody the subjective experience of truth-telling?

2. What representational transformations do feelings undergo as they are recognized, identified, and felt toward?
3. Are interventions empathic to the extent that they are formulated at a symbolic level and in a stylistic mode that is comprehensible to the other?
4. Do feelings pass through various preparatory or transitory stages before they appear in clear, conscious forms?
5. Does recognizing and actively mirroring patients' habitual styles of using and translating among the modes of representation promote the development of higher levels of integration between modes of information processing and the progressive differentiation of the body and its biological forces?

REFERENCES

Arlow, J., & Brenner, C. (1964). *Psychoanalytic Concepts and the Structural Theory*. New York, NY: International Universities Press.

Arnold, M.B. (1970). *Feelings and Emotions: The Loyola Symposium*. New York, NY: Academic Press.

Blatt, S.J. (1974). Levels of object representation in anaclitic and introjective depression. *Psychoanalytic Study of the Child* 29:107–157.

Bower, G.H. (1981). Mood and memory. *Am Psychol* 36:129–148.

Bruner, J.S. (1964). The course of cognitive growth. *American Psychologist* 19:1–15.

Denzin, N.K. (1981, September 8). *A Note on Emotionality, Self, and Interaction*. Paper presented at the annual meeting of the Society for the Study of Symbolic Interaction, San Francisco, CA.

Dorpat, T. (1981). Basic concepts and terms in object relations theory. In S. Tuttman, C. Kay, & M. Zimmerman (Eds.), *Object and Self: A Developmental Approach* (pp.149–178). New York, NY: International Universities Press.

Easser B.R., & Lesser, S.R. (1965). Hysterical personality: A reevaluation. *Psychoanalytic Quarterly* 34:390–405.

Ekman, P. (1972). Universals and cultural differences in facial expressions of emotion. In J.K. Cole (Ed.), *Nebraska Symposium on Motivation* (Vol. 19). Lincoln, NE: University of Nebraska Press.

———— & Levenson, R. (1983). Emotions differ in autonomic nervous system activity. *Science* 221:1208–1210.

Fenichel, O. (1954). The ego and the affects. In *Collected Papers of Otto Fenichel* (Vol. 2, pp. 215–217). New York, NY: Norton. (Original work published 1941.)

Gaylin, W. (1982). *Feelings: Our Vital Signs*. New York, NY: Ballantine Books.

Geller, J.D. (1978). The body, expressive movement, and physical contact in psychotherapy. In J.L. Singer & K.S. Pope (Eds.), *The Power of Human Imagination* (pp. 347–378). New York, NY: Plenum Press.

————, Cooley, R.S., & Hartley, D. (1981). Images of the psychotherapist: A theoretical and methodological perspective. *Imagination, Cognition and Personality* 1(2):123–146.

———— & Howenstine, R.A. (1980). Adult men as romantic lovers. In K. Pope (Ed.), *On Love and Loving* (pp. 61–89). San Francisco, CA: Jossey-Bass.

Gordon, S.L. (1981). The sociology of sentiments and emotion. In S.L. Rosenberg & R.H. Turner (Eds.), *Social Psychology: Sociological Perspectives* (pp. 562–592). New York, NY: Basic Books.

Guntrip, H. (1969). *Schizoid Phenomena, Object Relations and the Self*. New York, NY: International Universities Press.

Hartocollis, P., & Lester, E.P. (1982). New directions in affect theory. *JAPA* 30:197–211.

Hopkins, G.M. (1953). *Poems and Prose* (W.H. Gardner, Ed.). New York, NY: Penguin Press.

Horowitz, M.J. (1972). Modes of representation of thought. *Journal of the American Psychoanalytic Association* 20:793–819.

———— (1983). *Image Formation and Psychotherapy*. New York, NY: Jason Aronson.

Jacobson, E. (1957). On normal and pathological moods. In *The Psychoanalytic Study of the Child* (Vol. 12, pp. 73–113). New York, NY: International Universities Press.

James, W. (1890). *The Principles of Psychology*. New York, NY: Henry Holt.

Kernberg, O. (1976). *Object Relations Theory and Clinical Psychoanalysis*. New York, NY: Jason Aronson.

Klein, G.S. (1976). *Psychoanalytic Theory*. New York, NY: International University Press.

Krystal, H. (1974). The genetic development of affects and affect regression. *The Annual of Psychoanalysis* 2:98–126.

Langer, S.K. (1953). *Feeling and Form*. New York, NY: Charles Scribner's Sons.

Lewis, H.B. (1981). Shame and guilt in human nature. In S. Tuttman, C. Kaye, & M. Zimmerman (Eds.), *Object and Self: A Developmental Approach* (pp. 253–265). New York, NY: International Universities Press.

Lipowski, Z. (1977). Psychosomatic medicine in the seventies: An overview. *Am J Psychiatry* 134:233–243.

Loewald, H.W. (1962). Internalization, separation, mourning, and the superego. *Psychoanalytic Quarterly* 31:483–504.

Mahler, M.S. (1966). Development of basic moods. In R.M. Loewenstein, L.M. Newman, & M. Schor (Eds.), *Psycho-*

analysis: A General Psychology (pp. 152–166). New York, NY: International Universities Press.

Mandler, G., Mandler, J.M., & Uviller, E.T. (1958). Autonomic feedback: The perception of autonomic activity. *The Journal of Abnormal and Social Psychology 56*(3):367–373.

Meissner, W.W. (1981). *Internalization in Psychoanalysis*. New York, NY: International Universities Press.

Moffat, M.J. (1982). *In the Midst of Winter: Selections from the Literature of Mourning*. New York, NY: Random House.

Nemiah, J.C. (1978). Alexithymia and psychosomatic illness. *J Continuing Ed Psychiatry* 39:25–37.

Novey, S. (1958). A clinical view of affect theory in psychoanalysis. *Int J Psychoanal* 40:94–104.

———— (1961). Further considerations on affect theory in psychoanalysis. *Int J Psychoanal* 42:21–32.

Nowlis, V. (1968). Research with the mood adjective check list. In S. Tomkin & C. Izard (Eds.), *Affect: Measurement of Awareness and Performance*. New York, NY: Springer.

Pelletier, K.P. (1979). *Mind as Healer, Mind as Slayer*. New York, NY: Delta.

Piaget, J. (1954). *The Construction of Reality in the Child*. New York, NY: Basic Books.

Rapaport, D. (1954). On the psychoanalytic theory of affect. In R.P. Knight & C.R. Friedman (Eds.), *Psychoanalytic Psychiatry and Psychology* (pp. 274–310). New York, NY: International Universities Press.

Reich, W. (1949). *Character Analysis*. New York, NY: Orgone Institute Press.

Rosen, V. (1961). The relevance of "style" to certain aspects of defense and the synthetic function of the ego. *International Journal of Psychoanalysis* 42:447–457.

Schachtel, E.G. (1959). *Metamorphosis: On the Development of Affect, Perception, Attention, and Memory.* New York, NY: Basic Books.

Schachter, S. (1964). The interaction of cognitive and physiological determinants of emotional state. In L. Berkowitz (Ed.), *Advances in Experimental Social Psychology.* New York, NY: Academic Press.

———— & Singer, J. (1962). Cognitive, social, and psychological determinants of emotional state. *Psychol Rev* 69:379–399.

Schafer, R. (1964). The clinical analysis of affect. *JAPA* 12:275–299.

———— (1968). *Aspects of Internalization.* New York, NY: International Universities Press.

———— (1970). The psychoanalytic vision of reality. *International Journal of Psychoanalysis* 51(3):279–297.

———— (1976). *A New Language for Psychoanalysis.* New Haven, CT: Yale University Press.

Schwartz, G.E. (1983). Disregulation theory and disease: Applications to the repression/cerebral disconnection/cardiovascular disorder hypothesis. *International Review of Applied Psychology* 32(2):95–118.

Selye, H. (1956). *The Stress of Life.* New York, NY: McGraw Hill.

Shapiro, D. (1965). *Neurotic Styles.* New York, NY: Basic Books.

Sifneos, P.E. (1974). A reconsideration of psychodynamic mechanisms in psychosomatic symptom formation in view of recent clinical observations. *Psychother Psychosom* 24:125–132.

———— (1975). Problems of psychotherapy patients with alexithymic characteristics and physical disease. *Psychother Psychosom* 26:65–70.

Singer, J.L. (1974). *Imagery and Daydream Methods in Psychotherapy and Behavior Modification*. New York, NY: Academic Press.

Stanislavski, C. (1948). *An Actor Prepares* (E.R. Hapgood, Trans.). New York, NY: Theatre Arts Books.

Temoshok, L. (1983). Emotion, adaptation, and disease: A multidimensional theory. In L. Temoshok, C. VanDyke, & L.S. Zegans (Eds.), *Emotions in Health and Illness: Theoretical and Research Foundations* (pp. 207–233). Orlando, FL: Grune & Stratton.

Tomkins, S.S. (1962). *Affect Imagery Consciousness: Vol. 1. The Positive Affects*. New York, NY: Springer.

Weiss, J. (1959). Intensity as a character trait. *Psychoanal Quarterly* 28:64–72.

Werner, H. (1961). *Comparative Psychology of Mental Development*. New York, NY: Science Editions.

Youngblood, G. (1970). *Expanded Cinema*. New York, NY: Dutton.

Zetzel, E. (1964). Depression and the incapacity to bear it. In M. Schur (Ed.), *Drives, Affects, Behavior* (Vol. 2, pp. 243–274). New York, NY: International Universities Press.

CHAPTER 4

The Process of Psychotherapy: Separation and the Complex Interplay Among Empathy, Insight, and Internalization

[J.D. Geller (1987). In J. Bloom-Feshbach & S. Bloom-Feshbach (Eds.), *The Psychology of Separation and Loss: Perspectives on Development, Life Transitions, and Clinical Practice* (pp. 459–514). San Francisco, CA: Jossey-Bass.]

It is the image in the mind that binds us to our lost treasures,
but it is the loss that shapes the image.
—Colette

Psychotherapy has become one of the major resources in our culture for helping individuals come to terms with the accumulating experiences of separation and loss endured during a lifetime. Every day, psychotherapists provide consolation and understanding to individuals who have suffered separation by exclusion, rejection, abandonment, betrayal, and disillusionment. As the meanings and rituals associated with death have become more secularized, psychotherapists have increasingly assumed the solemn responsibility of enabling the bereaved to complete what Freud (1917) called the "work" of mourning. Therapists are regularly called on to help individuals manage the raw and often violent emotions that accompany the dissolution of a marriage or love affair. Many of their patients are people who are having difficulty dealing with externally imposed endings or transitions: receiving a promotion, graduation from a training program, the aftermath of compulsory retirement, inability to honor publication deadlines, curtailment of activities due to accidents and disease, the "empty nest," and so forth. Some come to therapy because they feel afraid whenever separated from the familiarity and security of their homes. Still others seek psychotherapy because they have lost faith in their capacity to achieve an autonomous feeling of identity (a "self") clearly marked off from the key persons in their lives.

The theories of psychopathology that guide the work of psychotherapists grant varying degrees of importance to the universal themes of separation and loss. Rank (1924/1952) was an early advocate of the view that all neurotic symptoms could be interpreted as an expression of the thesis and antithesis of separation and union. Freud (1926) came to regard separation anxiety as the primal, prototypical anxiety. Existential psychotherapists (e.g., May, 1961; Boss, 1963) have always given particular importance to the idea of separateness and its relation to loneliness, awareness of nonbeing, a sense of responsibility, and the struggle to achieve personal freedom. More recently, the processes of separation and individuation have been assigned new prominence among psychotherapists influenced by the object relations theorists within psychoanalysis (e.g., Fairbairn, 1952; Loewald, 1962; Winnicott, 1965; Guntrip, 1969; Mahler et al., 1975; Kernberg, 1976; Searles, 1977; Stolorow & Ross, 1978; Mahler, 1979; Meissner, 1981), the self psychology of Kohut (1971, 1977), and the attachment theory of Bowlby (1969, 1973).

My own efforts to grapple with the multiform ways in which separations present themselves in psychotherapy are based on a selective integration of psychoanalytic and existential teachings along with the contributions of developmental cognitive psychologists (Piaget, 1954; Werner, 1961; Bruner, 1964). Though differing in important respects, therapists working in these traditions share the belief that a phenomenologically based, developmentally informed, empathic appreciation of the ways individuals internally represent interactions with others and act on behalf of, or in response to, these representations is essential to understanding the diversity and complexity of the processes set in motion by separations and losses, whether actual or symbolic. The emerging view in the psychoanalytic literature is that the predominant emotional tone, painfulness, and duration of the feelings induced by the loss or threatened loss of a relationship as well as the meanings ascribed to those feelings are prefigured by the mental models of relationships that populate an individual's "representational world" (Sandler & Rosenblatt, 1962). There is growing consensus that, to the extent that individuals have failed to acquire realistic and cohesive representations of themselves as separate and different from others and feel incapable of functioning independently, they are vulnerable to severe and prolonged reactions to the conditions that would best promote the creation of "new" therapeutic cognitive/affective representations of the functional aspects and qualities of the therapy relationship. Psychotherapists guided by this concern make the fundamental assumption that when mental models of relationships develop in the direction of becoming increasingly embodied, differentiated, and hierarchically organized, they advance the journey toward a constructive acceptance of the separateness, uniqueness, autonomy, historicity, and finitude of the self and others.

The primary aim of this chapter is to extend the implications of these trends and assumptions for the individual psychotherapy of adult patients. I will argue for a model of psychotherapy that assigns complementary roles to insight and to that form of internalization known as introjection in explaining how events happening in the two-person psychotherapy relationship move patients toward successive levels of maturity in dealing with the crises of separation that prompted their entrance into therapy.

To illustrate the value of this perspective, I will focus on the therapeutic potential of sustained, empathically infused inquiries into the problematic nature and quality of patients' reactions to the spatial, temporal, and interpersonal boundaries that separate them from their therapists. Every issue to be discussed within this perspective is linked to the view that exploring patients' unique modes of negotiating the separations, losses, transitions, and endings woven into psychotherapy itself concurrently (1) facilitates the conscious recovery and reconstruction of damaging mental models of relationships (acquired as a function of early attachment- and separation-related events) so that they can be expressed in the form of differentiated feelings and memories, independent of overt behavior, and (2) activates, at the introjective level of symbolization, the processes that preserve and replicate, within self-experience, the beneficial actions originally experienced during therapy sessions.

For reasons that will become gradually apparent, the following questions can profitably serve to organize these inquiries: What characteristics does a patient ascribe to his or her therapist? What roles or functions does the therapist serve for the patient? What are the emotional consequences for the patient of the therapist's failure or unwillingness to meet his or her needs, expectations, or wishes? Can the patient maintain a durable, positive attachment to the therapist regardless of fluctuations in need states or externally imposed frustrations?

One cannot conceive of separation apart from attachment or from the interdependence of self and others. Similarly, attachment and separation, like frustration and gratification, are polar principles. Separations and attachments are also sources of frustration and gratification. When patients have been chronically separated from the affectionate and caring concern of valued others, they tend to respond in a particularly problematic way both to the frustrating aspects of separations and to the gratifications made possible by intimate attachments to others. Throughout this chapter, particular attention will be given to the therapeutic challenges posed by patients suffering from this two-fold difficulty. To conclude, I will briefly discuss the ways therapists define, order, and negotiate the tasks arising during the termination phase.

THE WORK STRUCTURE OF PSYCHOTHERAPY

Establishing and Regulating Boundaries

Psychotherapy can be differentiated from other forms of human relatedness in a variety of ways. From an open-systems perspective, the psychotherapeutic enterprise can be differentiated from other aspects of the interpersonal environment on the basis of discontinuities of time, space, and task definition (Astrachan et al., 1971). Temporal, spatial, and interpersonal boundaries of various kinds are also woven into the work structure of psychotherapy.

To begin with, all psychotherapies, whether explicitly time-limited or not, terminate. The very success of a psychotherapy signals the readiness of the relationship to end. Second, psychotherapy takes place only in an environment created, maintained, and sanctioned by the therapist. John Updike (1966) has commented that the settings where therapists work occupy an ambiguous terrain, midway between an office and a home. Therapists pledge confidentiality and protect the relationship from external interruptions and distractions. For example, within the intimate confines of individual psychotherapy, a patient's significant others are excluded from sessions. The role requirements of psychotherapy are such that therapists also have primary responsibility for defining the temporal parameters of the relationship, including length of sessions, interval between sessions, their availability during intersession intervals, timing and duration of their vacations, and in some instances the total duration of the psychotherapy. Sessions are typically scheduled at regular and therefore predictable intervals. Encounters with therapists are rhythmically spaced. Therapeutic sessions also have a more or less fixed duration, and therapists avoid or limit contact with their patients in extratherapeutic situations. Most therapists in private practice continue to follow Freud's (1913) recommendation of "leasing a definite hour" to each patient. Whether to charge, as Freud further recommended, full fee for missed or canceled appointments as a deterrent to motivated absences remains a source of perennial controversy.

Much needs to be learned about the management of the temporal parameters of psychotherapy. Current guidelines for the optimal duration and frequency of sessions are not empirically grounded, and recommendations tend to be idiosyncratic. Langs (1976) advocates a frequency of two sessions a week, with increases for patients who are psychotic or imminently so or who are "acting out." By contrast, Saul (1972) recommends a basic frequency of three sessions a week. In Weiner's (1975) view, a week is the maximum interval across which a patient is likely to work consistently on his or her problems. Writing of psychoanalysis, Glover (1955) suggests that after forty-eight hours there is a "dwindling" of responses to the "average current stimulus" of the analyst.

Therapists are empowered to establish, regulate, and limit transactions across the temporal and spatial boundaries that differentiate psychotherapy as a social system from the rest of the interpersonal environment. This empowerment highlights the status inequalities that separate the positions of patient and therapist. Psychotherapists not only function as symbols of authority but also occupy a *position* of authority. Most broadly stated, psychotherapists, in their roles as institutionally sanctioned experts, have the primary responsibility for defining the tasks and division of labor required to accomplish the work of psychotherapy (Geller et al., 1976). As conceptualized here, it is the imposition of these tasks that transforms a relationship between two individuals into a therapeutic situation and sets in motion a benignly influential and healing process.

The Search for Synthetic Solutions: The Importance of Empathy

The tasks that therapists impose on themselves require the synthetic resolution of a wide variety of polarities. Rhythmic oscillations between commitment and detachment, gratification and frustration, immediacy and deferral, passion and decorum, levity and gravity, emotional understanding and intellectual comprehension, talking and listening, and so on are required to practice psychotherapy creatively. In their search for a vocabulary to describe the coordinations or integrations required to optimize a patient's adaptation to the therapeutic process, therapists have invented such terms as "participant observation," "benign impartiality," "detached concern," "selective authenticity," and "disciplined subjectivity." In the terminology of Piaget (1954), therapeutic competence entails assimilating patients into one's existing conception of the rules, rituals, and roles of psychotherapy while, in a complementary fashion, accommodating the work structure to effect a better fit with the unique needs and circumstances of each patient.

Empathy provides a means for synthesizing Piaget's dual imperatives and makes an indispensable contribution to honoring the uniqueness of each individual. In his most recent statement, Rogers (1975) describes empathy as a

complex, demanding, strong, subtle, and gentle process...
of entering the private perceptual world of the other and
becoming thoroughly at home in it. It includes being sensitive, moment to moment, to the changing felt meanings which flow in this other person... delicately without
making judgments, seeing meanings of which he/she is
scarcely aware, but not trying to uncover meanings of
which the person is totally unaware, since this would be
too threatening. It includes communicating your sense of
his/her world as you look with fresh eyes at elements of
which the individual is fearful.... To be with another in
this way means that for the time being, you lay aside the
views and values you hold for yourself in order to enter
another's world without prejudice (p. 4).

Psychotherapists of diverse persuasions regard this way of
discovering and conveying the subjective meanings of an individual's experience as the most important element in their
concept of the ideal therapist (Raskin, 1974). Moreover, empirical research indicates that trying to comprehend and share
empathically in the psychological states of patients facilitates
self-exploration and correlates positively with various independent criteria of successful therapeutic outcomes (e.g., Bergin
& Strupp, 1972; Kurtz & Grummon, 1972; Kazdin, 1980).
What will be emphasized here is the ways in which empathically conveyed understandings move patients, via successive
approximations, toward the establishment of more meaningful, coherent connections between disparate, and perhaps
disavowed, aspects of experience. Empathic interventions so
conceived serve to combine, unite, and synthesize that which
has been kept apart.

Survival of the Enterprise

The decision to enter therapy is not made easily or once and for all. It is commonly preceded by lengthy, agonized conflict and a series of unsuccessful prior attempts to master a particular "problem in living" either self-reliantly or with the help of friends and relatives (Farber & Geller, 1977). Moreover, many patients begin therapy compromised in their ability to collaborate with therapists in a mutually satisfying pursuit of solutions to the troublesome aspects of their lives. These difficulties often make their first appearance in the form of dysfunctional responses to the tasks therapists impose on their patients. These tasks, in varying proportions, require self-reflectiveness, free recall of past events, intimate self-disclosure, the development of an emotional attachment to the therapist, cognitive processing of "new" information, attentiveness to nonverbal behavior, and accommodations to the ambiguities and work structure of therapy as defined by the therapist. Establishment of a genuinely collaborative and emotionally honest relationship often requires repeated clarification of the relevance of these tasks to the goals of therapy (Bardin, 1976). In order to erode obstacles to the development of what has been called a "working alliance" (Greenson, 1967) or a "therapeutic alliance" (Friedman, 1969), a therapist must consider patients' initial expectations of how the therapy relationship should or will proceed, as shaped by their characterologically based styles of help seeking (Rickers-Ovsiankina et al., 1971). Failure to attend empathically to this task can intensify a patient's suffering and jeopardize the continued existence of the enterprise, and it may prompt patients to leave psychotherapy before they can experience its benefits.

In actual practice, therapists often fall short of being empathic, and many therapies terminate before desired or planned-for outcomes are achieved. There is, in fact, a high attrition rate during the initial phase of psychotherapy, the first 10 sessions (Baekeland & Lundwall, 1975). Garfield's (1978) comprehensive review of the literature finds that clinics typically report that 50% or more of their patients withdraw from therapy before the eighth session and over 65% before the 10th. In some comprehensive mental health centers, over 50% of patients from minority group backgrounds drop out of therapy after only *one* interview (Sue, 1977; Geller, 1988).

Although "premature terminations" are commonplace and are a source of deep concern to clinicians, very few studies have sought out their determinants. One notable exception is a retrospective study of early terminators by Kline et al. (1974). These investigators found that ex-patients weighed the "perception" that their therapist was not interested in them most heavily in their decision to drop out of therapy. Moreover, about half the patients who were recontacted reported that they had sought help elsewhere after dropping out of therapy, leading the authors to conclude that many patients who terminate prematurely are not lacking in motivation to obtain help, as professionals often assume, but rather are reacting to the failure to find it.

That a psychotherapy may be in danger of ending prematurely can be inferred from the ways a patient responds to the external boundaries that encircle the therapeutic enterprise and the interpersonal boundaries that differentiate the positions of patient and therapist. Here I would include such warning signals as rigid accentuations of the status inequalities that separate therapist and patient, dependently demanding requests for extratherapeutic gratifications, tendencies to agree or disagree indiscriminately with the therapist, uncertainties about the privacy of bodily and mental experiences (and consequent withholding of "secrets"), confusion over the distinction between the therapist's professional role and his or her personality, and functional restrictions in the ability to retain the distinction between self and other while experiencing empathic closeness.

Insight and an Atemporal Perspective on Relationships

Empathic exploration of the nature, origins, and significance of these interactional phenomena plays a predominant role in some therapies, a lesser one in others, but is of some importance in all therapies. The pursuit of such understandings recommends itself for a variety of reasons. A focus on the patient's behavior *in* therapy is consistent with the widely held belief that for interpretations to be effective, they must be directed to the patient's concrete experience (Hammer, 1968). As Strachey (1934) said, "for an interpretation to be 'transmutative,' it must be 'emotionally immediate.' The patient must experience it as 'something *actual*'" (p. 136). Extending the implications of this technical principle, I would argue, following Gill (1982), that if patients are to benefit from insight into their methods of coping with the stress of separations in the essential relationships in their lives, they must experience and reflect on these methods within the "here and now" context of the transference. Reliance on transference interpretations derives from the assumption that, during the course of therapy, patients relive and reenact, rather than merely talk about, their prototypical reactions to the loss or threatened loss of relationships. Goleman (1984) expressed this conviction as follows:

> Of course, each kind of leave-taking is distinct in many ways from all others, with its own intrinsic problems, pain, and promise. Nevertheless, those who study the momentous departures in life often find common strands that

bind them, and it is possible to see in any goodbye the texture and the lessons of all those that preceded it and that will follow (p. C1).

As I understand the concept, transference is a particular instance and potential liability of the universal tendency to perceive and cognitively structure new experiences on the basis of the enduring and often unconscious schemata, or mental models, that people construct of persons and of transactions with them (Singer, 1985). All relationships, to varying extents, are influenced by spontaneously recurring attempts, made unknowingly, to perceive and feel toward others as if they represented important figures from the past. A psychoanalytically designed therapeutic situation distinguishes itself by providing patients with repeated and varied opportunities to learn how their efforts to collaborate with the therapist as a "real person" are distorted by the biasing influence of defensive displacements and the projection of mental models of relationships that are reacted to without awareness of their existence or significance.

Such inquiries help patients to discriminate more clearly between the past and the present and to develop a more integrated perspective on the evolution of persons and relationships over time. A stylistic analysis of a patient's use of language can reveal whether the patient is alienated from his or her personal past, lives in ceaseless transition, or appreciates that events and interactions have significance from the vantage point of the time at which they occurred. Patients whose sense of personal continuity is impaired have great difficulty in telling "stories" about themselves that have a clearly intelligible beginning, middle, and end. Statements are made about the self or others as if they were applicable at any point in time, whether past, present, or future.

By linking sessions together thematically, therapists can help patients to recognize their continuity in time as well as challenge directly and immediately an atemporal perspective on relationships. Interconnected narratives increase an awareness of the relations that exist between what was, what is, and what will be. This function can also be served by working within the context of a precise, time-limited therapy contract. Mann (1973) maintains that such a structural framework mobilizes the personal meanings that separations and endings have for patients with greater clarity than psychotherapies that leave open the question of duration. Whether or not a termination date is set early on, clinical experience supports the hypothesis that dealing with separation anxieties from the very beginning of therapy prevents overwhelming crises at the time of termination. Ends of hours, canceled sessions, and vacations as well as intra-hour ruptures of attachment, including pauses or breaks—actual or impending—in the flow of the therapeutic dialogue, are "apprenticeships" (Edelson, 1963) during which patients and therapists can struggle to acquire the understanding and skills to handle the end of therapy constructively.

I believe that when transference-based interpretations of patients' responses to these mini-separations are empathically and developmentally informed, they facilitate the growth and differentiation of the representational capacities that enable a patient to derive maximum benefit from the processes and results of insight and internalization. The rest of this chapter is devoted to the hypothesis that insight and internalization reactivate the processes of "representational differentiation and consolidation" (Schafer, 1973a) and, in so doing, conjointly bring about enduring changes in a patient's sense of self, capacity to organize conflicts, and ability to maintain secure and realistic "internal working models" (Bowlby, 1969, 1973) of attachment to individual beloved persons during their physical absence. According to the hybrid perspective that guides my work, the representational capacities underlying these sectors of the personality unfold according to developmental principles and timetables, are influenced by the phase-specific tasks, crises, and conflicts of early childhood, and shape the unique route that the individual travels in dealing with the recurrent crises of separation encountered during the life course. To clarify the implications of these assumptions, I will next compare the varying types of difficulty that neurotic, schizoid, and borderline patients have with the evocative challenges posed by the gratifying and frustrating aspects of psychotherapy. In responding to these diagnostic categories, the reader is encouraged to bear in mind that "every man is in certain respects (a) like all other men, (b) like some other men, (c) like no other man" (Kluckhohn & Murray, 1949, p. 53).

SEPARATION AND THE REPRESENTATION OF CONFLICT

Separations, as distinct from endings or permanent losses, initiate a process that is completed by the reunion of the participants in a relationship. Separation, in this sense, implies both moving away from and coming back together. That the therapist decides when, where, and for how long he or she will be available complicates this cycle and charges it emotionally. On the one hand, the rhythmic regularity with which therapists space therapeutic sessions can reintroduce a sense of congruent order into lives more accustomed to anarchy. It is not uncommon for patients in once-weekly psychotherapy to define the beginning and end of each week as occurring on the day of their therapy session. The regular recurrence of sessions presents concrete evidence of the therapist's reliability and trustworthiness. On the other hand, the time limitations and spatial restrictions that therapists impose on their patients are sources of conflict. They activate patients' problematic relations with "authority figures." Like the "abstinent" (Freud, 1917) therapist's neutrality, restricted rate of verbalization, impersonal diction, and refusals to provide advice or affirmations about actions taken, the spatial and temporal boundaries that separate patient and therapist are also *real* deprivations.

The very human imperfections of the "good enough" psychotherapist confront patients with still another potent source of conflict. All therapists make mistakes, perhaps the most important of which are the failures of empathy that inevitably occur during a lengthy and ambitious psychotherapy. In the ordinary conduct of psychotherapy, empathic failures take various forms, such as premature interpretations, accurate but narrowly apprehended interpretations, inadvertently intrusive assertions of certainty ("You *must* have felt..."), generalities that compromise a patient's uniqueness, and defensively prompted retreats from empathic immersion in a patient's psychic reality. Empathic failures such as these are, for patients, mini-experiences of separation and loss. They engender a feeling of not being recognized or understood and, hence, of being alone.

Individuals beginning therapy vary enormously in their readiness and ability to recognize, tolerate, and deal openly with the felt internality of the conflicts, depressive states, and memories of unempathic parenting precipitated by the varying sources of separation and frustration inherent in psychotherapy. Individuals who fall within the normal-neurotic range of functioning can usually be expected to experience the contradictory tugs of conflict exerted by feelings that can be localized, distinguished, and described. They tend to organize conflicts in terms of feelings that are differentiated with respect to their ideational and affective components and, when testing the limits of their therapist's authority or availability, do so within the work structure of therapy, as defined by the therapist. Once they have established an emotional attachment to their therapists, enforced separations occasionally arouse within them complex blends of love and hate, relief and regret, deprivation and longing. Intermittently, the status inequalities and power differentials that separate the positions of patient and therapist provoke similar conflicts as well as interpersonal struggles for mutuality and autonomy. And, in response to their therapists' failures of empathy, patients suffering from neurotic character disorders are apt, at varying levels of intensity, to feel sad, fearful, lonely, needy, helpless, self-hating, hostile toward others, apathetic, withdrawn, or hypochondriacal. In general, these feelings and struggles do not overwhelm the therapeutic alliance but rather serve to catalyze more or less frank discussions of the personal, especially unconscious, meanings for the patient of the inherently frustrating limits on the relationship with the therapist. These discussions bring conflicts that originated in childhood and the defenses associated with them into consciousness and, in an inseparable fashion, initiate qualitative changes in a patient's capacity to benefit from the opportunities for interpersonal learning made available in therapy. Gradually, these discussions uncover and attenuate a patient's a patient's resistances to being influenced by the nonspecific agents of healing by the "nonspecific" healing ingredients of psychotherapy (Frank, 1973; Strupp, 1976).

A therapist's empathy and interpretations, as offered, occur within a context in which information is concurrently being transmitted by voice quality, gaze, facial expressions, limb movements, posture, odor, touch, and the animate and inanimate objects that inhabit the therapist's office. These nonlexical contributions to the therapeutic situation convey, *indirectly*, the therapist's empathy as well as their calmness, nonintrusiveness, interest, hopefulness, gentleness, respect, and competence. Moreover, interpretations always contain implicit statements about the therapist himself and his emotional attitudes toward the patient. As Rycroft (1956) has noted, a "correct" interpretation says, in effect,

> I am still here. I have been listening to you. I understand what you are talking about. I remember what you said yesterday, last week, last month, last year. I have been sufficiently interested to listen, and remember, and understand. Also, you are not the only person to have felt this way. You are not incomprehensible. I am not shocked. I am not admonishing you or trying to get you to conform to any ideas of my own as to how you should feel or behave (p. 472).

As a totality, these implicit, nonlexically conveyed messages embody the therapist's so-called nonspecific contributions to the therapeutic dialogue.

Opinions differ on just what conditions must exist if the insights resulting from accurate interpretations are to initiate enduring changes in the ways patients cope with the stress of separations. The majority opinion among analytic therapists is that successful participation in an insight-oriented therapy demands the capacity to bring to awareness the simultaneity of the opposing feelings, impulses, beliefs, and goals that structure the inner experience of conflict (e.g., Krystal, 1979). Schafer (1973b) would additionally argue that it is not expanding awareness itself that promotes growth and change but, rather, the free and open communication of expanded awareness within the context of a relationship that is consistently experienced as benignly influential. My own view is that, for insights to achieve their desired ends, the patient must also be capable of storing, reproducing faithfully, and yielding to the "corrective emotional experiences" (Alexander & French, 1946) carried by the therapist's specific and nonspecific contributions to the therapeutic dialogue.

The Schizoid Dilemma

These various conditions are not prevailing during the opening phases of the treatment of patients who have defensively withdrawn into enduring maladaptive states of separateness. Patients whom Guntrip (1969) would call schizoid "stand apart" from their bodies, from conflicts, and from intimate relationships. A schizoid patient's characteristic orientation to the external world is never to become attached to anybody or anything that might become indispensable. Although such patients complain of feeling trapped inside a "plastic bubble" or a "cocoon" or behind a "sheet of glass," allowing nothing of emotional importance to leave or enter, they nevertheless rigidly attempt to maintain "an illusion of self-sufficiency" (Modell, 1976) early in therapy. Schizoid patients have pronounced needs for privacy and dignity. They experience the invitation to speak truthfully about themselves as inherently subversive and are extremely reluctant to acknowledge that they have "wishes" or that, for the gratification or relief of "needs," benign, predictable, and giving others must exist in the external world. In their efforts to avoid conflicts and disappointments, they may try to forsake all desires for unity, belonging, and love. Because "wishes are to the mind as needs are to the body" (Rieff, 1961, p. 79), pronounced schizoid tendencies alienate individuals from their bodies as well as from interpersonal relationships. Furthermore, schizoid patients experience an absolute contradiction between the state of being authentically involved *in* an experience and simultaneously bringing self-reflectiveness to bear on that experience.

Consequently, they are alienated as well from the concrete and palpable aspects of their own experience.

The conscious efforts of schizoid patients to attend to the "perceptual reality" of the therapeutic dialogue are also more or less disembodied. Schizoid patients are cut off from access to the physicality of the therapeutic situation. Like grief's self-absorption, schizoid detachment precludes receptivity to interpersonal influence or to the external cues that convey compassion. Though exquisitely sensitive to variations in their therapists' depth of involvement, schizoid patients cannot feel the animating presence of their therapists or the bodily closeness implicit in all forms of verbal intimacy. They are unable to tolerate subjective awareness of the therapist's caring concern and genuine interest. They cannot look directly at their therapists and risk seeing whether there is the possibility of gratifying chronically disavowed wishes for consolation or forgiveness. They cannot risk feeling with an empathic therapist who appreciates their loneliness, their stoic self-reliance, and their hyperdeveloped sense of irony. In brief, because of pronounced tendencies toward disembodiment and emotional inaccessibility, schizoid patients lack intimate knowledge of whether or not their therapists are conveying the nonspecific healing ingredients of psychotherapy. Given that the same processes make possible sensitivity to and awareness of one's own and another's bodily states, the insights produced by schizoid patients are therefore in danger of remaining colorless, sterile, and disappointingly nontransformative.

Equally formidable therapeutic challenges are posed by patients suffering from borderline personality disorders (Kernberg, 1976). Whereas schizoid patients begin each hour as if they were greeting a stranger, borderline patients, early in therapy, develop an intense addiction-like attachment to their therapist. They cling to their therapist's concrete presence as if the therapist were an irreplaceable object of use. Yet, like schizoid patients, they have great difficulty assimilating the sensuous fullness of the therapeutic dialogue. Consequently, they are significantly less capable of constructing, inwardly sustaining, and internalizing the realistic and comforting representations of their therapists than normal-neurotic patients. They seem to use their therapists like a drug whose positive effects wear off rapidly between sessions. Further complicating therapeutic work with borderline patients is that they have greater difficulty than neurotic patients coherently formulating and talking openly about the negative feelings, images, cravings, and ideas activated by the disappointments and separations intrinsic in psychotherapy.

The Borderline Condition and a Reduced Sense of Conflict

In order to preserve our illusions, certainty, and innocence, we all occasionally "keep apart" or actively dissociate mutually contradictory perspectives on ourselves or others. Investigations of the cognitive functioning of borderline patients indicate that they, by contrast, rigidly adopt an undialectical, either/or stance toward distinctions of all kinds—for example, yes/no, inside/outside, male/female, weak/strong, dependent/independent, self/nonself (Kernberg, 1976). Patients who chronically segregate positively and negatively charged attributes into such dichotomous categories do not, strictly speaking, experience intrapsychic conflict or ambivalence. Rather, they are vulnerable to emotional turmoil, emotional upheaval, and precipitous transitions between all-encompassing "good" and "bad" moods (Geller, 1984).

Borderline patients are particularly notorious for the radically discontinuous ways in which they alternate between extreme polarized and dissociated states of mind and roles vis-à-vis their therapists. Often within a single hour they will both pick a fight and demand proof of emotional support, only to refuse warmth when given. They may report suicidal feelings and immediately thereafter ask to reduce the frequency of their sessions. They may relate to the therapist first as a powerful, omniscient figure worthy of being supplicated, only to treat him or her, soon after, as an individual to be demeaned and depreciated. Concomitantly, they may rapidly fluctuate between a view of their situation as futile and of themselves as totally worthless, hopeless, and helpless and the megalomaniacal illusion that complete recovery or cure is imminent.

Though obvious to their therapists, these sudden shifts and contradictions are not apparent to patients, for whom there exist separate divisions of "good" and "bad" selves as well as actively kept-apart "good" and "bad" others. As Horowitz and Zilberg (1983) have observed, "the patient is the 'I,' the therapist is the 'you,' without the recognition of there being, simultaneously and potentially, another 'I' and another 'you'" (p. 289). Excessive reliance on defenses such as splitting, denial, and projective identification (Kernberg, 1976) can impair the ability to tolerate the felt experience of simultaneously activated, incompatible dispositions to action. Like the early stages of grief, an "authoritarian" (Adorno et al., 1950) style of information processing limits the distinctiveness, variety, and communicability of the feelings available to an individual. Accordingly, when patients habitually dissociate mutually contradictory self- and object representations, "regression" can be discerned in the nature as well as the handling and expression of the affects that are provoked by the stress of separations.

I regard affects as regressed to the extent that they are represented in awareness without significant psychic elaboration, symbolization, or ideation. Affects that are located in close proximity to the primitive trunk of emotion are almost totally somatic. They are "unstructured," are lacking in specific meanings, and are difficult to translate into emotion words. Like pervasive moods, affects in their regressed forms blur the distinction between the experienced self and the experienced world. During adulthood, affect regression does not generally manifest itself as a total or unchangeable phenomenon but as ever-changing in clinical picture and severity (Arlow & Brenner, 1964). However, regression may proceed to the point where an individual characteristically feels out of control, vulnerable to impulsive action, and "diseased" when dealing with ruptures of attachment from valued others.

These various tendencies can be discerned in the commonly reported observation that borderline patients respond to enforced separations from their therapists with suicidal gestures, morbid disturbances of self-esteem, and various psychophysiological disturbances, including psychomotor retardation or agitation. This constellation of symptoms has been found to differentiate "pathological grief" from the normal depressions that accompany acute bereavement (Jacobs & Kosten, 1983). When suffering in this way, borderline patients feel "entitled" to engage their therapists in transactions across the spatial and temporal boundaries that separate the therapist from the patient. During these hoped-for extratherapeutic interactions (e.g., telephone calls, unscheduled visits), they are given to expressing feelings of helpless distress, confusion, impotence, impending disintegration, or even death in a dependently demanding and/or paranoid fashion.

At times, even the most well-timed or accurate interpretation cannot contain borderline patients within the contractually agreed-upon temporal framework of the therapy relationship. When working with them on an outpatient basis, psychotherapists must therefore delicately integrate the explicit exercise of their "managerial" functions (Newton, 1973) and their empathic responsibilities. A therapist can remain empathically attuned to the borderline patient's efforts to cope with intersession intervals by bearing in mind that the length and breadth of time, as experienced, are relative. When the patient is experiencing imperious longings and uncertainties, even a momentary separation can feel like a prolonged or even permanent loss. A dysregulated conception of time, not simply entitlement, hostile impulses, or the wish to control the therapist, is visible in the borderline patient's efforts to cope with separations. Consequently, the work requires the ability to maintain a firm, programmatic, and objective stance toward transactions across the external boundaries between patient and therapist; otherwise, the therapy relationship could duplicate the chaos of the borderline patient's other relationships. Clinical experience substantiates that clear definition of the roles of patient and therapist, including an authoritative and predictable stance toward transactions "outside" therapy, is inherently reassuring to patients who are rendered confused and disorganized by separations, notwithstanding the storminess of their transactions at the ends of hours.

A therapist can infer from the "exit lines" (Gabbard, 1982) that he or she uses to indicate that a session is over how guilty or how comfortable he or she feels about imposing time limits and spatial restrictions on a particular patient. "We will continue next time" promotes a process-oriented view of therapy without the implicit coercion to be found in the concluding statement "We will talk more about that next week." By comparison, some exit lines obscure the therapist's authority (e.g., "We *have* to end now") or apologize for this authority (e.g., "I'm sorry, our time is up for today").

To effectively exercise one's authority while remaining empathically attuned to the psychic reality of patients suffering from the more profound forms of character pathology taxes the emotional maturity and technical skills of the most seasoned therapist. Borderline patients inevitably arouse intense and disquieting feelings of grandiosity, anger, and confusion in their therapists. However, when patients are relentlessly avoidant of intimacy and authenticity, the therapist faces struggles with boredom, sleepiness, and loneliness. Such countertransference reactions are implicated in precipitously ended as well as unnecessarily prolonged therapy relationships. However, like the mini-separations that punctuate the therapeutic process, therapists can turn to advantage countertransference-based ruptures of attachment by empathizing with their emotional consequences for a patient. In this regard, Kaiser (1965) placed the management and understanding of a therapist's inclination to withdraw emotionally from his or her patient(s) at the core of his theory of psychotherapy. My efforts in this direction are guided by the assumption that giving patients the opportunity to experience and express (at progressively higher levels of organization) their "disappointments" in the person of the therapist and the process of therapy opens up the possibility of nurturing the development of the representational capacities needed to reconcile the flaws, contradictions, and paradoxes inherent in *all* persons and relationships and to facilitate formation of more recognizable, desomaticized, and communicable memories of childhood attachments and separations. The conceptual starting point for this clinical strategy is the hypothesis that the processes that promote maturation of differentiated affects and those that give rise to creation of evocative memories are correlated and mediated by the process of introjection.

The Processes and Products of Introjection

Introjection is an evolving concept within psychoanalytic theory (Meissner, 1981) and bears many similarities to the proliferating array of schema-like concepts being advanced by social and cognitive psychologists (Singer, 1985). According to the theoretical model that guides this chapter, introjection is that form of internalization that gives rise to the creation of cognitive/affective representations of the reciprocally contingent nature and dyadic structure of the self in relation to others. This view is consistent with Loewald's (1962) hypothesis that what is internalized is relations with external objects, not the objects themselves. (In psychoanalytic parlance, an object may be a person, a psychological or physical part of a person, a tool, an inanimate aspect of the environment, or a symbol. When human objects are referred to here, I shall use the term "other.") The hypothesis that it is *relationships* to others rather than others themselves that are internalized suggests that whenever a person brings to awareness "evocative memories" (Fraiberg, 1969) of a significant other, discernible cues or signs that they are occurring, inextricably, against a background of evocative memories of the self should be present. The crux of Sullivan's (1953) theorizing pointed in this direction.

There is accumulating research data to support the conclusion that schematic representations of the self and others are not merely the imaginative by-products of fantasy but have the capacity to organize and directly influence attention, memory, and the felt appraisal of experience (Singer, 1985). In a similar vein, psychoanalytic theorists presume that introjects have the capacity to replace relations to an external object, to stabilize them, or to supplement them with relations to mental representations of an internalized object (Cameron, 1961; Giovacchini, 1975; Volkan, 1976; Dorpat, 1979). Though integral components of behavioral systems, the roles or functions that the objects of an introjected relationship serve for an individual are not necessarily consciously perceived. The available evidence suggests that the mental models of relationships acquired specifically as a function of early attachment- and separation-related events tend to operate outside conscious awareness and to resist dramatic change (Main et al., 1985).

When brought to awareness, the objects of introjected relationships are experienced as separate, to lesser or greater degrees, from the subjectively grasped sense of self. Temporary suspension of the reflective self-representation that one is daydreaming enables individuals to experience the objects of introjected relationships that are brought to consciousness as "imaginary felt presences" existing within the confines of the mind or body or both (Schafer, 1968). Individuals conceive of their relations with these presences as analogous to their relations to an external object, including those that have been lost in actuality. This tendency is implicated in the experience of conflict, including the contradictory nature of grief. Bereaved individuals often treat painful memories and constantly recurring images of loved ones who have been lost as "cherished burdens" (Moffat, 1982). Moffat describes as follows her own paradoxical reaction to the passing of grief:

> Feeling better, more frequently surprised by joy, as was Wordsworth, I also felt a sense of betrayal of my husband, even though I rationally knew that sustained grief would be morbid. Because grief may become a substitute for the dead one, giving up our grief can be the greatest challenge of mourning (p. xxvii).

Psychotherapy can be critical in assisting the process of mourning (see Chapter 12), in facilitating the surrendering of the internalized relationship (the introject), and in working through the natural ambivalence of loss (anger or repressed anger and guilt). A primary focus of a psychotherapy guided by these basic goals would consist in the "externalization" of mental models of relationships to the extent that differentiated conflicts and memories, with specific meanings, could materialize in the privacy of consciousness.

The Language of Conflict

The metaphors an individual uses to group and explain the opposing tendencies that constitute the experience of conflict provide a valuable avenue for exploring the emotional and conceptual maturity with which that person conducts relationships with mental representations of internalized others. At the introjective level of symbolization, action fantasies, varying in the extent to which they rely on the metaphor of internalized persons, arise during efforts to resolve or master emotional conflicts. Individual differences along this continuum tend to be correlated with the security of a person's attachments. Patients who are able to sustain contact and communication with absent others also tend to organize conflicts involving their separateness in terms of real and imagined transgressions against vividly constituted representations of autonomous, approving and/or disapproving whole human figures. In their fantasies, their differentiated strivings and wishes for autonomy are confronted with the antithetical values and prohibitions of persons, groups, and/or a vast array of nonhumans personified with human qualities, such as pets, institutions, and deities.

During development, abstractions and moral principles increasingly come to serve as symbolic substitutes for imagistic representations of persons in positions of authority. Some patients speak as if they were in bondage to moral absolutes such as duty or truth; others, as if they were being assailed, persecuted, or gratified by, and in passive relation to, imagistic representations of their parents' moral commands. Prior to the achievement of "secondary autonomy" (Hartmann, 1939/1958), either stylistic choice implies a diminished feeling of conscious self-determination.

Individuals who have great difficulty maintaining lively internal relationships with realistically conceived human beings tend to speak as if they were dominated and driven by the part properties of persons (e.g., the voice of conscience, a wagging finger) or quasihuman figures and creatures (e.g., monsters). When individuals who are functioning at the lower levels of "person constancy" imaginatively gaze within, they discover the presence of vague and unassimilated "pressures," "forces," and ameboid "things" or "shadows" that have the property of "otherness" and render them unable to perform various actions. At still more regressed levels, the other's felt presence can be unconsciously represented in the chronic persistence of rigidly held and stereotyped facial expressions, gestures, postures. Here, bodily pain may not be distinguishable from the painful feeling that conflicts inspire within and between people.

Self/Other Differentiation and the Narcissistic Condition

In some pathological states, the objects of an introjected relationship may be phenomenologically confused with or mistaken for the subjectively grasped sense of self. The link between incompletely differentiated self- and object representations and regressive reactions to ruptures of attachment is recognized in

Kohut's (1971) concept of the *selfobject*. Selfobjects are described by Kohut and Wolf (1978) as those

> objects which we experience as part of our self; the expected control over them is therefore closer to the concept of the control which a grown-up expects to have over his own body and mind than the concept of control which he expects to have over others (p. 414).

Kohut regards a person as suffering from a narcissistic personality disorder to the extent that he or she is dominated by the need to use the therapist as a selfobject in order to maintain self-esteem, vitality, a sense of purposiveness, personal coherence, and temporal stability.

According to Kohut, a tenuous or fragmented sense of self and the felt inability to perform these functions for oneself are diagnostic of the traumatic effects of childhood disillusionment with idealized parents. He believes that patients so impaired seek, in a regressive manner, to re-create within the context of selfobject transferences the subject-centered grandiosity of early childhood and the small child's belief in the possibility of merging with the calmness, infallibility, and omnipotence of perfect parental figures. Clinical manifestations of narcissism, so conceived, include the failure to acknowledge that the therapist exists outside the role of "my therapist" and the expectation that the therapist will serve as a symbiotic partner who totally shares and participates in the patient's experience. When functioning narcissistically, patients do not perceive their therapists as having a separate existence of their own; the therapist is perceived exclusively from the perspective of the satisfaction and frustration of the patient's wishes. For Kohut, empathic attunement requires of the therapist the capacity to allow for and respond flexibly to a patient's needs for such an idealizing relationship as well as to the patient's fears and defenses against merging with an idealized symbiotic partner. At the extremes, narcissistic patients manifest an inability to distinguish clearly between imaginative fantasies about the therapist and memories that are based on real events or the more objective characteristics of the therapist. In essence, narcissistic patients are embedded in their own point of view without clearly being aware that they have a point of view.

That a selfobject transference is emerging can be inferred from the emotions a patient experiences when the therapist fails or is unwilling to serve a function that the patient believes he or she should perform. When disappointed by their therapists, individuals who are moving toward individuation experience a variety of intelligible depressive states that are accompanied by a contemplative appreciation of imperfections or a willingness to forgive, with a wistful acknowledgment of the universal longing for preambivalent relationships. Levinson et al. (1978) coined the term "de-illusionment" to describe this constellation of focused, neutralized, and thoughtlike feelings and reactions. By contrast, when patients are in the throes of an idealizing selfobject transference, disappointments give rise to physiologically diffuse and conceptually vague feelings of devitalization, worthlessness, panic, despair, and inconsolability. Disappointments, experienced at such regressed levels of affectivity, call into question the overall acceptance or rejection of the relationship and are expressed either in hatefulness and excessive demands or in emotional withdrawal.

Central to Kohut's position is the belief that patients suffering from narcissistic personality disorders require the opportunity gradually and fully to experience an idealizing transference within the context of a relationship in which the therapist functions empathically as a selfobject and in which the patient experiences the therapist as unempathic at times, at conscious and preconscious levels. Kohut recommends neither the acceptance of idealizations nor their manipulation but, rather, an empathic exploration of real, imagined, and provoked disruptions of idealization and the discovery of the precipitating events that lead to the disruptions of the idealizing transference. He maintains that the pursuit of such empathic understandings promotes both the gradual appropriation to consciousness of the traumatic effects of unempathic parenting and the "transmuting internalizations" that bring about "structural leaps" in the development of a cohesive sense of self.

In adopting this position, Kohut echoes and expands on Freud's seminal hypothesis that activation of the processes of introjection requires the loss or threatened loss of an object as a precondition. Freud's (1917, 1923) investigations of moral development and mourning led him to this hypothesis. He invoked the concept of introjection to explain how the guiding, restraining, punishing functions originally imposed on children by their parents were re-created on the intrapersonal terrain of self-experience (that is, in the superego). Freud believed that the shift from regulation by the environment to self-regulation, as mediated by introjection, required as a precondition the relinquishment of ambivalently held aggressive and sexual impulses toward the parents.

The pivotal role of relinquished relationships in activating the processes of internalization reappears in Freud's overarching conclusion that "the character of the ego is a precipitate of abandoned object cathexes and contains the history of those object choices" (1923, p. 23). Schwaber (1971) summarizes the essence of Freud's views as follows:

> When we lose persons important to us or have to give up an earlier mode of relating to them, we try nonetheless to keep them with us by setting up a remembrance within the ego. If then we rage unconsciously at being deserted, or give vent to old ambivalences toward them, we suffer because we are angry at what has become an aspect of ourselves. The superego is a special grouping of identifications within the ego distilled from our earliest and most important loves and losses, our parents (p. 147).

In the context of therapy, these remembrances and identifications assume individual forms within the evolving transferential phenomena. In accord with classical psychoanalytic technique, idealizations are routinely interpreted as transference resistances against acknowledgment of components of the Oedipus complex such as hostile-rivalrous attitudes (Gedo, 1975). Kernberg (1976) alternatively regards idealizations as a defense against preoedipal primitive envy and aggression. According to Kohut's point of view, idealization transferences may defensively serve these functions, and they may also serve to prevent reactivation of unbearable states of rage, sorrow, helplessness, and other primitive residues of the traumatic effects of unempathic parenting.

It is extremely difficult to differentiate trauma from pathogenic influence in general. Inferences from clinical data have led me to the view that when patients seem driven to experience the therapeutic situation as necessarily and relentlessly disappointing, they may be demonstrating, as precisely as they can, lexically inexpressible memories of separations and losses that operated like traumas in their effects during childhood. In a similar vein, Lipin (1963) has reasoned that when patients rigidly hold the conviction that the therapist will be cold, unresponsive, unreliable, unpredictable, arbitrary, and deliberately humiliating, or when they repetitively interact with their therapists in ways that invite rejection, they may be doing so not only for defensive purposes but in order to produce replicas of memories that have never been fully conscious or capable of relatively organized expression. Cohen (1980) likewise believes that his research supports the view that memories of childhood traumas are not withdrawn from consciousness merely because of their offensive contents but, rather, because they overwhelm the capacity to form memory traces. He maintains that they "are not only unrecallable in the ordinary sense that repressed memories are. Rather, they are unavailable for recall because they do not employ adequate mental representations even in the unconscious" (p. 423).

The various psychotherapy literatures have emphasized clinical strategies for helping patients *recover* repressed representational memories and percepts that, at one time, were consciously known. Far less attention has been devoted to helping patients *construct* memories, revived and repeated in the transference, that are unconscious because they have never been coherently formulated.

Forms of Representing the Forgotten Past

My own efforts to discover and describe the structure of unconscious memories and fantasies draw heavily on the view that character-based cleavages and restrictions in gaining access to one's personal past often result from imbalances in the *forms* of representation that encode the affective and cognitive components of internalized interpersonal experiences. I am using the term "form" here to refer to the end products of the enactive or sensorimotor imagistic and symbolic modes or systems of processing new experiences, constructing inner models of experiences, and representing past experiences to awareness (Piaget, 1954; Bruner, 1964). Selective reconstructions of persons or events, in their physical absence, can take place in one or more of these modes of representation. For example, memories of the "weight" or "heaviness" of loss may be enacted behaviorally through the assumption of various postures, gestures, and facial expressions. Memories of losses encountered during the earliest stages of development are organized exclusively at a sensorimotor level of representation (Schimek, 1975). This aspect of the forgotten past is continuously presented to others in the form of an individual's personal style of bodily movement (Geller, 1978). When representations of an event find expression in the imagistic mode, individuals reexperience sensory/perceptual processes similar to those that were activated when the event actually occurred. There is growing evidence that it is in the imagistic mode that unresolved traumatic episodes, disavowed self-appraisals, and conflicted interpersonal fantasies may enter awareness after a prolonged period of repression (Singer, 1974). Such imaginings may include vivid nightmares, obsessively reviewed pictorializations of scenes involving an estranged other, and memories of the way the other smelled or tasted. Symbolic representations predominantly include intrusive repetitions of or reflections on the elements of a memory that are nameable by words and their grammatical organization. The process of recalling to mind a flow of verbal meanings that stand for a memory to which they are related can obviously arouse intense feelings. Nevertheless, enactive and imagistic representations stand in closer proximity to actual, immediate physical experience than do more abstract and symbolic forms of representation.

Bruner's (1964) studies of cognitive growth show that, during the course of development, the processes of differentiation result in the articulation of functional boundaries between the enactive, imagistic, and lexical modes of representation. Thus, not only do these modes acquire their own unique properties, but their relations may come to be either mutually facilitating and congruent or, to varying extents, disjunctive. Insofar as a memory is encoded in more than one of these modes of representation (Crowder, 1970), crucial aspects of that memory may be "lost" because of the inability to translate information from one mode to another. It is impossible for a unitary memory trace to materialize when the modes of representation that bring information to consciousness are dissociated from one another. When "enactive memories" (Dorpat, 1983) that are cut off from access to imagistic and symbolic representations of the "same" event are reactivated, unsuspectingly and without warning, in response to some stimulus, remembering is functionally equivalent to repeating the experience. Because each mode organizes the "reality" of an event differently, changes in the relations among modes can prompt far-reaching changes in the vividness, duration, intensity, amount of detail, and emotional meanings of a particular memory.

Like Horowitz and Zilberg (1983), I believe that "neurotic styles" (Shapiro, 1965) of information processing impose significant functional restrictions on one's capacity to explore, coordinate, and integrate the enactive, imagistic, and lexical modes of representation. Consequently, my working clinical model prominently includes strategies that initiate qualitative changes in the relations among the sensuous modes of representation that are called into play during the therapeutic dialogue.

In order to extend one's awareness of these forms of sentience, one must temporarily liberate the mind from practical purposes, including the search for hidden meanings. It requires a leap of faith for some patients and some therapists to attend to the aesthetic surface of experience as it emerges into consciousness. In order to gain intimate knowledge of the processes of formulation that culminate in mental contents and that precede speech, it is necessary, moreover, to allocate attention in a sensuously receptive manner (Deikman, 1976). I actively encourage patients to "recognize" or "sense" how they organize, selectively, the content of experience while using and translating among the enactive, imagistic, and symbolic modes of representation. With varying degrees of skill and anxiety, they begin to recognize how the process of recalling a memory can be aborted at various preparatory levels of formulation before the memory appears clearly in consciousness. They also discover how inhibitions to awareness, as revealed by discontinuities in experience, occur at the boundaries between these representational systems (Horowitz, 1972). In turn, progressive elaboration and integration of the relations between modes of representation help patients bring to awareness, more readily and vividly, dissociated and lexically inexpressible memories, some of which may never have been fully conscious or capable of being given relatively organized expression. Viewed from this perspective, the therapeutic process is not so much a matter of "lifting" repressions as a means of providing patients with structuralizing and humanizing experiences.

I have found metaphors particularly useful in stimulating multimodal memories—that is, in connecting or reconnecting modes and levels of expressive functioning. Recasting abstract statements (Patient: "I felt criticized when you said the hour was over...") into body-centered metaphors (Therapist: "You looked like I slapped you across the face when I...") strengthens the concreteness and palpability of subjective awareness. Promoting these changes enriches a patient's conscious efforts to attend to external reality and the state of the body itself. Appropriately chosen metaphors thus provide patients with emotionally significant information and increase the likelihood that they will "take in" and constructively remember recent interactions with the therapist. These two sources of gain make a required and inseparable contribution to the unfolding of the representational capacities that enable an individual to attain an integrated and constant sense of "self."

EMPATHY, INTROJECTION, AND THE JOURNEY TOWARD INDIVIDUATION

Many rival versions of what constitutes the "self" coexist without final reconciliation (Horowitz & Zilberg, 1983). Some theorists (e.g., Schafer, 1973a) regard the self as a superordinate self-representation, a summary formulation considering at once all of the following: the bodily me; the realization that one is not the other but a being in one's own right; narcissistic aspirations driven by and experienced as ambitions; the emotions of pride and humiliation; extensions of the self, including identifications with possessions (both animate and inanimate); loyalties to groups, nations, abstract moral values, and religious ideals; self-images of present abilities, statuses, roles; and the pursuit of long-range goals regarded as central to personal existence and the sense of futurity (Allport, 1955). Still others (e.g., Kohut, 1971) find it useful to postulate the existence of a synthesizer, or "self of selves," that transcends and is responsible for the inward unity among all the principal functions and properties that have been attributed to the self. Whether or not a distinguishable, substantive single self exists, the component elements of the selves of the patients seeking psychotherapy exist in varying degrees of contradiction, disjointedness, or integration.

A person can be said to be approaching individuation (Jung, 1965) when the representations that constitute his or her sense of self are coordinated, complexly organized, and coherently interrelated so that they add up effortlessly to form an indivisible whole. Persons who are moving toward individuation possess a valued, coherent, and stable identity that springs from and comprises all the "persons" within them. They live comfortably in and with the knowledge that a basically solid sense of self is not monolithic in nature (Searles, 1977). Their subjective experience is characterized, to borrow a phrase from Loewald (1978), by a sense of "unity within multiplicity." Moreover, when a person's identities are differentiated and hierarchically arranged, the distinction between the self and the external world feels substantial and natural.

Various benefits accrue to individuals who possess these attributes. Individuals who feel secure in their own identities are able to erect a firm line of demarcation between themselves and the pressures and influences of the external world. They know which experiences, feelings, and opinions are peculiarly their own. The consolidation of an *initial* adult identity also brings with it an increased capacity to reexperience symbiotic-like modes of relatedness for a variety of adaptive purposes.

Giving as well as receiving empathy presumes the ability to participate in intimate exchanges in which there is an interpenetration of self and other. Parents or therapists who can extend themselves, selectively and nonintrusively, into the experience of their children or patients are able to discover ways of providing care that are empathically attuned to the children's or patients' particular needs. When in need of help themselves, individuals who feel secure in their own identities can enter into and use relationships in which there is a blending or sharing of the functions and experiences of valued others. They can, for example, augment and alter their capacity for human relatedness through the medium of *identificatory love* (Loewald, 1978). According to Loewald, identificatory love is a form of mentation that "does not structure or divide reality into the poles of inner and outer, subject and object, self and others" (p. 39). This fluid and "symbiotic" mode of relatedness enables individuals who possess an overriding sense of identity to relinquish, in controlled and reversible ways, the burdens of defining the self in terms of separateness from others. In situations of deep intimacy, identificatory love enables individuals who have developed a stable sense of self to "take in," or introject, functional aspects of a caring relationship and, in so doing, expand or refine attributes that may not be adequately represented in their own personalities.

Internalization and the Psychotherapy Relationship

The development of new, more caring images of self and other is thus facilitated when patients constructively accept the relaxation of the boundaries between themselves and their therapists brought about by participating in reciprocal exchanges having the quality of rhythmic synchronization (Geller, 1985). Introjection takes advantage of the fact that rhythmic synchronization of the therapeutic dialogue inspires mutuality and co-oscillation and makes it easier (or at least possible) to cross the boundaries separating patient and therapist. When these conditions prevail, patients, without their knowledge or consent, begin to imitate, to mirror, the nonspecific healing ingredients of psychotherapy as embodied in their therapists' habits, mannerisms, facial expressions, and vocal qualities. Mirroring an empathic therapist's calm bodily state (or imagined calm bodily state) and warm facial expressions initiates changes in a patient's experience of diffuse and poorly localized sensations having to do with muscle tension, posture, temperature, equilibrium, vibration, rate and depth of breathing, and resonance. By yielding to the bodily changes brought about by such reciprocal coanesthetic (Spitz, 1965) stimulation, patients increasingly learn how to empathize with themselves. This form of softening ego boundaries, on a bodily level, provides, I believe, one of the bases that make possible nondefensively motivated forms of introjecting the "atmosphere" of being in the presence of an empathic therapist.

It will be recalled that psychoanalytic use of the concept of introjection is intertwined with the view that it is the structure of a disrupted or relinquished relationship that is preserved in the form of an introject. What is being suggested here is that introjection can also operate silently and spontaneously, like the incidental learning that occurs in conditioning paradigms, when patients do not need to cling rigidly to their sense of self. In a similar vein, Eagle and Wolitzky (1982, p. 353) quote Rangell as concluding that in the analysis of neurotic patients there is "a constant series of micro-identifications." What is further being suggested here is that the wish to reexperience symbiotic modes of relatedness is not in itself pathological or immature, nor does the need to suspend the boundaries that separate self and other necessarily entail a defensive retreat from intrapsychic autonomy. In fact, working with patients who expect that feeling and thinking with an empathic therapist will overwhelm, perhaps irreversibly, an already tenuous and fragmented sense of self necessitates clinical strategies that promote the maturation rather than the relinquishing of the wishes and capacities to participate in symbiotic modes of relatedness.

Individuals who are uncertain about their existence as separate beings are seriously threatened by their positive yearnings and unsatisfied longings for empathy. To be known, empathically, jeopardizes the precarious sense of individuality, cohesion, and stability of patients who feel that the distinction between self and others is illusory and artificial. Consequently, warmth, concern, consensus, and tenderness, expressed either by the therapist or by the patients themselves, are experienced as more threatening than gratifying. This need/fear dilemma achieves terrifying proportions in the lives of schizophrenic patients (Laing, 1965). Many "first breaks" with reality are precipitated by the dissolving sense of self brought about by the experience of "merging" or "fusing" with caring others.

When patients have never established a clearly delineated sense of self as separate from the external world, promoting access to symbiotic modes of relatedness requires as a precondition the progressive differentiation of the "bodily me." Developmental cognitive psychologists and clinical psychoanalysts agree that the process of emerging from "embeddedness" (Schachtel, 1959) originates in the acquisition of the ability to distinguish oneself as a physical body that is separate from the bodies of others. According to the epigenetic principle of development (Erikson, 1959), the emergence of the ability to recognize and localize coanesthetic representations of the "bodily me" serves as a lifelong anchor for self-awareness and forms a necessary foundation of a body image, which, in turn, resides at the core of the adult's efforts to become a whole self. Directing attention to the organic continuity of the stream of sensations that arise within the body can provide patients who are in doubt with the surest evidence of their separate existence.

Individuation in patients for whom reexperiencing symbiotic modes of relatedness with caring others is extremely difficult should prominently include repeated and varied opportunities to experiment with being close while maintaining comfortable access to the distinction between self and nonself. Such opportunities arise from the invitation to oscillate between experiencing and reflecting on fears of and defenses against taking in the therapist's empathy and interpretations. By drawing a patient's attention to the concrete, immediate, palpable presence of the therapist, transference-based interpretations temporarily attenuate or eliminate impediments to the flow of accurate information from therapist to patient. Concurrently, therapists can increase the fullness of the information flowing toward them by making greater use of clarifications and confrontations. These interventions can be used to bring into sharper focus patients' needs for and fears of empathic closeness. In making decisions about how to space apart sound and silence, I am guided by the view that dysrhythmic human interactions engender separation anxiety and that patients experience as unempathic, at conscious and preconscious levels, their therapist's inability or unwillingness to accommodate to their "obligatory rhythms" (Kestenberg, 1966). Consequently, I try to delicately adjust my rate of vocalization as well as my verbal utterances to meet the idiosyncratic rhythmic requirements of each patient. For example, the sounds of a therapist's voice reassure patients who feel alone when expected to speak at length about themselves under minimal guidance. Likewise, dependently demanding patients misconstrue their therapist's interest as disappointingly inadequate unless the therapist is frequently and expressively brought to speech. By contrast, in order not to feel intruded on or entrapped, emotionally inaccessible patients require a therapist who limits his or her verbal output as well as motility. Allowing and responding to these idiosyncratic patterns of the individual will make it possible to move the therapeutic dialogue in the direction of greater mutuality and reciprocity. Patients who have adopted the tactics of alienation are gradually encouraged to risk being close to their therapists and, indeed, even to go so far as to invite their therapists to become benignly influential introjected presences in their representational worlds.

Functional Significance of Introjection

The "new" cognitive/affective representations that patients create from their relations with their therapists vary in ease of evocation, affective tone, aliveness, felt proximity to actual experience, vividness, and a host of other formal properties (Geller et al., 1981). Their conscious manifestations are more or less vulnerable to "contamination" (Volkan, 1976) by preexisting mental models of relationships. Newly created representations can also be characterized in terms of their functional significance for a particular individual. As early as 1934, Strachey spoke of a patient's introjection of the analyst as an auxiliary superego that helps to modify the patient's harsh superego. More recently, object relations theorists have sensitized clinicians to the possibility that "therapist introjects" (Giovacchini, 1975; Dorpat, 1979) can serve a much wider variety of functions, from wish fulfillment to problem-solving (Atwood & Stolorow, 1980).

Let us briefly review some of the ways in which the ability to evoke in specific, perceptive detail, under conditions of relaxation, the felt presence of an empathic therapist can both provide temporary respite from the burdens of self/other differentiation and promote such differentiation. Introjected representations of the therapeutic situation can function similarly to the "transitional objects" of infancy (Winnicott, 1953). They can symbolically reunite a patient with soothing images of the therapist during separations. At the onset of therapy, the furniture, plants, paintings, and books in the therapist's office as well as the clothing worn by the therapist may have no personal meaning, except for the concrete, momentary pleasures they provide. By contrast, patients who are moving in the direction of personalizing and internalizing the therapeutic process may symbolically re-create the familiar surroundings in which the therapist is embedded in order to relieve the pain associated with the frustrations and real limits of the therapy relationship and to assuage more generalized feelings of loneliness. While using therapist introjects in order to be soothed or consoled, patients may, unwittingly, enter more comfortably what Winnicott (1953) calls the "transitional mode of experience." In this mode, the demarcation between the self and extrapersonal space is temporarily suspended rather than negated. Winnicott observes that

> it is an area not challenged, because no claim is made on its behalf except that it shall exist as a resting place for the individual engaged in the perpetual human task of keeping inner and outer reality separate yet interrelated (p. 91).

According to Winnicott, while functioning in this "intermediate area of experiencing," an individual can endow objects, concepts, or reevoked memories with lifelike qualities and roles while retaining an appreciation of their objective properties. Access to this mode of experiencing may be a psychic precondition for the "taking in" of empathy and makes possible the experience and appreciation of the therapist as simultaneously real and current as well as transferential and historical. Therefore, even as patients are using images of the therapist as an aid in avoiding, limiting, or curbing anxiety-laden fantasies, they may be strengthening their ability to form fantasies in which reliable representations of the self in relation to others are preserved.

The dyadic structure of introjected relations with the therapist provides patients with a way to contain clashing tendencies and entertain differing perspectives on the same event. Introjected images of the therapist may assert, deny, or question a state of affairs. They may be called forth like the imaginary companions of childhood in order to gratify wishes that might otherwise be repressed or squelched. While acknowledging such desires in the other, through the medium of creative play, patients have the opportunity to stand at a distance and discover new ways of sublimating their drives. As previously noted, en route to acquiring their own autonomous values and the capacity for self-regulation, children rely on the ethical standards—both approving and forbidding—of first real and then internalized parental figures. In a similar fashion, therapist introjects can serve as inner directives that shape decisions about goodness, safety, pleasure, and survival.

Though adaptive and reparative, these functions do not directly increase a patient's insight into the motivational and developmental origins of his or her problems in dealing with separation and loss. Rather, introjection strengthens the ego functions required for gaining emotionally intensified and intimate knowledge of oneself. In other words, the functions of observing, listening, thinking, remembering, judging, and recognizing are enhanced by the creation of introjected representations of the new modes of relatedness and information processing made available in psychotherapy.

A patient's capacity and motivation for gaining such emotionally charged self-knowledge can serve as an important guide in determining whether the termination of therapy for that individual is going to be a "prologue" (Ekstein, 1965) to further growth and development.

THE PROCESS OF TERMINATING THERAPY

For a variety of reasons, the *process* of terminating therapy, in itself, may be the most crucial aspect of a patient's treatment experience. During the extended leave-taking of the termination phase of therapy, highly influential role relationship schemes are revived, often for the first time, with clarity. The imminent ending of the relationship has the power to provoke the emergence of transference paradigms that may have been inaccessible during the initial and working-through stages of therapy. For example, the working out of the conflicts and coalitions between the "I's" and "you's" that structure the experience of separation guilt usually peak during the termination phase. (*Separation guilt* refers to the conviction that to become oneself, to be fully separate, will deprive, betray, damage, or even kill the "other." The other potentially includes former states of self that are left behind during the progressive development of a sense of self.) Moreover, it is during this phase of the relationship that patients and therapists confront most poignantly the limit on what therapy can accomplish.

Assessing Readiness for Termination

A systematic approach to the question of how to arrive at the decision to terminate a psychotherapy is still lacking. Kauff (1977) has observed that termination has been most often treated in the various psychotherapy literatures as an "isolated event" or as "the end point of the working-through phase of therapy." Kauff has recommended the use of Mahler's description of disturbances originating during a period extending from infancy to roughly 4 years of age, designated as the "separation/individuation" period, as a paradigm for understanding the meaning of termination as a continuing process within the total therapeutic experience. This perspective may be too restrictive. Recent investigations of adult development have revealed that the quest for individuation is far more lengthy and complex than has usually been imagined. Jung (1965) believed that individuation may not be achievable till the fifth decade of life. The work of Erikson (1959), Gould (1972), Vaillant (1977), and Levinson et al. (1978), however, also carries the implication that we are not condemned to repeat, perpetually and stereotypically, the nature and outcome of our earliest attachments to and separations from our parents. What evidence is available suggests that although the adult's reactions to attachments and separations reveal the enduring influence of childhood prototypes, the process of individuation is potentially carried forward by the ever-changing constellation of developmental tasks that confronts us as we age. Existing theories of psychotherapy have not as yet integrated an adult development perspective into their investigations of how the unique separations and losses of each developmental era can serve to reorganize the quality and substance of mental models of relationships.

The literature has focused mainly on developing criteria to assess readiness to terminate psychotherapy. Many criteria have been suggested. Frequently they reflect idealized conceptions of psychological health or the authors' values and personal philosophy of life (e.g., Rogers, 1961; Horney, 1966). Relief from symptoms is probably the most frequently cited criterion (Luborsky et al, 1980). But because symptomatic improvement is unreliable as a sole measure of successful treatment, therapists are apt to rely on supplementary criteria to assess whether a decision to consider termination is appropriate (Dewald, 1961).

Other criteria frequently mentioned in the psychoanalytic literature include the capacity for love, the capacity for work, the capacity for mourning, genital primacy, the changing nature of recurring dreams, and the removal of defenses and resistances by interpretation (see Firestein, 1978, for a review of this literature). An undercurrent of dissatisfaction is betrayed in every effort to find adequate criteria to document the efficacy of psychotherapy in ways that are acceptable to academicians and to institutions that financially support the professional practice of psychotherapy. I rely on multiple and patient-specific criteria to negotiate the fact that all endings are, more or less, arbitrary, and I accept the equally humbling realization that all therapies are "incomplete."[12]

The Therapist's Stance During the Termination Phase

Of increasing importance to some therapists are criteria that focus attention on the therapist's relationship with the patient as it changes during the process of termination or affects that process (Balint, 1950; Edelson, 1963). Expressive of this view is the hypothesis that the work of therapy is being successfully accomplished if, among other things, patients can assume roles and functions for themselves that their therapists had previously fulfilled for them. To this end, attention is devoted during the terminal phase of psychotherapy to working through the dependency elements in the relationship (Firestein, 1978). Among psychoanalytic therapists, there is considerable disagreement on whether this task is or should be facilitated by shifting the structure of the relationship in a more egalitarian direction. In order to foster a patient's perception of the therapist as a real person, Buxbaum (1950) advocates becoming more spontaneous and self-disclosing. Hurn (1971) maintains that the analyst has no need to present himself as a "human being," since the entire

---

12 Therapies that terminate prematurely for reasons external to the therapy relationship are commonplace. For example, the realities of clinical work are such that therapists-in-training often impose administratively dictated endings on their patients. Most psychotherapy training programs are organized in such a way that student therapists change settings once a year and therefore terminate annually with the majority of their patients. This educational policy deprives many therapists of the opportunity to learn how to bring a therapy relationship to a mutually agreed-upon "natural conclusion." In parallel, Keith (1966) has expressed concern over the iatrogenic consequences for patients of being left by one's therapist and/ or transferred to a new therapist. Despite their ubiquity and importance, externally imposed premature terminations have received relatively scant attention in the literature (Lenzer, 1955; Pumpian-Midlin, 1958; Dewald, 1965; Whitaker, 1966; Sher, 1970; Glenn, 1971; Mikkelson & Gutheil, 1979).

analytic process leads inevitably to the patient's perception of "the analyst as he is." Weigert (1952) takes yet another approach to this issue. She believes that when therapists find themselves no longer needing to maintain a cautiously objective and neutral stance, a timely termination is approaching because the resolution of the countertransference goes hand in hand with the resolution of transference. In other words, she does not advocate role-playing this shift for technical reasons but, rather, believes that a therapist's felt readiness to engage in a more egalitarian relationship parallels the disappointment in the resistances of transference and consequently provides an important barometer of the approaching successful end of treatment. Possibly the most extreme version of this attitude is found in Searles's belief that "a successful psychoanalysis involves the analyst's deeply felt relinquishment of the patient, both as being a cherished infant and as being a fellow adult who is responded to at the level of genital love" (1965, p. 297).

An alternative hypothesis is that such changes signal a patient's growing capacity to form or symbolically create, during and outside treatment hours, enduring introjected representations of real and imagined patient/therapist interactions. A patient's greater readiness to receive help tacitly encourages some therapists to become more expressive, open, active, and spontaneous—that is, increasingly egalitarian—at the outset of the termination phase. This shift entails a change in the rhythmic structure of the therapeutic dialogue. Therapists who limit themselves to correctly timed, sparingly employed interpretations implicitly set themselves above and apart from their patients; a give-and-take conversational style is more likely to induce feelings of equality in a patient. As previously posited, rhythmic coordination of patient/therapist relations may be one of the interactional bases that permit nondefensively activated forms of introjection.

Ideally, a therapist's orientation to termination should evolve out of an understanding of his or her relationship with the particular patient and what it has meant to that patient. Realization of this goal depends, in large part, on a therapist's ability to adapt his or her depth of involvement, activity level, and expressiveness to fit the unique needs and circumstances of each patient. Studies by Geller and Nash (1975) and Greene and Geller (1980) suggest that therapists, especially beginners, experience a change in their depth of involvement during the termination phase and that this shift may be expressive of an internally consistent and possibly generalized orientation to ending relationships. It appears that beginning therapists tend to move in the direction of seeking either greater intimacy with or increasing distance from their patients as termination approaches. Unrestrained expression of either disposition during the final weeks of therapy may seriously undermine a patient's efforts to achieve autonomy. For example, therapists who, in the extreme, "act out" their need to withdraw from the relationship and from the pain of termination might well be experienced as rejecting or as prematurely stopping the work of therapy, and those therapists who need to get closer to their patients prior to the imminent ending might unwittingly inhibit the expression of anger and resentment, arouse regressive urges within their patients, or make it more difficult for them to experience, without separation guilt, the desire to leave therapy.

Introjection and the Continuation of Therapy After Termination

Dorpat (1979) has written: "Identifications are made with the subject's representations of objects, not with the actual object. It is not correct to say that one identifies with a person. Rather,

one identifies with one's conscious or unconscious representation of that person" (p. 36). Following Dorpat, I assume that
introjection must logically precede identification if the functions and qualities originally ascribed to the therapist are to be
transformed into representations of the self as regulatory agent.
Nevertheless, in the absence of normative data, it is impossible to determine whether the use of fantasies of the therapeutic relationship is a transitional mode en route to autonomous
self-regulation or whether their continued use is *necessary* for
autonomous self-regulation.

In order to examine empirically this and other hypotheses
presented in this chapter, phenomenologically based models
of both the representational forms that organize and present to
awareness representations of the self in relation to others and
the corresponding affects that accompany such representational
forms must be created. As a first step in this direction, we have
developed a methodology for investigating the content, formal
properties, and functions of patients' representations of the therapeutic relationship (Geller et al., 1981). Data from a sample
of 206 psychotherapists (who themselves had been patients in
psychoanalysis, psychotherapy, or both) show that the creation
of multimodal representations of the therapeutic relationship
and those that are used for the purpose of continuing the therapeutic dialogue is correlated with self-perceived change and
growth. Moreover, our data indicate that, in situations of stress
and also during sleep, the need for visual, tactile, or auditory
contact with "personifications" of the therapist may continue to
appear long after termination. In addition, preliminary analyses
of the dreams of our subjects in which the therapist appears in
the manifest content suggest that the therapeutic relationship is
experienced differently according to the patient's sex. Consistent
with Gilligan's (1982) understanding of women's development,
the dreams of the female patients in our sample were infused

with a greater preoccupation with separation and loss and a greater acceptance of needs for relatedness than the dreams of the male patients.

Finally, our findings suggest that an assessment of a patient's motivational priorities to discover what functions therapist introjects can serve may prove to be a sensitive index of that patient's readiness to enter the terminal phase of psychotherapy. Edelson (1963) describes the relationship between internalization and the outcome of psychotherapy as follows:

> The problem of termination is not how to get therapy stopped, or when to stop it, but how to terminate so that what has been happening keeps on "going" inside the patient. The problem of termination is not simply one of helping the patient to achieve independence in the sense of willingness to function in the physical absence of the therapist. Most basically it is a problem of facilitating achievement by the patient of the ability to "hang on" to the therapist (or the experience of the relationship with the therapist) in his physical absence in the form of a realistic intrapsychic representation (memories, identification associated with altered functioning) which is conserved rather than destructively or vengefully abandoned following separation, thus making mastery of this experience possible (p. 23).

With this perspective in mind, I have become particularly attentive to the articulation and recurring use of fantasies of the therapeutic relationship to practice the "new" modes of looking at, listening to, talking to, and being with others that are made available during psychotherapy sessions. Symbolic re-creation of the therapeutic dialogue in the form of evocative memories provides patients with a model for continuing, in the privacy of consciousness, the work of expressive and exploratory psycho-therapy. The dyadic structure of introjected relations with the therapist provides patients with a sympathetic audience before which they can grasp and reveal that which, as yet, cannot be discussed with others. When cognitive/expressive fantasies are used in this way, they not only contribute to the temporary relief of inner turmoil but also promote acquisition of a generalizable skill for repairing affectional bonds and dealing with stressful situations, dysfunctional fears, and inhibitions in everyday life. If the psychotherapeutic process is to independently endure the physical absence of the therapist, it must have an afterlife in the form of such enduring, beneficial cognitive/affective represen-tations. Thus, introjection of the therapeutic dialogue not only helps to preserve the gains derived from therapy but ensures the survival of the process after termination.

REFERENCES

Adorno, T.W., Frenkel-Brunswik, E., Levinson, D.J., & Sanford, N. (1950). *The Authoritarian Personality*. New York, NY: Harper & Brothers.

Alexander, F., & French, T.M. (1946). *Psychoanalytic Therapy: Principles and Application*. New York, NY: Roland Press.

Allport, G.W. (1955). *Becoming*. New Haven, CT: Yale University Press.

Arlow, J., & Brenner, C. (1964). *Psychoanalytic Concepts and the Structural Theory*. New York, NY: International Universities Press.

Astrachan, B.M., Flynn, H.R., Geller, J.D., & Harvey, H.H. (1971). A systems approach to day hospitalization. In J.H. Wasserman (Ed.), *Current Psychiatric Therapies*. Orlando, FL: Grune & Stratton.

Atwood, G., & Stolorow, R. (1980). Psychoanalytic concepts and the representational world. *Psychoanalysis and Contemporary Thought* 3:267–290.

Baekeland, F., & Lundwall, L. (1975). Dropping out of treatment: A critical review. *Psychological Bulletin* 82:738–783.

Balint, M. (1950). On the termination of analysis. *International Journal of Psycho-Analysis* 31:196–201.

Bardin, E.S. (1976, September). *The Working Alliance: Basis for a General Theory of Psychotherapy*. Paper presented at the annual meeting of the American Psychological Association, Washington, DC.

Bergin, A.E., & Strupp, H.H. (1972). *Changing Frontiers in the Science of Psychotherapy*. Chicago, IL: Aldine-Atherton.

Blatt, S.J. (1974). Levels of object representation in anaclitic and introjective depression. *Psychoanalytic Study of the Child* 29:107–157.

Boss, M. (1963). *Psychoanalysis and Daseinsanalysis*. New York, NY: Basic Books.

Bowlby, J. (1969). *Attachment and Loss: Vol. 1. Attachment*. New York, NY: Basic Books.

———— (1973). *Attachment and Loss: Vol. 2. Separation: Anxiety and Anger*. New York, NY: Basic Books.

Bruner, J.S. (1964). The course of cognitive growth. *American Psychologist* 19:1–15.

Buxbaum, E. (1950). Criteria for the termination of an analysis. *International Journal of Psychoanalysis* 31:184–193.

Cameron, N. (1961). Introjection, reprojection, and hallucination in the interaction between schizophrenic patient and therapist. *International Journal of Psycho-Analysis* 42:86–96.

Cohen, J. (1980). Structural consequences of psychic trauma: A new look at beyond the pleasure principle. *International Journal of Psycho-Analysis* 61:421–432.

Crowder, R.G. (1970). The role of one's own voice in immediate memory. *Cognitive Psychology* 1:157–178.

Deikman, A.J. (1976). Bimodal consciousness. In R.E. Ornstein (Ed.), *The Nature of Human Consciousness*. New York, NY: Viking Press.

Dewald, P.A. (1961). Reactions to forced termination of therapy. *Psychiatric Quarterly* 39:102–126.

Dorpat, T.L. (1979). Introjection and the idealizing transference. *International Journal of Psychoanalytic Psychotherapy* 7:26–51.

——— (1983). Denial, defect, symptom formation—and construction. *Psychoanalytic Inquiry* 3(2):223–253.

Eagle, M., & Wolitzky, D.L. (1982). Therapeutic influence in dynamic psychotherapy: A review and synthesis. In S. Slipp (Ed.), *Curative Factors in Dynamic Psychotherapy*. New York, NY: McGraw Hill.

Edelson, M. (1963). *The Termination of Intensive Psychotherapy*. Springfield, IL: Thomas.

Ekstein, R. (1965). Working through and termination of analysis. *Journal of the American Psychoanalytic Association* 13:57–78.

Erikson, E.H. (1959). Identity and the life cycle. *Psychological Issues*, Monograph 1.

Fairbairn, W.D. (1952). *An Object-Relations Theory of the Personality*. New York, NY: Basic Books.

Farber, B.A., & Geller, J.D. (1977). Student attitudes toward psychotherapy. *Journal of the American College Health Association* 25:301–307.

Firestein, S.K. (1978). *Termination in Psychoanalysis*. New York, NY: International Universities Press.

Fraiberg, S. (1969). Libidinal object constancy and mental representation. *Psychoanalytic Study of the Child* 24:3–47.

Frank, J.D. (1973). *Persuasion and Healing* (Rev. ed.). Baltimore, MD: Johns Hopkins University Press.

Freud, S. (1913). On beginning the treatment: Further recommendations on the technique of psycho-analysis. *Standard Edition* 12:121–144.

———— (1917). Mourning and melancholia. *Standard Edition* 14.

———— (1923). The ego and the id. *Standard Edition* 19.

———— (1926). Inhibitions, symptoms and anxiety. *Standard Edition* 20.

Friedman, L. (1969). The therapeutic alliance. *International Journal of Psycho-Analysis* 50:139–153.

Gabbard, O. (1982). The exit line: A manifestation of heightened transference-countertransference at the end of the hour. *Journal of the American Psychoanalytic Association* 30:579–599.

Garfield, S.L. (1978). Research on client variables in psychotherapy. In A.E. Bergin & S.L. Garfield (Eds.), *Handbook of Psychotherapy and Behavior Change: An Empirical Analysis* (2nd ed.). New York, NY: Wiley.

Gedo, J. (1975). Forms of idealization in the analytic transference. *Journal of the American Psychoanalytic Association* 23:485–505.

Geller, J.D. (1978). The body, expressive movement, and physical contact in psychotherapy. In J.L. Singer & K.S. Pope (Eds.), *The Power of Human Imagination* (pp. 347–378). New York, NY: Plenum Press.

———— (1984). Moods, feelings, and the process of affect formation. In L. Temoshok, C. Van Dyke, & L.S. Zegans (Eds.), *Emotions in Health and Illness: Applications to Clinical Practice* (pp. 171–186). Orlando, FL: Grune & Stratton.

———— (1985, November). *The Role of Rhythm in Psychotherapy*. Paper presented at the conference of the National Coalition of Arts Therapy Associations, New York, NY.

——— (1988). Racial bias in the evaluation of patients for psychotherapy. In L. Comas-Díaz & E.E.H. Griffith (Eds.), *Clinical Guidelines in Cross-Cultural Mental Health* (pp. 112–134). New York, NY: Wiley.

———, Astrachan, B., & Flynn, H. (1976). The development and validation of a measure of the psychiatrist's authoritative domain. *Journal of Nervous and Mental Diseases* 162:410–422.

———, Cooley, R.S., & Hartley, D. (1981). Images of the psychotherapist: A theoretical and methodological perspective. *Imagination, Cognition and Personality* 1(2):123–146.

——— & Nash, V. (1975). Termination from psychotherapy as viewed by psychiatric residents. Unpublished manuscript.

Gill, M. (1982). *Analysis of Transference* (Vol. 1). New York, NY: International Universities Press.

Gilligan, C. (1982). *In a Different Voice: Psychological Theory and Women's Development*. Cambridge, MA: Harvard University Press.

Giovacchini, P.L. (1975). Self-projections in the narcissistic transference. *International Journal of Psychoanalytic Psychotherapy* 4:142–166.

Glenn, M.L. (1971). Separation anxiety: When the therapist leaves the patient. *American Journal of Psychotherapy* 25:437–442.

Glover, E. (1955). *The Technique of Psychoanalysis*. New York, NY: International Universities Press.

Goleman, D. (1984, April 3). Saying goodbye speaks volumes. *New York Times*, pp. C1, 12.

Gould, R.L. (1972). The phase of adult life: A study in developmental psychology. *American Journal of Psychiatry* 129:521–531.

Greene, L.R., & Geller, J.D. (1980). Effects of therapists' clinical experience and personal boundaries on termination of psychotherapy. *Journal of Psychiatric Education* 4:31–35.

Greenson, R.R. (1967). *The Technique and Practice of Psychoanalysis* (Vol. 1). New York, NY: International Universities Press.

Guntrip, H. (1969). *Schizoid Phenomena, Object Relations and the Self.* New York, NY: International Universities Press.

Hammer, E.F. (Ed.). (1968). *Uses of Interpretation in Treatment: Technique and Art.* Orlando, FL: Grune & Stratton.

Hartmann, H. (1958). *Ego Psychology and the Problem of Adaptation.* New York, NY: International Universities Press. (Original work published 1939.)

Horney, K. (1966). *New Ways in Psychoanalysis.* New York, NY: Norton.

Horowitz, M.J. (1972). Modes of representation in thought. *Journal of the American Psychoanalytic Association* 20:793–819.

———, Wilner, N., Marmar, C., & Krupnick, J.L. (1980). Pathological grief and the activation of latent self-images. *American Journal of Psychiatry* 137:1157–1162.

——— & Zilberg, N. (1983). Regressive alterations of the self concept. *American Journal of Psychiatry* 40:284–289.

Hurn, H.T. (1971). Toward a paradigm of the terminal phase. *Journal of the American Psychoanalytic Association* 19:332–348.

Jacobs, S., & Kosten, T.R. (1983). Depressive syndromes during acute bereavement: Indications for professional intervention. *Yale Psychiatric Quarterly* 6:4–13.

Jung, C.G. (1965). *Memories, Dreams, Reflections.* New York, NY: Vintage Books.

Kaiser, H. (1965). *Effective Psychotherapy: The Contributions of Helmuth Kaiser.* New York, NY: Free Press.

Priscilla F. Kauff, P.F. (1977). The termination process: Its relationship to the separation-individuation phase of development. *International Journal of Group Psychotherapy* 27(1)3–18.

Kazdin, M. (1980). *Research Design in Clinical Psychology*. New York, NY: Harper & Row.

Keith, C. (1966). Multiple transfers of psychotherapy patients. *Archives of General Psychiatry* 14:185–190.

Kernberg, O.F. (1976). *Object Relations Theory and Clinical Psychoanalysis*. New York, NY: Jason Aronson.

Kestenberg, J.S. (1966). Rhythm and organization in obsessive-compulsive development. *International Journal of Psychoanalysis* 47:151–159.

Kline, F., Adrian, A., & Spevak, M. (1974). Patients evaluate therapists. *Archives of General Psychiatry* 31:113–116.

Kluckhohn, C., & Murray, H.A. (1949). *Personality in Nature, Society, and Culture*. New York, NY: Knopf.

Kohut, H. (1971). *The Analysis of the Self*. New York, NY: International Universities Press.

——— (1977). *The Restoration of the Self*. New York, NY: International Universities Press.

——— & Wolf, E.S. (1978). The disorders of the self and their treatment: An outline. *International Journal of Psycho-Analysis* 59:413–425.

Krystal, H. (1979). Alexithymia and psychotherapy. *American Journal of Psychotherapy* 33:17–31.

Kurtz, R.R., & Grummon, D.L. (1972). Different approaches to the measurement of therapist empathy and their relationship to therapy outcomes. *Journal of Consulting and Clinical Psychology* 39:106–115.

Laing, R.D. (1965). *The Divided Self*. Baltimore, MD: Pelican Books.

Langs, R. (1976). *The Bipersonal Field*. New York, NY: Jason Aronson.

Lenzer, A.S. (1955). Countertransference and the resident on leaving his patient. *Journal of the Hillside Hospital* 4:148–157.

Levinson, D.J., Darrow, C.N., Klein, E.B., Levinson, M.H., & McKee, B. (1978). *The Seasons of a Man's Life*. New York, NY: Knopf.

Lipin, T. (1963). The repetition compulsion and "maturational" drive-representatives. *International Journal of Psycho-Analysis* 44:389–406.

Loewald, H.W. (1962). Internalization, separation, mourning, and the superego. *Psychoanalytic Quarterly* 31:483–504.

——— (1978). *Psychoanalysis and the History of the Individual*. New Haven, CT: Yale University Press.

Luborsky, L., Mintz, J., Auerbach, A.H., Christoph, P., Bachrach, H.M., Todd, T.C., Johnson, M., Cohen, M.L., & O'Brien, C.P. (1980). Predicting the outcome of psychotherapy: Findings of the Penn Psychotherapy Project. *Archives of General Psychiatry* 37:471–481.

Mahler, M.S. (1979). *The Selected Papers of Margaret S. Mahler: Vol. 2. Separation-Individuation*. New York, NY: Jason Aronson.

———, Pine, F., & Bergman, A. (1975). *The Psychological Birth of the Human Infant: Symbiosis and Individuation*. New York, NY: Basic Books.

Main, M., Kaplan, N., & Cassidy, J. (1985). Security in infancy, childhood, and adulthood: A move to the level of representation. *Monographs of the Society for Research in Child Development* 50(1/2):66–104. https://doi.org/10.2307/3333827

Mann, J. (1973). *Time-Limited Psychotherapy*. Cambridge, MA: Harvard University Press.

May, R. (Ed.). (1961). *Existential Psychology*. New York, NY: Random House.

Meissner, W.W. (1981). *Internalization in Psychoanalysis*. New York, NY: International Universities Press.

Mikkelson, E.J., & Gutheil, J. (1979). Stages of forced termination: Uses of the death metaphor. *Psychiatric Quarterly* 51:15–27.

Modell, A. (1976). "The holding environment" and the therapeutic action of psychoanalysis. *Journal of the American Psychoanalytic Association* 24:285–309.

Moffat, M.J. (1982). *In the Midst of Winter: Selections from the Literature of Mourning*. New York, NY: Random House.

Newton, P.M. (1973). Social structure and process in psychotherapy: A sociopsychological analysis of transference, resistance, change. *International Journal of Psychiatry* 11:480–509.

Piaget, J. (1954). *The Construction of Reality in the Child*. New York, NY: Basic Books.

Pumpian-Midlin, E. (1958). Comments on techniques of termination and transfer in a clinic. *American Journal of Psychotherapy* 12:455–459.

Rank, O. (1952). *The Trauma of Birth*. New York, NY: Brunner/Mazel. (Original work published 1924.)

Raskin, N. (1974). Studies on psychotherapeutic orientation: Ideology in practice. *AAP Psychotherapy Research Monographs*. Orlando, FL: American Academy of Psychotherapists.

Rickers-Ovsiankina, M., Berzins, J.I., Geller, J.D., & Rogers, G.W. (1971). Patients' role expectations in psychotherapy: A theoretical and measurement approach. *Psychotherapy* 8:124–127.

Rieff, P. (1961). *Freud: The Mind of the Moralist*. New York, NY: Doubleday.

Rogers, C.R. (1961). *On Becoming a Person*. Boston, MA: Houghton Mifflin.

———— (1975). Empathic: An unappreciated way of being. *Counseling Psychologist* 5:1–10.

Romey, K. (1966). *New Ways in Psychoanalysis*. New York, NY: Norton.

Rycroft, C. (1956). The nature and function of the analyst's communication to the patient. *International Journal of Psycho-Analysis* 37:469–471.

Sandler, J., & Rosenblatt, B. (1962). The concept of the representational world. *Psychoanalytic Study of the Child* 17:128–145.

Saul, L. (1972). *Psychodynamically Based Psychotherapy*. New York, NY: Science House.

Schachtel, E.G. (1959). *Metamorphosis: On the Development of Affect, Perception, Attention, and Memory*. New York, NY: Basic Books.

Schafer, R. (1968). *Aspects of Internalization*. New York, NY: International Universities Press.

———— (1973a). Concepts of self and identity and the experience of separation-individuation in adolescence. *Psychoanalytic Quarterly* 42:42–59.

———— (1973b). The termination of brief psychoanalytic psychotherapy. *International Journal of Psychoanalytic Psychotherapy* 2:135–148.

Schimek, J.G. (1975). A critical re-examination of Freud's concept of unconscious mental representation. *International Review of Psychoanalysis* 2:171–187.

Schwaber, P. (1971). Freud and the twenties. *Massachusetts Review* 10:133–147.

Searles, H.F. (1965). Oedipal love in the countertransference. In *Collected Papers on Schizophrenia and Related Subjects*. New York, NY: International Universities Press.

———— (1977). Dual and multiple-identity processes in border-line ego functioning. In P. Hartocollis (Ed.), *Borderline Personality Disorders: The Concept, the Patient, the Syndrome*. New York, NY: International Universities Press.

Shapiro, D. (1965). *Neurotic Styles*. New York, NY: Basic Books.

Sher, M. (1970). The process of changing therapists. *American Journal of Psychotherapy* 25:278–282.

Singer, J.L. (1974). *Imagery and Daydream Methods in Psychotherapy and Behavior Modification*. New York, NY: Academic Press.

———— (1985). Transference and the human condition: A cognitive-affective perspective. *Psychoanalytic Psychology* 2:189–219.

Spitz, R.A. (1965). *The First Year of Life: A Psychoanalytic Study of Normal and Deviant Development of Object Relations*. New York, NY: International Universities Press.

Stolorow, R., & Ross, J. (1978). The representational world in psychoanalytic therapy. *International Review of Psychoanalysis* 5:247–256.

Strachey, J. (1934). The nature of the therapeutic action of psychoanalysis. *International Journal of Psycho-Analysis* 15:127–159.

Strupp, H.H. (1976). The nature of the therapeutic influence and its basic ingredients. In A. Burton (Ed.), *What Makes Behavior Change Possible?* New York, NY: Brunner/Mazel.

Sue, S. (1977). Community mental health services to minority groups: Some optimism, some pessimism. *American Psychologist* 32:616–624.

Sullivan, H.S. (1953). *The Interpersonal Theory of Psychiatry*. New York, NY: Norton.

Updike, J. (1966). *The Music School*. New York, NY: Fawcett.

Vaillant, G.E. (1977). *Adaptation to Life*. Boston, MA: Little, Brown.

Volkan, V.D. (1976). *Primitive Internalized Object Relations*. New York, NY: International Universities Press.

Weigert, E. (1952). Contribution to the problem of terminating psychoanalyses. *Psychoanalytic Quarterly* 21:465–472.

Weiner, I.B. (1975). *Principles of Psychotherapy*. New York, NY: Wiley.

Werner, H. (1961). *Comparative Psychology of Mental Development*. New York, NY: Science Editions.

Whitaker, C. (1966). The administrative ending in psychotherapy. *Voices* 2:69–73.

Winnicott, D.W. (1953). Transitional objects and transitional phenomena: A study of the first not-me possession. *International Journal of Psycho-Analysis* 34:89–97.

———— (1965). *The Maturational Processes and the Facilitating Environment*. New York, NY: International Universities Press.

CHAPTER 5

Racial Bias in the Evaluation of Patients for Psychotherapy

[J.D. Geller (1988). In L. Comas-Díaz & E.E.H. Griffith (Eds.), *Clinical Guidelines in Cross-Cultural Mental Health* (pp. 112–134). New York, NY: Wiley.]

This chapter seeks to advance our understanding of the ways in which various historical, organizational, and interpersonal issues can interfere with a clinician's ability to evaluate accurately an applicant's capacity to participate in and benefit from various forms of treatment, especially in the context of outpatient services of community mental health centers (CMHCs). I will attempt to come to terms with the results of studies, mostly conducted during the late 1960s and 1970s, that revealed the existence among psychotherapists of negative biases prejudicial to lower-class and minority group patients, particularly Blacks, receiving long-term, dyadic, exploratory psychotherapy. At the center of this effort is a study conducted by Stevenson and Geller (1969) that sought to discover possible inaccurate generalizations or racial stereotypes among mental health professionals that might help to account for the underrepresentation of Blacks in psychotherapeutic treatment populations. Such underrepresentation, it should be emphasized, continues to exist even at institutions where efforts are made to recruit these patients, where minority groups are proportionately represented in the intake statistics, and where conscious efforts are made to give equal opportunity for treatment to all (Griffith & Jones, 1979). The relative contributions to these trends of patients, clinicians, and the organizations they represent have been heatedly debated within the mental health professions and the community at large (Smith et al., 1978).

It is now generally recognized that complex, multilayered relationships are set in motion when individuals who have defined themselves or who have been defined by others as needing help approach CMHCs. Contemporary writers emphasize that the prospective patient, his or her sociocultural matrix, and the philosophy, structure, and staffing patterns of mental health centers are *all* significantly involved in the decision-making process that leads to exclusion from individual psychotherapy (Levinson et al., 1967; Pinderhughes, 1973; Jones, 1974; Lazare et al., 1975). This has not always been the case. In the past, mental health professionals were more likely, as Ryan (1971) put it, to "blame the victim" (p. 3).

A HISTORICAL AND ORGANIZATIONAL OVERVIEW

Psychotherapy, as a profession, originated within the entrepreneurial context of the private practice of medicine. Today, psychotherapy is increasingly being practiced by a heterogeneous group of professionals and nonprofessionals within complex bureaucratic organizations, such as health maintenance organizations (HMOs) and CMHCs.

The CMHC movement, in its origins, was intimately related to changes taking place in the economic and sociopolitical sectors of the culture, for instance, the war on poverty and the Civil Rights Movement. These shifts challenged mental health professionals to reexamine critically various assertions that, during previous generations, were used to justify not treating whole classes of patients psychotherapeutically.

A relentless flow of unscreened applicants presenting with a heterogeneous group of problems—many of which do not easily lend themselves to official psychiatric diagnostic categories or psychodynamic formulations—seek entrance to community health centers (Feshbach et al., 1982). The great majority of these prospective patients cannot afford psychotherapy from private practitioners. In their efforts to satisfy urgent demands for psychotherapeutic services, mental health centers have greatly expanded the definition of what constitutes appropriate and beneficial outpatient care. The outpatient services of CHMCs are organized to provide a variety of psychotherapeutic resources that go far beyond the one-to-one doctor-patient relationship. In addition to offering long-term dyadic psychotherapy, mental health centers perform crisis intervention functions, facilitate reentry of previously hospitalized patients into the community, offer group and family therapy, dispense medication, and so on.

At the time of intake, individuals seeking entrance into these organizations must be evaluated for each of these forms of treatment. These treatment modalities vary in important respects, for example, duration, ambitiousness, cost-effectiveness, the therapeutic tasks they pose for patients and therapists, and the conceptualizations of behavioral and psychological symptoms from which they derive. Some of the more supportive forms of therapy encourage dependency; others promote more self-governance. Some strive to help patients adjust to their current situations; others attempt to effect fundamental changes in a patient's self or personality. Therapies also vary in their popularity or prestige. In many outpatient settings treatment modalities other than long-term exploratory individual psychotherapy still tend to be regarded as "second-class" treatment. For example, Grunebaum and Kates (1977) have observed that referrals to group therapy are often made only when the places for individual therapy are filled and not because group therapy is viewed as the treatment of choice.

Despite important differences in the organizational structures of mental health centers, the task of regulating the flow of patients both into and out of these various treatment modalities is typically assigned to clinicians working within a center's intake and evaluation unit. In the language of social systems theory, they are responsible for managing and controlling the boundaries that separate the mental health center's input and conversion systems (Rice, 1964). To this end, intake clinicians seek to determine, among other things, a patient's eligibility for treatment, the likelihood of continuation in treatment to a beneficial conclusion, and the appropriateness of a particular type of therapeutic setting, therapy, or therapist. When the admission criterion for a particular treatment modality is simply the existence of a target symptom (e.g., alcoholism, obesity, drug addiction), these tasks are relatively uncomplicated. In general, however, the realization of these goals requires a sophisticated understanding of what demands are made on a patient by a particular therapeutic situation and procedure and which features and resources of the patient's physical and psychological makeup will be called upon to meet these demands. In making these judgments, clinicians rely on a host of commonly held, although frequently unsubstantiated, beliefs regarding the prerequisites, requirements, and conditions necessary for successful therapy.

THE SELECTION CRITERIA FOR PSYCHOTHERAPY

When functioning as therapists, in the service of making empathic contact with a patient, mental health professionals try to set aside their prejudices. However, when selectively distributing limited psychotherapeutic resources, they must discriminate between more or less suitable candidates. With few exceptions, the emphasis in the psychotherapy literature has been on identifying undesirable or unsuitable candidates for a particular mode of therapy rather than on establishing clear indications for success-ful treatment. Yalom (1975) has observed, for example: "Almost all of the systematic studies of group psychotherapy selection have attempted to elaborate exclusion and failure criteria rather than success criteria" (p. 175). Consequently, the determination of which applicants are best qualified for admission to a par-ticular form of therapy often has the character of a qualifying examination or a selective admissions procedure. As Levinson et al. (1967) have observed, direct parallels can be found between the selection of applicants for a job or school and the procedures used for assigning applicants to psychotherapists in psychiatric clinics. What Levinson et al. further discovered was that the allocation of a clinic's psychotherapeutic treatment resources depends only in part on a patient's formal or medical diagnosis.

Although the allocation of psychotherapeutic resources may not be based on a patient's psychiatric diagnosis, diagnoses themselves are based on comparisons, many of which imply value judgments. For example, a diagnosis of personality dis-order implies greater and more long-standing psychopatholo-gy than a diagnosis of transient situational disturbance. As Sue (1977) found, Blacks are more likely to be placed in the former category than Whites. This is not an isolated finding. Despite some inconsistencies in research findings, epidemiological in-vestigations indicate that Blacks receive more diagnoses within the realm of major psychiatric disorders than do Whites (Mayo, 1974; Griffith & Jones, 1979).

It is more feasible from the standpoint of research methodol-ogy to establish failure criteria than to establish success criteria. However, as shall be more fully discussed later in this chapter, the observational biases inherent in such an approach can handicap a clinician in his or her efforts to honor the singularity of a stranger. What further complicates the work of intake clinicians is the fact that the literature on selection criteria abounds with inconsistencies. Clinical opinions and anecdotal reports can be found that contradict any of the purportedly established guidelines for patient selection.

In many settings psychotherapeutic work is no longer skewed in the direction of the psychoanalytic model. Yet the continuing influence of the psychoanalytic perspective on the "ideal" candidate for insight-oriented psychotherapy can be discerned in the selection criteria used to identify suitable patients for many of the newer forms of therapy. Freud (1937) emphasized the restricted applicability of psychoanalysis. The consensus view among contemporary psychoanalytic researchers is that verbal, anxious, neurotic, intelligent, educated, and psychologically minded individuals will benefit more from the therapy designed specifically to promote insight than people who are more seriously disturbed and/or impulsive in the psychopathic sense (Luborsky et al., 1971). During previous generations, whole classes of patients were deemed inaccessible to psychoanalytic therapy (e.g., addicts, criminals, chronic schizophrenics) because of the belief that they were suffering from severe and irreparable developmental deficits in the capacities required to form a therapeutic alliance and/or successfully resolve intrapsychic conflicts.

For several decades researchers have consistently found that mental health facilities tend to offer the poor different services than patients of higher social classes (e.g., Yamamoto et al., 1968; Lerner, 1972). For example, it has been revealed that lower-class patients are more apt to receive short-term supportive therapy and minimal-contact pharmacological therapy and are less likely to receive intensive insight-oriented therapy than are middle-class patients (Sue et al., 1974). Some have suggested that these trends point to the operation of negative biases toward lower-class individuals receiving the most beneficial and appropriate treatment (e.g., Meltzoff & Kornreich, 1970). Others would argue that, first and foremost, many lower-class patients require assistance from a wide range of social services, which might include financial aid, housing, medical care, and job rehabilitation, and that directly helping a patient deal with the overwhelming nature of a psychonoxious environment makes it all but impossible to engage in insight-oriented treatment. An extension of this argument is that, even in the absence of oppressive environmental conditions, lower-class patients do not hold the values, attitudes, and role expectations assumed to characterize individuals who can participate efficaciously in a psychotherapy centered around the development of introspection and self-understanding. In the historically dominant tradition, the differential treatment of lower-class patients has been primarily defended on the grounds that their styles of help seeking do not coincide with the role requirements and division of labor of exploratory psychotherapy as it is generally practiced.

RACE, SOCIOECONOMIC STATUS, AND PRETHERAPY EXPECTATIONS

Clinical lore and previous research are believed to support the view that patient expectations of the rules, techniques, and events that will occur in psychotherapy influence satisfaction, continuation, and improvement in psychotherapy and that, within broad limits, such expectations are predictable from personality and/or sociodemographic variables (Heine & Trossman, 1960; Frank, 1973; Geller et al., 1976).

An important origin of the hypothesis that lower-class patients predominantly demand a medically oriented authoritarian doctor and unrealistically expect immediate solutions to their problems can be traced to Hollingshead and Redlich's research into the relationship between social class and pretreatment expectations. Although published in 1958, Hollingshead and Redlich's findings are still quoted, with regularity, as evidence of the unsuitability of lower-class patients for exploratory psychotherapy. These investigations reported that, in comparison with patients of higher social classes, low-income patients had less faith in the efficacy of a "talking treatment" and greater difficulty understanding that their emotional troubles were not actually physical illnesses. Hollingshead and Redlich further observed that by comparison such patients were also more likely to demand, either tacitly or overtly, that their therapists adopt an active, medical, and supportive role in therapy.

The results of studies conducted during the 1960s supported the claim that low-income patients tend to hold an optimistically dependent view of the psychotherapist as a benignly authoritarian, medically oriented figure who will have the primary responsibility for the work of therapy (Overall & Aronson, 1963; Aronson & Overall, 1966; Williams et al., 1967). Such a passive-obedient-externalizing orientation to help seeking can be a critical obstacle to the establishment of a working alliance and must be dealt with early in evaluation and treatment. Whether the pretherapy expectations of low-income patients render them less suitable candidates for intensive psychotherapy has not, however, been empirically validated. Many types of patients begin therapy compromised in their ability to collaborate genuinely with their therapists, and various procedures have been created to facilitate the establishment of mutuality of expectations prior to the first hour (e.g., the role of the induction interview [Hoehn-Saric et al., 1964]). Moreover, in the aforementioned studies and in those done in the 1970s, no evidence was found to indicate that lower-class patients were significantly more likely to define their problems in physical rather than psychological terms (Fischer & Cohen, 1970; Lorion, 1972; Geller & Singer, 1976; Comas-Díaz et al., 1982). Members of all social classes appear to have become more knowledgeable about the conversational content and emotional atmosphere of psychotherapy. Irrespective of their social class membership, the patients in these studies appeared ready to participate in a psychotherapy that focuses on the discussion of emotionally charged and intimate matters, including thoughts and feelings about the therapist; they also showed an awareness that to do so might be anxiety arousing. Moreover, when data have been examined for interaction effects, variables related to social class (e.g., education, religion, race, ethnicity) are often found to be more influential determinants of patient expectations regarding the kind and degree of help psychotherapists will provide than is social class itself (Geller et al., 1976; Acosta, 1979; Comas-Díaz et al., 1982).

The experience of Blacks in our culture has been radically different from that of other groups, even those that are dispro-portionately represented in the lower socioeconomic classes (Cross, 1978). The obvious confounding of class and race in many of the reported studies makes suspect any generalizations as to whether there are observable and consistent differences in the modal personality patterns of Black and White individuals. In some studies, socioeconomic status accounts for a greater number of the effects that might otherwise be called racial (Harrison, 1975). Other studies, however, show Black-White effects on personality characteristics relevant to the psychotherapeutic process when demographic variables such as age, sex, and social class are controlled. For example, lower self-disclosure has been consistently found among Blacks in comparison with Whites of the same class and educational level (Ridley, 1984).

It is generally agreed that the socialization of Blacks in America has conditioned them to reveal themselves reluctantly to White therapists (Vontress, 1976). On the other hand, Blacks have been found to risk openness more willingly with Black as opposed to White therapists (Wetzel & Wright, 1983). Moreover, racially similar counselor-client dyads have resulted in greater self-exploration (Carkhuff & Pierce, 1967; Banks, 1972).

Multivariate studies and analyses are obviously needed to determine whether there are any important differences between Black and White individuals in their readiness to participate in particular forms of psychotherapy. Empirical clarification of this emotionally charged issue will benefit both patients and therapists, and it will also contribute to the creation of more effective delivery systems.

With these historical, conceptual, and organizational issues in mind, I will now discuss the detailed activities that go into arriving at an understanding of the appropriateness of a particular type of therapy, therapist, and setting for a particular patient. This is far from a purely rational, objective, or technical procedure.

THE EVALUATION INTERVIEW(S)

As conceptualized here, the diagnostic interview is a temporary open system that is created to accomplish work. The interviewer occupying the institutionally validated role of expert has primary responsibility for defining the tasks and division of labor required to accomplish this work.

To begin with, intake clinicians are expected to establish an emphatic, confidence-inspiring relationship with a stranger. As Bruch (1974) put it, a primary task of the initial interview is that of establishing "the possibility of meaningful exchange"

(p. 25). A skilled intake interviewer is capable of shifting flexibly between the pursuit of a variety of primary tasks during the initial or screening interviews. Because of the heterogeneity of the individuals seeking entrance into mental health centers, the diagnostic interview can never become a tightly scripted technical regime according to which the clinician behaves in a largely prescribed fashion. The sequencing of the tasks clinicians impose on themselves and their patients should in each instance be governed by the unique needs and circumstances of a particular patient. For example, an intake interviewer may also be called upon to respond helpfully to the immediate and often pressing suffering and disabilities of the prospective patient. Neglecting this task and/or failing to make empathic contact with a patient can intensify a patient's suffering and manifest psychopathology. Clinical experience also supports the hypothesis that such failures of empathy may be causally related to the distressingly high dropout rates reported by various mental health facilities (Baekeland & Lundwall, 1975).

The decision to seek psychotherapy is not made easily, nor is the decision binding. Psychotherapy is usually the treatment of last resort. Even individuals who value psychotherapy as a means of alleviating pain and promoting growth seek professional psychotherapeutic help only after they have failed to master a problem self-reliantly or exhausted their personal relationships (Farber & Geller, 1977). Consequently, a demoralization syndrome that includes feelings of powerlessness and hopelessness usually accompanies entry into psychotherapy (Frank, 1972). If an intake evaluator fails to mobilize faith or hope, or if the intake interview is experienced as a personal failure, the likelihood of a premature termination is heightened. The importance of this issue is testified to by the fact that in some comprehensive care centers more than 50% of Black clients drop out after only *one* interview (Sue, 1977).

Much of the work of the initial interview is devoted to obtaining information. The intake clinician is expected to conduct in a coherent, rational, and more or less systematic fashion a detailed inquiry into the more troublesome aspects of the prospective patient's personal-social-medical history as well as to obtain significant information regarding the individual's current desires, conflicts, defenses, resources, symptoms, and so forth. Since psychopathology within the diagnostic interview is often manifested in terms of difficulties in communication, obtaining such intimate data requires considerable tact and skill. Concurrently, the clinician is expected to maintain an awareness of his or her own contribution to the diagnostic interview, including an appreciation of the personal wishes, conflicts, and defenses that are stimulated by the prospective patient. In other words, a clinician's readiness to receive the uniqueness of each prospective patient alternates with a thoughtful scrutiny of his or her countertransference reactions to the patient. To do so, a clinician must harmoniously manage the dual roles of participant and observer.

The role of intake clinician also carries with it the burden of balancing the therapeutic needs of persons seeking entrance into mental health centers and the needs of the organization. Whereas some treatment modalities tend to be under-utilized (e.g., group psychotherapy), demand often exceeds the supply of individual psychotherapy slots. Besides providing the particular form of help that will most benefit an applicant and distributing the proper number and kind of patients to the various treatment modalities, the intake clinician's work must often be further accommodated to an organizational structure that attempts to assign optimally suitable teaching cases for the purpose of training a variety of mental health professionals and nonprofessionals.

SOURCES OF BIAS IN THE INTAKE PROCESS

More or less consciously adopted theoretical orientations (e.g., psychoanalytic, behavioral, existential) organize a clinician's expectations as to how the intake interview should or will proceed. These orientations provide clinicians with guidelines about what data to look for and how to interpret the data that are found. As with patients' expectations of the transactions that will take place during the intake process, a clinician's consciously endorsed role models can lead to *selectivity* in attention, encoding, representation, and retrieval of information. The difficult task of integrating and weighing the relative importance of the information obtained during the intake interviews with the aforementioned organizational constraints in order to arrive at a diagnosis and treatment recommendation potentially calls into play other, often less consciously recognized sources of bias.

A clinician's efforts to perceive and appraise the "reality" of an applicant's capacity to use psychotherapeutic resources can be compromised by the biasing influence of countertransference reactions and/or social stereotypes. Psychotherapists have devoted considerable attention to uncovering the irrational and idiosyncratic origins of their countertransference reactions and the ways in which conflictual relationships to persons from their own past have led them erroneously to ascribe traits to a particular patient. With tough-minded curiosity, they have also begun to explore the hypothesis that private, "subjective" fantasies and feelings about a patient, no matter how problematic, hateful, or neurotic in origin, often can provide invaluable information about the processes currently characterizing the relationship between patient and therapist.

Psychotherapists have not been as explicit in asking themselves whether and/or how social stereotypes have compromised their ability to recognize the uniqueness of a particular patient.

Within the clinical situation, stereotyping essentially involves the use of broad, oversimplified generalizations about categories of people as guidelines for the possible presence of character traits in a particular individual. Perhaps it has been seen as less ignoble to attend selectively to and interpret information about a patient for neurotic reasons than to do so on the basis of stereotypic preconceptions of social groups such as Blacks or women. I believe this unfortunate imbalance can be overcome by reconceptualizing countertransference and stereotyping as but two particular instances and potential liabilities of the universal tendency to perceive and cognitively structure new events and experiences schematically rather than in detail.

A proliferating array of vocabularies have been invented to discover and convey the ways in which the interpretation and remembrance of information contained in the social environment are affected by the enduring schematic cognitive-affective representations that people construct of persons and transactions between them (e.g., prototypes [Cantor & Mischel, 1979]; scripts [Abelson, 1981]; and introjects [Geller et al., 1981]). There is a growing consensus that, while essential to imputing structure and meaning to incoming data, schematic processing can also interfere with accuracy by inducing a bias to perceive new situations as old (Singer, 1985). On the one hand, the schemata individuals impose on their world enable them to "selectively" perceive relevant events, to fill in gaps when certain information is not readily available, and to recall essential aspects of an incident (Goldfried & Robins, 1983). On the other hand, when employed as shortcuts or heuristics that simplify or shorten the process of making evaluations of others, schemata may close off new definitions and solutions and lead to a loss of crucial information. There is abundant evidence from research in the area of social cognition that individuals tend to overlook objectively available information if this information is not representative of their generalized theory of how things should be (Nisbett & Ross, 1979; Taylor & Crocker, 1981). When generalized beliefs and current information are at odds, people tend to rely more heavily on their beliefs, ignoring current information. Individuals apparently resist information that runs counter to their prevailing mental models of the world and how it works.

A complementary line of investigation recently summarized by Snyder (1981) indicates that, when social stereotypes are used to predict others' behavior, they can actually induce the other to behave as predicted so as to have the prediction about them come true. In other words, stereotypes perpetuate themselves by exerting a powerful pressure on others to behave in ways that support and bolster the initially erroneous attributions. Thus, in several important respects, the schemata individuals have about personalities, social roles, and events function similarly to transference and countertransference paradigms.

In sum, whenever a clinician tries to construct an image of a particular patient and the kind of world he or she lives in, schemata bearing a more or less accurate relationship to the material or factual reality of that patient, who is seen as a member of a larger group or class, are called into play. Whether these acts of the imagination (1) impose functional restrictions on the information that is encoded (i.e., perceived, classified, stored) during an interview and (2) distort the retrieval of information when looking at the patient's reality from a distance are researchable questions. To this end, Dr. Karl Stevenson and I did the following study.

THE INFLUENCE OF RACE IQ ON JUDGMENTS REGARDING SUITABILITY FOR TREATMENT

During the spring of 1969, we asked the entire population of White psychiatric residents ($N = 77$) and younger faculty psychiatrists ($N = 13$) involved in outpatient treatment at a northeastern mental health center to participate in a study regarding the criteria used at intake to evaluate patients for psychotherapy. Each clinician was mailed a highly detailed, three-page summary of an intake interview of a 25-year-old, low-income male patient with marital and work adjustment problems and a three-part questionnaire that asked the therapists to describe, diagnose, and prescribe treatment for the patient. The protocol was a modified and abridged version of a case history written by Rogers (1955) to provide suggestions of psychotic illness while reflecting a basically neurotic character structure.

The patient's symptomatic picture was said to include loss of appetite, nausea, panic attacks, fears of loss of control, a preoccupation with suicide, and occasional homicidal thoughts directed toward his wife. He had been briefly hospitalized 3 years prior to the present contact because of similar problems, which seemed to arise after he had attempted to have intercourse with his wife-to-be. During the mental status exam, the patient was tense yet appropriate, orientated in all three spheres, and denied hallucinations, delusions, and ideas of reference. The biographical information revealed that the patient was a Catholic factory worker who had recently moved to the city and that he had been married for a year. The patient was described as having been an average student who had to drop out of school at 16 for financial reasons. It was further disclosed that he had had asthma as a child, was the only son and the oldest of four siblings, and that he perceived his mother as the dominant member of the family. Unbeknownst to the psychiatrists, they were randomly divided into three experimental groups ($N = 30$). They all received identical protocols except that the patient's alleged race and IQ were varied across the three experimental groups. The first group was led to believe that the patient was White and had an IQ of 120. The second group was told that the patient was Black and had an IQ of 120, while the third group was informed that the patient was White with an IQ of 85. The patient's IQ, which had been obtained during the previous hospitalization, was not mentioned until the last line of the intake protocol and was reported in terms of Wechsler Adult Intelligence Scale IQ. In contrast, the patient's race was mentioned twice, once in the first line and again toward the end of the protocol. A total of 75 out of our population of 90 psychiatrists returned completed questionnaires. All 30 therapists receiving the protocol that described the patient as White with an IQ of 85 responded. Twenty-four of the 30 receiving the protocol that said the patient was White with an IQ of 120 replied. Of the 30 who were told that the patient was Black with an IQ of 120, 21 returned completed questionnaires. Although this differential return rate is not statistically significant, its general trend is consistent with the results that were found.

A detailed presentation of the results of this study is beyond the scope of this presentation, especially those that deal with alleged psychometrically defined intelligence of the patient. For the present purposes, I will focus on the findings that bear upon Griffith and Jones's (1979) conclusion that "the mental health system does not serve the needs of blacks as well as it does those of whites" (p. 323).

Irrespective of race or IQ, the patient was diagnosed as having a functional neurotic disorder of intrapsychic-interpersonal origins. This finding is noteworthy given that epidemiological research suggests that Blacks tend to receive more severe diagnoses than Whites (Griffith & Jones, 1979). Neither did the therapists view the Black patient's difficulties as emanating more importantly from sociocultural influences than from intrapsychic conflicts, as was fashionable during the early 1970s (Jackson, 1972). Across the experimental groups, the patient was depicted as suffering from such characterological difficulties as rigidity, passivity, and intolerance of anxiety. Moreover, the Black patient was not described as significantly less complex or understandable, more guarded, or less familiar than the allegedly White patient. There was basic accord among the experimental groups that the patient was definitely in need of treatment, motivated to change, and had benefited somewhat from the initial interview.

Despite the decline in stereotyping suggested by these findings, the analyses also indicated that the experimental manipulation had influenced the therapists' judgments regarding several issues or questions that are crucial in the decision-making process that leads to treatment. For the purposes of discussion, these questions might be formulated as follows:

1. Does the patient have the skills and resources necessary to do the work of therapy?
2. Do I (the intake clinician) like the patient and want to get close to him or her?
3. Will the patient or his or her environment make trouble for the therapist?

The first cluster of items that significantly differentiated among the experimental groups appeared to deal with the therapists' evaluation of the patient's ability to do the work of therapy. The allegedly Black patient was consistently evaluated as being least endowed with the skills required of a good psychotherapy candidate. Thus, especially in contrast to the White IQ 85 experimental group, the Black IQ 120 group saw the patient as significantly less articulate, competent, introspective, self-critical, sophisticated about mental health centers, and psychologically minded. These results reveal the persistence of racially stereotyped thinking; they also suggest that the clinicians in our study were reevaluating the "evidence" and therapeutic truisms that have justified a skeptical view of the lower-class patient's accessibility to psychotherapy. The patient was represented in each experimental group as a poorly educated factory worker. Nevertheless, the therapists who were told that the patient was White, especially those in the White IQ 85 experimental group, did not conclude that he was deficient in the skills required of patients in intensive-dyadic modes of psychotherapy. He was regarded as neither too uninformed nor too impulsive to adapt to the work structure of the psychotherapeutic enterprise, nor too nonverbal and nonintrospective to engage in a therapeutic dialogue. Consequently, he was felt to have considerable ability to profit from treatment.

This greater optimism concerning the lower-class patient's ability to utilize long-term psychotherapy also characterized the therapists' responses to those items that bear upon the question, Do I like the patient and want to get close to him or her? Lower-class patients have traditionally been offered short-term, directive, supportive kinds of therapy because the evidence indicated that this is what they wanted and would use. Yet intensive, long-term dyadic forms of psychotherapy were considered to be appropriate referrals by both groups that thought the patient was White. Once again, this view was not extended to the patient when he was said to be Black. The allegedly Black patient was regarded as a significantly less suitable candidate for insight-oriented and psychoanalytically oriented psychotherapy than either of the allegedly White patients. Moreover, the most favored modality of treatment for the patient when he was said to be Black was chemotherapy.

Irrespective of ascribed race or IQ, the patient was regarded as a somewhat appropriate candidate for supportive, family, crisis-oriented, group, and directive therapies. On the other hand, the experimental groups tended to agree that environmental manipulation, behavior therapy, and somatic therapy were inappropriate referrals.

Although the three experimental groups were in basic accord regarding the patient's considerable need for treatment and did not differ significantly in the degree to which they felt that it was urgent to get the patient into treatment with a staff therapist, there was a definite tendency for the experimental manipulation to alter the therapist's willingness personally to assume the responsibility for treating the patient. The therapists were most willing to take the White IQ 85 patient into treatment and least willing to treat the patient when he was represented as Black. If one assumes that the experimental task set up a relationship, albeit presumptive, between the therapist and the patient, then it would seem reasonable to conclude that the need to maintain professional-personal distance was strongest in the group that was presented with the Black patient. That both groups who thought the patient was White seemed to feel far more comfortable with the prospect of getting close to him than did the therapists who thought the patient was Black is implied by the priority given to chemotherapy. Further support for this hypothesis is provided by the finding that the clinicians described the Black patient as significantly less responsive or warm than either of the groups that thought the patient was White.

In keeping with this argument, Sheatsley (1965) has documented that the closer a White person comes to having an intimate relationship with a Black person, the more likely he or she is to reject him or her. Moreover, the inferences that can be drawn from our data are consistent with Erikson's (1965) speculations regarding the role a group's communal identity plays in perpetuating stereotypic thinking. Erikson maintains that one's communal identity is composed of positive poles (i.e., which I am) as well as negative poles (i.e., which I am not, even though I may be tempted to be). He contends that the negative poles tend to become more salient when one gets too close to a member of another group and that as a result of this process the perceived differences between "your" group and "my" group are emphasized. According to Erikson, the mechanism reinforces the phenomenon of subspeciation, which also leads Whites and Blacks, in the United States, to focus on their differences rather than their similarities.

With respect to the third question, the results indicated that the clinicians maximized the possibility of adverse effects from the environment and the probability of acting out when the patient was said to be Black. It was anticipated by the subjects that the Black patient would be far more likely to drop out of treatment prematurely than either of the White patients. Furthermore, the Black patient was described as significantly more impulsive, intolerant of frustration, in need of immediate gratification, and intolerant of successful treatment than the White patients. While there was general agreement regarding the unsupportive nature of the patient's family, the Black patient was perceived as coming from a more chaotic environment than the White IQ 85 patient. Here one might wonder whether the complexities of the Black extended family system may be mistaken for signs of disorganization when compared to the nuclear type, which is more common among White Americans. Moreover, before generalizing unequivocally about the implications of these findings, it will be recalled that the patient was preoccupied with homicidal ideas toward his wife and had suicidal concerns. The potentially violent nature of the presenting complaints used in the protocols of our study might be particularly powerful in stimulating the regressive return of stereotypic thinking and/

or fantasies of the potential for violence in Black-White relations. A dominant hypothesis in the therapeutic literature is that internalized racist attitudes—inner-directed racism and frustrated rage toward Whites—constitute the central conflict and the core of the Black male's psychopathology (Grier & Cobbs, 1968). Familiarity with this hypothesis may be a potent source of countertransference anxieties leading to psychological withdrawal on the part of young White clinicians working at urban mental health centers. One question for future investigations is whether similar results would have been obtained irrespective of the symptomatic picture, or sex, or socioeconomic background presented by the patient.

THE QUEST FOR UNIQUENESS AND THE SELF-FULFILLING PROPHECY

In order to create an empirically grounded science of psychotherapy, the discovery of the similarities between between people, whether members of the same group or of different groups, is of first importance. Without the discovery of uniformities and commonalities, as Kluckhohn and Murray (1949) concluded, "there can be no concepts, no classifications, no formulations, no principles, no laws and without these no science can exist" (p. 53). As previously noted, the burden of distributing selectively limited therapeutic resources is complicated by the fact that there are no unequivocally established and empirically derived guidelines for patient selection. Moreover, although most practitioners readily concede that they are more successful with some patients than with others, there is at present no organized body of knowledge that could serve as a guideline for matching patients and therapists (Geller & Berzins, 1976; Gunderson, 1978).

Still another source of dilemmas faced by the clinicians during intake interviews, within any setting, derives from the fact that "every man is in certain respects (a) like all other men, (b) like some other men, (c) like no other man" (Kluckhohn & Murray, 1949, p. 53). For complex and interacting reasons it has become increasingly imperative to accent the uniqueness of the patients seeking psychological assistance from CMHCs.

Mental health services are becoming more available, but they are also becoming increasingly bureaucratized. Bureaucracies tend to treat individuals as instances of generalities. Concurrently, the diagnostic enterprise tends to have a conventionalizing influence on clinicians' portrayals of prospective clients. Kadushin (1963) has observed that intake workers are prone to writing diagnostic reports that fail to particularize generalizations so that a specific patient can be differentiated from all other patients. These diagnostic statements tend to be diagnostically valid but would be equally true of "Jane Doe." At best, an intake interview can only provide a rough and superficial outline of the major landmarks in a person's life. In general, those landmarks that are discussed spontaneously by the patient organize the direction taken by the inquiry. Consequently, when filling in gaps in information and reducing ambiguities inherent in the situation, clinicians must of necessity rely on schemata and expectations derived from previous experience with individuals from the particular group(s) from which the patient comes.

The results of the study presented here further suggest that, when evaluating Blacks, White clinicians are in danger of relying on cultural stereotypes that do not apply to specific individuals or that might not even be accurate characterizations of the group as a whole. Clearly the "facts" of the case did not dictate unequivocally the therapists' conclusions about the patient's strengths and weaknesses. Rather, they appear on various dimensions to have confused, unwittingly, the specific patient's abilities and problems with their probably unrecognized feelings and expectations about a whole class of patients.

Our findings therefore highlight the importance of recognizing the possibility that the deficiencies that we have observed in our patients may result from a failure to comprehend the operation of the self-fulfilling prophecy. Merton (1948) has written that "the self-fulfilling prophecy is, in the beginning, a false definition of the situation evoking a new behavior which makes the originally false conception come true" (p. 193). Established expectancies regarding how Black men will or should behave in the interview situation thus selectively influence particular Black men to behave as anticipated. The dangers of this mechanism are heightened because the diagnostic enterprise focuses on identifying whether the patient has certain deficiencies that weigh against admission to a particular form of treatment. Given that clinicians are subject to the same cultural stereotypes and biases found in the culture, it is likely that therapists have, in actual clinical contacts, unwittingly stimulated Blacks to behave in a manner that confirmed the therapists' possibly unrecognized attitudes toward Black people. Just as the expectations of White experimenters and classroom teachers have been shown to suppress the cognitive functioning and expressivity of Black subjects and students (Rosenthal & Jacobson, 1968), it is likely that clinicians' expectations have provoked docility, acquiescence, and/or wary, cynical, and cautious behaviors in Black applicants for psychotherapy. A series of experiments by Ward et al. (1974) suggest that in interracial interview situations self-fulfilling prophecies are mediated by nonverbal cues. They found, for example, that when naive White job interviewers interviewed trained White and Black applicants, the interviewers saw the Black applicants for shorter periods of time, made more speech errors, and demonstrated less immediacy—a measure consisting of physical distance, forward lean, eye contact, and shoulder orientation.

IMPLICATIONS AND RECOMMENDATIONS

In coming to terms with the question of who should bear the responsibility, even the guilt, for inequities in the allocation of limited treatment resources, it is necessary to bear in mind that the role or positions taken by persons in organizations that selectively grant resources to applicants can be defined independently of the particular persons occupying these roles. From an organizational perspective, the diagnostic enterprise is rooted in principles that both support and are antagonistic to the virtue of "equimindedness." Mental health centers, on the one hand, have attempted to extend the availability of psychotherapeutic resources to groups that have been excluded from these resources because of financial considerations. However, in an attempt to group patients so as to regulate effectively the flow of patients into and out of their treatment systems, mental health centers generate discriminatory social processes. Impulses toward brotherhood and bigotry are interwoven in the moral economy, as they are in the religious doctrines of election and revelation.

These organizational realities can arouse serious ethical dilemmas for the equiminded clinician as well as conflicts between clinicians and applicants. In general, a major barrier to effective communication is the tendency to evaluate others. The initial interview is a time of mutual evaluation. The evaluative transactions occurring directly between patients and clinicians evoke anxieties and their attendant defenses in both parties. If these conflicts are not addressed and negotiated (Levinson et al., 1967) to consensus, the cognitive and expressive skills of both participants will be impaired and manifested in disordered communication. When the needs of the patient and the needs of the organization exert strong and mutually conflicting influences, clinicians become particularly vulnerable to the evocation of subtle and covert prejudices.

Prejudices are beliefs and affective dispositions that are wholly or partially erroneous. They may be rooted in overgeneralizations that hold that *all* members of a group possess some alleged characteristic. Prejudices may also serve protective and defensive functions, as they do for authoritarian personalities (Adorno et al., 1950). In order to differentiate clearly and individualize the extent to which an intake clinician is subject to these differing forms of prejudice, it will be necessary to specify precisely the circumstances and contexts in which prejudicial behaviors are manifested, the strength or level at which a given prejudicial behavior occurs, and the frequency with which a given prejudicial act occurs. Otherwise, we shall be in danger of stereotyping clinicians.

Failures of communication cannot be laid exclusively at the door of the clinicians' prejudices. Although this chapter has focused essentially on the clinicians' contributions to difficulties in the intake process, it is taken here as a root principle that the processes of interpersonal influence are inherently bidirectional. Blacks are as likely to have as many fixed and stereotyped notions about Whites as Whites have about Blacks. Stereotyped conceptions held by either participant in the dyad can impose functional restrictions on the accuracy of the information that flows between them. As one might expect, a Black client being evaluated for admission in an outpatient clinic by a White intake worker will probably respond in the same way he or she has learned to respond to most other unknown Whites (Jones, 1978). She or he will quickly try to determine whether this White person's attitudes are anti-Black. Until convinced otherwise, he or she may appear to be guarded, secretive, and reluctant to reveal himself or herself. Failure to recognize that this type of behavior is reserved for Whites may lead to the erroneous conclusion that the patient lacks the ability to relate in an intensive one-to-one relationship (Jones et al., 1982; Jones & Gray, 1984). The insidious vicious cycle that is set in motion by such a relationship can deprive White therapists of ever having a corrective experience that might serve to modify their preexisting hypotheses about Blacks. It would appear that, if this cycle is going to be broken, it is incumbent upon those who organize and supervise mental health programs to foster a more open exploration of how sociocultural influences contribute to the ways in which psychotherapists emotionally experience and acquire knowledge about their patients. In order to learn to understand one Black patient and the unique resources and problems that he or she may present, sociopsychologically informed conceptions of countertransference must be developed.

CONCLUSION

This chapter has been concerned with the effects of race on the evaluation of patients for outpatient psychotherapy. In 1979, Griffith and Jones concluded that, since race relations in this culture continue to be in flux, descriptions concerning the effects of race in psychotherapy can do no more than capture a particular phase in time; they are by no means immutable and, in fact, are likely to change in important ways with the continued evolvement of the sociocultural context (p. 228).

Investigations of whether therapists tend to ascribe traits to Blacks on the basis of race alone have gone out of fashion. It is not known whether the forms of stereotyping we uncovered have substantially declined in the intervening years. However, most of what we know about the effects of *race* on the evaluation of patients for psychotherapy still comes from studies of latent *racism*, personal and institutional. As Sue (1977) concluded: "We know far more about inequities and discrimination than about setting up responsive services" (p. 623). Now we need more clinically sophisticated studies of the ways in which so-called demographic variables such as age, gender, ethnicity, and race influence the processes by which patients and therapists reciprocally qualify each other's experience.

REFERENCES

Abelson, R.P. (1981). Psychological status of the script concept. *American Psychologist* 36:715–729.

Acosta, F.X. (1979). Pretherapy expectations and definitions of mental illness among minority and low-income patients. *Hispanic Journal of Behavioral Sciences* 3:403–410.

Adorno, T.W., Frenkel-Brunswik, E., Levinson, D.J., & Sanford, N. (1950). *The Authoritarian Personality*. New York, NY: Harper & Brothers.

Aronson, H., & Overall, B. (1966). Treatment expectations of patients in two social classes. *Social Work* 11:35–41.

Baekeland, F., & Lundwall, L. (1975). Dropping out of treatment: A critical review. *Psychological Bulletin* 82:738–783.

Banks, W. (1972). The differential effects of race and social class on helping. *Journal of Clinical Psychology* 28:90–92.

Bruch, H. (1974). *Learning Psychotherapy: Rationale and Ground Rules*. Cambridge, MA: Harvard University Press.

Cantor, N., & Mischel, W. (1979). Prototypes in person perception. In L. Berkowitz (Ed.), *Advances in Experimental Social Psychology* (Vol. 12). New York, NY: Academic Press.

Carkhuff, R., & Pierce, R. (1967). Differential effects of therapist race and social class upon patient depth of self-exploration in the initial interview. *Journal of Consulting Psychology* 31:632–634.

Comas-Diaz, L., Geller, J.D., Melgoza, B., & Baker, R. (1982, August). *Attitudes and Expectations About Mental Health Services Among Hispanics and Afro-Americans.* Paper presented at the 90th annual meeting of the American Psychological Association, Washington, DC.

Cross, W.E., Jr. (1978). Models of psychological nigrescence: A literature review. *Journal of Black Psychology* 5:13–31.

Erikson, E.H. (1965). The concept of identity in race relations. Notes and queries. In T. Parsons & K.B. Clark (Eds.), *The Negro American.* Daedalus Library (Vol. 7). New York, NY: Houghton Mifflin.

Farber, B.A., & Geller, J.D. (1977). Student attitudes toward psychotherapy. *Journal of the American College Health Association* 25:301–307.

Feshbach, J., Quinlan, D., Geller, J.D., & Levine, M. (1982, October). *Psychopathology and the Life Course: Age and Sex Differences in a Psychiatric Population.* Paper presented at the seventh annual MSIS National Users Group conference, Rockland Research Institute, Orangeburg, NY.

Fischer, E.H., & Cohen, S.L. (1970). Demographic correlates of attitude toward seeking professional psychological help. *Journal of Clinical & Consulting Psychology* 35:19–90.

Frank, J.D. (1972). The bewildering world of psychotherapy. *Journal of Social Issues* 28:27–43.

———— (1973). *Persuasion and Healing* (Rev. ed.). Baltimore, MD: Johns Hopkins University Press.

Freud, S. (1937). Analysis terminable and interminable. *Standard Edition* 23:216–253.

Geller, J.D., Astrachan, B.M., & Flynn, H. (1976). The development of validation of a measure of the psychiatrist's authoritative domain. *The Journal of Nervous & Mental Disease* 162:410–422.

——— & Berzins, J. (1976). A-B distinction in a sample of prominent psychotherapists. *Journal of Consulting & Clinical Psychology* 44:77–82.

———, Cooley, R.S., & Hartley, D. (1981). Images of the psychotherapist: A theoretical and methodological perspective. *Imagination, Cognition and Personality* 1(2):123–146.

——— & Singer, T.J. (1976, August). *Social Class Differences in Attitudes and Expectations Toward Psychotherapy.* Paper presented at the 84th annual meeting of the American Psychological Association, Washington, DC.

Goldfried, M.R., & Robins, C. (1983). Self-schema, cognitive bias, and the processing of therapeutic experiences. In P.C. Kendall (Ed.), *Advances in Cognitive-Behavioral Research and Therapy* (Vol. 2). New York, NY: Academic Press.

Grier, W., & Cobbs, P. (1968). *Black Rage.* New York, NY: Bantam Books.

Griffith, M.S., & Jones, E.E. (1979). Race and psychotherapy: Changing perspectives. *Current Psychiatric Therapies* 16:225–235.

Grunebaum, H., & Kates, W. (1977). Whom to refer for group psychotherapy. *American Journal of Psychiatry* 134:130–133.

Gunderson, J.G. (1978). Patient-therapist matching: A research evaluation. *American Journal of Psychiatry* 135:1193–1197.

Harrison, D. (1975). Race as a counselor-client variable in counseling and psychotherapy: A review of the research. *The Counseling Psychologist* 5:124–133.

Heine, R.W., & Trossman, H. (1960). Initial expectations of the doctor-patient interaction as a factor in continuance of psychotherapy. *Psychiatry* 23:275–278.

Hoehn-Saric, R., Frank, J.D., Imber, S.C., Nash, E.H., Stone, A.R., & Battle, C.C. (1964). Systematic preparation of patients and psychotherapy: I. Effects on therapy behavior and outcome. *Journal of Psychiatric Research* 2:267–281.

Hollingshead, A.B., & Redlich, F.C. (1958). *Social Class and Mental Illness: A Community Study*. New York, NY: Wiley.

Jackson, J. (1972). Can White therapists treat Black patients? *Journal of the National Medical Association* 64:145–150.

Jones, B.E., Gray, B.A., & Jospitre, J. (1982). Survey of psychotherapy with Black men. *American Journal of Psychiatry* 139:1174–1177.

—— & Gray, B.A. (1984). Similarities and differences in Black men and women in psychotherapy. *Journal of the National Medical Association* 76:21–27.

Jones, E.E. (1974). Social class and psychotherapy: A critical review of research. *Psychiatry* 37:307–320.

—— (1978). Effects of race on psychotherapy process and outcome: An exploratory investigation. *Psychotherapy: Theory, Research & Practice* 15:226–236.

Kadushin, A. (1963). Diagnosis and evaluation for (almost) all occasions. *Social Work* 7:12–20.

Kluckhohn, C., & Murray, H.A. (1949). *Personality in Nature, Society, and Culture*. New York, NY: Knopf.

Lazare, A., Eisenthal, S., & Wasserman, L. (1975). The customer approach to patienthood. *Archives of General Psychiatry* 32:553–558.

Lerner, B. (1972). *Therapy in the Ghetto: Political Importance and Personal Disintegration*. Baltimore, MD: Johns Hopkins University Press.

Levinson, D.J., Merrifield, J., & Berg, K. (1967). Becoming a patient. *Archives of General Psychiatry* 17:385–406.

Lorion, R.P. (1972). *Social Class Differences in Treatment Attitudes and Expectations*. Unpublished doctoral dissertation, University of Rochester.

Luborsky, L., Chandler, M., Auerbach, A.H., Cohen, J., & Bachrach, H.M. (1971). Factors influencing the outcome of psychotherapy: A review of quantitative research. *Psychological Bulletin* 75:145–185.

Mayo, J.A. (1974). The significance of sociocultural variables in psychiatric treatment of Black outpatients. *Comprehensive Psychiatry* 15:471–482.

Meltzoff, J., & Kornreich, M. (1970). *Research in Psychotherapy*. New York, NY: Atherton.

Merton, R.K. (1948). The self-fulfilling prophecy. *Antioch Review* 8:193–210.

Nisbett, R.E., & Ross, L. (1979). *Human Inference: Strategies and Shortcomings in Social Judgment*. Englewood Cliffs, NJ: Prentice Hall.

Overall, B., & Aronson, H. (1963). Expectations of psychotherapy in patients of lower socioeconomic class. *American Journal of Orthopsychiatry* 33:421–430.

Pinderhughes, C.A. (1973). Racism and psychotherapy. In C.V. Willie, B.M. Kramer, & B.S. Brown (Eds.), *Racism and Mental Health*. Pittsburgh: University of Pittsburgh Press.

Rice, A.K. (1964). *The Enterprise in Its Environment*. London, UK: Tavistock.

Ridley, C.R. (1984). Clinical treatment of the nondisclosing Black client: A therapeutic paradox. *American Psychologist* 39:1234–1244.

Rogers, L.S. (1955). An adult neurotic. In A. Burton & R.E. Harris (Eds.), *Clinical Studies of Personality*. New York, NY: Harper & Brothers.

Rosenthal, R., & Jacobson, L. (1968). *Pygmalion in the Class-room: Teacher Expectations and Pupils' Intellectual Development*. New York, NY: Holt, Rinehart & Winston.

Ryan, W. (1971). *Blaming the Victim*. New York, NY: Vintage Books.

Sheatsley, P.B. (1965). White attitudes toward the Negro. In T. Parsons & K.B. Clark (Eds.), *The Negro American*. Daedalus Library (Vol. 7). New York, NY: Houghton Mifflin.

Singer, J. (1985). Transference and the human condition: A cognitive-affective perspective. *Psychoanalytic Psychology* 2:189–219.

Smith, W.D., Burlew, A.K., Mosley, M.H., & Whitney, W.M. (1978). *Minority Issues in Mental Health*. Reading, MA: Addison-Wesley.

Snyder, M. (1981). On the self-perpetuating nature of social stereotypes. In D.L. Hamilton (Ed.), *Cognitive Processes in Stereotyping and Intergroup Behavior*. Hillsdale, NJ: Erlbaum.

Stevenson, K.R., & Geller, J.D. (1969). The effects of race and borderline intelligence on the evaluation of patients for outpatient psychotherapy. Unpublished manuscript.

Sue, S. (1977). Community mental health services to minority groups: Some optimism, some pessimism. *American Psychologist* 32:616–624.

———, McKinney, H., Allen, D., & Hall, J. (1974). Delivery of community mental health services to Black and White clients. *Journal of Consulting & Clinical Psychology* 42:794, 801.

Taylor, S.E., & Crocker, J. (1981). Schematic bases of information processing. In E.T. Higgins, C.P. Hermann, & M.P. Zanng (Eds.), *Social Cognition: Cognitive Structure and Processes Underlying Person Memory and Social Judgment*. Hillsdale, NJ: Erlbaum.

Vontress, C. (1976). Racial and ethnic barriers in counseling. In P. Pedersen, W. Lonner, & J. Dragons (Eds.), *Counseling Across Cultures*. Honolulu, HI: University Press of Hawaii.

Ward, C.O., Zanna, M.P., & Cooper, J. (1974). The nonverbal mediation of self-fulfilling prophecies in interracial interaction. *Journal of Experimental Social Psychology* 10:109–120.

Wetzel, C., & Wright, W. (1983, August). *Reciprocity of Therapist's Self-Disclosure: Effects of Therapist's Race on Black Client's Disclosures*. Paper presented at the annual meeting of the American Psychological Association.

Williams, H.V., Lipman, R.S., Uhlenhuth, E.A., Rickels, K., Covi, L., & Mock, J. (1967). Some factors influencing the treatment expectations of anxious neurotic patients. *Journal of Nervous & Mental Disease* 145:208–220.

Yalom, I. (1975). *The Theory and Practice of Group Psychotherapy*. New York, NY: Basic Books.

Yamamoto, J., James, Q.C., & Palley, N. (1968). Cultural problems in psychiatric therapy. *Archives of General Psychiatry* 19:45–49.

CHAPTER 6

The Psychotherapist's Experience of Interest and Boredom

[J.D. Geller (1994). *Psychotherapy* 31(1):3–16.]

This article explores the clinical utility of conceptualizing the intensity and direction of psychotherapists' interest in their patients in terms of the interdependent aspects of the patient-therapist relationship. An evolving interpretive framework that takes into account the affective, cognitive, and motivational properties as well as the object-relational nature of interests is presented. It is hypothesized that the rise and fall of interest in particular patients is influenced by the complex interplay between patients' hopes and fears regarding their therapists' emotional availability, their expectations regarding how therapy should or will proceed, the distinctive ways they use the narrative mode of exposition, the styles in which they protect themselves against interpersonal anxiety, and therapists' theoretical commitments, personal preferences, conflicts, needs, values, and skills. The origins, meanings, and management of boredom in the therapeutic situation are given special consideration.

This article is concerned with the ways in which psychotherapists experience and express the emotion we call interest. My goal is to organize what is known about the affective, cognitive, and motivational properties of interest into an interpretive framework that can be used to think about the rise and fall of therapists' interest in their patients. I shall discuss the therapeutic possibilities and limitations of the hypothesis that the ebb and flow of a therapist's interest in a particular patient occurs within the context of a complex interaction in which both patient and therapist play important roles. For the present purposes, I will selectively focus on those aspects of the therapeutic situation that render therapists vulnerable to subtle and gross reductions of interest in their patients. I will also limit myself to a consideration of the challenges faced by therapists who, under ordinary circumstances, are abundantly endowed with a genuine interest in people and their welfare and who find the process of therapy inherently interesting. I will not be discussing the chronic dysfunctions of curiosity, concern, and commitment experienced by the so-called "turned-out" therapist (Farber & Heifetz, 1982).

THE CONCEPT OF INTEREST

"Interest" is a multi-purpose word. When used as a verb, "interest" refers to our intentions. Therapists are, for example, interested in helping their patients acknowledge and find relief from painful feelings. In *Webster's Ninth New Collegiate Dictionary* (1983), "interest" is defined first as "a feeling that accompanies or causes special attention to an object or class of objects." Psychologists have also given the name interest to the emotion that directs and sustains attention and exploration. My understanding of the affective, cognitive, and motivational properties of the state of experiencing what we call "interest" is based on a selective integration of the differential emotions theories of Tomkins (1962) and Izard (1977), Schachtel's (1959) notion of "activity affects," and Eagle's (1981) emphasis on the inborn basis for and object-relational nature of interests. Each of these theorists includes interest in his catalog of the "primary emotions" and assumes that interest typically functions as a generalized drive state. These psychologists also recognize that, like other distinguishable emotions, interest may be experienced at varying levels of intensity. To indicate that the subjective experience of interest spans a very broad range of intensities, Tomkins assigns it a joint name: interest-excitement. My basic premise is that varying points along this intensity continuum are associated with different modes of allocating attention and imply different forms of emotional involvement with the someone or something that stimulated the interest. In other words, a therapist's level of interest in a patient can be conjointly examined from an information processing perspective and in terms of its interpersonal implications.

Like the early psychophysicists, psychotherapists cannot define precisely "what is a difference, that makes a difference?" Consequently, there are no absolute standards against which to judge the therapeutic "dosage" or appropriateness of a particular level of interest. Moreover, DeChenne's (1988) review of findings and hypotheses from varied literatures would seem to suggest that there are individual differences in the level of intensity of involvement a therapist requires to feel "optimally responsive" (Bacal, 1985) and in the personally calibrated point on the intensity continuum below which interest gives way to boredom or sleepiness. Each therapist probably also relies on different strategies to maintain preferred levels of such experiences as excitement, tension, or alertness and calls upon different skills to obtain the types of information required to nourish his/her curiosity. In addition, therapists are likely to hold different views regarding the depth and breadth of interest patients have a "right" to expect from them. Throughout what follows, I will argue that these and other individual difference variables directly and indirectly influence a therapist's readiness and ability to take and show lively interest in a particular patient.

Optimal Levels of Interest

Interest finds its most intense expression in states such as awe, fascination, or enthrallment. Surprise is a short-lived form of intense interest. At the highest levels of intensity, the object of one's interest totally fills the field of attention. One virtually feels taken over, carried away by, or totally immersed in the person, activity, or event toward which very intense interest is directed. At the extremes of the intensity continuum, the distinction between "I" and "it" or the distance between "self" and "other" disappears in what Csikszentmihalyi (1975) refers to as the "flow" of experience. Theoretical advances and scandals have, in recent years, sensitized clinicians to the dangers associated with taking and showing "too much interest" in a patient (Pope & Bouhoutsos, 1986).

In its "purest" form, intense interest manifests itself in completely absorbing and sustained intellectual or creative activity (Wessman & Ricks, 1966). Artists and natural scientists have license to give single-minded expression to their curiosity. They are free to probe and analyze as fully as possible that which has excited their interest in ways that may be at turns passionate or detached. By contrast, the positive motivational thrust of interest exerts multiple and sometimes conflicting pulls on psychotherapists. By temperament and training, therapists are interested in obtaining new, varied, and emotionally charged knowledge about their patients. The effective practice of psychotherapy, however, requires the coordination of tough-minded curiosity about a patient, tender-minded concern for a patient's welfare, and a commitment to participate, responsively, in a relationship with a patient. Subtle and difficult discriminations are required to harmonize these conceptually distinguishable modes of expressing interest. For example, in order to lay the foundation for a therapeutic alliance, the intrusive thrust of a therapist's interest in discovering the "truth" about a patient must be softened and constrained by an empathic appreciation of the types and levels of curiosity a patient needs, can tolerate, and can use. Otherwise, a patient is apt to feel like a "case" that is being studied scientifically. Secretive patients do not take unconflicted pleasure in the knowledge that their therapists will be interested in the intimate details of their lives. Among patients who are hiding or who fear being "found out," a therapist's curiosity occasions anger, guilt, and shame, especially if it ventures into the unknown. Concern implies honoring a patient's privacy and his/her right "not to communicate" (Winnicott, 1965). Winnicott (1969) reports that he interprets mainly to let patients know the limits of his understanding. A reconciliation of the competing claims of curiosity and concern can be discerned in this stylistic choice.

Research on the nature and origins of play and exploration (Eagle, 1981) as well as evidence regarding the neuropsychological concept of activation (Fiske & Maddi, 1961) support the view that a therapist's investigatory activities are best served by operating within the midrange of the intensity continuum. Interest, as experienced at moderately elevated levels of intensity, is characterized by zesty curiosity, attentiveness, and intentness as well as by feelings of excitement and engagement. Such lively and spirited interest is required to remain alert to nuances, paradoxes, the particularity of a moment, and human specificity. To be effective, a therapist's understandings must be concrete, fresh, and ideographic. In order to discover that which is unique rather than conventional about a patient, a therapist must remain open to surprises and receptive to the multiple connotations of what is being heard, especially those meanings not consciously intended. When functioning at moderately elevated levels of interest, investigatory activities feel energized and animated, and consciousness of relating itself recedes from awareness. Izard (1977) observes that "even when relatively immobile, the interested or excited person has the feeling that he is 'alive and active'" (p. 233). When such vitalizing conditions prevail, therapists eagerly and efficiently engage in goal-directed listening, looking, understanding, remembering, problem-solving, and so on.

Interest exerts a pervasive motivational influence on a therapist's ability to exercise his/her supportive functions as well as his/her exploratory functions. On a day-to-day basis, interest typically precedes and makes a fundamental contribution to the activation of other emotional reactions to patients. Under optimal conditions, interest nonspecifically amplifies and blends with such distinguishable feelings as warmth, kindness, patience, and respect. When experienced in combination with these tender emotions, interest leads to the establishment of an emotionally safe atmosphere that strengthens the courage and ability of both participants to confront the inherently conflictual aspects of self-exploration. In turn, these positive emotions augment the modulated pleasures provided by interest.[13]

Thus, the work of therapy feels virtuous, meaningful, purposeful, and important when energized and guided by persistent, broad, and deep interest in a patient. According to Fromm (1976), this enlivening quality of the therapist is the "essential factor in psychoanalytic therapy. No amount of psychoanalytic interpretation will have an effect if the therapeutic atmosphere is heavy, unalive and boring" (p. 23). At an empirical level, these notions are supported by the Luborsky et al. (1985) finding that therapists who are judged by clinically experienced colleagues familiar with their work to be "unusually interested in helping

---

13 Interest, itself, is susceptible to nonspecific amplification by a host of other affects and motives, including sexuality. Nevertheless, evidence from a wide range of research areas supports the conclusion that, both developmentally and in terms of everyday functioning, interests do not necessarily represent a sublimation or channeling of more basic instincts, as is presumed by traditional psychoanalysts, but rather derive from the inborn propensity to establish cognitive and affective links to objects (Eagle, 1981).

patients" and persistent in these efforts tend to be the same ones who bring about positive therapeutic outcomes. Conversely, in a retrospective study of early terminators, Kline et al. (1974) found that ex-patients weighted the "perception" that their therapist was not interested in them most heavily in their decision to drop out of therapy.[14]

Losing Interest: A Call to Action

No therapist is immune to lapses of attention during therapy sessions. Because of their very human imperfections, "good enough" psychotherapists, moreover, experience transient and sustained episodes of attenuated or inhibited interest in their patients. As we move into the lower regions of the intensity continuum, curiosity lags. Curiosity that is experienced at low levels of intensity can be variously described as tepid, superficial, half-hearted, or perfunctory, and it yields understandings that are merely trite, stale, or formulaic. Moreover, when interest wanes, effort is required to resist the temptation to pay attention to competing distractions, including all those basic and "selfish" needs therapists suppress on behalf of their patients and their commitment to doing the work of therapy.

Withdrawal of interest from patients is laden with moral overtones, as is ignoring or denying this state of affairs. Both are in conflict with the values and goals to which therapists

---

14 About half of the patients who were recontacted by Kline et al. had sought psychotherapy elsewhere, leading the authors to conclude that many patients who terminate "prematurely" are not lacking in the motivation to obtain help, as professionals often assume, but rather are reacting to the failure to find it. Some therapists—because of greed, or a sense of duty, or external necessity under ordinary circumstances—force themselves to work at being interested but have no real enthusiasm for what they are doing. In some instances, boredom in a therapist is evidence of deep, unresolved conflicts that are best dealt with outside the patient's psychotherapy sessions.

aspire: Therapists feel they shouldn't lose interest in their patients. We feel obligated, ethically and technically, to give our
full attention to our patients every session; and that is the way it
ought to be. When subjected to self-scrutiny, therapists usually
discover that withdrawal of interest in a patient, whatever its
origins, is usually accompanied by feelings of personal failure.
The felt inability to take up this delicate issue with a patient and
the concomitant effort to conceal withdrawal of interest are particularly distressing to those therapists who regard authenticity
as essential to "virtue" (Trilling, 1972).

Anyone whose mind has wandered during a conversation
knows that the face of interest or attentiveness can be worn in-
authentically. In general, facial cues are ambiguous as indicators
of the full nature of a therapist's interest. Research indicates that
the facial cues that attest to the presence of activation of interest
are less clear-cut than they are for any other primary emotion
(Izard, 1977). Electromyographic mapping of facial tensions
reveals that interest may be expressed merely by the increased
tone of the facial muscles or by the raising or lowering of the
eyebrows and eyelids. Some people turn their heads toward and
fixate their eyes upon the person to whom they are listening. A
faraway look, however, may also be indicative of an excited
thinking about what one has just been told. Like the ambiguous
phrase "that's interesting," the bodily manifestations of listening
can accommodate a variety of plausible interpretations. My exploratory activities, especially during the early stages of therapy,
include efforts to gauge the accuracy of patients' interpretations
of the depth and breadth of my interest in them. This clinical
strategy is rooted in the view that patients' initial, often unformulated expectations regarding the types and levels of interest
they have a "right" to ask for or think are due them are highly
varied and exert a continuing influence on their ability to judge
accurately the cues that convey genuine interest. For example,

patients who can be described as secure in their attachments (Bowlby, 1973) enter therapy confident in the belief that their therapist will provide them with adequate levels of interest, particularly if what they say is plausibly related to the origins and fate of their problems-in-living. On the other hand, based on repeated experiences of indifference or ignorance on the part of caretaking others, some patients behave as if they have lost faith in ever finding anyone who would be interested in paying close attention to anything they have to say. To anticipate a later point, I am attentive to the possibility that these patients exert pressure, unwittingly, on their therapists to think, behave, and feel toward them in a manner congruent with their initially erroneous or minimal expectations. In other words, I regard patients' hopes and fears regarding their ability to excite and sustain interest in their therapists as derivatives of the transference paradigms that will shape the therapeutic relationship.

The feelings that are evoked in patients by the perception that their therapist is losing interest in them are also highly varied. A developmental perspective on the representational forms in which feelings and memories enter awareness guides my efforts to understand and manage the wide variety of ways in which patients react to these episodes (Geller, 1987). As conceived here, development in the sphere of emotionality leads to an increasing ability to recognize, tolerate, and deal with the flaws, contradictions, and limitations inherent to all persons and relationships.

To the extent that a patient has achieved the attitude Levinson et al. (1978) refer to as "de-illusionment," elements of forgiveness and humor reduce the strain placed on the therapeutic alliance by the perception that the therapist's interest is neither intense nor continuous enough. An advanced achievement of adult development, de-illusionment brings with it the capacity to empathize with the personal and professional pressures that reside in the circumstances of a therapist's life and to accept constructively the possibility that on occasion these pressures will render the therapist weary and preoccupied.

Patients who are functioning within the normal-neurotic range are apt to feel, in varying combinations, at conscious and preconscious levels, devalued, sad, criticized, rejected, unsafe, misunderstood, lonely, fearful, insulted, humiliated, and mistrustful when "disappointed" in their therapists' level of interest. In general, the contradictory tugs exerted by these emotional reactions can be expected to be tolerable and verbalizable and to initiate questions regarding the origins and meanings of the therapist's difficulties in maintaining high levels of interest. Predictions based on attribution theory (Jordan et al., 1988) are consistent with my observation that patients are biased toward blaming themselves when their usually empathic therapist appears to be losing interest in them. Moreover, because of some combination of timidity, conventionality, deference to authority, or schizoid tendencies, a neurotic patient may not signal, verbally or affectively, that he/she is aware of palpably visible evidence of boredom or sleepiness in the therapist, especially if the therapist's withdrawal of interest has been interpreted as a negative reflection upon the self. Unless attentive to the obscuring power of these inhibiting influences, a therapist might underestimate his/her patient's ability to recognize signs of waning interest.

The concept of disillusionment rather than unresolved ambivalence more closely approximates the ways in which patients who are functioning at borderline levels of pathology emotionally experience "disappointments" in their therapists. Failing to provide patients who are suffering from borderline personality disorders (Kernberg, 1975) with "adequate" levels of interest precipitates crisis reactions, shatters the therapeutic alliance, and calls into question the continued existence of the relationship. They are likely to interpret those occasions during which their therapist appears to be impatient, distracted, tired, or even in poor health in exclusively self-referential terms. At such times, they are given to severe and prolonged feelings of impotent rage, inconsolability, despair, futility, panic, betrayal, loss of energy, and worthlessness. Kohut (1971) recognizes in this constellation of negative states the primitive residues of unempathic parenting.

Obviously, insufficient interest is a call to action, a warning signal that the therapeutic relationship is in need of repair. Based on my experiences as a psychotherapy supervisor, therapists-in-training vary enormously in their readiness to recognize, manage, and respond effectively to transient and sustained experiences of attenuated interest. Case reports (e.g., Yalom, 1989) indicate that even very experienced therapists sometimes postpone dealing with markedly diminished levels of interest until they have reached the limits of their tolerance. Largely stimulated by Kohut's (1977) formulations, I assume that therapists can turn to advantage the real, imagined, and provoked occasions on which they lose interest by empathically exploring their meanings and consequences for the patient. As I have discussed at length elsewhere (Geller, 1987, 1992), nondefensively giving patients the opportunity to experience and express (at progressively higher levels of organization) their "disappointments" in the person of the therapist and the process of therapy provides a valuable avenue for pursuing a variety of therapeutic goals. To begin with, enabling a patient to more eloquently and boldly speak about the events that precipitated their negative reactions to waning interest nurtures the formation of more differentiated affects, for example, the transformation of intensely felt but conceptually vague feelings of disillusionment into more subtle, focused, and thoughtlike versions of disappointment. Devoting therapeutic attention to this task concurrently appears to facilitate the conscious recovery and reconstruction of previously disavowed memories of disappointments in the quality of maternal and paternal care. It is my contention that the process of mourning the real deprivations and ruptures of attachment that accumulate during the course of development cannot be completed unless memories of these experiences materialize in consciousness in forms that are specific, vivid, concrete, and meaningful. Thirdly, transference-based interpretations of a patient's reactions to variations in his/her therapist's level of interest draw attention to the therapist's presence or personhood and consequently can strengthen a patient's ability to perceive, judge accurately, and remember the nonverbal cues that convey curiosity, concern, and commitment. Even a small change in a patient's ability to recognize that the therapist is a "new" object or a "real" person increases the likelihood that he/she will benefit from the opportunities for interpersonal learning made available in therapy. Taken together, these enhanced abilities bring into existence the conditions that precede and pave the way for the activation of the processes whereby patients construct enduring and benignly influential "internalized" representations of the therapeutic relationship (Geller, 1987; Orlinsky & Geller, 1993).

BOREDOM IN THE THERAPEUTIC SITUATION

When the intensity of interest falls below a personally calibrated critical value, it turns into its opposite—that constellation of feelings commonly referred to as boredom. "Boredom" is a generic term that encompasses a variety of inherently aversive states or processes. According to Greenson (1953/1978), the five most commonly experienced elements of boredom are

a state of dissatisfaction with and a disinclination to action; a state of longing and an inability to designate what

> is longed for; a sense of emptiness; a passive expectant
> attitude with the hope that the external world will supply
> the satisfaction; a distorted sense of time in which time
> seems to stand still (p. 46).

In other words, when low levels of interest give way to boredom, therapists feel simultaneously alienated from the patient and from their own imaginative capacities.

To date, the dilemmas posed by boredom for psychotherapists have been dealt with in only a handful of papers and discussed primarily from the point of view of the patient's limitations. (For an overview of this literature see DeChenne, 1988.) The consensus opinion is that with some patients one can expect to be bored and that some patients are "simply" more boring than others (e.g., Modell, 1976). By contrast, I will next argue on behalf of the hypothesis that boredom in the therapeutic situation can never be fully understood without taking into account both participants' felt inability to talk about the conflictual aspects of their relationship and/or the "poorness of fit" between their cognitive, expressive, and interpersonal styles. In adopting this interactional position, I draw on evidence from a variety of sources (e.g., Jaffe & Feldstein's [1970] studies of the temporal features of social interaction and Beebe & Stern's [1977] analyses of patterns of mutual regulation between mothers and infants during the early months of life) as well as DeChenne's (1988) "modified activation model of boredom."

My basic premise is that neglect or mismanagement of boredom is antitherapeutic. Contemporary conceptions of countertransference charge therapists with the responsibility to adopt an investigatory attitude toward all of their emotional reactions to and affective judgments about their patients. The inner freedom to experience and reflect upon the meanings and implications of boredom requires, as a precondition, a durable view of oneself as capable of sustained and intimate involvement with others in task-oriented relationships. Young and relatively inexperienced therapists who feel insecure in this regard have great difficulty "distancing" themselves from boredom and anxiously avoid confronting patients with those aspects of their self-presentation that repel interest.

Many factors complicate even seasoned therapists' efforts to use boredom as an interpretive resource. Cognitive appraisal of countertransference-based reactions that are differentiated with respect to their ideational and affective components, such as hate or lust, direct therapists to specific courses of action. Reflections upon boredom do not. Like a bad mood or the feeling "upset," boredom indicates that something is wrong but does not suggest the kinds of choices that would change the situation (Geller, 1984). Because the bored therapist is alienated simultaneously from the patient as well as from his/her own imaginative capacities, boredom is represented in consciousness without significant psychic elaboration, symbolization, or ideation. Boredom is too diffuse, painfully somatic, and objectless to serve as an instrument of rationality. Second, some interludes of boredom can be understood as serving defensive functions for a therapist. Although inherently aversive, boredom's crude phenomenological properties can be used, albeit masochistically, to escape from knowledge that might induce conflict. "Dedifferentiation" is the term Jacobson (1957) uses to refer to the processes that transform feelings that are directed toward a specific object into vague and indefinite moods. I believe that, on occasion, therapists, consciously and unconsciously, use these processes to deny the knowledge and potential choices carried into awareness by specific negative feelings directed toward patients, for example, the wish that they would quit therapy, fantasies of hurting or rejecting them. What I am suggesting is that some forms of boredom are derivatives of and a means of camouflaging unacceptable motives and such feelings as guilt, shame, unexpressed anger, dread, despair, or even downright malice. On other occasions, the route to boredom may originate in the desire to retreat from empathic immersion in a patient's struggle with these aversive emotions. In the words of Fenichel (1934/1953), boredom arises when "we must not do what we want to do, or must do what we do not want to do" (p. 301).

THE INTERACTIONAL NATURE OF BOREDOM

Fundamental to my evolving framework is the hypothesis that everything that is felt during therapy sessions is, in part, a function of the interdependent aspects of the patient-therapist social system that uniquely characterizes a given therapy dyad. With respect to the issues being discussed here, I am guided by two interrelated assumptions: first, that patients embody or "actualize" (Sandler, 1976) their fears and expectations regarding their therapists' emotional availability through the medium of their expressive or communicative styles, and second, that therapists' differing emotional reactions to these styles exert a continuing influence as their felt readiness to take and show interest in a particular patient. As predicted by Merton (1948), when under the influence of the self-fulfilling prophecy, therapists feel unable to prevent themselves from becoming what their patients expect them to be.

These interactional phenomena are most poignantly enacted in the psychotherapy of patients who are guided by the expectation that efforts to gain their therapists' interest would threaten rather than strengthen the relationship. Like the anxious-avoidant children studied by Bowlby (1973), patients whom I shall designate here as schizoid attempt to minimize, control, or deny expressions of distress that generally elicit attachment and caretaking behaviors in others. Although exquisitely sensitive to variations in their therapists' depth of involvement, schizoid patients selectively ignore or defensively falsify information about their therapists that might activate long unmet wishes to receive and/or give affection. They defensively inhibit the explicit expression of interest in their therapists. They suppress behaviors indicative of curiosity about their therapists and avoid the direct behavioral expression of conflict. They defensively avoid communicative exchanges that might potentiate the wish to trust and rely on their therapists for support and understanding. In short, schizoid patients are afraid of opening themselves up to bold and potentially healing curiosity, concern, and commitment.

Even therapists who pride themselves on being capable of inexhaustible interest are apt to struggle with boredom in the presence of patients who rigidly adopt an avoidant style. La Rochefoucauld (1664/1957) anticipated this dilemma when he wrote that "we are almost always bored by just those whom we must not find boring." In order to "stay with" patients who appear to be emotionally inaccessible, I try to keep in mind that an anxious-avoidant stance is adopted by children to preserve relationships with rejecting and indifferent caretakers.

In other instances, a boring self-presentation may provide valuable clues regarding childhood experiences that may otherwise remain unspeakable, intangible, or preverbal. As the following vignette illustrates, even the monotony of lengthy silence may capture precisely the psychic reality of experiences that are inaccessible to self-reflection and verbalization.

A young man in psychoanalytic therapy gradually learned that his lengthy silences during therapy sessions represented the enactment of the inchoate and terrifying memory of watching and hearing his father having a grand mal seizure. The patient was 15 years old the night the seizure occurred; it purportedly was his father's first seizure, and he had never witnessed a convulsion. He and his father were sitting in the living room in chairs that faced each other, much like the seating arrangement in psychotherapy. His father had been sleeping for about 15 minutes when he "erupted" into the seizure. The patient heard "a bloodcurdling scream" and helplessly watched his father's radical metamorphosis. He thought his father was dying, and on different occasions described him as looking like "a demonic monster," "an exploding bear," and "a raging bull."

That night, and for the next several months, he kept a silent vigil. Late into the night, lying in his bed as still as possible, he tried to listen for signs that would let him know whether his father, sleeping in a bedroom down the hall, was about to have another seizure. He took changes in the rhythm of his father's breathing as a clue that a seizure was about to occur.

In therapy he was often silent, sometimes for an entire hour. He talked in an inhibited, tentative manner. Over time, he learned to recognize when his silences served defensive functions. On some occasions, he chose silence as a means of avoiding shame. Other episodes became recognizable as assertions of autonomy. What persisted, however, were inexplicable silences during which he felt as if a heavy pressure physically descended upon him. He felt embedded within silence. At these times he felt as if his tongue were swollen and choking off speech. In his nightmares he could not scream for help.

He reported that he felt lonely and frightened when silent and that he watched the therapist vigilantly during these episodes. Any hint of boredom or sleepiness in the therapist intensified his vigilance, his anxiety, and further inhibited his capacity to speak. When anger exceeded fearfulness, he would hesitantly ask his therapist, "Are you losing interest in me?" or cautiously confront him: "You are falling asleep." Answers that he regarded as false or inadequate drove him deeper into silence. However, when the therapist acknowledged that the lengthier silences did, in fact, render him vulnerable to sleepiness, fragments of the memories and images described above began to materialize in his consciousness. Honest interchanges about the actual and alleged times when the therapist's interest in him was compromised frequently led to the remembering of previously unnamed aspects of the night his father had his first seizure. He returned to this scene over and over again, accumulating more differentiated and meaningful details, for example, the newspaper that jumped wildly from his father's convulsing body, his own panicky scream and loss of breath. He also recalled how confused and frightened he felt when he telephoned his mother to tell her what had happened. She had been out playing cards in a neighbor's apartment. Eventually, with pride, he spoke about telephoning the family doctor before calling for his mother. His self-esteem was further strengthened by the realization that he had been interacting silently with the therapist in a way that invited sleepiness not only for defensive purposes but in order to produce "replicas" (Lipin, 1963) of memories that had never been fully conscious or capable of relatively organized expression.

To keep the interactional nature of boredom in sharp focus, I ask myself whether I feel that a patient is pursuing the therapeutic tasks that I have imposed on him/her "boringly" or "interestingly." These tasks might include self-reflectiveness, free recall of past events, intimate self-disclosure, attentiveness to nonverbal behavior, and accommodations to the ambiguities of etiquette woven into the work structure of psychotherapy. The adverbial form of interest carries with it the clear implication that my judgments about whether or not a person is boring do not describe a person but rather my personal reactions to what they are doing. Adverbial usage is a reminder that "affective judgments are always about the self. They identify the state of the judge in relation to the object of judgment" (Zajonc, 1980, p. 157). To call someone boring, on the other hand, implies that the wish to withdraw from them is objectively justifiable and exclusively attributable to their limitations. Assigning a patient to this status is contaminated with unequivocal pejorative connotations and a disparaging attitude. Calling a patient boring is inconsistent with any definition of neutrality or objectivity. Simply stated, the patient who is boring is too often viewed as a bad patient. Like Altshul (1977), I recommend discarding the self-serving and misleading concept of "the so-called boring patient."

"That's Interesting" and "Am I Boring?"

The question "Am I boring?" implicitly and explicitly plays a predominant role in some therapies, a lesser one in others, but is of some importance in all lengthy and ambitious psychotherapies. The question is not restricted to one "type" of patient. Like performing artists, exhibitionistic patients are haunted by the possibility that their audiences, including their therapists, will find them boring. Patients who suffer from chronic and pervasive feelings of "emptiness" and who project those feelings onto others can be expected to doubt that their therapist will listen to them with avid interest. Individuals from whom others typically withdraw in social situations understandably worry about boring their therapist. One need not look beyond these patients' individual dynamics or their definable attributes to understand why they anticipate boredom in the therapeutic situation. But why do patients who effortlessly bring their therapists to zesty curiosity and passionate concern also share the concern about being boring? I hear reverberations of broad social factors when patients who would excite and sustain interest in any therapist ask, "Am I boring you?" One possibility is that they are giving voice to the increasing awareness of the tenuousness of communication and the prevalence of unattractive forms of narcissistic self-absorption in our culture. I take as one manifestation of these sociohistorical trends the widespread and duplicitous use of the phrase "That's interesting" in ordinary speech. Like the bodily manifestations of listening, the phrase "That's interesting" is ambiguous with respect to the actual interest a listener may feel.

"That's interesting" serves many ends. When spoken truthfully, it is meant to acknowledge the novelty, evocativeness, cogency, complexity, and meaningfulness of what has just been heard. On such occasions, it is a reassuring or affirming way of saying, "That's something I'd like to think about" or, "I have never thought about that." Today, "That's interesting" is just as frequently used to conceal conflictual or noncommittal reactions to what has just been heard. On these occasions the phrase serves as a delaying tactic or replaces judgments felt to be inappropriate, such as "That's wrong" or "That's stupid." (In parallel, have you noticed how many people preface their anecdotes with comments such as "You're going to find this interesting" or "It is interesting to note that…"?)[15] Most people are unaware of how dependent they are on these phrases. When I have asked friends, colleagues, and students to forgo use of "That's interesting," it has engendered anxiety, disorganization, inarticulateness, and an embarrassed recognition of the frequency with which they use it duplicitously. I take it as axiomatic that phrases and words that are in vogue in a culture are a living mirror of its changing concerns. What I am specifically suggesting here is that "That's interesting" is used promiscuously because it is emblematic of the psychopathology of everyday life in our culture. Perhaps we

---

15 When making referrals, therapists frequently tell or promise their colleagues that they will find the patient "interesting." This prediction is most often made when the patient is otherwise "unattractive."

are all increasingly in need of reassurance that genuine dialogues are still capable of taking place.

STYLE AND CONTENT IN THE THERAPEUTIC DIALOGUE

The overall direction of a therapist's interest in what is going on in a particular therapy session flows from narcissistically invested theoretical commitments. Other things being equal, the wider the range of conceptually separable theory-derived questions a therapist can ask of clinical data, the more likely he/she will feel that there is an inexhaustible supply of interesting things to respond to in the therapeutic situation. All existent theories of therapy suggest what is necessary for a therapist to be interested in if he/she is to help a patient. Under the influence of interpretive biases, therapists selectively listen to and for some content areas, ignore others, and subtly impose their preferences on patients. Thus, the focusing power of theoretical convictions can narrow the range of things that are possible for a therapist to be interested in during therapy sessions.

Theoretical convictions that are taken for granted or too tightly held about the potential meanings of what one is hearing need not be consciously experienced as confining to exert a restrictive influence on a therapist's curiosity. Some aspects of psychoanalytic theory draw a therapist's attention to the covert and unconscious meanings of a patient's verbalizations and to the discovery of that which is not being verbalized. If this theory-driven interest plays itself out in a one-sided emphasis on interpreting the content of a patient's communications, it can handicap a clinician's ability to shift his/her attention to the style in which a patient speaks and the problems that this style poses for the therapy. In my experience as a supervisor, I have found that this interpretive bias is particularly characteristic of therapists-in-training who read a great deal of fiction in their youth. Moreover, recent research by Lehman & Geller (1992) suggests that early in their careers therapists tend to overemphasize what their patients say when constructing "working models" of their patients and their relationship with them. In comparison to those constructed by experienced therapists, their internalized representations of their patients tend to be abstract and sensuously impoverished.

During ordinary conversations, the participants usually focus their attention on what is being talked about. For many reasons, by contrast, psychotherapists are now trained to pay attention to the style as well as the content of their patients' communications. Therapists so trained are better prepared to cope with the sobering realization that the thematic surprises of psychotherapy are exhaustible. Therapists are expected to appreciate again and again, with curiosity, even wonder, stories that are apt to have become stale to others, including the patient. On first reading, a cleverly constructed detective story is suspenseful throughout. On second reading, there are no surprises, and so interest lags. In psychotherapy, as elsewhere, even the most fascinating story begins to pall on the nth retelling. Two friends, both of whom see the same therapist on the same day, decided to tell the therapist the same dream. The wily therapist responded to this test by saying to the second patient, "That's the third time I heard that dream today."

Although we all wish to be "special cases" (Camus, 1956), a limited number of universal themes underlie the diversity of our stories. Today, as always, the themes of psychotherapy repetitively revolve around the issues classically listed as the seven deadly sins—pride, lust, anger, greed, sloth, gluttony, and covetousness. I try to identify, early in therapy, whether preexisting restrictive assumptions about the conversational content of therapy are inhibiting a patient's expressivity. Sometimes the monotonous repetition of symptoms and current conflictual experiences reflects the misconception that these are the only legitimate topics for discussion. Expanding a patient's conception of what is "permissible" to talk about can have an immediate vitalizing impact on the therapeutic dialogue.

When the plot or theme that a patient is talking about becomes tedious and predictable, interest can be augmented by shifting one's attention to the suspense of character. Patients reveal some of the invariant aspects of character in their expressive styles. Everyone has a unique and definable expressive style that persists over time and contexts. In clinical situations, personal style can best be observed in the ways in which an individual uses language, gestures, postures, facial expressions, eye contact, voice qualities, and dress to express their thoughts and feelings. For example, patients use the narrative mode of exposition in distinctively consistent ways. Paranoid patients regularly link together the people and events in their lives as if they were detectives or prosecuting attorneys making a case. Those who fear sounding "irrational" just stick to the "facts." Hysterical patients recurrently sacrifice the "truth" to tell an "interesting" story, or "feed" their therapist with what they believe interests him/her. Still others weave their raw experiences into a personal history that resembles a heroic quest. In short, like writers of fiction, patients invoke the concepts and vocabularies of different genres to describe their lives. However, unlike the novelist who self-consciously uses these tools to create emotional atmospheres, patients are largely unaware of the ways in which their styles impact on others.

In some instances, it is impossible to consider the origins of boredom without taking into account therapists' differing emotional reactions to these styles, including those aspects of the patient's style that are typically outside of conscious control.

The following are illustrative of the types of incompatibility that are relevant to and may impede the mobilization of curiosity, concern, and commitment. The dysfunctional interaction between the cognitive-expressive styles of patients and therapists can be discerned in those dyads that include a patient that compulsively overproduces therapeutic material and a therapist who feels obligated to listen, passively, to everything the patient has to say. Therapists who don't feel they have the "right" to withdraw from or interrupt a flood of verbiage permit themselves to be depleted. Some therapists are particularly predisposed to boredom when working with affect-inhibited or "alexithymic" (Krystal, 1979) patients. They are also likely to have difficulty tolerating the monotony of chronic depression.

Either the form or content of a patient's communicative style can evoke boredom or other forms of emotional withdrawal. Some therapists feel manipulated by theatricality or seemingly "fraudulent" displays of affect and consequently withhold interest when a patient appears to be playing a part in a high drama. Still others are reluctant to mirror empathically the exhibitionistic and grandiose needs of narcissistic patients. Kernberg (1975) has observed that a common fantasy of narcissistic patients is that they are their therapists' most interesting patients and that the therapists prefer them above all others. Yet, Modell (1976) believes that boredom is an inevitable byproduct of entering into relationships with patients suffering from narcissistic personality disorders. This discrepancy is suggestive of the hypothesis that some therapists only partially and grudgingly give their interest to patients whose interest in others is dictated mainly or entirely by the aims of self-enhancement or self-aggrandizement.

Patients whose object relations are essentially egocentric, exploitative, and exhibitionistic tend to adopt a purely instrumental view of their therapists. They are intensely interested in what the therapist has to say about them. But they appear to be disinterested in who the therapist is as a person. When patients inhibit or repress their curiosity about both of these sources of knowledge, I find myself losing touch with my own "interesting" thoughts, memories, and images.

If a patient does not signal, either verbally or affectively, that he/she is interested in what the therapist has to say, it is plausible to assume that he/she is a poor listener. Some patients are unaware that they suffer from this "learning disability." Others shamefully hide the fact that their listening capabilities are impaired. One patient I had in therapy told me that based on his own limitations he assumed that I, too, would be an inadequate or incompetent listener. In addition to holding this initially erroneous expectation, he told lengthy monologues that focused on details that were scarcely relevant to the mainstream of the plot. His delivery was both breathless and objective. Providing him with a description of this style elicited guilt-ridden associations about "never listening" to his mother. During the course of therapy, he realized that he had been motivated by a strong, unconscious need to deny that he "spaced out" on his mother whenever she spoke. In time he learned that it was his mother's preoccupation with the singularly banal and inconsequential details of living that had originally repelled his interest. Further exploration led to the discovery that by adopting those aspects of his mother's expressive style (e.g., "She never got to the punch line"), he was exerting strong pressure on me to do to him what he had done to his mother (i.e., stop listening). In other words, he unsuspectingly sought to make me the "repository" of a quality he found unacceptable in himself and concurrently enacted the need to be punished for his fraudulence with his mother. What I am proposing here is an extension of Ogden's (1979) lucid discussion of the effects on recipients of so-called "projective identifications." As conceptualized by Ogden, under various conditions, the unsuspecting targets of projective identifications feel unable to resist being manipulated into playing the role or taking on the characteristics that are being projected onto and into them. Ogden has written cogently about the ways in which therapists can constructively deal with patients' efforts to "put into" them qualities they cannot tolerate as part of their conscious sense of self and need to disown. His writings have sensitized me to the implications of Tahka's finding that "a profound lack of concern for a patient on the part of the therapist often immediately precedes the patient's suicide" (quoted in Ogden, p. 359). Viewed from the perspective of projective identification, suicidal patients may attempt to induce in their therapists their own lack of concern for themselves or lack of interest in their own lives.

In order to observe and comment upon those occasions when I am feeling a reduced sense of interest in a patient, I am apt to ask myself, What stylistic choices is the patient making to access, organize, and speak about himself/herself? What defensive styles does the patient use to protect himself/herself against the perceived dangers of self-exploration? Does the patient have a distinct style of maintaining and repairing ruptures in the therapeutic alliance? These inquiries yield comments like, "You are under no obligation to entertain me, yet you work so hard to interest me"; "Perhaps you are showing me something you cannot put into words when you treat me like I am not here"; "Are you really interested in what you are talking about?"

It is a narcissistic injury to have one's attention drawn to those aspects of one's being that repel interest. Therefore, great tact, kindness, and something akin to connoisseurship are required of a therapist if he/she is to maximize the therapeutic benefits of familiarizing patients with the dysfunctional consequences of their interpersonal style. When infused with these qualities, patients are apt to find comments like those noted above both evocative and liberating. As Einstein reportedly once said, "Curiosity is a delicate little plant that, aside from stimulation, stands mainly in need of freedom."[16]

The Styles in Which Therapists Demonstrate Interest

The stylistic choices therapists make on behalf of their patients can reinforce or undermine the confident expectation that one is being listened to with lively and spirited interest. It is not enough to know what is true about a patient. In order to respond empathically, one must additionally be capable of gracefully exchanging the positions of listener and speaker. From moment to moment (under conditions of uncertainty), therapists have to decide not only what to say but also when and how to say it. The more practiced and better informed in these matters a therapist becomes, the more these decisions are made without having to think about them. At this stage of development, a therapist speaks with his/her own voice and has essentially created a personal style of doing therapy.

Each therapist's style is modeled, to a greater or lesser extent, on the styles of his/her predecessors (Geller & Schaffer, 1988). Today, many individuals who are preparing to become psychotherapists take on the difficult task of blending the styles in which their psychoanalytic and existential-humanistic teachers, supervisors, and therapists express interest in patients. Each tradition offers adherents broad guidelines to cope with the ambiguities posed by the improvisational nature of the therapeutic dialogue. As they are written about, deep differences appear to

16 ersonal communication. The author thanks Mr. Robert Parker for telling him this anecdote.

separate the ways in which therapists who are firmly grounded in these traditions "demonstrate" interest in patients.

Existential-humanistic models of the therapeutic action of psychotherapy take as their conceptual starting point the view that "real talk" sets in motion benignly influential and healing processes. The goal of establishing a "genuinely communicative relationship" is pertinent to the work of all therapists. It supersedes all others in the existential-humanistic tradition (Havens, 1974). The existential-humanistic psychotherapists' style is thus broadly shaped by the elusive ideal of authenticity. Authenticity is that state of being that exists when what is avowed and what is felt are one and the same. Incongruities between the content and the manner in which a person communicates are taken as evidence of some form of inauthenticity. Existential-humanistic therapists listen with a refined sensitivity for such disjunctions. With respect to their own utterances, authenticity implies simplicity, naturalness, spontaneity, and expressivity. These virtues or ego ideals have an expansive influence on a therapist's expressive options and emotional reactivity. They encourage therapists to enter into more active communicative exchanges with their patients than do the technical recommendations found in the psychoanalytic literature.

In discussions of psychoanalytic technique, the chief emphasis is upon the desirability of adopting a waiting, sentient, listening attitude. In order to practice psychoanalytic psychotherapy successfully, it is necessary to achieve the inner sense of waiting without waiting and the ability to allocate attention in a pan-directional fashion (Spence, 1984).[17] The stylistic pre-

---

17 McLaughlin (1975) has suggested that a free-floating, sensuously receptive stance is, itself, conducive to sleepiness. Although a gross reduction of interest results in sleepiness, sleepiness during therapy sessions does not always imply withdrawal from a patient. Occasionally, sleepiness is induced by participation in an experience that is pleasurable and soothing and may express the wish for bodily closeness and intimacy.

sentation of therapists who are firmly grounded in the psycho-analytic tradition is primarily shaped by the technical princi-ples of abstinence, neutrality, and objectivity and the notion of "analytic anonymity" (Freud, 1912). By adopting this form of "presence," Havens (1989) attempts to convey "an interest that does not itself attempt to be interesting" (p. 36). Although these methodological ideals do not necessarily imply detached cool-ness or lack of spontaneity, they nevertheless diminish overtly recognizable activity and "evidence" of personal involvement on the part of the therapist. They also tend to reduce to an in-dispensable minimum the "give and take" between patients and therapists. The prototypical psychoanalytic psychotherapist prefers to speak briefly, precisely yet evocatively, and only at certain decisive moments. In order to facilitate the creation of insights, psychoanalytic psychotherapists take great care to par-ticularize the timing of their clarifications, confrontations, and interpretations. The psychoanalytic dialogue is governed neither by the norm of reciprocity with respect to self-disclosure nor by the unwritten code that turn taking during conversations should be equitable. Patients in psychoanalytic forms of therapy are encouraged and pressured into speaking, at length and under minimal guidance, about the ongoing flow of their inner expe-rience. They are also provided with fewer instances of "proof" that their therapist is really interested in them. The psychoana-lytic dialogue thus departs more radically from the conventions of ordinary conversations than any other form of therapy.

Individuals who are secure in the belief that they are interest-ing and/or that their therapist will pay full attention to what they have to say can accommodate themselves to these conditions. Patients who doubt that anyone would be interested in paying close attention to anything they have to say, obviously, cannot. We are always asking and answering, tacitly, two questions when engaged in conversations. They are: How long can I speak before I have spoken too long? And, How long can I listen before I need to and/or should speak? These questions concern patients as well as therapists. "Am I talking too much?" is a common preoccupation among neophyte psychotherapists who have yet to answer for themselves the question, What stylistic choices are permissible and appropriate in the therapeutic situation? These questions also haunt patients who do not believe they have the "right" to speak at length about the ongoing flow of their inner experience. When such patients begin to speak "uninterestingly" about themselves or do not appear to have a lot to say, it may give expression to the fear that they have spoken too long.

The guidelines provided by the existential-humanistic and psychoanalytic traditions do not precisely define and delimit the kinds of activities and overt responses that are permissible in the therapeutic situation. Consequently, they have generated heated debate. To cope with the ambiguities posed by the question, How should interest be expressed in the therapeutic situation? I additionally rely on the guidance provided by the concept of rhythm.

Rhythmically Inspired Stylistic Choices

My decisions as to when and how to speak take into account the communicative significance of the flow of sound and silence. On initial reading, the rhyme and rhythm of a poem may have a more compelling impact than the actual meaning of the words. Similarly, during the anxiety-ridden early stages of therapy, patients may be influenced more by the predictability and the tonal qualities of the therapist's voice than by the content of what he/she says. Phrases and even sounds that recur regularly such as grunts, snorts, growls, and mm-hmms are reassuring to patients who are constantly in doubt regarding their therapist's interest. In other words, rhythmically inspired vocalizations can increase the "holding aspects" of the therapeutic environment. Pine (1985) recommends making this a primary task in the psychotherapy of "fragile" patients who are ordinarily unable to work in an insight-oriented mode. In order to convey his consistent presence, Winnicott is reported to have said to his prospective patient, Harry Guntrip (1975), near the end of their initial interview, "I've nothing particular to say yet, but if I don't say something, you may begin to feel I'm not here" (p. 152).

My decisions as to when and how to speak also take into account people's needs for, as well as their fears and defenses against, participating in communicative exchanges that are rhythmically synchronized. Synchronization of interaction rhythms is in evidence during conversations when the participants "mirror" each other's gestures, imitate each other's postures, and match each other's vocal behavior. Research indicates that, in general, vocal and postural convergence during conversations leads to harmonious feelings in the participants regardless of the content being discussed (Jaffe & Feldstein, 1970; Duncan & Fiske, 1977). Individuals who are able to move in unison with others and converge with respect to duration of speech, frequency of interruptions, pause length, speech rate, and loudness draw positive attention to themselves.

Patients whom I have referred to as schizoid are frightened by the feelings of closeness encouraged by rhythmically coordinated conversations. Obsessive patients rage against interference with what Kestenberg (1966) conceptualizes as their "obligatory rhythms." They welcome their therapist's participation in the therapeutic dialogue only to the extent that the therapist does not interfere with their strivings for autonomy. Pauses in the flow of the therapeutic dialogue—impending and actual—are experienced as ruptures of attachment by dependently demanding patients. They misconstrue a therapist's interest as disappointingly inadequate unless the therapist is frequently and expressively brought to speech. They have yet to achieve "the capacity to be alone" with a valued other (Winnicott, 1969). As these examples are meant to suggest, patients who are suffering from various forms of character pathology require a psychotherapist who can allow and respond flexibly to their dysrhythmic modes of participating in relationships.

By delicately adjusting one's rate of vocalization to accommodate the idiosyncratic rhythmic requirements of each patient, it is possible to gradually move the therapeutic dialogue by successive approximations in the direction of greater mutuality and reciprocity. Such changes signal a patient's growing capacity for intimacy and collaborative inquiry—the cornerstone of effective psychotherapy.

CONCLUSIONS

Countertransference reactions are no longer regarded primarily as a sign of professional or personal failings. This intellectual climate has encouraged therapists to explore with tough-minded curiosity the hypothesis that "negative" feelings about a patient, no matter how hateful or neurotic in origin, can provide invaluable information about the processes currently characterizing the relationship between patient and therapist. Therapists, nevertheless, continue to be reluctant to discuss, especially in print, incisively and insightfully the therapeutic challenges posed by transient and persistent loss of interest in their patients. In order to encourage more open discussion of this delicate clinical issue, I have presented the beginnings of an interactional framework that clarifies those occasions when insufficient interest in a patient is not attributable exclusively to the personal limitations of either the patient or the therapist. It is respectful and helpful to conceptualize boredom in the therapeutic situation as coauthored. It is also energizing to ask whether a patient is engaging in the tasks of psychotherapy boringly than to conclude that he or she is boring. I have argued in this paper that transient episodes of boredom arise when both patient and therapist anxiously avoid the burdens of making choices and taking actions that might induce shame or guilt in one or both participants. Stalemated therapies may arise because of the vicious cycles set in motion by mutual withdrawal from the risks of truth-telling. A therapy may also arrive at an impasse because of a therapist's prolonged failure to acknowledge that his/her boredom is reflective of basic incompatibilities. Early identification of and candid discussions about the "poorness of fit" between the expressive, cognitive, and expressive aspects of a patient's and therapist's styles are required if crises and the need for dramatic and forceful confrontations are to be avoided.

Finally, facing up to the boredom that keeps one from functioning optimally with a given patient does not ensure the return of interest and revitalization of the treatment. It would be naive to assume that with sufficient self-reflection a therapist should be able to treat anyone. A therapist cannot provide more interest than he/she feels is reasonable or personally acceptable. On some occasions, an optimal outcome of disciplined self-examination of the origins and meanings of one's boredom would be the referral of the patient to someone who can provide the patient with what he/she needs, perhaps because of that therapist's therapeutic zeal, youth, or special skills and interests.

REFERENCES

Altshul, V.A. (1977). The so-called boring patient. *American Journal of Psychotherapy* 31:533–545.

Bacal, H.A. (1985). Optimal responsiveness and the therapeutic process. In A. Goldberg (Ed.), *Progress in Self Psychology* (pp. 202–206). New York, NY: Guilford Press.

Beebe, B., & Stern, D.N. (1977). Engagement-disengagement and early object experiences. In N. Freedman & S. Grand (Eds.), *Communicative Structures and Psychic Structures* (pp. 35–55). New York, NY: Plenum Press.

Bowlby, J. (1973). *Attachment and Loss: Vol. 2. Separation: Anxiety and Anger.* New York, NY: Basic Books.

Camus, A. (1956). *The Fall.* New York, NY: Vintage Books.

Csikszentmihalyi, M. (1975). *Beyond Boredom and Anxiety: The Experience of Play in Work and Games.* San Francisco, CA: Jossey-Bass.

DeChenne, T.K. (1988). Boredom as a clinical issue. *Psychotherapy* 25:71–81.

Duncan, S., & Fiske, D.W. (1977). *Face-to-Face Interaction: Research, Methods, and Theory.* Hillsdale, NJ: Erlbaum.

Eagle, M.N. (1981). Interests as object relations. *Psychoanalysis and Contemporary Thought* 4:527–565.

Farber, B.A., & Heifetz, L.J. (1982). The process and dimensions of burnout in psychotherapists. *Professional Psychology* 13(2):293–301.

Fenichel, O. (1953). On the psychology of boredom. In *The Collected Papers of Otto Fenichel* (First Series, pp. 292–302). New York, NY: Norton. (Original work published 1934.)

Fiske, D.W., & Maddi, S.R. (1961). *Functions of Varied Experience.* Homewood, IL: Dorsey.

Freud, S. (1912). Recommendations on psychoanalytic technique. *Standard Edition* 12:111–171.

Fromm, E. (1976). *To Have or to Be?* New York, NY: Bantam Books.

Geller, J.D. (1984). Moods, feelings, and the process of affect formation. In L. Temoshok, C. Van Dyke, & L.S. Zegans (Eds.), *Emotions in Health and Illness: Applications to Clinical Practice* (pp. 171–186). Orlando, FL: Grune & Stratton.

———— (1987). The process of psychotherapy: Separation and the complex interplay among empathy, insight, and internalization. In J. Bloom-Feshbach & S. Bloom-Feshbach (Eds.), *The Psychology of Separation and Loss: Perspectives on Development, Life Transitions, and Clinical Practice* (pp. 459–514). San Francisco, CA: Jossey-Bass.

———— (1992). *The Meanings and Uses of Misunderstandings in Psychotherapy.* Paper presented at the 24th annual meeting of the Society for Psychotherapy, Berkeley, CA.

———— & Schaffer, C.E. (1988, June 23). *Internalization of the Supervisory Dialogue and the Development of Therapeutic Competence.* Paper presented at the 21st annual meeting of the Society for Psychotherapy Research, Santa Fe, NM.

Greenson, R.R. (1978). On boredom. In *Explorations in Psychoanalysis.* New York, NY: International Universities Press. (Original work published 1953.)

Guntrip, H. (1975). My experience of analysis with Fairbairn and Winnicott. *International Review of Psychoanalysis* 2:145–156.

Havens, L.L. (1974). The existential use of self. *The American Journal of Psychiatry* 131:1–10.

———— (1989). *A Safe Place: Laying the Groundwork of Psychotherapy.* Cambridge, MA: Harvard University Press.

Izard, C.E. (1977). *Human Emotions.* New York, NY: Plenum Press.

Jacobson, E. (1957). On normal and pathological moods. In *The Psychoanalytic Study of the Child* (Vol. 12, pp. 73–113). New York, NY: International Universities Press.

Jaffe, J., & Feldstein, S. (1970). *Rhythms of Dialogue*. New York, NY: Academic Press.

Jordan, J.S., Harvey, J.H., & Weary, G. (1988). Attributional biases in clinical decision making. In D.C. Turk & P. Salovey (Eds.), *Reasoning, inference, and judgment in clinical psychology* (pp. 90–106). New York, NY: Free Press.

Kernberg, O. (1975). *Borderline Conditions and Pathological Narcissism*. New York, NY: Jacob Aronson.

Kestenberg, J.S. (1966). Rhythm and organization in obsessive-compulsive development. *International Journal of Psychoanalysis* 47:151–159.

Kline, F., Adrian, A., & Spevak, M. (1974). Patients evaluate therapists. *Archives of General Psychiatry* 31:113–116.

Kohut, H. (1971). *The Analysis of the Self*. New York, NY: International Universities Press.

——— (1977). *The Restoration of the Self*. New York, NY: International Universities Press.

Krystal, H. (1979). Alexithymia and psychotherapy. *American Journal of Psychotherapy* 33:17–31.

La Rochefoucauld, F. (1957). *The Maxims of the Duc de la Rochefoucauld* (C. FitzGibbon, Trans.). London, UK: Wingate. (Original work published 1664.)

Lehman, A., & Geller, J.D. (1992, June 23–27). *Psychotherapists' Representations of Their Patients*. Paper presented at the 23rd annual meeting of the Society for Psychotherapy Research, Berkeley, CA.

Levinson, D.J., Darrow, C.N., Klein, E.B., Levinson, M.H., & McKee, B. (1978). *The Seasons of a Man's Life*. New York, NY: Knopf.

Lipin, T. (1963). The repetition compulsion and "maturational" drive-representatives. *International Journal of Psycho-Analysis* 44:389–406.

Luborsky, L., McLellan, A.T., Woody, G.E., O'Brien, C.P., & Auerbach, A. (1985). Therapist success and its determinants. *Archives of General Psychiatry* 42:602–611.

McLaughlin, J.T. (1975). The sleepy analyst: Some observations on states of consciousness of the analyst at work. *Journal of the American Psychoanalytic Association* 23:363–382.

Merton, R.K. (1948). The self-fulfilling prophecy. *Antioch Review* 8:193–210.

Modell, A. (1976). "The holding environment" and the therapeutic action of psychoanalysis. *Journal of the American Psychoanalytic Association* 24:285–309.

Ogden, T.H. (1979). On projective identification. *International Journal of Psychoanalysis* 60:357–373.

Orlinsky, D.E., & Geller, J.D. (1993). Psychotherapy's internal theater of operation: Patients' representations of their therapists and therapy as a new focus of research. In N.E. Miller, J. Doherty, L. Luborsky, & J. Barber (Eds.), *Psychodynamic Treatment Research: A Handbook for Clinical Practice* (pp. 423–466). New York, NY: Basic Books.

Pine, F. (1985). *Developmental Theory and Clinical Process*. New Haven, CT: Yale University Press.

Pope, K.S., & Bouhoutsos, J. (1986). *Sexual Intimacy Between Therapists and Patients*. New York, NY: Praeger.

Sandler, J. (1976). Countertransference and role-responsiveness. *International Review of Psychoanalysis* 3:43–47.

Schachtel, E.G. (1959). *Metamorphosis: On the Development of Affect, Perception, Attention, and Memory*. New York, NY: Basic Books.

Spence, D. (1984). Perils and pitfalls of free floating attention. *Contemporary Psychoanalysis* 20:37–59.

Tomkins, S.S. (1962). *Affect Imagery Consciousness: Vol. 1. The Positive Affects*. New York, NY: Springer.

Trilling, L. (1972). *Sincerity and Authenticity*. Cambridge, MA: Harvard University Press.

Webster's Ninth New Collegiate Dictionary. (1983). Springfield, MA: Merriam-Webster.

Wessman, A.E., & Ricks, D.E. (1966). *Mood and Personality*. New York, NY: Holt, Rinehart & Winston.

Winnicott, D. (1965). *The Maturational Processes and the Facilitating Environment*. New York, NY: International Universities Press.

——— (1969). The use of an object and relating through identifications. *International Journal of Psychoanalysis* 30:86–94.

Yalom, I.D. (1989). *Love's Executioner*. New York, NY: Basic Books.

Zajonc, R.B. (1980). Feeling and thinking: Preferences need no inferences. *American Psychologist* 35:151–175.

CHAPTER 7

Thank You for Jenny[18]

[J.D. Geller (1996). In B. Gerson (Ed.), *The Therapist as a Person: Life Crises, Life Choices, Life Experiences, and Their Effects on Treatment* (pp. 119–139). New York, NY: Analytic Press.]

My wife Ruth and I have two daughters, Elizabeth (31) and Jennifer (25). Jennifer was born profoundly deaf. The discovery of this cruel fact in 1973 confronted me with a series of crises unlike anything I had ever encountered before. Two decades later, in the spring of 1993, Dr. Gerson invited me to write an essay about the ways in which our efforts to cope with the crises triggered by Jennifer's deafness have influenced the way in which I do psychotherapy and think about my work. Even after obtaining Jennifer's permission to do so, I said yes only ambivalently. The balance of my feelings was initially tipped in a negative direction.

The conflicts I was experiencing at the outset derived from several sources. Objectifying my relationship with Jenny is repugnant to me. I feared that writing about her for a professional audience would alienate me from the most private and precious meanings of my relationship with Jenny. I also tend to be suspicious of parents who portray their children's disabilities as "gifts," "messages," or even as "opportunities for learning." I usually find their tone to be too sentimental, too heroic, or too self-congratulatory. In fact, I am wary of all retrospective attempts to specify direct and inevitable lines of influence between

---

18 The title is borrowed from an article my mother (Geller, 1984) wrote about Jenny.

early and subsequent events. Very different narratives could have been fashioned out of the facts, events, and anecdotes that are included in this chapter. Nevertheless, as I discovered while writing this, I believe that the continuing process of learning to be a father to Jenny has influenced my views of just about everything of importance that happens in psychotherapy. (In distinctive ways, each of my daughters has had a decisive impact on what I hear, see, feel, think, and say during therapy sessions.) For the present purposes, however, I will restrict myself to discussing the influence of Jenny's deafness on my attitudes toward the nature and functions of communication and miscommunication in the therapeutic situation.

WHO IS JENNY?

My representation of Jenny and the meanings that I ascribe to her deafness have changed many times over the course of our lives together. Where once I construed Jenny's deafness as her most defining feature, I now conceive of her deafness as only one aspect of her highly distinctive and inspiring personhood. I made the following "slip of the tongue" the week Jenny was diagnosed. I mistakenly told a friend she was "profoundly retarded" rather than profoundly deaf. Today, I regard her as a highly intelligent, creative young woman. She is a college junior at the Rochester Institute of Technology. She is trying to decide whether to become a teacher, a social worker, or a graphic designer/artist. Jenny embodies an affirmative answer to my brother Norman's question, Is it possible to be both real and cool at the same time? Her vitality is contagious. She is the Picasso of lip readers. She signs with eloquence and style. Her voice is aesthetically pleasing. She is making a life for herself in the "Deaf" community[19] and, if she chooses, can "pass" in the hearing world. Like her older sister, Liz, Jenny is a loving and lovable person. She is generous, empathic, and sensible. Her sense of irony is well-developed. Her courage and successes deserve to be celebrated. This chapter is, in part, a thank you for all that Jenny has taught me.

To understand why and how Jenny exerted a positive and pervasive influence on my work requires some knowledge about the barriers to contact and communication resulting from profound deafness. Because profound deafness is a rare occurrence, I assume that most therapists are unfamiliar with the emotional, interpersonal, and cognitive consequences of being born without the ability to hear the human voice. Deafness is far more than simply a loss of hearing. So before proceeding, I will provide some basic information about the diagnosis of deafness, hearing aids, the misleading notion of lipreading, residual hearing, and the developmental difficulties Jenny has endured as she proceeded from infancy, through childhood, and into her adolescence.

DEAFNESS: SOME FACTS AND THEIR IMPLICATIONS

The diagnosis of deafness is usually determined by the degree of hearing loss in the speech range. Auditory loss is measured in decibels, or units of sound. A slight hearing loss is 20 decibels or less. With this limitation, one may experience strain in hear-

---

19 Following a convention proposed by Woodward (1972), an increasing number of deaf people distinguish, conceptually, between the audiological condition of not being able to hear (spelled with a lowercase "d") and the "culture" of Deafness (spelled with a capital "D"). The latter concept is especially important to those Deaf people who do not consider themselves disabled or handicapped but who identify themselves as members of an "ethnic" community that has a distinctive language, sensibility, and culture of its own. Jenny is currently struggling, heroically, to define her relationship to Deafness.

ing when tired or inattentive, in distant theater seats, or when articulation is soft or poor. Persons whose hearing loss averages 40–60 decibels in the speech range struggle to decipher even shouted conversations. Without the help of hearing aids, they cannot learn speech or language normally.

Jenny suffers from a profound degree of hearing loss. A child whose hearing loss averages 80 decibels (about the volume of a garbage disposal) in the speech range is considered to be profoundly deaf. Jenny's first audiological examination indicated that she had a "sensori-neural" hearing loss of 95 decibels in her right ear and 100 in her left ear. This means that without a hearing aid she can detect only sounds that are louder than a lawn mower, food blender, or jet plane. Jenny's deafness was not diagnosed until she was 19 months old.

My wife Ruth "knew" something was "wrong" with our baby's development by the time Jenny was 5 months old. Pediatric ignorance, incompetence, and arrogance, as well as the power of a family system in denial, postponed the diagnosis of Jenny's "invisible" handicap. Ruth and I watched through a one-way mirror as the first audiologist tested Jenny in a cold room in the basement of Yale–New Haven Hospital. We could not tell what the results were indicating. We were traumatized when he told us that Jenny was profoundly deaf because of physical damage to either her inner ear or to the nerves leading to the auditory cortex. The audiologist then predicted that Jenny would not benefit from hearing aids and that she would never acquire usable speech. He also claimed that not providing Jenny with "sign language"[20] immediately would retard her intellectual develop-

---

20 "Sign language" is a broad term that encompasses a variety of sign languages used with and among the deaf, for example, Seeing Essential English, Manual English, finger spelling, and American Sign Language (ASL). In contrast to the other systems, ASL is not a mere transliteration or visual representation of spoken English. Until recently, it was viewed by the hearing merely as a way of pantomiming using gestures. Thanks to the research of William

ment and inevitably lead to serious mental illness. He presented these conclusions coldly, as if they were incontrovertible facts rather than the biased opinion of a "manualist."

Centuries-old questions about how best to educate prelingually deaf children are still being debated acrimoniously by deaf educators. The polarized positions taken by the so-called "oralists" and "manualists" resemble religious wars. I quickly lost faith in their "expertise." There is an appalling lack of objective data to help parents decide whether a child who is deaf from birth or who lost his/her hearing before learning to talk should be taught speech or sign language. There is, for example, still no reliable method to determine the nature and extent of a prelingually deaf child's "residual hearing" or how much it could be amplified. "Residual hearing" is the term audiologists use to refer to the hearing that remains after a hearing loss. This hearing may be limited to the ability to detect the presence of sound, or it may also include the ability to discriminate between sounds. People with similar audiograms may have very different speech discrimination abilities.

Three months after she began wearing a hearing aid, Jenny uttered her first word. It was "baby." Our joy was immense. This developmental landmark indicated, contrary to the first audiologist's predictions, that the new computerized hearing aids could provide Jenny with some usable sound. It also signaled that she was rapidly learning how to connect lip shapes to concepts. It appeared as though she might even be abundantly endowed with the talents required to transform noise into the sounds of speech. And so, in full knowledge that we were playing Russian

---

Stokoe (1960), it is now recognized that ASL satisfies every linguistic criterion of a genuine language. It has a distinct lexicon and syntax as well as the capacity to generate an infinite number of propositions. Oliver Sacks (1989) discusses ASL in *Seeing Voices* in a way that can provide psychotherapists with a highly illuminating perspective on the emotional and cognitive development of the deaf as well as the hearing.

roulette with Jenny's future, we decided to educate her orally. We dared to hope that someday Jenny might achieve linguistic competence and intelligible speech.

Owing to many factors, ambitious goals such as these can be realized only after many years of arduous effort, if at all. Binaural hearing aids amplify sound but do not, themselves, discriminate between messages, competing messages, or background noise. Even with maximum amplification, Jenny can hear only low-frequency sounds, mostly vowels. Thus, for example, the word "impossible" might sound to her like "i-a-i-al." Imagine trying to learn a foreign language by listening to it spoken over a static-filled radio station. Under optimal circumstances, this is somewhat akin to the challenges Jenny experiences when trying to listen. A further complication is the fact that the linguistic information that can be extracted from the movements of a speaker's lips, even by experts, is often incomplete or misleading.

Sacks (1989) has likened lipreading to "a complex art of observation, inference and inspired guesswork" (p. 15). These mental abilities are a major component of lipreading because many speech elements and words look identical on the lips, although they sound quite different. To cite just a few examples, the letters "m," "p," and "b" look alike on the lips, as do "s" and "z." Unstressed syllables, articles, some prepositions, and many other entire words (e.g., "a," "the," "in," "at") are not usually visually detectable in speech presented at a normal conversational rate. To a lip reader, the words "baby" and "paper" are indistinguishable, as are "mama" and "papa." Even when a sentence provides contextual cues, it is maddeningly difficult to distinguish by lipreading the words "but," "bad," "ban," "mat," "mad," "man," and "pad." It has been estimated that, at best, deaf persons recognize three or four words for every 10 that are spoken. Dolnick (1993) has, therefore, likened lipreading to filling in the blanks in a fast and ongoing crossword puzzle.[21]

Looking back, Ruth and I now agree that it was "irrational" faith in Jenny that sustained our optimism during the many and recurrent periods when there seemed to be no visible progress toward linguistic competence and intelligible speech. I am convinced that, if it had not been for Ruth's untiring perseverance and unselfish devotion, Jenny would never have acquired the listening and speaking abilities that enable her to participate in our world, the hearing world. In the next section, I will begin to examine how the difficult tasks we imposed on Jenny, ourselves, Liz, our friends, and our relatives contributed to my continuing education as a therapist. To paraphrase an African proverb, the raising of a deaf child is so difficult that it requires the contributions of the entire village.

PERSONAL TRANSFORMATIONS

In 1973, the year Jennifer's deafness was confirmed, I was 34 years old. I was still very much in the process of personalizing and integrating the theoretical viewpoints of my teachers. My first psychotherapy supervisors were influenced primarily by Helmuth Kaiser (1965) and David Shapiro (1965), who in turn acknowledge their indebtedness to Wilhelm Reich (1949). My supervisors encouraged me to develop a refined sensitivity to the ways in which patients and therapists withdraw from intimate and collaborative dialogues. Kaiser placed authenticity of communication rather than the creation and working through of insights at the center of his theory of therapy. My own view,

---

21 More extensive discussions of the information summarized above can be found in the works of Meadow (1980), Padden and Humphries (1988), Sacks (1989), and Peterson (1994).

after many years of practice, is that the search for the "truth" and the subjective experience of "truth-telling" each make a positive contribution to the success of psychotherapy and that they jointly set in motion various forms of experiential and interpersonal learning. Thus, I assume that, while promoting insight and/or authenticity, therapists provide their patients with repeated experiences of feeling understood, which in turn activate the processes of internalization (Geller, 1987, 1994). Most broadly stated, a single, efficacious communicative exchange can be conceived of as serving multiple therapeutic functions simultaneously.

When Jenny was born, a durable sense of myself as a "good enough" therapist was in the process of becoming a more stable aspect of my professional identity, thanks in part to my experiences raising our daughter, Liz. With Liz, I was already learning that I was capable of loving unambivalently and unselfishly. The love I gave and the love I received from her supported my striving for maturity and virtue. I took to fathering Liz rather intuitively. Our first infant thrived on what came naturally and spontaneously to Ruth and me. Liz permitted us to nurture, comfort, and protect her. From birth onwards, she provided me with palpable evidence that I was capable of providing her with experiences that promoted her growth and development.

These affirmations were especially important to me during the earliest stages of my career, for they made it easier for me to tolerate the feelings of incompetence and fraudulence that inevitably accompany training to become a psychotherapist. They counteracted my inclination to interpret my difficulties in mastering the roles and functions of a psychotherapist as a negative reflection upon my character development. As my confidence regarding my capacity to be benignly influential grew, it became increasingly possible for me to use diminished as well as amplified feelings of therapeutic competence as information about the particular patient with whom I was working.

By contrast, raising Jenny from the very outset was often grueling, painful, and difficult. Early on, before Jenny's deafness was diagnosed, Ruth feared that there was something inaccessible, perhaps even "autistic," about her. Jenny seemed to disregard our efforts to soothe her. Liz loved eating. Jenny was lactose intolerant and suffered from severe colic. Liz was joyously active. Jenny was hyperactive. When frustrated, Liz got angry, while Jenny, on the other hand, became rageful. Liz cried. Jenny screamed. Liz enjoyed going to sleep at night. Jenny had serious problems falling and staying asleep. Often, Jenny stayed up past midnight until she virtually collapsed. From ages 3 to 10, she regularly was awakened by nightmares and insisted on spending the rest of the night in our bed.

In short, our home felt like a residential treatment center under siege. The stress and fatigue Ruth and I had to deal with inevitably took their toll upon our marriage. So, too, did our frequent quarrels about the meaning and management of Jenny's sleep disorder. Ruth advocated the comfort provided by structure and routines and the setting of limits. I insisted that going to sleep fueled Jenny's intense separation and annihilation anxieties. Both perspectives were valid. Both were also incomplete, and as I came to realize, my own interpretation reflected to some degree the projection onto Jenny of the unfinished business of my own childhood. For example, my reactions to Jenny's deafness were anticipated by my reactions to her colic. I am told that, like Jenny, I suffered from severe colic during the first 6 months of my life. While little is known about the long-term developmental consequences of colic, my own speculations have led me to believe that, whatever its origins, colic diminishes an infant's trust in his/her caretakers and leaves behind a legacy of sensory-dominated, presymbolic memories of being both alone and afraid. When activated, these memories enter awareness in the form of diffuse, intense, and "unnamed" somatic sensations. Like the inability to hear our loving voices, I believe Jenny's colic further diminished her capacity to call forth self-soothing representations when separated from us.

What remained constant throughout these chaotic years was Ruth's and my shared love for Jenny, our commitment to Jenny, and our faith in Jenny. Moreover, Ruth and I were in agreement that Jenny's deafness retarded her acquisition of the representational capacities required to differentiate, describe, and regulate emotional experiences. Jenny had not, after all, heard the human voice until she was almost 20 months old. She did not know that words existed or that everything—objects, actions, and abstractions—has a name. She did not begin speaking in syntactically organized sentences until she was 3½. (Some analysts take this developmental achievement as signaling the beginnings of secondary process thought.) Furthermore, it took many years before Jenny could participate comfortably in the interactions that take place when we tell each other stories. For these and other reasons, misunderstandings and miscommunications were daily occurrences in our home.

MISUNDERSTANDING EVENTS IN PSYCHOTHERAPY

Misunderstandings are an ever-present danger when trying to communicate verbally with a profoundly deaf person. I shudder to think about the number of times that Jenny interpreted what we were asking of her "inaccurately" or "incorrectly." In turn, Jenny frequently experienced us as not understanding her needs and/or as being unresponsive to them. From infancy until she was about 8½, Jenny had severe and prolonged temper tantrums in response to our perceived lapses of understanding. Efforts to console Jenny after these misunderstanding events often inadvertently intensified her frustration at not being understood. Her raging inconsolably until she collapsed in exhaustion was a recurrent feature of our average expectable environment. Like the girl in the nursery rhyme, when Jenny was good, she was very, very good, and when she was bad, she was horrid. Lacking a shared vocabulary, I believe, exacerbated the expression of the more selfish and aggressive aspects of her nature and delayed her emergence from the "egocentrism" (Piaget, 1965) of early childhood.

Difficult as they were, these experiences impressed upon me how important it is for therapists and patients to attend with exquisite care to patients' reactions to feeling misunderstood (Geller, 1992; Geller & Rhodes, 1993). The analysand in Judith Rossner's (1983) novel *August* put it this way: "With a shrink, a little mistake goes a long way" (p. 23).

Much remains to be learned about how to turn to advantage the interactional phenomena and intrapsychic processes set in motion by lapses of understanding on the part of therapists who are usually perceived as understanding. My evolving approach draws upon Greenson's (1967) discussion of mistakes or technical errors and on Kohut's (1971) formulations regarding empathic failures. It includes the following working clinical hypotheses.

I assume that therapists, for varying reasons, underestimate the frequency with which their patients feel misunderstood. Early in my career, I was sensitized to this possibility by Reich's (1949) assertion that every patient, without exception, begins therapy with a more or less explicit attitude of distrust or cynicism that, as a rule, remains hidden. More recently, Rennie (1985) has documented that many patients do not signal, either verbally or affectively, that they are preoccupied with negative reactions to the therapists' characteristics or with their therapists' way of working because of timidity, deference to authority, and stereotyped politeness.

There is ample clinical evidence to indicate that there are consistent and psychologically important differences in the recognizability, intelligibility, and communicability of the feelings and memories triggered by empathic failures, narcissistic injuries, and the stresses of separation and loss (Geller, 1984, 1987). These reactions can span the range from the "object-less" and impotent rage of the frustrated infant to the subtle, refined, thoughtlike blend of anger and forgiveness experienced by adults who have achieved that attitude Levinson et al. (1978) refer to as "de-illusionment." The present-day consensus among psychoanalytically informed clinicians is that patients who are suffering from narcissistic and borderline, as compared to normal-neurotic, levels of character pathology are vulnerable to experiencing disorganizing, grossly unmodulated, and conceptually obscure states of emotional upheaval when "disappointed" by valued others. In a like manner, I have found that much of what enters the awareness of such patients when they perceive that they have been misunderstood by their therapists is inchoate or undifferentiated with respect to its ideational and affective content rather than merely disguised or denied.

Thus, a crucial diagnostic distinction that a therapist must make, at any given moment, is between reactions to feeling misunderstood that are being kept "private" for fear of jeopardizing the relationship and those for which patients genuinely have no words. Incorrect assessment of these independent sources of silence and secrecy can further intensify a patient's suffering and reinforce the conviction that one's feelings are incomprehensible. As these diagnostic formulations are meant to further suggest, the precise framing of a therapist's verbal responses requires an ongoing assessment of the levels of symbolic functioning at which the patient's reactions to lapses of understanding are being experienced and expressed.

HELPING PATIENTS TO COMMUNICATE

Especially during her early years, Jenny often felt as if she couldn't make herself comprehensible or understood. Until she could produce words intelligible to strangers, we served as Jenny's interpreters. As in the movie *Johnny Belinda*, people in our community often treated our little girl as if she were "a dummy." Even now, despite her remarkable academic successes, Jenny often refers to herself as "stupid." I feel actual sensations of pain whenever I think of how often Jenny had to reckon with feeling ignorant and learning disabled en route to acquiring linguistic competence.

These experiences impressed upon me the importance of inquiring as to whether a patient feels that he/she is participating in therapy competently and intelligently. What I am discovering is that many patients feel like "failures" at therapy itself. Feeling like a failure as a patient is, as I now realize, a normative aspect of the experience of individuals whom investigators refer to as "alexithymic" (Krystal, 1979; Geller, 1984). Alexithymic individuals suffer from extreme difficulties distinguishing feelings from body sensations and putting them into words. Consequently, like Jenny during her childhood, much of their experience remains "unformulated" (Stern, 1983). I am especially likely to observe Jenny's presence in my conscious and preconscious processes when I listen to such patients. It is she who has made it possible for me to identify directly and immediately with patients who are unable to describe their wishes and feelings vividly and "interestingly" (Geller, 1994). These identifications then find expression in the ways in which I help patients talk about the what, when, how, and why of the more troublesome aspects of their lives.

Whenever possible, I try to help my patients achieve greater clarity and specificity regarding what they are experiencing. Not surprisingly, Ruth and I made prominent use of "clarifications" when conversing with Jenny. Clarifications essentially paraphrase, reflect, or summarize what has been communicated. At first, we found ourselves using clarifications when we were trying to make what was incomprehensible comprehensible. We used them to reassure her that what she had intended had actually been communicated. We used clarifications to validate her perception of "reality." Our clarifications would, we hoped, provide her with the reassurance that we took upon ourselves the primary responsibility for the failure of a communicative exchange.

Providing patients with clarifying descriptions of inner states strengthens their feeling that they are competently or successfully engaging in psychotherapy. For example, I rely on a clinical strategy Loewald (1978) refers to as "active mirroring" when patients' reactions to real and alleged lapses of understanding are inaccessible to self-reflection and verbalization. Active mirroring essentially refers to verbal responses that restate or translate the felt meanings inherent in a patient's communications into statements that are more explicit, concrete, "hot," and intimate or more well organized than those used by the patient. By going beyond what a patient has said, active mirroring thus blends the qualities of clarifications with those of interpretations. I give center stage to this clinical strategy when I am trying to help a patient transform vaguely apprehended negative reactions (e.g., "I felt upset... bad... weird... when you misunderstood me") into more precise emotion words (e.g., "angry," "afraid," "embarrassed," "hurt"). Nurturing the formation of affects that are recognizable as being of one kind, and not another, helps the patient to feel capable of expressing his/her pain articulately. Increased eloquence reduces the intensity of painful emotions and makes them more available for self-exploration. As Fenichel (1953) put it, words "tame" affects.

Active mirroring can, furthermore, be used to lend vitality to patients who express their negative reactions to feeling misunderstood in a "disembodied" fashion. When clinically indicated, I will translate words such as "anger" or "fear" into body-centered metaphors that stand closer to the physicality of immediate experience. As an example, I will speak of "a broken heart," "a lump in the throat," or "a pain in the neck" when an intellectualizing patient speaks about failed love, sadness, or anger.

In order to foster the creative and responsible use of language—two of the cornerstones of effective psychotherapy—I try to voice all interventions so that they affirm and highlight what a patient is trying to accomplish rather than what he/she is trying to avoid. For example, when commenting on what a patient is resisting, I do not use terms such as "running away" or "hiding" but rather talk about retreating to a safe place.

The following vignette can be used to illustrate how these technical principles inform my work as a psychotherapy supervisor. The dialogue is an excerpt from the final minutes of the fourth hour of a course of psychotherapy being conducted within the Yale Psychological Services Clinic. The therapist (T) is a 5th-year clinical psychology graduate student whom I am supervising. The patient (P) is a 21-year-old single man who recently returned home after spending 10 years in another city to take a managerial position in his father's very successful real estate business. His father, whom he idealizes, is about to retire, and he and his brothers are competing for power and the father's approval. What do you hear in the following exchange?

P: I was thinking on the ride home last week that it feels like I just scratch the surface and then it's time to go. What are your thoughts or your policy here about meeting more often?

• T: Do you feel like the issues you're bringing to therapy don't have the chance to get addressed adequately?

• P: No. It's that there's a lot of background stuff that I feel like it's going to take a while to get through. Later on, I'd probably want to go back to meeting once a week.

• T: So you feel in a hurry to get to some later phase of therapy?

• P: I don't know. Maybe not. You're the boss: You tell me.

• T: I don't think of myself as a boss. I view our work here as a collaborative endeavor. But that said, I'd like to suggest that we wait another 2 weeks, and then let's reevaluate this issue again. I can understand how you might be impatient with this process, but it's often a slow one—and we really are in the beginning stages.

• P: I am the kind of person who doesn't like to wait too long for things.

• T: Uh-huh. At the same time, the therapy doesn't end at 8:30. Look at all of the thoughts and memories that were generated in here last week that you've been working over since then.

• P: Sounds good. See you next week.

Because of the ambiguities inherent in language and the sheer number of possible meanings of any complex statement, the patient's metaphorical reference to "scratching the surface" and subsequent request for clarification regarding the therapist's thoughts or policy about increasing the frequency of visits can be variously interpreted. Does his question represent a retreat from the direct expression of the wish to meet more frequently? Is he deferring to the therapist's legitimate authority or presumed greater knowledge about the benefits of various dosages of therapy? Is he expressing impatience and disappointment in the process of therapy? Is he criticizing the therapist for being superficial?

The therapist chose to ask the patient whether the issues he is bringing to therapy are not getting adequately addressed. Alternative affirmative wordings of this intervention might have been, "You are really eager to get to the heart of things" or, "Perhaps you both wish and fear that our sessions will cut to the bone." Even interventions that challenge or call into question a patient's expectations about how therapy works can be stated affirmatively (Schafer, 1983). For example, in response to the patient's saying that there is a lot of "background stuff" that he must get through and that, once this is accomplished, he would want to go back to meeting once weekly, the therapist decided to ask another question: "So you feel in a hurry to get to some later phase of therapy?" Once again, a less "accusatory" formulation of this idea is possible, for example: "Perhaps you feel that my knowing a lot about your background (early childhood?) is crucial to the success of your therapy? Maybe there are other ways of thinking about this."

A follower of Kohut (1971) probably would argue for an intervention that affirmed the patient's feeling that it is important to him that the therapist understand what led up to his current predicaments. What I wish to emphasize here is that changes in stylistic choice might have strengthened the patient's confidence in his ability to use psychotherapy and his sense of self-determination. I wonder what the fate of the session might have been if the therapist had inquired whether the patient felt somehow misunderstood rather than asking him if his issues were not getting adequately addressed. The question, as posed, is an invitation to criticize the therapist's competence or expertise.

Let me weave in here a related issue raised by this clinical vignette. The patient reacted to the therapist's second question by retreating from his implied proposal and by emphasizing the inherently hierarchical nature of the patient-therapist relationship with respect to issues of authority and power: "You're the boss." My supervisee and I agreed that his reactions to the patient's deferring to his authority included a host of his own uncertainties about how to coordinate the exploratory, supportive, and managerial responsibilities inherent in the role of psychotherapist. In my experience, therapists-in-training tend to be more comfortable interpreting their patient's reactions to them as "authority figures" than with managing the fact that they are persons in positions of authority who are empowered to define when, where, and for how long they will meet with their patients.

DEAFNESS AND ALIENATION

The stance of "alienation" has always appealed to me. My exemplary sufferers include Holden Caulfield, James Dean, Jack Kerouac, and the anti-heroes of Paul Simon's songs. I have romanticized the role of "outsider." With Jenny, the gravitational pull exerted upon me by these positive images of alienation began to lessen.

In her autobiography, Helen Keller (1905/1990) wrote that "blindness cuts one off from things. Deafness cuts one off from people" (p. 48). Jenny has experienced alienation in all of its painful incarnations. To me, Jenny's inability to hear the human voice is at the heart of the alienation she suffered during infancy. During adulthood, voice qualities are usually thought of as serving primarily to enhance or modify the meanings of words.[22] During infancy, vocal qualities are one of the primary vehicles through which parents communicate with their hearing offspring. Jenny was deprived of the pleasure-giving, protective, and adaptation-enhancing sounds of lovingness and the soothing tones of lullabies. I still feel the sadness of these facts in my throat and chest.

At the heart of Jenny's alienation during childhood was her severely curtailed ability to learn by listening to and telling stories. It wasn't until age 7 that she discovered the difference between TV programs and commercials. Before she came to understand that plots organize stories, she created her own kinetic montages by rapidly changing TV channels.

Narration involves far more than the exchange of information. Stories make it possible to express the idea of "necessity" or, in contrast, of "possibility." Negotiating endings or making transitions with Jenny was very difficult because we were unable to convey to her the temporal order of things. Trilling (1972) has observed: "It is in the nature of narration to explain; it cannot help telling how things are and even why they are that way" (p. 135). We could not enlist the aid of stories to serve these didactic purposes. For example, we could not read Jenny fairy tales or cautionary tales that illustrated our values.

When Liz was 4, she began to ask her grandmother (my mother) to tell her "stories from her mouth" (not from a book). Their narrative content usually concerned my family's history. Liz loved most to hear anecdotes about my childhood or about the time my mother told my brother, Norman, that his

---

22 Research indicates that in many instances the acoustic properties of the voice are far more important than the actual words chosen in conveying attitudes and emotions. Voice qualities tell us, more or less precisely and directly, the extent to which an interactant is energized by, invested in, and moved emotionally by what he/she has said or heard (e.g., Rice & Kerr, 1986).

great-grandfather was a Black slave to counteract a racist comment he had just made. Jenny was ignorant of this family tradition. This limited her sense of "kinship" and deprived her of the myths that organize my family's saga. Jenny's delayed language acquisition also deprived her of the opportunity to laugh with us at my father's jokes. Many of his jokes contained Yiddish expressions that signaled our family's religious heritage and cultural identity. This, too, was unknown to Jenny. At age 10, she asked me what the "Holly Bibble" was. I was stunned. She did not know about the existence and importance of the Holy Bible. This forced me to recognize, once again, the magnitude of Jenny's estrangement from the hearing world.

My efforts to combat Jenny's isolation, her underdeveloped sense of personal continuity, and her limited storytelling capacities took many forms. For instance, in order to help Jenny develop a more integrated perspective on the evolution of persons and relationships over time, we created family photograph albums. Like interconnected narratives, photographs that are arranged chronologically can reveal the relations that exist between what was, what is, and what will be. Most importantly, I became much more attentive to the informative and rhetorical, as compared to the merely expressive, functions of the nonverbal channels of communication. I do not think that I am overstating the case when I say that these experiences and experiments had a substantial impact on the evolution of my therapeutic style and on my abiding interest in harnessing those agents of therapeutic change that are less dependent on the more purely linguistic aspects of language.

THE EVOLUTION OF MY THERAPEUTIC STYLE

In therapy, as elsewhere, there are identifiable and broadly categorizable "styles" of communicating the fruits of one's listening. A therapist's communicative style and its variations can be discerned in the way in which he/she formulates answers to the following types of questions: How often should I speak? When and how should I exchange the positions of listener and speaker? How expressive can I permit my face to be? In what proportions should my presence express warmth or coolness, informality or formality, activity or passivity, spontaneity or restraint? To what extent should my communications expand on what patients have already said as opposed to offering a new and different perspective on their experiences?

I struggle with these questions differently today than I did in 1971, the year my daughter Jenny was born. At the time, I called into question the value of all "techniques." Like most existential analysts, I believed that a preoccupation with technique led to the "stylization" of the therapeutic dialogue and to a resultant dilution of its authenticity. On the other hand, I often felt uncertain about what stylistic choices to make for my patients, especially if they were "fragile" or "difficult." I frequently knew what I wanted to say to them before I found the appropriate voice for the occasion. Today, in order to maximize the possibilities of interacting authentically with my patients, I think consciously and systematically about the proper timing, sequencing, and use of clarifications, confrontations, and interpretations. This shift was parallel to and congruent with my very different experiences raising Liz and Jenny. Liz seemed to thrive on what came naturally and spontaneously to Ruth and me as parents, while extraordinary effort and a great deal of conscious strategizing were required to accommodate to Jenny's communicative requirements.

During communicative exchanges that are proceeding optimally, the activities of listening and talking are themselves taken for granted. They recede from awareness. This makes it possible to focus one's attention exclusively on the content of the conversation. Communicating with Jenny always did, and still does, bring into sharp focus the problematic aspects of the activities of listening and speaking themselves. Jenny's ongoing struggle, moreover, is a constant reminder that our capacity to understand one another is always incomplete and imperfect.

Jenny titled one of her recent paintings *I Hear with My Eyes*. Vision is her principal source of knowledge about speech. Once I fully understood this, I became increasingly attentive to the positioning of my face vis-à-vis Jenny during communicative exchanges. Looking down or turning away severely curtails the clarity and intelligibility of the information received through lipreading. Concurrently, I became much more attentive to the ways in which I used gestures, postures, and facial expressions to communicate to her my thoughts and my feelings.

I can trace my greater facial expressiveness as a therapist to my efforts to find visual equivalents for the vocal qualities Jenny could not hear. I tried to communicate with my face the grunts, sighs, tones, murmurs, and other vocal qualities through which we give form to our feelings. I brought to awareness the didactic possibilities inherent in the games I had played, unselfconsciously, with Liz. For example, having a game of catch with Jenny became an opportunity to practice reciprocity. Like jazz singers, we sang scat and babbled together in rhythmic synchrony. I taught Jenny how to box and dance.[23] As previously noted,

---

23 I find it almost karmic that I brought to my experiences with Jenny a working knowledge of the ways in which dance therapists use sensorimotor dialogues to establish a sense of relatedness with otherwise noncommunicative schizophrenic patients (Geller, 1978).

I also took primary responsibility for the success or failure of a communicative exchange with her.

At this point in my career as a psychotherapist, I possess a distinctive, consistent, and personally satisfying style of communicating with my patients. It can be characterized as "responsive," "expressive," "demonstrative," and "conversational. "I do not think that I am deceiving myself in suggesting that the experiences described above moved me in this direction. I also do not think it is too fanciful to claim that Jenny stimulated my interest in the formidable technical challenges posed by patients who are unable to receive the sensuous fullness of the therapeutic dialogue. Jenny alerted me to the possibility that patients' problems processing sensory information are an often overlooked impediment to therapeutic progress. Her inability to hear the human voice sensitized me to the importance of assessing my patients' capabilities for receiving, storing, and recalling the verbal and nonverbal aspects of the therapeutic dialogue. I began posing to myself such questions as, How many sensory systems are effectively called into play when X is in the presence of his/ her therapist? What range of sensory experiences are aroused in X when listening to his/her therapist? What do patients look at while they are listening? How does X coordinate looking and listening? What sensory modalities does X rely on when constructing mental models of the therapeutic relationship?

I now accord patients'[24] difficulties processing sensory information a prominent place in my evolving theory of therapy. One of its conceptual starting points is that the cognitive styles

---

24 My experience as a psychotherapy supervisor suggests that the sensory processing of therapists-in-training tends to favor incoming auditory stimulation. A concern with understanding what patients are saying or are hesitant or unable to verbalize may inherently bias therapists' sensory awareness in the direction of audition. Moreover, in the psychotherapy literature, information that is available to therapists' eyes tends to be regarded merely as an ancillary source of data about patients. I believe the well-educated therapists' observational skills are as well-developed as are his/her listening skills.

patients bring to therapy can exert a restrictive influence on the distinctiveness and variety of their sensory experiences.

In the therapeutic situation, psychopathology often reveals itself in the form of difficulty "listening." Difficulties with listening are, for example, commonplace among patients whom Bowlby (1973) would designate "insecurely attached." Compulsively self-reliant patients experience themselves, for example, as turning to their therapists more fully for help when they are listening, as compared to when they are talking. In order to deal with their anxieties about becoming dependent on their therapist, compulsively self-reliant patients tend to impose, prematurely, their own meanings on what their therapists are saying. I do not take it for granted that they are open to receiving the "supportive" aspects of my communications. On the other hand, I now often take it as a signal of a growing readiness to ask for and to take in help when a compulsively self-reliant patient tells me, "I'm not getting any better."

A compulsively care-seeking attachment style also interferes with effective listening. Compulsive care-seekers feel under constant pressure to pay close attention to everything their therapists have to say. This makes it particularly difficult for them to think about what has already been heard or to attend to the felt internality of their own experience. To paraphrase Lacan (1966), whereas compulsively self-reliant patients begin therapy by listening to themselves without listening to their therapists, compulsive care-seekers begin therapy listening to their therapists without listening to themselves.

Variations can also be discerned in the ways in which patients process information available to their eyes. Some are "blind" to the meanings, attitudes, and feelings conveyed by their therapists' facial expressions, gestures, and postures. Those who are fearful of affect-laden face-to-face contact cannot see whether or not their therapists' facial expressions say, "Yes, I am listening," "Yes, I am present," "Yes, we are together," and "Yes, I am interested in you." Deprived of this information, they remain uncertain as to whether their therapist is conveying "serious interest" and "sympathetic understanding." This uncertainty can significantly undermine the therapy. Indeed, Freud (1912) proposed that offering patients serious interest and sympathetic understanding laid the groundwork for what we now call the "therapeutic alliance."

Jenny has told me that, when she turns off her hearing aids, the way things look to her is also transformed. Her return to silence is often accompanied by a reduction in the speed with which objects and persons appear to be moving. At the extremes, this slowing down process feels to Jenny as if the world is "dying." What these anecdotes are meant to suggest is that the interdependence of looking and listening must be taken into consideration when trying to understand a patient's experience of the therapeutic dialogue. To illustrate: A female patient recently told me a dream in which a former teacher is reading her a poem. In the dream, she is seated behind him, and they are facing away from each other. Her first association to the back-to-back seating arrangement was that it felt both "highly personal and impersonal." She stated further that the positioning of their bodies made it easier for her to attend to the "message" and "not the messenger." What we are coming to understand is that the anxieties associated with seeing and being seen interfere with her ability to listen.[25] Furthermore, it was only when she was relieved of the anxieties of looking at me—after we'd arranged the furniture during a therapy session so that she was facing away from me—that she could begin to look within. As she is

---

25 Another female patient taught me that, when speaking, a patient may paradoxically feel invisible. According to my patient, she compulsively engaged in lengthy monologues when feeling anxious or ashamed in order to create the illusion that she was hidden behind a wall of sound.

further realizing, when wishing to look in on her own thoughts and feelings, she sometimes merely looks at her behavior evaluatively. The difference between these modes of self-observation is as great as the distance traveled between saying, "I'm not dead" and, "I am alive."

TRAGEDY, PITY, AND ACTIVE MIRRORING

Psychotherapists are frequently called upon to help patients face and deal with the tragic aspects of living. My current caseload includes a mother who is grieving the death of a beloved infant daughter, a social worker who was sexually abused by her father, an impaired physician who sexually abused one of his patients, and a young musician who is dying from a rare and incurable heart disease. I take it as an a priori assumption that who I *am*, or what I am capable of experiencing, is as important as what I *do* in determining whether I will be able to help these patients move through the process of mourning. To illustrate this conviction, I offer the hypothesis that, to the extent that a therapist is threatened by experiencing "pity," his/her capacity to clarify or give meaning to suffering and misfortune will be curtailed. I doubt whether I would have come to this particular belief if Jenny hadn't put me in touch with my most vulnerable "selves." Unless I am deceiving myself, Jenny taught me something about how not to shrink away from problems that can neither be altered by doing nor avoided by not doing. Like inoperable deafness, some forms of psychopathology cannot be "cured." Their devastating consequences can, however, be mitigated if we can learn to manage and contain the painful feelings that they awaken.

Until I had to reckon with Jenny's deafness, I had little appreciation of what I didn't know about the emotional consequences of being caught up in a tragic situation. Prior to

Jenny's diagnosis, I had experienced, during my adulthood, only superficial levels of despair, disappointment, and terror. I paid lip service to the notion that "bad things happen to good people, for no good reason, all the time." But since that time, I have learned to live with the awful burden of unanswerable questions. The origins and causes of Jenny's deafness are not known. On occasion, I fill the vacuum with self-punitive/blaming fantasies about the unforeseen consequences of my actions. In my youth, I inhaled.

Seneca (quoted in Moffat, 1992) was right: "Great grief is dumb" (p. 21). In the weeks following Jenny's diagnosis, I was rendered mute by the intensity of my sorrow. I felt wordless in the face of my raw emotions. I felt like a helpless "victim." I felt condemned and abandoned by God. I fell prey to intense self-pity, and for the first time in my adulthood, I felt that people were making me, not only Jenny, the object of their pity.

As defined by dictionaries, the word "pity" literally means "to suffer with," as do its synonyms, "sympathy" and "compassion." Nevertheless, antipathy toward pity and self-pity are recurrent themes in our culture. The positive meanings once ascribed to pity are nowadays attributed only to sympathy and compassion. For example, the deaf poet David Wright (1969) has written that pity

> is a sentiment that deceives its bestower and disparages its recipient.... Its acceptance not only humiliates, but actually blunts the tools needed to best the disability. To accept pity means taking the first step towards self-pity, thence to the finding, and finally the manufacture, of excuses. The end-product of self-exculpation is the failed human being, the "victim" (p. 8).

Jenny helped me to reclaim the original, positive meaning of pity. My bias is that all human beings need both to pity and to be pitied throughout their lives. Wisdom, according to Jewish thought, is associated with an all-forgiving pity toward humanity and a wry sense of humor regarding human weaknesses. Jenny's disability forced me to recognize that we are all bound together by shared vulnerability. I feel a certain kind of solidarity with those whose suffering is caused by vice, depravity, and deficiencies of will. To die alone is, in a sense, everybody's fate. As Coleridge (1977) put it, "Pity is best taught by fellowship in woe." In becoming the object of pity, I began to realize that one can feel pity toward someone who is not otherwise pitiful or pathetic. That others "felt sorry" for me did not undermine my sense of self-as-agent. Because I evoked pity in others, I took my own suffering more seriously. Sometimes my self-pity represented the first step toward empathizing with the enormity of my predicament. Nothing softens a man's sense of ironic detachment more than the felt inability to protect his handicapped child.

Although it is not the full explanation, I recognize a connection between these transformative experiences and my current interest in the technical problems and countertransference issues encountered in the psychotherapy of patients who are unable to receive, without conflict, their therapists' help or caring concern. I have begun to explore whether patients and therapists are capable of distinguishing between pity, sympathy, and compassion. My own emotional reactions to a patient's suffering or misfortunes usually include a complex blend of pity, sympathy, and compassion. Although conceptually and introspectively distinguishable, pity, sympathy, and compassion all seem to emerge from the same matrix of biophysiological states. I cannot detect a highly distinctive pattern of autonomic activity for each of these emotional states. On any particular occasion, they may be of equal strength or aggregate in various configurations. Pity tends to be salient when patients are in the grip of powers and forces they cannot control, and I am resonating with the magnitude of their misfortune rather than with their strengths, sensitivities, and resilience. Whether experienced singularly or in combination with sympathy and compassion, I have found that pity can facilitate my efforts to understand, empathically, a patient's suffering.

Responses to my inquiries about such experiences seem to indicate that most of my colleagues share the modern disdain for pity, and consequently, they are threatened when they recognize that they are experiencing pity toward a patient. My experiences as a psychotherapy supervisor have led me to conclude that therapists-in-training who hold a predominantly negative view of pity have particular difficulty empathizing with their patients' suffering, especially if they believe that the suffering was "caused" by the patients' own actions or is being used strategically to "manipulate" others.

I have also been trying to determine whether or not there are subtle "meta-messages" that enable recipients to determine whether the other is expressing pity, sympathy, or compassion. At present, I am moving toward the conclusion that all expressions of caring and concern, regardless of how they are intended, are potentially ambiguous with respect to the respective strength of these feeling states. Some patients' difficulties in receiving their therapists' empathy, I now believe, cannot be fully understood without taking into account that there are no unequivocal cues that distinguish the expression of pity, sympathy, and compassion. To the extent that a patient fails to make these distinctions, he/she may experience any expression of caring concern as disempowering, patronizing, stigmatizing, foreboding, limiting, demeaning, or belittling. In my experience, devoting attention to uncovering the meanings, functions, and consequences of this potent source of misunderstandings—for both patients and their therapists—may be the first step toward the establishment of a therapeutic alliance. Conversely, neglecting this task can give rise to therapeutic impasses or to the breaking off of treatment.

EPILOGUE

In this chapter, I have attempted to establish linkages between my experiences raising my daughter Jenny and my views about the barriers to contact and communication encountered in psychotherapy. While struggling to bring it to a natural conclusion, I recalled that psychoanalyses are rarely, if ever, "complete" (Freud, 1937) and that the termination of a particular therapy should not imply the cessation of the therapeutic process. I also paused, remembering the day I delivered an earlier version of the chapter.

On that occasion, Jenny and five of her deaf college friends were in the audience, as were Ruth and Liz. I had hired an interpreter who translated my lecture into American Sign Language. Love and work came together on that triumphant day. Since then, we have been humbled again by the emergence of the new and ever-changing tasks that are being dealt with by each of the members of our family. It is for this reason that I aspire to practice psychotherapy in a way that honors Kafka's (1961) overarching conclusion that "the decisive moment in human development is continuous" (p. 55).

Today Jenny works as a masters-level clinical social worker and co-parents her 13-year-old hearing, bilingual son Elliot with her partner Kay in their own home.

REFERENCES

Bowlby, J. (1973). *Attachment and Loss: Vol. 2. Separation: Anxiety and Anger*. New York, NY: Basic Books.

Coleridge, S.T. (1977). *Portable Coleridge*. New York, NY: Viking Press.

Dolnick, E. (1993). Deafness as culture. *Atlantic Monthly* 272:37–53.

Fenichel, O. (1953). *The Collected Papers of Otto Fenichel* (First Series). New York, NY: Norton.

Freud, S. (1912). Recommendations to physicians practicing psychoanalysis. *Standard Edition* 12:109–120.

———— (1937). Analysis terminable and interminable. *Standard Edition* 23:216–253.

Geller, J.D. (1978). The body, expressive movement, and physical contact in psychotherapy. In J.L. Singer & K.S. Pope (Eds.), *The Power of Human Imagination* (pp. 347–378). New York, NY: Plenum Press.

———— (1984). Moods, feelings, and the process of affect formation. In L. Temoshok, C. Van Dyke, & L.S. Zegans (Eds.), *Emotions in Health and Illness: Applications to Clinical Practice* (pp. 171–186). Orlando, FL: Grune & Stratton.

———— (1987). The process of psychotherapy: Separation and the complex interplay among empathy, insight, and internalization. In J. Bloom-Feshbach & S. Bloom-Feshbach (Eds.), *The Psychology of Separation and Loss: Perspectives on Development, Life Transitions, and Clinical Practice* (pp. 459–514). San Francisco, CA: Jossey-Bass.

———— (1992). *The Meanings and Uses of Misunderstandings in Psychotherapy*. Paper presented at the 24th annual meeting of the Society for Psychotherapy, Berkeley, CA.

———— (1994). The psychotherapist's experience of interest and boredom. *Psychotherapy* 31(1):3–16.

————— & Rhodes, R. (1993). A task analytic approach to studying the resolution of misunderstanding events in psychotherapy. Grant application: Fund for Psychoanalytic Research.

Geller, T. (1984). Thank you for Jenny. *Parents Magazine* 59:66–67.

Greenson, R.R. (1967). *The Technique and Practice of Psychoanalysis* (Vol. 1). New York, NY: International Universities Press.

Kafka, F. (1961). *Parables and Paradoxes*. New York, NY: Random House.

Kaiser, H. (1965). *Effective Psychotherapy: The Contributions of Helmuth Kaiser*. New York, NY: Free Press.

Keller, H. (1990). *The Story of My Life*. New York, NY: Bantam Books. (Original work published 1905.)

Kohut, H. (1971). *The Analysis of the Self*. New York, NY: International Universities Press.

Krystal, H. (1979). Alexithymia and psychotherapy. *American Journal of Psychotherapy* 33:17–31.

Lacan, J. (1966). *Écrits*. London, UK: Tavistock.

Levinson, D.J., Darrow, C.N., Klein, E.B., Levinson, M.H., & McKee, B. (1978). *The Seasons of a Man's Life*. New York, NY: Knopf.

Loewald, H.W. (1978). *Psychoanalysis and the History of the Individual*. New Haven, CT: Yale University Press.

Meadow, K.P. (1980). *Deafness and Child Development*. Berkeley, CA: University of California Press.

Moffat, M.J. (1992). *In the Midst of Winter: Selections from the Literature of Mourning*. New York, NY: Vintage Books.

Padden, C., & Humphries, T. (1988). *Deaf in America: Voices from a Culture*. Cambridge, MA: Harvard University Press.

Peterson, P. (1994). *Mother Father Deaf: Living Between Sound and Silence*. Cambridge, MA: Harvard University Press.

Piaget, J. (1965). *Moral Judgments of the Child.* New York, NY: Free Press.

Reich, W. (1949). *Character Analysis.* New York, NY: Orgone Institute Press.

Rennie, D.L. (1985, June). *Client Deference in the Psychotherapy Relationship.* Paper presented at the 16th annual meeting of the Society for Psychotherapy Research, Evanston, IL.

Rice, L.N., & Kerr, G.P. (1986). Measures of client and therapist vocal quality. In L.S. Greenberg & W.M. Pinsof (Eds.), *The Psychotherapeutic Process: A Research Handbook* (pp. 73–105). New York, NY: Guilford Press.

Rossner, J. (1983). *August.* New York, NY: Houghton Mifflin.

Sacks, O. (1989). *Seeing Voices: A Journey into the World of the Deaf.* Berkeley, CA: University of California Press.

Schafer, R. (1983). *The Analytic Attitude.* New York, NY: Basic Books.

Shapiro, D. (1965). *Neurotic Styles.* New York, NY: Basic Books.

Stern, D.B. (1983). Unformulated experience. *Contemporary Psychoanalysis* 10:71–99.

Stokoe, W.C. (1960). *Sign Language Structure: An Outline of the Visual Communication System of the American Deaf. Studies in Linguistics. Occasional Papers* (Vol. 8). Buffalo, NY: University of Buffalo Press.

Trilling, L. (1972). *Sincerity and Authenticity.* Cambridge, MA: Harvard University Press.

Woodward, J. (1972). Implications for sociolinguistic research among the deaf. *Sign Language Studies* 1:1–7.

Wright, D. (1969). *Deafness.* New York, NY: Stein & Day.

CHAPTER 8

What Does It Mean to Practice Psychotherapy Scientifically?

[J.D. Geller (1998). *Psychoanalysis and Psychotherapy* 15:187–215.]

ABSTRACT: This paper is concerned with the scientific status of psychoanalytic therapy. The first half focuses on the question, Have empirical investigations of the process and outcome of psychotherapy strengthened or weakened the claim that psychoanalytic psychotherapy is an applied clinical science? The second half presents an argument on behalf of the hypothesis that empirical research on the processes of internalization can advance our efforts to practice psychoanalytic psychotherapy scientifically. The paper concludes with a discussion of joint technical implications of the hypothesis that the processes of introjection and identification make their own independent contributions to the success or failure of psychotherapy and to the maintenance of therapeutic gains following termination.

Where does one draw the lines between the sciences and the arts, the sciences and the humanities, and the arts and the humanities? I am inclined to the view that there are no absolute distinctions among them and that these interrelated perspectives are all needed to comprehend and deal therapeutically with the human predicaments encountered daily by psychotherapists. This view provides the framework within which I shall pose two questions: Does psychoanalytic psychotherapy have a legitimate claim to being called an applied clinical science? And can empirical research on the processes encompassed by the concept of internalization advance our efforts to practice psychoanalytic psychotherapy significantly? In tandem, we'll consider the technical and educational implications of practicing a psychotherapy in which insight and the processes of internalization are accorded equal status as agents of change. It is a central tenet of this paper that these issues must be approached historically and that the evolution of psychotherapy as a scientifically based enterprise is intimately linked to the fact that the profession of psychotherapy originated within the entrepreneurial context of the solo private practice of medicine.

A HISTORICAL PERSPECTIVE

Psychotherapeutic endeavors of one kind or another have been continuously practiced since ancient times. Every culture requires "experts" to perform psychotherapeutic functions. I believe the publication of Breuer and Freud's "The psychotherapy of hysteria" in *Studies on Hysteria* (1895) ushered in the modern era of psychotherapy in two interrelated ways. First, their novel approach to the treatment of neuroses was based on the knowledge revealed to them by the application of the scientific methods that were becoming available at the end of the 19th century. Prior modes of healing had been formulated primarily within the context of all-encompassing mythological, religious, and philosophical frameworks. Second, Freud and Breuer laid down the foundations for a new profession (which in time became the cornerstone of an industry dictated to by merchants and corporate executives).

Freud went on to successively extend and revise his theory and therapeutic practices on the basis of the phenomena brought to light by his clinical observations and introspective analyses of himself, his individual cases, and the cases brought to him by his colleagues. His revolutionary studies brought into existence, simultaneously, a general psychology, an investigative tool, and a therapeutic method. As Shevrin (1995) put it, Freud's initiatory creations included a "basic science of mind" and an "applied clinical science." Although both bear the name "psychoanalysis," they are by no means identical. For example, while the goals of treatment follow directly from the psychoanalytic theory of mind, the intervention strategies required to realize these goals do not. The task of delineating how these changes can or should be brought about is assigned to the psychoanalytic theory of technique. Contrary to expectations, advances in psychoanalytic theories of mental functioning and change have not consistently led to corresponding technical innovations or to the development of more specific guidelines for the implementation of the intervention strategies that characterize traditional psychoanalytic technique. I shall return to this issue when discussing the technical implications of recent efforts to assign increased prominence to internalization-based models of psychoanalytic psychotherapy.

Opinions as to whether or not psychoanalysis is a basic science, in its own right, have always varied. I shall not grapple with this thorny question in this paper. My conceit here is with seeking answers to two questions: Does psychoanalytic psychotherapy, as it is currently practiced, have a legitimate claim to being called an applied clinical science? And can empirical research on the processes encompassed by the concept of internalization advance our efforts to practice psychoanalytic therapy scientifically? This task is complicated by the fact that there is no universally accepted definition of what constitutes an applied science. I take the position that, in order to qualify as an applied clinical science, an approach to psychotherapy must satisfy the following fundamental requirements. First of all, insofar as it is an applied science, it will provide its practitioners with a set of guidelines and techniques that are based on a body of knowledge and theoretically driven beliefs that are capable, at least in principle, of being empirically confirmed or refuted. Meeting this requirement entails a commitment to establishing standards of excellence for therapeutic work that draw on the findings provided by basic research on psychopathology, psychotherapy outcome research, and studies of the nature and impact of therapist-patient interactions, what is known as psychotherapy process research. Second, in order to qualify as an applied science, the profession of psychotherapy must be committed to training practitioners who are armed with this cumulative knowledge base, who can implement therapeutic techniques in a competent and autonomous manner, and who recognize the limits of applicability of these techniques.

A fundamental scientific tenet is that the search for "truths" can only proceed in minds that aspire to be independent and objective. To this end, psychotherapists need to be trained to recognize those times when their personal problems are interfering with their objectivity or with their professional effectiveness. The well-educated psychotherapist engages in disciplined self-examination in order to fulfill ethical as well as scientific obligations. He or she appreciates that listening therapeutically presumes the ability to transcend or temporarily set aside one's own prejudices and values. I believe that in order to practice psychotherapy scientifically, therapists must also be able to verbalize their theory-driven expectations regarding what will occur during the course of therapy and articulate the hypotheses that shape what they hear, see, and feel during therapy sessions. In other words, the applied scientist at work is able to give solid reasons for his actions while remaining sensitive to the potential obscuring effect on listening of his or her theory-based interpretive biases.

With this goal in mind, I ask my psychotherapy supervisees to organize their clinical thinking and presentations in terms of the following questions: What did you attempt to accomplish during this therapy session? What factors entered into your decision to arrive at these particular goals (e.g., patient characteristics, theoretical considerations, phase of therapy)? What techniques or clinical strategies did you call upon to realize these treatment goals? What relationships exist between the treatment goals you pursued and the patient's life goals? In my work I seek to establish linkages between treatment goals and life goals. The former include such things as promoting insight or strengthening the therapeutic alliance. The latter refer to such things as achieving symptomatic relief, completing the work of mourning, or improving occupational functioning. For example, increasing a patient's ability to recognize, tolerate, and deal openly with his or her reactions to lapses of understanding on the part of therapists who are usually perceived as understanding is a treatment goal that contributes to the achievement of an invaluable life goal, that is, the capacity to constructively accept the flaws, limitations, and contradictions inherent to all intimate and task-oriented relationships (Geller, 1992, 1996).

Before examining the extent to which psychoanalytic psychotherapy is practiced in accord with the principles outlined above, let me weave in two important distinctions. It is important not to confuse the psychoanalytic method of investigation and psychoanalytic treatment. Whereas Freud attempted to rule out suggestion, persuasion, love, attachment, and the personality of the psychoanalyst as biases to the findings generated by psychoanalytic investigations, he took it as a matter of course that these forces would unavoidably and powerfully influence the outcome of psychoanalytic treatment (Friedman, 1978).

Grounding one's therapeutic techniques in the sciences does not obligate a therapist to adopt as his or her major reference role with patients that of "scientist." In my own opinion, it is both appropriate and commendable to draw on other role models besides that of scientist when conceptualizing one's posture or basic attitude vis-à-vis patients. In the practice of science, everything is subservient to the rigors of finding out what is true with respect to facts and their interrelations. Practicing scientists have the license to pursue their interest in acquiring knowledge single-mindedly. By way of contrast, the competent practice of psychotherapy requires citations of conflicts among three conceptually distinguishable forms of taking and showing interest in patients. These are curiosity, caring concern, and a commitment to participating responsively in a relationship (Geller, 1994).

Freud wrote: "We serve the patient in various functions, as an authority and a substitute for his parents, as a teacher and educator..." (1940, p. 181). I would add the following qualification: Successful therapeutic outcomes depend upon a patient's prevailing capacity to perceive the therapist as genuinely possessing the qualities of a "good enough" parent, mentor, teacher, or leader rather than upon the artificial or manipulative adoption of these roles.

THE SCIENTIFIC STATUS OF PSYCHOTHERAPY

For complicated economic, political, and sociocultural reasons, contemporary psychotherapists are under increasing pressure to demonstrate that their practices are grounded in the sciences. Whether or not a particular therapy is judged to be scientifically based depends, in large part, on the methods that have been used to obtain evidence that it "works."[26] What is considered to be scientific evidence is indissolubly linked with what is considered to be a scientific method.

In the psychoanalytic literature, clinical observations, introspection, and case reports of several "successful" therapies have been the methods most heavily relied upon to secure and present evidence on behalf of the beneficial effects of psychoanalytic therapy (Spence, 1982). These research tools are currently regarded, on methodological grounds, as inadequate vehicles for answering, scientifically, the question, Does psychotherapy work? (Fonagy & Moran, 1993).

One of the defining features of scientific methodologies is that they are devoted to acquiring knowledge that is publicly confirmable. As they have been traditionally written, case histories do not satisfy this requirement. The "story schemas" (Mandler, 1983) that organize the typical case study include only the highlights of clinical encounters. Only their authors have access to all the "facts." Consequently, case reports do not lend themselves to replication and cross-validation by individuals other than their originators.

In the traditionally written case report, therapists attribute patients' positive outcomes to the effects of their own clinical work without taking into consideration a host of possible confounding variables as a means of ruling out rival plausible explanations. Consequently, it is not possible to infer "causal agency" on the basis of the data and findings included in case reports. And, as Edelson (1988) has reminded us, the prevailing view among philosophers of science is that "enumerative inductionism" (i.e.,

---

26 Proving scientifically that psychotherapy "works" doesn't necessarily mean that psychotherapy itself is a scientific enterprise. Prayer, which is based on faith rather than science, has also been shown to be an important factor in both the prevention and treatment of disease (Levin, 1990).

offering a list of positive instances) does not suffice as a criterion of proof.

No matter how penetrating the insights presented in case reports may be, they can only suggest, rather than prove, scientific hypotheses. A belief qualifies as a scientific hypothesis to the extent that directly testable statements (e.g., predictions, postdictions) can be derived from it, whether or not it has yet to be confirmed. By way of contrast, scientific knowledge or "truths" refer to those conclusions and propositions that are regarded as at least reasonably well confirmed by a community of scholars working at a given time.

Contemporary psychotherapy researchers take it as axiomatic that therapy outcomes vary as a function of complex interactions between a fluctuating matrix of the variables that inhere in patients, therapists, and the therapeutic situation. Beutler (1990) has estimated that there are nearly 1½ million potential combinations of these determinants. Consequently, psychotherapy research alone can at best provide us with incomplete knowledge about the therapeutic action of psychotherapy. We must content ourselves with holding what we regard as scientific knowledge about psychotherapy as tentatively as we hold our scientific hypotheses. In acknowledgment of the importance of adopting this stance, Boswell (1980) begins his book on our changing beliefs about homosexuality by quoting the Belgian educator Pirenne:

All those whose lives are spent searching for truth are well aware that the glimpses they catch of it are necessarily fleeting, glittering for an instant only to make way for new and still more dazzling insights. The scholar's work, in marked contrast to that of the artist, is inevitably provisional. He knows this and rejoices in it, for the rapid obsolescence of his books is the very proof of the progress of scholarship (p. 3; Boswell cites Gérardy [1962] for the Pirenne quote).

Having set the stage, let us next consider whether the scientific status of psychoanalytic psychotherapy has been strengthened or weakened by the investigations conducted by psychotherapy outcome and process researchers.

PSYCHOTHERAPY RESEARCH

An essential belief of the 20th century is that experimentation is the preeminent method of securing scientific knowledge. Conducting an experiment essentially involves "the manipulation of variables and the systematic observation of their effects on other variables" (Campbell & Stanley, 1963, p. 1). The distinctive power of experiments, particularly those that include contrasts (i.e., controls), rests on their ability to detect whether there is a causal relationship between a therapeutic intervention and the changes observed in outcome criteria. Successive generations of psychotherapy outcome researchers have developed increasingly rigorous experimental and quantitative techniques, including meta-analyses (Smith & Glass, 1977), to evaluate the comparative effectiveness of different approaches to therapy. Whereas early researchers asked whether psychotherapy was effective in relieving suffering and in producing personality change, over time more precisely formulated questions took center stage, such as which specific therapy interventions are more effective in dealing with various target symptoms, for example, phobias, depression, lack of assertiveness, and anxiety (Lambert & Bergin, 1994; Lambert & Hill, 1994).

This shift stimulated the development of operationalized measures of specific disorders, and, during the 1980s, culminated in the view, largely held by academic clinicians and especially by behavior therapists, that the evidence provided by "randomized clinical trials" represented the best or only method of settling disputes regarding rival theories and therapeutic practices (Seligman, 1995). This type of investigative method originated in drug studies (Elkin et al., 1985). Its major features are as follows: First, patients are selected according to highly specific inclusion-exclusion criteria. In the ideal randomized clinical trial, only those patients who meet criteria for a single disorder, preferably a specific DSM-IV Axis I diagnosis (APA, 1994), are included, and patients with multiple problems are excluded. Second, randomization procedures are used to ensure the pretreatment comparability of both the treatment and control groups. This strategy is intended to increase one's confidence that the "cause" of any observed differences in outcome criteria are due to the treatment conditions. In the most rigorously conducted studies, efforts will also be made to control for the influence of so-called nonspecific variables, such as rapport and expectancy of gain. In order to further increase internal validity, treatment conditions, including the duration of treatment, are clearly specified in highly detailed treatment manuals (Wilson, 1996). These manuals are used to train study therapists, whose adherence to the manual is closely monitored by taping sessions; wayward implementers are asked to correct their ways.

Long-term psychoanalytic psychotherapy has not proven its efficacy under such rigorously controlled experimental conditions. It is, moreover, unlikely that it ever will be empirically validated by controlled comparisons of its beneficial effects with those of other therapies. As it is practiced in most settings, psychoanalytic therapy does not lend itself to verification by studies in which patients are randomized into manualized, fixed-duration treatments or into control groups. For example, generally speaking, patients choose therapists because they are known to be psychoanalytically oriented. They stay in treatment for varying lengths of time, and the problems that brought them to treatment are often characterological in nature rather than specifically symptomatic. Moreover, for several reasons, psychoanalytic therapy can be "manualized" only to a limited extent.[27] To begin with, the moment-to-moment conduct of psychoanalytic therapy is based on an array of methodological principles (e.g., abstinence, neutrality) rather than on specific rules of procedure. Moreover, psychoanalytic recommendations regarding the implementation of these basic operating principles are far from standardized. Following the introduction of the structural model, the analysis of patients' transferences and resistances became the premier methods of psychoanalytic therapy. There is currently no unanimously agreed-upon "best" approach to eliciting phenomena. Neither is there a generally accepted approach to dream interpretation, the introduction of supportive techniques, therapist self-disclosure, and other basic components of psychoanalytic technique. In short, psychoanalytic therapy is a "low-technology" enterprise, the practice of which requires improvisational skills and refined sensitivities.

In the end, if the professional practice of psychotherapy is to survive, it has to be, above all, financially viable (Cummings, 1995). Based on the assumption that it is justifiable to define as scientific only those modalities that have been tested and sufficiently confirmed on the basis of randomized clinical trials,

---

27 Treatment manuals are essential for defining each form of therapy so that controlled comparisons of its benefits with those of other therapies can be conducted. General manuals for dynamic psychotherapies have been written by Luborsky (1984) and by Strupp and Binder (1984). A specific manual for borderline patients has been produced by Kernberg and Clarkin (1993), and an adaptation of Luborsky's general manual for supportive-expressive psychotherapy has been written for depression (Luborsky & Mark, 1991). Moreover, operational measures are being developed for guiding clinical judgments and the use of transference-related concepts. Effective efforts in this direction include Luborsky's method for identifying core conflictual relationship themes (Luborsky & Crits-Christoph, 1990) and Horowitz et al.'s (1989) consensual response formulation method.

businesspeople are making policy decisions that are unfavorable to practitioners of long-term psychoanalytically informed psychotherapy.[28] However, a swelling chorus of scholars is beginning to call this assumption and its restrictive implications into question (e.g., Stiles et al., 1986; Howard et al., 1994; Lambert & Bergin, 1994). Their opposition is based on a growing recognition that the conclusions drawn from randomized clinical trials may lack "generalizability" to other patients, therapists, and settings because they omit many crucial elements of treatment as it is actually practiced in the "field." Furthermore, even those who advocate the use of randomized clinical trials to determine whether one treatment is better than another for a given disorder are calling for a reevaluation of the evidence provided by "effectiveness studies." Seligman (1995) proposes using this term to distinguish systematic empirical studies of whether or not a particular therapy works in actual practice or for a particular patient from experimental studies.

The findings generated by this body of literature indicate that psychotherapy, by a generic process, is effective (Smith et al., 1980; Lambert & Hill, 1994). Virtually hundreds of studies and subsequent meta-analyses have demonstrated that people who undergo psychotherapy of one form or another benefit from it. Most recently, *Consumer Reports* (1995) published a pioneering, large-scale survey of people who chose to go into a particular form of therapy for their problems. Among other things, the data indicated that not only did patients benefit "very substantially"

---

28 Interprofessional conflicts and profit-seeking motives have repeatedly complicated psychoanalytic psychotherapy's evolution as a scientifically based enterprise. For example, although Freud (1926) clearly asserted that psychoanalysis "is a part of psychology" and "is not a medical specialty," the New York State Legislature passed a bill in 1926 declaring illegal any analysis conducted by a non-M.D. The American Psychoanalytic Association did not decide to give up this restrictive policy on the basis of scientific considerations. Lawsuits sponsored by clinical psychologists in the 1980s were required to extend the practice of psychoanalysis to appropriately trained non-M.D.s.

from psychotherapy, but patients in long-term therapy did better than patients in short-term therapy, and patients whose length of treatment or choice of therapist was limited by insurance or managed care did worse.

Another conclusion shared by the cadre of scholars who have reviewed the experimental and correlational literatures is that the outcomes of purportedly distinct, that is, technically diverse, therapies with clinical populations are generally equivalent. For example, the research findings have not consistently pointed to the superiority of cognitive-behavioral therapy over interpersonal therapy in the treatment of unipolar depressive disorders (Frank & Spanier, 1995; VandenBos, 1996).

Such findings are having a double-edged influence on the field of psychotherapy. On the one hand, they are stimulating a reordering of research priorities. Instead of investigating treatments at the level of global effectiveness, researchers are turning their attention to the impact of subunits of therapy, such as sessions, events within sessions, and specific interventions. To realize these goals, new research paradigms, including replicable single-subject experiments (Hilliard, 1993) as well as more sophisticated process measures, are being developed to study the helpful and hindering consequences of various techniques (Orlinsky & Geller, 1993). These advances are permitting researchers to engage in increasingly fine-grained analyses of moment-to-moment interactions between patients and therapists. If future research proceeds in this direction, it will become increasingly relevant to those who practice psychoanalytic psychotherapy and consequently will narrow the gap that has traditionally separated psychotherapy researchers and psychoanalytic practitioners. My belief is that as process research becomes more rigorous and precise it will increasingly provide a scientific basis for the practice of psychoanalytic psychotherapy.

NONSPECIFIC AGENTS OF CHANGE

The phenomenon of approximately equal-outcome effects for different approaches to psychotherapy, despite marked differences in their assumptions and emphases, is also reinforcing a growing dissatisfaction with single-school approaches to psychotherapy. There appears to be increasing interest in isolating the "generic" or "nonspecific" agents of change that may be operative in all forms of therapy (Strupp & Hadley, 1979; Orlinsky & Howard, 1986). An early sign of this shift is the transtheoretical importance now assigned to the "therapeutic alliance" (Bordin, 1979). The most robust finding to emerge during the last decade of establishing and maintaining a "therapeutic alliance" makes a positive contribution to the success of both short- and long-term psychotherapies (Lambert & Bergin, 1994). As measured in different ways, with varying types of patients and in different forms of therapy, the quality of the therapeutic alliance has consistently emerged as a powerful predictor of outcomes (Horvath & Symonds, 1991).

Empirical recognition of the transtheoretical importance of the therapeutic alliance opens up the possibility of establishing conceptual and technical bridges between rival approaches to therapy. The therapeutic alliance represents a common ground for discussion between psychoanalytic, cognitive, interpersonal, and existential therapists. Psychoanalysis introduced the notion of the therapeutic alliance into the literature. In essence, the therapeutic alliance coincides with what Freud (1913) called "rapport." However, the cumulative progress that psychoanalytic theorists have made in understanding the effective management of the therapeutic alliance remains largely unknown to members of other schools of therapy.

For the most part, the psychoanalytic edifice of knowledge has developed in parallel with that of other relevant "discourse communities" (Bizzell, 1986). I believe the wish to stand alone, on the basis of its own vocabulary and scholarship, has contributed to the marginalization of psychoanalytic therapy in the therapeutic marketplace. Outsiders do not know that the psychoanalytic literature is rich in hypotheses regarding those technical problems presented by difficult and fragile patients that cannot be solved purely on empirical grounds. Nor is it widely appreciated that psychoanalytic therapists no longer view themselves as "blank screens" upon which patients project endogenously generated sexual and aggressive impulses and fantasies. More so than ever before, psychoanalytic theories of technique are taking into consideration the interpersonal (Levenson, 1991) and intersubjective (Stolorow et al., 1983) aspects of the relationships that therapists establish with their patients. Concomitantly, most nonanalytically trained therapists and researchers seem not to know that psychoanalytic therapists have shown a growing receptivity to assigning therapeutic value to mechanisms of change other than the promotion and working through of insights. A growing number of contemporary therapists influenced by psychoanalytic object relations theory, attachment theory, and self psychology and by Piaget's cognitive developmental psychology are more systematically studying a paradigm of psychotherapy in which insight plays a role secondary to the complex interplay between empathy and the internalization of patient-therapist relations (e.g., Loewald, 1960, 1962; Dorpat, 1974; Geller, 1984, 1987; Pine, 1985; Behrends & Blatt, 1985; Kantrowitz et al., 1990; Quintana & Meara, 1990; Geller & Farber, 1993).[29]

---

29 Although basic agreement as to terminology has yet to be achieved, internalization is generally conceptualized as encompassing all those processes whereby individuals transform real or imagined regulatory interactions with their environments, and real or imagined characteristics of their environment into their own self-generated functions and characteristics (Schafer, 1968; Meissner, 1981).

At the center of this enlarged view is the hypothesis that patients are likely to benefit from therapy and preserve these gains following termination to the extent that they construct, sustain, use, and identify with benignly influential internalized representations of the functional aspects and qualities of the therapeutic relationship. In 1981, my colleagues and I initiated a research project that is devoted to testing, empirically, this and related hypotheses. Following a brief overview of our evolving theoretical perspective, I will summarize our major findings and then discuss their technical and educational implications.

INTERNALIZATION–BASED MODELS OF PSYCHOTHERAPY

For clinical as well as research purposes, we align ourselves with those theorists who have adopted a two-stage model of the processes of internalization (Kohut, 1971; Atwood & Stolorow, 1980). Broadly stated, the first phase, hereafter referred to as "introjection," consists of the transformation of the emotional and motivational states experienced and actions taken within the context of particular naturally occurring social situations into mental models of what people are like and how relationships with them proceed. According to our hybrid theoretical perspective, introjection is a special instance of what Piaget (1954) refers to as "interiorization." It is that form of interiorization that gives rise to memory structures or inferred "schemas" (Orlinsky & Geller, 1993) that are interpersonal in content and dyadic in structure. When these schemas appear in awareness, they take the form of emotionally charged self-representations, representations of others, and representations of interactions with them. There is a growing consensus among psychoanalytic and cognitive investigators that mental representations of human interactions may be as varied in their complexity, emotional coloring, and functional significance as those relationships existing between actual persons (Baars, 1986; Singer & Salovey, 1991). Perhaps this is what is implied in Freud's (1921) statement:

> In the individual's mental life, someone else is invariably involved, as a model, as an object, as a helper, as an opponent, and so from the very first individual psychology, in this extended but entirely justifiable sense of the words, is at the same time social psychology as well (p. 69).

Following introjection, the second phase of the internalization process, hereafter referred to as identification, may or may not take place. Broadly stated, identification consists of the transformation of human qualities and functions that were originally experienced as "other" into possessions of the "self." As conceptualized here, to identify with another essentially involves the transformation of self-representations in the direction of increasing their felt resemblance to one or more mental representations of another person. While under the influence of the processes of identification, individuals come to represent as their *own* the characteristics that they earlier ascribed to representations of others (some of which owe their existence to the prior processes of introjection). Presumably, at the deepest levels of internalization, self-representations are rendered functionally equivalent to and substitute for representations of the self in relation to others.

Identification may be a deeper form of internalization than introjection and may promote self-reliance more so than introjection, but is it also a more mature form of internalization, as is generally assumed in the psychoanalytic literature? The received wisdom is that it is less mature to symbolically reconstruct the therapeutic dialogue for the purposes of engaging in self-reflection than it is to engage in autonomous self-analysis or reflection (Meissner, 1981). I discern in this essentially untested notion several biases or values that are implicit in psychoanalytic theory, for example, the belief that ideas rather than persons should be the ultimate authorities as well as an inordinately individualistic conception of human nature.

Another basic postulate of psychoanalytic theory is that introjection and identification are essentially unconscious processes, even when they are activated by conscious wishes to emulate the valued characteristics of others. But evidence from a variety of sources (Nisbett & Wilson, 1977) indicates that although they typically tend to operate outside of focal awareness, the mental models that populate an individual's "representational world" are to some extent phenomenologically knowable. Participation in psychotherapy, moreover, prepares individuals to narrow the gap between experience as it is experienced and experience as it is described or reported.

Our research strategy is based upon the assumption that once they have been established in long-term memory, representations of therapy-with-the-therapist can be expressed, more or less flexibly, in overt behavior, in the cognitive processes that underlie, precede, and accompany overt action, or in the form and content of evocative memories and action fantasies. Consequently, behavioral, self-report, and projective measures can all be used to study the processes and products of introjection as they manifest themselves in psychotherapy. We began our studies by constructing the Therapist Representation Inventory (TRI; Geller et al., 1981)—a network of self-report measures that systematically solicit quantifiable information about what current and former patients remember, think, fantasize, or dream about their therapist and therapy. How often? On what occasions? In what forms? With what feelings? And to what ends?

Repeated administrations of the TRI and related measures (Tarragona & Orlinsky, 1987, 1988) have strengthened our conviction that it is possible to obtain valid, reliable, and useful, as compared to academically interesting, information about whether and how the processes of introjection bring into existence representations of the patterns of listening and talking, seeing and being seen, feeling and being with, that recurrently characterize the communicative exchanges that occur during the course of therapy. Detailed presentations of our slowly accumulating findings are reported elsewhere (Orlinsky & Geller, 1993). For the present purposes, I will briefly summarize those findings that bear upon the hypothesis that the processes of introjection make their own independent contributions to the success or failure of psychotherapy and to the maintenance of therapeutic gains following termination.

Normative data from a variety of samples indicate that mental activities involving positively and negatively charged representations of the therapeutic relationship are a recurrent and often integral aspect of the subjective experiences of current and former patients. The phenomenological properties of these experiences vary widely. There is great variation in their ease of evocation, duration in awareness, vividness, sensory intensity, intelligibility, and communicability. When voluntarily or involuntarily brought to awareness, representations of therapy-with-the-absent-therapist tend to be composed, in varying proportions, of pictures, sounds, words, odors, body movements, and somatic sensations. Individual differences in this regard tend to be associated with the cognitive styles patients bring to therapy. Not surprisingly, visual, auditory, and lexical representations are the primary vehicles whereby patients replicate what it feels like to be in the physical presence of their therapists.

Regardless of the gender of their therapists, men and women, whether currently in therapy or former patients, are most likely to experience the felt presence of their absent therapists by visually imagining the therapist sitting in his or her office, by imagining the particular tonal qualities of the therapist's voice, or by recalling specific statements made by the therapist. Nevertheless, our findings indicate that representations that are kinesthetically felt, as distinguished from those that are experientially localized "in one's head," play a vital role in enabling some patients to remain "in touch" with their therapist's presence and to "sense" the emotional atmosphere that accompanies the experience of being empathically understood. Moreover, it appears that patients' modes of constructing representations of their unfolding therapy experiences do not become progressively more conceptual and less sensory in nature over the course of therapy.

With respect to the circumstances under which these representations appear in awareness, our findings indicate that patients are most likely to evoke them when experiencing painful emotions (e.g., anxiety, depression, guilt, loneliness), when feeling uncertain about the choices they are expected to make in ambiguous or conflictual situations, and when desiring their therapist's approval. In addition, patients use these representations, with varying degrees of awareness, to serve a wide variety of wish-fulfilling, defensive, reparative, and adaptive functions. In their benign forms, therapist representations are pleasure-giving, supportive, and clarifying, and they enhance adaptive functioning. In their problematic forms, they are experienced as threatening, disapproving, disappointing, malevolent, or persecutory. It is noteworthy that it is in the manifest content of their dreams about their therapists that patients are most likely to express the critical, confusing, and exploitative influences they experience as embodied in their representations of their therapists in relation to themselves (Rohde et al., 1992).

From the point of view of the outcome of psychotherapy, the most important findings to emerge from our studies are that self-perceived improvement among both current and former patients is positively and significantly correlated with the vividness of patient representations of the therapist and with the tendency to use these representations for the specific purpose of continuing the therapeutic dialogue in the privacy of consciousness (Rohde et al., 1992). What we are consistently finding is that among the variety of functions that mental representations may serve, it is in those instances in which representations are used to retain, rehearse, and accumulate the mutative "impact" of successive sessions that patients report that they are satisfied with their therapist and are benefiting from treatment. Finally, it is encouraging to note that benignly influential representations of the therapeutic relationship do not seem to dissipate over time. Indeed, long after termination, former patients who perceived their therapy to be successful report that they enter into imaginative dialogues with their therapists in order to engage in self-reflection and problem-solving activities similar to those learned in therapy (Wzontek et al., 1995). It is on the other hand plausible to hypothesize that the post-termination "fate" (Bergmann, 1988) of negatively charged representations of the therapeutic relationship would be a basis for "deterioration effects" (Strupp et al., 1977; Lambert & Bergin, 1994). In sum, for better or for worse, from the perspective of internalization, therapy may be in a very real sense "interminable."

DOING THE WORK OF PSYCHOTHERAPY

I think about the technical implications of our findings in terms of the tasks that therapists impose on themselves and their patients. Each form of therapy selectively emphasizes some tasks and ignores others. In order to liberate patients from the influence of past relationships on current behavior, insight-oriented therapists give priority to two interrelated sets of tasks. The first cluster includes such things as the search for meanings, the discovery of truths, the telling of stories, the recovering and placing of traumatic memories in a causal context, the construction of a personal past, and the translation of images into words. The second constellation of tasks take as their primary aim fostering those subjective experiences and states of relatedness that enable patients to collaboratively pursue these definable projects with their therapists. In other words, the second constellation encompasses all those tasks that are primarily relational in nature.

The initial task in any therapy is the creation of a "safe place" (Havens, 1989). Much of the work of the psychoanalytic therapist is devoted to promoting the development of a mutually trusting and respectful relationship. There is nearly universal agreement that it is impossible to derive therapeutic benefits from the performance of the first constellation of tasks in the absence of a durable and positive therapeutic alliance. It is concomitantly acknowledged that resistances to doing the work of exploratory psychotherapy stem not only from desires not to know one's conflict-laden desires and fears but also arise when patients do not feel safe with and valued by their therapists.

The progressive internalization of the therapeutic relationship can be conceptualized as a byproduct of the successful performance of the two sets of tasks described above. It is also possible to reconceptualize the therapeutic functions that they serve from the perspective of internalization-based models of the therapeutic action of psychotherapy. Taking this step brings into sharper focus the relationship-transforming functions of key components of analytic technique. For example, Kohut's (1971) therapeutic approach is premised on the assumption that, apart from any value they might have in furthering self-understanding, properly timed transference interpretations foster and augment the subjective experience of feeling empathically understood. According to Kohut, the experience of feeling empathically understood paves the way for the activation of the processes of internalization early in therapy, and during later stages, the repeated working through of optimal failures of empathy is required to harness the therapeutic potential of "transmuting internalizations." Kohut's working assumption is that internalizations are transmuting to the extent that they bring about structural changes in the self.

As an extension of these technical principles, I have argued elsewhere that empathically and developmentally informed inquiries into patients' problematic reactions to the spatial, temporal, and interpersonal boundaries that separate them from their therapists similarly enable them to derive benefit from the processes of internalization (Geller, 1987). Our empirical findings suggest that, in order to skillfully implement these techniques, therapists will need to be trained to be more attentive to the interaction between their patients' styles of processing sensory information and their own styles of listening and speaking.

The learning that takes place while under the influence of the processes of internalization is primarily sensory, as compared to conceptual, in nature. Such learning is, in other words, ultimately grounded in the physiological-biological "reality" of the senses of hearing, sight, bodily movement, touch, smell, and taste. In order to maximally benefit from the processes of internalization, patients must, therefore, be able to receive accurately the sensuous fullness of their therapists' verbal and nonverbal contributions to the therapeutic dialogue. There is now abundant evidence that the ways in which persons attend to the information that is available to their senses is influenced by self-maintaining "cognitive styles" that typically operate outside of conscious awareness (Baars, 1986). These broadly identifiable cognitive styles have been shown to bias and distort the acquisition of new information. Consequently, I attempt early in the therapy to determine whether or not a patient's attentional focus is exerting a restrictive influence on the variety and vividness of his or her sensory experiences. What I have been discovering is that "neurotic styles" (Shapiro, 1965) of processing sensory information play a role equal to or greater than transference paradigms in interfering with those forms of experiential learning that provide the raw materials to the processes of internalization. For this reason, I now more systematically employ intervention strategies that are meant to promote parity, or equity, between "sensuously receptive" and "actively rational" modes of allocating attention (Deikman, 1976). To illustrate: Without having the slightest conscious intention of doing so, obsessional patients overemphasize self-directed, deliberate, sharply focused modes of allocating attention. The sensory biases inherent to this style have an impoverishing effect on the mental models that obsessional patients create of the events and interactions that take place during therapy sessions. Alternatively stated, an obsessional cognitive style weakens a patient's ability to recognize that the therapist is a "new object." I therefore give cardinal importance to expanding and refining their access to more impressionistic, immediate, and softly focused modes of allocating attention. Dedication to this task goes a long way toward strengthening an obsessional patient's ability to recognize and remember those aspects of a therapist's style that convey genuine interest, caring concern, and a commitment to participating responsively in a relationship.

In parallel, each therapist has a habitual and typical style of using language, vocal qualities, facial expressions, gestures, postures, interaction rhythms, and so forth to express their thoughts and feelings. Its recurrent and predictable aspects are broadly shaped by that therapist's preferred theoretical orientation and by identifications with the conversational styles of valued therapists and supervisors (Geller & Schaffer, 1988). Psychoanalytic theories of technique derived from a concern with promoting insight encourage therapists to speak briefly and only at certain decisive moments. The prototypical psychoanalytic therapist tends to reduce to an indispensable minimum all forms of active verbal participation in the therapeutic dialogue. This minimalist stance is well illustrated by Mayman's advice (personal communication, 1987): "Never a paragraph when a sentence will do. Never a sentence when it could be a word. Never a word when it could be a gesture." By way of contrast, there are no generally accepted guidelines for specifying what stylistic choices are required to facilitate the creation of new benignly influential representations of the therapeutic relationship. Our findings are consistent with the hypothesis that the relatively invariant aspects of therapists' nonverbal styles of communicating are more likely to be stored in long-term memory and re-presented to awareness than are the specific comments he or she made on a particular occasion. This finding leaves me wondering whether it is "authentic" and therapeutically useful to consciously regulate one's nonverbal contributions to the therapeutic dialogue. Empirical clarification of this controversial question will benefit patients and therapists alike.

CONCLUSION

.Scientific investigations of patient-therapist relations have traditionally focused on what takes place when patients and therapists are in each other's presence. The research we have conducted underscores the feasibility and importance of also studying the ways in which patients interact with the felt presence of their therapists between sessions, during vacations, and after termination. Furthermore, the accumulating findings lend support to the hypothesis that there is clinical value in devoting increased attention to the interpersonal and experiential learning that takes place while patients and therapists are pursuing the definable projects that characterize particular approaches to therapy. I anticipate that this shift in focus will deepen our understanding of the therapeutic processes that are shared by all approaches to therapy and will consequently provide a comprehensive way of conceptualizing the phenomenon of approximately comparable outcome effects for different approaches to therapy. If such changes take place, I believe that therapists of all persuasions will also become more receptive to the view that there are many ways of practicing psychotherapy scientifically.

REFERENCES

American Psychiatric Association. (1994). *The Diagnostic and Statistical Manual of Mental Disorders* (4th ed.) (DSM-IV). Washington, DC: American Psychiatric Press.

Atwood, G., & Stolorow, R. (1980). Psychoanalytic concepts and the representational world. *Psychoanalysis and Contemporary Thought* 3:267–290.

Baars, B. (1986). *The Cognitive Revolution in Psychology*. New York, NY: Guilford Press.

Behrends, R.S., & Blatt, S.J. (1985). Internalization and psychological development throughout the life cycle. *The Psychoanalytic Study of the Child* 40:11–39.

Bergmann, M.S. (1988). On the fate of the intrapsychic image of the psychoanalyst after termination of the analysis. *The Psychoanalytic Study of the Child* 43:137–152.

Beutler, L. (1990). Methodology: What are the design issues involved in the defined research priorities? *National Institute on Drug Abuse Research Monograph* 104:105–118.

Bizzell, P. (1986). What happens when basic writers come to college? *Coll. Composit. & Commun.* 37:294–301.

Bordin, E.S. (1979). The generalizability of the psychoanalytic concept of the working alliance. *Psychotherapy: Theory, Research & Practice* 16:252–260.

Boswell, J. (1980). *Christianity, Social Tolerance and Homosexuality*. Chicago, IL: University of Chicago Press.

Breuer, J., & Freud, S. (1895). Studies on hysteria. *Standard Edition* 2.

Campbell, D.T., & Stanley, J.C. (1963). *Experimental and Quasi-Experimental Designs for Research*. Chicago, IL: Rand McNally.

Consumer Reports (1995, November). Mental health: Does therapy help?

Cummings, N.A. (1995). Impact of managed care on employment and training: A primer for survival. *Prof. Psychol: Res. & Prac.* 26:10–15.

Deikman, A.J. (1976). Bimodal consciousness. In R.E. Ornstein (Ed.), *The Nature of Human Consciousness*. New York, NY: Viking Press.

Dorpat, T.L. (1974). Internalization of the patient-analyst relationship in patients with narcissistic disorders. *J. Internat. Psycho-Analytic Association* 55:183–191.

Edelson, M. (1988). *Psychoanalysis: A Theory in Crisis*. Chicago, IL: University of Chicago Press.

Elkin, I., Parloff, M.B., Hadley, S.W., & Autry, J.H. (1985). NIMH Treatment of Depression Collaborative Research Program: Background and research plan. *Arch. Gen. Psychiatry* 42:305–316.

Fonagy, P., & Moran, G. (1993). Selecting single case research designs for clinicians. In N.E. Miller, J. Doherty, L. Luborsky, & J. Barber (Eds.), *Psychodynamic Treatment Research: A Handbook for Clinical Practice* (pp. 62–95). New York, NY: Basic Books.

Frank, E., & Spanier, C. (1995). Interpersonal psychotherapy for depression: Overview, clinical efficacy, and future directions. *Clin. Psychol. Sci. & Prac.* 2:349–369.

Freud, S. (1913). On beginning the treatment: Further recommendations on the technique of psycho-analysis. *Standard Edition* 12.

———— (1921). Group psychology and the analysis of the ego. *Standard Edition* 18:65–143.

———— (1926). The question of lay analysis. *Standard Edition* 20:177–250.

———— (1940). An outline of psycho-analysis. *Standard Edition* 23:139–208.

Friedman, L. (1978). Trends in the psychoanalytic theory of treatment. *Psychoanalytic Quarterly* 67:524–568.

Geller, J.D. (1984). Moods, feelings, and the process of affect formation. In L. Temoshok, C. Van Dyke, & L.S. Zegans (Eds.), *Emotions in Health and Illness: Applications to Clinical Practice* (pp. 171–186). Orlando, FL: Grune & Stratton.

———— (1987). The process of psychotherapy: Separation and the complex interplay among empathy, insight, and internalization. In J. Bloom-Feshbach & S. Bloom-Feshbach (Eds.), *The Psychology of Separation and Loss: Perspectives on Development, Life Transitions, and Clinical Practice* (pp. 459–514). San Francisco, CA: Jossey-Bass.

———— (1992). *The Meanings and Uses of Misunderstandings in Psychotherapy.* Paper presented at the 24th annual meeting of the Society for Psychotherapy, Berkeley, CA.

———— (1994). The psychotherapist's experience of interest and boredom. *Psychotherapy* 31(1):3–16.

———— (1996). Thank you for Jenny. In B. Gerson (Ed.), *The Therapist as a Person: Life Crises, Life Choices, Life Experiences, and Their Effects on Treatment* (pp. 119–139). New York, NY: Analytic Press.

————, Cooley, R.S., & Hartley, D. (1981). Images of the psychotherapist: A theoretical and methodological perspective. *Imagination, Cognition and Personality* 1(2):123–146.

———— & Farber, B.A. (1993). Factors influencing the process of internalization in psychotherapy. *Psychotherapy Research* 3(3):166–180. https://doi.org/10.1080/10503309312331333769

———— & Schaffer, C.E. (1988, June 23). *Internalization of the Supervisory Dialogue and the Development of Therapeutic Competence.* Paper presented at the 21st annual meeting of the Society for Psychotherapy Research, Santa Fe, NM.

.Gérardy, G. (1962). *Henri Pirenne, sa vie et son oeuvre.* Brussels: Ministère de l'Éducation Nationale et de la Culture.

Havens, L. (1989). *A Safe Place: Laying the Groundwork of Psychotherapy.* Cambridge, MA: Harvard University Press.

Hilliard, R.B. (1993). Single-case methodology in psychotherapy process and outcome research. *J. Consult. & Clin. Psychol.* 61:373–380.

Horowitz, L.M., Rosenberg, S., Ureno, G., Kalehzan, B., & O'Halloran, P. (1989). Psychodynamic formulation, consensual response method, and interpersonal problems. *J. Consult. & Clin. Psychol.* 57:599–606.

Horvath, A.O., & Symonds, B.D. (1991). Relation between working alliance and outcome in psychotherapy: A meta-analysis. *J. Counsel. Psychol.* 38:139–149.

Howard, K., Orlinsky, D., & Lueger, R. (1994). Clinically relevant outcome research in individual psychotherapy. *Brit. J. Psychiatry* 165:4–8.

Kantrowitz, J.L., Katz, A.L., & Paolitto, F. (1990). Followup of psychoanalysis five to ten years after termination: II. Development of the self-analytic function. *Journal of the American Psychoanalytic Association* 38:637–654.

Kernberg, O.F., & Clarkin, J.F. (1993). Developing a disorder-specific manual: The treatment of borderline character disorder. In N.E. Miller, J. Doherty, L. Luborsky, & J. Barber (Eds.), *Psychodynamic Treatment Research: A Handbook for Clinical Practice* (pp. 227–247). New York, NY: Basic Books.

Kohut, H. (1971). *The Analysis of the Self.* New York, NY: International Universities Press.

Lambert, M.J., & Bergin, A.E. (1994). The effectiveness of psychotherapy. In A.E. Bergin & S.L. Garfield (Eds.), *Handbook of Psychotherapy and Behavior Change: An Empirical Analysis* (4th ed., pp. 143–189). New York, NY: Wiley.

Lambert, M.J., & Hill, C.E. (1994). Assessing psychotherapy outcomes and process. In A.E. Bergin & S.L. Garfield (Eds.), *Handbook of Psychotherapy and Behavior Change: An Empirical Analysis* (4th ed., pp. 72–113). New York, NY: Wiley.

Levenson, E.A. (1991). *The Purloined Self: Interpersonal Perspectives in Psychoanalysis.* New York, NY: Contemporary Psychoanalytic Books.

Levin, J.S. (1990). Religion and health: Is there an association, is it valid, is it causal? *Social Science Medicine* 38:1475–1482.

Loewald, H.W. (1960). On the therapeutic action of psychoanalysis. *International Journal of Psychoanalysis* 41:1–18.

———— (1962). Internalization, separation, mourning, and the superego. *Psychoanalytic Quarterly* 31:483–504.

Luborsky, L. (1984). *Principles of Psychoanalytic Psychotherapy: A Manual for Supportive-Expressive Treatment.* New York, NY: Basic Books.

———— & Crits-Christoph, P. (1990). *Understanding Transference: The Core Conflictual Relationship Theme Method.* New York, NY: Basic Books.

———— & Mark, D. (1991). Short-term supportive-expressive psychoanalytic psychotherapy. In P. Crits-Christoph & J.P.

Barber (Eds.), *Handbook of Short-Term Dynamic Psychotherapy* (pp.110–136). New York, NY: Guilford Press.

Mandler, J. (1983). Representation. In P.H. Mussen (Ed.), *Handbook of Child Psychology* (Vol. 3, 4th ed.). New York, NY: Wiley.

Meissner, W.W. (1981). *Internalization in Psychoanalysis*. New York, NY: International Universities Press.

Nisbett, R.E., & Wilson, T.D. (1977). Telling more than we can know: Verbal reports on mental processes. *Psychology Rev.* 84:231–259.

Orlinsky, D.E., & Geller, J.D. (1993). Psychotherapy's internal theater of operation: Patients' representations of their therapists and therapy as a new focus of research. In N.E. Miller, J. Doherty, L. Luborsky, & J. Barber (Eds.), *Psychodynamic Treatment Research: A Handbook for Clinical Practice* (pp. 423–466). New York, NY: Basic Books.

———— & Howard, K.I. (1986). The relation of process to outcome in psychotherapy. In A.E. Bergin & S.L. Garfield (Eds.), *Handbook of Psychotherapy and Behavior Change: An Empirical Analysis* (3rd ed.). New York, NY: Wiley.

Piaget, J. (1954). *The Construction of Reality in the Child*. New York, NY: Basic Books.

Pine, F. (1985). *Developmental Theory and Clinical Process*. New Haven, CT: Yale University Press.

Quintana, S.M., & Meara, N.M. (1990). Internalization of therapeutic relationships in short-term therapy. *J. Counsel. Psychol.* 37:123–130.

Rohde, A.B., Geller, J.D., & Farber, B.A. (1992). Dreams about the therapist: Mood, interactions, and themes. *Psychotherapy: Theory, Research, Practice, Training* 29:536–544.

Schafer, R. (1968). *Aspects of Internalization*. New York, NY: International Universities Press.

Seligman, M.E.P. (1995). The effectiveness of psychotherapy: The Consumer Reports study. *Amer. Psychologist* 50:965–974.

Shapiro, D. (1965). *Neurotic Styles*. New York, NY: Basic Books.

Shevrin, H. (1995). Psychoanalysis as science. *Journal of the American Psychoanalytic Association* 43:963–986.

Singer, J.L., & Salovey, P. (1991). Organized knowledge structures and personality: Person schemas, self schemas, prototypes, and scripts. In M. Horowitz (Ed.), *Person Schemas and Maladaptive Interpersonal Patterns* (pp. 33–79). Chicago, IL: University of Chicago Press.

Smith, M.L., & Glass, G.V. (1977). Meta-analysis of psychotherapy outcome studies. *Amer. Psychologist* 32:752–760.

———, ———, & Miller, T.I. (1980). *The Benefits of Psychotherapy*. Baltimore, MD: Johns Hopkins University Press.

Spence, D.P. (1982). *Narrative Truth and Historical Truth: Meaning and Interpretation in Psychoanalysis*. New York, NY: Norton.

Stiles, W.B., Shapiro, D.A., & Elliott, R. (1986). Are all psychotherapies equivalent? *American Psychologist, 41*(2):165–180.

Stolorow, R.D., Brandchaft, B., & Atwood, G.E. (1983). Intersubjectivity in psychoanalytic treatment: With special reference to archaic states. *Bulletin of the Menninger Clinic* 47(2):117–128.

Strupp, H., & Binder, J.L. (1984). *Psychotherapy in a New Key: A Guide to Time-Limited Dynamic Psychotherapy*. New York, NY: Basic Books.

——— & Hadley, S.W. (1979). Specific vs nonspecific factors in psychotherapy: A controlled study of outcome. *Archives of General Psychiatry* 36(10):1125–1136.

———, ———, & Gomes-Schwartz, B. (1977). *Psychotherapy for Better or Worse: The Problem of Negative Efffects*. New York, NY: Jason Aronson.

Tarragona, M., & Orlinsky, D.E. (1987). *Patients' Experiences of Therapy Between Sessions*. Paper presented at the 18th annual meeting of the Society for Psychotherapy Research, Ulm, F.R.G.

———— & ———— (1988). *During and Beyond the Therapeutic Hour: An Exploration of the Relationship Between Patients' Experiences of Therapy Within and Between Sessions*. Paper presented at the 19th annual meeting of the Society for Psychotherapy Research, Santa Fe, N.M.

VandenBos, G.R. (1996). Outcome assessment of psychotherapy. *American Psychologist 51*(10):1005–1006.

Wilson, G.T. (1996). Manual-based treatments: The clinical application of research findings. *Behaviour Research and Therapy 34*(4):295–314.

Wzontek, N., Geller, J.D., & Farber, B.A. (1995). Patients' post-termination representations of their psychotherapists. *Journal of the American Academy of Psychoanalysis 23*:395–410.

CHAPTER 9

Self-Disclosure in Truth-Telling Talk Therapies

[J.D. Geller (2003). Self-disclosure in psychoanalytic-existential therapy. *Journal of Clinical Psychology* 59(5):541–554.]

ABSTRACT: This article is an effort to integrate contemporary psychoanalytic and existential perspectives on intentional therapist self-disclosure. It offers a two-stage decision-making model that considers self-disclosure from the vantage points of style and internalization. Clinical and research findings are presented to support the notion that the meanings a patient attributes to a particular self-disclosure and its power to move him or her toward greater health are the product of a fluctuating matrix of interpersonal and intrapsychic variables. Special consideration is given to the challenges that arise during the early and termination stages of treatment and to the psychotherapy of therapists.

> *I like two types of conversations—*
> *gossip and real talk.*
> *—Jimmy Cannon*

In this article, I will present interrelated ideas that I have been using to think about the following questions: When is it therapeutically beneficial to choose self-disclosure as the means of performing particular psychological functions on a patient's behalf? What stylistic choices are required to individualize, as far as possible, the content of my communications? Are there occasions when revealing personal information can accomplish therapeutic aims that may not be possible otherwise?

I begin by embedding my views within a historical context. Then I will introduce a two-stage decision-making framework that distinguishes between the mental activities that enter into the decision to pursue certain therapeutic goals and the mental activities that enter into the choice of self-disclosure, rather than another verbal response, to try bringing about these goals. A central assumption is that a full understanding of therapist self-disclosure cannot be achieved by isolating that interaction outside the sequence of interactions when patients speak and therapists listen. The remaining sections of the article offer a sampling of the contextual factors that impact on my choices about when, what, and how to say something personal about myself to a patient. In the spirit of integration, I rely on clinical observations, clinical vignettes, and research findings to argue that the meanings a patient attributes to a particular self-disclosure and its power to move him or her toward health are the product of a fluctuating matrix of intrapsychic and interpersonal variables.

AN EVOLVING PERSPECTIVE ON THERAPIST SELF-DISCLOSURE

This article grows out of my ongoing efforts to reconcile existential-humanistic and contemporary psychoanalytic perspectives on the tasks and division of labor required to realize the goals of long-term expressive-exploratory psychotherapy (Geller, 1974, 1984, 1987, 1996, 1998).

A historical overview of the literature reveals an ongoing struggle on the part of successive generations of psychoanalytically informed therapists to grapple with Freud's (1912) prophetic mandate on therapist opacity—"The analyst should remain opaque to his patients, like a mirror and show them nothing but what is shown to him" (p. 118)—and his warning against too much intimacy on the part of the analyst. Freud's own writings about technique are at best skeletal in terms of what they have to say about therapist self-disclosure. Moreover, by his own admission, Freud's technical recommendations were essentially negative. In a letter to Sandor Ferenczi, who was at the time experimenting with "mutual analyses," Freud wrote:

> I thought it most important to stress what one should not do, to point out the temptations that run counter to analysis. Almost everything one should do in a positive sense I left to tact. What I achieved thereby was that the obedient submitted to those admonitions as if they were taboos and did not notice their elasticity. This would have to be revised someday but without setting aside the obligations (as cited in Grubricht-Simitis, 1986, p. 270).

I began my psychotherapy training in the late 1950s. During that era, therapists tended to read Freud's "recommendations" as obligating them to verbally disclose as little personal information as possible and to limit their expressivity as far as possible. My earliest readings focused on the dangers and pitfalls of revealing personal information to patients. Like many contemporary psychoanalytic therapists (e.g., Davies, 1994; Renik, 1995), I have gradually and cautiously liberated myself from the view that I ought to present myself as a blank screen upon which patients project their sexual and aggressive impulses and fantasies. Classical interpretations of such notions as abstinence, neutrality, and analytic anonymity no longer play a starring role in determining what I do and do not reveal about myself to psychotherapy patients.

My basic stance is primarily shaped by concepts such as reciprocity, mutuality, responsiveness, and symmetry and by a concern with the intersubjective aspects of the therapeutic relationship (Aron, 1996). Advocacy of these relational principles is congruent with a commitment to a therapeutic stance marked by authenticity, transparency, realness, and egalitarianism. These are the standards against which my existential teachers encouraged me to judge the quality of my work (Yalom, 1980).

Identifying myself with these principles has exerted two influences on my inclination to self-disclose: first, my inclination to use intentional self-disclosure as a therapeutic technique, and second, my nonlinguistic contributions to the therapeutic dialogue. I conceive of my emotional expressivity as operating both as a vital source of information for my patients and as a simultaneous contributor to an interpersonal context that anticipates and modifies the manner in which any particular self-disclosure is expressed and experienced.

I believe that I self-disclose more frequently than the prototypical psychoanalytically informed therapist. Still, for me, self-disclosure remains a low-frequency intervention. I believe that self-disclosures are all the more powerful if used sparingly. Less is (sometimes) more.

In contrast to previous generations of psychoanalytic therapists, I do not regard my commitment to using self-disclosure sparingly as obligating me to be muscularly vigilant or to inhibit the nonlinguistic expressions of my emotional reactions. For me, entering into an authentic dialogue has more to do with presenting myself in a way that is congruent with what I am feeling than with absolute verbal honesty. I believe that a therapeutic stance that combines judicious self-disclosure and relaxed, warm, spontaneous behavior yields an optimal therapist-patient relationship style. The distinction I am making is comparable to the difference between adopting a supportive posture/attitude toward a patient and deciding to use a supportive technique (e.g., reassurance) with him or her on a particular occasion.

I recognize that my style is only partly predictable from my theoretical allegiances. Data from various sources indicate that the personal styles and character traits of therapists who share the same theoretical point of view lead to substantial differences in our application of basic principles and techniques, including self-disclosure.

THINKING ABOUT SELF–DISCLOSING

Intentional self-disclosures require interpersonal skills such as tact, timing, patience, humility, perseverance, and sensitivity. These soft skills cannot be learned from a manual. What can be taught are the precepts, rules, criteria, and cognitive processes that guide effective clinical decision-making. To this end, I have been developing a two-stage decision-making model that considers the interaction between intentional self-disclosures and the expressive styles from which they emerge and in which they are embedded. For purposes of analysis, I follow Rosen (1977) in defining style, in the sense of craftsmanship, as a "progressing synthesis of form and content in an individually typical manner and according to the individual's sense of appropriateness" (p. 288).

I conceive of self-disclosure as a form of communication in its own right (Geller, 1984). Self-disclosure plays a role comparable to clarifications, interpretations, and questions in the repertoire of therapeutic tools. It is one more way to deliver a message, and perhaps as adaptable as traditionally recognized therapeutic techniques. As used here, therapeutic techniques exist independently of the particular contents or messages that they communicate. Self-disclosure understood in this way offers the possibility of uncoupling its use from decisions that are made primarily on the basis of questions regarding content. Self-disclosures are both a what and a how. They can be used in the service of making interpretations, clarifying patients' experiences, and posing questions.

Figure 1 illustrates the first phase of the decision-making and the hypothesis that internalized representations of the therapeutic dialogue, like the communicative exchanges from which they arise, can serve a wide range of psychological functions (Geller & Farber, 1993). As can be seen, the outer circles contain the names of a broad spectrum of therapeutic aims and purposes, ranging from those that are more closely identified with the definable "projects" that characterize a particular approach to therapy (e.g., cocreating insights, meanings, and narratives) to those that are of agreed-upon transtheoretical importance (e.g., conveying empathic understanding). A review of the literature would reveal that psychotherapists have called upon self-disclosures to serve most, if not all, of the communicative and psychological functions found in Figure 1.

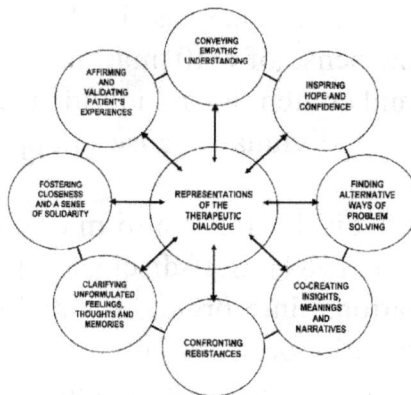

Figure 1. Internalization of the therapeutic dialogue. The lines connecting the circles indicate that a single efficacious communication can simultaneously serve multiple therapeutic functions.

According to this conceptual rationale, a therapist first decides which treatment goals have priority and then selects from among various techniques in an effort to realize these goals. In my two-stage decision-making model, questions relevant to the intentional use of self-disclosure enter the picture after a therapist decides which treatment goals should be given priority. So conceived, choosing self-disclosure is the assertion of a stylistic preference.

Therapists who have found their own voice may experience the coming together of these conceptually distinguishable stages of decision-making as an organic event. One can experience the decision to self-disclose as inherent in the decision to pursue a particular treatment goal. Beginners, by contrast, often find themselves trying to choose between conflicting modes of realizing a particular goal, all of which feel as if they have a legitimate claim.

To illustrate the distinction between form and content, let us consider the decision to provide a patient with feedback regarding his or her impact on others, including the psychotherapist. It would be hard to find a contemporary therapist who disagrees that pursuing this goal can make a vital contribution to psychotherapy. What remains after prioritizing this goal is whether self-disclosure represents the optimal form to reach this laudable goal. Here are contrasting forms of confronting a patient with the consequences of his or her verbosity: "If I'm to speak, I feel I have to interrupt you"; "I feel shut out by your nonstop talking"; "You speak like a runaway train that no one can stop"; "Are you afraid to stop talking?" There are patients who react negatively to self-involving statements, irrespective of their content. They object to the form itself. I take such (aesthetic) preferences into account when selecting the combinations of forms of communicative exchanges that I encourage during therapy sessions.

FORMS OF PATIENT SELF-DISCLOSURE

In one form or another, psychotherapists ask their patients to reveal personal information about themselves. The medium of communication most frequently authorized is spoken language. Patients tend to use only those modes of communication that their therapists have explicitly or implicitly authorized for use. Patients taking the talking cure tend to limit themselves to syntactically organized words. Creative arts therapists do not share this bias. They authorize patients to self-disclose in many different formats. For example, dance therapists view expressive movements as an alternative mode of communication rather than as an accessory or as preliminary to verbal self-disclosure. Similarly, art therapists do not regard thought and communication in images as more primitive than thinking and speaking in words.

Their work has strengthened my conviction that personal disclosures and the creation of meaning through the symbolization of experience can occur in any medium or channel of communication. Words are only part of the communicative exchanges that take place during therapy sessions. So much of what is communicated in therapy is visual or nonverbal. These truths have encouraged me to explore the therapeutic possibilities of looking at family pictures with my patients, having them draw the rooms they lived in as children, and inviting them to take on the postures, gestures, and facial expressions of their parents.

In varying degrees, the content of psychotherapy is furnished by patients' narrative accounts of the personal and private lives of others. Therapists are told things about others that these others might prefer to keep hidden. In other words, psychotherapists are privy to what in ordinary conversations would be considered the classic form of gossip. In a smoothly flowing therapeutic dialogue, talk about the flaws, limitations, and morally suspect activities of others steadily mutates into open-ended exploration and acceptance of one's own secrets and foibles. But therapies rarely run smoothly, not by any means.

Talking about others is one way of taking the spotlight off the self. It can be a means of trying to persuade or convince the therapist to accept and emotionally participate in one's personal evaluation of the other. When the content is related to a moral offense, talking about others may be an invitation to share in something forbidden. The sharing and keeping of secrets is also a way of establishing closeness. The sociologist Simmel (1950) observed with respect to secrets that they "put a barrier between men ... but at the same time create the tempting challenge to break through it, by gossiping or confessing" (p. 123).

To discover ways of transforming patients' portraits of others into vehicles for their gaining intimate knowledge of their own personal experiences, I listen to revelations about others with Richter's (1962) aphorism somewhere active in my mind: "A man never reveals his character more vividly than when portraying the character of another" (p. 80). For example, I will listen with a mind toward understanding the extent to which the patient is capable of experiencing his or her parents as unique, complex, flawed persons, existing external to the self, and as having an inner life and a history, and not merely as sources of gratification and frustration. My attentiveness is rooted in the assumption that bringing to awareness these aspects of patients' internalized representations of caregivers and authority figures and subjecting them to constructive modification is an important agent of change (Geller, 1987).

RESISTANCES TO SELF-DISCLOSURE

One of the few things that unites the different versions of psychotherapy is a belief that patients resist self-disclosure and self-exploration vigorously, persistently, and often with great subtlety. In the usual sense of the word, resistance connotes oppositionality. What distinguishes psychoanalytic therapy is that patients are told, instructed, exhorted to disclose to the therapist everything that comes to mind regardless of how insignificant or shameful it might be. No other therapy so explicitly and so authoritatively tells patients what and how they are required to communicate during therapy sessions. In place of free association, existential-humanistic therapists prescribe another kind of verbal honesty—speaking authentically (Yalom, 1980). By definition, a dialogue ceases to be authentic if one or both participants present themselves at variance with what they are feeling.

To narrow the gap between experience as it is experienced and experience as it is described, I begin by listening for what a patient considers to be the subject matter or conversational content of therapy. By leaving their task with respect to self-disclosure ambiguous, I have a chance to gradually expand my patients' conception of what constitutes therapeutic material. Some enter therapy assuming we are only interested in what is sick, wrong, or sinful about them.

I find it useful to think of self-revelation and self-concealment as co-occurring inclinations that stand in a dialectical relationship. Patients simultaneously approach and avoid the ideals of authenticity and free-associating. Therefore, our comments on resisting should not be phrased as if self-revelation and self-concealment were polar principles. Statements beginning, "You seem to be avoiding..." are half-truths, at best. Conflicts are inevitable, given the degree of candor and affective freedom expected of patients. To honor the structure of conflict, sentence constructions such as, "On the one hand... yet, on the other hand..." are required. For example, I once told a patient who was struggling to protect his precarious sense of autonomy while trying to be cooperative that he repeated my questions before answering them: "On the one hand, you always try to answer my questions conscientiously. On the other hand, by restating them out loud, before answering them, you seem to be trying to answer your own questions: I feel as if I am overhearing a conversation you are having with yourself." With him I took care to acknowledge that resistances are a function of the interdependent aspects of the therapeutic relationship, and I phrased my comments so as not to convey the impression that I "knew more" and he "knew less" about himself: "It seems as if we are getting into power struggles about who is right and who is wrong. What do you make of this?"

THE TEMPORAL CONTEXT OF SELF-DISCLOSURE

As previously stated, my working assumption is that the meaning and value of self-disclosures only can be understood in context. Beginnings and endings are temporal contexts. Psychotherapists approach self-disclosure differently during the opening and closing phases of therapy.

I am particularly attentive to the communicative importance of my vocal qualities and facial expressions during the early stages of therapy. Early in therapy, patients may be too anxious to take in the lexical/conceptual meanings of a therapist's communications. They may hear and remember little more than the acoustic properties of their therapists' voices or the information written on their therapists' faces. To accommodate the idiosyncratic communicative requirements of "listening-challenged" patients (Geller, 1996), I am prepared to adjust the ways in which I space silence and sound, stillness and movement. Winnicott clearly appreciated the communicative significance of the flow of sound and silence. He demonstrated this appreciation when he told his prospective patient, Harry Guntrip (1975, p.

152), near the end of their initial interview, "I've nothing particular to say yet, but if I don't say something, you may begin to feel I'm not here."

I have found variations of "If I ... you will ..." a valuable format in which to express my reactions to the kinds of impact patients have on me, especially if they are bringing about the very hurt they are trying to avoid. One of my patients watched me, hypervigilantly, for feedback about how his performance as a patient was being evaluated. At the same time, with characteristic worry, he scrutinized me to detect whether I was physically present but emotionally absent. Before we were ready to submit the meanings and origins of these inclinations to therapeutic scrutiny, I used the following self-involving statements to acknowledge their consequences for our relationship: "I fear that if I don't completely agree with you, you will feel as if I am insulting your intelligence," and, "I fear that if I don't say, 'I'm sorry, my attention lapsed for a second,' you'll think you were boring me."

THE LISTENING CURE

During the early stages of therapy, I limit myself to self-disclosures that are meant to convey acceptance, empathy, and encouragement. This task was successfully accomplished when I revealed to a distraught mother/patient of a handicapped child how difficult it was to raise my deaf daughter, Jenny (Geller, 1996). Moreover, I did not try to conceal the tears that spontaneously welled up in my eyes when she spoke, stoically, of her father's death. She lost him when she was a child. I have noticed that I am sometimes brought to visible tears when a patient describes, unemotionally, his or her own legitimate suffering. Analogously, when a patient persistently describes painful feelings in terms of raw bodily sensations, I will name the painful feelings that I associate with my somatic reactions. For example, when a hypochondriacal, panic-stricken, and alexithymic divorcée told me, "I thought my pounding heart was going to explode when I saw my ex-husband," I recall saying, "I take it as a sign that I am feeling anxiety or fear when my heart pounds."

But as I have come to learn, there are no risk-free self-disclosures, nor is there such a thing as "just listening" in psychotherapy. This commonly heard phrase implies that it is possible to "not communicate" when in the role of listener. Therapists convey as much comprehensible content about themselves when listening as when they are talking. Each therapist unavoidably and uniquely reveals who he or she is in ways of being and listening that are publicly observable.

One patient interpreted my relative stillness while listening as signifying "selfless devotion" to her welfare. She felt I had given her a gift when I told her the destination of my vacation. By contrast, another patient told me, "You just sit there like a bump on a log," and resented my telling him that I was going to a Caribbean island he had previously visited. As we subsequently learned, he feared that I would die in a plane crash and wanted to avoid recognition of the ways in which we were alike. It is important to identify early on those patients who feel burdened by the responsibilities that accompany knowing about their therapist's private life. In my experience, they tend to be the same patients who cannot take in positive feedback about their impact on people, including therapists, without feeling "intruded upon," "invaded," "penetrated," or "engulfed."

There are many reasons why a patient might not express any curiosity about the therapist. Some patients are only interested in what their therapists can do for them while in the role of therapist. Some are afraid that their curiosity will be experienced as an invasion of their therapist's privacy and as an act of disrespect. Still others bring to therapy the unformulated assumption that there are prohibitions or taboos about asking therapists personal questions.

A related, unwritten rule is that patients are to explore their reasons for asking the therapist personal questions before the therapist answers them. Insisting on this sequence is not technically correct. It is rigid. There are clearly patients with whom one should first answer a question, and then, if possible, try to understand its associated meanings. This stance was first recommended as a way of dealing with the special challenges posed by adolescents as well as by paranoid and narcissistically vulnerable individuals (Miletic, 1998). My patients usually have an accurate sense of the limits beyond which I will not disclose information in response to a request. I have come to expect that their questions are linked to their implicit theories of healing. I take it as a sign that I am with a deeply disturbed person if his or her questions betray a disordered or deficient guiding sense of the appropriate.

Therapists are perhaps most in doubt about what is the "right" thing to do when a patient asks their opinion about their personal characteristics: "Am I pretty?" "Am I smart?" "Am I talented?" "Am I sexy?" "Was I right?" When it comes to any intervention, the best safeguard against making a mistake is choosing a response that reflects the individuality of each patient. Necessary first steps are taken in this direction by demonstrating a willingness to learn from and with a patient through dialogue and by relinquishing the need to be "right." Moreover, educated therapists have devoted serious study to the question, What personal questions evoke in me defensiveness, hostility, and withdrawal? Until this inquiry has been conducted, it is very difficult to distinguish between evasiveness and a grounded decision to reflect a personal question.

Given the limits of understanding human specificity, therapeutic mistakes are inevitable. But there is no more powerful way of demonstrating that therapy is a process of mutual discovery than by openly acknowledging one's mistakes. It is therefore encouraging to note that preliminary data indicate that revealing one's mistakes is a common practice among psychotherapists (Geller & Farber, 1997). This practice is compatible with the widely held view that a consistent focus on threats to and ruptures of the therapeutic alliance contributes to the success of therapy.

TIMING AND SELF-DISCLOSURE

An essential prerequisite for the effectiveness of any therapeutic intervention is timing. I have found that it is inadvisable to wait to make one's first self-disclosure until one is doing so as a means of dealing with a difficult resistance. Patients' reactions to the novelty of the event may override their reactions to the message's content. If a novel stimulus is too novel, it will be experienced as frightening and noxious. By contrast, individuals tend to move toward and explore with pleasure moderately novel stimuli.

Whenever highly charged feelings are involved, I check their strength and persistence before searching for words to describe them. The inclination to self-disclose must return several times during a session after it has been dismissed or has dissipated before I give it serious consideration. The disciplined practice of psychotherapy requires finding the optimal balance between restraint and relaxed spontaneity. So-called "spontaneous disclosures" often are made in the throes of a disturbing countertransference reaction. They are blurted out when a therapist has reached the limits of tolerance of what is going on in therapy.

At these times, the inclinations to self-disclose may be a form of self-indulgence. When it comes to countertransference disclosures, it is best to "strike when the iron is cold."

Patients need to be prepared to listen to self-involving statements that bring the resisted aspects of their experience of therapy to awareness without hearing them as "uncomplimentary." There are various ways of preparing a patient to receive more intimate self-disclosures. Providing patients with information about one's training and method of treatment can serve this function and enables them to make more informed decisions about whether to continue in therapy. Revealing some "innocuous" details of one's life early in therapy (e.g., vacation plans, age) is especially important if one anticipates revealing a "special event" (e.g., pregnancy and birth, serious illness in the therapist) during the course of therapy. If a patient has difficulty with my revealing any personal information, I rely on two alternative modes of preparation. The first way is to describe a decisive moment in the life of a prominent public figure. I do so to indicate that we are members of the same community and to concretize otherwise abstract ideas. For example, I recently told an author whose inability to tolerate the excitement and anxiety that accompany striving to create about Philip Roth's telling an audience that he was having a panic attack, how he left the stage uncertain if he would return, and how he came back and finished his lecture. Recounting scenes from emblematic films and television programs known to the patient and myself is another form of quasi–self-disclosure. An emotionally isolated ex-addict who reflexively reacted against my describing an experience parallel to his in my own life accepted our common humanity when we discovered that we were both moved by a son's longing for a respected father, as portrayed in the film *Field of Dreams*. Like many men, he confused fearfulness and cowardice. To highlight my respect for his courage and to clarify what courage means to me, I recounted the following scene from the film *The Three Kings*: An Army sergeant, fighting in the Gulf War, asks an inexperienced private, "You're scared, right?" Reluctantly, the private answers, "Maybe," to which the sergeant replies, "The way this thing works is you do the thing you're scared shitless of and you get the courage afterwards, not before you do it."

There is always something I admire, effortlessly, about my psychotherapy patients. When they find it unacceptable to be self-congratulatory or self-promoting, I will be on the lookout for opportunities to praise their accomplishments in therapy and elsewhere. Moreover, my offerings of praise are typically voiced personally (e.g., "That's great") rather than impersonally (e.g., "You must be very proud of yourself"). Similar considerations enter into my work with patients who disqualify or invalidate their own feelings. With them, I will find occasions to say such things as, "I like the way you put it," "You hit the nail on the head," "Can I quote you on this one?" "You're oh so right," and "It's so true."

KNOWING ABOUT AND EXPERIENTIAL KNOWING

Broadly speaking, patients have two potential sources of knowledge about their therapists: knowledge that is dependent on what the therapist chooses to verbally reveal and knowledge that is dependent on receiving the information that is available to the senses during therapy sessions. Therapists have less conscious awareness of and control over the messages conveyed by their characteristic level of expressivity than over the messages conveyed by intentional self-disclosures. Analogously, patients have far less awareness of what they are learning about their therapists by receiving information during therapy sessions. In other words, the knowledge that patients acquire from encounters with the "perceptual reality" of their therapist often remains at a tacit or subliminal level. Consequently, a patient may know much more about the therapist than he or she is aware of knowing and much more than either the patient or the therapist is willing to acknowledge.

I draw on this distinction to deal with a variety of technical challenges. There are patients who benefit from feeling understood but who react negatively if they are supplied with knowledge about themselves. Similarly, there are patients who can accept their therapist's empathic understandings but who have a reduced ability to feel safe if autobiographical information about their therapist is known to them. During the course of exploring a patient's complaint that I volunteer too little personal information about myself, I will try to inquire how the patient is feeling about what he or she does know about me. Such inquiries are a valuable source of information about a patient's prevailing capacity to recall, use, and identify with influential representations of our therapeutic dialogue. I take this capacity as an important sign that a great deal of significant therapeutic work has been accomplished.

SELF–DISCLOSURE AND THE THERAPIST–PATIENT

Psychotherapy with patients who are themselves psychotherapists offers a unique perspective from which to examine questions about therapist self-disclosure. Therapists have less control over what their therapist-patients know about their private lives than they do with lay patients. Nontherapist-patients usually begin therapy not knowing very much about their therapists. In some cities, therapist-patients begin their own treatment uneasy about the "information" they already have about their therapist's reputation, lifestyle, marital history, and the like. If they live and work in the same community as their therapists, therapist-patients are likely to know if their therapist's status is that of teacher, supervisor, administrator, scholar, guru, or sage. In some professional communities, therapist-patients have the opportunity to observe their therapists at conferences, business meetings, and parties. Moreover, much more than is true for lay patients, therapist-patients have post-termination social and professional contact with their therapists. There is a tradition in psychoanalytic circles for therapist-patients to transform their therapy relationships into supervisory relationships and vice versa.

Therapist-patients whom I have treated are frequently perplexed about how to talk about what they have been told about me, in confidence, when "gossiping" with colleagues. They also have acknowledged feeling awkward about expressing opinions about people we know in common, especially if they assume we hold conflicting opinions. In short, the therapy of therapist-patients takes place in interpersonal and organizational contexts different from those encountered with lay patients.

I recognize that these differences influence my decisions regarding the expressiveness of my conversational style and the use of self-disclosure. The findings from our national study of psychologists' experiences conducting psychotherapy with mental health professionals (Norcross et al., 2001) indicated that my experience overlaps with that of "therapist-therapists." In contrast to therapists who treat mental health professionals rarely or intermittently, the self-designated therapist-therapists in our study tended to be more forthcoming about personal information and more emotionally expressive with their therapist-patients. Statistical analyses revealed that therapist-therapists are more likely to disclose information about their own therapy and to apologize for mistakes and technical errors when treating therapist-patients. The therapist-therapists also characterized their self-presentation as being less guarded as well as more collaborative and egalitarian when the patient is a fellow therapist. Even those therapists who claimed to be no more self-disclosing with their therapist-patients than with lay patients of comparable intelligence, socioeconomic status, and diagnosis reported enjoying being with therapist-patients more than their nontherapist-patients and feeling less detached from and friendlier toward them.

Whether or not they share the same profession, my patients have described the occasions on which I spoke of my own experiences as a patient as dramatic, intense, and memorable. They also have frequently characterized these exchanges as turning points in the course of their therapy. I recall one patient who was able to speak for the first time without knowing exactly what he was going to say when I told him about how I had rehearsed what I was going to tell my first therapist.

Psychologists in our study acknowledged that they were more likely to discuss research and professional matters with their therapist-patients than with lay patients. If excessive intellectualizations that might be used defensively are avoided, frank discussions of scientific issues are a respectful way of dealing with the inherent tension between the formal roles of therapist and patient and the collegial aspects of the relationship. Like shoptalk and inside jokes, there are self-disclosures that make reference to the practice of psychotherapy itself that only a fellow therapist would fully understand. For example, a colleague was able to counteract the interfering consequences of his therapist-patients overidealizing transference—she thought he would make the ideal husband—by saying, "As you know, we present our best selves when in the role of therapist." A cognitive-behavioral therapist deeply appreciated and benefited from my quoting his mentor, Marsha Linehan, when he bitterly blamed himself for resisting making progress in therapy: "You are doing as well as you can *and* you can do a lot better."

Self-disclosures about affiliating with different theoretical orientations also can lead to fruitful and emotionally charged interactions. In the 2nd year of therapy, I said to a therapist-patient who espoused a theoretical orientation other than my own: "Somehow when we talk about our ideas about therapy, you seem to not only need to be right, but right in such a way as to prove me wrong." I encouraged him to notice how frequently he began sentences with "Yes, but..." rather than "Yes, and..." when discussing matters of theory and practice with his colleagues. What he discovered was that he was antagonizing his colleagues by structuring scientific conversations as if they were debates between adversaries.

That self-disclosure is particular to the treatment of patients who are themselves therapists is consistent with my argument that self-disclosures should be relative to the specific context and the individual patient. The psychotherapy of therapists also offers a unique perspective from which to examine a question that is relevant to the psychotherapy of all types of patients: Does access to information about one's therapist's personal affairs interfere with the development and observation of transference reactions? My own view is that ambiguity is far more capable of stimulating analyzable fantasies than the total absence of information.

SELF-DISCLOSURE AND TERMINATION

Owing to a variety of reasons, for therapists the inclination to self-disclose intensifies during the termination phase of therapy. Some therapists advocate becoming more self-revealing for technical reasons. They call upon self-disclosures to facilitate a working through of the transferential aspects of the relationship. This strategy is premised on the assumption that self-disclosures are required to narrow the status inequalities and emotional distance separating therapist and patient.

By contrast, like the majority of therapists we have interviewed (Greene & Geller, 1980), I am naturally inclined to move closer to my patients and to democratize the relationship as the final sessions approach. I am temperamentally given to deepening my involvement with persons with whom I am saying goodbye, especially if we have had a warm, meaningful, and productive relationship. Self-awareness and restraint are required to modify this generalized orientation to ending relationships according to the needs of one's patients. Failure to manage this task undermines a therapist's ability to be intimate with a patient while in role.

Concurrently, over the years I have come to trust that an increase in my readiness to become more spontaneous and self-disclosing is a sign that I am becoming for the patient more of a "real person" to remember and identify with. I believe that the entire therapeutic process, if effective, leads inevitably to the patient's perception of the therapist-as-he/she-is. I further believe that, like the obverse and reverse of a coin, the achievement of this therapeutic goal goes hand in hand with the approaching realization of a patient's life goals.

During the ending phase of therapy, self-disclosures are called upon to serve a different constellation of tasks than those that predominated during earlier stages. During the middle phases of therapy, self-involving statements play a vital role in identifying those problematic aspects of the therapeutic relationship that prevent the realization of treatment goals. It is quite a different order of things to self-disclose to celebrate the achievement of these goals, to reciprocate the tender feelings expressed by an appreciative patient, and to say goodbye. Intimacy replaces power and authority as the focal point of therapist self-disclosures during termination. Within this context, the question, Is it appropriate for me to ask my patients to risk sharing their most intimate feelings if I am unwilling to take the same risk? takes on new meaning.

The cumulative effect of these changes is to increase uncertainties about the optimal location and management of the boundary between the "professional self" and the personal self. The tension between spontaneity and restraint peaks once the decision to terminate has been made. I would not be surprised if fears of saying and doing more than one intended become more salient when ending a therapeutic relationship that is emotionally charged for both participants. Worries about overstepping the ethical boundaries of contact with patients can lead to a defensive avoidance of the ambiguities of intimacy. Resisting the temptation to express loving feelings for technical reasons and the fear of boundary violations must be clearly distinguished. This is no easy task, for as Rieff (1961) concluded, "Freud conceived of abstinence both as a scientific principle and as a moral injunction" (p. 23).

THE FATE OF SELF-DISCLOSURES AFTER TERMINATION

Patients usually remember very little of what was actually said during a course of therapy. Our studies suggest that therapist self-disclosures tend to be among the few utterances that can be recalled by patients after they have terminated (Wzontek et al., 1995). Moreover, as the following example illustrates, therapist self-disclosures can have a delayed or continuing influence on patients after termination.

When interviewed 1 year after he had ended a therapy that he regarded as "successful" but "incomplete," an obsessional lawyer and film buff recalled with great vividness that "Dr.__

recommended that I go see Albert Brooks's movie entitled *Defending My Life*.... I took it as a sign of trust in me." He savors and benefits from the assumption that his therapist knew he would enjoy the film and find it instructive. Yet, he still hasn't watched the movie. He explained: "I feel like it's like dessert, like you know, sometimes you want to save dessert, and I feel I'm not quite ready to give myself that pleasure."

CONCLUSION AND SUMMARY

In this article, I have reasoned that competent use of self-disclosure in psychoanalytic-existential psychotherapy depends on a therapist's ability to flexibly accommodate his or her activity level, depth of involvement, and expressivity to meet the idiosyncratic requirements of individual patients at each phase of therapy. I have sampled a few of the intrapsychic and interpersonal variables that have an immediate impact on patients' and therapists' attitudes toward self-disclosure.

Before concluding, let me place the therapeutic situation in its broader cultural context. Very different attitudes toward privacy and modesty held sway when Freud formulated his notions of repression, resistance, and anonymity. His early discoveries were made during a time when people's erotic secrets were a walled-off realm. We live in a culture that encourages public displays of real and imagined openness. Baring it all is a staple of today's television shows, movies, memoirs, and novels. Human suffering has increasingly become a source of entertainment. In one form of media after another, the unsavory secrets of our leaders, heroes, and celebrities surface as gossip. Have these changes in our sociocultural attitudes between what is public and what is private weakened the constraints that inhibit confessing personal secrets in psychotherapy? Have they increased the probability of patients' talking about the intentionally concealed secrets of others? Have they weakened therapists' efforts to resist the temptations of gossiping?

Professional codes and oaths have very little to say about the circumstances that justify overriding the principle of confidentiality when talking with a colleague. Although they would be loath to acknowledge it, what would be deemed as gossip in other contexts clearly takes place when mental health staff gather behind closed doors. Concurrently, new forms of interagency collaboration and new forms of record keeping are making it ever more difficult for therapists to keep the secrets they have been entrusted with by their patients from third parties.

One hundred years from now, how will psychotherapists evaluate our efforts to maximize the therapeutic potential of the intentional use of self-disclosure? Hopefully, they too will be guided by the proposition that deciding what, when, and how to reveal one's self to patients is not something we can get straight once and for all but is an ongoing task of reaching toward ever more exact formulations in an ever-changing field.

REFERENCES

Aron, L. (1996). *A Meeting of Minds: Mutuality in Psychoanalysis*. Hillsdale, NJ: Analytic Press.

Davies, J. (1994). Love in the afternoon. *Psychoanalytic Dialogues* 4:153–170.

Freud, S. (1912). Recommendations to physicians practicing psychoanalysis. *Standard Edition* 12:109–120.

Geller, J.D. (1974). Dance therapy as viewed by a psychotherapist. *American Dance Therapy Association Monograph* 3:1–21. [Reprinted in *A Collection of Early Writings: Toward a Body of Knowledge* (Vol. 1, pp. 63–80). ADTA, 1989.]

———— (1984). Moods, feelings, and the process of affect formation. In L. Temoshok, C. Van Dyke, & L.S. Zegans (Eds.), *Emotions in Health and Illness: Applications to Clinical Practice* (pp. 171–186). Orlando, FL: Grune & Stratton.

———— (1987). The process of psychotherapy: Separation and the complex interplay among empathy, insight, and internalization. In J. Bloom-Feshbach & S. Bloom-Feshbach (Eds.), *The Psychology of Separation and Loss: Perspectives on Development, Life Transitions, and Clinical Practice* (pp. 459–514). San Francisco, CA: Jossey-Bass.

———— (1996). Thank you for Jenny. In B. Gerson (Ed.), *The Therapist as a Person: Life Crises, Life Choices, Life Experiences, and Their Effects on Treatment* (pp. 119–139). New York, NY: Analytic Press.

———— (1998). What does it mean to practice psychotherapy scientifically? *Psychoanalysis and Psychotherapy* 15:187–215.

———— & Farber, B.A. (1993). Factors influencing the process of internalization in psychotherapy. *Psychotherapy Research* 3(3):166–180. https://doi.org/10.1080/10503309312331333769

———— & ———— (1997, August). *Why Therapists Do and Don't Disclose*. Paper presented at the annual meeting of the American Psychological Association, Chicago, IL.

Greene, L.R., & Geller, J.D. (1980). Effects of therapists' clinical experience and personal boundaries on termination of psychotherapy. *Journal of Psychiatric Education* 4:31–35.

Grubricht-Simitis, I. (1986). Six letters of Sigmund Freud and Sándor Ferenczi on the interrelationship of psychoanalytic theory and technique. *International Review of Psychoanalysis* 13:259–277.

Guntrip, H. (1975). My experience of analysis with Fairbairn and Winnicott. *International Review of Psychoanalysis* 2:145–156.

Miletic, M. (1998). Rethinking self-disclosure. *Psychoanalytic Inquiry* 18:580–600.

Norcross, J.C., Geller, J.D, & Kurzawa, E.K. (2001). Conducting psychotherapy with psychotherapists: II. Clinical practices and collegial advice. *Journal of Psychotherapy Practice and Research* 10:37–45.

Renik, O. (1995). The ideal of the anonymous analyst and the problem of self-disclosure. *Psychoanalytic Quarterly* 64:466–495.

Richter, J. (1962). In W.H. Auden & L. Kronenberger (Eds.), *Viking Book of Aphorisms*. New York, NY: Dorsey.

Rieff, P. (1961). *Freud: The Mind of the Moralist*. New York, NY: Doubleday.

Rosen, V. (1977). *Style, Character and Language*. New York, NY: Jason Aronson.

Simmel, G. (1950). The secret and the secret society. In K. Wolf (Ed.), *The Sociology of George Simmel* (pp. 211–229). New York, NY: Free Press.

Wzontek, N., Geller, J.D., & Farber, B.A. (1995). Patients' post-termination representations of their psychotherapists. *Journal of the American Academy of Psychoanalysis* 23:395–410.

Yalom, I. (1980). *Existential Psychotherapy*. New York, NY: Basic Books.

CHAPTER 10

My Personal Tiresias:
A Geographer of the Inner World

[J.D. Geller (2002). In R. Lasky (Ed.), *Symbolization and Desymbolization: Essays in Honor of Norbert Freedman* (pp. 511–533). New York, NY: Other Press.]

Let man's soul be a sphere.
—John Donne

INTRODUCTION

This essay is concerned with the spatial properties of the representational world. It was inspired by the intimate privilege of reading a valued friend's works in progress. Last year I began reading two of Norbert (Bert) Freedman's (1997a, b) unpublished essays. The ultimate aim of these essays is the development of a model of the intricate and constantly changing ways in which varying kinds of space are experienced, particularly in the therapeutic situation.

Taken together, these essays are an invitation to think systematically about the network of relations that link the representations of the spaces that separate self and others, the representations of the spaces within the body, the representations of the spaces within the mind, and the overall physicality of a situation or event. Bert assumes that these three domains of experience, which he refers to as "object relational space," "body-self space," and "symbolizing space," are in constant dialogue with one another and with the physical actuality of the forces and spaces outside of our bodies. He uses the term "inner psychic space" to refer to an inclusive framework, or functional

387

composite, within which are arranged the interrelations among these representational domains. At the center of his still provisional model is the hypothesis that "psychic content needs a place in which to live—we cannot move physically without a concept of space, nor can we do so psychically. The inhabitants of such a space are inner objects, affects, and self-representations" (Freedman & Lavender 1997, p. 83).

Bert's innovative ideas about the spatialization of the representational world are a dazzling synthesis of psychoanalytic thought (Lewin, 1946; Bion, 1963; Viderman, 1970; Winnicott, 1971; Grotstein, 1978; Anzieu, 1989), body-image theory (Schilder, 1950; Wapner & Werner, 1965; Fisher & Cleveland, 1968), anthropological studies of variations in personal space (Hall 1959, 1966; Sommer, 1969), and Susanne Langer's (1942) philosophical perspective on symbolizing. These ideas represent an extension of his keenly observed kinesthetic-linguistic studies of the nonverbal facilitation of verbalized symbolic thought (e.g., Freedman & Bucci, 1981; Freedman, 1983). Bert's insights are also a product of his efforts to understand what his blindness can teach us about the origins, nature, functions, and modifiability of the psychological experience of inner space.

Here, the fate of Tiresias might be recalled. Legend has it that Hera, Zeus's wife, blinded Tiresias because he saw too clearly and spoke the truth about female and male sexuality. Then, according to the myth, Zeus compensated Tiresias for his loss by giving him the gift of "inner sight," which Tiresias, in turn, called upon to foresee and reveal to Oedipus the King the true origin of the tragedies confronting Thebes (Sophocles, 429 B.C.E./1971). Like Tiresias, Bert has unflinchingly gazed upon the truths that are revealed when the eyes are open and those that are revealed when the eyes are closed. It is only because of knowing Bert personally that I have come to appreciate, and now write about, the psychic geography of the inner world.

First, I will address the question, What does the notion of psychic inner space actually mean? I will present what my therapist colleagues have been revealing to me about their own experiences of inner space. Then, I will present the broad outlines of Bert's theorizing about the emergence and evolution of the spatial qualities of the representational world. And finally, I will discuss how Bert's ideas have led me to new kinds of thinking about the therapeutic action of the processes of introjection.

WHAT IS INNER SPACE?

Consider the following modes of self-reference: My mind is racing. I couldn't put the thought out of my mind. I must have been out of my mind. I couldn't keep my mind on my work. My mind plays tricks on me. I couldn't wrap my mind around it. Thoughts of suicide entered my mind. I am of two minds about that. I'm losing my mind. You've been on my mind. My mind feels like a sieve.

These common expressions point to two deeply ingrained human inclinations: the tendency to objectify processes by transforming them into autonomous things or thing-like entities, and the tendency to conceive of the mind as its own "place," as if it were an imaginary container in which thinking, remembering, feeling, fantasizing, and other mental activities take place.

The idea that the mind actually has an "inside" is basically the concretization of a metaphor. Modern philosophers of knowledge agree that substantive designations implying that the mind actually has an inside that exists within a person are not a sound basis for thinking, theoretically, about psychological processes and events. Bert concurs. At the same time, he recognizes that it is legitimate and desirable to retain phenomenologically based uses of the terms "internal" and "external." In other words, he does not confuse the subjective differentiation of the experiential field into inner and outer regions and the localization of psychological activities in physical space.

In order to differentiate Bert's own phenomenologically based investigations of psychic inner space from the idea that the mind has an actual inside, I will hereafter speak of "the experience of inner psychic space." My primary focus will be upon that quality or activity of mind that Bert has named "symbolizing space."[30]

Representations of Inner Space

Some aspects of Bert's evolving understanding of what constitutes psychic inner space find expression in the following definition: "a *mode* of spatial representation that exists side by side, or is coordinated with, mental content but is not reducible to this content" (1997a, p. 11, italics added). The meanings and implications of this working definition reside in the convergence of a network of ideas. As a whole, the statement can be read as an answer to the question, What (activity or quality of mind) remains when you have eliminated the emotionally charged self-representations, representations of the other, and representations of interactions with him or her that comprise an internalized object relationship? Bert's notion of representation applies equally to words, pictures, postures, gestures, sounds, tastes, and odors; and the term "mode" can be understood as a synonym of "form," which in this context refers to the distinct and constantly changing representational configurations that structure and organize the experience of inner space.

---

30 At times, Bert appears to use the terms "listening space," "associative space," and "representational space" as synonyms of "symbolizing space."

Bert's working definition leaves open the question of whether one can sever psychic contents and the inner spaces in which they reside. The phrases "side by side" and "coordinated with" suggest that inner space can be likened to the file icon on the computer screen before items have been added. So conceived, inner space exists as a potentiality, a virtual space. An alternative view, and the one to which I subscribe, is that one cannot exist without the other and that inner spaces both shape and are molded by their contents.

The distinction I am making is comparable to the difference between a bottle of water and a drop of water.[31] A bottle of water is a "real" container. It does not change its shape when emptied of its contents. It can stand alone or apart from its contents. A drop of water cannot. The "drop" and the "water" do not exist independently of one another. Their relationship is one of co-determination.

The connection between moods and feelings, as experienced qualities, provides me with yet another model for thinking about the ways in which varying types of psychic contents and inner spaces mutually influence each other. As I have discussed elsewhere (Geller, 1984), moods permeate and envelop our existence, whether experienced for shorter or longer periods of time. To a lesser or greater degree, they provide the background against which other contents of consciousness stand out. It is as if we were embedded in our moods. When the subject of introspection pertains to bad moods, we speak of being "in a black cloud" or "down in the dumps," "surrounded by a fog." Styron (1990) described his depression as resembling "the diabolical discomfort of being imprisoned in a fiercely overheated room"

---

31 The idea of a drop of water and the notion of inner space are both examples of what Whorf (1956) refers to as "container-ingredient metaphors."

(p. 2). In other words, moods are experienced as happening around us in a contextual surround but not necessarily within us.

Consequently, insofar as they are enduring, moods provide the frameworks or contexts that anticipate and modify the manner in which emergent feelings are experienced and expressed. I believe this is what Kundera (1984) had in mind when he wrote, "The sadness was form, the happiness content. Happiness filled the space of sadness" (p. 314) to describe his hero's feelings about returning home in *The Unbearable Lightness of Being*.

The Gestalt psychologists' conceptualization of the relations between figure and ground resembles in almost every respect what art critics refer to as the relations between "positive shapes and negative space" (Blom & Chaplin, 1982). In graphic works of art, negative space is defined as the surrounding areas created by, around, and in between the spaces formed by images (i.e., positive shapes). The interaction between these design elements can be clearly seen in the optical illusion of the vase/face profile drawing. As can be seen in Figure 1, the viewer has a choice of perceiving either the black or white as the positive shape and designating the opposite color the negative space.

Focusing attention on the negative or empty spaces reveals that they are not, in fact, "dead spaces." Rather, negative spaces are as important as positive images, for they, too, occupy and mold a given amount of space, and they are malleable as well. Moreover, any change in the foreground or background results in a specific and accommodating change in the other. In a similar vein, I am proposing that the thoughts and feelings a person is capable of experiencing and the shapes taken by the inner spaces that contain his or her thoughts and feelings are inseparably related.

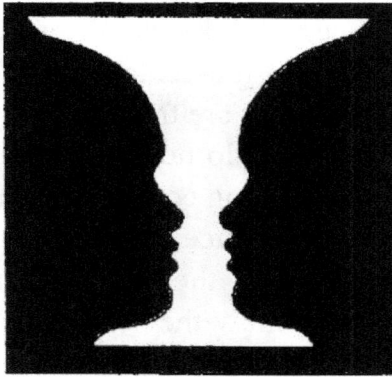

Figure 1.

Most people seem to be unaware that inner space is an integral and omnipresent aspect of their subjective experience. For a variety of reasons, we are interested in the "what" or content of our experiences. Unless we're specifically asked about them, there is no obvious reason we should pay attention to the spatial attributes and qualities of our thoughts and feelings. Doing so requires shifting attention away from the symbolic content, or explicit function, of an experience and bringing into focal awareness its structural or formal properties. This would entail a reversal of foreground and background.

Furthermore, without access to a vocabulary that permits one to speak about the structure of sensory experiences, it is extremely difficult to tell others about the ways in which one experiences psychic inner space. I anticipate that if introspective investigations were conducted with individuals who were disciplined and refined observers of their own subjectivity, the results would reveal that the forms taken by inner space are capable of being apprehended and described in terms of the same spatial dimensions and orientations that are used to perceive and describe physical spaces: size, height, distance, up/down, front/back/left/right, and here-in-the-center.[32]

Psychoanalytic therapists are trained to pay attention to and talk about experiences that do not readily lend themselves to description. I have been asking colleagues who are also friends to tell me about their experiences of inner space. With varying degrees of skill and anxiety, they have been able to "know," "sense," and "recognize" how they experience inner space. In an informal experiment of my own, I provided colleagues who were unfamiliar with the notion of inner space with Bert's working definition of it (see above). If they had difficulty grasping it or were resistant to performing the task, I asked them to relax, close their eyes, and imagine a painting or a photograph and the frame that surrounds it.

Decorative frames can draw one toward or away from the works of art they contain. Unadorned picture frames fade into the background of experience as attention is brought by the work of art to itself, while other frames are experienced as an integral part of the subject matter portrayed. I presume that the cognitive structuring of functions performed by psychic inner space are comparable to the unnoticed organizing influence unobtrusive picture frames have upon the viewing of a painting or photograph; that is, frames, whether real or imaginary, provide the windows, lenses, perspectives, and points of view that arrange the information presented to the mind. They contain, limit, and direct one's attentiveness and do so at a prereflexive level of symbolic functioning.

---

32 Theoretically, time can be added to these dimensions, making inner psychic space time, a single continuum within which movements and directions could be perceived and described. The common expression "I need space" carries two meanings: "I need to increase the distance between us," which is equivalent to "I need time away from you," and "I need to expand the sense of space within my mind."

To date, I have conducted approximately twenty introspective inquiries. My preliminary findings suggest that (1) the human head is the primary, but not necessarily the exclusive, site of psychic inner space; (2) the fundamental constituents of psychic inner space are constellations of visual, kinesthetic, proprioceptive, and auditory representations; and (3) discursive explicitness about the sense of inner space inevitably requires the use of metaphors.

Some Preliminary Findings

Innumerable mental activities take place within the brain, and most of the sensory apparatus is high up on the human face. The head probably owes its special status as the most frequently chosen landmark for the location of inner space to these facts. Objectively speaking, adults know that the brain is a material substance. Nevertheless, according to Bloomer and Moore (1977), it is represented, in many people's imaginations, as more of a void than a filled entity.

The notion of physical space, as most of us understand it, refers to voids, that is, to those portions of a place that are empty of solids. We see the walls, or the objects between which empty space exists. Space itself is not directly perceived. It is mostly apprehended and emotionally felt in relation to ourselves as standing, sitting, walking, lying down (on the earth, which holds us down). All of these forms of movement are tacitly thought of as domains separate from their existence in space.

Theoretically, mental activities are describable in terms of the spatial and temporal dimensions that are used to describe the directions and magnitude of movements in physical space. When someone moves in and through physical spaces, two changes can be observed: change in the shape of the body and change in the place where the body is located. That the flow of thought is not unlike the paths the body travels in movement or the route the eyes take when scanning the landscape is for Bert an experiential reality. In recognition of this phenomenon, William James coined the phrase "the stream of consciousness" many years earlier (1890). While reading or thinking about James's phrase, I am apt to see in my mind's eye images of a river's flowing dark waters moving across, within, and beyond. When she is reading novels, my wife imagines the words "snaking through my right ear and going out through my left ear like a pen-and-ink Saul Steinberg cartoon of a moving train." The poet Lux (1997) tells us that he hears his voice speaking while reading silently in the "dark cathedral of his skull" (p. 15).

A colleague told me, "When I can't retrieve a memory, or even the words for something, I feel suspended in space, ungrounded. But when I am feeling organized, focused, motivated, I experience my thoughts as moving through a circle that is moving in on itself. It's like I can picture the hole in a powdered donut." Another colleague envisioned his brain as "full of stuff" but as attached at its base to an "empty bubble where thoughts go and play with one another." He associated the image of a bubble to the ways in which thinking and dialogue are portrayed in comic books and cartoons.

Inner space is not necessarily experienced as located within the confines of the head. A Jungian therapist described her experience of inner space as located in her chest, as oval in shape, and as varying in the extent to which it felt "full, busy, and crowded." In order to convey the feeling of a "crowded mind" that is "not big enough to hold all of my ideas," a social worker told me that it "feels as if a vise is attached to my temple and is squeezing my mind narrower and narrower." As this and the previous example suggest, the psychological experience of inner space can expand and contract, like the postures taken by the body, and can vary in the extent to which it is hospitable to memories, fantasies, and the attributes of the reflective self.

To be sure, that which encloses can also exclude. Schizoid patients speak of feeling trapped inside "a plastic bubble" or a "cocoon" or behind a "sheet of glass," barriers that allow nothing of emotional importance to leave or enter. One can feel supported and comforted—or confined and shut in—by an embrace or by the current status of one's sense of psychic inner space.

A Scene from *Five Easy Pieces*

I consider the following scene from *Five Easy Pieces* (Rafelson, 1970) a fine illustration of the failure to separate a "container" from that which it "contained" (Bion, 1963). The character portrayed by Jack Nicholson (JN) is speaking to a waitress in a diner (W):

JN: I'd like a plain omelet, no potatoes, tomatoes instead, a cup of coffee, and wheat toast.

W: No substitutions.

JN: What do you mean? You don't have any tomatoes?

W: Only what's on the menu. You can have a number two—a plain omelet. It comes with cottage fries and a roll.

JN: I know what it comes with, but it's not what I want.

W: I'll come back when you make up your mind.

JN: Wait a minute. I have made up my mind. I'd like a plain omelet, no potatoes on the plate. A cup of coffee, and a side order of wheat toast.

W: I'm sorry, we don't have any side orders of toast. An English muffin or a coffee roll.

JN: What do you mean you don't make side orders of toast? You make sandwiches, don't you?

W: Would you like to talk to the manager?

JN: You've got bread and a toaster of some kind?

W: I don't make the rules.

JN: OK. I'll make it as easy for you as I can. I'd like an omelet, plain, and a chicken salad sandwich on wheat toast, no mayonnaise, no butter, no lettuce, and a cup of coffee.

W: A number 2. A chicken salad sandwich. Hold the butter, the lettuce, and the mayonnaise, and a cup of coffee. Anything else?

JN: Yeah, now all you have to do is hold the chicken, bring me the toast, give me a check for the chicken salad sandwich, and you haven't broken any rules.

W: You want me to hold the chicken, huh?

JN: Yeah, I want you to hold it between your knees.

W: You'll have to leave, sir. I've had enough of you.

If we focus on the waitress in the above scene, we can see that her insular and rigidly held view that a menu contains immutable descriptions of what constitutes a meal makes it impossible for her to separate the bread that surrounds a sandwich from the sandwich's ingredients. She is embedded in her own narrow point of view without being aware that she has a point of view. This raises the question, Do narrow- and broad-minded people differ in the structure of their symbolizing spaces?

FORMS TAKEN BY INNER SPACE

Visual images are the predominant mode of representing the spatial attributes of physical reality. It also appears as if individuals rely heavily on visual images and metaphors when asked to describe their sense of inner space. If an interviewee included visual images in his or her description, I asked, "Do the shapes taken by your visual images of inner space resemble anything?" Invariably the answers came back to me in metaphoric form. The metaphors chosen by my sample of therapists were drawn from a wide variety of domains: architecture, mathematics, anatomy, geography, astronomy, and so on. Some likened their sense of inner space to the visible properties of the land forms found in nature (such as caves, craters, and the hollow habitats animals create by burrowing into the earth). Others characterized the shapes taken by their sense of inner space as resembling the shelters and structures created by humans (like houses, rooms, molds, scaffoldings, tunnels). For several respondents, the notion of inner space brought up images of the proscenium arch or film screens of which we are vaguely aware in the semidarkness of a theater. I would not be surprised if the shapes taken by inner space have, in our culture, come increasingly to resemble television and computer screens with their four sides at right angles. Did Lewin's (1946) clinically based finding that dream images, especially if they are visual, tend to be experienced as if they were being projected onto blank surfaces anticipate this trend? Still earlier, Proust (1913/1989) opined that "when a man is asleep, he has in a circle round him the chain of the hours, the sequence of the years, the order of the heavenly host" (p. 5).

THE UNIVERSE AS CONTAINER

Space (and time)[33] on a cosmic scale are commonly conceived of as immense containers of a universe in which all of nature and organic life exist and move. For several members of my informal sample, the notion of inner space evoked immediate associations to the universe. These people tended to be individuals for whom inner space is more felt than seen. A music therapist told me that as a boy he was haunted by two questions: If the universe is bounded, what is on the other side? And if it is unbounded (infinite), what does it mean that it can go on forever? Whether he conceived of the universe as infinite or finite, his questions about the unknown immensities of the solar system left him feeling small, weak, and vaguely terrified.

He then described the essential constituents of his adult sense of inner space as a "matrix of psychophysical or body-centered sensations" and translated these sensations into an image of inner space that was not radically different from his boyhood thoughts about interplanetary space. "I have the feeling that I am standing in the center of a circle that turns above and around my head and body. It seems to radiate axes in all directions that extend outward into a vast darkness." In comparison to his childhood view of his place in the universe, he feels at home

---

33 Bert takes into account the fact that while time is usually regarded as an aspect of reality differing from space, they are experienced and described in much the same way. A moment in time is analogous to a point in space. A time span can be subdivided infinitely, as a line in space can be. Time includes such relations as before and after. We speak of the distant future and of temporal schedules that are long or short. By analogy with rising and falling in space, successive musical tones can be interpreted as rising and falling. Silence, as a period of time without noticeable sounds, is somewhat analogous to empty space. Neither silence nor empty spaces are merely absences of stimuli; they provide the frames of reference within which actions, perceptions, and thoughts start, continue, or stop. For these and other reasons, the temporal ordering of auditory events that are bounded by the onset and cessation of stimulation—that is, the "open spaces" that separate sound and silence—provide yet another model for the creation of "inner spaces."

in this enclosure; he experiences himself as the center of his cosmos. His image reminded me of the comforting idea of an earth-centered cosmos and of the mandala, in Jungian psychology a symbol representing the effort to reunify the self.

Another respondent, a dance therapist, recognized that her experience of inner space was fluid, and its changeable characteristics seemed to depend upon how centered or grounded she felt. At her best, this person feels as if she is "standing in the middle of my circle." Here we see that the visualizations of what is at first experienced kinesthetically and proprioceptively do not always yield descriptions of inner space that are limitless or indeterminate with respect to their form or shape. On the other hand, when under stress, she could discern that her kinesthetic experiences of inner space yielded images of "being unhinged and floating through eternity, or of falling through a black hole." She also observed that "good and bad introjects seem to be experientially located in different parts of my body—the bad ones are in my stomach and the good ones in my chest."

ORIGINS OF INNER SPACE

Bert's theorizing about the emergence and evolution of the representational capacities required to create and maintain symbolizing spaces that are hospitable to those forms of mentation that aid in adaptation takes into account the contributions of geography, biology, culture, and psychology. He assigns fundamental importance to the fact that psychological experience always takes place within the context of two physical actualities: the ever-present body and the environmental surround. Being in a body is always also about being located in a place.

Following Schilder (1950), Bert would characterize an adult's confrontation with the world outside his body as the simultaneous encounter of an inside world occurring within an outside world, each dependent on the other for its existence and complexity. As a developmentalist, Bert presumes that the most primordial source of our representations of space is the body itself. As Adrienne Rich (1984/1986) has so beautifully phrased it, the body is "after all, the geography closest in" (p. 212).

Surely, long before infants reach any degree of articulate visual or verbal representations of space, they are sensing, codifying, and storing knowledge about the distinction between an inside world and an outside world on a body-felt level (Geller, 1978). An early first step is taken when infants use their sensorimotor intelligence to detect, organize, and respond to sensations coming from inside and outside the body. Piaget (1956) has hypothesized that, over the course of development, we gradually learn to coordinate the tactile, visual, auditory, buccal, and postural spaces formed by our bodies. For example, at the beginning of life, sucking objects promotes the coordination of the buccal and tactile-kinesthetic spaces. Spitting food out of the mouth, purposely, perhaps signals the arrival of the discovery of the distinction between the feeling of inside and all of that stuff "out there."

Another developmental landmark in the spatialization of experience is the acquisition of the representational capacities that underlie the sense of being bounded and three-dimensional. There are many more directions in which to move or look than merely proceeding outward and inward in three-dimensional space (e.g., here and there; near and far; between, through, and around; right and left; east and west; above and below.)[34] It is well documented that representations that aim at boundedness or defining the limits of self and nonself are subject to wide

---

34 Everyday speech reveals that spatial positions tend to acquire connotative meanings; for example, "above" and "below" tend to suggest rank or status.

variation, and this is, of course, pertinent to Winnicott's (1971) important notion of transitional space.

The discovery that there are sealed and unsealed enclosures in the physical world lends credence to the preverbal sense that there is a space that extends from the core of the body to the surface. Bachelard (1964) has argued that the forms ultimately taken by our sense of inner space bear the fundamental imprint of the body of images provided by the homes of our childhood and their "spaces of intimacy." Opening and closing drawers and closets, entering and exiting the interior of rooms, houses, cars, and so on, does, at a minimum, reinforce our body-based sense of inside and outside. My catalog of intimate spaces includes the primal roundness of the cups and plates in our kitchen, our king-size bed, the bathroom mirror and toilet bowl. High on my list of intimate spaces is the structural wholeness of the "witness circle" in which I practice Authentic Movement (Pallaro, 1999).

One interviewee described her sense of inner space as an "upside down vase." She produced the following drawing, Figure 2, to clarify what she was saying. She felt as if it ended at her neck.[35] She characterizes the vase as having "fluffy gray borders" that are "arranged harmoniously" and as being "a rich dove gray" in color. She added that the clouds, "not having a discrete edge, signified that things aren't settled." Her first association was to a classical Greek urn. Mine was to the contours of a beech or maple tree in full bloom. For both of us, the shape then brought up images of the folds created by the gray matter of the brain and of the uterus. Life begins in an enclosure.

---

35 I am given to thinking of the neck as a transitional space that, in people's imaginations, separates the mind and the body.

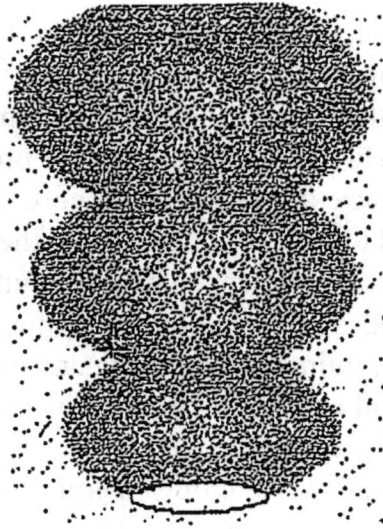

Figure 2.

The human body contains numerous openings and cavities (e.g., the throat, the nostrils, the ears, the anus, the belly). Women additionally possess the containing spaces of the vagina, the womb, and breasts. My granddaughter calls her mother's breasts "nursies," that is, containers of milk. Do these anatomical differences influence how men and women apprehend boundedness and construct representations of inner psychic space?[36]

The developmental trajectory Bert is suggesting is that the forms taken by the body, in stillness and when in motion, representationally prefigure and provide the nonverbal substrate for our psychological experiences of inner space. Like Anzieu (1989), Bert also believes that the sense of boundedness provided by representations of the skin as a sheath or outer en-

---

36 In 1950, Erikson (1963) described the contrasting play configurations of girls and boys. The boys tended to use blocks to build towers; the girls tended to use them to construct enclosures. Many changes have taken place with regard to gender distinctions since these data were collected. Thus, I believe that his data can no longer be cited as evidence of gender differences in the construction of psychic inner space.

velope that surrounds and contains the bodily self is another fundamental source of our sense that representational boundaries surround the mind. In other words, conceiving of the self as a three-dimensional bounded entity anticipates and contributes to experiencing the mind as a container that holds our thoughts and feelings.

At the same time, as we begin to experience ourselves as three-dimensional bounded entities, the formation and establishment of representations of the spaces that separate self and others are also occurring. Much anthropological and psychological research indicates that there are cultural and characterological differences in the ways people respond to the felt experience of being close to and far away from the other. Hall's (1959, 1966) studies of proxemics indicate that we usually try to maintain a personal envelope of space around our bodies and that any violation or infringement upon this sense is acutely experienced. I believe that shifts in the location and permeability of "personal space" (Sommer, 1969), like variations in the experience of transitional space, are pertinent to activation of the process of introjection.

INTROJECTION AND THE THERAPEUTIC PROCESS

For the past 20 years, my colleagues and I have been studying the therapeutic action of the processes of introjection (Geller et al., 1981). Since being introduced to Bert's ideas about psychic inner space, I have been rethinking some of the most important findings that our ongoing project has yielded (Geller, 1998). Currently, I am intrigued by the idea that the processes of interiorization, of which introjection is a particular instance, make a fundamental contribution to the formation and reshaping of the psychological experience of inner space.

For research purposes we define the concept of introjection as those processes that bring into existence, modify, and re-organize emotionally charged schemas of human interactions. In our model, interpersonal schemas, as such, are not directly knowable or available to consciousness; they are the inferred memory structures whose activation gives rise to emotionally charged representations of the self, others, and interactions be-tween them.

We work with the assumption that, within the context of therapy, patients acquire or construct representations that rep-licate within subjective experience the patterns of listening and talking, seeing and being seen, feeling and being with the ther-apist that recurrently organize the therapeutic dialogue. Once such schemas are firmly established in long-term memory, pa-tients are no longer dependent on the actual presence of the therapist to continue the therapeutic dialogue, and they do so representationally, in the privacy of consciousness. For example, when we are daydreaming, interpersonal schemas may appear or reappear in awareness in the form of imaginary "felt presenc-es" that exist within the confines of the body or mind or both but are not experienced as an expression of the subjective self. In other words, the person about whom the fantasy refers may be experienced as if he or she were objectively present; in this sense, they are "inner experiences."

Thus far, our results indicate that patients' representations of the therapeutic process tend to be more imagistic than con-ceptual (Geller & Farber, 1993). Psychotherapy clients drawn from diverse samples typically report that, when interacting with the felt presence of their therapists (between sessions and after termination), they do so in the form of images of being in the presence of their therapist sitting in his or her chair, in his or her office. We have also found that access to vivid, detailed, sensorially rich visual, auditory, and kinesthetic images of a continuing dialogue with one's therapist, in his or her office, increases the probability of a positive therapeutic outcome and its preservation after termination (Orlinsky & Geller, 1993).

Psychotherapy sessions typically or solely take place within the intimate confines of an environment created, maintained, and sanctioned by the therapist. Moreover, encounters with the therapist are typically scheduled at regular and predictable intervals. In short, they are rhythmically spaced apart. Do the spatial boundaries and temporal parameters of the work structure of psychotherapy contribute to the creation of a "holding environment" (Winnicott, 1971) or "frame" (Langs, 1976) that, when introjected, serves as the raw materials for the reshaping of the psychological experience of inner space?

Opinions differ as to which interpersonal conditions set in motion the processes of introjection. The repair of ruptures in the therapeutic alliance, the working through of nontraumatic empathic failures, and the process of mourning all have their share of advocates. My opinion is that in situations of deep intimacy, participating in reciprocal exchanges having the quality of rhythmic synchronization ultimately leads to a blending and sharing of the functions and experiences of the other. This, in turn, makes it possible to "take in" or introject qualities of a caring person, and, in so doing, expand or refine attributes that may not be adequately represented in the patient's own personality.

The novel angle of vision provided to me by Bert's ideas has led me to ponder the following questions: What do patients remember of the places in which their therapists work? Do images of one's therapist inhabiting his or her office replicate the sense of being in a private and protective enclosure? Do aesthetically pleasing images of the therapist's workplace play an influential role in the conscious and preconscious mental activities that occur when patients are attempting to achieve further self-understanding, resolve conflicts, problem solve, or regulate affect?

Does the creation of mental models of the spatial configurations encountered in the therapy room (e.g., the arrangement of the chairs) promote an internal climate that makes verbal representation of that which must be spoken about in therapy possible? Does the body of images provided by evocative memories of sitting with the therapist in his or her office facilitate or interfere with adaptive utilization of verbalized symbolic thought?

I have many other questions, including the following: Is progress in therapy marked by transformations in the forms taken by inner space? What is the route back to the road not taken? What is the shape of a sense of inner emptiness? Does it make a difference whether one's self-representations are higher or lower, larger or smaller, further to the left or right, than one's representations of the therapist? Do patients' representations of the physical identifying properties of the therapists' offices and their contents have iconic properties, similar to those of maps? (In semiotics, an icon is a sign that stands for something else by virtue of being similar to it.)

In an earlier publication (Geller, 1984), I argued on behalf of the idea that the processes of introjection can play a vital role in the structuralization of feelings as experienced qualities. I reasoned that by bringing into existence benignly influential representations of relationship episodes with a trusted therapist, the processes of introjection strengthened the capacity to engage in what Bert refers to as "discursive symbolization." Grappling with the questions posed above has led me to hypothesize that a patient's capacity for "dynamic symbolization" will be strengthened when the processes of introjection give rise to representations of benignly influential relationship episodes with the therapist that concern self-reflection. "Dynamic symbolization" is the name Bert has given to those forms of mentation that underlie subjective awareness of irreconcilable conflicts, the ability to take oneself as an object of consciousness and to reflect upon consciousness of consciousness.

QUESTIONS FOR PONDERING

If we are to learn whether and how the processes of introjection contribute to the formation and reshaping of inner space within the context of psychotherapy, we will have to develop tools to study questions that are even more fundamental.

1. Do the spatial properties of the representational world take on different qualities when we are retrieving memories, problem solving, theorizing, and so on?
2. What spatial properties of an individual's representational world persist over time and across changes in circumstance?
3. What do representations of the places in which memorable events occurred and their affective valences contribute to our sense of inner space?
4. Do the representational boundaries that surround the mind regulate what potentially can be brought into the mind?
5. Are the cohesiveness and integrity of the self correlated with the forms taken by inner space?
6. Can spatial representations be characterized in terms of their mimetic complexity?
7. Are there connections between the ways in which we move through spaces outside our bodies and the ways in which our thoughts move through inner space?
8. Like the stars and planets, do thoughts move in regular paths according to discoverable laws?

9. Are there psychologically important linkages between the forms taken by psychic inner space and the ability to perform different mental functions?
10. Do some spatial representations have a referential meaning in their own right? That is, do they themselves signal mental content?
11. Are the forms taken by inner space predictive of the quality of the symbolizing processes taking place within these representational boundaries?
12. Can one infer from the thinness or thickness of the contours of its silhouette the degree to which a particular sense of inner space feels coherent, substantial?
13. Are there resemblances between the visible properties of the physical world and the forms taken by pictorial representations of inner space?
14. What forms of symbolizing space pave the way for the production and consideration of conflictual ideas from multiple perspectives?

One of the most sophisticated developments in the evolution of the human mind is the capacity for reflexive consciousness. As defined by Humphrey (1984), "reflexive consciousness means not merely observing from outside but from within, not merely looking at one's behavior, but looking in on it—in on the thoughts and passions which accompany consciousness" (p. 210). Bert Freedman has deepened my understanding of what is required to conduct such introspective inquiries. Tiresias warned Oedipus that "wisdom is a dreadful thing if it brings no profit to the man who is wise" (Sophocles, 429 B.C.E./1971, p. 23). I have consistently profited, personally and professionally, by a very wise man whom I have affectionately come to think of as my personal Tiresias.

REFERENCES

Anzieu, D. (1989). *The Skin Ego* (C. Turner, Trans.). New Haven, CT: Yale University Press.

Bachelard, G. (1964). *The Poetics of Space* (M. Jolas, Trans.). Boston, MA: Beacon Press.

Bion, W.R. (1963). *Elements of Psychoanalysis*. London, UK: Tavistock.

Blom, L.A., & Chaplin, L.T. (1982). *The Intimate Act of Choreography*. Pittsburgh: Pittsburgh University Press.

Bloomer, K.C., & Moore, W.M. (1977). *Body, Memory, and Architecture*. New Haven, CT: Yale University Press.

Erikson, E.H. (1963). *Childhood and Society* (2nd ed.). New York, NY: Norton. (Original work published 1950.)

Fisher, S., & Cleveland, S.E. (1968). *Body Image and Personality* (2nd. ed.). New York, NY: Dover.

Freedman, N. (1983). On psychoanalytic listening: The construction, paralysis, and reconstruction of meaning. *Psychoanalysis and Contemporary Thought* 6(3):405–434.

——— (1997a). On spatialization—personal and theoretical reflections. Unpublished paper.

——— (1997b). The spatialization of the representational world. Unpublished paper.

——— & Bucci, W. (1981). On kinetic filtering in associative monologues. *Semiotica* 34:225–249.

——— & Lavender, J. (1997). On receiving the patient's transference: The symbolizing and desymbolizing countertransference. *Journal of the American Psychoanalytic Association* 45:79–103.

Geller, J.D. (1978). The body, expressive movement, and physical contact in psychotherapy. In J.L. Singer & K.S. Pope (Eds.), *The Power of Human Imagination* (pp. 347–378). New York, NY: Plenum Press.

————— (1984). Moods, feelings, and the process of affect formation. In L. Temoshok, C. Van Dyke, & L.S. Zegans (Eds.), *Emotions in Health and Illness: Applications to Clinical Practice* (pp. 171–186). Orlando, FL: Grune & Stratton.

————— (1998). What does it mean to practice psychotherapy scientifically? *Psychoanalysis and Psychotherapy* 15:187–215.

—————, Cooley, R.S., & Hartley, D. (1981). Images of the psychotherapist: A theoretical and methodological perspective. *Imagination, Cognition and Personality* 1(2):123–146.

————— & Farber, B.A. (1993). Factors influencing the process of internalization in psychotherapy. *Psychotherapy Research* 3(3):166–180. https://doi.org/10.1080/10503309312331333769

Grotstein, J.S. (1978). Inner space: Its dimensions and its coordinates. *International Journal of Psycho-Analysis* 59:55–61.

Hall, E.T. (1959). *The Silent Language*. Garden City, NY: Doubleday.

————— (1966). *The Hidden Dimension* (1st ed.). Garden City, NY: Doubleday.

Humphrey, N. (1984). *Consciousness Regained*. Oxford, UK: Oxford University Press.

James, W. (1890). *The Principles of Psychology*. New York, NY: Henry Holt.

Kundera, M. (1984). *The Unbearable Lightness of Being*. New York, NY: Harper & Row.

Langer, S.K. (1942). *Philosophy in a New Key*. Cambridge, MA: Harvard University Press.

Langs, R. (1976). *The Bipersonal Field*. New York, NY: Jason Aronson.

Lewin, B.D. (1946). Sleep, the mouth, and the dream screen. *Psychoanalytic Quarterly* 15:419–434.

Lux, T. (1997). *New and Selected Poems*. Boston, MA: Houghton Mifflin.

Orlinsky, D.E., & Geller, J.D. (1993). Psychotherapy's internal theater of operation: Patients' representations of their therapists and therapy as a new focus of research. In N.E. Miller, J. Doherty, L. Luborsky, & J. Barber (Eds.), *Psychodynamic Treatment Research: A Handbook for Clinical Practice* (pp. 423–466). New York, NY: Basic Books.

Pallaro, P. (Ed.). (1999). *Authentic Movement: Essays by Mary Starks Whitehouse, Janet Adler and Joan Chodorow*. London, UK: Jessica Kingsley.

Piaget, J. (1956). *The Child's Conception of Space*. London, UK: Routledge and Kegan Paul.

Proust, M. (1989). *Swann's Way: Remembrance of Things Past*. New York, NY: Vintage International Books. (Original work published 1913.)

Rafelson, B. (Director). (1970). *Five easy pieces* [Film].

Rich, A. (1986). Notes toward a politics of location. In *Blood, Bread and Poetry: Selected Prose 1979–1985* (pp. 210–232). London, UK: Virago. (Original work published 1984.)

Schilder, P. (1950). *The Image and Appearance of the Human Body*. New York, NY: International Universities Press.

Sommer, R. (1969). *Personal Space*. Englewood Cliffs, NJ: Prentice Hall.

Sophocles (1971). Oedipus the king. In D. Greene & R. Lattimore (Eds.), *The Complete Greek Tragedies* (7th ed.). New York, NY: Washington Square Press. (Original work published 429 B.C.E.)

Styron, W. (1990). *Darkness Visible*. New York, NY: Random House.

Viderman, S. (1970). *La construction de l'espace analytique*. Paris: Denoël.

Wapner, S., & Werner, H. (Eds.). (1965). *The Body Percept*. New York, NY: Random House.

Whorf, B.L. (1956). *Language, Thought, and Reality*. Cambridge, MA: M.I.T. Press.

Winnicott, D.W. (1971). *Playing and Reality*. New York, NY: Basic Books.

CHAPTER 11

My Experiences as a Patient in Five Psychoanalytic Psychotherapies

[J.D. Geller (2005). In J.D. Geller, J.C. Norcross, & D.E. Orlinsky (Eds.), *The Psychotherapist's Own Psychotherapy: Patient and Clinician Perspectives* (pp. 81–97). New York, NY: Oxford University Press.]

I am currently 62 years old. I have become introspective again. I welcome reminiscing with old friends about the persons and events that have contributed significantly to our development. I approached writing this chapter about my experiences as a patient in five different psychoanalytic psychotherapies with hopes similar to the ones I bring to these intimate conversations. I was not disappointed. I took another look at what I learned about my symptoms and my character pathology. Like my experiences in therapy, this effort yielded new self-discoveries. I will not dwell on these matters in this chapter; I have no interest in producing what Joyce Carol Oates (1999) would call an "exercise in pathography."

I also retrospectively evaluated whether and how each of my therapies contributed to my growth as a therapist and as a human being. What I realized is that I have no settled opinions about these matters. My understanding of the ways I have changed over time keeps changing. Moreover, my current estimates of how much I have benefited, personally, from my various therapies is different, in some important respects, from the remembered estimates I took in my 40s and 50s. If I had written this retrospective report during those decades, my estimates would have been biased in a more negative direction.

Still, I strongly believe that the illustrative experiences related here are the same ones I would have included if I had written this chapter earlier in my life. For me, they represent the decisive moments that took place in each of my therapies. Memories of these critical incidents are somehow emblematic of something that stood at the emotional center of each of my therapies. I seem to return to them over and over again when reflecting on the continuing and particular roles each of my therapies has played in determining what I do and what I do not do as a therapist. The primary purpose of this chapter is to further explore these connections in some detail.

ON BECOMING A PSYCHOTHERAPY PATIENT

The gateway into my first therapy was by way of seeking vocational guidance. I arrived at the City College of New York in 1956 poorly educated, learning disabled, and math phobic. I took a bus and the subway into Manhattan from Flushing, Queens, where I lived with my parents and shared a bedroom with my two younger brothers. I feared I would flunk out and would have to join the army like the majority of my friends. I have been ill-prepared for every major undertaking in my life. I was convinced that I would have to perform well beyond my "intelligence" if I were to remain in college.

In the hopes that I would be told what my interests and talents were and what I should become, I went, at the beginning of my sophomore year, for vocational guidance at the college's counseling center. I was interviewed and took a battery of psychological tests. To my surprise, I was told that I needed psychotherapy, not vocational guidance, and that the school would provide me with free psychotherapy if I chose to go.

I was assigned to Dr. A. I had very little idea of what to expect. I didn't know how to ask him for help. I was too proud to ask him for help. I was afraid of asking him for help. As I was to learn, I was searching for someone to help me develop what I would have called courage, in particular the courage to face and conquer my fears of failure, weakness, disease, accidents, an early death, and after death.

LEARNING HOW TO USE THERAPY

Dr. A introduced me to experiences that were previously unknown to me. I was the first person I knew who'd ever gone to therapy. I never knew anyone who dressed in three-piece tweed suits and smoked a pipe, as Dr. A did most hours. I had never had a productive conversation with an adult, in private, about matters that were important to me. My father and I had never had a heart-to-heart talk. He would become angry and impatient when his efforts to teach me how to tie my shoelaces or solve an arithmetic problem repeatedly failed. I estimate that by age six I had stopped asking him for help, reassurance, or instruction.

With Dr. A, I took my first tentative steps toward learning how to learn with a "trusted companion" (Bowlby, 1973) through the medium of dialogue. I talked with Dr. A, as I could talk to no other adult, about the helpless terrors of early childhood. I owe my acute "sense of place" (Bachelard, 1964) to having grown up in a Bronx basement apartment whose foyer door opened onto the building's furnace, discarded furniture, garbage cans, and the superintendent's savage German shepherd. I had grown accustomed to feeling anxious and alone in an ugly environment.

Dr. A helped me to find names and metaphors for my feelings. He provided me with clarifying descriptions of my "unformulated" (Stern, 1983) experiences. He helped me translate what had been "fits of anxiety" into particular fears. Fears can be met with courage. Anxieties, having no definable object, cannot. Unfortunately, I experienced my fears as a form of cowardice. I was ashamed that my mind lacked the power to overcome my acute fears of an early death. Bravery was the preeminent value in my neighborhood.

My most vivid memory of therapy with Dr. A is the following communicative exchange: "Jesse, you've often spoken about feeling angry at your father and the things that make you angry with him. Yet, you never talk about feeling angry with your mother. Is there anything that she does that gets you angry?" I shrugged my shoulders, hesitated, and then answered, "I can't think of anything." He replied, "How about her having poisoned your view of your father?" I doubt that this is what we actually said, but this representation of it has the feel of truth. He was right. I tended to see my father through my mother's often disrespectful eyes. With this remark, Dr. A opened me up to the possibility of reenvisioning how I was treated by each of my parents. With this primal insight, Dr. A earned my respect. Nonetheless, I never felt deep affection for him. I reserved this feeling for my teachers.

MY DIFFICULTIES WITH BEING A PATIENT

I did not enjoy being Dr. A's patient and, as it turns out, wrongly assumed that I wasn't benefiting from therapy. In fact, to anticipate a later point, I might have dropped out of therapy if I hadn't concurrently been studying psychology, literature, and philosophy with teachers whom I admired and wished to emulate and whose approval meant a great deal to me. For the most part, I hated going to my weekly, 50-minute sessions when I first began seeing Dr. A. I had to overcome many obstacles in order to use my relationship with Dr. A for personal benefit.

My conception of what a patient is supposed to do was something like, "I have to be a good soldier." A misguided sense of bravery required me to face unflattering truths about myself, however humiliating, while maintaining the facade of "taking it very well... like a man." I counterphobically revealed what I wished to conceal.

The idea that my self was intrinsically worthwhile was alien to me. I believed doctors only gave you bad news about yourself. I did not trust that Dr A would be nonjudgmental or respectful. In the absence of trust, it takes courage to become aware of and to admit to the raw, unexpressed, and unknown aspects of one's personality.

I had trouble being the focus of Dr. A's "serious interest" and "sympathetic understanding" (Freud, 1912). I was incapable of unselfconscious consciousness of myself. I had trouble taking my own suffering seriously. It felt weird speaking with seriousness of purpose about myself. I was constantly watching him watching me. I rarely made eye contact with him. I especially dreaded it when we looked at each other during silences, and there were many.

I also dreaded his asking, "What are you thinking?" to break a silence. I could usually be found taking inventory of whatever I felt I should be telling him—my pathetic vanities, my unkept promises, my mind-boggling grandiosity, my self-hatred, my sexual fantasies, and so on. It was particularly difficult when he asked this question while I was thinking that I preferred my psychology teachers to him. Like my unvoiced bad habits, this secret alienated me from Dr. A.

I hated it even more when he would ask me, "What are you feeling (right now)?" as he was disposed to do. I often didn't know. The question left me speechless. He seemed to believe me when I said, "Words fail me," but I assumed that he experienced me as a secretive and unrewarding patient. I didn't know if he really liked me.

In hindsight, it occurred to me that I was able to endure the hardships of being in therapy stoically because of what I was learning in the classroom, in the theater, at the movies, and in Greenwich Village. I persisted in therapy because my intellectual heroes advocated the view that self-understanding was intrinsically worth pursuing whether or not it "cured" one's neurosis. My psychology professors taught me that being in an insight-oriented therapy would turn one into a better, smarter, more cultured person, if not a healthier one. This conviction was especially important to me because I felt I was failing to transform my "intellectual insights" into "emotional insights," to use the jargon of that time. Being concurrently a psychology major and a psychotherapy patient provided me with an "identity" (Erikson, 1963).

Psychoanalysis and psychotherapy offered the alienated/secular college students of my time and place, New York in the 1950s, standards and values regarding our unanswered questions about meaning and morality. I came to the study of psychology and my first therapy seeking guidance about masturbation, romantic love, premarital sex, conventional cultural mores, and the ethical conduct of life. Moreover, studying developmental and abnormal psychology reassured me that my "symptoms"—agonizing self-consciousness, vocational disorientation, rebellion, preoccupation with health, heightened ambivalence, elusive mood swings, and identity confusion—were regarded by the experts as the "typical" manifestations of adolescence. Studying Freud and the neo-Freudians reassured me that beneath the surface of socially acceptable behavior of even the most mature person existed patricidal and incestuous wishes. At the same time, I was becoming aware that the psychoanalytic theories of the day were molding the taste, opinions, language, and life-styles of serious (e.g., intellectual, artistic, and bohemian) New Yorkers. I wanted to be one of them. I saw psychoanalysis as an ally in my struggle to establish myself as a cultural rebel, a defiant individualist, an American existentialist. I was attracted to the tension between the pro- and antisocial forces found in the teachings of Freud. My studies, my psychotherapy, and the conversations that dominated my social life were being integrated into a way of being in the world.

I decided to go to graduate school to study clinical psychology while in therapy, but I believe this choice grew primarily out of my identifications with my teachers. Once this decision was made, I began to see psychotherapy as a way of sharpening the knowledge I required to be an outstanding student. I discovered that while paying close attention to what was on *my* mind, I was learning how *the* mind works. As I have gotten older, it has become clearer to me that there is a direct continuity between the questions and concerns I have struggled with in therapy and my scholarly interests.

A BRIEF ENCOUNTER

After graduation and before starting graduate school, I was in a psychotherapy that I terminated unilaterally after six sessions. I had been referred to Dr. B by Dr A. Dr. A was opposed to transferring me into his private practice after having treated me "for free" for more than 2½ years. He told me that Dr. B was a Horneyian, as he himself was, and that he would see me for a reduced fee. At the time I terminated with Dr. A, there was still a possibility I would get into NYU's clinical PhD program. My favorite college professors were all graduates of NYU. I didn't want to leave New York or my girlfriend, Ruth. As it turned out, I was rejected by NYU. I chose to go to the University of Connecticut (1960–66) because it was closer to New York than the other schools that had accepted me. And that has made all the difference.

Two things about my therapy with Dr. B stand out in my memory—the overall physicality of the therapeutic situation and a particular piece of dialogue.

Dr. B sat eight to 10 feet away from me. He felt too far away. I was distracted by the voices of his wife and children, who lived next door to his posh Upper West Side office. I felt he was oblivious to matters of taste and style, as was revealed by the furniture, paintings, and lamps that inhabited his consulting room. I couldn't see him clearly because of the glare and shadows created by the late afternoon sun that poured through the large windows located directly behind his chair. All in all, I was disappointed because I did not find signs of expertise and healing authority when I submitted his office to semiotic and aesthetic scrutiny.

I am, however, indebted to Dr. B in one respect. In the fifth session, Dr. B said to me, "You seem to be comparing me unfavorably to Dr. A." I replied, "No, I think you are a very good *psycholoshits*." I dropped out of therapy at the next session, but I took away an unshakable conviction that parapraxes provide an especially compelling vantage point from which to explore conflicts and their transformations. My Freudian slip convinced me of the existence and creativity of unconscious processes.

THE DECISION TO BECOME A PSYCHOTHERAPIST

When I entered graduate school, I had only the vaguest idea about how I was going to earn a living. The men in my family had jobs. I was going to be the first one that had ever had a career. During my 2nd year at the University of Connecticut, I began to think that the practice of psychotherapy was a suitable and viable career aspiration. I could imagine no higher calling than to free others from their suffering. But my principal motives for seeking training as a psychotherapist lay elsewhere. I was drawn to the field by the realization that becoming a therapist would essentially involve the professionalization of my interests and talents. I saw earning some of my living by doing psychotherapy as a valid response to various conflicts, for example, the practical versus the idealistic. I regarded the private practice of therapy as a way of being what the Dalai Lama and Cutler (1998) describe as "wisely selfish." The profession appealed to me because in the early 1960s psychotherapists were still seen as being in the vanguard of social change.

THE CORNERSTONES OF MY APPROACH TO THERAPY

During my 6 years at the University of Connecticut, all of my supervisors and psychotherapy teachers identified themselves, first and foremost, as "Kaiserians." They had all been treated or trained by Helmuth Kaiser. Kaiser had begun his career in Europe as a classically trained Freudian analyst. In his maturity, he arrived at a position that radically departed from psychoanalytic insight-seeking psychotherapy as it was practiced during the 1950s and early 1960s. Kaiser's theory is basically founded on the notion that what is healing about psychotherapy can be found in the degree of "communicative intimacy" that the participants have been able to achieve (1965).

Kaiser's teachings have been labeled in several ways—namely, as existential, humanistic, and interpersonal and as an extension of Reich's (1949) psychoanalytic writings about character analysis. Not surprisingly, my supervisors interpreted his ideas in various ways. Ross Thomas taught my first practicum. He instructed us: "See what happens when you make engaging in authentic dialogues with your patients your sole and exclusive concern." Harvey Wasserman emphasized the importance of being able to estimate the congruence between what a patient is feeling and avowing. For Wasserman, the basic intent of a Kaiserian therapist was to promote in patients a feeling of responsibility for their words and deeds. Alan Willoughby advocated a nondirective but highly interactive therapy that focused on the patient's immediate and concrete experience in the "here and now."

These broad and ambiguous mandates held for me what Yeats (1959) called "the fascination of the difficult." Although they were scary as hell, they suited my temperament and values. The Kaiserian point of view was for me a great place from which to begin training as a therapist. It appealed to me intellectually, emotionally, and aesthetically. Its emphasis on authenticity and personal responsibility was consistent with the existential values I embraced in college. It pleased me that Kaiser's key concepts anticipated what were to become the dominant concerns of the late 1960s and early 1970s. It was during my generation that authenticity became a virtue. Taking a revisionist position vis-à-vis psychoanalysis appealed to my need to see myself as irreverent and as a maverick. I received my graduate education in an era when psychotherapists essentially had two choices—you either followed or reacted against psychoanalysis. I resonated with Kaiser's use of artistic means to convey his scientifically based views about the effectiveness of psychotherapy. In an allegorical play called *Emergency* (1965), he called into question fundamental aspects of psychoanalytic therapy. From a distance, it is clear to me that another crucial motive was at play. Identifying with a radical minority of Kaiserian therapists enabled me, at one and the same time, to remain an outsider and to join a community of believers.

THE QUEST FOR AUTHENTICITY

It was inevitable that I would go to see a Kaiserian when I decided to return to therapy, which I did during my 3rd year of graduate school. I conceived of this choice as essential to my "initiation" into the group of therapists who were known to be Kaiserians, or who acknowledged being influenced by him (e.g., Shapiro, 1975). Although this "pseudocommunity" existed only in my imagination (even Kaiser insisted he wasn't a Kaiserian), going into therapy with Dr. C felt like my idea of the "training analyses" offered within the context of psychoanalytic institutes. I entered treatment with Dr. C to grapple with the key choices I had made during my transition into early adulthood (e.g., marrying Ruth and starting a family) and to deal with my conflict between the need to succeed and my desire to be loving and loved. During an argument, without realizing the fullness of what she was saying, Ruth described me as becoming "ruthless" whenever I undertook a writing project.

I came to therapy with Dr. C wanting to reveal myself without artifice, without self-dramatization, without fictionalizing myself or uglifying my past. I wished to reveal myself (as I really was). But I knew all too well that I would have to overcome a variety of obstacles in order to speak with Dr. C spontaneously, authentically, and expressively—to name a few: Having grown up surrounded by people I experienced as "too pushy," "too vulgar," "too demonstrative," in effect "too much" inhibited me from speaking expressively. I had spent much of my youth "pretending" everything was all right, although I knew something was dreadfully wrong. At home I'd always kept my worries to myself. By the time I got to college, I had arrived at the Buddhist position that much of my suffering was caused by wishing and wanting. I tried, willfully, to disavow the desire to have what I didn't already have. I operated under the assumption that you were more likely to get what you wanted if you didn't let the other know what you wanted. I acted as if my hurts and disappointments were unimportant. To counteract my boyish and, so I was told, "cute" appearance, I developed the ability to assume the physiognomy of seriousness. In high school this required presenting an image of myself as "cool." In college, my preferred persona was that of a beatnik or a bohemian intellectual like the melancholy young men I admired in foreign films and existential novels.

DR. C AND HIS THERAPY STYLE

I was painfully aware of the myriad occasions in which my behavior was at variance with what I felt. With Dr. A, I had learned how difficult it is to resist resisting. Not surprisingly, I began therapy with Dr. C feeling somewhat fearful about looking closely at the contradictions that existed between the "images" I sought to project and my insider's view of what was "really" going on.

Dr. C saw clearly those aspects of myself that I found difficult to accept. He seemed to emphasize, in a highly selective way, what was left unsaid but was conveyed by my postures, gestures, facial expressions, and voice qualities. It was a therapy in which the "form" rather than the "content" of what I said was given priority. His approach with me seemed to conform most closely to the psychoanalytic notion of confronting and analyzing resistances. Bringing a patient's attention to the expressive behaviors that accompany speech requires considerable tact and must be done compassionately. From my own difficult firsthand experience with Dr. C, I know that focusing on the nonlinguistic aspects of a patient's utterances will provoke shame, and little else, if these qualities are lacking.

Sadly, Dr. C did not interpret and enact the principles of Kaiser in a style that was congruent with my sensibility. Dr. C prided himself on his sense of irony. I found him too glib, droll, and sarcastic. As a neophyte adult, embarking on an uncharted course, I needed to be taken seriously. Dr. C's approach seemed to be in the service of not taking what I said "too seriously." He did not give my suffering its due. I felt he did not acknowledge its magnitude. I felt caricatured by him. He seemed insufficiently grounded in a tragic perspective on the human condition. I felt he could have benefited from Paul Simon's (1973) advice: "Try a little tenderness. There is no tenderness beneath your honesty."

During my 1½ years of therapy with Dr. C, I took further steps toward learning how to say "I think... ," "I feel... ," "I believe... ," "I want..." directly and straightforwardly. Not finding in Dr. C the idealized model of the Kaiserian therapist I hoped to become, I felt greater affection for and identified more with my teachers than my therapist, as I had in college. In fact, much of what I took away from my therapy with Dr. C was the conviction that I would develop a therapy style that was gentle, kind, and nonironic.

COMING TO NEW HAVEN

In graduate school I was taught mainly what was wrong with psychoanalysis. When I arrived in New Haven in 1967, almost all of the therapy being practiced was derived from and judged against psychoanalysis. Here, the prevailing view was that psychoanalysis was the deepest and most thorough form of therapy.

New Haven is a city in which psychoanalytic theory and practice continues to flourish. Then, and to a lesser extent now, the most intellectually rigorous and admired figures were and are psychoanalysts. As an assistant professor in the Yale Department of Psychiatry, I was supervised by men such as Sid Blatt, Marshall Edelson, and Borge Lofgren, who persuasively argued that a four- or five-times-a-week psychoanalysis was inherently superior to all other therapies and a necessary training requirement. I read their typed manuscripts and sat in at seminars and lectures with Roy Schafer and Hans Loewald. I could say of Roy Schafer (1983) what he said of his relationship to Erik Erikson:

> I was absolutely enamored of his way of thinking, his way of integrating social psychological, biological, and anthropological material with psychoanalytic material. I then found myself in a position of a kind that I think is not rare among young analysts. I was imitating my hero, thinking and talking like him. It was only when I tried writing like him that I became aware that it was as though I was trying to be Erikson himself (p. 284).

It was practically and politically wise to think and speak in the vocabulary shared by therapists working in the psychoanalytic tradition. Concurrently, I had grown distrustful of the ways Kaiser's ideas were being interpreted by the handful of clinicians in New Haven who espoused this point of view. And so, when I felt the need to return to therapy, I decided to be psychoanalyzed. A friend who was being trained as a psychoanalyst recommended that I see Dr. D. He described him as bright and unflappable and as having had a lot of experience treating hospitalized adolescents.

MY DISAPPOINTMENTS IN DR. D

I am aware of representing all of my therapists in a twofold manner. First, they are represented as the persons with whom

I engaged in psychological development. Second, they are the source of disappointments and negative transference reactions, perhaps originating in my troubles with significant others. The latter peaked during my psychoanalysis.

I took it as a matter of course that Dr. D would draw anger and disappointed reactions toward himself through no fault of his own. I was intellectually prepared for him to become the target of displacements from significant male authority figures of my past. But by the 6th or 7th month of analysis, I was beginning to fear that Dr. D and I were a poor fit. I felt at times that he was studying me like a "case." This suspicion was confirmed years after I terminated, when I stumbled on an article he had published. I was shocked when I found myself being described by him, "disguised" of course. He had never sought my permission.

Dr. D was a very proper, textbook analyst. With me he never seemed to deviate from "correct" technique. I felt his therapeutic stance and stratagems were unduly influenced by obeisance to orthodox interpretations of Freud's recommendations regarding anonymity, abstinence, and neutrality. However technically expert he may have been, he never said anything that I found evocative or exciting. He never dazzled me with the depth of his insights or led me to feel as if I had been enriched by new ideas. I wanted an analyst who had the qualities of inventiveness and originality. I felt he did not grasp the unpredictable specifics of my life. He did not have a creative edge about him. He seemed to value my efforts of arriving at interpretations of myself, but all too often I felt as if I was teaching myself what I had come to learn from and with him.

Like the film stereotype of the rigid analyst, he was not responsive to my "realistic" questions. I felt he was duplicating my family's secrecy by scrupulously avoiding all forms of self-disclosure. He remained silent when I needed an empathic reflection of my feelings. Whereas Dr. C had delivered his confrontations in tones of irony, the tonal qualities of Dr. D's voice did not convey liveliness or vitality. I remember him as slouched over in a director's chair that seemed too small for his large and burly body.

Dr. D did not tell me if he agreed or disagreed with my interpretations, with one major exception. We disagreed about my interpretation of his management of the business aspects of our relationship. When my VA insurance benefits for outpatient therapy ran out during the 3rd year of my analysis, I asked if we could renegotiate the fee. We disagreed about what I should pay. I felt he wanted more than I could afford. I don't know if he bought into Menninger's (1962) then-influential assertion that for therapeutic purposes the fee should be a "definite sacrifice" for the patient. I regarded my position as consistent with my commitment to the values of the community mental health center movement (Geller & Feirstein, 1974). In the Outpatient Department of the Connecticut Mental Health Center, where I worked, our mission was to offer long-term psychodynamic psychotherapy to people who could not afford the fees charged by therapists in private practice. A study published in 1975 by Pope et al. documented that neither the amount nor the source of the money paid for therapy bore a significant relationship to positive outcomes among the patients seen in our clinic. I was rooting for this finding.

Whatever their meanings, our conflicts over the economics of therapy were never resolved, and I left the analysis prematurely. The shocking discovery that he had made extensive use of material from my analysis to illustrate his theoretical convictions in a published article, without first consulting me, transformed my disappointments in him into disillusionment. I have forgiven my father, but I still have not forgiven Dr. D.

RECLAIMING MY PAST

In each of my therapies I have especially treasured the sessions during which I recovered memories that seemed to have been permanently lost. With Dr. A I learned that I pictured myself walking forward in a straight line. One step behind me, a tall, red brick wall was following me. It moved forward as I did. Its monolithic presence made it impossible for me to look to see where I had come from. We extracted many meanings from this metaphor. Doing so awakened me to the possibility of thinking historically about myself. Dr. A encouraged me to be curious about myself, and I took pleasure in identifying the "originators" of my problems-in-living.

I began my analysis in the hope of recovering many more formative childhood experiences. As my therapy with Dr. B was essentially focused on the here and now, I had not progressed very far in my quest to overcome my "childhood amnesia." With Dr. D I reconstructed far less of my childhood than I had hoped but perhaps no less than would have been predicted by Ernst Schachtel (1959), one of my favorite authors.

On the other hand, as with all my therapies, analysis did bring about beneficial changes in unforeseen directions. One such unexpected, but greatly appreciated, change was the discovery of the constant flux of visual images that stream through my "inscape" (Hopkins, 1998). While lying on the couch, I often closed my eyes in order to make contact with the kaleidoscopic flow of flickering, often grainy, and silent visual images. My memory medium is film montage, not the narratives found in novels. Psychoanalysis strengthened my ability to disallow the censorship of the images that are evoked during regressive and disorganizing experiences. As I was to learn, once one has achieved the ability to "stay with" objectionable fantasies, "an inescapable gap" (Berger, 1972) between imagery and spoken language still remains. Only a pale version of dreams as they are experienced can be reported.

THE LANGUAGE OF DREAMS

I do not think I am deceiving myself by suggesting that my therapies contributed to the transformation and extinction of a nightmarish dream that had tormented me since childhood. In its original form I am running away in fear from two anonymous men. Sometimes I find temporary sanctuary in the tenement apartment of a middle-aged African American woman. Just as I am about to fall asleep on the cot in her kitchen, the two men forcibly gain entrance into the apartment by climbing up the fire escape and breaking in a window. The next generation of dreams was signaled by the disappearance of one of the men. I was still running away, but I interpreted the dream more optimistically as suggesting that the magnitude of my fears was diminishing.

The final dream in this series took place during my analysis. This time the action occurred at the front door of my house in New Haven. The man was banging on the door and yelling at me. We could see each other through the glass and oak door that separated us. He was wearing a navy blue suit, a white shirt, and a tie. I didn't know who he was. That night, instead of taking flight, I grabbed a baseball bat, opened the door, and said, "Come on in, you motherfucker. I'm ready for you."

Obviously, this dream can be interpreted in multiple ways. I would like to think it meant I had developed the courage to face and conquer whatever fears "he" symbolized. Perhaps it signified that I was prepared to integrate into my sense of self the aggressive and destructive qualities that I had previously projected onto him. For me, all interpretations contain an irreducible element of fiction. What is important, though, is the fact that after that night I no longer had dreams that were so scripted.

THE DEVELOPMENT OF BODY AWARENESS

During and after my psychoanalysis, I experienced the benefits of a variety of practices whose basic operating premise is that changes in personality can be brought about directly by modifying the body structure and its functional motility. These educative or growth-oriented approaches included Feldenkrais's (1949) system of postural and neuromuscular relearning, therapeutic massage, Rolf's (1963) structural integration, and yoga. I also began my ongoing participation in Authentic Movement groups (Pallaro, 1999) and my study of treatment modalities derived from the creative arts (Geller, 1974, 1978; Clarkson & Geller, 1996). These largely nonverbal, noncognitive practices have complemented and reinforced the benefits I have derived from the "talking cure."

In tandem with psychoanalysis, my involvement in these practices has taught me how to pay attention to the subtle and localized physical sensations that accompany various experiential states, including those altered states of consciousness that occur while free-associating. They provided me with alternative modes of communicating the "truths" that even the poets find difficult to express in words. It was deeply reassuring to learn that artists' descriptions of the creative process closely resembled my struggles as a patient.

Singly and in combination, these experiential approaches enabled me to "embody" the insights I derived from therapy. In psychoanalysis I explored conflicts between "the urge to let go" and the felt necessity to maintain self-control, but it required neuromuscular relearning for me to surrender to passive weight and to experience trust kinesthetically. I learned about the many meanings and functions served by my addiction to cigarettes in analysis, but I learned how to breathe naturally, and without the aid of cigarettes, by doing body-movement work. (I had unconsciously held my breath—a legacy of childhood fears—and thus paradoxically lit cigarettes in order to reinitiate the cycle of inhaling and exhaling.) In analysis I sought further understandings of my hyperactivity, but I learned how to sit in stillness, without getting muscularly bound, by doing yoga and other forms of meditation. In psychoanalysis I examined the ways I was at one and the same time an amoral sensualist and a bashful prude, but it required direct body work to melt my "physical armor" (Reich, 1949) so that I could take unconflicted pleasure in sensory experiences.

WRITING AND PSYCHOTHERAPY

Each of my therapies can be characterized in terms of the developmental tasks I was dealing with when I entered treatment. For example, Dr. A accepted my adolescent pretensions while supporting my adult aspirations. He helped me to leave my home and New York City. There is, however, one theme that has recurrently surfaced in all of my psychotherapies—my relationship to writing academic papers, especially those concerning psychotherapy.

In my first therapy, I discovered that the obligation to write term papers within a specified period of time invariably awakened annihilation anxieties. Somehow, I had acquired the view that I would perish before reaching my goals or because of my efforts to reach my goals. My inability to accept as valid comforting religious beliefs that could only be explained on the basis of faith intensified my acute fears of death and what happens after death. As a youth, my deepest connection to other Jews was linked to an intense awareness of the Holocaust and the dangers of anti-Semitism. No one in my family accepted the faith of Judaism or ever went to a synagogue to pray. None of the men on either side of my family were bar mitzvahed. We did not participate in any organized aspects of Jewish life. My favorite uncles mocked the idea that the Jews were the chosen people of the most powerful God. I both envied and felt sorry for those who had a benign vision of the eternal and could apprehend a divine presence at work in the world. My parents were admirably principled but were analytically skeptical about the existence of God. They brought me up to believe in the classical "virtues"—courage, wisdom, justice, and temperance.

Although it is not the full explanation, I recognize a deep connection between having grown up as a nonobservant and unaffiliated Jew and the inchoate spiritual yearnings I brought to each of my therapies, my reluctance to join any school of therapy, and my ongoing struggle to find a theoretical vocabulary in which to write about therapy.

Dread of doing a dissertation figured prominently in my therapy with Dr. C. With him I dealt with the peculiar disappointment that I was not a "genius" and my fears of being mediocre. With him I dealt with my rebellious wish to challenge the strictures of academic formalism. I came to understand that my search for respect and self-worth depended too heavily on what and how much I wrote.

I am deeply committed to providing my patients with unconditional positive regard. But, for as long as I can remember, I have felt that my ultimate value as a man depended on the quality of what I created. Eight and a half- by eleven-inch lined, yellow pieces of paper have been the battleground on which I have struggled with this contradiction. I was compelled to publish so as not to "perish" at Yale. I broodingly anticipated that my productivity would be insufficient to get tenure. At the same time, I felt that I had chosen the wrong medium in which to express my imperious need to create. I considered going to drama school to become a theater director. These issues were an important focus of self-exploration during my analysis. Within this context I learned a great deal about the ways my perfectionism, competitiveness, aggressiveness, narcissism, and exhibitionistic motives complicated my efforts at writing.

DR. E AND VIOLATIONS OF DISTANCE

I deliberately chose Dr. E as my next therapist, in part because I knew he, too, was conflicted about writing. It was rumored that he had a closet filled with unpublished manuscripts. While in therapy with Dr. E, to keep my ambivalences about continuing to write in the foreground of my awareness, I posted Yeats's (1959, p. 242) poem "The Choice" on our refrigerator door. It begins: "The intellect of man is forced to choose, / Perfection of the life, or of the work."

Dr. E was thought to be one of the premier psychoanalytically oriented therapists' therapists in my area. He was widely respected for his intelligence and his clarity of thought. At conferences that I attended, he spoke expertly and eloquently about his work. He impressed me as the kind of man I could respect. He is a European man and has maintained a European style. It pleased me that, like myself, he wore comfortable shoes, corduroy pants, cotton shirts without ties, and sweaters made of soft fabrics. There was a kind of aura about him that was not present in my American therapists, whether they were Jewish (Drs. A, B, and C) or Christian, psychologist or psychiatrist. (Dr. D was the only psychiatrist.) Dr. E's aura seemed to suggest that he had achieved "wisdom." I could imagine that he was a highly evolved, mature, unusually creative, scholarly, probing yet gentle therapist. I hoped to find in him the idealized model of the type of therapist I hoped I was becoming.

Sadly enough, being Dr. E's patient did not match the fantasy as much as I had hoped. He frequently seemed tired, distracted, inattentive, and melancholy. There were occasional flashes of brilliance and insight that renewed my hope that he was returning to the top of his game. I still meditate on the meanings of his koan-like interpretation: "Jesse, you don't pretend to be who you are not; you pretend you are not who you are." His finest moments seemed to take place when he said goodbye at the end of a session. His exit lines (e.g., "Till next time") had in them the promise that maybe next time things would get better.

When I felt Dr. E enjoyed my presence, I was able to relax and turn my attention to my inner life. If I felt his presence could not be taken for granted, I became preoccupied instead with our relationship. While in therapy with Dr. E, I belonged to an informal network of his current and former patients. We were all therapists. Comparing our experiences with him was reassuring. We admitted to one another that Dr. E seemed to fall asleep occasionally during therapy sessions. We compared the differing ways we reacted to his eyes glazing over and his unwillingness to acknowledge his obvious fatigue. Some feared that he found them boring. I deeply resented the times he acted as if I could not make impartial judgments about his lapses of interest.

We speculated about how his personal life was affecting his work. Some details were known to us. This knowledge softened our disappointments in Dr. E. There are no objective or absolute standards against which to judge the intensity, breadth, and persistence of a therapist's interest in a patient. Therefore, it is very difficult to locate the boundary beyond which the felt inability to take and show lively interest in a patient warrants an apology or an inquiry. Our inner circle of therapist-patients of Dr. E found these ambiguities a hardship.

In a previously published article (Geller, 1994), I used clinical material from my therapy with Dr. E (I disguised my identity) to illustrate how to understand the temptation to emotionally withdraw from a patient. What I wish to underscore here is the following proposition: Like getting "too close" to a patient, markedly diminished interest in a patient carries with it ethical as well as technical implications. I believe a boundary violation occurs when the depth and breadth of a therapist's interest falls below the levels a patient has a "right" to expect. Gross reductions of interest constitute a violation of distance (Katherine, 1991).

TERMINATION THERAPY WITH DR. E

During the 2nd year of my therapy with Dr. E, I experienced a major episode of writer's block. I was trying to finish a paper on the role of separation and loss in psychotherapy (1987). My life was in turmoil because of the continuing crises triggered by our younger daughter's deafness (Geller, 1996) and the decision of the Yale Department of Psychiatry not to promote me. Dr. E gave me permission to stop writing. "Jesse, you don't have to finish this paper if you don't want to." But, for reasons I still only incompletely understand, I persisted. It therefore seemed fitting that Dr. E would say to me, in a dream that I took as a signal that I was moving toward termination, "Jesse, you can have a room of your own." In the dream, we are standing face-to-face in a well-lit but unfurnished attic. As you may recall, *A Room of One's Own* is the title of Virginia Woolf's (1929) essay on what is required for a writer's life.

CONCLUSION

I approached writing this chapter in the spirit of those who discover what they believe and wish to say in the act of writing. While writing this chapter, I made connections that were not evident to me before. I was surprised to see how much I had triangulated my teachers and therapists, thereby re-creating a pattern that was laid down when I felt caught between my father and my uncles. Looking back and seeing from whence I came has deepened my appreciation of the ways identifications and counteridentifications with my therapists have shaped my attitudes toward those aspects of therapeutic practice that are not covered in formal training programs and are not readily manualized. These include, but are not limited to, my conversational style, the fees I charge for my services, the importance I assign to embodying consciousness, and the centrality of presence.

Autobiographical accounts of therapists' experiences in therapy can be written in various genres. We don't need more confessionals. As a result of writing this chapter, I have come to the conclusion that it would be advantageous to set for ourselves the task of finding narrative formats that would enable therapists to explore the nonrational and irrational sources of their handling of the ambiguities and unscripted aspects of therapy.

Psychotherapy theories are, at best, skeletal and only loosely based on empirically grounded information. I would, therefore, recommend that writing an essay devoted to the question, How has my biography influenced my theoretical and clinical dispositions? should become an integral part of the professional education of all therapists. Armed with this knowledge, therapists would, I believe, practice the "applied science" (Geller, 1998) of psychotherapy more effectively.

REFERENCES

Bachelard, G. (1964). *The Poetics of Space* (M. Jolas, Trans.). Boston, MA: Beacon Press.

Berger, J. (1972). *Ways of Seeing*. London, UK: Penguin Books.

Bowlby, J. (1973). *Attachment and Loss: Vol. 2. Separation: Anxiety and Anger*. New York, NY: Basic Books.

Clarkson, G., & Geller, J.D. (1996). The Bonny method from a psychoanalytic perspective: Insights from working with a psychoanalytic psychotherapist in a guided imagery and music series. *Arts in Psychotherapy* 23(4):311–319.

Dalai Lama & Cutler, H.C. (1998). *The Art of Happiness*. New York, NY: Riverhead Books.

Erikson, E.H. (1963). *Childhood and Society* (2nd ed.). New York, NY: Norton. (Original work published 1950.)

Feldenkrais, M. (1949). *Body and Mature Behavior*. New York, NY: International Universities Press.

Freud, S. (1912). Recommendations on psychoanalytic technique. *Standard Edition* 12:111–171.

Geller, J.D. (1974). Dance therapy as viewed by a psychotherapist. *American Dance Therapy Association Monograph* 3:1–21. [Reprinted in *A Collection of Early Writings: Toward a Body of Knowledge* (Vol. 1, pp. 63–80). ADTA, 1989.]

——— (1978). The body, expressive movement, and physical contact in psychotherapy. In J.L. Singer & K.S. Pope (Eds.), *The Power of Human Imagination* (pp. 347–378). New York, NY: Plenum Press.

——— (1987). The process of psychotherapy: Separation and the complex interplay among empathy, insight, and internalization. In J. Bloom-Feshbach & S. Bloom-Feshbach (Eds.), *The Psychology of Separation and Loss: Perspectives on Development, Life Transitions, and Clinical Practice* (pp. 459–514). San Francisco, CA: Jossey-Bass.

————— (1994). The psychotherapist's experience of interest and boredom. *Psychotherapy* 31(1):3–16.

————— (1996). Thank you for Jenny. In B. Gerson (Ed.), *The Therapist as a Person: Life Crises, Life Choices, Life Experiences, and Their Effects on Treatment* (pp. 119–139). New York, NY: Analytic Press.

————— (1998). What does it mean to practice psychotherapy scientifically? *Psychoanalysis and Psychotherapy* 15:187–215.

————— & Feirstein, A.R. (1974). Professional training in community mental-health centers. In G.F. Farwell, N.R. Gamsky, & P. Mathieu-Coughlan (Eds.), *The Counselor's Handbook* (pp. 449–471). New York, NY: Intext.

Hopkins, G.M. (1998). *The Selected Poems of Gerard Manley Hopkins*. New York, NY: Oxford University Press.

Horney, K. (1966). *New Ways in Psychoanalysis*. New York, NY: Norton.

Kaiser, H. (1965). *Effective Psychotherapy* (L.B. Fierman, Ed.). New York, NY: Free Press.

Katherine, A. (1991). *Boundaries: Where You End and I Begin*. New York, NY: Hazelden.

Menninger, K. (1962). *Theory of Psychoanalytic Technique*. New York, NY: Basic Books.

Oates, J.C. (1999, July 19). Writers on writing. *New York Times*, p. 10.

Pallaro, P. (Ed.). (1999). *Authentic Movement: Essays by Mary Starks Whitehouse, Janet Adler and Joan Chodorow*. London, UK: Jessica Kingsley.

Pope, K.S., Geller, J.D., & Wilkinson, L. (1975). Fee assessment and outpatient psychotherapy. *Journal of Consulting and Clinical Psychology* 43(6):835–841.

Reich, W. (1949). *Character Analysis*. New York, NY: Orgone Institute Press.

Rolf, I.P. (1963). Structural integration. *Systematics* 1:66–83.

Schachtel, E.G. (1959). *Metamorphosis: On the Development of Affect, Perception, Attention, and Memory.* New York, NY: Basic Books.

Schafer, R. (1983). *The Analytic Attitude.* New York, NY: Basic Books.

Shapiro, D. (1975). Dynamic and holistic ideas of neurosis and psychotherapy. *Psychiatry* 33:218–226.

Simon, P. (1973). Tenderness [Song]. On *There Goes Rhymin' Simon.* BHI.

Stern, D.B. (1983). Unformulated experience. *Contemporary Psychoanalysis* 10:71–99.

Woolf, V. (1929). *A Room of One's Own.* London, UK: Harcourt Brace.

Yeats, W.B. (1959). *The Collected Poems of W.B. Yeats.* New York, NY: Macmillan.

CHAPTER 12

Boundaries and Internalization in the Psychotherapy of Psychotherapists

[J.D. Geller (2005). In J.D. Geller, J.C. Norcross, & D.E. Orlinsky (Eds.), *The Psychotherapist's Own Psychotherapy: Patient and Clinician Perspectives* (pp. 379–404). New York, NY: Oxford University Press.]

CLINICAL AND RESEARCH PERSPECTIVES

The word "boundary" has been used as a metaphor by individual, group, couples, and family therapists, of varying theoretical persuasions, to serve multiple and overlapping ends (e.g., Minuchin, 1976; Bowen, 1978; Greene & Geller, 1980; Framo, 1982; Hartmann, 1991; Gutheil & Gabbard, 1993; Ruttan & Stone, 1993; Epstein, 1994; Gabbard & Lester, 1995; Smith & Fitzpatrick, 1995; Johnston & Farber, 1996). "Boundaries" has been used to describe and understand (1) the discontinuities of time, space, and task definition that separate psychotherapy, as a social system, from the rest of the interpersonal environment; (2) the role requirements that are specific to the positions of patient and therapist; (3) the ethical standards and codes of conduct that arise out of therapists' efforts to protect patients from harm and exploitation; and finally, (4) the mental activities that enable individuals to construct and preserve personally significant distinctions between self and nonself, fantasy and reality, "inside" personal space and "outside" extrapersonal space, and other aspects of personality functioning that affect the course and outcome of psychotherapy.

This research-informed chapter brings to the foreground the relevance of these interrelated figurative applications of the notion of boundaries to the psychotherapies offered to and experienced by psychotherapists and therapists-in-training. Experience and science support two propositions that shall serve as the primary focus of this chapter. First, there are "reality" factors that are more or less specific to the psychotherapy of therapist-patients that must be taken into account when dealing with the contractual, interpersonal, ethical, and intrapersonal boundaries that arise during the beginning, termination, and post-termination phases of the process of therapy. Second, internalization-based models of the therapeutic action of psychotherapy offer an illuminating vantage point from which to examine the ways psychotherapy contributes to the personal and professional development of psychotherapist-patients.

Our research (e.g., Geller, 1987, 1998) has focused primarily on those internalization processes that transform the patterns of listening and talking, seeing and being seen, feeling and being-with that recurrently characterize the communicative exchanges that occur during the course of therapy into aggregates of enduring representations of interactions-with-the-therapist. It is a central tenet of this chapter that patients are likely to benefit from therapy—and maintain these gains following termination—to the extent that they construct, preserve in long-term memory, use, and identify with positively toned representations of the "self-in-relation-to-my-empathic-therapist." I further assume that the processes that bring these benignly influential representations into existence are operative in all therapies in which patients and their therapists communicate responsibly and creatively within the context of an increasingly collaborative and intimate relationship.

Unless otherwise specified, I shall be writing about long-term expressive-exploratory individual therapy. Sometime in my 50s,

I sensed that I was selectively integrating existential-humanistic and psychodynamic ideas into my own uniquely derivative blend (Geller, 2003). If I am feeling glib, I will refer to myself as a "Gellerian." Concurrently, I began treating therapist-patients with greater regularity. For the past 7 years, I have usually had three to five therapist-patients in my caseload at any one time. Although there are important exceptions, the majority of these individuals are in their early 30s and aspire to become competent and autonomous therapists. One of my first therapist-clients was a 72-year-old retired clinical social worker. At termination, she left me with an indelible remark: "How great it is to peak in my 70s." I think of her when I need to be reminded about the ongoing possibilities of adult development.

THERAPISTS AND NONTHERAPISTS AS PATIENTS

There is obviously a great deal of overlap between patients who are therapists and those who are not. Perhaps most saliently, therapist- and nontherapist-patients are subject to the same agents that contribute to therapeutic change. Like lay patients, therapist-patients vary widely in their estimates of the relative amounts of catharsis, guidance, cognitive restructuring, reassurance, coaching, mentoring, role modeling, confrontation, and self-exploration they will "need." They vary, too, in their fears as to what they might not receive. Therapist- and nontherapist-patients are also subject to the same forces that can interfere with therapeutic progress. For example, no matter how intellectually well prepared therapist-patients may be to view themselves as actively implicated in their own difficulties or to rationally cooperate with their therapists, unconsciously motivated resistances intrude into the therapy of therapist-patients as pervasively as they do in the psychotherapy of lay patients.

Nevertheless, it is also true that therapist- and nontherapist-patients can differ in ways that are clinically relevant and that such differences often bear upon boundary-related issues (Geller et al., 2005). For instance, whatever their original reasons for seeking therapy, their choice of therapist is based on sources of information that are more readily available to mental health professionals. Therefore, therapist-patients are likely to know more about their prospective therapists' personal characteristics, professional reputation, and theoretical orientation and what these factors imply about what will or should occur during the course of therapy than equally well-educated patients drawn from the general clinical population. They are more familiar with the physical settings in which therapists work and have more detailed information about the contractual arrangements of therapy prior to becoming patients. Therapist-patients begin their own treatments with greater awareness of the customs, conventions, and language of psychotherapy than do lay patients. Thus, they are more likely to detect those moments when their therapists deviate from accepted practices. At the same time, they are also more likely to be aware when they themselves deviate from behaving like a "good patient."

Lay patients frequently know very little about their therapists' private lives. They are also less likely than therapist-patients to encounter their therapists outside of therapy, especially if they live in large urban areas. By comparison, in small cities such as New Haven, extratherapeutic contact between therapist-patients and their therapists is often unavoidable. In places like these, therapist-patients have the opportunity to observe their therapists at seminars, parties, academic conferences, and organizational meetings.

Even if both therapist and patient strictly avoid social or professional contacts during the course of treatment, therapist-patients are often privy to gossip about their clinicians. The upshot is that many therapist-patients begin treatment knowing more about their therapist's reputation, status in professional organizations, and lifestyle than either may be willing to consciously admit. For example, in departments of psychiatry, junior faculty often select therapists from the senior members of their departments. In contrast, it is not uncommon for lay patients to complain about not knowing enough about their therapist "as a person."

Most therapies end with the understanding, implicit or explicit, that the patient is free to recontact the therapist if the need arises (Schachter, 1992). For those lay patients who do not avail themselves of this opportunity, the termination of therapy represents a total and permanent separation. By way of contrast, when patient-therapists and their former therapists continue to live and work in the same community, there are often many opportunities for posttherapy contact. In some communities, mental health professionals transform therapeutic relationships into supervisory relationships and vice versa. Analytic candidates are destined to become the colleagues of their training analysts. Gestalt training programs are similarly organized (Lichtenberg, 2005).

DO THESE DIFFERENCES MAKE A DIFFERENCE?

Clearly, the therapy of therapists takes place in interpersonal and organizational contexts that are potentially quite different from those that are encountered with lay patients. The cumulative effect of these differences is at least twofold. When the patient is also a therapist, one expectable consequence would be a heightened awareness of the therapeutic tasks that revolve around the temporal, spatial, and interpersonal boundaries woven into the work structure of psychotherapy. The second major consequence would be the introduction of an interpersonal boundary that is missing when the patient is a nontherapist. This boundary is created by the dynamic tension between the formal roles of therapist and patient and the collegial aspects of the relationship. Treating a therapist-patient effectively requires protecting and preserving the professional therapeutic relationship while honoring shared membership in the same profession. Reconciling the sometimes competing claims of these dual imperatives further complicates therapeutic tasks that are in themselves quite thorny. These include locating the optimal placement of the boundaries that separate the therapist-patient's and therapist's "professional" and "personal" selves and choosing a clinical stance regarding the poles of expertise and egalitarianism. Not surprisingly, the therapists we surveyed ranked understanding and managing boundary issues as one of the most challenging aspects of their work with therapist-patients (Geller et al., 2005).

INTERSUBJECTIVITY

Earlier generations of psychoanalytic therapists downplayed the influence of sharing the same profession on training analyses and personal analyses (Fleming, 1987). This view is a particular instance of a more fundamental assumption. According to classical psychoanalytic theorizing, as long as analysts fulfill the principles of abstinence, anonymity, and neutrality, transference reactions will start with and reside solely in the patient (Freud, 1940).

My approach to the therapy of therapists rests on an opposing point of view. I believe that sharing the same profession as one's patient influences the interactive processes reverberating in both patient and therapist in much the same way that gender, age, race, and social class shape the day-to-day and transferential aspects of the therapeutic relationship. I presume that, like these self-evident sociopsychological realities, the importance of sharing the same profession as one's patient to the course and outcome of therapy varies from patient to patient and from time to time with a particular patient.

This perspective is compatible with converging trends in the psychoanalytic (e.g., Mitchell, 1993; Gabbard, 1995), existential (Heery & Bugental, 2005), and feminist (Brown, 2005) psychotherapy literatures. Today's therapists take it as an a priori assumption that interpersonal and intrapersonal processes affect each other and cannot be sharply separated (e.g., Aron, 1991). In this vein, transference reactions and resistances have come to be regarded as interactive processes that go on between patient and therapist; their activation depends, in part, on the personal "reality" of the therapist, including his or her personal experience of a therapy relationship (e.g., Ehrenberg, 1992; Hoffman, 1998).

Nothing is more characteristic of contemporary theorizing than challenges to the notions of "objective reality" and the reality of "objective truth" (Shevrin, 1995). For example, it would appear from debates about the evidential status of "case histories" that it has become increasingly difficult to locate the boundaries that separate imaginative literature from scientific writing (Spence, 1982). The emerging consensus is that "inter-being" (Mahoney, 1991) or what Atwood and Stolorow (1980) call "intersubjectivity" is the fundamental context for human knowing.

In keeping with an increased emphasis on the interdependent aspects of the therapeutic relationship, such basic principles as mutuality, reciprocity, symmetry, and optional responsiveness are coming to be regarded as the proper baselines for participation in the therapeutic relationship (e.g., Bacal, 1985; Mitchell, 1993; Greenberg, 1995; Aron, 1996). These methodological ideals, like the orthodox Freudian triumvirate of anonymity, abstinence, and neutrality, to which Freud himself evidently did not adhere (Lohser & Newton, 1996), can be interpreted more or less restrictively. Nevertheless, their endorsement tends to encourage therapists to be both more emotionally expressive and self-disclosing of feelings and attitudes toward patients. This shift has intensified heated debates about what a therapist should and should not reveal to a patient and has heightened ambiguities regarding the optimal placement of the boundary between therapeutic intimacy and personal intimacy.

Concurrently, an emphasis on the precise timing of transference interpretations is being subordinated to the establishment of a "healing" relationship in psychoanalytic theories of technique (e.g., Renik, 1993). An important manifestation of this conceptual shift is the increased emphasis being given to the sequence of empathy, failures of empathy, and their reparation by therapists who conceive of the processes of internalization as making an independent and positive contribution to the outcome of therapy (e.g., Loewald, 1962; Kohut, 1971; Dorpat, 1974; Blatt & Behrends, 1987; Mitchell, 1988). For example, Kohut (1984) has hypothesized, and we concur, that empathizing with a patient's negative reactions to narcissistic injuries activates the processes of internalization that will strengthen his or her self-esteem, vitality, sense of coherence, and continuity. What will be emphasized in the pages that follow is the hypothesis that clinical strategies designed to harness the therapeutic potential of the processes of internalization gain effectiveness to the extent that they are informed by an empathic appreciation of the nature and functioning of a patient's psychological boundaries.

THE IDEA OF PSYCHOLOGICAL BOUNDARIES

As defined by the dictionary, a boundary is that which delineates one entity as separate from another (*American Heritage Dictionary of the English Language*, 4th ed., 2002). I have chosen the term "psychological boundaries" to refer to the complex network of intrapersonal processes that presumably underlie and regulate the ability to make distinctions between various domains of experience and to establish linkages among them. In other words, I designate as psychological boundaries the representational capacities that provide the nonverbal substrate for such experience-based distinctions as inside and outside; self and nonself; the past, present, and future; remembering and imagining; fantasy and perception.

Some psychological boundaries operate at the juncture between the interpersonal and intrapersonal domains of experience. I infer their existence from individual differences in the distinction between the physical body and ever-present "body image" or "body schema" (Fisher, 1970) and from variations in what anthropologists refer to as "personal space" (Hall, 1966).

Each of us constructs and maintains, unconsciously, a psychic image that envelops, more or less cohesively, one's entire body (e.g., Fisher, 1970). This body image is quite separate from what we know, objectively, about our physicality. Were it not so, eating and body dysmorphic disorders would not be so prevalent. Introspective inquiries indicate that body images vary along multiple continua, for example, size, shape, and three-dimensionality, as well as their "penetration" and "barrier" characteristics (e.g., Bloomer & Moore, 1977). In complex combinations these attributes form the basis for the sense of there being an "inside me" and an "out there." And to anticipate a later point, they create a containing or symbolizing space, like the "mind," in which psychological experiences can occur.

Anthropologists were first to discover the existence of a psychological boundary that further differentiates "out there" into "inside" personal space and "outside" extrapersonal space (Hall, 1966). Apparently, without necessarily being aware of it, we locate ourselves within an intangible and invisible boundary that extends beyond and surrounds our psychic image of our bodies. The experiential reality of this interpersonal boundary is most acutely sensed when an uninvited other trespasses or intrudes on our "personal space." Research indicates that there are cultural, characterological, and situational differences in the distances at which individuals feel that they are "too close to" or "too far away from" others with whom they are interacting (e.g., Hall, 1966; Sommer, 1969).

Equally important to adaptation are the psychological boundaries that operate when interacting with internalized others, most notably when they are not physically present. It falls to these psychological boundaries to serve differentiating, integrating, and dedifferentiating functions vis-à-vis the representations of self and nonself that emanate from *within* us. One of the primary functions of the psychological boundaries that reside within "the representational world" (Sandler & Rosenblatt, 1962) is to subdivide experiences taking place "inside me" into those that are "lived bodily" and those that are known cognitively. This function manifests itself in the deeply ingrained tendency to treat the mind as if it actually had an "inside" that holds and contains thoughts, feelings, and all the persons within us. As the following common expressions indicate, we tend to un-self-consciously speak of the mind as a more or less enclosed "place" of its own from which subjective experiences leave and enter: for example, "My mind is too filled up to take in anymore," "I can't get my mind around it," "My mind feels like a sieve," "I couldn't get you out of my mind," "I put her in the back of my mind." As the last two statements illustrate, varying degrees of "spaciousness" can separate the others who are represented in interaction with the subjectively grasped sense of self.

Apart from their content and the functions they serve, representations of human interactions can be described in terms of the "forms" in which they take shape in conscious and preconscious experiences (Geller, 1984). Any single instance of remembering or fantasizing about an absent other varies in the extent to which it finds expression in pictures, sounds, a flow of word meanings, tastes, odors, body sensations, and enactments. My work has been deeply influenced by Bruner's (1964) model of cognitive growth. The conceptual starting point of his model is the assumption that psychological boundaries are laid down between the sensorimotor, imagistic, and verbal symbolizing systems during the course of development by the processes of representational differentiation and integration. A person is psychologically advantaged insofar as he or she can travel back and forth freely across the boundaries that separate these functionally differentiated modes of organizing, storing, and expressing knowledge. Early on, I try to learn whether a patient is equipped with the representational capacities that will enable him or her to keep apart or establish linkages between concrete, physicalized, and affect-laden memories and fantasies and abstract and verbalizable ideas about the interactions to which they refer—depending on the clinical needs of the moment. The work of exploratory-expressive therapy is facilitated when a patient's psychological boundaries function like the synaptic connections that make possible the transmission of information across the spaces that separate adjacent neurons. Inferences from clinical data suggest that this work will be stifled if the boundaries separating a patient's analytical intelligence and his or her sensuously receptive modes of knowing function more like the fortified geographical borders that encircle countries at war.

Individuals appear to vary widely in their ability to separate these varied incarnations of psychological boundaries from everything that accompanies and surrounds them. The psychological boundaries that keep self-representations and representations of others separate yet related are integral aspects of subjective experiences. But they typically operate at a prereflective level of symbolic functioning. Their phenomenological properties are rarely brought into focal awareness.

Preliminary research (Geller, 2002) indicates that, if consciously thought of, the boundaries that structure the experience of "inner space" tend to be described primarily in terms of visual images and metaphors. As for my patients, they tend to draw on the same metaphors when describing experienced variations in the boundaries that define and delineate their psychic images of their minds and their bodies. Those aspects of psychological boundaries that are potentially reportable tend to be described as varying with respect to such properties as their location, size, hardness, intactness, fluidity, permeability, transparency, and capability of expanding or contracting or of being moved backward and forward. Furthermore, qualitative changes in these properties tend to be understood as occurring in a range between opposite extremes. Rigidity-flexibility, fluidity-stability, and transparency-opaqueness are three such polarities. If the pitfalls of reification can be avoided, these metaphors provide a useful vocabulary for thinking and talking about the boundary-related issues that may arise during the course of therapy.

THE BOUNDARIES BETWEEN PSYCHOTHERAPY AND PSYCHOTHERAPY SUPERVISION

Whatever their presenting complaints, and however reluctant they may be to take on the identity of patient, therapists typically conceive of personal therapy as operating on two fronts simultaneously—the therapeutic and the educational (e.g., Geller & Schaffer, 1988). Many of the analysts Shapiro (1976) interviewed cited identifications and counteridentifications with their therapists' approach as the single most important determinant of their attitudes toward what it means to be a therapist and do the work of therapy. Similarly, it has long been recognized by psychoanalytic educators that "teaching and healing are not clearly differentiated dichotomies, but tend to cross their ill-defined boundaries" (Wolf, 1996, p. 253). Furthermore, our research indicates that many therapist-patients use internalized representations of their therapists as models to be imitated, perhaps only in fantasy, when they are experiencing difficulties in coping with the unscripted, stressful, novel, and unpredictable aspects of practicing therapy (Geller & Farber, 1993). Whether they are experienced as comforting or threatening or serve as stimuli for conformity or rebellion, representations of one's therapist's conversational style appear to have direct functional significance for a therapist's choices regarding expressivity, spontaneity, and the limits of self-disclosure.

A POTENTIAL FOR CONFUSION

Quite understandably, the teaching methods of psychotherapy supervisors who focus attention on the understanding of problematic countertransference reactions tend to be regarded by student therapists as models of the ways therapy is conducted. This is particularly true when a supervisor goes so far as to explore the ways a supervisee expresses indirectly or reenacts, within the supervisory relationship, temporary identifications or unresolved and unarticulated issues he or she has with the patient under consideration (Doehrman, 1976). The learning that takes place when such "parallel processes" (Caligor, 1981) are subject to inquiry can be as affectively based, as compared to cognitively based, as the experiential and interpersonal learning that takes place in exploratory therapy. Consequently, within this supervisory context, an educational enterprise itself can begin to feel like a therapeutic undertaking. When such conditions prevail, a therapist-patient may unconsciously equate the experience of being in therapy and being in supervision.

Given the potential for confusion, early in therapy I listen for opportunities to achieve mutual understanding of the similarities and differences between the learning and self-exploration that take place in psychotherapy and psychotherapy supervision, especially if the therapist-patient is in training and has never been in personal therapy.

There are limits to what a supervisee will tell a supervisor about his or her problematic emotional reactions and attitudes toward particular patients (Yourman & Farber, 1996). Therapists-in-training tend to reveal to their therapists what they "hide" from their supervisors. This includes their difficulties understanding and managing patient "enactments" that evoke defensiveness, hostility, and withdrawal. Trying to understand, in therapy, the difficulties of conscience involved in making this choice can prompt very useful discussions about the boundaries that separate privacy and secrecy. Even if brought into supervision, such countertransference reactions are not as likely to be as thoroughly explored as they would be in psychotherapy.

The importance of clearly distinguishing between psychotherapy and psychotherapy supervision is particularly urgent when a therapist seeks "supervision" with a former therapist while in a state of crisis regarding his or her emotional overinvolvement with a particular patient. If the former therapist-patient's psychopathology renders him or her vulnerable to "boundary violations" (Gabbard & Lester, 1995), it is essential to propose that the contract be one of purchasing psychotherapy and not supervision. Otherwise, a clinician is at risk of being held equally responsible for any ethical misconduct of which his or her patient might be accused.

PREPARING PATIENTS FOR THERAPY

Research conducted in the early 1960s strengthened my conviction that socializing individuals into the role of patient and educating them about how to use therapy for personal benefit promotes positive outcomes (e.g., Hoehn-Saric et al., 1964). To prepare "naive" patients for the exploratory work to come, I will try to underscore the courage it takes to speak truthfully about one's "vulnerable selves." I will also emphasize the inevitability of reluctances about speaking "truthfully," given the degree of candor and affective freedom required of patients. I will often find occasion to mention that so-called resistances and negative transference reactions are inevitable and that they may bring to light otherwise inaccessible knowledge of fears and defenses against hostility and hatred.

From the opening moments of the first session, I can implement these clinical strategies with therapist-patients in ways that convey another message: I accept our shared professional identity. For example, I can phrase my comments by making reference to persons only a fellow therapist would recognize. I draw on the quotes and anecdotes that are parts of the largely undocumented "oral history" of our profession. To illustrate the interdependence of transference and countertransference, I might quote a statement a supervisor of mine attributed to Jung: "The therapy has not begun until it is problematic for both participants." If the patient is an inexperienced therapist struggling, for the first time, with a "negative transference reaction," I might quote what a teacher told me H.S. Sullivan said: "God save me from a therapy that is going well."

Quoting our intellectual ancestors is a way of affirming that we share membership in a professional community and a common history passed on from one generation of therapists to the next. This clinical strategy isn't always successful. A therapist-patient of mine informed me that my Jung quotation was, for him, an "empathic failure, because it could be applied to many others besides myself." Another patient betrayed his displeasure with my choosing an anecdote from my own career to illustrate a point. Thinking he was going to say, "I hate your anecdote," he found himself saying, "I hate your antidote." I take these as examples of the repeatedly obtained finding that acceptance of a therapist's comments depends not only on their accuracy or truthfulness but also on how well these communications integrate with a patient's stylistic and aesthetic preferences.

With respect to matters of style, investigations of the "fit" between therapists and patients (Kantrowitz et al., 1989) and autobiographical accounts of analysts who have been treated by two or more analysts (e.g., Guntrip, 1973; Hurwitz, 1986; Simon, 1993; Couch, 1995), plus my own experiences as a patient, converge with respect to a variety of generalizations. The foremost of these is that both therapists and patients inevitably possess distinctive and potentially quite different conversational styles. Second, from a patient's point of view, it may be difficult to distinguish between a therapist's perceived competence and one's positive or negative feelings about his or her conversational style. Third, a distinctive feature of therapeutic competence is the ability to speak in a "voice" that is attuned to a patient's communicative requirements. Fourth, giving thoughtful attention to a patient's communicative requirements with regard to matters of style is experienced as an affirmative and empathic answer to questions that frequently thematize interactions between therapist-patients and their therapists: Is my therapist able to recognize and respond flexibly to my individuality? Can he or she understand my concrete and immediate experiences? Is he or she available and prepared to learn from and with me? Is he or she insistent on controlling the entire therapy? How powerful should each of us be in deciding what needs changing and how these changes should be brought about?

THE POWER DYNAMICS OF THERAPY

There is more power and authority inherent in the role of therapist than in the role of patient. This emotionally charged fact is clearly evident in the following potentially potent sources of frustration and gratification. Therapists are in charge of defining and controlling where and when therapy will take place. They have the legitimate authority to impose geographical restrictions and temporal limitations on their availability. Therapists also have the primary responsibility for conceptualizing and assigning the tasks and division of labor required to accomplish the goals of therapy.

Early on, in any course of therapy, it is important to gauge how a patient's reactions to the power differentials that separate the positions of patient and therapist will influence the separation-reunion cycles woven into the work structure of therapy and the establishment of a therapeutic alliance (Geller, 1987). For some patients, clarity regarding the boundaries that separate "inside" and "outside" of therapy sessions has an organizing influence in regard to their feelings of safety and expressivity. For others, the temporal and spatial arrangements of therapy engender ambivalence. As a therapist-patient of mine put it, "I experience the therapeutic situation as equal parts cage and sanctuary." For still others, issues of "leadership" and "followership" provoke power struggles, some fueled by unresolved conflicts with "authority figures."

I am most keenly aware of the power dynamics that are inherent in psychotherapy when attempting to differentiate between requests for technique modifications that organically flow from a seasoned therapist-patient's theory of therapeutic change and efforts to induce conformity with transference-driven motivations. This challenging task has arisen most frequently while working out a "therapeutic contract" (Orlinsky & Howard, 1986) regarding the use of self-disclosure as a therapeutic technique. It is a quite negative thing to share personal information with a therapist-patient who views self-disclosure as a form of acting out that contaminates the transference and subverts the therapeutic process. It is quite another if a therapist-patient believes the indications for self-disclosure are ever present during the course of therapy.

Among other considerations, I take a therapist-patient's basic position along this continuum into account when deciding whether to voluntarily reveal personal information to achieve a therapeutic goal (Geller, 2003). I believe that as long as there are "levelers" and "sharpeners" (Witkin & Goodenough, 1981), there will never be agreement regarding the precise location of the place beyond which one should not self-disclose. Reconciling divergent views regarding matters of technique in the direction of the therapist-patient is a subtle way of introducing greater "symmetry" into the relationship.

Moreover, patients often benefit from recognizing that their therapist believes that learning to learn with another through the medium of dialogue is as important for the therapist as it is for the patient. As an example of these principles, I accommodated a Jungian analyst's request that we focus primarily on the interpretation of his dreams and that I share my associations to his dream images. These are standard practices among Jungian therapists. To express respect for his approach, I extended the limits beyond which I characteristically self-disclose. Not to have done so, he later told me, would have been a "mistake" and an "empathic failure."

A QUESTION OF TECHNIQUE

Seventy-nine percent of the participants in Pope and Tabachnick's (1994) sample of therapist-patients reported that they felt their therapists had made clinical and therapeutic errors. Comparable norms are not available for lay patients. Whatever the global percentage may be, both lay patients' and therapist-patients' evaluations of their therapists' competence range from complete admiration to utter disdain. It is, however, specific to the therapy of therapist-patients that they can voice their positive and negative judgments in the language of the profession.

Empathizing with a therapist-patient who is complaining in the language of "science" or "ethics" about what one is doing or not doing is perhaps the greatest technical challenge of all. Sometimes it is the first step toward helping such patients develop the capacity to speak about hateful feelings in a constructive and responsible manner. Working toward this therapeutic goal is a predominant focus in some therapies, less so in others, but it is of some importance in all therapies. In my experience it is a particularly powerful therapeutic tool when the therapist-patient has considerable conflicts about his or her critical/sadistic impulses or tends to be masochistic and underentitled. Patients suffering from these characterological problems begin therapy with a reduced ability to recognize and accept their therapist's empathic understandings. Working through reactions to the disappointing, enraging, and frustrating aspects of the process of therapy prepares them to take pleasure in the actuality of their therapist's caring concern.

In the next two sections, I illustrate how I apply these ideas. For the sake of confidentiality and continuity, I have blended clinical examples that actually occurred with different therapist-patients into working clinical models of two prototypical therapist-patients.

THE HANDLING OF EMPATHIC FAILURES

A patient can feel that a therapist has taught him or her new "truths" about himself or herself without feeling empathically understood by that therapist. This was the legacy of K's first therapy. Like other therapist-patients who have had previous therapies, K, a brilliant 33-year-old clinical psychologist and self-diagnosed "obsessive compulsive with schizoid tendencies," arrived with an elaborate psychodynamic formulation of his presenting complaints. He came to therapy knowing that his unwanted but irresistible "perfectionism" and "diminished capacity for loving" were the result of growing up with a mother who "didn't enjoy being nurturant." But his hard-won insights had not led to behavioral change, and he felt neither liked nor respected by his former therapist.

During the initial stage of therapy, he could not release himself from the burden of being "the responsible one," "the rational one," "the one-in-charge," nor could he explicitly reveal his "disowned dependency needs." He wanted to be a "good" patient but could not avail himself of the regressive inducements of patienthood. As a compromise, he defensively clung to the therapeutic alliance. He acted "as if" we could work together as "equal partners" to bring about therapeutic change, but it quickly became clear to both of us that he was unable to continue collaborating with me if I started a session two or three minutes late. He reacted to these occasional lapses of punctuality as if they signified "incompetence and a lack of integrity." He took my policy of extending the length of such sessions beyond the prearranged ending as further evidence of my "flagrantly careless mismanagement of the therapeutic frame." He quoted Langs (1976) to impress on me that even minor departures from the maintenance of invariant temporal boundaries represented a failure to live up to the ego ideals and values of the profession. His eloquent critiques collapsed the distinction between the technical principles and the moral norms that regulate the professional boundaries between patients and therapists. Moreover, he experienced his explanations single-mindedly, as if they were factual and concrete realities.

At the time of intake, he could only tolerate hearing echoes of the meanings inherent in what he said. Efforts on my part to make inferences beyond the meanings he gave for our problematic interactions were resentfully disregarded. Initially, even my questions were experienced as "interruptions" and "disruptive." It wasn't until the 2nd year of treatment that he could turn his curiosity to issues that I deemed in need of exploration. As we were to learn, needing help in making meaning of his experiences induced in him a humiliating sense of being "foolish" and "stupid." He was guided by the belief that I only listened to find out what was "wrong" with him and what he "didn't know" about himself.

His unflattering interpretations of my handling of the beginnings and endings of sessions provoked in me a great deal of soul-searching. What sustained me was the hypothesis that responding nondefensively to his criticisms would ultimately strengthen his ability to recognize, tolerate, and benefit from being empathically understood. To do this, I found a way of conducting therapy that allowed for and upheld his need to discover his own personalized meanings for the problematic aspects of our relationship. This required choosing comments that highlighted the limits of my understanding. I restricted myself to questions that could be asked by both patient and therapist: "How do you want to use the time today?" "How do you understand this?" Another way of avoiding narcissistic injuries was to invite him to elaborate on *how* he experienced *what* he experienced. Dealing respectfully with his communicative requirements entailed giving priority to interventions that widened and deepened the immediacy of what he heard, thought, saw, and felt.

Our work together was not so much about adding new insights to those he had taken away from his first therapy but rather about concretizing and energizing insights that had previously remained disembodied. Along the way, he gained access to his imaginative capacities. He extended "bridges" across what were once the barriers to awareness that separated his verbal and imagistic modes of knowing. Establishing meaningful connections between these distinct spheres of experiencing proved to be the gateway through which he could enter a new and transformative stage of therapy. It laid the groundwork for a major turning point in his therapy. This transition took place during a session in which he both recalled how his mother alternated between being withdrawn and verbally abusive and realized that he expressed his disavowed longings to be dependent on me in the form of criticisms. His lists of "shoulds" for me were thereafter seen as "enactments of desire." A correlated step forward was taken when he also acknowledged that questioning and complaining about my techniques—"Why are you doing it that way?" "What are you trying to do?"—were driven as much by aggressive competitiveness and by the need to cover up his own searing doubts about how best to conduct therapy as by the high value he placed on scientific skepticism. From that time forth, he found the "intellectual courage" to begin talking about how his morally perfectionistic orientation was exerting a restrictive influence on his functioning as a therapist and compromising his own sense of "goodness."

BALANCING SELF-CONCERN AND CONCERN FOR OTHERS

In diverse vocabularies, mystics, Zen Buddhists, poets, parents, lovers, and therapists have offered boundary-based explanations of variations in the ability to give and receive empathy (e.g., Rogers, 1975). They all share the assumption that trying to understand what another person feels, empathically, is one of the most mature variants of the capacity to enter into relationships in which there is a movement toward the experience of two persons becoming "one." Phenomenologically speaking, empathy is a mode of knowing the other that comes about by softening or blurring the boundaries separating self and nonself without actually losing awareness of the distinction. Similarly, mature dependency requires a certain level of comfort in reexperiencing "symbiotic" modes of relatedness on one's own behalf.

A basic tenet of "relational" perspectives on psychoanalytic theory (e.g., Blatt & Behrends, 1987) is that the acquisition of psychological boundaries promotes the development more or less simultaneously in an interactive dialectic of three fundamental aspects of psychological functioning—feeling secure in one's identity, the ability to function independently, and the freedom to relax the burdens of self-determination and self/other differentiation. Under ideal circumstances, a person develops the representational capacities that both uphold the sense that he or she is clearly separate, autonomous, and unique in relation to others and yet enable him or her to take pleasure and benefit from experiences of "merging" or "fusing" with valued others.

A particularly poignant variant of the inconsistencies possible involves therapist-patients whose capacity to give their patients empathy far exceeds their capacity to receive empathy from their own therapists. Sometimes the very boundary-related personality characteristics that enable therapists to be empathic with their patients may leave them vulnerable to difficulties regulating the distinction and distance between self and nonself in other intimate interpersonal contexts. In listening to my own therapist-patients and hearing about those discussed by supervisees and colleagues, I have been struck by the frequency with which these inconsistencies surface during the course of therapy when the therapist-patient is struggling with the conflict between unselfish sacrifice of personal desires, selfishness, and healthy self-interest. To illustrate, I turn next to B, a 32-year-old psychoanalytically oriented therapist for whom psychological matters and questions of value often merged into one another.

PRIDE AND RESPECT

The statement "I want my therapist to be proud of me" received the highest degree of endorsement in my study with Farber of the themes that organize therapist-patients' involvements with mental representations of their therapists (Geller & Farber, 1993). The polar principles of admiration/pride and disillusionment have been key affective components of my experiences treating therapists who have struggled in an ongoing way with serious "mental illnesses." However talented these individuals may have been as therapists, they all began therapy fearful that I would regard them as "unfit" to be therapists. To the contrary, their intimate familiarity with terror, despair, futility, and chaos seemed to have prepared them to "stay with" patients who are in the throes of such awful experiences.

Patient B was further burdened by what he called "maturity morality"—the superego-driven conviction that he had to be "healthier" than his patients. Shame was the penalty he paid for having failed to profit from the year-and-a-half-long psychoanalytic therapy he had undergone while in graduate school. His reasons for coming to therapy this time included guilt about not "coming out" and "joining the gay pride movement."

The following communicative exchange took place between me (T) and the patient (P) during the ninth session:

P: I've been thinking a lot about coming out. I have a lot of guilt for not doing my part.

• T: Guilt?

P: I feel like I'm passing... like a light-skinned Black person who is pretending to be White. It's like I'm going against my people.

T: It feels cowardly keeping your homosexuality a secret... especially in professional circles?

P: Yeah, I'd like to be more courageous. It would help a lot of people too, give them hope. I could be used as a resource. People could pick my brain. But I just don't know if I could bear the shame. What is this fear of what other people think? Why do I wrestle with it?

T: Let me add another question. Are you worried about what I will think of you and your sexuality and the choice you are trying to make?

• P: Yes. I am afraid you will see all my behavior through that lens... and that you'd view parts of my personality as part of my pathology.

In therapy, as elsewhere, B was hyperaware of the gap that separated the public image he sought to project "out there" from his "insider's view" of what was "really going on." He was troubled, morally, by his ability to "simulate authenticity." His facade of normalcy had been created so that he would not appear effeminate, but it alienated him from his body and diminished his capacity for pleasure. K had likened his body to that of the Tin Man in *The Wizard of Oz*. By contrast, B likened his "false self" to a "wall that separates public from private spaces."

Building on this metaphor, we arrived at the realization that he spent a great deal of time "looking at" himself, evaluatively, but rarely "looked in" on his own thoughts and feelings contemplatively. Although very curious about the subjective experiences of others, he felt "immodest" whenever he devoted himself to self-exploration. During the initial phase of therapy, without being conscious of it, he avoided feeling "selfish" by rapidly applying what he learned about himself in therapy to his work as a therapist.

Responsiveness to nonverbal cues, the ability to project oneself into the consciousness of others, sensitivity to people's stated and unstated needs—these attributes strengthen one's access to the empathic mode of knowing. B was abundantly endowed with them. They enabled him to excel as a therapist, but they also made it difficult for him to retain his own perspective while entering the point of view of others. His interpretive bias was to identify with the other person's view of a problematic situation. If he himself was dealt with hurtfully, he tended to "blame" himself and to believe that he must have "done something wrong or bad."

B said of himself, "I feel like a cliché... the therapist who is masochistic because of the caretaking role he adopted in his family." But it eventually proved liberating when he discovered that his felt inability to join the gay pride movement was directly related to and analogous with his generalized inhibitions about carving out an identity separate from his family of origin. Following this insight, he began to relinquish the burdens of defining himself as an "outsider" or "displaced" person, as had his parents, who felt like "devalued exiles." He no longer felt compelled to protect them by remaining silent when they drew sharp and repugnant distinctions between "them" (i.e., homosexuals and "the goyim") and "us" (i.e., heterosexuals and Jews).

Before B arrived at the point where he could "come out," a major focus of our conversations was his deep shame about his own dependency needs. In truth, B was raised to be a provider, not a recipient of caring concern. From early childhood he had adopted a parental role vis-à-vis his Eastern European immigrant parents and his mentally retarded younger sister. Besides valuing himself almost exclusively for what he could do to protect his family, B feared he would be regarded as "childish," "infantile," and "clinging" if he risked expressing his unsatisfied yearnings to be empathically understood. Saying "I want" made him feel like a "helpless child."

We devoted ourselves to expanding the range of desires that could be articulated with those with whom he wished to be intimate or aggressive. Within the microcosm of the therapeutic situation, we took special notice of how and why he disavowed negative reactions to my mistakes and empathic failures. Allowing himself to "complain" about the ways I didn't meet his needs advanced the work of therapy in several ways. On these occasions he benefited from the experience of "truth-telling," from confrontations with his wishes to devalue my idealized qualities, and he came to a greater understanding of the meanings of his fears and defenses against expressing anger. In a previous therapy, B had learned that his intense conflicts about his own aggressive strivings had developed as a result of defensive counteridentifications with his competitive, combative, and intermittently rageful father.

As his wishes became more fully known to himself, B became more comfortable experiencing my actual physical presence and his previously dissociated hope of finding a therapist who could serve as an idealized model of the therapist he hoped to become. A major turning point occurred when he was finally able to tolerate looking at me when my silent presence gave evidence of patience and compassion. The listening presence of the empathically responsive therapist communicates tender emotions that may never be put into words. A great deal of what we regard as being empathic is only conveyed through gestures, postures, and facial expressions.

Expanding the range of perceptual capacities B brought into therapy made it more possible for him to "take in" those aspects of my empathy that were carried by my nonverbal contributions to the therapeutic dialogue. The cumulative impact of these changes started a ripple effect that brought together the "supportive" and "exploratory" aspects of his therapy. Generally speaking, once this kind of integration has been consolidated, there is no end in sight to the potential collaborative and intimate conversations that are possible.

THE TERMINATION PHASE OF THERAPY

Knowing when and how to end a lengthy and ambitious therapy that is going well is a most difficult task for both therapist and patient. If patient and therapist have shared a close and productive relationship, there will be intimations of arbitrariness in their (final) goodbye. With respect to assessing termination, most therapists are likely to reply that multiple and patient-specific criteria should be used (Firestein, 1978). I have found a variety of markers to be sensitive indices for recognizing a patient's progress in therapy and readiness to enter the termination subphase of the therapeutic process.

Among the most important intratherapy markers are (1) the ability to work together with the therapist in exploring personal qualities that present obstacles to change; (2) the ability to use language responsibly and constructively when feeling hateful toward the therapist; (3) an enhanced sense of competence about one's participation in therapy; (4) the ability to oscillate between regressive and progressive forms of mental activity; (5) the fullest and freest expression of previously unacknowledged and unmourned losses; (6) the ability to smoothly exchange the positions of listener and speaker; (7) the ability to choose what to "take in" and what to "keep out" of what the therapist has to offer; and finally, (8) the ability to place the bodily experience and not merely the eyes and the ears at the center of the perceptual and representational experience of therapy.

In varying combinations, these diverse achievements seem to go hand in hand with the approaching realization of a patient's "life goals" (e.g., symptomatic relief and enhanced self-esteem). At the same time, they seem to indicate that the therapy will also have an "afterlife" in the form of evocative and benignly influential representations of therapy-with-the-therapist. At this juncture, the patient is growing increasingly capable of continued self-analysis.

THE CAPACITY TO ENGAGE IN SELF-ANALYSIS

From the perspective of the processes of internalization, one can distinguish between introjective and identificatory forms of self-reflexiveness (Orlinsky & Geller, 1993). At the introjective level of internalization, patients symbolically reconstruct the therapeutic dialogue in order to reflect on and interpret their own experience. The research cited earlier in this chapter found that therapist-patients are most likely to engage in imaginary conversations with the "felt presence" of their therapist for the purposes of self-reflection when carrying out the tasks of therapeutic work and organizing the experience of being a therapist. At the identificatory level of symbolization, the manner in which a patient engages in self-analysis is modeled on representations of the therapist's abilities and personal qualities but excludes conscious representations of what has been shown or given to them by their therapists. Who is listening when you talk to yourself?

In the classical psychoanalytic tradition, the received wisdom has been that self-analytic abilities that derive from constructive identifications associated with altered functioning are more "mature" than those based on calling forth introjected representations of the self-in-relation-to-the-therapist. This essentially untested assumption is of more than theoretical interest to psychoanalytic therapists who wish or need to interact with personifications or introjected representations of their analysts following termination. The psychoanalyst Martinez (Martinez & Hoppe, 1998) tells us she felt ashamed of her inclination to interact intermittently with her "analyst introject" because she had been taught that doing so implied "immaturity," the prolongation of a dependent relation to the analyst, and therefore cast doubt on the completeness of her analysis. Obviously, such theoretical subtleties are of little or no concern to nontherapist-patients, or for that matter, to nonanalytic therapist-patients.

THE POST-TERMINATION PHASE OF PSYCHOTHERAPY

At every stage of therapy, distinctions must be made between those personal attributes that are role relevant and those aspects of the self that must be suppressed in the interest of successful task accomplishment. In the psychotherapy of therapist-patients, this task is complicated by the inherent tension created by straddling the interpersonal boundary between the formal roles of patient and therapist and the collegial aspects of the relationship. Nowhere are the ambiguities posed by these tasks more apparent than in the therapist's efforts to deal with the largely unexamined question, How can I continue to interact with my former patients in ways that fulfill my therapeutic and ethical responsibilities to them following the termination of therapy?

All major mental health professional codes of ethics contain proscriptions against so-called boundary violations (Pope & Vasquez, 1998). The American Psychological Association (1992) did not classify having sex with a former patient as a boundary violation until 1977 (Pope & Bouhoutsos, 1986). Currently, there are no explicit guidelines regarding the ethics of nonromantic and nonsexual relationships following the discontinuation of therapeutic services other than those that are clearly exploitative and destructive. Moreover, professional codes still have little to say about a question that is of particular concern to therapists' therapists: Beyond termination, are standards of conduct regarding "dual relationships" equally applicable to lay patients and members of the same professional community? Dual or multiple relationships are those in which additional role relations are established in conjunction with or in succession to the professional therapeutic relationship.

The extreme position is that the restrictions on extratherapeutic contact that applied during therapy should extend to the post-termination phase of the relationship. A major reason given for this policy is that to do otherwise would make it difficult for a former patient to resume therapy at some point in the future. Most therapies do, in fact, end with the agreement that the patient is free to return to therapy whenever his or her judgment indicates its usefulness (Schachter, 1992). Hartlaub et al. (1986) found that it is not uncommon for former analysands to recontact their former analysts for a brief or even for an extended therapy. Such contacts tend to increase as time elapses after termination, irrespective of the patient's diagnostic category or age.

Unless a lay patient renews professional contact with his or her therapist, termination of therapy potentially represents a total and permanent separation. Psychotherapists who continue to live and work in the same professional group as their former therapists markedly diverge from lay patients in this respect. Treating a fellow therapist significantly increases the possibility that a social or professional relationship will "replace" the therapeutic relationship after termination. Hence the question, following termination, of how one can continue to interact with one's former patients in ways that fulfill one's therapeutic and ethical responsibilities to them arises more frequently in the psychotherapy of therapists than in the psychotherapy of lay patients.

ONCE A PATIENT, ALWAYS A PATIENT

When I unavoidably encounter former patients in public settings, I aspire to behave in ways that are disciplined by attentiveness to the following questions: Is the person still mourning the loss of the therapeutic relationship? Will my behavior confirm or disconfirm his or her preexisting mental models of our relationship? Does he or she use representations of the therapeutic dialogue

to continue the work of therapy in the privacy of consciousness? Are these representations still transference laden? Did the
therapy leave behind a legacy of malevolent and persecutory
introjects? Does he or she call me forth like an "imaginary companion" (of childhood) to avoid or curb anxiety and loneliness?
How ready is he or she to reexperience the transferential aspects
of our relationship? Will he or she view my behavior as deviat-
ing from the standards that define the ideals of our profession?

The standards I hold myself to when interacting with former patients at such events as seminars, parties, and professional meetings have been heavily influenced by the convergent
findings of clinical research on the persistence of transference
reactions after termination (Pfeffer, 1963; Schlessinger & Robbins, 1974; Oremland et al., 1975; Kantrowitz et al., 1990) and
empirical studies of the form, content, functions, and affective
coloration of the internalized representation of the therapeutic
relationship that lay and therapist-patients retain and recall after
termination (Orlinksy & Geller, 1993; Wyzontek et al., 1995;
Arnold et al., 2004). Both lines of inquiry strongly support the
conviction that a post-termination phase (Rangell, 1966) of the
therapeutic relationship must be considered to be an integral
part of the therapeutic process itself and not just as the time
after therapy ends.

Studies of the transformations that representations of the
therapeutic relationship undergo after termination are few. Our
studies indicate that former therapist-patients are apt to recall
representations-of-therapy-with-my-therapist more frequently
and vividly than former nontherapist-patients (Wyzontek et al.,
1995). As previously noted, representations of the missed or
yearned-for former therapist can appear in awareness in various
forms. They can be "visualized." They can be "heard." They can
materialize in consciousness in the form of verbal thought. They
can also include proximal imagery, that is, kinesthetic, proprio-

ceptive, and tactile representations. Initial findings suggest that former therapist-patients' evocative memories of their therapists are more highly saturated with proximal imagery than are those of lay patients.

Therapist-patients' written descriptions of their former therapists, in comparison to those authored by lay patients, tend to give greater emphasis to the therapists' "inner life." The lay patients focused their portraits primarily on their therapists' observable behaviors, especially those that gratified or frustrated their needs. Far more than lay patients, former therapist-patients' portraits expressed greater interest in their therapists' feelings, values, and attitudes.

With respect to the ability to use representations of the therapeutic dialogue for adaptive and reparative purposes, lay patients and therapist-patients have not differed significantly in our studies. We have obtained significant positive correlations between ratings of self-perceived benefits from therapy and two representational activities. These are the tendency to use representations of the therapeutic dialogue to continue the work of therapy into the future and the tendency to use representations to give expression to missing therapy and the therapist. By way of contrast, the tendency to evoke representations of the therapist to engage in sexual and aggressive fantasies has been found to correlate negatively with self-perceived improvement.

These findings are consistent with the results of the previously referenced follow-up research interviews with therapist and nontherapist analysands. On the one hand, these studies support Loewald's (1960, 1962) contention that the ending of a beneficial analysis ushers in a gradual relinquishment or "mourning" of the relationship and its internalization. On the other hand, they indicate that successful terminations do not result in the complete resolution of transference reactions but in their modulation to the point that the patient can deal with them more effectively. Remaining mindful that transference wishes and dispositions persist beyond termination can go a long way toward easing the awkwardness and ambiguities of etiquette that arise during contacts with therapist-patients after the discontinuation of regularly scheduled sessions.

From the point of view of the processes of internalization, therapy can make people "worse" to the extent that the experience leaves behind a legacy of disappointing, malevolent, or persecutory images of the therapist. On a case-by-case basis, this outcome can be assessed by scheduling therapist-initiated "follow-up" (as compared to therapeutic sessions) visits with patients during the post-termination phase of the relationship. Schachter (1992) has been experimenting with planned-for patient-analyst post-termination contact to review how the patient has fared and to reevaluate the gains and limitations of the analytic process. He has found the risk/benefit ratio for such contact to be highly favorable and that patients do benefit from experiencing a reaffirmation of the therapeutic alliance. These follow-up sessions might prove to be an ideal "anthropological laboratory" (Kundera, 1984) for studying the fate of the transference residues that linger after termination, the work of mourning, the afterlife of the therapeutic process, and relapse prevention strategies.

CONCLUSION

In this chapter, I have attempted to identify some of what is unique about the psychotherapy of therapists from the standpoint of the complex interplay between the notion of psychological boundaries and the processes of internalization. I have drawn on the concepts and data of body image theorists, anthropologists, cognitive developmental psychologists, and psychoanalysts to develop a framework that therapists could use to think and talk about the psychological boundaries that are operative in interpersonal contexts and in the privacy of consciousness. I have cited clinical experiences and psychotherapy research findings that support the hypothesis that internalization-based models of the therapeutic action of therapy offer an illuminating vantage point from which to examine whether there are clinically significant differences in the therapies offered to and experienced by therapist- and nontherapist-patients. At the end of it all, I have arrived at the conclusion—to paraphrase Kluckhohn and Murray (1949, p. 53)—that every psychotherapist-patient is in certain respects (a) like all other patients, (b) like some other patients, and (c) like no other patient. To be continued....

REFERENCES

American Heritage Dictionary of the English Language. (4th ed.). (2002). New York, NY: Houghton Mifflin.

American Psychological Association. (1992). Ethical principles of psychologists and code of conduct. *American Psychologist* 49:1597–1611.

Arnold, E.G., Farber, B.A., & Geller, J.D. (2004). Termination, post-termination, and internalization of therapy and the therapist: Internal representation and psychotherapy outcome. In D.P. Charman (Ed.), *Core Processes in Brief Psychodynamic Psychotherapy* (pp. 289–308). Hillsdale, NJ: Erlbaum.

Aron, L. (1991). The patient's experience of the analyst's subjectivity. *Psychoanalytic Dialogues* 1:29–51.

——— (1996). *A Meeting of Minds: Mutuality in Psychoanalysis*. Hillsdale, NJ: Analytic Press.

Atwood, G., & Stolorow, R. (1980). Psychoanalytic concepts and the representational world. *Psychoanalysis and Contemporary Thought* 3:267–290.

Bacal, H.A. (1985). Optimal responsiveness and the therapeutic process. In A. Goldberg (Ed.), *Progress in Self Psychology* (202–206). New York, NY: Guilford Press.

Blatt, S.J., & Behrends, R.S. (1987). Internalization, separation-individuation, and the nature of therapeutic action. *International Journal of Psychoanalysis* 68:279–297.

Bloomer, K.C., & Moore, W.M. (1977). *Body, Memory, and Architecture*. New Haven, CT: Yale University Press.

Bowen, M. (1978). *Family Therapy in Clinical Practice*. New York, NY: Jason Aronson.

Brown, L.S. (2005). Feminist therapy with therapists: Egalitarian and more. In J.D. Geller, J.C. Norcross, & D.E. Orlinsky (Eds.), *The Psychotherapist's Own Psychotherapy: Patient and Clinician Perspectives* (pp. 265–281). New York, NY: Oxford University Press.

Bruner, J.S. (1964). The course of cognitive growth. *American Psychologist* 19:1–15.

Caligor, P.C. (1981). Parallel and reciprocal processes in psychoanalytic supervision. *Contemporary Psychoanalysis* 17:1–27.

Couch, A.S. (1995). Anna Freud's adult psychoanalytic technique: A defense of classical analysis. *International Journal of Psychoanalysis* 76:153–171.

Doehrmann, M. (1976). Parallel processes in supervision and psychotherapy. *Bulletin of the Menninger Clinic* 40:3–104.

Dorpat, T.L. (1974). Internalization of the patient-analyst relationship in patients with narcissistic disorders. *J. Internat. Psycho-Analytic Association* 55:183–191.

Ehrenberg, D.B. (1992). *Extending the Reach of Psychoanalytic Interaction*. New York, NY: Norton.

Epstein, R.S. (1994). *Keeping Boundaries: Maintaining Safety and Integrity in the Psychotherapeutic Process*. Washington, DC: American Psychiatric Press.

Firestein, S.K. (1978). *Termination in Psychoanalysis*. New York, NY: International Universities Press.

Fisher, S. (1970). *Body Experience in Fantasy and Behavior*. New York, NY: Appleton-Century-Crofts.

Fleming, J. (1987). *The Teaching and Learning of Psychoanalysis*. New York, NY: Guilford Press.

Framo, J. (1982). *Explorations in Marital and Family Therapy*. New York, NY: Springer.

Freud, S. (1940). An outline of psycho-analysis. *Standard Edition* 23:139–208.

Gabbard, G.O. (1995). When the patient is a therapist: Special challenges in the psychoanalytic treatment of mental health professionals. *Psychoanalytic Review* 82:709–125.

———— & Lester, F.P. (1995). *Boundaries and Boundary Violations in Psychoanalysis*. New York, NY: Basic Books.

Geller, J.D. (1984). Moods, feelings, and the process of affect formation. In L. Temoshok, C. Van Dyke, & L.S. Zegans (Eds.), *Emotions in Health and Illness: Applications to Clinical Practice* (pp. 171–186). Orlando, FL: Grune & Stratton.

———— (1987). The process of psychotherapy: Separation and the complex interplay among empathy, insight, and internalization. In J. Bloom-Feshbach & S. Bloom-Feshbach (Eds.), *The Psychology of Separation and Loss: Perspectives on Development, Life Transitions, and Clinical Practice* (pp. 459–514). San Francisco, CA: Jossey-Bass.

———— (1998). What does it mean to practice psychotherapy scientifically? *Psychoanalysis and Psychotherapy* 15:187–215.

———— (2002). My personal Tiresias: A geographer of the inner world. In R. Landy (Ed.), *Symbolization and Desymbolization* (pp. 511–533). New York, NY: Other Press.

——— (2003). Self-disclosure in psychoanalytic-existential therapy. *Journal of Clinical Psychology* 59(5):541–554.

——— & Farber, B.A. (1993). Factors influencing the process of internalization in psychotherapy. *Psychotherapy Research* 3(3):166–180. https://doi.org/10.1080/10503309312331333769

———, Norcross, J.C., & Orlinsky, D.E. (2005). Research findings: Providing personal therapy to other therapists. In J.D. Geller, J.C. Norcross, & D.E. Orlinsky (Eds.), *The Psychotherapist's Own Psychotherapy: Patient and Clinician Perspectives* (pp. 345–364). New York, NY: Oxford University Press.

——— & Schaffer, C.E. (1988, June 23). *Internalization of the Supervisory Dialogue and the Development of Therapeutic Competence*. Paper presented at the 21st annual meeting of the Society for Psychotherapy Research, Santa Fe, NM.

Greenberg, J.R. (1995). Psychoanalytic technique and the interactive matrix. *Psychoanalytic Quarterly* 64:1–22.

Greene, L.R., & Geller, J.D. (1980). Effects of therapists' clinical experience and personal boundaries on termination of psychotherapy. *Journal of Psychiatric Education* 4:31–35.

Guntrip, H. (1973). *Psychoanalytic Theory, Therapy, and the Self*. New York, NY: Basic Books.

Gutheil, T.G., & Gabbard, G.O. (1993). The concept of boundaries in clinical practice: Theoretical and risk management dimensions. *American Journal of Psychiatry* 150:188–196.

Hall, E.T. (1966). *The Hidden Dimension* (1st ed.). Garden City, NY: Doubleday.

Hartlaub, G.H., Martin, G.C., & Rhine, M.W. (1986). Recontact with the analyst following termination: A survey of seventy-one cases. *Journal of the American Psychoanalytic Association* 34:885–910.

Hartmann, E. (1991). *Boundaries in the Mind: A New Psychology of Personality*. New York, NY: Basic Books.

Heery, M., & Bugental, J.F.T. (2005). Listening to the listener: An existential-humanistic approach to psychotherapy with psychotherapists. In J.D. Geller, J.C. Norcross, & D.E. Orlinsky (Eds.), *The Psychotherapist's Own Psychotherapy: Patient and Clinician Perspectives* (pp. 282–296). New York, NY: Oxford University Press.

Hoehn-Saric, R., Frank, J.D., Imber, S.C., Nash, E.H., Stone, A.R., & Battle, C.C. (1964). Systematic preparation of patients and psychotherapy: I. Effects on therapy behavior and outcome. *Journal of Psychiatric Research* 2:267–281.

Hoffman, I.Z. (1998). *Ritual and Spontaneity in the Psychoanalytic Process*. New York, NY: Analytic Press.

Hurwitz, M.R. (1986). The analyst, his theory, and psychoanalytic process. *Psychoanalytic Study of the Child* 41:439–466.

Johnston, S.H., & Farber, B.A. (1996). The maintenance of boundaries in psychotherapeutic practice. *Psychotherapy: Theory, Research, Practice, Training* 33:391–402.

Kantrowitz, J.L., Katz, A.L., Greenman, D.A., Morris, H., Paolitto, F., Sashin, J., & Solomon, L. (1989). The patient-analyst match and the outcome of psychoanalysis: A pilot study. *Journal of the American Psychoanalytic Association* 37:893–920.

———, ———, & Paolitto, F. (1990). Followup of psychoanalysis five to ten years after termination: II. Development of the self-analytic function. *Journal of the American Psychoanalytic Association* 38:637–654.

Kluckhohn, C., & Murray, H. (1949). *Personality in Nature, Society, and Culture*. New York, NY: Knopf.

Kohut, H. (1971). *The Analysis of the Self*. New York, NY: International Universities Press.

───── (1984). *How Does Analysis Cure?* Chicago, IL: University of Chicago Press.

Kundera, M. (1984). *The Unbearable Lightness of Being.* New York, NY: Harper & Row.

Langs, R. (1976). *The Bipersonal Field.* New York, NY: Jason Aronson.

Lichtenberg, P. (2005). Group therapy for therapists in Gestalt therapy training: A therapist-trainer's perspective. In J.D. Geller, J.C. Norcross, & D.E. Orlinsky (Eds.), *The Psychotherapist's Own Psychotherapy: Patient and Clinician Perspectives* (pp. 307–322). New York, NY: Oxford University Press.

Loewald, H. (1960). On the therapeutic action of psychoanalysis. *International Journal of Psychoanalysis* 41:1–18.

───── (1962). Internalization, separation, mourning, and the superego. *Psychoanalytic Quarterly* 31:483–504.

Lohser, B., & Newton, P.M. (1996). *Unorthodox Freud: The View from the Couch.* New York, NY: Guilford Press.

Mahoney, M.J. (1991). *Human Change Processes: The Scientific Foundations of Psychotherapy.* New York, NY: Basic Books.

Martinez, D., & Hoppe, S.K. (1998). *The Analyst's Own Analyst: Other Aspects of Internalization.* Paper presented at the 27th annual meeting of the Society for Psychotherapy Research, Snowbird, UT.

Mitchell, S.A. (1988). *Relational Concepts in Psychoanalysis: An Integration.* Cambridge, MA: Harvard University Press.

───── (1993). *Hope and Dread in Psychoanalysis.* New York, NY: Basic Books.

Minuchin, S. (1976). *Families and Family Therapy.* Cambridge, MA: Harvard University Press.

Oremland, J.D., Blacker, K.H., & Norman, H.F. (1975). Incompleteness in "successful" psychoanalyses: A follow-up study. *Journal of the American Psychoanalytic Association* 23:819–844.

Orlinsky, D.E., & Geller, J.D. (1993). Psychotherapy's internal theater of operation: Patients' representations of their therapists and therapy as a new focus of research. In N.E. Miller, J. Doherty, L. Luborsky, & J. Barber (Eds.), *Psychodynamic Treatment Research: A Handbook for Clinical Practice* (pp. 423–466). New York, NY: Basic Books.

———— & Howard, K.I. (1986). Process and outcome in psychotherapy. In A.E. Bergin & S.L. Garfield (Eds.), *Handbook of Psychotherapy and Behavior Change: An Empirical Analysis* (3rd ed., pp. 311–381). New York, NY: Wiley.

Pfeffer, A.Z. (1963). The meaning of the analyst after analysis: A contribution to the theory of therapeutic results. *Journal of the American Psychoanalytic Association* 11:229–244.

Pope, K.S., & Bouhoutsos, N. (1986). *Sexual Intimacy Between Therapists and Patients*. New York, NY: Praeger.

———— & Tabachnick, B.G. (1994). Therapists as patients: A national survey of psychologists' experiences, problems, and beliefs. *Professional Psychology: Research and Practice* 25:247–258.

———— & Vasquez, M.J.T. (1998). *Ethics in Psychotherapy and Counseling*. San Francisco, CA: Jossey-Bass.

Rangell, L. (1966). An overview of ending an analysis. *Journal of the American Psychoanalytic Association* 11:229–244.

Renik, O. (1993). Analytic interaction: Conceptualizing technique in light of the analyst's irreducible subjectivity. *Psychoanalytic Quarterly* 62:553–571.

Rogers, C. (1975). Empathic: An unappreciated way of being. *The Counseling Psychologist* 5:2–10.

Ruttan, J.S., & Stone, W.N. (1993). *Psychodynamic Group Psychotherapy*. Toronto: Coll Amore Press.

Sandler, J., & Rosenblatt, B. (1962). The concept of the representational world. *Psychoanalytic Study of the Child* 17:128–145.

Schachter, J. (1992). Concepts of termination and post-termination patient-analyst contact. *International Journal of Psychoanalysis* 73:137–154.

Schlessinger, N., & Robbins, F. (1974). Assessment and follow-up in psychoanalysis. *Journal of the American Psychoanalytic Association* 22:542–567. https://doi.org/10.1177/000306517402200305

Shapiro, D. (1976). The analyst's own analysis. *Journal of the American Psychoanalytic Association* 24:5–42.

Shevrin, H. (1995). Psychoanalysis as science. *Journal of the American Psychoanalytic Association* 43:963–986.

Simon, B. (1993). In search of psychoanalytic technique: Perspectives from on the couch and behind the couch. *Journal of the American Psychoanalytic Association* 41:1051–1081.

Smith, D., & Fitzpatrick, M. (1995). Patient-therapist boundary issues: An integrative summary of theory and research. *Professional Psychology: Research and Practice* 26:499–506.

Sommer, R. (1969). *Personal Space*. Englewood Cliffs, NJ: Prentice Hall.

Spence, D.P. (1982). *Narrative Truth and Historical Truth: Meaning and Interpretation in Psychoanalysis*. New York, NY: Norton.

Witkin, H.A., & Goodenough, D.R. (1981). *Cognitive Styles: Essence and origins*. New York, NY: International Universities Press.

Wolf, E.S. (1996). How to supervise without doing harm: Comments on psychoanalytic supervision. *Psychoanalytic Inquiry* 15:252–267.

Wzontek, N., Geller, J.D., & Farber, B.A. (1995). Patients' post-termination representations of their psychotherapists.

Journal of the American Academy of Psychoanalysis 23:395–410.

Yourman, D.J., & Farber, B.A. (1996). Nondisclosure and distortion in psychotherapy supervision. *Psychotherapy* 33:567–575.

CHAPTER 13

Style and Its Contribution to a Patient-Specific Model of Therapeutic Technique

[J.D. Geller (2005). *Psychotherapy: Theory, Research, Practice, Training* 42:469–482.]

ABSTRACT: The vocabulary of style is used in this article to address the following questions: How can the authors improve on our methods of teaching therapists to attune the ways in which they listen and speak to meet the communicative requirements of each patient? What does it mean to practice psychotherapy scientifically? Are the technical and relational aspects of therapy interdependent and overlapping? What forms of presence have facilitating effects on the process of therapy? How does a therapist's overall level of expressiveness anticipate and modify the manner in which any particular intervention is experienced by a patient? What does it mean to confront a patient's therapy-interfering behaviors tactfully? What is it about the therapeutic relationship that is healing?

> *The best we can expect in psychology is that everybody*
> *puts his cards on the table and admits: "I handle*
> *things in such and such a way, and this is how I see them."*
> —C.G. Jung

Psychotherapy is, at its core, a special form of conversation that aims to bring about psychological and behavioral changes. As Freud (1926) said of psychoanalytic therapy, "Nothing takes place between them [patient and analyst] except that they talk to each other" (p. 187). This report is concerned with the basic listening, looking, and speaking skills that lie at the heart of therapeutic competence. It constitutes yet another effort on my part to articulate a form of expressive-exploratory therapy that is both a source of change-promoting insights and a catalyst for the activation of various forms of experiential and interpersonal learning (Geller, 1984, 1987, 1994, 1998, 2003, 2005).

I approached the writing of this paper with the following questions in mind: What kind of education would best prepare the next generation of psychotherapists to improve and expand upon the therapeutic techniques offered to them by their pre-decessors? How can we improve the ways in which we teach therapists to participate in conversations that honor the unique qualities of each patient?

I begin by declaring my position regarding the role of ther-apist and the venerable distinction between the technical and relational aspects of therapy. The first of the paper's three main sections deals with the information-processing capacities that are required for empathic listening. The second section explores the ways in which the therapist's "presence" broadly influences the experiential and interpersonal learning that occurs during therapy sessions. The third section is focused upon the subtleties of communication that heighten the likelihood that a therapist's interventions will have their intended effect. What connects the separate sections is the belief that competence in attaining therapeutic goals is importantly linked to the ability to attune one's conversational "style" (Geller, 1994, 1996, 1998) to the communicative requirements of each patient. The main thesis of this paper is that in order to be truly individualized, a treatment plan should specify the optimal style in which to use the set of techniques that have been chosen to realize the goals that have been prioritized.

THE THERAPIST'S ROLE

My ideal is to practice a psychotherapy that has a legitimate claim to being called an "applied clinical science" (Geller, 1998). Meeting this requirement means relying on guidelines and techniques that are grounded in a cumulative knowledge base and on theoretically derived ideas about people and how they change that can be, at least in principle, confirmed or refuted. As I teach my students, however, it is important not to confuse basing the professional practice of psychotherapy on the findings provided by scientific research with adopting the role model of a scientist vis-à-vis patients.

The scientist role model is one in which technical and intellectual competencies dominate all other aspects of the personality; scientists can single-mindedly and dispassionately pursue facts and truths. Not so the psychotherapist. He or she must soften the hard edges of scientific objectivity and curiosity with caring concern. I, therefore, encourage students to look beyond the role model of scientist in their efforts to create an understanding for themselves of what it means to *be* a psychotherapist.

Beginning with Freud (1940), the role of therapist has been repeatedly analogized to that of parent. Understandably, student therapists who are single and in their 20s often have difficulty imagining themselves inhabiting this role. Identifying themselves with the equally appropriate roles of teacher, mentor, or coach comes more easily and feels more legitimate.

My search for alternatives to the classical role models of clergyperson and physician has led me to the role model of healer. As portrayed by Bakan (1967), healers are concerned with suffering and things only partially comprehended. Their primary tool is communication. I recognize my own work in Bakan's description of the healer's major function, which is "enhancing communication among regions of existence, whether this be between the holy and mundane, between one person and another, between conscious and unconscious, or between the scientist and the laymen" (p. 126). Whereas the role of healer has intrinsic appeal to so-called new age therapists, academically trained therapists have shied away from adopting this identity, even if they speak of therapy as a healing experience. For me, one of the compensations of turning 65 is being viewed by my students and patients as a wise elder who can draw on a wealth of personal experience to heal and advise members of our community.

I believe that a therapist's education is incomplete if he or she has not considered the ways in which metapsychological and nonscientific sources of influence have entered into his or her selection of a theoretical position and style of conducting therapy. Accordingly, in my ideal training program, student therapists would be provided with the questions and tools necessary to examine how their ideas about what advances and what interferes with the realization of therapeutic goals are linked to their ideological, cultural, aesthetic, and political predilections. Recognizing that one's clinical judgments are grounded, to one degree or another, in matters of taste, articles of faith, and acts of the imagination is a humbling experience. Autobiographical accounts of therapist-patients indicate that it is within their own personal therapies that therapists explore the linkages between the clinical judgments that they make at any moment in time and their efforts to master basic problems of childhood and to find solutions to fundamental existential questions (Geller, 2005; Pinsof, 2005; Wittine, 2005).

WHAT ARE THERAPEUTIC TECHNIQUES?

Most broadly stated, techniques are the means or procedures used in attaining a goal. Therapeutic techniques are the methods of performing the tasks I impose on myself and my patients. My technical choices are strategic. They are motivated by a set of interrelated "intentions" (Stiles et al., 1996). I speak to console, to clarify, to exemplify, to motivate, to inspire, to explain, and so forth. Some of my utterances are meant to move the therapeutic dialogue toward greater levels of collaboration, intimacy, trust, and mutual respect (Geller, 1984). Others aim to stimulate the creative and responsible uses of truth-telling (Geller, 2003). My overriding therapeutic intention is to enter into a relationship that permits a patient to "use" what I have to offer for reparative and adaptive purposes. I proceed on the assumption that patients benefit from therapy to the extent that they come to view the therapeutic situation as a "safe place" (Havens, 1989) in which to try out *new* ways of thinking, feeling, and behaving. If all goes well, a wide range of surprises await patients: experiencing startling insights; being taken seriously for the first time; receiving feedback without blame; taking calculated risks; having feelings previously unexperienced at a conscious level; discovering that talking about dangerous, difficult, and painful emotions can make them feel good rather than anxious; no longer feeling that they have to be perfect; and so forth. An unwelcome but potentially transformative surprise for an undetermined number of patients is the disappointing realization that understanding the origins of one's old ways is not a guarantee of discovering new ways of behaving. Nevertheless, I know we are moving in the right direction when a patient says, "I never thought I could ever tell you about my disappointments in you and this therapy."

RELATIONSHIP-TRANSFORMING TECHNIQUES

The ideal of some therapists is to practice a "psychotechnolo-gy" in which specific and clearly defined symptoms would be treated expediently in a prescribed and systematized fashion. In spite of this, all techniques are processes of interaction. Thera-peutic techniques do not function separately from the particular relationship in which they are being used, whether they are be-havioral, cognitive, imaginative, or emotive in nature. In other words, the technical and relational aspects of therapy neither occur nor function independently. This becomes most apparent when a technique is specifically designed to bring about changes in the therapeutic relationship itself.

Relationship-transforming techniques are derived from an interest in promoting the capacities required to participate ef-ficaciously in intimate and task-oriented relationships. Two of the most promising and provocative relationship-transforming techniques are providing feedback regarding a patient's self-de-feating impact on others, including the therapist, and confronting patients with their resistances. I will present a detailed consid-eration of these techniques when we shift our attention from listening to speaking therapeutically. In my opinion, the devel-opment of empirically grounded and experience-near guidelines for performing these general clinical strategies is pertinent to the work of all therapists who treat patients suffering from various forms of character pathology. Furthermore, I accept the fact that "borrowing" techniques generated by theories other than one's own may be necessary when trying to facilitate the grad-ual development of a therapeutic relationship with patients who "enact" their "salient maladaptive relationship predispositions" (Strupp & Binder, 1984) in the relationship with the therapist. Beck and Butler (2005) have similarly acknowledged that cog-nitive therapists "use a wider range of strategies and techniques, including psychodynamic-like and experiential ones" (p. 256), when the patient brings Axis II interpersonal problems into therapy. I take this as a sign that our profession is arriving at a point where the ideal of establishing one final, absolute, incontestable set of therapeutic techniques is vanishing. Perhaps the earliest manifestation of this shift was the growing acceptance of the trans-theoretical importance of the "therapeutic alliance" (Greenson, 1967). If these trends continue, future generations of therapists might be better prepared to transcend the counterproductive rivalries of the past. What would the field be like if all therapists shared a common and agreed-upon vocabulary?

Before proceeding, let me weave in yet another reason why I find the distinction between the technical and relational aspects of therapy to be somewhat artificial and misleading. Techniques that are specifically designed to bring about changes in self-contained states experienced by a patient set in motion a variety of interpersonal and intrapsychic processes. For example, accurate and properly timed clarifying descriptions of vague and lexically inexpressible feelings of somatic distress serve to promote the formation of more differentiated, recognizable, and manageable affects and memories. In addition to serving pedagogic functions, such interventions provide feedback to the effect that what one has intended has actually been communicated. Restating in more precise phenomenological terms what the patient is already saying also offers evidence that the therapist is making a sincere effort to be understanding and reinforces a patient's confidence in the competence and caring concern of his or her therapist. These reactions, in turn, inspire "hope" (Frank & Frank, 1991), which may also be understood as serving a dual role. First, hope can be understood as providing a favorable context in which to pursue the work of therapy. Second, the comfort derived from feeling hope can also serve as a healing experience itself.

ON LISTENING THERAPEUTICALLY

Let me next turn my attention to the forms of listening that enable a therapist to understand the world from a patient's point of view, nonjudgmentally, on a moment-to-moment basis, which is the essence of the empathic mode of knowing (Rogers, 1975; Kohut, 1984). At the center of my evolving theory of technique is the hypothesis that providing patients with empathic understanding of the origins, subjective meanings, and consequences of their problems sets in motion two interrelated agents of change. The first is the progressive *externalization* and constructive modification of the dysfunctional self-representations, representations of others, and representations of interactions with others that are stored in long-term memory. The second and simultaneous agent is the progressive *internalization* of the benignly influential functions of the therapeutic relationship (Geller, 2003). Consequently, in my ideal training program, much of the teaching would be devoted to strengthening each student's access to the forms of attentiveness that are required to listen empathically to the oft-repeated stories patients tell about themselves.

The curriculum and practicum would provide students with the tools required to study the ongoing nature of listening from multiple perspectives. Thus, their inquiries would focus on such domains as the capacities required to receive, store, and retrieve the verbal and nonverbal aspects of the therapeutic dialogue; the cognitive styles in which meanings are constructed from what patients say and do; variations in the width of attentional focus; the strategies used for overcoming distractions; and the observable behaviors that embody variations in how therapists listen.

In supervisions and seminars, student therapists would explore a key determinant of the depth and quality of a person's listening during dyadic interactions, namely, the ability to shift back and forth, as the situation requires, between sensuously receptive and actively rational modes of paying attention to internal and external stimuli (Deikman, 1977). I believe that therapists who possess this skill are better prepared to create highly individualized case conceptualizations and treatment plans. I speak of these matters in terms of the alternation between two experientially distinguishable modes or phases of listening. For pedagogic purposes, I refer to them, following Freedman (1983), as "receiving" and "restructuring."

Receiving: A Form of Listening

Receiving and restructuring are, at one and the same time, approaches to processing multiple channels of information and forms of relatedness. Receiving is an effort to maintain one primary focus of attention—the patient's experience. As depicted by Freedman (1983), receiving involves "an openness to the intent of the other, out there" (p. 409). Receiving is an endeavor to take what is given to us in its "giveness," as May (1959) put it. Like the phenomenological method, receiving implies a willingness to suspend one's theory-based assumptions about the potential meanings of what is being heard. Receiving can be understood as an attempt to surrender, temporarily, the need to objectify, the use of selectivity, and the tendency to seek closure. During the receiving phase, a listener aims to broaden his or her attentional focus to include mental activities that are carried out at the periphery of consciousness. Receiving is an effort to achieve attentional states that allow a wide variety of nonverbal and sensory information to enter awareness. This requires cultivation of a moment-to-moment "willingness not to will" (Langan, 1997). These qualities of listening open a listener to images of his or her own desires, fears, memories, and associations. In this way, receiving is akin to Freud's (1912) notion of "evenly suspended attention" and that form of meditation known as "choiceless awareness" (Safran, 2003).

Restructuring: Another Form of Listening

The transition from receiving to restructuring involves the reactivation of directed consciousness, the reintroduction of objectivity, and the reassertion of one's critical judgment. This shift may be triggered by the felt need to understand the stream of preconscious images, symbols, and fantasies elicited while listening in the receptive mode. Whatever the catalyst, upon entering the restructuring mode of listening there are two attentional foci: the patient's experience and the therapist's experience.

For educational purposes, I describe restructuring as a three-phase process. In the first phase, the therapist begins following the patient with a "running commentary" (Heimann, 1977). Here a therapist begins talking to himself or herself about what has been said and left unsaid while also hearing what the patient is saying. Basescu (1990) describes himself as "listening to the other person and listening to myself, or listening to myself listening to the other" (p. 56).

During the second phase, the mental activities that enter into the decision to pursue certain therapeutic goals or intentions are activated. Listening becomes increasingly geared toward monitoring and remembering patient utterances that illuminate one's theory-driven expectations regarding what will or should occur during therapy sessions. It is here that ideas about how to respond to the possible meanings of what one is hearing arise and become more available for contemplation. These ideas and intentions may never be verbalized because in further listening they may be relinquished or revised.

The task of deciding how the goals one has selected to pursue can or should be brought about belongs to the third phase of listening. The distinguishing feature of the third phase of listening in the restructuring mode is arriving at a judgment regarding the content, form, and timing of a therapeutic intervention. At this point, a therapist prepares to make the transition from listening to speaking.

Educational Implications of Receiving and Restructuring

To recapitulate, receiving and restructuring are, at one and the same time, the cognitive and perceptual foundations of listening and the modes of interacting with patients. My efforts to understand the interpersonal impact of these modes of relatedness are based on a dyadic systems view of communication (Beebe et al., 2004). According to this bidirectional formulation of the nature of communication, in face-to-face conversations, people simultaneously send and receive information whether they are listening or speaking. From this perspective, there is no such thing as "just listening." A silent therapist's listening presence may convey or express as much comprehensible information to a patient as his or her verbalizations.

Using this model as a guiding framework, I encourage students to investigate the forms of attentiveness that they bring to the experience of listening. In proportions that vary from student to student, I ask them to give serious consideration to the following types of questions: What length of time do I spend in receiving and restructuring? How do I sequence through these forms of listening with different patients? What are the consequences of prolonged immersion in the receptive mode? To what extent can I resist the temptation to stop listening? Do I restrict my listening to the content of my patients' verbalizations? Can I connect with that which lies outside the reach of language? Can I transcend the sequential linearity of verbal thought? Do I listen to how it feels to be in relation to a particular patient? How do I, nonverbally, communicate evidence of personal "interest" in a patient while listening? How does my preferred style of listening impact the subjective experience of my patients?

The educational yield of conducting such thought experiments can strengthen a student therapist's access to a wider range of modes of knowing his or her patients. Some students learn how to temporarily set aside their theory-based interpretive biases about the potential meanings of what they are hearing. Others come to realize that listening has been restricted to monitoring their patients' syntax, themes, and story lines. Still others expand and refine the distinctiveness and variety of the sensory experiences that accompany listening, and they learn to create more vibrant and vital working clinical models of their various patients. In this regard, it is noteworthy that research suggests that, with increased experience, therapists come to rely more extensively on knowledge brought to awareness in the form of multimodal images and bodily felt experiences when thinking about their patients during intersession intervals (Geller et al., 2002). Our data further suggest that inexperienced therapists, relative to their more experienced colleagues, tend to include fewer of the nonverbal and noncognitive aspects of the therapeutic dialogue in their working clinical models of their patients.

Research methods have also been developed to determine whether a therapist can identify repetitive interactional patterns as they are evidenced in verbatim transcripts of therapy sessions. I believe these operational measures can make an important contribution to educating student therapists. For example, I have recommended the use of Luborsky and Crits-Christoph's (1990) method for identifying core conflictual relationship themes when students have difficulties extracting such themes from their patients' narratives.

The Interdependence of Listening and Looking

Because of the auditory bias of the "talking cure," the development of therapists' observational skills is an often-neglected component of psychotherapy training programs. To counteract this imbalance, my educational program would have students conduct movement analyses of the facial expressions, gestures, and postures that they and their patients exhibit when listening and speaking. (Do you raise or lower your eyebrows when paying serious attention?) (Geller, 1978, 1996). I advise my students to ask themselves, What does my patient need to see in order to feel that I am "optimally responsive" (Bacal, 1985) to his or her communicative requirements?

Ekman's (1982) research indicates that the facial muscles can make 43 distinct movements. These "action units," as they are called by Ekman, can serve as visual equivalents of a therapist's words and vocal qualities. Calling upon more complex variations in the movements of the facial muscles to give form to one's feelings about a patient may be advisable when the patient finds it difficult to listen to the linguistic content of the therapist's utterances. I assume that it is within their own personal therapies that therapists feel most free to examine the question, Are the relatively invariant aspects of my characterologically based communicative style exerting a restrictive influence on the expressive options that are available to me as a therapist?

THE LISTENING PATIENT

For patients as well as therapists, listening is a multisensorial experience. In order to gain intimate knowledge of the new modes of relatedness made available in therapy, a patient must be capable of faithfully receiving and reproducing the sensuous fullness of the therapeutic dialogue. There is now abundant evidence that patients bring to therapy personality dispositions that can either facilitate or interfere with their capacity to recognize whether their therapists are manifesting the "facilitating human qualities" (Rogers, 1975) of the "good enough" parent, teacher, mentor, physician, clergyperson, or healer. For example, "neurotic styles" (Shapiro, 1965) of processing sensory information, which typically operate outside of conscious awareness, have been found to exert an impoverishing influence on patients' receptivity to encounters with therapists that could provide the basis for what have been characterized as "corrective emotional experiences" (Alexander & French, 1946).

Accordingly, I give high priority to determining whether patients have the ability to perceive accurately the meanings, attitudes, and feelings that therapists convey acoustically, facially, gesturally, and posturally. For certain patients, many obstacles will have to be overcome before they can gain intimate knowledge of and consistently benefit from the functional aspects of their therapists' verbal and nonverbal contributions to the therapeutic dialogue. Consequently, I encourage students to bear in mind that what is heard cannot be fully understood without taking into consideration the fact that in face-to-face conversations listening is powerfully influenced by what is being observed. Until (self-) consciousness about seeing and being seen recedes from awareness, it is difficult to pay adequate attention to what is being heard. Patients who are fearful of making extended eye contact with their therapists remain uncertain about whether their therapists' faces are saying, "Yes, I am listening," "Yes, I am present," "Yes, I am interested and care about you." These truths may never be put into words.

THE INTERPERSONAL IMPACT OF A THERAPIST'S PRESENCE

From the opening moments of therapy, predictable degrees of expressiveness and muscular exertion accompany all that therapists do and say. There are wide individual differences in the degree to which a therapist's actions while listening include facial expressions, head movements, postural shifts, and various forms of self-touching. I haven't done a statistical analysis, but my impression is that cradling the chin in one's hand and crossing the arms and holding them at chest level are two forms of self-touching that therapists do not feel obligated to restrain. The meaning a patient attributes to any form of self-touching is quite another matter. Holding oneself at chest level, for example, can accommodate a variety of plausible interpretations. One person might feel as though this activity represented a barrier that shielded the other. Another might take this action as a comforting sign of stillness and solidity. A friend of mine might well have been speaking of psychotherapy rather than an abstract painting when he observed, "There is not much to look at but there is a great deal to see."

One can use variations in expressiveness strategically, but these variations are also a unique and defining feature of each person's presence. By "presence" I mean far more than impression management. Presence has far more to do with the subtle and organic features of a person than with selling an image of oneself. The deepest sources of presence can be found in processes that move through our bodies and take place, more or less, below the threshold of conscious awareness. Here I would include the combined effect of the physical actions associated with breathing, the micromovements of the facial muscles, the pitch of voice, the stillness of posture, and temperature regulation. These action tendencies are initiated by "aliveness" itself. They are a primary quality of "being-in-the-world" (May, 1959).

The Presence of Calmness in the Therapeutic Situation

To illustrate the importance of energetic expressions of being present, let us consider the interpersonal impact of a fundamental constituent of a person's presence—his or her level of calmness. Recently my wife, Ruth, referred a female patient she had seen for an initial interview to a very seasoned therapist. The therapist had received specialized training in the treatment of patients with the young woman's presenting complaint. The patient accepted the referral but after several sessions decided that she wanted to be in therapy with Ruth. When asked why, the patient answered, "Because I feel more comfortable and calm in her presence." In this instance, it was Ruth's calm presence that produced a sense of calm in the patient. I am confident that expert witnesses would agree that Ruth's presence embodies a blend of calmness and vitality. I also believe it would have been very difficult for the patient to describe and explain how the calming influence of Ruth's presence was transmitted.

Calmness insinuates itself into those aspects of subjective experiences that are apprehended primarily in the form of felt sensations moving through the body. Like the steady, grounded musical rhythms laid down by the bass, a therapist's calmness registers on a patient's body kinesthetically. In other words, calmness transmits sensory qualities that are perceived "directly" and have a phenomenological "immediacy" but do not call attention to themselves. Consequently, sometimes, without either patient or therapist being aware of it, a therapist's calm presence can reawaken regenerative states of relaxation in otherwise "tense" individuals. Energetic expressions of a therapist's calm presence may have the power to slow down and deepen a patient's breath and relax his or her muscles, blood vessels, and organs so that the flow of body fluids becomes easier, smoother, fuller. These are the bodily changes that occur when the activity of the parasympathetic component of the autonomic nervous system is in ascendancy. Perhaps calmness serves as a constructive force in therapy by restoring the balance between the sympathetic and parasympathetic components of the nervous system. Quieting an overactive sympathetic nervous system has direct relevance to the healing of the affective symptoms of traumatized individuals and those suffering from psychosomatic disorders. Certain patients, however—for example "intensity junkies" (Geller, 1984)—may fear giving in to the sedating influence of a therapist's calm and easy manner of being.

INTERNALIZED REPRESENTATIONS OF THE THERAPEUTIC RELATIONSHIP

Thus far I have been discussing how the "perceptual reality" of the therapist's presence impacts a patient when the therapist is actually present in the physical world of the patient. At this point, I want to underscore how the emergence of the symbolic function during the course of development makes it possible for patients to employ images, words, and objects to stand for or represent interactions with their therapists when they are not immediately available to the senses. When dreaming and daydreaming, patients can create the "illusion" of being somewhere (e.g., in the therapist's office) and with someone (e.g., the therapist) when they are not. The significance of this developmental achievement for psychotherapy is that it makes it possible for patients to learn new behaviors by imitating or "modeling" (Bandura, 1977) behaviors and attitudes of their therapists between sessions, during vacations, and after termination.

Clinical research and empirical findings (Orlinsky & Geller, 1993) indicate that many patients, at varying levels of consciousness, use representations of their therapist's verbal and nonverbal contributions to the therapeutic dialogue for the purposes of self-soothing, problem-solving, and decision-making and when trying to further self-understanding. These patients tend to be the same ones who report positive therapy outcomes and the maintenance of therapeutic gains following termination. Conversely, current and former patients who are unable to continue the therapeutic dialogue at varying levels of consciousness for adaptive and reparative purposes are the same ones who tend to report that therapy has been disappointing, unhelpful, or at worst, harmful (Geller & Farber, 1993).

In previous publications I have explored the technical implications of these findings for the empathic exploration of patients' reactions to feeling misunderstood by their therapists (1996) and to the separation-reunion cycles woven into the work structure of therapy (1987). At the center of these investigations was the hypothesis that whoever is to acquire competent knowledge of the practice of psychotherapy must be prepared to respond nondefensively to unflattering interpretations of what one is doing or not doing, especially if they are fueled by negative transference reactions. I reasoned that this therapeutic tool is of primary importance if we are to help patients develop the capacity to speak about hateful feelings in a constructive and responsible manner. What I wish to emphasize in the next section of the paper are the technical implications of the possibility that what seems to be most enduring in patients' memories is the particular cast of their therapists' conversational style rather than the content of any particular intervention.

THE IMPORTANCE OF STYLE

I am committed to the view that the value of a therapeutic technique is not independent of the "style" in which it is performed (Geller, 2003). The term "style" is useful shorthand for evoking a distinguishable mode of performing a particular activity. The essential features of a therapist's communicative style are the patterned and consistent ways in which he or she uses words, vocal qualities, facial expressions, postures, gestures, and interaction rhythms, consciously and unconsciously, when listening, speaking, and exchanging the roles of listener and speaker.

A therapist's communicative style and its variations can be discerned in the ways in which he or she answers the following types of questions: How often should I speak? How expressive can I permit my face to be? How much therapeutic attention can I devote to direct communication about the affective qualities of the therapeutic relationship? In what proportions should my demeanor express warmth or coolness, informality or formality, activity or passivity, spontaneity or restraint, passion or decorum, levity or gravity?

A therapist's judgments about the permissibility of showing tears, laughter, anger, horror, pity, fear, or pride are in part predictable from his or her theoretical allegiances. Narrative accounts of psychotherapists who have had multiple experiences of psychoanalysis indicate, however, that there are substantial differences in the styles in which psychoanalysts who supposedly share the same theoretical position perform basic techniques

(Guntrip, 1975; Hurwitz, 1986; Simon, 1993). I assume that this is also true of therapists of other theoretical persuasions.

Clinical and research findings have strengthened my conviction that such stylistic differences will have a decided effect in determining whether a particular intervention will benefit a patient, prove ineffective, or in the worst cases, augment suffering (Norcross, 2004). I anticipate that research will indicate that the "fit" or lack thereof between particular patients and particular therapists' investigatory styles has direct relevance for the outcome of therapy. For example, the American Psychological Association Division of Psychotherapy Task Force on evidence-based practices reported that in 80% of the studies they reviewed, matching therapist directiveness to client level of resistance improved therapeutic efficiency and outcome (Norcross, 2004). Norcross summarized the findings as follows: "Specifically, clients presenting with high resistance benefited more from self-control methods, minimal therapist directiveness, and paradoxical interventions. By contrast, clients with low resistance benefited more from therapist directiveness and explicit guidance" (p. 2). Consequently, much of my teaching is devoted to helping students discover the kinds of stylistic choices that increase the probability that their therapeutic interventions will have their intended impact. I ask students to ground their decision-making in the question, What stylistic choices are required to individualize, as far as possible, the content of my communications?

TRANSLATING INTENTIONS INTO TECHNIQUES

With increased practice and training, much of the decision-making that enters into prioritizing a therapeutic intention and the choice of one technique rather than another to bring about this intention is done preconsciously and with an effortlessness that makes it seem as though the therapist did not have a "technique." A recurrent theme in the autobiographical literature on therapy is that the most striking characteristic of expert therapists is the complete naturalness of their clinical approach. For example, in writing about his analysis with Anna Freud, Couch (1995) notes:

> She seemed not to know the orthodox rules of technique. She was just herself; there were no signs of learned technique or of any imposed "system" of rules and unresponsiveness. She was always her real self and analyst at the same time, not like a trained professional person who took on the analytic role in sessions, leaving the real self behind during the therapeutic work (p. 158).

I believe that therapists who are seen as *not* relying on techniques trust that they will find what they are thinking of achieving in the speaking. Therapists who have a relaxed, natural, and spontaneous manner during sessions seem to experience the coming together of what is to be said and how it is to be said as an organic event. Prior to this advanced developmental achievement, more conscious deliberation is required to manage the interplay between the ostensible content of an intervention and the form in which it is conveyed. In fact, before learning to speak in their own voice, some novice therapists are plagued by doubts about how "best" to implement their intentions.

When is it appropriate to reveal one's personal feelings and countertransference reactions to a patient in order to achieve a therapeutic goal? This question is perhaps the one most frequently and anxiously asked by students in my seminars and in supervision. In response, I help students develop more heuristic rationales for choosing to self-disclose. My decision-making model takes into account the ways in which a therapist's conversational style anticipates and modifies the meanings and consequences of any particular self-disclosure (Geller, 2003).

THE EDUCATIONAL ROLE OF THERAPY MANUALS

Therapists of my generation had very little access to accurate descriptions of the techniques actually used by experienced clinicians. Even extensive clinical case reports are rarely detailed enough to convey what "actually" had transpired between the therapist and the patient. Fortunately, today's students have access to much fuller accounts of what happens in therapy and a growing number of therapeutic manuals that provide detailed information about specialized procedures and methods derived from scientific principles. Notable examples for guiding dynamically oriented therapies include those by Luborsky (1984) and Strupp and Binder (1984), and for borderline patients there is Kernberg and Clarkin's (1993) manual. These manuals are making an important contribution to the education of psychoanalytically informed psychotherapists. They are a useful starting point for teaching basic therapeutic techniques; but still, they have limitations. Manuals confine themselves almost entirely to the therapists' verbal efforts. They have very little to say about the ambiguities that arise when dealing with the unscripted and unpredictable aspects of therapy.

Manuals are not adequate for the purposes of teaching students about improvisation, creative problem-solving, or the pragmatics of communication. In other words, they do not pay much attention to *how* language is used by patients or how language *should* be used when implementing the interventions recommended in the manual. To supplement the guidance provided by therapy manuals, we will need to develop particularizing and nuanced models of the wide range of styles in which any technique can be performed.

THE STYLISTIC CHOICES OF STUDENT THERAPISTS

Student therapists narrow the range of their stylistic options without being fully aware of or in control of it. For example, a patient may speak about his or her struggles to bring to awareness and accept his or her conflictual past. In response, the therapist can either expand on what the patient has already said through the use of clarifying comments or can offer a new and different perspective on what has been said through interpretations and explanations. I have noticed that there are beginning therapists who overemphasize one mode of communicating the fruits of their listening. Deeply empathic student therapists who have considerable difficulty initiating discussions about what is being concealed or not talked about tend to limit themselves to reflective comments. I encourage these students to rely more heavily on what Loewald (1960) refers to as "active mirroring." Active mirroring blends the qualities of clarification and interpretation. This technique restates or translates the felt meanings inherent in a patient's communications into words that are more explicit, concrete, hot, and intimate than those used by the patient. I have found that actively mirroring a patient's painful emotions nurtures the formation of affects that are more accessible to self-reflection and verbalization (Geller, 1984).

In order to communicate one's empathic understanding of what a patient is feeling, one can make an observation or pose a question. Some patients welcome hearing, "Are you feeling sad?" and react negatively to, "You seem sad." Others welcome being provided with names for vaguely comprehended feeling states but react negatively to being questioned. In my experience, young therapists also tend to favor either the interrogative or the declarative mode of helping patients gain insight into what they are feeling.

Every therapeutic intention can be communicated via verbal and nonverbal means. Having decided the moment is right to express "compassion" (Geller, 2006), a therapist might paraphrase a patient's words of grief, lean forward in the chair, touch the patient's hand, self-disclose, or remain silent. Patients have distinct, often unrecognized preferences, including some based on aesthetic considerations, when it comes to the styles in which they wish to have their suffering acknowledged. In turn, student therapists will often exclude one or more of these options. Prohibitions against self-disclosing or touching patients are not uncommon among students who have been influenced by orthodox psychoanalytic interpretations of such concepts as abstinence and neutrality. The same students frequently seem to believe that there are "taboos" about providing advice or affirmations of a patient's achievements. Outmoded stereotypes of the surgeon-like detached psychoanalyst have an especially tight hold upon the imaginations of students who identify with cognitive-behavioral forms of therapy. Whatever their professed orientation, I ask all of my students to give serious consideration to the question, Why do certain techniques count as psychoanalytic while others do not? Although certain techniques may be used more frequently by psychoanalysts (e.g., transference interpretations), there is no technique used exclusively by psychoanalysts, and there probably are no general therapeutic techniques that psychoanalysts would never use (e.g., self-disclosure).

I have experimented with various research-based methods of familiarizing students with the selective preference and gaps in their technical repertoires. Some have benefited from coding transcripts of their therapy sessions on the basis of Hill's (1986) rationally derived system for categorizing response modes independently of their content. Hill's system includes the following range of therapeutic responses: approval, information, direct guidance, closed question, open question, paraphrase, interpretation, confrontation, self-disclosure, and minimal encouragement. As stated earlier in this paper, I regard the ability to choose the response modes that accommodate a patient's communicative requirements as an important component of therapeutic competence.

USING CONFRONTATIONAL TECHNIQUE TACTFULLY

It is vitally important to learn how to formulate comments that move patients toward greater awareness of personal characteristics that interfere with therapeutic progress without provoking shame, self-consciousness, and more defensiveness. But it is impossible to offer specific rules of procedure for making the finely honed discriminations required to transmit this knowledge. Like knowing how to balance closeness and distance, the ability to use confrontational techniques tactfully is the prototype of an interpersonal skill that can be manualized only to a limited extent. Perhaps Freud had these difficulties in mind when he wrote in a letter to Ferenczi, "Almost everything one should do in a positive sense I left to tact" (Grubricht-Simitis, 1986, p. 270). Sledge observed in 1989 that the technical and educational implications of this provocative assertion had yet to be systemically explored. This is still the case. In *The American Heritage Dictionary* (2002), "tact" is defined as "acute sensitivity to what is proper and appropriate in dealing with others, including the ability to speak or act without offending" (p. 323). This definition incompletely captures the essence of therapeutic tact. As I understand it, therapeutic tact is that form of "personal intelligence" (Gardner, 1983) that enables a clinician to speak about matters that would be considered inappropriate and hurtful in most social contexts.

The importance of tact is perhaps most apparent when initiating conversations about patient personality characteristics that interfere with the ability to ask for or receive help from caretakers and authority figures. Describing a patient as resisting the therapy or as being defensive would be immediately recognized as judgmental in the course of common social discourse. Tact implies a keen sense of what a patient is ready to hear. Tact is a feeling for how much pain and frustration a patient can tolerate. To paraphrase Cocteau (1981), tactful therapists are capable of "knowing how far to go in going too far" (p. 51). In these various respects, therapeutic tact is comparable to Kohut's (1984) conceptualization of the empathic mode of knowing.

Acquiring these refined sensitivities requires combining tough-minded curiosity and candidness with receptiveness and softness. Synthesizing these often-competing inclinations into an efficacious and personally viable investigatory style is inherently difficult. This task is particularly difficult for student therapists who have unresolved conflicts about their aggressive impulses, especially if they view the resistant patient as struggling against them or as not cooperating in the therapy in a way that they would wish or expect. To ease their burdens, I offer them an alternative perspective on overcoming resistances.

ON RESISTING

Contemporary analytic, cognitive, and behavioral therapists have acknowledged that bringing the resisted aspects of a patient's experience to his or her attention is especially important when treating patients with Axis II disorders. Many different forms of behavior have been categorized as resistances in the therapy literature. A brief sampling of commonly reported resistances would include excessive flattery, relentless self-depreciation, concealing problems, remaining aloof, intellectualizing, discussing tangential matters, role reversal, submissiveness, and so forth. It is generally agreed that these diverse behaviors are all unconscious self-protective responses to feeling threatened. Two of the most frequently cited threats are the fear of knowing oneself and feeling unsafe with and devalued by the therapist. Whether these behaviors should be interpreted as a form of "fighting against" the therapist or as efforts to "fight for oneself" is, however, a source of lively debate.

During the initial stages of therapy, I give high priority to determining what feelings and thoughts a patient believes are too painful or frightening to endure, much less talk about. My inquiries are guided by the assumption that characterological issues such as those having to do with basic trust, security of attachments, struggles for autonomy, an insufficiently developed sense of self, and shame-based narcissistic injuries are likely to provoke different forms of resistance and to require different therapeutic strategies. I find it useful to think of patients as simultaneously approaching and avoiding candor and affective freedom. Within the context of psychotherapy, self-revelation and self-concealment are co-occurring inclinations; they are not polar opposites. From this perspective, interpreting a resistant patient's responses to perceived threat as "avoidant" or "oppositional" is, at best, a half-truth. If self-revelation and self-concealment stand in a dialectical relationship, then comments regarding the resisted aspects of a patient's experience of therapy should be constructed with this duality in mind.

Consequently, I translate signs of resisting into messages such as, "Are you telling me that you both desire to come to therapy and wish to avoid it by coming late to your sessions?" and, "On the one hand, you say you wish to be free to pursue your own aims, yet on the other hand, you turn silent and angry when I don't give you advice about how to live your life." Whatever format is chosen, therapists need to remain alert to the fact that intentions are not always reliable predictors of accomplishments. What a therapist thinks of as well-intentioned, constructive, and generous in spirit may be regarded as an "unhelpful empathic failure."

PERCEIVED HELPFULNESS AND USABILITY

On the one hand, I give the highest priority to repairing ruptures in the therapeutic alliance precipitated by real and imagined empathic failures. On the other hand, I distinguish between the ultimate value of a therapeutic intervention and a patient's immediate subjective experience of being its recipient. Therapeutic interventions that can be used to relieve pain are subjectively experienced as helpful. But what a therapist regards as useful, perhaps essential, may initially be experienced as unhelpful by a patient. The helpfulness of interventions that are chosen to increase the capacity to tolerate painful feelings and conflict may not become apparent to patients until later in the course of therapy. This tends to be true of interventions that make it more difficult for a patient to call upon habitually used defenses. Curtis et al. (2004) make much the same point: "It may take several weeks, months, or even years for a patient to realize an intervention was helpful" (p. 200).

Like the principles of specificity theory (Bacal, 1985), the notion of usability gives legitimacy to attempts to adjust one's choice of techniques to fit the changing capacities and limitations of a particular therapeutic dyad. Viewing therapeutic interventions as tools that are more or less useful to patients offers an ecumenical way of judging the work of colleagues whose clinical theory and technical practices are different from one's own. Adopting the notion of usability facilitates mutual respect in seminars among cognitively and psychoanalytically oriented student therapists who begin their careers valuing a different assortment of technical options. Moreover, there are times when a therapist feels the need to look beyond the technical options generated by his or her chosen theory of therapy. The criterion of usability reduces the awkwardness therapists feel when "borrowing" techniques generated by theories of therapy other than their own. Consequently, in supervision and seminars I encourage student therapists to apply the notion of "usability" as an overarching criterion when seeking answers to the question, What techniques shall I call upon to realize the therapeutic goals I have prioritized?

SUMMARY AND CONCLUSIONS

Fifty years of increasingly sophisticated empirical investigations have yielded convincing documentation to the effect that psychotherapy helps many people. But the evidence also indicates that we can still do better. For example, substantial numbers of patients are at risk for premature termination. Drop-out rates average about 47% and range as high as 67% (Wierzbicki & Pekarik, 1993). It has been my thesis that we can identify ways of improving on promising therapeutic interventions by creating educational models that strengthen the listening, looking, speaking, and being-with capacities that lie at the heart of therapeutic competence. In this report, I have presented a sample of the principles and strategies that would guide the teaching in my ideal psychotherapy training program.

To summarize, I am committed to the development of a theory of therapy in which the strictures of a therapist's adopted technique and the therapeutic relationship are conceptualized as interdependent and overlapping. My presentation has attempted to lay the groundwork for integrating the concepts of style, presence, tact, and usability and two experientially distinguishable modes of listening into our efforts to learn more about what it is about the complex interplay between the technical and relational aspects of therapy that promotes growth and development. In the practice of psychotherapy, technical skills do not exist apart from the personality dispositions and values of the therapist who is employing them. I have argued that many questions about technical matters remain even after a therapist has learned to adhere to the techniques found in prescriptive therapy manuals. Lying beyond the duties detailed in manuals are uncertainties and challenges that cannot be mastered on the basis of intellect alone. I have arrived at the view that whatever theory a therapist currently professes when making technical decisions, he or she would be well-advised to ask, What stylistic choices are required to individualize, as far as possible, the content of my communications? I believe that doing so would advance our efforts to discover scientific principles that illuminate the specificity of personal experience and the distinctive uniqueness of each therapeutic dyad.

REFERENCES

Alexander, F., & French, T.M. (1946). *Psychoanalytic Therapy: Principles and Application.* New York, NY: Roland Press.

American Heritage Dictionary of the English Language. (4th ed.). (2002). New York, NY: Houghton Mifflin.

Bacal, H.A. (1985). Optimal responsiveness and the therapeutic process. In A. Goldberg (Ed.), *Progress in Self Psychology* (pp. 202–206). New York, NY: Guilford Press.

Bakan, D. (1967). *On Method.* San Francisco, CA: Jossey-Bass.

Bandura, A. (1977). *Social Learning Theory.* New York, NY: General Learning Press.

Basescu, S. (1990). Show and tell: Reflections on the analyst's self-disclosure. In G. Stricker & M. Fisher (Eds.), *Self-Disclosure in the Therapeutic Relationship* (pp. 47–59). New York, NY: Plenum Press.

Beck, J.S., & Butler, A.C. (2005). Treating psychotherapists with cognitive therapy. In J.D. Geller, J.C. Norcross, & D.E. Orlinsky (Eds.), *The Psychotherapist's Own Psychotherapy: Patient and Clinician Perspectives* (pp. 254–264). New York, NY: Oxford University Press.

Beebe, B., Jaffe, J., & Lachmann, F. (2004). A dyadic systems view of communication. In J. Auerbach, K. Levy, & C. Schaffer (Eds.), *Relatedness, Self-Definition and Mental Representation: Essays in Honor of Sidney J. Blatt* (pp. 23–42). New York, NY: Routledge.

Cocteau, J. (1981). In W.H. Auden & L. Kronberger (Eds.), *Aphorisms: A Personal Selection.* New York, NY: Viking Press.

Couch, A.S. (1995). Anna Freud's adult psychoanalytic technique: A defense of classical analysis. *International Journal of Psychoanalysis* 76:153–171.

Curtis, R., Field, C., Knaan-Kostman, I., & Mannix, K. (2004). What 75 psychoanalysts found helpful and hurtful in their own analyses. *Psychoanalytic Psychology* 21(2):183–202.

Deikman, A.J. (1977). Bimodal consciousness and the mystical experience. In P.R. Lee & R.E. Ornstein (Eds.), *Symposium on Consciousness* (pp. 123–132). Baltimore, MD: Penguin.

Ekman, P. (1982). Methods for measuring facial action. In K.R. Scherer & P. Ekman (Eds.), *Handbook of Methods in Nonverbal Behavior Research* (pp. 45–90). Cambridge, MA: Cambridge University Press.

Frank, J.D., & Frank, J.B. (1991). *Persuasion and Healing: A Comparative Study of Psychotherapy* (3rd ed.). Baltimore, MD: Johns Hopkins University Press.

Freedman, N. (1983). On psychoanalytic listening: The construction, paralysis, and reconstruction of meaning. *Psychoanalysis and Contemporary Thought* 6(3):405–434.

Freud, S. (1912). Recommendations to physicians practicing psychoanalysis. *Standard Edition* 12:109–120.

——— (1926). The question of lay analysis. *Standard Edition* 20:177–250.

——— (1940). An outline of psycho-analysis. *Standard Edition* 23:139–208.

Gardner, H. (1983). *Frames of Mind: The Theory of Multiple Intelligences*. New York, NY: Basic Books.

Geller, J.D. (1978). The body, expressive movement, and physical contact in psychotherapy. In J.L. Singer & K.S. Pope (Eds.), *The Power of Human Imagination* (pp. 347–378). New York, NY: Plenum Press.

——— (1984). Moods, feelings, and the process of affect formation. In L. Temoshok, C. Van Dyke, & L.S. Zegans (Eds.), *Emotions in Health and Illness: Applications to Clinical Practice* (pp. 171–186). Orlando, FL: Grune & Stratton.

——— (1987). The process of psychotherapy: Separation and the complex interplay among empathy, insight, and internalization. In J. Bloom-Feshbach & S. Bloom-Feshbach (Eds.), *The Psychology of Separation and Loss: Perspectives on Development, Life Transitions, and Clinical Practice* (pp. 459–514). San Francisco, CA: Jossey-Bass.

——— (1994). The psychotherapist's experience of interest and boredom. *Psychotherapy* 31(1):3–16.

——— (1996). Thank you for Jenny. In B. Gerson (Ed.), *The Therapist as a Person: Life Crises, Life Choices, Life Expe-*

riences, and Their Effects on Treatment (pp. 119–139). New York, NY: Analytic Press.

———— (1998). What does it mean to practice psychotherapy scientifically? *Psychoanalysis and Psychotherapy* 15:187–215.

———— (2003). Self-disclosure in psychoanalytic-existential therapy. *Journal of Clinical Psychology* 59(5):541–554.

———— (2005). My experiences as a patient in five psychoanalytic psychotherapies. In J.D. Geller, J.C. Norcross, & D.E. Orlinsky (Eds.), *The Psychotherapist's Own Psychotherapy: Patient and Clinician Perspectives* (pp. 81–97). New York, NY: Oxford University Press.

———— (2006). Pity, suffering, and psychotherapy. *American Journal of Psychotherapy* 60(2):187–205.

———— & Farber, B.A. (1993). Factors influencing the process of internalization in psychotherapy. *Psychotherapy Research* 3(3):166–180. https://doi.org/10.1080/10503309312331333769

————, Lehman, A.K., & Farber, B.A. (2002). Psychotherapists' representations of their patients: *Journal of Clinical Psychology* 58(7):733–745.

Greenson, R.R. (1967). *The Technique and Practice of Psychoanalysis* (Vol. 1). New York, NY: International Universities Press.

Grubricht-Simitis, I. (1986). Six letters of Sigmund Freud and Sándor Ferenczi on the interrelationship of psychoanalytic theory and technique. *International Review of Psychoanalysis* 13:259–277.

Guntrip, H. (1975). My experience of analysis with Fairbairn and Winnicott. *International Review of Psychoanalysis* 2:145–156.

Havens, L. (1989). *A Safe Place: Laying the Groundwork of Psychotherapy*. Cambridge, MA: Harvard University Press.

Heimann, P. (1977). Further observations on the analyst's cognitive process. *Journal of the American Psychoanalytic Association* 25:313–333.

Hill, C.E. (1986). An overview of the Hill counselor and client verbal response modes category systems. In L.S. Greenberg & W.M. Pinsof (Eds.), *The Psychotherapeutic Process: A Research Handbook* (pp. 131–159). New York, NY: Guilford Press.

Hurwitz, M.R. (1986). The analyst, his theory, and psychoanalytic process. *Psychoanalytic Study of the Child* 41:439–466.

Jung, C.G. (1968). *Analytical Psychology: Its Theory and Practice*. London, UK: Routledge.

Kernberg, O.F., & Clarkin, J.F. (1993). Developing a disorder-specific manual: The treatment of borderline character disorder. In N.E. Miller, J. Doherty, L. Luborsky, & J. Barber (Eds.), *Psychodynamic Treatment Research: A Handbook for Clinical Practice* (pp. 227–244). New York, NY: Basic Books.

Kohut, H. (1984). *How Does Analysis Cure?* Chicago, IL: University of Chicago Press.

Langan, R. (1997). On free-floating attention. *Psychoanalytic Dialogues* 7:819–839.

Loewald, H.W. (1960). On the therapeutic action of psychoanalysis. *International Journal of Psychoanalysis* 41:1–18.

Luborsky, L. (1984). *Principles of Psychoanalytic Psychotherapy: A Manual for Supportive-Expressive Treatment*. New York, NY: Basic Books.

——— & Crits-Christoph, P. (1990). *Understanding Transference: The Core Conflictual Relationship Theme Method*. New York, NY: Basic Books.

May, R. (1959). Contributions of existential psychotherapy. In R. May (Ed.), *Existence* (pp. 37–91). New York, NY: Basic Books.

Norcross, J.C. (2004). Tailoring the therapy relationship to the individual patient: Evidence-based practices. *Clinician's Research Digest, Supplemental Bulletin* 30:1–2.

Orlinsky, D.E., & Geller, J.D. (1993). Psychotherapy's internal theater of operation: Patients' representations of their therapists and therapy as a new focus of research. In N.E. Miller, J. Doherty, L. Luborsky, & J. Barber (Eds.), *Psychodynamic Treatment Research: A Handbook for Clinical Practice* (pp. 423–466). New York, NY: Basic Books.

Pinsof, W.M. (2005). A shamanic tapestry: My experiences with individual, marital, and family therapy. In J.D. Geller, J.C. Norcross, & D.E. Orlinsky (Eds.), *The Psychotherapist's Own Psychotherapy: Patient and Clinician Perspectives* (pp. 145–162). New York, NY: Oxford University Press.

Rogers, C. (1975). Empathic: An unappreciated way of being. *The Counseling Psychologist* 5:2–10.

Safran, J.D. (2003). *Psychoanalysis and Buddhism: An Unfolding Dialogue*. Boston, MA: Wisdom Publications.

Shapiro, D. (1965). *Neurotic Styles*. New York, NY: Basic Books.

Simon, B. (1993). In search of psychoanalytic technique: Perspectives from on the couch and behind the couch. *Journal of the American Psychoanalytic Association* 41:1051–1081.

Sledge, W. (1989). The psychoanalyst's use of tact. *The Psychoanalytic Study of the Child* 44:137–147.

Stiles, W.B., Startup, M., Hardy, G.L., Barkham, M., Rees, A., Shapiro, D.A., & Reynolds, S. (1996). Therapist session intentions in cognitive-behavioral and psychodynamic-interpersonal psychotherapy. *Journal of Counseling Psychology* 43:402–414.

Strupp, H., & Binder, J.L. (1984). *Psychotherapy in a New Key: A Guide to Time-Limited Dynamic Psychotherapy*. New York, NY: Basic Books.

Wierzbicki, M., & Pekarik, G. (1993). A meta-analysis of psychotherapy dropout. *Professional Psychology: Research and Practice* 24:190–195.

Wittine, B. (2005). The I and the self: Reminiscences of existential-humanistic therapy. In J.D. Geller, J.C. Norcross, & D.E. Orlinsky (Eds.), *The Psychotherapist's Own Psychotherapy: Patient and Clinician Perspectives* (pp. 114–128). New York, NY: Oxford University Press.

CHAPTER 14

Pity, Suffering, and Psychotherapy

[J.D. Geller (2006). *American Journal of Psychotherapy* 60(2):187–205.]

ABSTRACT: Every day, psychotherapists are called upon to assuage and give meaning to human suffering. This report examines the ways in which therapists' and patients' attitudes toward giving and receiving "pity" can advance or interfere with the realization of these goals. Clinical observations, introspective analyses, interviews, and questionnaires are used to investigate the following questions: What feelings and thoughts are encompassed by the state of pitying a person or an aspect of a person? What are the similarities and differences between pity and compassion? How do pity and empathy interact in the therapeutic situation? When is taking and showing pity therapeutically beneficial? Is pity a force that brings people together, or is it a way of distancing ourselves from those whom we regard as "other"? Based on the phenomena brought to light by investigating these questions, the author proposes that pity is an inevitable and integral component of our reactions to the ordeals suffered by individuals facing tragic situations. As a background, an overview of the two radically different conceptions of pity that coexist in our culture is presented.

Pity is a rare and fleeting virtue
whose essence is freedom: to be
freely given, it must remain unsought or
accidental, even fought against.
—Leslie Farber

Psychotherapy holds the promise of helping people come to terms with their traumas and tragedies. Great responsibilities are inherent in this promise. The primary aim of this paper is to bring into sharp focus the ways in which patients' and psychotherapists' attitudes toward "pity" influence therapists' attempts to fulfill these responsibilities.

First, I will present an overview of the varied and contradictory meanings "pity" has acquired over time and circumstances. Then I will consider the distinctions and connections between pity, compassion, and empathy. I believe that a clarification of the relations among them would advance efforts to provide our patients with optimally effective forms of "caring concern" (Geller, 1994b; Pope & Vasquez, 1998). Following that, I will distinguish between the bondage imposed by nonproductive forms of self-pity and the occasions when self-pity is the first step that victims of traumas and tragedies take toward feeling empathy for themselves. My basic assumption is that anxieties about experiencing and expressing pity exert a restrictive influence on the capacities required to assuage and give meaning to human suffering.

In order to study pity and its place in the therapeutic situation, I have relied on a variety of methods—interviews with therapists, a questionnaire survey of therapists (1994b), and my own clinical and introspective reflections. The motivational roots of my concern with this topic are both professional and personal. My family became the target of pity, and I fell prey to self-pity, when my younger daughter was diagnosed as profoundly deaf. I have written about these experiences in "Thank You for Jenny" (1996).

I have also drawn heavily upon the insights of theologians (e.g., Augustine, early 5th century/1958; Nouwen, 1976; Houlden, 1984; Boteach, 1995), ethical philosophers (e.g., Aristotle, ca. 335 B.C.E./1961; Cioran, 1963; Goldstein & Kornfeld, 1987; Worthour, 1991; Boleyn-Fitzgerald, 2003), poets (e.g., Dante Alighieri, 14th century/1954; Yeats, 1959; Stevens, 1982; Bishop 1983), literary critics (e.g., Scheff, 1979; Slatoff, 1985; Ulrich, 1989), and social historians (e.g., Rieff, 1966; Jackson, 1994) in preparing this paper. From ancient times to the present, written works have explored the modes of relatedness that lead to the arousal of pity, the feeling aspects of pity, the functions that pity serves, and the moral judgments it implies. The themes of these works are varied and include the intimate linkages that exist between pity and the inevitability of death, pity and forgiveness, pity and status, pity and shame, pity and love, and pity's relationship to acts of kindness.

Given this extensive history, it is surprising to find that pity has been largely ignored in the psychotherapy literature. There are only a few brief and incidental references to the cognitive, affective, and motivational properties of pity as they manifest themselves in the therapeutic situation. Moreover, on the few occasions when pity is mentioned at all, the emphasis has been decidedly negative. Representative of the opinions expressed is Horney's (1937) notion that neurotic patients use "appeals to pity" in a covertly hostile fashion to disclaim responsibility for their actions or to demand affection from others, as illustrated by the directive, "You ought to love me because I suffer and am helpless" (p. 141).

By way of contrast, I will give special attention to the occasions in which pity may have some unique therapeutic value. I shall advocate the view that recognition and constructive use of what Farber (1996) chose to call "unsolicited pity"—pity that is not sought after, or that is even resisted—can make a vital contribution in helping traumatized patients address the tragic aspects of their lives and undo the maladaptive consequences of aspiring to a radical lack of pity for the self. As a background, let us first consider the drastic and remarkable changes the notion of pity has undergone since it was first introduced to Western thought.

PITY: A HISTORICAL OVERVIEW

"Pity" is a word with many meanings. It has been variously regarded as a feeling, a capacity, an attitude, a state of mind, and a moral stance. Like the notion of piety, pity comes to us by way of *pietas*, the Latin term for "due respect for Gods and man" (Hainsworth, 1991). Original users of the word "pity" intended it to mean sorrow felt for another's suffering or misfortune and the attendant desire to be of help. For the ancients, pity in the strict sense of the word meant to "suffer with."

My readings suggest that up until the early part of the 20th century, serious authors used the word "pity" to refer to the feeling states and modes of relatedness that the ancients had in mind when they brought the word into common usage.

In the teachings of Judaism and Christianity, pity has always been presented as a precious ideal to which a good person should aspire. At the heart of Rabbinic Judaism is an all-forgiving form of pity known as *rachmones* (Boteach, 1995). Rachmones denotes a constellation of feelings and thoughts expressing compassion, mercifulness, respect, and a wry sense of humor about human frailty and corruptibility.

In the Old Testament, "Job is the suffering servant of God" (Jung, 1965). In the New Testament, it is Jesus. Job cries out, agonizingly, "Have pity on me, have pity on me, O you my friends" (*Holy Bible: New Revised Standard Version*, 1989, Job 19:21). Pity is repeatedly referred to in the New Testament as the originating source of Jesus' efforts to bear the sufferings of all humanity in his body, as if all of mankind's were his own. According to the Gospels, it was this universal pity that motivated Jesus to heal the blind, to cleanse the leper, to teach the ignorant, to feed the hungry, and to raise the dead.

This is very different from ancient Greek dramas, where the objects of pity were tragic heroes, kings, and noble individuals who possessed qualities equal to or greater than that of the imagined audience. Aristotle (ca. 335 B.C.E./1961) describes these larger-than-life figures as "innocent victims" who brought about their own downfall "by some error or frailty" and as somewhat "better" but not too much better than the implied spectators in their efforts to face moral choices. One can perhaps feel the greatest pity for those who are not essentially pitiable—or so it seemed to Aristotle. In ancient Greece, as in the Christian and Jewish religious traditions, pity was regarded as a deep source of humanitarian inclinations; like the classical "virtues"—courage, wisdom, justice and temperance—one couldn't have too much pity.

Michelangelo's sculptural image of the Virgin Mary supporting the body of her dead son, Jesus, in her lap, is widely regarded as the ultimate artistic representation of Christianity's positive valuation of pity (Tolnay, 1956). It is known in America as the *Pietà*. The French call it *la Vierge de Pitié*. Since the Renaissance, Mary's posture and facial expression have been interpreted not only as signifying maternal grief and love but as embodying an empathic appreciation that her son's suffering offered mankind the hope of redemption. Among poets, the intermingling of love and pity continued to be a common theme up until the middle part of the 20th century. For example, Heine

(1848/1996) wrote, "To be wholly loved with the whole heart one must be suffering. Pity is the last consecration of love, or is perhaps love itself." And Yeats (1959) wrote, "A pity beyond all telling is hid in the heart of love" (p. 40).

Today, pity is rarely used when seeking to express pure and deep feelings of tenderness for the suffering of those whom we know *personally*. On the contrary, contemporary usage indicates that there is a strong pull in our society toward thinking of pity as being primarily expressive of a condescending or even contemptuous form of feeling sorry for another, especially those who have brought misfortune upon themselves. At this moment in history, "pity" is predominantly spoken in phrases of censure. Consider the affective meanings of the following colloquial sayings: A misanthropic conception of pity can be heard in "I pity you." It is usually uttered in a disdainful fashion and directed toward persons who are regarded as pathetic, inferior, or reprehensible in some way. Impatience and indignation are carried by the phrase "for pity's sake...." The television character Mr. T. popularized the usage of "I pity the fool" as a way of expressing contempt. In recovery-speak, alcoholics are told to get off the "pity pot" when seeking to use their "poor me" stories as an alibi or as an excuse for a relapse.

In brief, deep differences separate the core of ideas the premoderns intended when they spoke of pity from our culture's understanding of what it means to have or to take pity on the self or another. "Pity" is still very much a part of our living language, but its original positive meanings have receded into the background, and they have been superseded by essentially mean-spirited uses of pity.

It is not the purpose here to trace the changes in the meaning of "pity" into more modern times. The reasons for the progressive devaluation of pity, like its neglect in the literature on psychotherapy, are undoubtedly complex and overdetermined.

My own readings suggest that Nietzsche (1885/1996) may have been among the first authors to give published voice to the view that giving and receiving pity was undesirable. For Nietzsche, pity, whether arising from Christian motives or otherwise, was a vulgar and shameless intrusion into the lives of others. "'Pity is obtrusive'—you, O Zarathustra, whether it be God's pity or man's—pity offends the sense of shame" (p. 123). Consequently, he objected strongly to receiving pity:

> Verily, I like them not, the merciful ones, whose bliss is in their pity: too destitute are they of bashfulness. If I must be pitiful, I dislike to be called so: and if I be such, it is preferably at a distance. (p. 124)

As a psychotherapist, my primary concern is with the ways in which the existence of two disparate and contradictory conceptions of pity complicates efforts to provide patients with benignly influential caring concern. Let us next turn our attention to these matters.

BEING THE RECIPIENT OF PITY

During the course of my career, I have encountered only one patient who consciously and unashamedly wished to be pitied. He was a 73-year-old, retired Catholic school teacher of English. In response to his worsening Parkinson's disease, he had become very depressed. On those occasions when he wished to both express and take some distance from his worries, he would quote a line from Dante Alighieri's *Inferno* (14th century/1954): "Have pity on me." The line is spoken to the Three Beasts of the Wilderness, who are meant to symbolize the sins of lust, violence, and fraudulence (Durling, 1996). At our last session he read to me from Milosz's (1995) poem "Body." The final stanza is:

> Julia, Isabel, Luke, Titus!
> It's us, our kinship and mutual pity.
> This body so fragile and woundable,
> Which will remain when words abandon us. (p. 60)

A week doesn't go by when I don't hear someone objecting to being or refusing to be pitied. How often do therapists hear a person say, either in session or in a nonclinical context, "Don't pity me under any circumstances!" or, "I hate being pitied"? Antipathy toward pity and self-pity are recurrent themes in the movies, on television, and in the autobiographies of individuals who are physically challenged in some way. For poet David Wright (1969), who is deaf, pity

> is a sentiment that deceives its bestower and disparages its recipient.... Its acceptance not only humiliates, but actually blunts the tools needed to best the disability. To accept pity means taking the first step towards self-pity, thence to the finding, and finally the manufacture, of excuses. The end-product of self-exculpation is the failed human being, the "victim" (p. 8).

Helen Keller (1905/1990), an archetypal sufferer, simply wrote: "I hate pity" (p. 53).

PSYCHOTHERAPISTS' ATTITUDES TOWARD PITY

Public expressions of pity's original meanings can still be heard in two present-day contexts. These meanings survive in declarations of pity for humanity. For example, Bertrand Russell (1951) claimed that "three passions simple but overwhelmingly strong have governed my life: the longing for love, the search for knowledge, and the unbearable pity for the suffering of mankind" (p. 23). This form of pity is impersonal, an abstraction. Pitying the millions of Jews who died in the Holocaust has far less immediacy and palpability than pitying the specific sons and daughters of the survivors of Auschwitz whom we know personally.

Echoes of sorrowful pity can also be heard when people speak about the victims of the devastating catastrophes lawyers refer to as "acts of God"—fires, earthquakes, famines—whom they have witnessed from afar. But what about the feelings and thoughts that accompany a therapist's pitying a patient in the privacy of his/her office?

Remarkably, there have been no systematic, empirical examinations of therapists' attitudes toward pity and the roles it plays in therapy. As a first step in this direction, I constructed a self-administered interview that asks therapists to describe their personal definition of pity, to list their immediate associations to the word "pity," to specify the frequency with which they experience pity toward their patients, and to indicate their opinions about the meanings and functions of pity on various Likert scales. This investigation (Geller, 1994a) of 40 psychotherapists (23 women, 17 men, all psychologists from a mid-size city in the northeast) revealed that therapists' attitudes toward pity are remarkably diverse. Although the small size and geographical limitations of this sample preclude any definitive conclusions, the patterning of the findings (see Table 1) nonetheless suggests that therapists differ in their attitudes toward pity in ways that mirror and reflect those found in the wider culture. These preliminary findings, then, are consistent with the hypothesis that no single definition of pity can encompass the spectrum of contradictory ways in which therapists conceive of this concept. Replication is obviously required to establish the reliability of all the preliminary normative data presented in this report.

When asked to estimate the frequency with which they felt pity for the pain and misfortune of their patients, 10% reported never, 30% reported rarely, 43% reported sometimes, and 17% reported often. The arousal of pity is not a low-frequency event. Interviews with therapists-in-training indicate that they are reluctant to tell their supervisors when they feel pity for patients, including those who have suffered traumas and tragic events. One supervisee told me that his reticence derived from the fear that his pity would be interpreted by his supervisors as serving to defensively distance him from his patients. Another traced the origins of his secrecy to the belief that he would be criticized for excitedly and excessively overidentifying with his patients' suffering. Whether or not these supervisees' expectations were justified, I believe that their anxieties about experiencing and expressing pity exerted a restrictive influence on their ability to empathize with their patients' suffering. I also believe that their divergent motives for not self-disclosing point to pity's confusing relationship to the central human dramas of closeness and distance, sameness and difference.

Once aroused, rarely is pity and pity alone experienced in relation to psychotherapy patients. Only 5% of the participants reported that they experience pity in the absence of other co-occurring emotions. Sixty percent of the therapists reported that, for them, pity is typically experienced in combination with negative emotions, for example, anger, anxiety, lack of respect, frustration. Aristotle (ca. 335 B.C.E./1961) anticipated these findings when he wrote that viewing tragedies gives rise to variably ambivalent blends of pity, horror, and fear.

Although very much in the minority, there are therapists (17%) whose overall attitude toward pity is positive. Thirty-five percent indicated that they tend to experience pity primarily in combination with positive emotions, for example, sympathy, loving kindness, generosity, and especially compassion. Parenthetically, it is noteworthy that Farber (1966) seems to have come to his positive view of pity as a result of receiving the pity of a patient he had been treating unsuccessfully for many years, a man who was unable to speak and was hospitalized with schizophrenia. After many years of remaining silent, the patient inexplicably began speaking to Dr. Farber. Several months later, the patient explained that he began speaking because he felt pity for Dr. Farber when he saw how despairing Dr. Farber was of never being able to reach him.

Standard dictionaries (e.g., *American Heritage*, 2000) and *Roget's Thesaurus* (1996) continue to define "pity" as closely equivalent in meaning to compassion, especially when pity is deeply felt and accompanied by strong feelings of wanting to alleviate pain and suffering. But "pity" and "compassion" are no longer used interchangeably in everyday speech or by a majority of psychotherapists. Sixty percent of the therapists in my sample emphasized the differences rather than the similarities between pity and compassion. These therapists were inclined to think that compassion always favorably connotes broad or profound feelings for the misfortunes of others, an emotional sharing of their distress, and a desire to aid them. For them, compassion has come to be equated with "suffering with" another, and pity with merely "feeling sorry" for another.

Table I.　THERAPISTS' ATTITUDES TOWARD PITY

Attitude*	% (n = 40)	
	Agree	Disagree
1. Pitying a patient places him/her in a one-down position	80	20
2. A therapist who lacks the capacity for pity cannot empathize with his/her patients	43	47
3. I am inclined to think of pity as encouraging patients to surrender to the role of "victim"	48	52
4. Pity is a counter-therapeutic emotional reaction that must be "overcome"	35	65
5. All human beings need both to pity and to be pitied throughout their lives	25	75
6. I have difficulty receiving pity	75	25
7. I equate psychological health with a lack of self-pity	70	30
8. Inequality is an inherent aspect of the relationship between the giver and recipient of pity	63	37
9. Pity impedes or hinders productive understanding of a patient and the ongoing process of therapy	45	55
10. I tend to react negatively to "appeals" for pity	75	25

*Note. Respondents expressed their opinions regarding each statement using the following scale: 1 = strongly agree, 2 = agree, 3 = mildly agree, 5 = mildly disagree, 6 = disagree, 7 = strongly disagree. Reproduced from Geller (1994), presented at the Society for Psychotherapy Research 26th Annual Meeting.

These divisions are based on the following types of comparisons. First, they tend to interpret compassion, symmetrically, as evidence of fellow feeling among equals, and pity, asymmetrically, as offered to those whom we regard as "other" or as somewhat inferior in worth or quality to ourselves. In their imaginations, the voice of compassion says, "I suffer too; it is part of our life," while the voice of pity says, "Oh, that poor person over there is suffering." As reported in Table 1, 80% of the sample holds the view that pity implies a relation between someone who is "one up" and someone who is "one down." This conviction tends to be correlated with two other interpretive biases. The first is that compassion dignifies suffering, whereas pity is condescending, insulting, or degrading. The second is that compassion is empowering, while pity symbolizes futility and impotence. According to this view, compassion holds out glimpses of hope to those who are suffering, while pity carries with it somber forebodings, such as the prediction that one is condemned to a horrible fate.

In short, the positive qualities once ascribed to both pity and compassion are now attributed solely to compassion by the majority of the therapists surveyed. Several colleagues recommended that I should only use the word "compassion" when writing about the feeling states and modes of relatedness the ancients had in mind when they spoke of pity.

This terminological solution recommends itself for a variety of reasons. In non-Western cultures, compassion played (and still plays) the same roles that pity and rachmones played in the Christian and Jewish religious traditions. Cultivating compassionate feelings and knowledge is an essential aspect of Buddhism (Goldstein & Kornfield, 1987). Some sectors of the therapeutic community have already begun to use the vocabulary and practices of Buddhism (e.g., meditation; Safran, 2003). In some places, "compassion fatigue" (Figley, 2002) has replaced "burnout" as the fashionable way to refer to the long-term consequences of listening daily to the stories of suffering caused by rape, fatal or incurable illnesses, child abuse, the death of a child, and so forth. I was surprised to learn that "pity" is also being systematically replaced by "compassion" in recent translations of the Bible (personal communication, Lancaster, 1999). But the problems posed by pity's linguistic ambiguities will not disappear by banishing "pity" from our vocabulary or by finding a more acceptable name for the capacity to "suffer with" others.

COMPASSION AND EMPATHY

The data and concepts of attribution theory (Heider, 1958; Kelley, 1967; Weiner et al., 1982) indicate that people, generally speaking, are likely to distinguish between sufferers who are deserving of compassion and those who are undeserving of compassion. Compassion appears to be reserved for those who cannot be held responsible or accountable for their suffering and withheld from those who are seen as bringing misfortune upon themselves because of their vices or other deficiencies of will. At best, people "feel sorry" for individuals who look as if they ought to be in control of the activities that led to their suffering. This is a way of saying that people are more likely to feel compassion for a hemophiliac who contracted AIDS during a blood transfusion than an IV drug user.

Withholding compassion from those among our patients whose suffering is perceived as being "caused" by their own actions or as perhaps avoidable runs counter to the ethical principles and clinical concepts of scientifically-based psychotherapy. Indeed, some of the most difficult moments in therapy revolve around the question, How do I hold a patient responsible for the life he/she created yet join with him/her in agreeing that he or she was harmed—perhaps unalterably—by crippling influences that could neither be altered by doing something nor avoided by not doing something?

We therapists must be simultaneously attentive to the damage caused by destructive forces that were beyond our patients' power to control and to the ways in which "reality" has been exploited to justify apparent helplessness. My efforts to resolve this dilemma are strengthened by maintaining a commitment to understanding patients empathically (Schafer, 1983).

Empathy, as I understand it, is a call to transcend blame-based systems of morality, and it offers a way of achieving this ideal. As used here, "empathy" refers to a mode of relatedness that enables a therapist to enter into and share a patient's needs, thoughts, and feelings on a moment-to-moment basis. An empathic grasp of a patient's situation presupposes a setting aside of one's own prejudices and the values one holds for oneself. To be with a patient empathically means aspiring to a nonjudgmental, or at least merciful, moral stance regarding patients who appear to have brought misfortune upon themselves. The empathic therapist does not demand "reasonable grounds" for supposing that a patient's suffering is deserving of caring concern. Doing so would constitute a failure to honor the ethical responsibilities of "caring" (Pope & Vasquez, 1998). The point here is that being deeply empathic widens the circle of compassion to include acceptance of and a readiness to "suffer with" patients whose actions do not conform to one's sense of how they *should* behave.

For the ethical and empathic therapist, compassionate concern potentially arises from two reliable sources. The first involves imagining oneself in a patient's place or summoning up personal memories that are of a sort similar to the experiences he/she is describing. A therapist need not, however, identify with a patient in the sense of the feeling that "he/she is like me" in order to gain access to the empathic mode of knowing. Compassionate concern can also be inspired by contrasting one's good fortune with the "undeserved misfortunes" that befall individuals with exceptional qualities. Both of these sources of caring were activated when I listened to the ordeals and suffering endured by a patient who was facing an imminent death.

My patient was a 43-year-old musician who was dying of a rare heart disease. He was a proud, dignified human being—someone who was deeply imbued with a tragic view of life long before his illness. During the course of therapy, he rarely complained or expressed feeling unjustly singled out by a cruel fate. I imagined that he identified with the restraint and manliness of Humphrey Bogart on the tarmac at the end of the film *Casablanca*. He asked "Why me?" ruefully, not ragefully.

Placing myself "in his shoes" awakened in me pity that he did not seek and put me in touch with my most vulnerable selves. Sitting face-to-face with him bent my thoughts to a terrifying awareness of my own mortality. (If one accepts Freud's [1930] view that every person is convinced, unconsciously, of his/her own "immortality," we all die prematurely.)

On the one hand, learning that he was dying stirred in me strong feelings of wanting to alleviate his pain and suffering. On the other hand, his deteriorating condition served as a constant reminder of the impossibility of being able to affect the outcome of his fatal illness. Contrasting my blessings with his "undeserved misfortunes" also provoked the feeling "There but for the grace of God go I," which in turn led to reflections on basic spiritual and philosophical questions: Why not me? Why have I been lucky, so far? How much control do I *actually* have over my destiny?

What I am trying to convey are the unwanted burdens, unanswerable questions, and deep ambivalences that can accompany empathizing with suffering of tragic proportions. I can feel both attracted to and repelled by the suffering of someone I genuinely care about. With this dual potentiality in mind, Nietzsche (1851/1996) wrote of his relationship to beggars, "Verily, it annoyeth one to give to them, and it annoyeth one not to give to them" (p. 94).

Aristotle (ca. 335 B.C.E./1961) would have predicted that my bearing witness to my patient's suffering would give rise to blends of pity, fear, and horror. My experience is also congruent with the finding that therapists typically experience pity within the context of a network of co-occurring positive and negative emotions. Pity's essence depends on whether the balance is tipped in the later or former direction.

Sometimes pity aimed me toward sympathizing with and feeling compassion for my patient. There were other moments when pity potentially awakened problematic or conflictual emotional reactions such as shame and despair. Psychologically, it is quite possible for one reaction to precipitate a compensatory reaction in the other direction. In other words, compassion can sour into pity, or pity can be transformed into compassion. Broadly speaking, a therapist can struggle against or suppress the inner experiences brought to awareness by pity or acknowledge and work nondefensively with them. The direction taken will have a decided effect in determining whether subsequent interventions will benefit a patient, prove ineffective, or, in the worst cases, augment harm. As long as a therapist is open and alert to the meanings of pitying a particular patient, pity can be used as a valuable source of information, like any other emotional reaction. What is of utmost importance is adopting an investigative attitude toward one's experience of pity whether or not one regards pity as an untoward countertransference reaction that needs to be "overcome."

A CLINICAL EXAMPLE

The following vignette (Moses, 1988) illustrates the lost opportunities that arise in therapeutic dyads in which both therapist and patient unquestionably agree that giving and receiving pity is inherently undesirable and to be avoided.

During the 1st year of a psychoanalytic psychotherapy, a female patient, communicating in a detached style, tells her male therapist:

My mother went to give me some medicine, but the bottle was not my medicine, it was some enamel paint for the kitchen appliances. I tried to tell her it was paint, but she refused to listen to me and made me take a teaspoon. I was afraid to tell my father about it because he might get angry at her and then I'd get in trouble again, but I didn't feel much else. I know when I'm telling it to you now I don't feel much either except my heart is beating very quickly (p. 578).

The therapist tells us that in response to hearing this he "conveyed to her how terrifying, helpless, and hopeless it *must* have been for her" (p. 579). Contrary to his expectations, the patient did not feel empathetically understood. Instead, she "scolded him" as she felt he was "pitying her." His reflections upon this incident included the following question: "Should I have inquired as to her motive for demeaning my observation and diminishing my response to one of pity?" (p. 579).

By contrast, I would have assumed that I was not listening empathetically if I had not been "brought to" pity and outrage by the magnitude of her calamitous experience. From the empathic vantage point, pity is a natural, appropriate, perhaps inevitable component of our emotional reactions to hearing patients describe severely traumatizing experiences. What I am suggesting is that pity is not aroused by some calculation concerned with its utilitarian consequences, as is the commitment to being with a patient empathically. Therapists strive conscientiously to be empathic because of a belief in its beneficial effects. Not so with pity. For me, pity arises spontaneously or is to some extent not directly subject to volition once I have made the decision to listen empathically. I further believe that in some instances (e.g., hearing of the death of a beloved infant) not to feel pity signals a loss of humanity, as is implied by pity's antonym. Pitilessness continues to be linked with indifference, cruelty, disrespect, and ruthlessness. In other words, those who are pitiless are incapable of empathy.

This perspective on pity opens up a wide range of exploratory possibilities. What did the therapist do or say that led the patient described above to believe that her therapist was feeling pity and not compassion, or sympathy, or empathy? What meanings did she, consciously and unconsciously, ascribe to being pitied? There are many reasons why she might assume that receiving pity is undesirable, for example, because for her pity implies being damaged beyond repair, or because it implies unfavorable judgments about one's strength of character. Did she believe that the acceptance of pity meant taking the first steps toward self-pity? In our culture, expressions of pity have somehow become associated with the idea of reinforcing "learned helplessness" (Seligman, 1975). The following stanza of a poem by Wallace Stevens (1982) expresses the belief that accepting even Jesus's pity can undermine one's sense of personal agency:

If only he [Jesus] would not pity us so much,
Weaken our fate, relieve us of woe both great
And small, a constant fellow of destiny,
A too, too human god, self-pity's kin
And uncourageous genesis... (p. 315).

Yet another possibility is that she was antagonized by the sense of certainty carried by his use of "must." For supportive utterances to be experienced as supportive, they must be accommodated to a patient's communicative requirements (Geller, 2003). Perhaps the patient would have been more receptive if Dr. Moses had spoken in a style that was more tentative. In a similar vein, I have found that the use of impersonal diction increases the probability that a prideful individual will take in and benefit from expressions of caring concern. For example, I will say,

"It's a pity" or, "It's a shame" or, "It's too bad" to convey my appreciation of the magnitude of their suffering.

I also wondered whether the patient took issue with her therapist's caring concern because she was unable to recognize whatever genuine differences separate expressions of pity and compassion. My clinical experience suggests that an important, often undetected source of a patient's prevailing capacity to accept offerings of genuine caring concern are related to individual differences in this regard. Among the most difficult patients to treat are those who interpret all expressions of caring concern as "evidence" that their therapist finds them pitiful and who hold the view that pity is an unsympathetic form of emotion that is felt toward a person who is to "blame" for his or her misery.

Systematic studies have yet to examine the extent to which pity and compassion can be differentiated by observers on the basis of contextual nuances and expressive cues or "meta-messages." I am moving toward the conclusion that such studies would reveal that all expressions of caring concern, irrespective of how they are intended, are ambiguous with respect to the presence of pity. In my experience, subtle stylistic differences separate the facial expressions and vocal qualities that accompany and reflect the emotional states of pity and compassion.

In my opinion, systematic studies will also be required in order to determine the extent to which pity and compassion are introspectively distinguishable. My introspective observations suggest that they interact and interpenetrate in complex ways and that the experiential boundaries that separate pity and compassion are neither clear nor fixed.

As for the therapist, did his prejudices against pity render him prone to avoidant forms of countertransference? Did he have the inner freedom to feel sorry for his patient? If he didn't, the therapeutic dyad was deprived of a potentially valuable source of information and an important avenue of exploration. Did he feel that bringing "science" to bear on her suffering required him to distance himself from a concept with religious overtones?

According to Rieff (1966), Freud refused even to ask the religious question, "How are we to be consoled for the misery of living?" and consequently, as he put it, "There is no theology at the end of Freudian therapy" (Riefff, 1966 p. 372).

In a similar vein, pity may have fit uneasily into Dr. Moses's lexicon because he associates it with earlier stages of cultural development. The introduction of pity as an ideal into Western civilization clearly advanced communal efforts to deal with life's "inequities." The role relations that pity implies were laid down within the context of tightly and hierarchically organized economic and political institutions. As such, appropriating pity may feel like a betrayal of the democratic and egalitarian values that interpersonalists such as Dr. Moses uphold. My hunch is that the failure to give scholarly attention to pity in the literature on psychotherapy derives from these same interrelated sources.

THE THERAPEUTIC USES OF SELF-PITY

The object of pity can be the self or another. In our culture, to be called "self-pitying" is one of the worst criticisms one can receive. It's often assumed that it means one is wallowing in suffering, neurotic, and unwilling to take initiative in bringing about improvements in one's life (Stöber, 2003). Therapists are not immune to this interpretive bias. Groves (1978) included the "whining self-pitier" in his system for classifying hateful patients. In the psychoanalytic literature, self-pity has been variously described as a "narcissistic orgy tinged with masochism" (Milrod, 1972), as a manifestation of "depletion depression" (Wilson, 1985), as a subtle but potent expression of "self-righteous rage" (Horowitz, 1981), and as a means of adopting a martyr's persona for the purpose of "exhibitionistic display" (Kahn, 1965).

Along with most of my colleagues, I believe that psychological health, like genuine spirituality, is marked by an absence of self-pity as a *dominant* part of one's characterological adaptation and by a deep gratitude for one's blessings (Goldstein & Kornfeld, 1987). I also believe that when self-pity becomes a *modus operandi*, or a characterological mechanism, it can serve as a resistance to self-exploration in certain stalemated therapies. However, I do believe that a one-sided negative view of self-pity can obscure the maladaptive consequence of aspiring to a radical lack of self-pity.

Despite the current emphasis on "victimization" in the popular media, most of the patients I have treated hold themselves "accountable" for their suffering. It is not even uncommon for incest survivors and rape victims to somehow "blame" themselves for having been traumatized. This conviction is often coupled, consciously and unconsciously, with the "pathogenic belief" (Sampson & Weiss, 1986) that they are undeserving of caring concern.

My work with patients such as these has led me to the hypothesis that helping them to develop the inner freedom to feel self-pity may be a fundamental first step toward developing self-care, self-concern, and empathy for themselves. One of my patients, the daughter of survivors of the Holocaust, is prone to severe agitated depressions and has a markedly diminished capacity for pleasure. Nevertheless, she ridicules and trivializes her own suffering and idealizes the ordeals her parents suffered through in concentration camps. She experiences all expressions of personal pain as histrionic or melodramatic. The trivialization of her distress is further reinforced by an overdeveloped sense of irony. Even when it is tempting or would be relieving to do so, she will not cry. She stifles any hint that she is surrendering to feeling sorry for herself and responds with intense shame and guilt whenever there is a suggestion that she is doing so. At the same time, she maintains her suffering because of unconscious identifications with her parents' "survival guilt" and as a strategy to avoid future calamities. She especially resists interventions that are intended to diminish her avoidance of gratification. As we are coming to understand, the dominant aim of her "moral masochism" (Berliner, 1947) is not the idealization of the role of suffering martyr but rather a persistent search for the love of her parents. Both of her parents, she now realizes, demanded suffering and the renunciation of pleasure as the price for their love.

Another patient maintained his Spartan stoicism even during the acute stages of grieving the death of a beloved friend. He experienced being depressed as immoral and self-indulgent. He grew up in a home in which there were strong prohibitions against crying, whining, whimpering, and other expressions of distress. His parents, also survivors of the Holocaust, regarded all expressions of distress as "childish." Like the previous patient, he considered it disrespectful and unfaithful if he questioned his parents' values or their internalized representations, to which he responded with loving submission. His father taught him that the sharing and comparing of vulnerabilities, even with friends, weakens one's efforts at survival. Like Maya Angelou (1994), he came to believe that "whining is not only graceless, but can be dangerous. It can alert a brute that a victim is in the neighborhood" (p. 87). He was haunted by the image of pleading with a Nazi soldier to "have pity on me."

The idea of receiving the pity of others was also repugnant to my patient. A very prideful man, he analogized pity to a "cheap gift" that is given to "losers" and to the "consolation prizes" given to "failures." Although Jewish, his assumptions about what constitutes being "pitiful" or "pitiable" were primarily derived from the imagery found in the Gospels. It will be recalled that

Christ's pity was directed toward the blind, lepers, the destitute, the terminally ill, and the dead. My patient also confused the wish to rely on me for support and understanding with being a "beggar." As a result of having internalized their parents' views, neither patient was able to avail themselves of the cathartic relief of "complaining." For decades, they suffered alone and in silence. Moreover, by aspiring to a radical lack of self-pity, they stifled the development of the capacity to have empathy for themselves.

To counteract their taboos against "complaining," I devote much attention to identifying the occasions when they disguise or deny their "disappointments" in my lapses of understanding and empathic failures. Alternatively stated, I give complex consideration to the defensive styles they adopt in order to protect themselves against the perceived and imagined dangers of speaking truthfully about the ungratifying aspects of therapy. As I have discussed at length elsewhere (Geller, 1994b), helping patients to become more eloquent critics of the process of therapy can serve a variety of therapeutic ends. This means that I express consistent caring concern not only for the misery suffered outside of therapy but also for the frustrations, difficulties, and sacrifices imposed within the therapeutic situation. Throughout this process, I am attentive to a piece of advice quoted by a clergyman friend: "Take pity on them, who cannot take pity upon themselves" (Charles Lemert, personal communication). My hope is that our explorations will lead to the insights the shipwrecked Robinson Crusoe achieved as depicted in Elizabeth Bishop's (1983) poem "Geography":

"Do I deserve this? I suppose I must. / I wouldn't be here otherwise. Was there / a moment when I actually chose this? / I don't remember, but there could have been." / What's wrong about self-pity anyway? / With my legs dangling familiarly / over a crater's edge, I told myself / "Pity should begin at home." So the more / pity I felt, the more I felt at home (p. 162).

CONCLUSION

My inquiries suggest that therapists' attitudes toward pity reflect and mirror the range of views found in the culture. Those who report feeling a blend of tender and loving feelings when experiencing pity are in the minority, and those who report experiencing pity primarily in combination with negative emotions are in the majority. Like the psychoanalyst Greenson (1967), members of the latter group are more likely to regard the arousal of pity as a conflict-laden countertransference reaction. Either set of attitudes can impede or facilitate productive understanding of a patient and the ongoing process of therapy. Giving and receiving pity are dense with meanings.

To encourage inquiry, I will leave with some questions that might help therapists think about resistances to acknowledging and appropriating pity into therapeutic work:

- What obstacles do you encounter in your efforts to "stay with" and use as interpretive resources personal reactions to giving and receiving pity?
- What forms of suffering do you turn away from in aversion?
- Who are your "exemplary sufferers"?
- How do notions of accountability, responsibility, free will, and determinism enter into your decisions about whom to pity?
- What is your reaction to patients who present themselves, initially, as passive and helpless victims of circumstances?

- In order to empathize with a patient who uses illegal substances to get high, do you have to lower your superego standards?
- How do you know if you are experiencing compassion or sympathy rather than pity?

REFERENCES

Alighieri, D. (1954). *The Inferno* (J. Ciardi, Trans.). New York, NY: New American Library. (Original work published 14th century.)

American Heritage Dictionary of the English Language. (4th ed.). (2000). Boston, MA: Houghton Mifflin.

Angelou, M. (1994). *Wouldn't Take Nothing for My Journey Now.* New York, NY: Bantam Books.

Aristotle. (1961). *The Poetics of Aristotle* (S.H. Butcher, Trans.). New York, NY: Hill and Weingarten. (Original work published ca. 335 B.C.E.)

Augustine, St. (1958). *City of God* (G.G. Walsh, D.B. Zema, G. Monahan, & D.J. Honan, Trans.). New York, NY: Doubleday. (Original work published early 5th century.)

Berliner, B. (1947). On some psychodynamics of masochism. *Psychoanalytic Quarterly* 15:459–471.

Bishop, E. (1983). *The Complete Poems: 1927–1979.* New York, NY: Farrar, Straus, and Giroux.

Boleyn-Fitzgerald, P. (2003). Care and the problem of pity. *Bioethics* 17:1–20.

Boteach, S. (1995). Wrestling with the Divine: A Jewish Response to Suffering. Northvale, NJ: Jason Aronson.

Cioran, E.M. (1963). *The Temptation to Exist.* New York, NY: Quadrangle Books.

Durling, R.M. (1995). Introduction and notes. In R.E. Marty (Ed.), *The Divine Comedy of Dante* (p. 36). New York, NY: Oxford University Press.

Farber, L.H. (1966). *The Ways of the Will.* New York, NY: Basic Books.

Figley, C.R. (2002). *Treating Compassion Fatigue.* New York, NY: Bruner-Routledge.

Freud, S. (1930). Civilization and its discontents. S*tandard Edition* 21:64–145.

Geller, J.D. (1984). Moods, feelings, and the process of affect formation. In L. Temoshok, C. Van Dyke, & L.S. Zegans (Eds.), *Emotions in Health and Illness: Applications to Clinical Practice* (pp. 171–186). Orlando, FL: Grune & Stratton.

———— (1994a, June 19–23). *Psychotherapists' Attitudes Toward Pity* [Poster session]. 26th annual meeting of the Society for Psychotherapy Research, Amelia Island, FL.

———— (1994b). The psychotherapist's experience of interest and boredom. *Psychotherapy* 31(1):3–16.

———— (1996). Thank you for Jenny. In B. Gerson (Ed.), *The Therapist as a Person: Life Crises, Life Choices, Life Experiences, and Their Effects on Treatment* (pp. 119–139). New York, NY: Analytic Press.

———— (2003). Self-disclosure in psychoanalytic-existential therapy. *Journal of Clinical Psychology* 59(5):541–554.

Goldstein, J., & Kornfield, J. (1987). *Seeking the Heart of Wisdom.* Boston, MA: Shambhala.

Greenson, R.R. (1967). *The Technique and Practice of Psychoanalysis* (Vol. 1). New York, NY: International Universities Press.

Groves, J.F. (1978). Taking care of the hateful patient. *New England Journal of Medicine* 298:883–887.

Hainsworth, J.B. (1991). *The Idea of Epic.* Berkeley, CA: University of California Press.

Heider, F. (1958). *The Psychology of Interpersonal Relations*. New York, NY: Wiley.

Heine, H. (1848). *Wit, Wisdom, and Pathos*. Quoted in Seldes, G.C. (1996). *The Great Thoughts* (Rev. ed.). New York, NY: Ballantine Books.

Holy Bible: New Revised Standard Version. (1989). Grand Rapids, MI: Zondervan.

Horney, K. (1937). *The Neurotic Personality of Our Time*. New York, NY: Norton.

Horowitz, M.J. (1981). Self-righteous rage and the attribution of blame. *Archives of General Psychiatry* 38:1233–1238.

Houlden, L. (1984). Pity, blame and toil. *Theology* 87:321–323.

Jackson, S.W. (1994). Catharsis and abreaction in the history of psychological healing. *Psychiatric Clinics of North America* 17(3):471–491.

Jung, C.G. (1965). *Memories, Dreams, Reflections*. New York, NY: Vintage Books.

Kahn, E. (1965). Self-pity. *American Journal of Psychiatry* 122:447–451.

Keller, H. (1990). *The Story of My Life*. New York, NY: Bantam Books. (Original work published 1905.)

Kelley, H.H. (1967). Attribution theory in social psychology. *Nebraska Symposium on Motivation* 15:192–238.

Milosz, C. (1995, April 10). Body. *The New Yorker*, p. 60.

Milrod, D. (1972). Self-pity, self-comforting, and the superego. *The Psychoanalytic Study of the Child* 27:505–528.

Moses, I. (1988). The misuse of empathy in psychoanalysis. *Contemporary Psychoanalysis* 24:511–594.

Nietzsche, F.W. (1996). *Thus Spake Zarathustra* (W. Kaufmann, Ed. and Trans.). New York, NY: Vintage Press. (Originally published 1885.)

Nouwen, H.J.M. (1976). Compassion: Solidarity, consolation and comfort. *America* 19:195–200.

Pope, K.S., & Vasquez, M.J. (1998). *Ethics in Psychotherapy and Counseling*. San Francisco, CA: Jossey-Bass.

Rieff, P. (1966). *The Triumph of the Therapeutic: Uses of Faith After Freud*. New York, NY: Harper & Row.

Roget's Thesaurus. (1996). New York, NY: Random House.

Russell, B. (1951). *The Autobiography of Bertrand Russell*. Boston/Toronto: Little, Brown.

Safran, J.D. (2003). *Psychoanalysis and Buddhism: An Unfolding Dialogue*. Boston, MA: Wisdom Publications.

Sampson H., & Weiss, J. (1986). *The Psychoanalytic Process: Theory, Clinical Observation and Empirical Research*. New York, NY: Guilford Press.

Schafer, R. (1983). *The Analytic Attitude*. New York, NY: Basic Books.

Scheff, T.J. (1979). *Catharsis in Healing, Ritual, and Drama*. Berkeley, CA: University of California Press.

Seligman, M.E.P. (1975). *Helplessness: On Depression, Development, and Death*. San Francisco, CA: W.H. Freeman.

Slatoff, W.J. (1985). *The Look of Distance: Reflections on Suffering and Sympathy in Modern Literature*. Columbus, OH: Ohio State University Press.

Stevens, W. (1982). *The Collected Poems*. New York, NY: Vintage Books.

Stöber, J. (2003). Self-pity: Exploring the links to personality, control beliefs, and anger. *Journal of Personality* 71:183–220.

Tolnay, C. (1956). *The Art of Michelangelo*. Princeton, NJ: Princeton University Press.

Ulrich, S. (1989.) Pity and terror: Christianity and tragedy. *Literature and Theology* 4:240–241.

Weiner, B., Graham, S., & Chandler, C. (1982). Pity, anger, and guilt. An attributional analysis. *Personality and Social Psychology Bulletin* 8:226–232.

Wilson, S.I. (1985). The self-pity response: A reconsideration. In A. Goldberg (Ed.), *Progress in Self Psychology* (pp. 178–190). New York, NY: Guilford Press.

Wright, D. (1969). *Deafness*. New York, NY: Stein & Day.

Yeats, W.B. (1959). *The Collected Poems of W.B. Yeats*. New York, NY: Macmillan.

CHAPTER 15

A Psychotherapist's Education: Lessons Learned from Both Sides of the Couch

[J.D. Geller (2012, August 2–5). Presented as an invited address at the American Psychological Association's annual convention, Orlando, FL.]

In this article, an autobiographical and narrative format is used to explore the connections between receiving personal therapy and providing it. It describes the multiple origins and evolution of my psychoanalytically informed framework for thinking about what it means to be a therapist and to do the work of therapy. He draws on his own experiences as a psychotherapy patient, being psychoanalyzed, and treating fellow therapists, as well as the teachings of body-movement therapists, internalization-based models of the sources of therapeutic change, and empirical research in order to argue on behalf of three propositions: (a) the cornerstones of effective therapy are ever-increasing collaborative inquiry and communicative intimacy, (b) effective personal therapy contributes to the continuing development of the interpersonal and communication skills that are widely regarded as the core components of therapeutic competence, and (c) effective personal therapy can make a vital contribution to the education of psychotherapists.

The thing is not to write what no one else could have written,
but to write only what you could have written.
—Saul Bellow

I have experienced the psychotherapy of psychotherapists from four perspectives—as a patient, a therapist's therapist, an educator/supervisor, and an empirical investigator of the connections between receiving and offering therapy. Since 1980, my colleagues and I have relied on anonymously completed questionnaires as a source of quantitative information about the ways in which therapists use internalized representations of communicative exchanges with their therapists to guide clinical decision-making (e.g., Geller et al., 1981; Orlinsky & Geller, 1993). One of our primary goals has been to document how the processes of imitation and identification enable therapists to apply what they learned as patients in their work with their own patients. More recently, I have been relying on a mode of inquiry that resembles a literary form—usually referred to as a memoir—to obtain seasoned therapists' narrative accounts of how their experiences as patients influence what they do and do not do with their patients (Geller, 2011).

In the pages that follow, I will describe how the trajectory of my career as a psychotherapist has been influenced by the complex interplay between the times and places in which my life has been embedded and the above sources of influence. Along the way, I hope to convey the many reasons why I believe personal therapy, if effective, can make a vital contribution to the education of psychotherapists.

MY INITIAL EXPERIENCE OF PSYCHOTHERAPY

My career as a patient has been distinguished by participating in five verbal therapies rooted in the psychoanalytic tradition

(Geller, 2005b) as well as exploring the healing potential of psychotherapies based on the arts of movement (Geller, 1974; Sandel et al., 1993) and music (Clarkson & Geller, 1996).

In 1957, I sought the free vocational counseling services provided by Downtown City College, The Bernard M. Baruch School of Business and Public Administration. I was a 17-year-old sophomore who had gone to college to avoid going into the army. I had no idea what I was interested in and believed I would have to perform well beyond my capabilities if I were to graduate. I was told by the vocational counselor that the tests I had taken revealed that I was "very anxious" and that "psychotherapy would help cure you of this symptom." I agreed to be assigned to Dr. A, a recent graduate of the Karen Horney Psychoanalytic Institute. As I was to learn, Horney's (1941) approach to therapy was rooted in the belief that neurotics suffered from "basic anxiety... the feeling a child has of being isolated and helpless in a potentially hostile world" (p. 41). Yes, that is how I felt much of the time as a child. Moreover, I regarded my fears as a form of cowardice.

I began my first therapy hoping that I would find a safe place in which to talk about my true feelings, but I expected otherwise.

As a boy, I experienced the gaze of others as inevitably charged with objectifying judgments about my physical being and as a source of unacknowledged shame. Because I was so vigilantly attentive to my physical self and the dangers in the environment, I had very little knowledge of what was going on in my inner life.

Fortunately, Dr. A, while listening to me, focused his eyes primarily in the direction of the large windows in his office. When I fell silent, as I often did, he continued to look away. Otherwise, I would have felt his eyes were boring into me. I will never know if his decision to look at me through the periphery of his vision had been influenced by Sullivan's (1954) recommendation that, when treating schizophrenic patients, it is best to arrange the chairs at a 45-degree angle.

With Dr. A, I took my first awkward steps toward learning how to learn about myself through the medium of dialogue with a trusted and valued adult. And as I was quickly learning, Freud was right (1900): Every advance on my part toward truth-telling was preceded by resistances. It was both thrilling and frightening telling Dr. A things I could not say to anyone else. The reward was feeling courageous.

Dr. A took a frank and straightforward approach to talking about my irrational fears, immaturities, sexual desires, inhibitions, moral failures, romantic disasters, and anxieties about nonbeing. As was to be true in all my therapies, we also often spoke about the difficulties I encountered writing academic prose. I panicked whenever I had to write a term paper. Dr. A provided me with the words and empathic understanding I needed to transform my sensory-dominated bad feelings into coherent narratives. He offered me explanations of my childhood terrors and chronic anxiety that did not induce further guilt or shame—just the opposite. He supported my efforts to purge my self-inquiries of harsh judgment. For the first time in my life, I permitted myself to complain.

With a Jungian therapist (e.g., E.N. Aron, 2006), I might have also learned that I was born highly sensitive and have suffered because of this innate sensitiveness. I was genetically predisposed to react negatively to the ugliness, foul odors, urban decay, and violence in my South Bronx neighborhood because of an innate sensitivity to disgusting and disillusioning experiences that was not in itself pathological.

Dr. A's cramped and book-filled office was on the ninth floor of a building in which all of my classes were held—23rd Street and Lexington Avenue—within walking distance of the neighborhood in which I hoped to live and work—Greenwich Village, the Paris of my generation. Two floors separated Dr. A's office from the psychology department's classrooms. There, I was learning about the Delphic oracle's injunction "Know thyself," the Socratic ambition to live an examined life, the discoveries the introspectionists and Gestalt psychologists were making about how our senses perceive the world, and the self-knowledge prized by Freud and successive generations of psychoanalysts.

In the 1950s in New York City, psychoanalysis had a great deal of cachet, especially among those who valued self-reflexiveness and among aspiring intellectuals like me. In fact, in the culture to which I was seeking membership, being psychoanalyzed was both highly valued as an end in itself and regarded as the best way of curing one's neuroses. Even a cursory review of the serious plays, movies, novels, and social criticism being produced while I was an undergraduate reveals that psychoanalysis permeated the cultural life of New York City. Broyard (1993) felt as if "psychoanalysis was in the air; like humidity, or smoke" (p. 43). Or, as Auden (2007) put it in his memorial poem to Freud: "To us he is no more a person now, but a whole climate of opinion under whom we conduct our differing lives" (pp. 100–101). In some respects, I experienced being in therapy with Dr. A as an initiation rite into the cultural life of New York City. This added incentive made the difficulties and painful aspects of therapy with Dr. A more tolerable.

THE BOUNDARIES BETWEEN HEALING AND TEACHING

The nearness of my therapist's office to the classrooms in which I was studying psychology probably reinforced my emerging sense that personal therapy operated on two fronts simultaneously—the therapeutic and the educational. Today, when a patient is also a therapist-in-training, I am particularly attentive to the porousness of the boundary between teaching and healing. I believe an effective therapy has inherent supervisory value. In turn, I am aware of feeling that I am crossing some ill-defined boundary when, as a psychotherapy supervisor, I give priority to the learning that occurs when I ask a student therapist to scrutinize the nature and consequences of his or her problematic emotional reactions to patients (e.g., boredom, sexual excitement, hateful feelings) or his or her difficulties in the supervisory relationship itself. I am especially prone to feel this way with therapist-patients who fear they have a psychotic core and who harshly diagnose themselves as borderline or narcissistic.

Over the past 25 years, since I began regularly treating therapist-patients, I have come to believe that sharing membership in the same profession as a patient plays a variably important role in shaping the process and outcome of therapy in a manner comparable to the influence exerted by sharing the same age, gender, ethnicity, social class, or disciplinary background. Additionally, I agree with the therapist's therapists who have been surveyed that one of the most challenging technical aspects of treating therapist-patients is finding the optimal placement of a boundary that, at one and the same time, honors the collegial aspect of the relationship and protects and preserves the professional relationship (Geller, 2005a). The complexity of this clinical and ethical responsibility is especially apparent when dealing with the possibility that a social or professional relationship will replace the therapeutic relationship after termination.

Professional codes of ethics have little of value to say about standards of conduct regarding nonromantic and nonsexual relationships following the termination of therapy other than those that are clearly exploitative (Pope & Vasquez, 1998). An extreme position would be that transforming a therapy into supervision constitutes a "boundary violation" (Gabbard & Lester, 1995). I aspire to interact with my former patients in ways that are disciplined by the findings of two complementary lines of inquiry: clinical investigations of the persistence of transference reactions after termination (Pfeffer, 1963; Schlessinger & Robbins, 1974; Oremland et al., 1975; Kantrowitz et al., 1990; Tessman, 2003) and studies of the ways in which former patients interact with internalized representations of their therapists after the discontinuation of regularly scheduled sessions (Geller & Farber, 1993; Wzontek et al., 1995; Arnold et al., 2004).

All of the investigators who have conducted interview-based follow-up studies have concluded that successful terminations of psychoanalyses do not result in the complete resolution of transference reactions but in their modulation to the point that the patient can deal with them more effectively, while the anonymously completed questionnaires that we have collected indicate that former therapist-patients are apt to recall representations-of-therapy-with-my-therapist more frequently and more vividly than former nontherapist-patients after termination. These convergent findings are consistent with the view that there is "a post-termination phase of therapy" (Rangell, 1966; Geller & Freedman, 2011) that should be considered to be an integral (and perhaps essential) part of the therapeutic process itself and not just as the time after the end of therapy. Given our limited knowledge about the psychological consequences of the afterlife of the therapeutic process, I hold myself to the standard "once a patient, always a patient."

GRADUATE SCHOOL, KAISERIAN THERAPY, AND IMITATIVE LEARNING

The interpersonal and communication skills I acquired during my 2½-year therapy with Dr. A benignly and enduringly influenced my relationships to love and work and eventually served me well as a therapist. Thanks largely to being identified as well-endowed with analytical and emotional intelligence by Dr. A and my psychology professors, I decided to apply to clinical psychology PhD programs. My preference was to study psychoanalytic psychology (with Morris Eagle and Lloyd Silverman) at New York University and live with my fiancée in Greenwich Village. I was not accepted by New York University. Unexpectedly, what at first felt like a disaster proved to be a blessing in disguise. I am not sure why I chose to go to the University of Connecticut rather than the University of Massachusetts, where I had been offered a scholarship. I knew very little about either school. I told friends I was going to UConn rather than UMass because it was a shorter bus ride from Manhattan. It was a joke, but not entirely.

I did not know before leaving home and arriving at the University of Connecticut that the director of the clinical psychology PhD program—Dr. Maria Rickers-Ovsiankina, a Russian émigré, colleague of Kurt Lewin, Rorschach expert, graphologist, and admirer of Vigotsky, Werner, Piaget, and Goldstein—had created a psychotherapy training clinic in which all the supervisors were either supervised or treated by Helmuth Kaiser, a little-known European-trained psychoanalyst who, for 8 years, had practiced in Hartford, Connecticut. Kaiser graduated as a psychoanalyst from the Psychoanalytic Institute in Berlin, having been treated by Wilhelm Reich and supervised by Sandor Rado, Hans Sachs, and Karen Horney.

While working at the Menninger Clinic, Kaiser (1965) came to believe that psychoanalysis, as it was being practiced in America, diluted the direct, concrete, sensuous immediacy and transformative powers of what he called *communicative intimacy*. Like the indigenously American strand of theorizing embodied in Carl Rogers's (1951) client-centered approach to therapy, Kaiser called into question the then-fashionable idea that insight was the essential agent of therapeutic change.

I was intrigued by Kaiser's view that the achievement of communicative intimacy is a necessary and sufficient means of realizing the goals of therapy and not merely a means of setting the stage for the reconstruction of the forgotten past. I also resonated with Kaiser's existentialist concerns. His basic analytic concepts are authenticity, the fear of one's separateness and aloneness, and the importance of taking responsibility for decisions made and actions taken. As an undergraduate, I was drawn to these ideas and values by two of my intellectual heroes— Kafka and Camus. My enthusiasm grew when I read that the president of the American Psychological Association's (APA's) Division of Clinical Psychology, Nicholas Hobbs, shared Kaiser's view that insight may be one among a number of possible consequences or by-products of therapeutic change rather than a cause of change. In his presidential address, Hobbs (1962) posited that the acceptance of insight as the sovereign remedy for all neuroses represented an unwarranted extrapolation from Freud's position that psychoanalysis worked best, if not solely, in cases of massive repression with accompanying conversion symptoms. This point of view appealed to me because I felt that the many insights I acquired in therapy with Dr. A did not cure me of my basic anxieties. In the jargon of the times, I had "failed" to transform my "intellectual insights" into life-transforming "emotional insights."

The conceptual starting point of Kaiser's skeletal theory of therapy is the belief that therapy is, first and foremost, an *experience in living* that will have lasting benefits for the patient if he or she learns how to say, "I believe... ," "I want... ," "I feel... ," "I think... ," shorn of shame, guilt, or self-consciousness. In other words, in his maturity, Kaiser (1965) abandoned classical psychoanalytic terminology in favor of a vocabulary that focused on the forms of communication that were causes and diagnostic of symptomatology or indicative of psychological maturity and inner freedom. Like H.S. Sullivan (1953), he believed that a large part of psychopathology was caused and perpetuated by inadequate communication, the communicative process being interfered with by anxiety.

Concomitantly, echoes of Reich (1949) can be heard in Kaiser's view that the uniqueness of each patient is to be found in his or her characterologically based conversational style and not in the subject matter (or content) of what he or she says. He also posited that interest in *how* a patient is speaking tends to supersede interest in *what* he or she is saying when strains are weakening the therapeutic alliance.

What I share with other Kaiserian-trained therapists is not a repertoire of manualizable techniques but the conviction that a course of therapy will be effective if therapist and patient speak authentically with one another, remain fully present to one another, and use language in ways that promote a feeling of responsibility for one's choices and actions. Today I routinely teach aspiring therapists that forming a positive emotional attachment to a therapist whose relational stance embodies the traits of kindness, courage, patience, genuineness, humility, flexibility, vitality, and integrity creates the interpersonal conditions that allow patients to acquire or strengthen the modes of listening and talking that make possible a robust sense of intimacy in nontherapeutic relationships (Geller, 1987, 2005b, 2005c, 2006).

KAISERIAN THERAPY WITH DR. C

In New York City, my friends had become "trusted companions" (Bowlby, 1973). We could talk for hours about everything, and we took each other's problems-in-living seriously. I did not make those kinds of friendships in graduate school. But I needed to talk to someone about my mounting fears that I would not be able to write a dissertation or that doing so would destroy my fragile marriage. So, in my 4th year of graduate studies, when I was in the grip of anxiety again, I hesitantly consulted a respected Kaiserian therapist in West Hartford, Connecticut. I left the initial appointment feeling uneasy about meeting with Dr. C on a weekly basis. I felt I could not afford his fees. It was more than an hour's drive from my home in Storrs, Connecticut, to his office. I had confidentiality concerns. My friends on internship were being supervised by him.

In accord with Kaiser's teachings, early in therapy, Dr. C placed his emphasis on the defensive functions of my conversational style rather than on the meanings of what I said. For example, he regarded my "intellectualizing ways" as worthy of comment. He was right in bringing to my attention the restrictions I imposed on my emotional expressivity. I inhibited the direct expression of my negative feelings, including those I had about him. There existed an uneasy alliance between the thinking me and the feeling me. I had not fully shed the persona that I had adopted as an adolescent to look cool at all times, to hide my shyness, and to appear more grown up than I felt or looked. I anticipated that Dr. C would comment on the façade I maintained to obscure my fears of affectivity and expressivity. But I was ill-prepared for his sardonic style of using confrontational techniques.

The substance of Dr. C's comments about my self-restraint and preference for thought over feared emotions, so characteristically obsessional, were usually accurate, but they did not leave me feeling empathically understood. It was not that he was incorrect when he cautioned me against taking myself too seriously; rather, I felt he did so recklessly, without regard for my dignity. I felt he took Kaiser's recommendations regarding *spontaneity* as a license to forego the constraints of tactfulness. His comments about the restraint I imposed on my expressivity did not get me to speak more freely or to feel more natural, more present, or more authentic. Instead, they brought out my insecurities and my shyness. I wished he would make more judicious use of countertransference self-disclosures about his subjective experiences of, and associations to, my discomfort in making eye contact with him. I wished that he was more of a mensch. I gradually gave up the hope of being told things about myself that were both true and kind.

To this day, whenever I engage in imaginary conversations with Dr. C, what stands out for me are the nasal and sarcastic qualities of his voice, his smug or cynical facial expressions, the fastidiousness of his gestures, and the preppy Brooks Brothers blue blazers, well-pressed gray slacks, and red ties that he wore. I think of him as a self-hating Jew who had artificially cultivated the persona of a patrician Wasp. In short, I disliked his style and terminated therapy in the 12th month of my relationship with him.

IMITATION AND LEARNING TO DO PSYCHOTHERAPY

I continue to believe that it was fortuitous and fortunate that I began my professional training to become a therapist with Kaiserians, but, not surprisingly, I did not adopt Dr. C as an exemplary model of how to practice Kaiserian therapy. I did not see in him the characteristics I wanted to see in myself. With Dr. C,

I found myself in a position similar to Bion, who purportedly quipped, "I learned what not to do with my patients during my analysis with Melanie Klein" (M. Edelson, personal communication, August 1986).

By contrast, early in my career, imitation of my valued Kaiserian supervisors played an important role in helping me grapple with the anxieties I felt dealing with the nonmanualizable aspects of doing therapy, of which there are many. Prescriptive therapy manuals can play an important role in preparing beginners to deal with their more tightly scripted responsibilities and tasks. But there is much about therapy that is improvisational and cannot be learned by adherence to a manual. Uncertainties are inherent in the decisions that must be made about waiting room etiquette, greetings, exit lines, emotional expressivity, self-disclosures, silences, interaction rhythms, the grammatical forms in which to articulate interventions, monetary transactions, the setting of limits when patients are acting out, and so forth.

With lingering embarrassment, I recall borrowing my supervisor's words, especially when formulating interventions that were likely to be experienced as painful or difficult. I am no longer aware of using representations of my supervisors or therapists as interpretive resources when with my patients. But I can discern their enduring influence on my conversational style with patients, on the ways in which I listen to myself, and on the ways in which I engage in self-analysis. It is noteworthy that every therapist who contributed to the narrative accounts of personal therapy found in our book, *The Psychotherapist's Own Psychotherapy* (Geller et al., 2005), and in a recent issue of *In Session* (Geller, 2011) has acknowledged that a great deal of what they do or do not do with their patients is based on identifications or counteridentifications with their former therapists.

Following graduation from the University of Connecticut, I turned down assistant professorships at the University of Buffalo and the University of Miami, above all because of geographical considerations. Instead, I went on to Clark University, where I did a 1-year postdoctoral fellowship with Dr. Morton Wiener—a fan of Kaiserian therapy. With him, I began my ongoing study of nonverbal communication (Wiener et al., 1972; Geller, 1978). Luckily, this led to being offered a job at Yale University in 1967.

PSYCHOANALYSIS WITH DR. D

I willingly entered psychoanalysis when I was a husband, a father, and an assistant professor in the Yale Department of Psychiatry 6 years after I arrived in New Haven. I was spending my days as the assistant director of the Connecticut Mental Health Center's outpatient clinic. When I arrived in New Haven, there were only six such centers in the United States. Much of my early career was devoted to developing psychotherapeutic services that met the needs of a relentless flow of prospective patients who could not afford therapy from private practitioners (e.g., Geller & Feirstein, 1974; Pope et al., 1975; Geller et al., 1976; Geller, 1988). An extraordinarily generous insurance policy— the equivalent of the GI Bill—paid for my 2½-year, four-times-a-week psychoanalysis.

Neither the need to find relief from symptoms nor the desire to make life-changing decisions prompted my desire to be psychoanalyzed. Consciously, my primary motives were educational and professional, although I also hoped that psychoanalysis would bring about characterological changes that moved me further toward what has been variously called "self-actualization," "maturity," and "individuation."

I have high regard for psychoanalysis as a means of laying bare the complex motivations that restrain or inhibit direct and spontaneous communication. Then, as now, I believe that free-associating in a safe place is a royal road to gaining experience-based knowledge of transference and resistance—the theoretical cornerstones of the talking cure. Moreover, when I arrived in New Haven, two of the most respected psychoanalysts—Hans Loewald and Roy Schafer—were theorizing about the clinical applications of psychoanalysis in ways that were supportive of my evolving version of Kaiserian therapy. They also enabled me to rediscover my youthful romance with psychoanalysis.

Loewald's (1962) and Schafer's (1968) theorizing about the processes whereby patients internalize the functional qualities of the therapeutic relationship provided me with the conceptual tools required to describe and empirically understand how the benefits of in-session communicative intimacy endure after termination in the form of benignly influential representations of the verbal and nonverbal aspects of the therapeutic dialogue. Additionally, Loewald (1960), like Kaiser, was proposing the existential view that whatever else *ego development* is, it entails taking responsibility for one's life. Concurrently, Schafer's (1973) affirmative perspective on the concept of resistance strengthened my ability to confront patients when they were being defensive in a style opposite to that which Dr. C had employed with me. Freud (1915/1959) originally conceived of resistance as anything that interfered with the progress of analysis. But over time, the concept took on the connotation of oppositionality. By contrast, Schafer (1973) encouraged analysts to think about what patients are trying to *accomplish* rather than what they are *avoiding* when resisting uncensored talk.

THE EDUCATIONAL VALUE OF FREE ASSOCIATION

My analyst's office was located in the attic of a gray-and-white-painted Victorian house next door to the offices of the Western New England Psychoanalytic Institute. What stands out for me when I remember being with Dr. D are images of his sparsely furnished office—aesthetically the opposite of Freud's, whose office was sensuously rich and evocative. Dr. D is bathed in the melancholy, late-afternoon light that I associate with the films of Ingmar Bergman. He is sitting behind and to the left of me in a director's chair that seemed too small for his large and burly body.

As I anticipated, Dr. D practiced psychoanalysis with me in a nondirective manner that was clearly grounded in Freud's (1915/1959) recommendations regarding abstinence, anonymity, and neutrality. Mostly, he was silent, except when he asked questions or made interpretations. For at least 6 months, I found his relational stance with me liberating. His lengthy silences gave me the inner freedom to "be alone with myself, in his presence" (Winnicott, 1965, p. 32). But over time, I gradually began to feel that I was being left alone with my thoughts and feelings.

My analyst did not instruct or invite me to free-associate. I assumed that he knew that I was already very familiar with the role requirements that are specific to analysands and analysts. I used the minimal guidance he provided as an opportunity to totally immerse myself in the living and unpredictable present of my stream of consciousness. Initially, I felt freer and more relaxed not having to look at my unseen analyst. I preferred not seeing his reactions to what I was saying. I enjoyed shifting my attention away from the outside world and tracking what was spontaneously emerging from inside my body. I found lying on his couch under the eaves of his dimly lit office conducive to stimulating dreamlike and meditative states of consciousness.

I gained access to visual images that existed on the fringes of consciousness that would have otherwise eluded my grasp. I observed that my images passed through various preparatory or transitory stages before they emerged clearly into consciousness. I took pleasure in transforming my unformulated visual images into memories and fantasies. I revisited, with interest and curiosity, the once terrifying nightmares that I had silently endured as a child. Gradually, I came to understand what Schafer (1983) meant when he said that subjective experiences are constructed rather than merely introspected.

When appropriate, I encourage patients with alexithymic tendencies to silently pay sensuously receptive attention to the making, unmaking, and remaking of images before they are transformed into speech. Uncensored *thought* precedes uncensored *talk*. Hopefully, like me, they discover that it is possible to increase the sensory richness and vividness of one's subjective experiences and to strengthen one's ability to retain and reflect upon stable images of oneself in relation to others.

DR. D AND THE MEANING OF RESISTING

When I fully immersed myself in my private experiences, I became less aware of Dr. D's listening presence. Sometimes I forgot that I was supposed to be free-associating. I was also becoming aware of the impossibility of communicating the fullness of my kaleidoscopic experiences. However honest and candid one aspires to be, only a small portion of what is actually experienced can be translated into syntactically organized sentences.

When I stopped free-associating and fell silent, my analyst waited (patiently, I hope) for me to speak again or interpreted my silence as a refusal to speak that derived from my still-unresolved conflicts about patriarchal authority. In other words, Dr.

D interpreted my silences as a form of oedipal defiance—rightly so, some of the time. Yes, as a boy, I stubbornly refused to talk to my father or accept his apology after he had explosively raged against me. Yes, in adults' eyes, my friends and I were juvenile delinquents. Yes, as a late adolescent, my role models were nonconformists and beatniks. Yes, as a young adult, I was drawn to countercultural lifestyles—I inhaled—and supported the values of what Trilling (2001) called "the adversarial culture."

Not surprisingly, my negative transference reactions to Dr. D's silence and his interpretations of my silences bore the imprint of my lifelong rebellious ways. But as I have since come to believe, two other impulses coexisted in my silences—the legacy of witnessing my father having a grand mal seizure and the loss of a "good enough mother" (Winnicott, 1965).

I was 15 and alone with my father when he had his first known grand mal seizure. We were sitting face-to-face in the living room. He had just fallen asleep while reading the sports section of the *Daily News*. My two younger brothers were asleep in the bedroom we shared. My mother was in a neighbor's apartment playing mah-jongg. He screamed. His eyes rolled up into their sockets. He frothed at the mouth. His body shook convulsively. And then he collapsed on the floor. I thought he had died. I called 911 and then my mother.

In a previous essay (Geller, 1994), I wrote about how my traumatic reactions to seeing my father's sleep morph into a grand mal seizure were revived when I saw my fifth therapist fall asleep and struggle to remain awake more than once during our therapy sessions. In that essay, my primary interest was in using Dr. E's sleepiness to illustrate the emotional and technical challenges therapists face when they find a patient boring and psychologically withdraw from being fully present.

What I wish to emphasize here is that for years after my father's first seizure, I would stop breathing in my bed at night to listen more carefully for signs that another seizure was imminent. In retrospect, I wish my analyst had seen me when I was silent as the boy who felt terrified and alone lying in his bed at night.

Another equally plausible source of my silences was that I was reenacting the loneliness I felt as a very frightened boy who could not ask for reassurance or comfort from his mother. In a letter written by my father to my mother when I was 6 months old, he asks her to "please be patient with Jesse when he gets colicky." According to my wife, my mother was uncomfortable being physically affectionate and had difficulty comforting her sons when they were crying. Dr. D did not understand that I began to feel entirely on my own again when he did not reach out to me after 15- to 20-minute episodes of silence.

I needed Dr. D to see my silences as a form of remembering the times when I felt solely responsible for taking care of myself. I needed him to reach out to me and gratify my previously disowned longings to be dependent on a nurturing caretaker. I yearned for comforting words. I required an analyst who behaved more like Winnicott, who said to Guntrip, "I have nothing new to say to you, but I'm afraid that if you don't hear my voice you will think I haven't been present and listening" (Guntrip, 2005, p. 74).

That Winnicott deeply understood Guntrip's communicative requirements is supported by the oft-replicated finding that, when experiencing painful emotions, some current and former patients recall internalized representations of the soothing "sound" of their therapists' voices. Still others rely more heavily on comforting visual images of their therapists sitting in their offices (Geller & Farber, 1993).

In the psychoanalytic literature, representations of absent others that are infused with quasiperceptual qualities, have a sense of immediacy, and are capable of serving psychological functions are usually referred to as *introjects* (Schafer, 1968). To date, psychoanalysts have devoted far more attention to explicating the functional significance of introjects that are experienced as problematic (i.e., threatening, disapproving, malevolent) than introjects that are pleasure giving, supportive, and capable of serving reparative and adaptation-enhancing functions. By contrast, using a variety of measures, researchers have consistently obtained positive correlations between the tendency to use multimodal representations of one's therapist's felt presence to promote self-acceptance and self-understanding and successful treatment outcomes (Geller et al., 2010; Geller et al., 2011).

Ending Psychoanalysis and Beginning Authentic Movement

As the months passed, more and more I felt as if Dr. D was treating me like a puzzle or riddle to be solved, as if he were a Holmesian detective. I felt he was behaving like a detached spectator of my silences because of his one-person view of transference. He took the position that my feelings of aloneness and alienation were uninfluenced by his strict adherence to the Freudian triumvirate of abstinence, anonymity, and neutrality. I argued that his stance toward me needed to be softened by such methodological principles as empathic attunement (Kohut, 1971), mutuality (L. Aron, 1996), optimal responsiveness (Bacal, 1985), and the use of noninterpretive techniques. To this day, I wonder what it was like for him to have me criticize his approach by advocating technical recommendations reflective of what Mitchell (1988) referred to as the post-Freudian era of psychoanalysis.

I recognize that my disappointment that Dr. D did not accommodate his relational stance to meet my communicative requirements is an idiosyncrasy of my character. For example, Pinsof (2005) has recently written a compelling memoir in which he constructively used his analyst's lengthy silence to surrender to the regressive pleasure of falling asleep on the couch. He is persuaded that allowing himself to take catnaps in his analyst's invisible presence was an important antidote to his compulsive ambitiousness and need to always be productive.

My growing disappointment in Dr. D peaked when he refused to lower my fee when my insurance benefits ran out. I used his refusal to renegotiate the financial aspects of our relationship as a justification to terminate analysis. Terminating with Dr. D coincided with my decision not to become a candidate in the Western New England Psychoanalytic Institute, no doubt for complexly overdetermined reasons. I react negatively to organizational barriers of any kind. When I came to New Haven, clinical applications of psychoanalysis were still the sole prerogative of medically trained psychiatrists. I have no appetite for the politics and polemics of the relations between orthodox and relational psychoanalysts. Mine is an integrationist agenda. I was raised in a family that rejected the idea that there was one true religion or absolute truth. As my brother Mark recently put it, "We are attracted to people who search for the truth, repelled by those who think they have found it." The competitive and hostile relations between the growing numbers of schools of therapy that were flooding the marketplace in the 1960s reminded my brother and me of the intolerance members of one religion have for members of other forms of institutionalized religions. Perhaps most importantly, I wished to continue my education by studying with teachers who were developing forms of therapy in which movement, sight, and touch were given as much or more importance than spoken language. Learning more about nonverbal communication took on added weight because of desperate attempts by my wife and me to connect with and educate our profoundly deaf daughter, Jennifer (Geller, 1996).

To this end, I served as a participant observer for the next 1½ years in a dance therapy group that Dr. Susan Sandel (Geller, 1974) was conducting with psychiatrically hospitalized adolescents. I was inspired by her ability to use the art of movement to establish communicative relationships in which seeing and being seen, rather than speaking and listening, were the primary modalities of communicating. Watching video recordings of the nonverbal exchanges that took place during the dance therapy sessions strengthened my ability to see how a person's movement repertoire influenced the range of emotions he or she was capable of experiencing. Dr. Sandel helped to refine my observational skills by teaching me Laban's (1976) system for describing the flow of movement in terms of a mover's relationship to time, space, weight, and gravity (Sandel et al., 1993).

I am indebted to Dr. Sandel for another reason. She intuitively understood that the preoedipal origins of my problems being a body were beyond the reach of language-centric modalities of therapy. Because of her advice, for the past 23 years I have participated in an Authentic Movement group whose original teacher/therapist was Janet Adler (2002). Space limitations preclude a detailed description of Authentic Movement. Most broadly stated, as an outgrowth of her experiences treating verbally inaccessible autistic children, Adler was developing a movement-based form of self-exploration that extended the reach of the talking cure.

PSYCHOANALYSIS AND AUTHENTIC MOVEMENT

Psychoanalysis and Authentic Movement have many things in common. They are both methods of learning how to pay attention, with compassion, to the ongoing multisensory nature of the stream of consciousness. Like psychoanalysis, this aspect of Authentic Movement can be used as a method of scientific inquiry or a form of therapy. I found psychoanalysis particularly well suited to expanding and enriching my access to imagistic thinking and remembering. And I found Authentic Movement particularly well suited to strengthening my awareness of the somatic sensations arising from the muscles, tendons, and joints that remain largely unnoticed under ordinary circumstances. I acquired this knowledge by free-associating in movement, with my eyes closed, in the witnessing presence of the other members of my group. Giving uncensored expression in movement to the kinesthetic and proprioceptive sensations that arose organically out of stillness rooted the lessons I learned in my previous verbal therapies more deeply in my body.

The ability to extract clinically relevant information from the somatosensory aspects of one's countertransference reactions is a valuable interpretive resource. Interactions with fragile, difficult, seductive, destructive, and paranoid patients inevitably stimulate *bodily* experiences in therapists, irrespective of their years of experience. I presume that those therapists who have achieved a sense of peace with being a body are best prepared to find important and clinically helpful meanings in these bodily experiences.

There are aspects of one's private experience that are beyond the reach of everyday speech. Freud (1900) believed that poetry might be the most appropriate medium when it came to trying to put into words one's most private subjective experiences, for example, love. In Authentic Movement, one is encouraged to use any art form to reflect on the experiential yield of having searched for authenticity by free-associating in movement. Over the years I have used poetry, drawing, sculpture, and choreography to contemplate and communicate what I was experiencing while moving with my eyes closed. These experiences have deeply reinforced my conviction that there is no one best way of symbolizing problematic experiences for therapeutic purposes.

In my experience, many therapists' observational skills are far less well-developed than their listening skills because of the auditory bias of verbal therapies. What I hope is becoming apparent is that I believe that the two-person nature of the psychotherapeutic enterprise is as much a looking cure as it is a talking cure, at least for some patients.

DR. E AND WRITING THIS ESSAY

Only one of my five individual therapies came to a timely, mutually agreed-upon, natural conclusion. I reluctantly had to say goodbye to Dr. A when I graduated from college. The school's policy prohibited him from treating me within the entrepreneurial context of his independent practice. As described elsewhere (Geller, 2005b), I dropped out after four sessions with Dr. B. Dr. A had referred me to him for a low-fee therapy when I thought I would go to NYU to obtain my PhD. I unilaterally left my therapy with Dr. C because I felt we were not a good fit stylistically, and I ended my analysis with Dr. D with a good deal of unfinished business because a stalemate or impasse had been reached regarding the financial aspects of our relationship. Thankfully, my fifth therapy, with Dr. E, ended on a happier note.

I sought therapy with Dr. E for two reasons—the cruel fact that my second daughter was born profoundly deaf was taking an emotional toll on all the members of our family, and I was once again having great difficulty writing an essay in which I would propose my own uniquely derivative version of psychoanalytically informed expressive-exploratory psychotherapy.

I was attracted to Dr. E's presence (Geller, 2005b). His expression was melancholy, but his smile was warm. He impressed me as the kind of man who took sensuality seriously and encouraged a lustful relationship to the aesthetic aspects of life. At his finest, Dr. E showed me that you could be completely spontaneous and rigorously disciplined at the same time. When he was at his best, he could trigger the kind of astonished "Whoa!" reactions I had not experienced with a therapist since Dr. A.

I felt privileged and closer to him knowing that he, too, grappled with the specialized problem of writing academic prose, but I felt burdened by knowing that he was dealing with serious problems in his family. It is the rare lay patient who knows about their therapist's life outside their office.

Unfortunately, as I previously mentioned, Dr. E fell asleep during my sessions with him more than once. Moreover, I felt as though my therapy with Dr. E was being conducted in a "fishbowl" (Gitelson, 1954). Dr. E's office was in the Yale Health Center, where I attended lectures, seminars, case conferences, and group therapy supervision with Dr. Marshall Edelson. Sitting in the hallway that served as a waiting room for the Mental Hygiene Clinic, of which Dr. E was a staff member, I felt very exposed, and I had awkward, brief, unavoidable encounters with colleagues as they walked to their offices and classrooms.

Having had therapy in five different organizational and architectural contexts has sensitized me to the importance of creating a physical environment that supports the therapeutic enterprise. I have submitted the neighborhoods, buildings, and offices in which my therapists practiced to semiotic and aesthetic scrutiny. What I saw or did not see either enhanced or diminished my confidence in their ability to have a healing influence on me. I am not aware of any training program that devotes systematic attention to teaching students how to transform empty rooms into environments that can themselves serve as agents of change.

When consulting with novice therapists who are opening their own offices, I encourage them to take into account the sensorial effects of their choices regarding color, lighting, fabrics, and the shapes, sizes, and placement of furniture and to think about the potential symbolic meanings that their aesthetic choices might have for patients of varied ages, races, ethnicities, and social classes.

A ROOM OF MY OWN

During each of my therapies, I acquired new knowledge about the predictable crises that I experience while writing clinical-theoretical essays. I have come to anticipate that organizing and reorganizing sentences into coherent narratives or sustained arguments will reactivate deep-seated doubts about my intelligence, on the one hand, and, on the other, the shame I feel in wishing to exhibit my talents in order to win the respect of my intellectual heroes and have idealizing interactions with them. I also know that I am obsessed with singularity, with being unclassifiable, and with the extravagant claim of seeking originality. I understand that my grandiosity will morph into doubt-ridden perfectionism as I approach real and self-imposed deadlines.

As I learned in analysis, "publish or perish" was, for me, more than a metaphor. While writing this article at the kitchen table with Bic pens, there were hours when I felt that I would die before completing it. In the final weeks before I had to present a lecture version of this paper at the APA annual conference, I relied on my former addiction—smoking cigarettes—to focus my increasingly restless mind. I have been willing to endure bodily abuse on behalf of trying to master the intellectual discipline of writing academic prose.

What I wish to highlight here is that relatively soon after having and talking about the following dream, I finished my manuscript (Geller, 1987) and brought my therapy with Dr. E to a natural conclusion. In the dream, we are standing face-to-face in an unfurnished attic about 6 feet apart. He says to me, "Jesse, you can have a room of your own." *A Room of One's Own* is the title of Virginia Woolf's (1929) highly influential memoir. In it, Woolf equates achieving legitimacy as a writer with acquiring "a room of one's own." With pleasure, we interpreted his utterance as a sign that I was capable of imagining a future in which I would be taken seriously as a writer. I doubt that I would have been able to appreciate others for reading this essay if it had not been for the cumulative benefits I have derived from therapy. Unless I am deceiving myself, I think my identity is catching up with who I have become (and am still becoming).

Since terminating with Drs. D and E, we have encountered one another on many occasions at social and professional events. These unplanned meetings have invariably reminded me of the previously noted finding that transference reactions can persist long after termination. Representations of the unresolved, conflict-laden aspects of my relationship with Dr. D are still in ascendancy, but I now forgivingly recognize that, like my own approach, his style of conducting therapy was a product of the time and place in which he was trained. And, then again, with respect to the outcome of my psychoanalysis, is it possible that I failed to distinguish between its painfulness and its benefits?

CONCLUSIONS

In this essay, I have attempted to write clearly and in an orderly fashion about how I acquired my ideas about what it means to be a therapist and do the work of therapy. It is my second attempt

(Geller, 2005b) to grapple with the following questions in writing: How helpful did you find your own personal therapy? What about it was helpful? What didn't you find helpful? What disappointed you? What aspects of your own personal therapy do you (try to) repeat or avoid when treating your own patients? Do you experience the way in which you conduct therapy as similar or different from the way your therapist(s) conducted therapy with you? In what way? What comes back to you first or most vividly when you remember your psychotherapist and session(s) with him or her? How would you describe your termination process and the inner presence of your former therapist(s) when you terminated? Has it changed since then? Why or why not? What kinds of professional and/or social contact have you had with your former therapist(s) since ending the therapy? Have you hoped for such encounters or wanted to minimize them? What role should personal therapy play in the education and development of psychotherapists? What lasting lessons about the theory and practice of psychotherapy did you take away from your personal treatment?

I hope I have demonstrated that a first-person account of the connections between receiving and offering psychotherapy can contribute usable knowledge about what patients of all types find helpful, unhelpful, and harmful. I believe the narrative mode of exposition is especially well suited to presenting clinician-friendly research that illuminates the question, Why do therapists do what they do with their patients? The tortured joys of producing this text also reaffirmed my belief that writing a personal history of the situational, characterological, and cultural conditions that were in ascendancy when one first came under the sphere of influence of psychotherapy has great educational value. In my ideal psychotherapy training program, students would write and read to their classmates an answer to the question, How have my genetic predispositions, family's provisions, and the historical context into which I was born contributed to my ideas about what it means to be a therapist and do the work of therapy?

REFERENCES

Adler, J. (2002). *Offerings from the Conscious Body: The Discipline of Authentic Movement*. Rochester, VT: Inner Traditions.

Arnold, E.G., Farber, B.A., & Geller, J.D. (2004). Termination, post-termination, and internalization of therapy and the therapist: Internal representation and psychotherapy outcome. In D.P. Charman (Ed.), *Core Processes in Brief Psychodynamic Psychotherapy* (pp. 289–308). Hillsdale, NJ: Erlbaum.

Aron, E.N. (2006). The clinical implications of Jung's concept of sensitiveness. *Journal of Jungian Theory and Practice* 8:11–43.

Aron, L. (1996). *A Meeting of Minds: Mutuality in Psychoanalysis*. Hillsdale, NJ: Analytic Press.

Auden, W.H. (2007). In memory of Sigmund Freud. In *W.H. Auden: Selected Poems* (pp. 100–101). New York, NY: Vintage International.

Bacal, H.A. (1985). Optimal responsiveness and the therapeutic process. In A. Goldberg (Ed.), *Progress in Self Psychology* (pp. 202–206). New York, NY: Guilford Press.

Bellow, S. (2010). *Saul Bellow: Letters* (B. Taylor, Ed.). New York, NY: Viking Press.

Bowlby, J. (1973). *Attachment and Loss: Vol. 2. Separation: Anxiety and Anger*. New York, NY: Basic Books.

Broyard, A. (1993). *When Kafka Was the Rage: A Greenwich Village Memoir*. New York, NY: Vintage Books.

Clarkson, G., & Geller, J.D. (1996). The Bonny method from a psychoanalytic perspective: Insights from working with a psychoanalytic psychotherapist in a guided imagery and music series. *Arts in Psychotherapy* 23(4):311–319.

Freud, S. (1900). The interpretation of dreams. *Standard edition* 4–5.

——— (1959). Observations on transference-love: Further recommendations on the technique of psychoanalysis. In J. Strachey (Ed.), *The Collected Psychological Papers of Sigmund Freud* 1:377–391. New York, NY: Basic Books. (Original work published 1915)

Gabbard, G.O., & Lester, F.P. (1995). *Boundaries and Boundary Violations in Psychoanalysis*. New York, NY: Basic Books.

Geller, J.D. (1974). Dance therapy as viewed by a psychotherapist. *American Dance Therapy Association Monograph* 3:1–21. [Reprinted in *A Collection of Early Writings: Toward a Body of Knowledge* (Vol. 1, pp. 63–80). ADTA, 1989.]

——— (1978). The body, expressive movement, and physical contact in psychotherapy. In J.L. Singer & K.S. Pope (Eds.), *The Power of Human Imagination* (pp. 347–378). New York, NY: Plenum Press.

——— (1987). The process of psychotherapy: Separation and the complex interplay among empathy, insight, and internalization. In J. Bloom-Feshbach & S. Bloom-Feshbach (Eds.), *The Psychology of Separation and Loss: Perspectives on Development, Life Transitions, and Clinical Practice* (pp. 459–514). San Francisco, CA: Jossey-Bass.

——— (1988). Racial bias in the evaluation of patients for psychotherapy. In L. Comas-Díaz & E.E.H. Griffith (Eds.), *Clinical Guidelines in Cross-Cultural Mental Health* (pp. 112–134). New York, NY: Wiley.

——— (1994). The psychotherapist's experience of interest and boredom. *Psychotherapy* 31(1):3–16.

————— (1996). Thank you for Jenny. In B. Gerson (Ed.), *The Therapist as a Person: Life Crises, Life Choices, Life Experiences, and Their Effects on Treatment* (pp. 119–139). New York, NY: Analytic Press.

————— (2005a). Boundaries and internalization in the psychotherapy of psychotherapists: Clinical and research perspectives. In J.D. Geller, J.C. Norcross, & D.E. Orlinsky (Eds.), *The Psychotherapist's Own Psychotherapy: Patient and Clinician Perspectives* (pp. 379–404). New York, NY: Oxford University Press.

————— (2005b). My experiences as a patient in five psychoanalytic psychotherapies. In J.D. Geller, J.C. Norcross, & D.E. Orlinsky (Eds.), *The Psychotherapist's Own Psychotherapy: Patient and Clinician Perspectives* (pp. 81–97). New York, NY: Oxford University Press.

————— (2005c). Style and its contribution to a patient-specific model of therapeutic technique. *Psychotherapy: Theory, Research, Practice, Training* 42:469–482. https://doi.org/10.1037/0033-3204.42.4.469

————— (2006). Pity, suffering, and psychotherapy. *American Journal of Psychotherapy* 60(2):187–205.

————— (2011). The psychotherapy of psychotherapists. *Journal of Clinical Psychology: In Session* 67:759–765.

—————, Astrachan, B., & Flynn, H. (1976). The development and validation of a measure of the psychiatrist's authoritative domain. *Journal of Nervous and Mental Diseases* 162:410–422.

—————, Bender, D.S., Freedman, N., Hoffenberg, J., Kagan, D., Schaffer, C., & Vorus, N. (2011). Patients' representations of the therapeutic dialogue: A pathway towards the evaluation of psychotherapy process and outcome. In N. Freedman, M. Hurvich, R. Ward (Eds.), J.D. Geller, & J. Hoffenberg (Collaborators), *Another Kind of Evidence* (pp. 17–28). London, UK: Karnac Books.

———, Cooley, R.S., & Hartley, D. (1981). Images of the psychotherapist: A theoretical and methodological perspective. *Imagination, Cognition and Personality* 1(2):123–146.

——— & Farber, B.A. (1993). Factors influencing the process of internalization in psychotherapy. *Psychotherapy Research* 3(3):166–180. https://doi.org/10.1080/10503309312331333769

———, ———, & Schaffer, C.E. (2010). Representations of the supervisory dialogue and the development of psychotherapists. *Psychotherapy: Theory, Research, Practice, Training* 47:211–220.

——— & Feirstein, A.R. (1974). Professional training in community mental-health centers. In G.F. Farwell, N.R. Gamsky, & P. Mathieu-Coughlan (Eds.), *The Counselor's Handbook* (pp. 449–471). New York, NY: Intext.

——— & Freedman, N. (2011). Representations of the therapeutic dialogue and the post-termination phase of psychotherapy. In N. Freedman, M. Hurvich, R. Ward (Eds.), J.D. Geller, & J. Hoffenberg (Collaborators), *Another Kind of Evidence* (pp. 55–66). London, UK: Karnac Books.

———, Norcross, J.C., & Orlinsky, D.E. (Eds.). (2005). *The Psychotherapist's Own Psychotherapy: Patient and Clinician Perspectives*. New York, NY: Oxford University Press.

Gitelson, M. (1954). Therapeutic problems in the analysis of the "normal" candidate. *The International Journal of Psychoanalysis* 35:174–183.

Guntrip, H. (2005). My experience of analysis with Fairbairn and Winnicott: How complete a result does psychoanalytic therapy achieve? In JD. Geller, J.C. Norcross, & D.E. Orlinsky (Eds.), *The Psychotherapist's Own Psychotherapy:*

Patient and Clinician Perspectives (pp. 63–80). New York, NY: Oxford University Press.

Hobbs, N. (1962). Sources of gain in psychotherapy. *American Psychologist* 17(11):741–747. https://doi.org/10.1037/h0040135

Horney, K. (1941). *Our Inner Conflicts*. New York, NY: Norton.

Kaiser, H. (1965). *Effective Psychotherapy* (L.B. Fierman, Ed.). New York, NY: Free Press.

Kantrowitz, J.L., Katz, A.L., & Paolitto, F. (1990). Followup of psychoanalysis five to ten years after termination: II. Development of the self-analytic function. *Journal of the American Psychoanalytic Association* 38:637–654.

Kohut, H. (1971). *The Analysis of the Self*. New York, NY: International Universities Press.

Laban, R. (1976). *The Language of Movement*. Boston, MA: Plays.

Loewald, H.W. (1960). On the therapeutic action of psychoanalysis. In H.W. Loewald, *Papers on Psychoanalysis* (pp. 123–137). New Haven, CT: Yale University Press.

———— (1962). Internalization, separation, mourning, and the superego. *Psychoanalytic Quarterly* 31:483–504.

Mitchell, S.A. (1988). *Relational Concepts in Psychoanalysis: An Integration*. Cambridge, MA: Harvard University Press.

Oremland, J.D., Blacker, K.H., & Norman, H.F. (1975). Incompleteness in "successful" psychoanalyses: A follow-up study. *Journal of the American Psychoanalytic Association* 23:819–844.

Orlinsky, D.E., & Geller, J.D. (1993). Psychotherapy's internal theater of operation: Patients' representations of their therapists and therapy as a new focus of research. In N.E. Miller, J. Doherty, L. Luborsky, & J. Barber (Eds.), *Psychodynamic Treatment Research: A Handbook for Clinical Practice* (pp. 423–466). New York, NY: Basic Books.

Pfeffer, A.Z. (1963). The meaning of the analyst after analysis: A contribution to the theory of therapeutic results. *Journal of the American Psychoanalytic Association* 11:229–244.

Pinsof, W.M. (2005). A shamanic tapestry: My experiences with individual, marital, and family therapy. In J.D. Geller, J.C. Norcross, & D.E. Orlinsky (Eds.), *The Psychotherapist's Own Psychotherapy: Patient and Clinician Perspectives* (pp. 145–162). New York, NY: Oxford University Press.

Pope, K.S., Geller, J.D., & Wilkinson, L. (1975). Fee assessment and outpatient psychotherapy. *Journal of Consulting and Clinical Psychology* 43(6):835–841.

———— & Vasquez, M.J. (1998). *Ethics in Psychotherapy and Counseling*. San Francisco, CA: Jossey-Bass.

Rangell, L. (1966). An overview on the ending of an analysis. *International Journal of Psycho-Analysis* 49:195–201.

Reich, W. (1949). *Character Analysis*. New York, NY: Orgone Institute Press.

Rogers, C.R. (1951). *Client-Centered Therapy*. Boston, MA: Houghton Mifflin.

Sandel, S.L., Chaiklin, S., & Lohn, A. (1993). *Foundations of Dance/Movement Therapy: The Life and Work of Marian Chace*. Columbia, MD: American Dance Therapy Association.

Schafer, R. (1968). *Aspects of Internalization*. New York, NY: International Universities Press.

———— (1973). The idea of resistance. *The International Journal of Psychoanalysis* 54:259–285.

———— (1983). *The Analytic Attitude*. New York, NY: Basic Books.

Schlessinger, N., & Robbins, F. (1974). Assessment and follow-up in psychoanalysis. *Journal of the American Psychoanalytic Association* 22:542–567. https://doi.org/10.1177/000306517402200305

Sullivan, H.S. (1953). *The Interpersonal Theory of Psychiatry.* New York, NY: Norton.

———— (1954). *The Psychiatric Interview.* New York, NY: Norton.

Tessman, H. (2003). *The Analyst's Analyst Within.* Hillsdale, NJ: Analytic Press.

Trilling, L. (2001). *The Moral Obligation to Be Intelligent: Selected Essays* (L. Niseltier, Ed.). New York, NY: Farrar, Straus, and Giroux.

Wiener, M., Devoe, S., Rubinow, S., & Geller, J.D. (1972). Nonverbal behavior and nonverbal communication. *Psychological Review* 79(3):185–214. https://doi.org/10.1037/h0032710

Winnicott, D.W. (1965). The capacity to be alone. In D.W. Winnicott (Ed.), *The Maturational Processes and the Facilitating Environment: Studies in the Theory of Emotional Development* (pp. 29–36). London, UK: Hogarth.

Woolf, V. (1929). *A Room of One's Own.* London, UK: Harcourt Brace.

Wzontek, N., Geller, J.D., & Farber, B.A. (1995). Patients' post-termination representations of their psychotherapists. *Journal of the American Academy of Psychoanalysis* 23:395–410.

CHAPTER 16

Attachment Style, Representations of Psychotherapy, and Clinical Interventions with Insecurely Attached Clients[37]

[J.D. Geller & B.A. Farber (2015). *Journal of Clinical Psychology* 71(5):457–468.]

ABSTRACT:

The primary aim of this article was to demonstrate the clinical utility of an empirically grounded perspective on the complex interplay between patients' attachment styles and their ability to create, remember, and use benignly influential representations of their experiences with their therapists. We focused on two interrelated questions: Are there significant attachment-related differences in the thematic content of the remembrances and fantasies that patients have about therapy? And, if so, what are the implications for practice? Results of a study of individuals currently in therapy ($N = 176$) indicated that although all the patients with different insecure attachment styles struggled to evoke positively valenced therapist representations, the specific nature of their representational patterns varied as a function of specific attachment styles. We offer several clinical strategies that may increase insecure patients' abilities to form adaptive representations of their therapist and therapy. We illustrate our

---

37 We acknowledge the help of Dr. Carrie Schaffer in the implementation of this study.

recommendations by presenting case material from the psychotherapy of a compulsively self-reliant man.

The primary aim of this report is to demonstrate the clinical
utility of developing empirically grounded knowledge of the
linkages between attachment theory (AT) and the ways in which
patients create and use representations of the therapeutic relationship. AT has been one of the most generative perspectives on
interpersonal relationships and their internalized legacies over
the past several decades.

From the pioneering work of Bowlby and Ainsworth to the
current mentalization-based studies of Fonagy et al., attachment researchers have investigated the ways in which internal
working models (IWMs) of relationships to primary caregivers
influence expectations, memories, and perceptions of oneself
and others. They have consistently demonstrated that securely
attached adults, relative to those who are insecurely attached,
not only display greater ease in obtaining support from others
when anxious but also are more able and likely to evoke comforting and calming representations of others when alone and
experiencing painful emotions. By contrast, insecurely attached
adults appear to be less adept at using caring relationships or
their symbolic representations (IWMs) to serve vital psychological functions, including the regulation of dysphoric emotional
experiences.

There have been various attempts to extend the ideas of AT to
the practice of psychotherapy, beginning with Bowlby's (1978)
efforts to delineate the ways in which AT could be understood
and used clinically. In particular, Bowlby emphasized the potential importance of strengthening the client's ability to use the
therapist as a secure base for self-explorations and, relatedly, as
a source of support (a "safe haven") in times of distress. In a
related vein, Farber et al. (1995) explicated the ways in which

the relationships created by effective therapists offer a set of interpersonal conditions that are analogous to the secure base paradigm originally intended as a model for parent-infant relationships.

More recently, there have been several attempts to derive attachment-informed variants of psychodynamic psychotherapy (e.g., Fonagy et al., 2004; Wallin, 2007; Mallinckrodt et al., 2009) and cognitive-behavior therapy (McBride & Atkinson, 2009). In addition, theorists and researchers are beginning to investigate the extent to which psychotherapeutic processes (e.g., the establishment and maintenance of the therapeutic alliance) and outcomes are influenced by therapist and client attachment styles (e.g., Mallinckrodt et al., 2005; Berant & Obegi, 2009; Farber & Metzger, 2009; Levy et al., 2011).

As an extension of this line of inquiry, we will here explore whether patients' attachment patterns are associated with their capacity to create and use adaptation-enhancing cognitive-affective representations of their experiences with their therapists in between sessions—an empirically documented agent of therapeutic change (e.g., Geller & Freedman, 2011). We bring to this task an integrationist agenda and the results of a study that tested principles derived from AT by examining the relational themes that organize secure and insecure patients' remembrances of interactions with their therapists.

This study grew out of our ongoing efforts—through studying patients' memories, fantasies, and dreams of therapy—to understand the interpersonal, intrapsychic, and contextual factors that influence the ways patients benefit from the transformative powers of the processes of internalization (e.g., Geller, 2006). The conceptual starting point of these studies and all that follows is the empirically derived hypothesis that, when conversational exchanges in therapy take place within the context of a stable and positive therapeutic relationship, they inspire the creation of representations of the self in relation to one's therapist that exert a positive influence on a patient's well-being (e.g., Geller & Farber, 1993; Geller & Freedman, 2011).

CLIENT REPRESENTATIONS OF THERAPY AND THE THERAPIST

Data from varied sources indicate that patients construct multiple and enduring representations of "my therapist as a person" or "my therapist in relation to me or a part of me" over the course of psychotherapy. An integrative summary of the available findings via case reports, surveys, and interviews (e.g., Geller et al., 1981; Rosenzweig et al., 1996; Knox et al., 1999; Geller et al., 2011; Atzil-Slonim et al., 2014) support three interrelated propositions:

- The themes that organize the manifest content of current and former patients' remembrances, fantasies, and dreams about therapy vary from individual to individual.
- These themes range from those that portray the therapeutic relationship as a source of gratification and help to those that portray therapy as a frustrating and unhelpful experience.
- There are identifiable themes that bear a statistically significant relationship to patients' perceptions of both positive and negative therapeutic outcomes. Patients who report being satisfied with what they are accomplishing in therapy are those who continue, in between sessions, to work on the problems they discussed in therapy by engaging in imaginary conversations in which the therapist serves as a "dialogic partner." Conversely, self-perceived negative therapeutic outcomes tend to be associated with patients'

felt inability to call upon benignly influential representations of the therapist when experiencing intrapersonal
distress and interpersonal conflicts.

In the hopes of building upon this database, we investigated whether patient attachment styles are associated with the
prevalence of specific thematic representations of therapy and
therapist. In the balance of this article, we will present a brief
summary of the findings of this study and then consider their
implications for clinical practice.

METHOD

Participants

A total of 176 adults in individual weekly psychotherapy, drawn
from eight outpatient clinical settings in the northeast part of
the United States, participated in this study. The mean age of
this sample was 35.8 (standard deviation [SD] = 9.8). Most participants were female (74%) and Caucasian (94%); most had
completed high school (95%), and a substantial minority had
completed college (40%). Per our request, patients were asked
by their therapists if they would be willing to participate in a
study "designed to collect information about the ways that people in psychotherapy think about their relationships with others
and their emotional experiences."

Instruments

A subscale of the Therapist Representation Inventory (Geller
et al., 1981) was used to measure the salience of the themes

that characterize participants' involvement with mental representations of their therapists. The Therapist Involvement Scale (TIS), a 33-item instrument, asks participants to rate the extent to which specific topics or themes characterize their thoughts, feelings, and fantasies about their therapists in his or her physical absence and is scored on a 9-point scale ranging from 1 (not at all characteristic) to 9 (highly characteristic). A principal components analysis of this data set essentially replicated the results of previous factor analyses (e.g., Geller et al., 1981) and indicated that these representations could be grouped and compared with respect to the prevalence of five themes:

- The *wish for reciprocity* reflects two related themes: (a) the wish for a personal relationship with one's therapist that transcends the roles of patient and therapist, such as becoming friends; and (b) a preoccupation with the person of the therapist, including doubts as to whether anyone could replace the therapist in the patient's life. Example: "I imagine our talking to each other outside of therapy."
- *Failure of benign internalization* reflects doubts about the helpfulness of therapy and the felt inability to recover and to use representations for personal benefit. Patients with high scores on this factor seemingly experience disappointment in their therapist and therapy. Example: "I don't seem to be able to use what I learned in therapy."
- *Longing for the gratifying aspects of the therapy relationship* reflects a desire to be in the physical presence of the therapist, including a wish to recapture the gratifying aspects of the therapy relationship in future sessions. Example: "I miss my therapist."
- *Continuing the therapeutic dialogue* reflects the felt readiness to rely on representations of the therapeutic dialogue to cope with difficult situations or internal conflicts. Ex-

ample: "When I am having a problem, I try to work it out with my therapist in mind."
* *Negative involvement* reflects malevolent or persecutory images of the therapist. Example: "I imagine my therapist hurting me in some way."

Respondents also completed the Reciprocal Attachment Questionnaire (RAQ; West et al., 1987; West & Sheldon-Keller, 1994), a 43-item scale that assesses an individual's attachment style to a specific, current attachment figure. As operationalized by the RAQ, an attachment figure is the person that the patient would most likely depend on and turn to for comfort, help, advice, love, or understanding. The scale yields dimensional scores on four insecure attachment patterns based on Bowlby's (1978) theorizing:

* Compulsive care-giving (e.g., "I put my attachment figure's needs ahead of mine.")
* Compulsive care-seeking (CCS; e.g., "My life is so full of problems that I have to depend a lot on my attachment figure.")
* Compulsive self-reliance (CSR; e.g., "I feel it is best not to depend on my attachment figure.")
* Angry withdrawal (e.g., "I get frustrated when my attachment figure is not around as much as I would like.")

The first two dimensions overlap (significant correlation of .57) and are broadly analogous to the more traditional anxious-ambivalent pattern and to the preoccupied classification of attachment. The CSR pattern is more closely aligned to anxious-avoidant and dismissive classifications. The angry withdrawal pattern reflects a mixture of ambivalent and avoidant attachment styles. In addition to the dimensional scores, individuals may be classified categorically into one of these four insecure attachment groups or into a secure attachment group.

Table 1

Analyses of Variance Comparing Attachment Groups on TIS Factors (Representational Themes)

| IS Factors | Attachment Groups | | | | | F | p |
	Self-Reliant (n = 42)	Angry with-drawal (n = 41)	Care-seeking (n = 32)	Care-giving (n = 31)	Secure (n = 29)		
I. Wish for reciprocity	2.20	2.17	2.80	2.20	1.98	1.83	.13
II. Failure of benign internalization	2.41	2.48	3.00a	2.22b	2.15b	3.08	.02*
III. Longing for gratifying involvement	3.85	4.08	4.35	4.48	3.99	84	.50
IV. Continuing therapeutic dialogue	3.27a	4.45b	4.25	3.65	3.94	2.68	.03*
V. Negative involvement	2.08	2.37	1.77	1.73	1.55	2.32	.06

Note. TIS = Therapist Involvement Scale.
Significant Tukey test group differences are noted by differing letters in each row.
*$p < .05$.

RESULTS

Discussion

CATEGORICAL DATA

We were interested in investigating the relationship between membership in these different attachment groups and scores on each of the five factors of the TIS. Our analyses indicate that at least some of the discrete themes (factors) that organize the manifest content of patients' representations with their therapists vary significantly as a function of different attachment patterns.

In Table 1, we present two significant findings for the categorical data: Those patients categorized as securely attached as well as those categorized as compulsive care-giving had lower scores on the failure of benign internalization factor than those categorized as CCS; that is, patients in these first two groups were less likely to evoke representations of their therapists that reflect doubts about the efficacy of psychotherapy.

The data in Table 1 further show that patients in one of the insecure attachment categories—angry withdrawal—had significantly higher mean scores on the continuing the therapeutic dialogue factor than those categorized in another insecure pattern, CSR. It is also noteworthy that there were no significant differences between scores of securely attached patients on the continuing the therapeutic dialogue factor and scores on all the insecure attachment categories, or even differences on this factor among those in most of the insecure attachment categories. This "nonfinding" is consistent with the results of previous studies that have documented that patients may rely on representations of the therapeutic dialogue to serve diverse and even contradictory functions (Geller & Farber, 1993).

DIMENSIONAL DATA

In Table 2, we present the correlations of factors on the TIS with scores on the insecure attachment styles (the dimensional rather than categorical means of assessing attachment). As can be seen, the pattern of significant correlations was different for each of the insecurely attached styles. For example, patients' tendencies to be care-seeking correlated significantly with scores on four of the five TIS factors, including the wish for reciprocity, failure of benign internalization, longing for gratifying involvement, and negative involvement. Thus, higher scores on this attachment style are associated with a highly complex representational profile that comingles, on the one hand, the longing to both recover the gratifying aspects of the relationship and extend the boundaries of this relationship, and, on the other hand, a disappointment in therapy, an inability to sustain images of therapy outside of sessions, and a sense of the therapist as a persecutory figure.

Table 2

Correlations of TIS Factors with Styles of Attachment

	Attachment Styles			
TIS Factor	Self-Reliant	Angry with-drawal	Care-seeking	Care-giving
I. Wish for reciprocity	.07	.12	.25***	.00
II. Failure of benign internalization	.19**	.19**	.42***	−.00
III. Longing for gratifying involvement	.06	.10	.24***	.02
IV. Continuing therapeutic dialogue	−.02	.15*	.10	−.08
V. Negative involvement	.31***	.27***	.15*	−.06

Note. TIS = Therapist Involvement Scale.
*p < .05. **p < .01. ***p < .001.

Inspection of the data in Table 2 further reveals that those high on the angry withdrawal dimension of attachment tended toward high scores on three factors: failure of benign internalization (associated with disappointment with therapy), negative involvement factor (reflecting a persecutory image of the therapist), and continuing the therapeutic dialogue (the tendency to evoke representations of communicative exchanges with one's therapist in between sessions). Seemingly, those patients with higher scores on this attachment dimension are given to experiencing representations of the therapeutic dialogue that reflect an ongoing struggle with their doubts about therapy and the painful aspects of their therapeutic relationship.

Notably, too, scores on the CSR type of insecure attachment are not significantly correlated with scores on the continuing the therapeutic dialogue factor. This finding is consistent with the data from Table 1 indicating low scores on this factor among individuals categorized in this group. Taken together, these findings lend credence to the hypothesis that self-reliant patients are unable (or unwilling) to evoke or sustain representations that imply that their therapists play an emotionally important role in their lives.

Finally, two representational themes emerged as significant across three of the four attachment styles. Scores on the CSR, angry withdrawal, and CCS attachment styles (but not compulsive care-giving) were significantly correlated with scores on failure of benign internalization and negative involvement, indicating that patients who struggle more intensely with these insecure attachment dimensions have greater difficulty constructing, recalling, and using positive, adaptive images of their therapists and therapy. These results are consistent with those of Calabrese et al. (2005), who reported an "inability of borderline patients ... to evoke and sustain representations of their analyst as a benign, trusted, available, responsive figure" (p. 524).

Our findings are also congruent with the emerging consensus that therapists can expect to encounter various obstacles in their attempts to establish a positive and durable therapeutic alliance with insecurely attached patients, and that these obstacles will vary as a function of a patient's specific attachment style. Most broadly, we are guided by the hypothesis that those who fear living autonomously and fear being abandoned by those on whom they depend (e.g., preoccupied or CCS clients) pose different challenges from those who fear intimacy and fear having their independence taken from them (e.g., avoidant or CSR clients).

CLINICAL IMPLICATIONS

Different paradigms, research strategies, and terminology have rendered integration of the burgeoning literature on the relevance of AT to psychotherapy difficult. We have used Bowlby's (1978) description of attachment-based pathology in adulthood (dysfunctional patterns of anxious care-seeking, compulsive care-giving, and CSR) as our conceptual frame. Other theorists and researchers have adopted Bowlby and Ainsworth's traditional classification system (secure, anxious-avoidant, anxious-ambivalent attachments) as a basis for thinking about targeted therapeutic strategies.

Still others have preferred using newer models that feature either Bartholomew's (1990) four-category classification system (secure, preoccupied, fearful, dismissing) of adult attachment or Shaver and Mikulincer's (2010) paradigm, in which individuals are assessed via independent dimensions of security seeking and hyperactivation-deactivation attachment strategies. These strategies are viewed as defenses against frustration caused by attachment figures' unavailability in times of need, the former (hyperactivation) representing anxious, intense desires to maintain contact, and the latter (deactivation) reflecting inhibition or suppression of proximity -eeking.

There is imperfect concordance among these systems. Consequently, recommendations on how to best work with anxious-ambivalent clients, for example, may or may not map onto the same population as those categorized in other systems, such as CCS or preoccupied attachment style. Further muddying the conceptual waters is the inexact correspondence between attachment style and patient diagnosis. For example, as Scott et al. (2013) note, "There does not appear to be any single category of insecure attachment that encompasses all individuals with BPD" (p. 473).

Despite conceptual divergences, virtually all attachment-informed therapists, including ourselves, ascribe to several fundamental propositions regarding therapeutic techniques. First and foremost, we are in agreement that therapists need to provide insecurely attached clients with a secure base within which to safely explore and disclose their thoughts and feelings, especially those related to prior and present relationships. "This sense of safety is facilitated, within sessions, by the therapist's constancy, availability, sensitivity, and responsiveness to the patient's expressions of distress and anxiety" (Farber et al., 1995, p. 207). The expectation is that patients will experience new ways of relating within the safety of the therapeutic relationship, try out these new ways of functioning in the world at large, and then return to the safety of the therapeutic relationship to further discuss the feelings engendered by these new behaviors and new possibilities for further change.

Concurrently, there is widespread agreement that patients will relive and reenact their prototypical reactions to attachment figures within the context of the therapeutic relationship, and that insofar as their relationships with their attachment figures are insecure, they will have great difficulty perceiving that their therapist is reliable and trustworthy and offers a safe place for therapeutic exploration. For example, CCS patients are apt to develop an intense and addiction-like relationship with their attachment figures, including their therapist. They compulsively cling to their therapists' concrete presence and, like a drug whose positive effects wear off, they crave contact between sessions. By contrast, individuals who are CSR can be expected to disavow that they have wishes directed toward their therapist.

Similarly, CCS and CSR patients can be expected to ascribe different meanings to the therapist's handling of the spatial and temporal arrangements of therapy. A CCS attachment style predisposes a patient to interpret the stability and predictability with which his or her therapist manages the timing and duration of sessions as direct and immediate evidence of the therapist's reliability and trustworthiness. On the other hand, CSR patients tend to be negatively and selectively reactive to the fact that the therapist has more power than they do to control when and where they meet.

Second, like other therapists influenced by AT, we believe that it is clinically advisable to encourage clients to devote serious and sympathetic attention to the felt internality of their working models of themselves and others. We prioritize promoting these patients' awareness and understanding of the mental states of self and others. For example, when treating insecurely attached clients who employ deactivating strategies (essentially avoidance) in response to perceived interpersonal discomfort, we invite them to explore why the therapeutic setting seems unsafe. We might ask, What is it that you're experiencing now as I ask you to explore this issue in greater depth? Or, What is it that I or we do that makes you fearful of getting closer? In this vein, too, here is an interchange between a therapist (T) practicing a mentalization-based treatment and a 16-year-old patient (P) who is full of feelings of self-loathing (Rossouw, 2015):

T: I wonder if you think I have the same thoughts in my mind about you as what you are having?

P: Yes, I think that and I have had enough experience to know that people don't like me.

T: I don't have the same feelings in my mind. I have my own feelings about you; I don't have your feelings about you. If someone else comes into the room now and they listen to our conversation and look at my facial expression and hear my tone of voice, what do you think they will think I feel about you? Will they think I dislike you?

P: I don't know. You could smile and not mean it.

T: Or I could smile and mean it. And maybe other people coming in here may think I care about you. And to me it is really sad that this cold thing in your mind makes you have cold feelings about yourself and it makes you convinced that everyone around you also has cold feelings. And I just wonder whether you then tend to push people away a bit?

P: I don't allow anyone close to me. If people get close to you, they hurt you or take advantage. I don't want anyone to know what I feel inside.

T: But if you keep people at such a distance, what do you think they feel?

A third common strategy is consistent with what Bowlby initially suggested: to react to the demands, expectations, and behaviors of clients in ways that challenge their relational assumptions, "to resist the pull to respond in ways that are consistent with expectations and complementary to behavioral strategies" (Dozier & Tyrrell, 1998, p. 237). For example, therapists working with clients who rely on hyperactivating strategies (typically manifest as energetic, frantic attempts to get the therapist to continually engage with them) must avoid the pull to be overly available and protective; they must also make this pattern an explicit focus of therapeutic discussion. Or, to use Kohut's (1971) concept of selfobjects, therapists must contend with the possibility that insecurely attached patients will treat them as an extension of themselves to serve functions that they feel they cannot perform for themselves.

Therapists of various theoretical persuasions are in agreement that they need to closely monitor the extent to which insecurely attached patients react problematically to the very human imperfections of their "good enough" therapist. There is also widespread agreement that therapists should attend to their own disquieting feelings—for example, boredom, loneliness, and anger—that are inevitably aroused when patients are relentlessly conflicted around issues of intimacy, collaboration, and/or authenticity.

Therapists must keep in mind that insecurely attached patients are especially sensitive to issues of separation and loss and, similarly, to dyadic connections and disconnections; to perceived empathic misattunements and ruptures in the alliance; to variations in their therapists' depth of involvement, self-disclosure, and apparent compassion; and to changes in the structure or boundaries of therapy, including canceled sessions, breaks in sessions (e.g., vacations), fee changes, and small variations in the time and length of scheduled appointments.

These patients may also have conflictual reactions to the rules of therapy, including those that regulate interpersonal discourse and are seemingly distinct from the rules of the rest of their interpersonal world. In a similar vein, they may have strong reactions to the status inequalities (i.e., power differentials) that separate the roles of therapist and patient. Thus, therapists can and should initiate discussions, beginning in the earliest stages of therapy, about the personal meanings for the patient of the real deprivations and uncertainties that are integral to the process of therapy. Discussions of patients' reactions to the spatial, temporal, and interpersonal boundaries that separate them from their therapists, difficult as they may be, can facilitate the construction or strengthening of representational models of therapy that reflect safety, trust, and connection—a pathway, we hypothesize, to greater security of attachment.

Fourth, a commonly held clinical conviction is that there is substantial value in exploring the extent to which and the conditions under which insecurely attached patients are capable of maintaining secure and realistic IWMs of the important people in their lives as well as determining the conditions that give rise to clients' fragmented and unsupported representations of others.

Our data further suggest that therapists would be well advised to use clinical strategies that strengthen the readiness and ability of patients with patterns of insecure attachment to create new, more realistic, and/or more positive representations of the functional aspects of the therapeutic relationship. There are multiple ways of implementing this goal. For example, a therapist might inquire about the frequency and nature of clients' intersession thoughts and dreams about their relationship. Thus, therapists might ask the following questions: What have you been thinking about in terms of what we've been working on? Do images or thoughts of our sessions occur to you in between our sessions? When you were feeling that way, struggling with that, were you able to use some of what we were working on? Is it difficult to allow thoughts of our work to enter your consciousness when we're apart? What kinds of emotions do you experience when you anticipate coming to therapy? To what extent do you think about the topics you'd like to talk about before we meet? Do you have dreams about therapy? If so, what do they tend to be about and how is each of us represented in these dreams?

Furthermore, therapists' knowledge of the representational themes that are associated with different attachment styles may enable them to create personally tailored and secure therapeutic contexts—safe enough spaces within which insecurely attached patients may be more likely to construct adaptive therapist representations, including those that evoke a sense of connection with the therapist in his or her physical absence. For example, as indicated by the pattern of results on the failure of benign internalization factor, CCS patients (akin to preoccupied patients) tend to evoke representations that reflect significant doubts about the effectiveness of psychotherapy. Therapists, then, would do well to repeatedly explore with these patients the nature of their relationship and their perceptions of the progress (or lack thereof) of their therapy. These patients may need considerable reassurance, extra "doses" of positive regard, and greater processing of the work done to begin to hold more securely and continuously images of the therapist as benign, caring, and helpful (e.g., Farber & Metzger, 2009; Mallinckrodt et al., 2009).

CSR patients, as indicated by their lower scores on the continuing the therapeutic dialogue factor, struggle to call forth representations of their therapist that continue the work of psychotherapy in between sessions. Their attachment to and representations of their therapist tend to be tinged with fears of intimate connection and of rejection. As a consequence, they may struggle to disclose to their therapists, take longer than other patients to develop a strong therapeutic alliance, and fight against the inclination or beginning awareness that their therapist is a meaningful figure in their lives—their actual lives and their intrapsychic (representational) lives. Thus, for CSR patients, like the patient in the case study below who defensively withdraws into enduring maladaptive states of separateness, it is especially important for a therapist, beginning early in treatment, to initiate discussions about autonomy, privacy, and dignity and how these apparent needs play out in the therapeutic relationship.

What unites these otherwise diverse techniques is that they all initiate qualitative changes in patients' representational worlds in two constructive ways. First, they bring about revisions of the representations of relationships that have exerted a longstanding dysfunctional influence on their lives. Second, they inspire the creation of new adaptation-enhancing representations of therapy-with-my-therapist. Therapy is most significant when it operates on these two fronts simultaneously. In other words, we believe that when patients and therapists cocreate insights about internalized attachment figures from the past, they establish the interpersonal conditions that stimulate the construction of functional representations of the therapeutic relationship. In doing so, they help clients modify their assumptions, beliefs, and behaviors to reflect a more securely attached pattern of interacting with multiple others (e.g., Mallinckrodt et al., 2009).

CASE EXAMPLE

To illustrate and expand upon these ideas and findings, we will briefly describe the case of a CSR patient who began psychotherapy (with the senior author of this paper, JG) in the hope of "finding a cure for my workaholism." The patient, "R," is a middle-aged, married university professor (biographical details have been altered in the service of confidentiality).

R came to therapy reluctantly at the urging of a colleague when a book he published did not become the triumph he expected. His intolerance of not achieving a national reputation rendered him depressed and anxious. I (JG) learned that he felt as if there was "never enough time to devote myself to my own scholarly work." He was anxiously preoccupied with time, finitude, and mortality. He rarely felt gratified by his relationships yet felt extremely greedy and selfish when he expressed his desires. He presented with some features of anhedonia: While he felt driven by an imperious quest for respect, he failed to experience much pleasure from his accomplishments. He rigidly attempted to maintain an "illusion of self-sufficiency" (Modell, 1986) and had great difficulty with having to reveal the intimate details of his life. Consequently, when he began therapy, he experienced intense shame whenever he expressed the need for help, and I anticipated that he would have great difficulty acknowledging and taking in what securely attached patients welcome and find helpful, such as the tender gaze of an empathic therapist.

During the course of our 2-year work together, I employed most of the clinical strategies noted in the previous section of this article in an attempt to help him overcome the inhibiting influences of his excessively autonomous, self-reliant attachment style. While negotiating the therapeutic contract, I appealed to his analytic and intellectual abilities by analogizing psychotherapy to an educational experience. I explained why I believed he would benefit from learning about his attitudes and feelings about the difficulties, frustrations, and deprivations inherent in therapy.

Consistent with his attachment style, when R began therapy, he resented that I was empowered to control where, when, and for how long we would meet for his therapy sessions. My approach to dealing with his negative feelings about the power differentials that separated us was dual-edged: On the one hand, I empathized with his feeling diminished by the status inequalities inherent in our relationship; on the other hand, I voiced my comments so as to underscore my intent to establish a collaborative relationship with him. To this end, I invited him to openly share his reactions to the time limitations and spatial restrictions I placed on our relationship. I chose a variety of clinical strategies to help him gain access to his disavowed yearnings to accept a dependent relationship with me. I said things like, "Help me to understand what angers you about my having more control than you about the length and endings of our sessions." In a similar vein, I pointed out to him that he typically stopped working as the final minutes of each session approached, assuming the position of "I will leave you before you leave me."

Over the course of therapy, R came to understand that his insecure relationships with attachment figures resulted from early life experiences in which he had no other means of attaining his parents' attention than by getting perfect grades in school. I, by contrast, found opportunities to thoughtfully compliment him on his non-achievement-oriented qualities. For example, I showed my appreciation for his admirable, self-deprecating sense of humor and his ironic sense of the "absurdity" of his irrational fears. I also relied on a variety of complimentary strategies to move the relationship in a more egalitarian direction.

First, I said things like, "Well said. I couldn't have found the words you just did to describe your fear of getting close to people." I also remarked, "We make a good team when it comes to discovering what undermines your sense of dignity and self-respect." Second, I openly admitted my doubts about being able to help him while remaining fully committed to the conviction that it was in our best interests to continue our work. Third, I asked his permission before offering him feedback about his therapy-interfering behaviors (Linehan, 1993). As a result of these discussions, R learned how exquisitely sensitive he was to perceived variations in my depth of emotional involvement with him despite the fact that he concomitantly was unable to tolerate awareness of and take pleasure in my caring concern and genuine interest in him.

R had overdeveloped his intellectual and verbal skills to succeed academically and concomitantly paid little attention to the information conveyed by vision. To counteract this imbalance, I encouraged him to strengthen his visual literacy by paying attention to what was revealed by my gaze, posture, and gestures. As I had observed and eventually told him, R rarely looked at me and never made eye contact. I initiated discussion of this "enactment" of his attachment style by quipping, in a quasieducational style, that "therapy can be a looking cure as well as a talking cure." As a cultured academic, R took pride in knowing that an early psychoanalytic patient, Anna O, had coined the term "the talking cure." My remark was intended to lay the foundation for our subsequent explorations of the anxiety he felt when seeing and being seen by me, when, for example, we shared moments of intimacy during our sessions or when he dreamt I was spying on him when he was at home.

Normatively, when therapists appear in the manifest content of their patients' dreams, the themes tend to be charged with fears and negativity (Rohde et al., 1992). I was therefore reassured when, in the 9th month of his therapy, R reported a dream in which he was smilingly looking at me as I cared for the plants in my office. Around this time, I noticed that R's capacity to coordinate listening, speaking, and looking had been strengthened. This enabled him to more fully receive the sensuous fullness of my offerings, thus rendering the IWMs of the therapeutic relationship that he was creating more realistic and vivid and therefore more accessible to conscious awareness and usage in extratherapeutic situations.

Although highly articulate, R's attempts to give a coherent narrative account of his past experiences were quite limited when he began therapy. Like other insecurely attached patients whose sense of personal continuity (temporality) is often impaired, he needed to develop a more integrated perspective on the evolution of relationships over time. To increase his awareness of the relationships that exist between what was, what is, and what will be, I strove to link our sessions together thematically and helped him to construct interconnected narratives, to "tell" cohesive stories. Narratizing techniques, like other previously noted clinical strategies, render patients' attachment patterns more vivid and accessible, enabling working models of self and others to be scrutinized and modified. Constructively modifying old patterns makes it less likely that they will contaminate new attachment models (i.e., of the patient-therapist relationship).

When he began therapy, R said of himself, "It's hard to imagine myself as being loved if I have any flaws. . . . I thought anyone who depended on others to feel good about themselves was weak." In the final weeks of therapy, R said, "Paradoxically, your giving me the space to complain about what you weren't giving me has helped me to accept what you have so generously offered me." I believe that enabling R to be an eloquent critic of psychotherapy promoted the emotional and conceptual development of his oftentimes intense and inchoate experience of "disappointment" (Geller, 1987).

In turn, I believe this change signaled that R had also begun to feel better about creating, remembering, and using functional representations of the healing ingredients of psychotherapy. In accord with this hypothesis, 6 months after termination, R wrote me a letter: "Time and again I find myself thinking about our conversations when I am seeking relief from painful feelings, especially those that arise when I feel that I am falling prey once again to the terribly all-consuming need to be productive."

CONCLUSION

In sum, we have attempted to convey why we believe that well-educated therapists, whatever their theoretical persuasion, can benefit from an empirically informed understanding of the clinical needs and resources of patients who experience difficulty maintaining secure IWMs of attachment figures. Our presentation has selectively emphasized several themes. First, consistent with previous observations and data, we have argued that different types of insecurely attached patients (e.g., CCS vs. CSR; anxious-ambivalent vs. anxious-avoidant) pose different emotional burdens and clinical tasks for therapists. Second, we have suggested that many of the challenges therapists face in treating insecurely attached individuals arise because of these patients' two-fold difficulties: On the one hand, they become painfully disappointed when their needs (whether conscious or disavowed) for caring and affection are frustrated; on the other hand, they have great difficulty accepting the caring concern and affection of their therapists.

Third, we have tried to specify some of the interpersonal conditions and clinical strategies that make it possible for insecurely attached patients to benefit from the experiential learning that takes place when they internalize the functional aspects of their therapist and the therapeutic relationship. Finally, our findings suggest that therapists, whatever their theoretical orientation, would be well-advised to keep in mind the following questions when undertaking therapy with a new patient, especially one whose presentation suggests an insecure attachment:

- Is this patient's characteristic pattern of relating to attachment figures going to facilitate or impede his or her ability to benefit from treatment?
- Is he or she able to create representations of therapeutic conversations that will enhance his or her efforts to make constructive changes in life?
- Will this patient be able to build on what was accomplished during sessions to use in the post-termination phase of treatment?

REFERENCES

Atzil-Slonim, D., Tishby, O., & Shefler, G. (2014). Internal representations of the therapeutic relationship among adolescents in psychodynamic psychotherapy. *Clinical Psychology & Psychotherapy* 22(6):502–512. https://doi.org/10.1002/cpp.1903

Bartholomew, K. (1990). Avoidance of intimacy: An attachment perspective. *Journal of Social and Personal Relationships* 7(2):147–178.

Bowlby, J. (1978). Attachment theory and its therapeutic implications. *Adolescent Psychiatry* 6:5–33.

Calabrese, M.L., Farber, B.A., & Westen, D. (2005). The relationship of adult attachment constructs to object relational patterns of representing self and others. *Journal of the American Academy of Psychoanalysis and Dynamic Psychiatry* 33:513–530.

Dozier, M., & Tyrrell, C. (1998). The role of attachment in therapeutic relationships. In J.A. Simpson & W.S. Rholes (Eds.), *Attachment Theory and Close Relationships* (pp. 221–248). New York, NY: Guilford Press.

Farber, B.A., Lippert, R.A., & Nevas, D.B. (1995). The therapist as attachment figure. *Psychotherapy: Theory, Research, Practice, Training* 32:204–212.

———— & Metzger, J.A. (2009). The therapist as secure base. In J.H. Obegi & E. Berant (Eds.), *Attachment Theory and Research in Clinical Work with Adults* (pp. 46–70). New York, NY: Guilford Press.

Fonagy, P., Gergely, G., Jurist, E.L., & Target, M. (2004). *Affect Regulation, Mentalization, and the Development of the Self.* New York, NY: Other Press.

Geller, J.D. (1987). The process of psychotherapy: Separation and the complex interplay among empathy, insight, and internalization. In J. Bloom-Feshbach & S. Bloom-Feshbach (Eds.), *The Psychology of Separation and Loss: Perspectives on Development, Life Transitions, and Clinical Practice* (pp. 459–514). San Francisco, CA: Jossey-Bass.

———— (2006). Research-informed reflections on the processes of introjection and identification: Commentary on Olds. *Journal of the American Psychoanalytic Association* 54:59–66.

————, Bender, D., Freedman, N., Hoffenberg, J., Kagan, D., Shafffer, C., & Vorus, N (2011). The RTD coding system and its clinical application: A new approach to studying patients' internalized representations of the therapeutic dialogue. In N. Freedman, M. Hurvich, R. Ward (Eds.), J.D. Geller, & J. Hoffenberg (Collaborators), *Another Kind of Evidence* (pp. 29–54). London, UK: Karnac Books.

———, Cooley, R.S., & Hartley, D. (1981). Images of the psychotherapist: A theoretical and methodological perspective. *Imagination, Cognition and Personality* 1(2):123–146.

——— & Farber, B.A. (1993). Factors influencing the process of internalization in psychotherapy. *Psychotherapy Research* 3(3):166–180. https://doi.org/10.1080/10503309312331333769

——— & Freedman, N. (2011). Representations of the therapeutic dialogue and the post-termination phase of psychotherapy. In N. Freedman, M. Hurvich, R. Ward (Eds.), J.D. Geller, & J. Hoffenberg (Collaborators), *Another Kind of Evidence* (pp. 55–66). London, UK: Karnac Books.

Knox, S., Goldberg, J.L., Woodhouse, S., & Hill, C.E. (1999). Clients' internal representations of their therapists. *Journal of Counseling Psychology* 46:244–256.

Levy, K., Ellison, W.D., Scott, L.N., & Bernecker, S.L. (2011). Attachment style. *Journal of Clinical Psychology* 67:193–203.

Mallinckrodt, B., Daly, K., & Wang, C.-C.D.C. (2009). An attachment approach to adult psychotherapy. In J.H. Obegi & E. Berant (Eds.), *Attachment Theory and Research in Clinical Work with Adults* (pp. 234–268). New York, NY: Guilford Press.

Rosenzweig, D.L., Farber, B.A., & Geller, J.D. (1996). Clients' representations of their therapists over the course of psychotherapy. *Journal of Clinical Psychology* 52:197–207.

Shaver, P.R., & Mikulincer, M. (2010). *Attachment in Adulthood: Structure, Dynamics, and Change.* New York, NY: Guilford Press.

Rossouw, T.I. (2015). The use of mentalization-based treatment for adolescents (MBT-A) with a young woman with mixed personality disorder and tendencies to self-harm. *Journal of Clinical Psychology* 71(2)178–187.

Wallin, D.J. (2007). *Attachment in Psychotherapy.* New York, NY: Guilford Press.

West, M., & Sheldon, A.E. (1988). Classification of pathological attachment patterns in adults. *Journal of Personality Disorders* 2:153–159.

———, ———, & Reiffer, L. (1987). An approach to the delineation of adult attachment: Scale development and rehabilitation. *Journal of Nervous and Mental Disease* 175:738–741.

——— & Sheldon-Keller, A.E. (1994). *Patterns of Relating: An Adult Attachment Perspective.* New York, NY: Guilford Press.

CHAPTER 17

Adult Development and the Transformative Powers of Psychotherapy

[J.D. Geller (2014). *Journal of Clinical Psychology* 70(8):768–779.]

ABSTRACT: This article explores the ways in which receiving, providing, and teaching others to do psychotherapy have influenced my adult development. In my 70s, I arrived at the conviction that at every stage of adulthood, practicing psychotherapy has had a direct and causal influence on my efforts to fill my personal life with meaning, virtue, and maturity. The first section of this article focuses on the ways in which learning to be a particular kind of psychoanalytic therapist facilitated my transition into early adulthood. The middle sections describe how I have used the professional practice of psychotherapy to integrate or dissolve the boundaries between work and play and between science and art in the everyday conduct of my life. My psychobiographical analysis concludes with some reflections on a professional failure and the compensations of being an aging therapist.

> *My object in living is to unite*
> *My avocation and my vocation*
> *As my two eyes make one in sight.*
> —Robert Frost

I enthusiastically welcomed Dr. Knox's invitation to write an article in response to the question, How does providing psychotherapy affect therapists themselves? I believe that when written in accord with the ideals of truthfulness and integrity, detailed narrative answers to this multilayered question can advance our scientific understanding of the experiences and processes that promote psychological and moral development. I am accustomed to thinking systematically about the effects that receiving psychotherapy has on the ways patients' personalities continue to develop through adulthood. But I have rarely asked myself to examine whether providing psychotherapy has exerted a distinctive influence on my own adult development.

Dr. Knox's invitation gave me the opportunity to think about myself moving through time. I welcomed the permission to "reminisce," a vital function and compensation for elders like myself. While preparing to write this article, I asked my therapist friends to think with me about such questions as these: How has my professional career as a therapist influenced the personal aspects of my life? What are the rewards and costs of cultivating high levels of psychological mindedness on behalf of learning to listen empathically to patients who are suffering? Has providing psychotherapy influenced what I believe is of value in life—what I regard as important and not important? Has the practice of psychotherapy shaped my standards and values regarding the moral conduct of our lives? Are memories of how I functioned as a therapist in the past exerting an influence on my current experiences inside and outside of psychotherapy?

By the time I sat down to write this final draft, I had come to the conclusion that there isn't an important aspect of my life that hasn't been influenced by my experiences receiving, offering, and teaching others how to do psychotherapy. In my 70s, I have arrived at the conviction that my experiences as a psychotherapy patient, psychotherapist, and psychotherapy supervisor have pervasively and positively influenced who "I am" (Erikson, 1964) and what I am "becoming" (Allport, 1955) as a husband, father, brother, friend, and citizen in a pluralistic democratic society. At the center of all that follows is the thesis that the never-ending process of learning to do psychotherapy effectively has served me well in my efforts to face and deal with the ever-changing developmental tasks that confront us as we age.

I begin by telling how, as a college student, I first came under the sphere of influence of psychotherapy and the allure of a "psychoanalytic vision of reality" (Schafer, 1976). Proceeding chronologically, I next catalog the ways that learning a particular kind of psychoanalytically informed therapy in graduate school influenced my transition into early adulthood. I will focus on the ways I attempted to integrate the interpersonal skills I was developing as a therapist into my marriage and family relationships. The third section focuses on two conspicuous features of my middle adulthood: the vital role psychotherapy has played in my efforts to integrate work and play and science and art into the everyday conduct of my life; and my difficulties making room in my life for sensuality, spontaneity, playfulness, and intimate time with my wife when I am writing scientifically about psychotherapy.

I conclude the article by arguing on behalf of the hypothesis that providing psychotherapy during one's later adulthood provides needed opportunities to move toward intimacy and generativity in one's relationships rather than toward isolation, stagnation, and self-absorption (Erikson, 1964). The story I tell does not focus solely on the question, How does providing therapy affect therapists? Rather, it is an effort to describe how psychotherapy is at the epicenter of my being-in-the-world. Following Levinson et al. (1978), I conceive of my life structure as a "tapestry" that weaves psychotherapy into interconnections with all that is important to me.

1956–1960: LATE ADOLESCENCE

Freud (1915/1959) recommended that psychoanalysts should seek their own personal therapy every 5 years. My first of five psychoanalytic therapies began when I was a sophomore at the City College of New York and still living with my parents. I sought therapy for "vocational counseling." Elsewhere (Geller, 2005b), I have written about the ways my therapist, Dr. A, a clinical psychologist trained at the Karen Horney Psychoanalytic Institute, facilitated my entrance into adulthood by strengthening my efforts to deal with the three overriding developmental tasks of late adolescence: separating from one's family of origin, taking fuller responsibility for one's choices, and forging an adult identity with respect to work and love.

In my therapy, as in my classrooms, I was impregnated with the view that the pursuit of self-understanding is inherently worthwhile. My most admired psychology professors were Freudian, existential, and Jungian in orientation. Like my therapist, they endorsed the view that one should lead an examined life and that personal therapy was the deepest and most rigorous way of acquiring truths about what it means to be a "human being." They encouraged me to develop the inner freedom to explore the irrational aspects of my fears and their inhibiting consequences. The more radical among them piqued my curiosity about the unapologetic exploration of the use of mind-altering drugs as a source of knowledge about consciousness. They legitimized my psychologizing about myself and relieved me of the stigma of being a "mental patient." In fact, in my classrooms I learned that "neuroses" were in vogue among the urban bohemian literary intellectuals with whom I sought solidarity (Broyard, 1993).

During my years in college, psychoanalysts (e.g., Fromm, 1956) and existential philosophers (e.g., Sartre) were widely read public intellectuals and major cultural arbiters. I was emotionally attracted to their shared vision of man forever trying to gain control over his impulses and autonomy from the penetrating thrust of cultural, especially puritanical and bourgeois, expectations. I was excited by their view that life should be a highly individualized quest to give uninhibited expression to one's talents, values, and proclivities. Studying their ideas about what constitutes "psychological maturity" and "inner freedom" offered me answers to questions about love and the ethical conduct of human affairs. My parents were atheists, and so I did not have a "language of faith" (Rieff, 1966). In the study of the science of psychology, I found the functional or secular equivalent of the wisdom and values my religious friends obtained from clergymen and sacred texts.

I went to college primarily to avoid being drafted into the military. I decided to become a psychology major for multiple reasons. At that time, I might have pretentiously said that I wanted to devote myself to exploring and expanding consciousness, especially consciousness of consciousness. Becoming a psychology major gave me an "identity" (Erikson, 1964) and a seriousness of purpose I had never known before. In my therapist's office and in my classrooms, I was taken seriously by adults whom I admired and who accepted my adolescent need for their encouragement. Thankfully, my therapist and teachers identified me as well endowed with the analytical and emotional intelligences required to succeed in graduate school. In my senior year, they provided me with much-needed evidence of deserved respect, encouraging me to obtain my PhD in clinical psychology. The decision to follow their advice catapulted me into adulthood, and their teachings continue to influence the ways I think about what it means to be a therapist and to do the work of a psychotherapist.

EARLY ADULTHOOD AND GRADUATE SCHOOL

I am a particular "kind" of therapist because I obtained my PhD at the University of Connecticut in the 1960s. When I entered the program, Dr. Maria Rickers-Ovsiankina was the director of clinical training. A Russian-born Rorschach expert, she encouraged her students to seek theoretical frameworks that integrated the findings and ideas of developmental cognitive psychology (e.g., Werner, 1961; Piaget, 1954; Vygotsky, 1978), Kurt Lewin's (1963) field theory, and Harry Stack Sullivan's (1953) conception of the therapist as "participant observer." An enduring legacy of my study of these theorists, both in graduate school and as a postdoctoral fellow at Clark University, is the conviction that personality development is propelled by the mutual interplay between the processes of differentiation and integration, and that when development occurs at the highest levels, it is manifested in hierarchically organized and harmonious relations between separate spheres of functioning.

What I hope to illustrate in the story that follows are the ways in which the practice of psychotherapy has facilitated my efforts to integrate the professional and personal aspects of my life.

LEARNING KAISER'S THEORY OF THERAPY

I was emotionally and intellectually attracted to the version of psychoanalytic therapy authored by Helmuth Kaiser (1965), a European-trained psychoanalyst. (Indeed, I am indebted to Dr. Rickers, as I call her respectfully, for creating a psychotherapy training program that was supervised and administered by clinical psychologists and psychiatrists who identified themselves as "Kaiserians.") In the early 1960s, two important things separated Kaiser from other psychoanalysts. First, whereas traditional analysts emphasized the transformative powers of the discovery of truths about oneself per se, Kaiser, in his maturity, arrived at the conviction that the transformative powers of psychotherapy are activated by the subjective experience of truth-telling within the context of an intimate relationship. His central tenet is that psychotherapies are healing to the extent that the participants learn how to engage in an "authentic dialogue" with one another. He taught that authenticity does not mean expressing whatever one is feeling or thinking; rather, it means saying exactly what one is feeling and thinking and taking responsibility for one's utterances.

Second, he proposed a radically new "style" (Geller, 2005c) of doing psychoanalytic therapy. He advocated adopting a relational stance vis-à-vis patients that was marked by naturalness, responsiveness, mutuality, and expressiveness. These methodological ideals anticipated those currently advocated by therapists who share an "intersubjective" or "relational" perspective on the clinical applications of psychoanalysis (e.g., Mitchell, 1988).

The Impact of Learning Kaiserian Therapy

In some respects, my professional training as a Kaiserian therapist allowed me to give uninhibited expression to what were already pronounced personality characteristics, and in other respects, it proved to be a powerfully transformative experience.

Kaiserian therapy appealed to my sensibility and my aesthetic. Like the jazz musician Shelley Manne, I am naturally inclined to "never do the same thing once" (quoted in Crow, 1999, p. 8). I become restless when I am not artfully engaged in a creative activity. I am thankful that my Kaiserian teachers' primary interest was in strengthening the listening, looking, and speaking skills that enable one to master the improvisational aspects of the therapeutic dialogue. They also encouraged me to exercise initiative in extending and refining Kaiser's skeletal theory of therapeutic technique. This liberating mandate was congruent with my need to view psychotherapy as an opportunity to be "endlessly creative" (Jung, 1963). I would have chafed under the pressure to accommodate to the self-limiting expectations of a manual-driven therapy or obeisance to Freud's (1915/1959) technical "recommendations" regarding abstinence, neutrality, and anonymity.

The sublimations required to bestow dignity and find meaning in lives that are filled with suffering "professionalized" another one of my basic inclinations. I am innately drawn to a "tragic" perspective (Schafer, 1976), to the fact that life is bounded by death and that there is so much suffering, cruelty, and evil in the world. For as long as I can remember, I have had the capacity to bear witness to the terrible things that happen to people and that people do to one another. Even at an early age I felt a sense of physical identification with sufferers (Geller, 2006). Unexpectedly, trying to "do good" at all times for my patients released me from worrying about myself. To this day, I find that engaging my mind in the task of assuaging the suffering of others holds in check the threatened breakthrough of my own worldly concerns.

The Personal Benefits of Doing Therapy

Even in my 20s, I still looked like a boy. Being perceived by my patients as an "authority figure" and as a "caretaker" supported my efforts to feel more like an adult. Moreover, in addition to allowing me to give expression to some already-established aspects of my character, being educated to assume the responsibilities of a Kaiserian therapist served as a vehicle for developing interpersonal skills that did not come naturally or easily to me.

Like all psychoanalytically informed therapists, I was trained to explore the informative potential of my subjective experiences of patients, no matter how hateful or neurotic in origin these reactions might be. Although I tend to look at life psychologically, I am not temperamentally given to psychologizing about my "inner life." The obligation to reflect calmly and objectively on the meaning of my countertransference reactions legitimized and strengthened my readiness and ability to be "psychologically minded" (Farber & Golden, 1983) about myself. Conducting psychotherapy in accord with Kaiser's methodological ideals, I became better able to recognize the specific and unique qualities of the feelings that arise in the concrete "presence" of others (Geller, 2012) and grew more comfortable evaluating my current and remembered subjective experiences.

Trying to move patients toward experiencing themselves as working closely with me in a collaborative endeavor provided me with repeated opportunities to understand my own conflictual patterns of relating to others and to take fuller responsibility for my own authentic emotional reactions. Learning to familiarize patients with their "resistances" served comparable functions. I am inclined to think that finding ways of speaking with my patients about matters that would be considered hurtful, judgmental, or inappropriate in most social situations strengthened my capacity to face and deal with the conflictual aspects of all intimate relationships. Moreover, what I have learned about the irrational and unconscious forces that drive people to inflict harm on others has extended my capacity to remain compassionate and nonjudgmental, even with people who antagonize or alienate others. Similarly, learning to take responsibility for my clinical mistakes and empathic failures encouraged me to do the same when I disappointed my loved ones.

Since graduate school, I have judged the quality and maturity of my personal relationships on the basis of many of the same standards and ideals that I rely on when evaluating my competence as a therapist. In short, I believe that learning how to view human relationships from multiple, even contradictory, psychological perspectives as a neophyte therapist set in motion constructive changes in my relationships with myself and loved ones. I think my wife would agree that the aforementioned lessons prepared me for marriage and parenthood.

But, to anticipate a later focus of this article, it pains me to acknowledge now, as it did earlier in my career, that I still haven't fully exported my relational skills as a therapist into my intimate personal relationships. Moreover, according to my politically savvy friends, my highly refined ability to perceive facts and phenomena from a psychological perspective has resulted in a "trained incapacity" (Veblen, 1919) to think about issues, problems, and ideas from alternative perspectives. They believe that what has enabled me to succeed professionally has had a limiting or biasing influence on my perception of and response to such things as world affairs. They are correct. Relying too heavily on a psychological outlook on life has narrowed the range of what I attend to. In comparison to my more knowledgeable friends, I often feel that I lack the information needed to express educated opinions about complex economic, political, and diplomatic issues. In the words of John Dewey (1910), my professional training has resulted in an "occupational psychosis." Or to paraphrase the art critic John Berger (1972), a way of seeing is also a way of not seeing.

1967–1985: MIDDLE ADULTHOOD

In the two decades that followed my postdoctoral studies at Clark University, I practiced a variety of forms of therapy as an assistant and then associate professor of psychology in the Yale Department of Psychiatry within the context of the Connecticut Mental Health Center (CMHC). From the beginning, the CMHC proved to be a favorable setting in which to continue my education as an individual and group therapist, clinical teacher, administrator, and researcher. The humanitarian philosophy of the CMHC and its staffing patterns supported my need to feel that I was living in accord with the ideals of a pluralistic democratic society and participating in the Civil Rights Movement and the war on poverty. I felt I was right in the midst of all the important liberation movements that were flourishing in New Haven in the late 1960s and early 1970s.

To fulfill the mandate of the Community Mental Health Act of 1963, namely, "giving equal opportunity for treatment to all," my colleagues and I sought to create innovative ways of offering mental health services to a relentless flow of financially and educationally challenged patients who could never pay for the services of private practitioners (Geller & Feirstein, 1974). Like our colleagues across the country, we were discovering that the preferences of economically and educationally disadvantaged patients for an active, highly structured, benignly paternalistic form of treatment were in conflict with the style of therapy preferred by classically trained psychoanalytic therapists and that this discrepancy put such patients at risk of disappointments that led them to drop out of therapy prematurely (Geller et al., 1976).

Thus, my early research ambitions were to discover the factors that might be causally related to the fact that in many mental health centers over 50% of the patients dropped out of therapy after one session. For example, we found that there were therapists who held negative biases prejudicial to minority groups that interfered with their clinical decision-making (Geller, 1988). Other findings called into question then-prevalent assumptions about the fees that should be charged by therapists, assumptions that were based on the fact that psychoanalysis originated within the context of the entrepreneurial context of medicine (Pope et al., 1975). I will later have more to say about my attitudes toward money and psychotherapy.

From the beginning, the CMHC and the Yale Department of Psychiatry also proved to be favorable settings in which to dissolve the boundaries between work and play and between science and art, lifelong ambitions of mine. Some examples follow. For pleasure, I prefer seeing movies to reading novels. Movies are fun, and I take their educational value and socializing influence seriously. Since college I have sought to sophisticate my knowledge of other cultures by religiously going to see foreign films. The films created by Bergmann, Fellini, Truffaut, Fassbinder, Rohmer, Ray, Hertzog, and so forth are filled with wise observations and reflections on the essential issues therapists grapple with on a daily basis, such as love, sex, power, cultural mores, and loyalty. By contrast, until recently the therapists portrayed in American films were simplistic, clownish, or evil. Even the early exception, *Ordinary People*, followed the Hollywood convention of representing the pivotal point in the hero's therapy as involving the dramatic recovery of a repressed, emotionally cathartic memory.

I am inclined to think that prospective patients' assumptions about what actually happens in therapy are shaped by such media portrayals of therapists. To serve as a corrective influence, my friend Dr. Marc Schwartz and I wrote, produced, and acted in a film, *An Introduction to Psychotherapy* (1973). The film portrays two working-class men having a conversation while in the waiting room of an outpatient clinic. Among other things, they talk about the stigma associated with mental illness, the conversational content and storminess of psychotherapy, the importance of the open expression of feelings in psychotherapy, and the importance of achieving mutuality of expectations with one's therapist. The film nondidactically explains the ways in which psychotherapy relationships differ from the relationships patients are accustomed to having with medical doctors.

Making our film was a source of fun and strengthened our friendship, and the film was used to serve two serious purposes. First, at the CMHC we regularly showed it to prospective patients who were at high risk of dropping out of therapy to teach them how to use psychotherapy for personal benefit. And second, in seminars we used it to strengthen the cultural competence of young therapists by familiarizing them with the fears, uncertainties, and misconceptions working-class men have about the rationale and procedures underlying psychotherapy.

In 2009, Barry Farber and I updated *An Introduction to Psychotherapy* by refilming it with our Teachers College, Columbia University graduate students. My son-in-law was the cinematographer and editor. We call the new version *Ready When You Are* and are providing it at no charge to interested viewers, in the spirit of the 60s. I would not have had the opportunity to play in this way if I hadn't spent much of my career providing psychotherapy.

I'd Rather Be Dancing

Throughout my career, I have also sought ways of integrating what I do for pleasure during leisure time—making music with friends and dancing—into my professional activities as a therapist. From 1978 until his death in 1998, William Fitch taught me how to play Afro-Cuban jazz on the conga drum. In his youth, before he became psychiatrically disabled, Bill had been a highly respected jazz musician and composer. I began taking paid conga lessons from Bill in his tenement apartment when he was psychotically grieving the death of his mother, drinking heavily, and suffering from cognitive deficits that had resulted from trauma to his head. Someday, I hope to write about our relationship at length.

For the present purpose, I will briefly note that Bill reclaimed his identity and dignity while teaching me, and I enjoyed the delicious pleasure of making music with him and the other musicians who gathered around us. As I've written elsewhere about another collaboration, I believe deeply in the healing powers of music (Clarkson & Geller, 1996). For example, my conversational style inside and outside of therapy is rooted in the idea of "rhythm" (Geller, 1994). I believe that rhythmic synchronization of the verbal and nonverbal aspects of the therapeutic dialogue paves the way for and is a reliable marker of the establishment of a positive therapeutic alliance.

The mutual shaping of my vocational and avocational pursuits can also be discerned in the continuous interplay between my love of movement and my psychotherapy-related interests and activities. While at the CMHC, I joined a dance therapy group as a "participant observer" to continue the research on nonverbal communication that I had begun as a postdoctoral fellow (Wiener et al., 1972). The patients were verbally inaccessible and psychiatrically hospitalized adolescents. Moving improvisationally with them, under the guidance of Dr. Susan Sandel, I learned to recognize the ways in which rigid and restrictive styles of moving interfere with developing a respectful attitude toward one's body, an accurate body image, and a pleasurable sense of being in a body (Geller, 1974, 1978).

To extend and refine the serious pleasure of expressing myself in movement, I regularly practice yoga and the exercises

Feldenkrais (1949) created to promote neuromuscular aware-ness. Most importantly, I have personally benefited from being a member of an Authentic Movement collective (Adler, 2002) for the past 23 years. Within the context of a circle, we free-associate, in movement, with our eyes closed, in the witnessing presence of one another. In our roles as movers and witnesses, we help each other forge connections between that which is lived bodily and that which is known imagistically and linguistically. Thus, I have used Authentic Movement both as a meditation and as a source of knowledge about creativity and embodied consciousness. In other words, practicing Authentic Movement, like receiving and offering psychotherapy, has advanced my youthful goal of learning to pay attention, with compassion, to the multisensory "stream of consciousness" (James, 1890). Moreover, my daily practice of yoga and my decision to walk or ride my bicycle to work each day have protected me from developing the all-too-common back problems of psychotherapists.

Friendship and Scholarship

I deeply enjoy dissolving the boundaries between my work as a psychotherapist and play by collaborating with my pals on scholarly projects. Because patients from all social classes seek psychotherapy to deal with failures in love, I felt my education would be advanced by giving serious thought to the origins, meanings, and functions served by love at varying stages of the life cycle. To this end, I asked my friend Richard Howenstine to cowrite an essay on the unfolding of romantic love in the lives of adult men (Geller & Howenstine, 1980). Doing justice to the elusive concept of love required us to speak candidly to one another about how we have loved romantically and dealt with the consequences of our romantic choices. Our trust and respect for one another made honesty possible and deepened our friendship.

Later, I once again found a way of forging connections between the personal and professional aspects of my life by asking my friend Paul Spector to co-edit an anthology of short stories about psychotherapy (Geller & Spector, 1987). I believe that the fictional portrayals of therapy created by serious artists may stand closer to the experience of a lived psychotherapy than the elegant abstractions of scientists. And I believe that there is much to be learned from comparing the creative process and the processes that mediate positive therapeutic outcomes.

Midway into my tenure at Yale, I flirted with the possibility of devoting some of my career to directing plays. For more than 10 years as a member of a community theater group, I acted in or directed plays that dealt with psychotherapy-related themes. In our production of Sophocles's (429 B.C.E.) tragic drama *Oedipus the King*, I played the role of Tiresias, the blind prophet. He greets Oedipus by warning him of the dangers of seeking "insight." He tells him, "Wisdom is a dreadful thing if it brings no profit to the man who is wise." As a patient and as a therapist, I too have had to confront the limitations of "insight" into the origins of one's problems in living as an agent of change. For personal and professional reasons, I was motivated to find agents of change other than insight. I feel most fortunate that in the late 1970s I found a "generative idea" (Langer, 1942) that continues to inspire my clinical, theoretical, and empirical work to this day. It is the concept of *internalization* (Geller, 1987).

INTERNALIZATION

Most broadly stated, the concept of internalization is an answer to the question, What symbolic transformations do people and our interpersonal relationships with them undergo en route to becoming enduring and functional cognitive-affective representations of the self in relation to others who are physically absent (Geller, 1987)? Placing the concept of internalization at the center of my theorizing about why psychotherapy "works" has had numerous salutary consequences. Until I found the concept of internalization, I felt that I had nothing to say about psychotherapy that hadn't already been written by countless others smarter, better educated, and more eloquent than I. Creating new methods (Geller et al., 1981; Geller & Freedman, 2011) to test the hypothesis that patients benefit from constructing and using adaptation-enhancing internalized representations of the therapeutic dialogue led me to feel I was making an original contribution to the science of psychotherapy.

My reformulations of the concept enabled me to remain true to Kaiser's emphasis on the therapeutic benefits of communicative intimacy and to reappropriate my youthful romance with psychoanalysis. I also felt more at home at Yale because two of the most admired psychoanalysts on the faculty—Hans Loewald (1960) and Roy Schafer (1968)—were advocating internalization-based models of the therapeutic action of psychotherapy that were consistent with Kaiser's emphasis on the experiential learning that takes place when patient and therapist engage in an authentic dialogue. My studies of the concept of internalization have also enabled me to transform friends into colleagues and colleagues into friends.

All of my empirical research on the roles played by internalization processes in psychotherapy (e.g., Geller & Farber, 1993; Orlinsky & Geller, 1993; Geller & Freedman, 2011) and psychotherapy supervision (e.g., Geller et al., 2010) has been done with good friends. Doing collaborative research with Barry Farber, David Orlinsky, and Norbert Freedman dissolved the boundaries between work and play. Without their knowledge, skills, patience, and vitality, I would never have been able to sustain a commitment to tackling the conceptual and methodological challenges involved in trying to empirically study the ways in which internalized representations of therapy-with-my-therapist originate, evolve, and exert a regulatory influence on patients' experiential states and behavior between sessions and after termination. Our accumulating findings lend strong support to the hypothesis that the benefits of in-session communicative intimacy endure in the form of benignly influential representations of the verbal and nonverbal aspects of the therapeutic dialogue.

A Curiously Contradictory Relationship

Programmatic research bolsters one's sense of psychic continuity. Now more than ever, our ongoing research provides me with a sense of "futurity." I have a "project" (Levinson et al., 1978) that is an antidote to the despair of knowing that my space-time is narrowing. The good news is I'm 74. The bad news is I'm 74. The good news is that I am thankful for what my pals and I have accomplished. The bad news is that as the specter of mortality draws ever closer, it pains me to acknowledge that because of my fierce devotion to the arduous discipline of writing scientifically about psychotherapy, I still haven't fully exported my relational skills as a therapist into my personal relationships. As my loving wife, Ruth, recently put it, "There are times that I wish I were one of your patients so that I could reap the benefits of your patience, kindness, and empathy."

We have been married for over 50 years. By today's standards, I was exceptionally young when I married (22) and concurrently began my training as a therapist. Like most men of my generation, I was ill-prepared to deal with the challenges of a dual-career marriage. My young bride's identification with the goals of the women's movement, her efforts to emancipate me from narrowly defined gender roles, and her fear that my search for self-respect depended too heavily on the success or failure of my career as a writer about the science of psychotherapy strained our relationship.

An addiction to the "megalomaniacal power of creation" (Bergler, 1949) has fueled my ambition to write works that are ranked as "major contributions" or "essential papers." I have been willing to endure interpersonal and intrapsychic conflicts trying to achieve what few among us achieve in a lifetime. Although my marriage gratifies my basic strivings, there are structural flaws in even the most suitable and viable marriage. A recurrent source of conflict in my marriage has been my felt inability to reconcile the competing claims of giving and receiving love and the pursuit of what William James (1890) called the "pursuit of the bitch-goddess SUCCESS."

In graduate school, my young wife (Ruth) told me I was "ruthless" when trying to complete an academic paper within a specified period of time. Not surprisingly, taking my own ambitions too seriously or selfishly took its toll on my marriage and the quality of my daily life. When doing therapy, the "feeling me" and "thinking me" coincide. When writing scholarly papers, they are at odds with one another, and I revert to an "obsessional way of living" (Salzman, 1968). Throughout my career, an undiagnosed mild case of attention deficit disorder has exacerbated my difficulties organizing sentences into a sustained and coherent argument or narrative that is articulated in a logical and orderly fashion. When writing the final draft of a manuscript,

I predictably grapple with the "anxiety of influence" (Bloom, 1973), vanity, feelings of competitiveness, dread of mediocrity, self-doubt, hubris, ascetic levels of discipline, and fatigue.

I still find it difficult to make room in my life for sensuality, spontaneity, intimacy, and playfulness when trying to bring an essay to completion. But, writing this article, I discovered that I no longer share Yeats's (1959) conviction that "the intellect of man is forced to choose between the perfection of the work and the perfection of life" (p. 73). Moreover, thankfully, my need for solitude when creating no longer places strains on my marriage as it did earlier in my career. I learn slowly, and usually the hard way. I am still trying to balance my wishes to give and receive love and my need to achieve worldly success.

My wife and I have raised two daughters, both of whom are married, live in our neighborhood, and have children of their own. We agree that protecting our children from harm, teaching and guiding them, enduring their suffering during illnesses and after accidents, and welcoming their gestures of intimacy have had a maturing influence on our own psychological and moral development (Geller, 1996). We also share the opinion that learning to be effective parents for our children and grandparents to our grandchildren as they proceed from infancy through adulthood has exerted a positive influence on our ability to deal comfortably with the emotional challenges of doing therapy. Therefore, we were not surprised by the recent finding that therapists who are parents feel they are better prepared to deal with the stressful aspects of doing therapy and also perhaps less vulnerable to the disruptive influence of countertransference reactions than therapists who are not parents (Geller & Orlinsky, 2010). My hunch is that there has been a continuous reciprocal interplay between and mutual shaping of the ways we assume the responsibilities of parenting and of doing psychotherapy.

1985–1995: PRIVATE PRACTICE AND THE MEANING OF MONEY

In 1985, when he learned that I was not given tenure in the Yale Department of Psychiatry and was planning to take a full professorship in another city, Dr. Jerry Singer asked me to create and direct an outpatient clinic staffed by Yale clinical psychology graduate students and postdoctoral fellows. Sadly, although the Yale Psychological Center was financially, clinically, and educationally successful for a decade, its doors were closed in 1995, and my life structure changed dramatically.

For the first time in my career, I faced the prospect of earning most of my income by doing psychotherapy in a private practice. I had previously supplemented my income by treating three to five patients on a low-fee weekly basis in offices provided first by the Yale Department of Psychiatry and then by the Yale Department of Psychology. My principal motive for treating patients was the belief that I had to continue my education as a therapist if I was to function as a psychotherapy supervisor and leader of psychotherapy seminars.

I have complicated feelings about the economics of the mental health "industry." My father taught me never to measure success in monetary terms. Compared to my peers, the fees I charge for psychotherapy then and now are modest. I am troubled by the exorbitant fees some therapists charge for their services. I fear that a profession that once belonged to the "moral economy" as compared to the "entrepreneurial economy" (Levinson, personal communication, 1970) has been corrupted by the profit motive and the excesses of capitalism. I am also troubled by the belief that few therapists can fulfill the highest ideals of our profession if they treat eight or more patients a day, 5 days a week; in that regard, I'd welcome research that identified the factors that influence the optimal size of a psychotherapist's caseload.

1995–PRESENT: THE COMPENSATIONS OF AN AGING THERAPIST

I am "growing old," and I am still "growing up." Nowadays, in later adulthood, I have come to agree with Bette Davis that "growing old is not for sissies." But I also believe that there are compensations if one's relationships are seasoned with wisdom, integrity and humility. According to Erikson (1964), these character strengths are the last and highest achievements of adult development, and their attainment is dependent on having opportunities to participate in relationships that are intimate and generative. I am deeply thankful that, in my eighth decade, my professional and personal relationships are shielding me from the despair, isolation, stagnation, and self-absorption felt by the elderly who are deprived of opportunities for intimacy and generativity.

On a daily basis, I have the privilege of getting paid well to engage in lively, purposeful, and intimate encounters with individuals of different ages, races, ethnicities, disciplinary backgrounds, and countries of origin. Today, as in 1995, I limit myself to doing 15 to 17 hours of therapy a week. Then as now, my caseload includes some patients who will attend relatively few sessions, those whose treatment will last between 6 and 12 months, and those who engage in truly lengthy therapies.

The novelty of doing and teaching psychotherapy has never worn off because there is no "story" that is the same as anyone else's. I feel wide-awake with my patients and students. I am capable of putting my whole self into the work I am doing with them, without pretense, and with a sense of wonder. They engage my still inquisitive mind with problems to solve, mysteries to be understood, and possibilities to be imagined. I feel that it does not require effort on my part to offer them a "presence"

(Geller, 2012) that is infused with high levels of empathy and acceptance.

On my best days, I feel I have become the therapist and teacher I hoped to become when I began my career. But gaining expertise as a therapist is not a process that comes to an end at some point; it is a process that is resumed again and again with each patient. Like adult development itself, the project of mastering the "impossible profession" is never finished. This is fine with me. At every age, my enduring commitment to learning how to conduct psychotherapy effectively has strengthened my sense of psychic continuity. Now more than ever I need "works in progress" to support my hope of having a meaningful future.

Failure and Repair

At the same time, I am starting to feel that it is possible to take pride in one's gifts, abilities, and accomplishments and yet remain true to humility. I can celebrate my claim to therapeutic expertise without feeling narcissistic or as if I am showing off. And, for the first time, I feel that I can write with dignity and integrity about a professional failure that infused my life with despair.

Till now, the story I've told is representative of a generation of ambitious, areligious Jewish men from poor backgrounds who accumulated financial, social, and cultural capital by practicing psychotherapy in accord with the Boulder model of the scientist-practitioner. But the story would be incomplete if I didn't acknowledge a humbling and humiliating crisis in my career.

In 2005, in a chapter I wrote (Geller, 2005a) in a book I coedited, *The Psychotherapist's Own Psychotherapy* (Geller et al., 2005), I discussed the challenges that arise when doing psychotherapy with fellow psychotherapists from the perspective of the concept of boundaries. I would never have obtained the knowledge required to write this chapter if 20 years ago two of my therapist-patients, strangers to one another when my therapy with each began, hadn't become conflictually entangled in each other's lives because of a convoluted series of coincidences. During our psychotherapy sessions together, one repeatedly expressed rage about the alleged misconduct of the other and acknowledged knowing that that person was working with me. After many attempts to not respond to these statements about my alleged professional relationship with the other individual, in a moment of weakness, I did disclose to this client the nature of my role with the other individual.

While evaluating the alleged offenses of that person, the Department of Health decided that I had committed a "boundary violation" by clarifying my role relationship with him or her. I was placed on probation until I completed an 18-month tutorial with an expert ethicist because my disclosure had betrayed the patient's confidentiality. I am deeply indebted to a former student of mine, Dr. Kenneth Pope (see, e.g., Pope & Vasquez, 1998). He offered me a seminar that was both educational and healing. With him I began the journey of transforming a crisis into an opportunity. Many calendar years later, writing about this awful time in my career has further detoxified my memories of failure and enabled me to reclaim more of what I have created and will have left behind.

CONCLUSIONS

Writing this autobiographical account of my career as a psychotherapist has provided me with the joy of finding more of myself. I reclaimed memories of decisive experiences I hadn't thought about for decades, including a professional crisis that

I wish had never occurred. Insofar as I am a scientist, I have no settled opinion as to whether I have over- or underestimated the width and depth of psychotherapy's influence on my adult development. Nevertheless, I am inclined to think that I have written honestly about the ways in which psychotherapy has served me well in my efforts to achieve meaning, maturity, and virtue at every stage of my adulthood.

Moreover, exploring the trajectory and nature of the interconnection between the professional and personal aspects of my life has reaffirmed my belief that Kafka (1961) was right in asserting that "the decisive moment in human development is continuous" (p. 23).

REFERENCES

Adler, J. (2002). *Offerings from the Conscious Body: The Discipline of Authentic Movement*. Rochester, VT: Inner Traditions.

Allport, G.W. (1955). *Becoming*. New Haven, CT: Yale University Press.

Berger, J. (1972). *Ways of Seeing*. London, UK: Penguin Books.

Bergler, E. (1949). *The Writer and Psychoanalysis*. Garden City, NY: Doubleday.

Bloom, H. (1973). *The Anxiety of Influence*. New York, NY: Oxford University Press.

Broyard, A. (1993). *When Kafka Was the Rage: A Greenwich Village Memoir*. New York, NY: Vintage Books.

Clarkson, G., & Geller, J.D. (1996). The Bonny method from a psychoanalytic perspective: Insights from working with a psychoanalytic psychotherapist in a guided imagery and music series. *Arts in Psychotherapy* 23(4):311–319.

Crow, B. (1999). *Jazz Anecdotes*. New York, NY: Oxford University Press.

Dewey, J. (1910). *How We Think*. Lexington, MA: D.C. Heath.

Erikson, E. (1964). *Insight and Responsibility*. New York, NY: Norton.

Farber, B.A., & Golden, V.M. (1983). Psychological mindedness in therapists. In M. McCallum & W.E. Piper (Eds.), *Psychological Mindedness: A Contemporary Understanding* (pp. 211–235). Hillsdale, NJ: Erlbaum.

Feldenkrais, M. (1949). *Body and Mature Behavior*. New York, NY: International Universities Press.

Freud, S. (1959). Observations on transference-love: Further recommendations on the technique of psychoanalysis. In J. Strachey (Ed.), *The Collected Psychological Papers of Sigmund Freud* 1:377–391. New York, NY: Basic Books. (Original work published 1915)

Fromm, E. (1956). *The Art of Loving*. New York, NY: Harper & Brothers.

Geller, J.D. (1974). Dance therapy as viewed by a psychotherapist. *American Dance Therapy Association Monograph* 3:1–21. [Reprinted in *A Collection of Early Writings: Toward a Body of Knowledge* (Vol. 1, pp. 63–80). ADTA, 1989.]

——— (1978). The body, expressive movement, and physical contact in psychotherapy. In J.L. Singer & K.S. Pope (Eds.), *The Power of Human Imagination* (pp. 347–378). New York, NY: Plenum Press.

——— (1987). The process of psychotherapy: Separation and the complex interplay among empathy, insight, and internalization. In J. Bloom-Feshbach & S. Bloom-Feshbach (Eds.), *The Psychology of Separation and Loss: Perspectives on Development, Life Transitions, and Clinical Practice* (pp. 459–514). San Francisco, CA: Jossey-Bass.

――――― (1988). Racial bias in the evaluation of patients for psychotherapy. In L. Comas-Díaz & E.E.H. Griffith (Eds.), *Clinical Guidelines in Cross-Cultural Mental Health* (pp. 112–134). New York, NY: Wiley.

――――― (1994). The psychotherapist's experience of interest and boredom. *Psychotherapy* 31(1):3–16.

――――― (1996). Thank you for Jenny. In B. Gerson (Ed.), *The Therapist as a Person: Life Crises, Life Choices, Life Experiences, and Their Effects on Treatment* (pp. 119–139). New York, NY: Analytic Press.

――――― (2005a). Boundaries and internalization in the psychotherapy of psychotherapists: Clinical and research perspectives. In J.D. Geller, J.C. Norcross, & D.E. Orlinsky (Eds.), *The Psychotherapist's Own Psychotherapy: Patient and Clinician Perspectives* (pp. 379–404). New York, NY: Oxford University Press.

――――― (2005b). My experiences as a patient in five psychoanalytic psychotherapies. In J.D. Geller, J.C. Norcross, & D.E. Orlinsky (Eds.), *The Psychotherapist's Own Psychotherapy: Patient and Clinician Perspectives* (pp. 81–97). New York, NY: Oxford University Press.

――――― (2005c). Style and its contribution to a patient-specific model of therapeutic technique. *Psychotherapy: Theory, Research, Practice, Training* 42:469–482. https://doi.org/10.1037/0033-3204.42.4.469

――――― (2006). Pity, suffering, and psychotherapy. *American Journal of Psychotherapy* 60(2):187–205.

――――― (2012, May 26). *Therapeutic Presence and the Looking Cure*. Paper presented at the 28th annual meeting of the Society for the Exploration of Psychotherapy Integration, Evanston, IL.

―――――, Astrachan, B., & Flynn, H. (1976). The development and validation of a measure of the psychiatrist's authoritative domain. *Journal of Nervous and Mental Diseases* 162:410–422.

———, Cooley, R.S., & Hartley, D. (1981). Images of the psychotherapist: A theoretical and methodological perspective. *Imagination, Cognition and Personality* 1(2):123–146.

——— & Farber, B.A. (1993). Factors influencing the process of internalization in psychotherapy. *Psychotherapy Research* 3(3):166–180. https://doi.org/10.1080/10503309312331333769

———, ———, & Schaffer, C.E. (2010). Representations of the supervisory dialogue and the development of psychotherapists. *Psychotherapy: Theory, Research, Practice, Training* 47:211–220.

——— & Feirstein, A.R. (1974). Professional training in community mental-health centers. In G.F. Farwell, N.R. Gamsky, & P. Mathieu-Coughlan (Eds.), *The Counselor's Handbook* (pp. 449–471). New York, NY: Intext.

——— & Freedman, N. (2011). Representations of the therapeutic dialogue and the post-termination phase of psychotherapy. In N. Freedman, M. Hurvich, R. Ward (Eds.), J.D. Geller, & J. Hoffenberg (Collaborators), *Another Kind of Evidence* (pp. 55–66). London, UK: Karnac Books.

——— & Howenstine, R.A. (1980). Adult men as romantic lovers. In K. Pope (Ed.), *On Love and Loving* (pp. 61–89). San Francisco, CA: Jossey-Bass.

———, Norcross, J.C., & Orlinsky, D.E. (Eds.). (2005). *The Psychotherapist's Own Psychotherapy: Patient and Clinician Perspectives*. New York, NY: Oxford University Press.

——— & Orlinsky, D.E. (2010, June). *Parenting and Psychotherapy*. Paper presented at the 25th annual meeting of the Society for Psychotherapy Research, Asilomar Conference Center, Monterey, CA.

————— & Spector, P. (Eds.). (1987). *Psychotherapy: Portraits in Fiction*. Hillsdale, NJ: Jason Aronson.

James, W. (1890). *The Principles of Psychology*. New York, NY: Henry Holt.

Jung, C.S. (1963). *Memories, Dreams, Reflections* (A. Jaffe, Ed.; R. Winston & C. Winston, Trans.). New York, NY: Random House.

Kafka, F. (1961). *Parables and Paradoxes*. New York, NY: Random House.

Kaiser, H. (1965). *Effective Psychotherapy* (L.B. Fierman, Ed.). New York, NY: Free Press.

Langer, S.K. (1942). *Philosophy in a New Key*. Cambridge, MA: Harvard University Press.

Levinson, D.J., Darrow, C.N., Klein, E.B., Levinson, M.H., & McKee, B. (1978). *The Seasons of a Man's Life*. New York, NY: Knopf.

Lewin, K. (1936). *Principles of Topological Psychology*. New York, NY: McGraw Hill.

Loewald, H.W. (1960). On the therapeutic action of psychoanalysis. In H.W. Loewald, *Papers on Psychoanalysis* (pp. 123–137). New Haven, CT: Yale University Press.

Orlinsky, D.E., & Geller, J.D. (1993). Psychotherapy's internal theater of operation: Patients' representations of their therapists and therapy as a new focus of research. In N.E. Miller, J. Doherty, L. Luborsky, & J. Barber (Eds.), *Psychodynamic Treatment Research: A Handbook for Clinical Practice* (pp. 423–466). New York, NY: Basic Books.

Pope, K.S., Geller, J.D., & Wilkinson, L. (1975). Fee assessment and outpatient psychotherapy. *Journal of Consulting and Clinical Psychology* 43(6):835–841.

————— & Vasquez, M.J. (1998). *Ethics in Psychotherapy and Counseling*. San Francisco, CA: Jossey-Bass.

Rieff, P. (1966). *The Triumph of the Therapeutic: Uses of Faith After Freud*. New York, NY: Harper & Row.

Salzman, L. (1968). *The Obsessive Personality*. New York, NY: Science House.

Schafer, R. (1968). *Aspects of Internalization*. New York, NY: International Universities Press.

———— (1976). *A New Language for Psychoanalysis*. New Haven, CT: Yale University Press.

Sullivan, H.S. (1953). *The Interpersonal Theory of Psychiatry*. New York, NY: Norton.

Veblen, J.B. (1919). *Comparative Psychology of Mental Development*. New York, NY: Science Editions.

Vygotsky, L.S. (1978). *Mind in Society. The Development of Higher Psychological Processes*. Cambridge, MA: Harvard University Press.

Werner, H. (1961). *Comparative Psychology of Mental Development*. New York, NY: Science Editions.

Wiener, M., Devoe, S., Rubinow, S., & Geller, J.D. (1972). Nonverbal behavior and nonverbal communication. *Psychological Review* 79(3):185–214. https://doi.org/10.1037/h0032710

CHAPTER 18

Ready When You Are: Answering Your Questions About Psychotherapy

[J.D. Geller & B.A. Farber (2020). *Journal of Clinical Psychology* 76(8):1438–1446.]

ABSTRACT: Psychotherapeutic treatment tends to have a high attrition rate ("premature termination"), and there have been multiple efforts to help new patients, including those considering treatment, better understand the nature and expectations inherent to this process as a means to improve retention and outcome. These efforts are often grouped under the term "role induction." This script, from a DVD produced in 2010, was written to help prepare new psychotherapy clients for this new role in their lives—specifically, to educate prospective patients about the unique and sometimes surprising features of psychotherapy and to empower them to ask questions of their therapist about the process. This script presents a conversation that takes place between three patients in the waiting room of a psychotherapy clinic who speak about common fears, misconceptions, and uncertainties surrounding psychotherapy.

It has now been amply documented that psychotherapy is an effective means of helping patients make constructive changes in their lives (e.g., Lambert, 2013). But many patients still do not benefit from therapy and/or drop out of therapy prematurely (Swift & Greenberg, 2015). To combat premature termination, several procedures and interventions have been developed (e.g., Swift & Greenberg). One of the most promising is educating prospective patients about how to derive maximal benefits from their experiences in therapy (e.g., Strassle et al., 2011). To achieve this goal, Geller, Farber, and their students produced the (2010) film *Ready When You Are: Answering Your Questions About Psychotherapy*.

We and our colleagues, in various settings, have been providing prospective patients with the opportunity to view the film alone or in groups, at home or in their therapist's office after intake and before their first session. Although we have yet to do the requisite statistical analysis, in our experience viewing this film appears to be positively associated with patient satisfaction, continuation, and improvement of therapy.

WALTER:	(voice-over as he enters building) Man, I need to remember to tell my therapist about what happened at work yesterday.
DONNA:	(voice-over as she enters building) OK, here we go. I don't know if this is working.... Four sessions. Has anything changed? Should I see a change? What am I supposed to be doing here?
WALTER:	(voice-over) You know, my girlfriend has really been getting on my nerves lately. I don't know what her problem is.... Or is it me? (sighs) This is something else I need to talk about with my therapist.

DONNA:	(voice-over) I was pretty anxious, but I was still getting along okay.... I don't know. Why did I even start this? It just seems like a big deal.... Maybe I don't really need this?
Camera POV:	WALTER walks into waiting room. Donna approaches receptionist. As WALTER approaches the chairs, he speaks to a nervous LOUISA, already sitting.
WALTER:	Excuse me, do you have the time?
LOUISA:	It's about ten of.
WALTER:	OK, cool! They really start on time here, like right on the dot. Usually they come out and get you at a certain time. It's not like at regular doctors' offices where you can wait a long time to be seen.
LOUISA:	Yeah, you can wait for hours for them....
WALTER:	Fortunately, it's not that way here. When they say you have a 4 o'clock appointment, it really means 4 o'clock. And it always lasts 50 minutes.
LOUISA:	Good, I'm glad you told me about that.... I'm not always on time. Or ... what if I can't get here at all?
WALTER:	Then you really should call to let them know. They really do set aside that time for you. And another thing.... They really try hard to end on time too.

LOUISA: Yeah, I was surprised last time when I was in the middle of something, but my therapist told me our time was up. I really wanted to keep talking, but she said it was time to end. I think that's gonna take a little getting used to.

Camera POV: DONNA standing at the receptionist's desk asking questions.

DONNA: (to RECEPTIONIST) I'm just wondering if my, like, medical insurance is gonna cover these sessions?

RECEPTIONIST: Let me check on that.

DONNA: I'm worried about being able to afford this. I mean, I don't make a lot of money.

RECEPTIONIST: Well, if the insurance doesn't cover you, there is another option. See, we have a regular fee here, but there's something called a "sliding scale." What you can do is fill out some forms, and we may be able to bring down the regular fee for you. Even the regular fee is pretty affordable. It was set up that way so people could get the treatment they need. But we know that people have different incomes, and that's what the sliding scale is for. We don't want to turn anyone away who needs help. Here are the forms....

DONNA: Thanks.

Camera POV:	Follows DONNA walking to sitting area where LOUISA and WALTER are engaged in light conversation. Both look up at DONNA and nod hello. DONNA returns the nod without smiling and sits in a nearby chair. Camera swings to LOUISA and WALTER.
LOUISA:	I have a friend who takes medication. Can I get medication here?
WALTER:	There is a psychiatrist here who can prescribe medication, if that's what you and your therapist decide might help you.
LOUISA:	So then I don't see a psychiatrist as my regular therapist?
WALTER:	No, the person you would see here is probably a clinical psychologist or social worker in training.
The phone RINGS.	
LOUISA:	Oh, okay.... I'm sorry to ask you all these questions....
WALTER:	Not a problem.
Camera POV:	Focus moves to DONNA. Phone RINGS. DONNA picks up the phone. The others glance furtively as she talks.

DONNA: Hello? Yeah, therapy again.... I can't talk to you now. But I can probably hang out this time next week. (pauses, listens, glances at WALTER) Well, because I'm thinking of stopping the therapy. (pause) 'Cause it just doesn't seem to be working for me. (pause) Right, look, I can't talk to you now. I'll catch up with you later. (hangs up phone, quietly starts crying)

Camera POV: WALTER and LOUISA look at each other. Camera goes back to intermittently covering the faces of each individual talking and wide group shots. LOUISA passes DONNA a tissue.

WALTER: (to DONNA) I couldn't help but overhear. I'm sorry.

DONNA: That's okay. (cries a bit more)
(pause)

WALTER: Wow! This isn't working out for you, huh?

DONNA: I don't know. I'm just not sure if it's right for me. (to LOUISA) Are you just starting, or what?

LOUISA: Yeah, this is my first time. I've never been to a therapist before.

DONNA: Your first session?

LOUISA: No, my fifth. But this is my first time in therapy.

DONNA: I am sorry, but I am just not sure about this whole thing. I don't know. It's just not going anywhere... and, I just don't know....

LOUISA: I know. During the first few sessions my therapist had a lot of questions. It wasn't till the third session that I started just coming in and talking about what I wanted to talk about.

DONNA: I don't know. I've been coming here for 4 weeks, and my problems with my boyfriend haven't gotten any better. Like, we're still fighting as much as we were before.

WALTER: Yeah, I remember feeling in the beginning like, what is this doing for me? I came to therapy because I was really angry and had all these problems at work. They didn't seem to change right away.

LOUISA: But eventually did it change?

WALTER: Yeah, but it was funny how, once it did start changing, it wasn't like it got better and better every day. I'd have one session where, afterwards, I felt like I could be less angry at work, talk to people more easily.... Then, there were times when I felt like I was back at square one.

LOUISA: I can't imagine having to come to therapy when after all that time you just felt like nothing had changed. And that's another thing: Do you have to come every week?

WALTER: Yes.... It's important that you do. I used to not want to come when I was feeling better. I would feel like I had nothing to say, but then I would be surprised to find I actually had a lot to say once things got going. And a lot of times too my therapist helped me find things to talk about.

DONNA: Hmm. I guess it's not that I don't have enough to talk about. In fact, sometimes I have too many different things to talk about. But there's also times that I just don't really feel like coming. I'm so busy, and sometimes I just don't see the point.

WALTER: That's probably especially when you should come! I know for me, I don't want to come when we get to the tough stuff. You know, like part of me wants to avoid the tough stuff. But that's when I know I really need to be here.

LOUISA: It sounds like you really have to find a way to get here every week.

DONNA: Yeah, I guess you really have to commit to it. (pause) And here's another thing: I was expecting my shrink to immediately give me answers to what my problems are. But he doesn't give me advice or tell me what to do to solve my problems. (pause) So, I'm wondering what I'm supposed to do... what he expects me to say.

WALTER:	It was hard not getting advice. She didn't say things just to make me feel better. Sometimes my therapist waits for me to say something.
DONNA:	So what did she do?
WALTER:	Well, sometimes she was quiet. Sometimes she'd ask me questions. Sometimes she'd reassure me about things. Sometimes she'd challenge the way I was thinking or acting. Sometimes she'd give me a new way of thinking that I hadn't thought of before.
LOUISA:	What are your guys' therapists like?
DONNA:	Mine is, I don't know, in his late 20s/early 30s or something. I don't really know. (pause) I'll admit… I'm not sure I really like him. (to WALTER) Do you like yours?
WALTER:	Yeah, my therapist is at least 10 years younger than me, and from a very different background. I mean, she's White. And it seems like I couldn't possibly relate to this person, and she could never understand me. But it was different with my first therapist. In the beginning, I didn't like him, but it turned out that trying to understand why I didn't like him was an important part of the therapy. I learned things about myself I never realized.
LOUISA:	What do you mean?

WALTER: Well, for example, I found that the way I was getting angry at my therapist was the same way I was getting angry at my co-workers. It was exactly the same problem as I was having in other areas of my life. The helpful thing was that my therapist and I were able to talk about it as it was happening between us.

DONNA: Well I don't like mine. He pisses me off.

LOUISA: I doubt if he can imagine what you're going through. I mean, he's a guy.

DONNA: Yeah . . . what's that? Shouldn't I have a woman for a therapist? How can he understand how a woman feels about stuff? I mean, I'm here 'cause some of the problems I'm having with my boyfriend have to do with, you know, "woman stuff" that (looking at WALTER) no offense. . . .

WALTER: No problem.

DONNA: . . . I don't think men get it.

LOUISA: So how can someone who's so different from you help you?

WALTER: I've found that you don't have to be similar in those ways, and that actually those differences can be something you talk about. I talked to her about my worries that she doesn't know what it is like to be Black, and it actually made our relationship stronger to... you know... acknowledge that. My therapist was really open to learning about me and my experiences. It didn't seem to matter as much that she didn't have those same experiences.

DONNA: Do you think I'd feel better if I talked to my therapist about doubts I'm having about staying in therapy? I mean, I feel like I'm really struggling.

LOUISA: (quickly) No, you can't do that, can you? I mean, that might offend them....

WALTER: It is a little weird. We're not used to... we don't talk to people in this way, you know? But what they do is help us to talk about things that are very difficult to talk about.

LOUISA: You mean like sex?

DONNA: So you're saying that I can go in there and be like, "Look, I was like really upset before I came in here, and then I talked to these people and created this huge scene where I'm like upset and crying and an emotional mess," and they're going to hear that? That's okay?

WALTER: (shrugs) I mean, yeah! They're trained to deal with people's feelings and their thoughts about stuff—you know, what you're talking about.

LOUISA: So she should tell her therapist she's thinking about stopping therapy?

WALTER: Yeah, I mean... they are trained to not take things personally and to deal with your needs, not their own. Actually, it's kind of like how we're talking about it right now. I mean, you've shared with us some really tough feelings... and how do you feel, having done that?

DONNA: I guess I do feel a little better. Talking to you guys has helped me see things in a different way.

WALTER: Let me tell you: A few years ago, before I was in therapy, I don't think I even could have had a conversation with you guys. I was angry all the time. I worked it out in talking to my therapist. It took some time to realize it was depression.

LOUISA: Wow, that's really interesting.

DONNA: Hmm. Maybe I can try that... like, try talking to my therapist about my feelings. This other thing that's really been bugging me, and maybe I should know this by now, but I'm really worried that... is what I say, like, going to be talked about? Does my therapist talk to other people about what I'm saying in there? 'Cause sometimes I've felt like I'm not telling him everything because I'm not sure, you know? What if I say something that... I just, I don't know.

LOUISA: Don't worry, what you say is confidential. I know. It's very personal stuff and so it's an important concern. My therapist explained this. Because it is a training clinic here, your therapist gets help from colleagues and more experienced therapists, which helps with your treatment. In fact, sometimes they might ask for your permission to be videotaped so they can show their work to the more experienced therapists. That's only if you want to though. But the important thing is that everything that you say stays here. Everyone who works here knows how important that is.

DONNA: That makes me feel better. But I have to say, I'm still a little uncomfortable with the process of therapy itself. It makes me feel like a helpless kid. I mean, I'm an adult! Shouldn't I be able to deal with this stuff on my own?

LOUISA: Sometimes everyone needs a little help.

DONNA: But what if you just don't like them?! Do you have to stay with your therapist?

WALTER: If you really, really didn't like your therapist and didn't think you could work with them, then probably, if it were me, I would try to change. But I've experienced conflicts with mine, gotten angry at them and felt not so sure if I was going to like them in the beginning. And at times I felt convinced that it wasn't going to work. But I've always been able to work it out.

DONNA: Okay, that sounds okay. But... how long am I going to be in therapy?

WALTER: It's hard to say. I mean, there are so many different kinds of problems. I've been in therapy for 2 years now. I don't know if it's that my stuff is particularly difficult, you know, or how quickly I'm ready to go through it. But it really depends; it depends so much on what your goals are in the therapy, what you're struggling with.

LOUISA: How do you know if therapy is working?

WALTER: Well, it's not like in the movies, where everything gets better all at once. Over time you begin to feel better. It's like you start to believe that you're making better decisions. And sometimes it does get worse before it starts to get better. I mean, you're talking about really difficult stuff. It can sometimes get overwhelming or confusing. But it gets better. For example, my relationship with my family has gotten better since I've worked things out in therapy. (pause)

DONNA: So you just get 50 minutes a week?

LOUISA: Yeah, what if something comes up and you really need to talk?

WALTER: It depends. Usually they try to keep everything in the session, but if you're in crisis, you can call them. I even met twice a week for a year when I was going through a lot of stuff. And that helped.... It's a special relationship.

LOUISA: (to WALTER) Does your therapist tell you stuff about her too? Like, do you talk about her problems too, or is it just about you?

WALTER: No, we really don't talk about her prob-
                 lems at all.... From what I've experi-
                 enced, some therapists seem to be more
                 talkative than others, but you still won't
                 know a lot about their personal lives.
                 Some might tell you their thoughts and
                 feelings about some things, but others
                 really don't talk that much. It's different
                 from a friendship: You won't get to know
                 them as well as they know you. It's really
                 a space for you.

Camera POV: Looking past the three characters, a door
                 opens to an office. Out walks a therapist,
                 who calls for DONNA.

Camera POV: On three characters, the camera swings to
                 focus on DONNA, who stands to leave.

DONNA: Well, take care, you two. Maybe I'll see
                 you guys here next week.

WALTER: (with a brief wave) See ya.

LOUISA: Bye, and thanks for everything.

Camera POV: DONNA walks up and says hello to ther-
                 apist as they enter the office and close
                 the door.

Credits start rolling on the door to the office.

END

ACKNOWLEDGMENTS

We gratefully acknowledge the contributions of several graduate students in writing this script and in acting in the production of the DVD: Sherrie Kim, Inessa Manevich, Jesse Metzger, Erica Saypol, and David Vaughns.

REFERENCES

Lambert, M.J. (2013). Outcome in psychotherapy: The past and important advances. *Psychotherapy* 50(1):42–51. https://doi.org/10.1037/a0030682.

Strassle, C.G., Borckardt, J.J., Handler, L., & Nash, M. (2011). Video-tape role induction for psychotherapy: Moving forward. *Psychotherapy* 48(2):170–178. https://doi.org/10.1037/a0022702

Swift, J.K., & Greenberg, R.P. (2015). *Premature Termination in Psychotherapy: Strategies for Engaging Clients and Improving Outcomes*. Washington, DC: APA Books.

The Transformative Powers of Aesthetic Experiences in Psychotherapy

[J.D. Geller (2018). *Journal of Clinical Psychology* 74:200–207.]

ABSTRACT: This issue of the *Journal of Clinical Psychology: In Session* contains seven essays that give expression to three basic convictions. The first is that therapists who are consistently able to help their patients make constructive changes in their lives practice psychotherapy creatively, whether or not they conceive of therapy as an applied science or as an art form. The second is that cultivating an aesthetic perspective on the communicative exchanges that take place in therapy can enhance a therapist's capacity to serve creatively as an agent of change. The third is that therapists can make better choices on behalf of their patients if they take inspiration from what artists have to teach us about the aesthetic domain of existence.

INTRODUCTION

The primary aim of this issue of the *Journal of Clinical Psychology: In Session* is to encourage readers to think of therapy as a creative enterprise and to move beyond the science versus art dichotomy that has burdened therapists beginning with Freud. It was inspired by the conviction that acquiring a working knowledge of the origins, nature, and effects of aesthetic experiences can enhance a therapist's ability to help patients make enduring constructive changes in their lives, whether or not the therapist conceives of therapy as an "applied science" (Geller, 1998) or essentially as an art form.

To produce this issue, we recruited eight potential participants whose reputations and/or published works indicated that they had integrated aesthetic concepts into their theorizing about psychotherapy and/or had cultivated their aesthetic sensibilities by practicing a traditional form of art to further develop their therapeutic skills. The recruitment e-mail informed potential authors that we were interested in soliciting clinical-theoretical essays for an issue of the *Journal of Clinical Psychology: In Session* that addressed the following types of questions: What can therapists learn about how to do the work creatively by thinking about what happens in therapy from the perspective of the concepts that were originally used to describe and explain people's aesthetic responses to nature and works of art? Are aesthetic judgments about what is valid and valuable about works of art relevant to judging how a person practices psychotherapy? What potential benefits accrue to patients and therapists when they develop their aesthetic capacities and receptivity to being influenced by aesthetic experiences?

We were deeply gratified when none of the individuals that we approached declined to participate in this project. Seven of their essays are included in this volume. All of the authors acknowledge that they have been influenced by psychoanalytic ideas. But only four identify themselves as psychoanalytic therapists: Billie Pivnick, Karen Schwartz, Matt Steinfeld, and Joan Wexler. David Johnson is the founder of an international network of drama therapy institutes. David Orlinsky is a founder of the Society for Psychotherapy Research and has dedicated his career to formulating a generic, empirically grounded theory of therapy that would appeal to therapists of all persuasions.

Devlin Jackson is a 3rd-year clinical psychology doctoral student. Like her peers, she is searching for a way to personalize and synthesize the competing theories of therapy that coexist in the therapeutic marketplace.

There are many moving and well-told stories in this issue that explain why their authors believe that the meanings and truths expressed in poetry and novels (Orlinsky), in the visual arts (Schwartz), in music (Johnson and Steinfeld), in dance (Wexler), and in the design of buildings and offices (Pivnick and Jackson) are useful tools for thinking and talking about the processes that give rise to divergent therapeutic outcomes. Their essays are examples of how creative therapists go about blending the objectivity and rigorous logic of scientific writing and the subjectivity and artistic qualities of well-told stories. I believe their contributions are worthy of being described as being at one and the same time scientific works of art and artistic works of science.

PRELIMINARY CONSIDERATIONS

To provide a context for reading the papers that follow I will briefly summarize how scholars from disciplines ranging from the cognitive and neurosciences (Kandel, 2012) through art history (Berger, 1972) and psychoanalytic phenomenology (Kohut, 1957; Stern, 2010) define and think about the aesthetic domain of existence.

For many centuries, learned scholars have grappled with the questions, What are the sources, characteristics, and functions of aesthetic experiences? and, What distinguishes works of art that are merely entertaining or decorative from those that are capable of inducing life-changing aesthetic experiences? Today's leading experts from diverse fields of inquiry share the view that works of art are merely a specialized means of activating aesthetic experiences. The prevailing consensus is that all forms of sensory stimulation—scents, tastes, sounds, sights, and being touched—can serve as catalysts for aesthetic experiences and their contemplation. There is wide agreement that aesthetic experiences are first and foremost the pleasurable and unpleasurable "feelings" that are spontaneously elicited by the senses we catalog as touch, taste, smell, seeing, and hearing.

I presume that the capacity to experience the world aesthetically is biologically grounded in an innate disposition that expresses itself in the tendency to seek out experiences with pleasurable stimuli and to avoid or withdraw from stimuli that evoke displeasure or pain. Some of our earliest aesthetic experiences are triggered by the foods we like and dislike, swallow, and spit out. The infantile experience of being fed, tenderly seen, touched, and spoken to by a loving caretaker is one of the great aesthetic pleasures of life. Life would be dull, colorless, shallow, and boring if we were unresponsive to what is sensuously pleasurable about people, places, and things. But the inborn disposition to encounter the world aesthetically is twofold in nature. The feelings of disgust and repulsion that are activated by nauseating foods, foul odors, and ugliness are the price we pay for being hardwired to experience the sensory properties of the world aesthetically. In short, aesthetic experiences can be a source of suffering, or they can make one's suffering easier to bear.

For analytic purposes, pleasurable and unpleasurable aesthetic experiences in adulthood can be grouped and compared with respect to which of their sensory qualities lend themselves to "disinterested contemplation" and are distinguishable, detailed, intelligible, and translatable into words (Kant, 1790/1966). Although aesthetic preferences that are shared are an important source of interpersonal compatibility, disagreements about matters of "taste" are an important source of sometimes irreconcilable interpersonal conflicts. Not surprisingly, the ways in which sensory experiences are interpreted varies greatly from culture to culture (e.g., Masai women use excrement as a hair dressing; Ackerman, 1990) and from person to person in the same culture. Moreover, in everyday conversations, the positive and negative aesthetic qualities that are attributed to physical objects and substances are also commonly used to characterize our subjective experiences of the personal characteristics of people. To cite a few examples: He is a sweet guy. She is a sourpuss. He stinks and is slick and slippery. She is softhearted. He blows hot and cold. She has a silky voice. You are a sight for sore eyes. She is food for the eyes. He has rough edges.

WHAT DO THE AUTHORS SHARE IN COMMON?

In all of the papers, readers will encounter the conviction that each patient uses therapy and the therapeutic relationship in a different way that is in part predictable from his or her aesthetic preferences. Second, all the authors embrace the view that they and serious artists share the following things in common: Like artists, therapists are interested in broadening and refining what can be heard and seen, thought, and felt. Like artists, therapists are interested in harnessing the creative and constructive powers of the imagination. Like artists whose creations address religious, moral, and ethical dilemmas, therapists encourage their patients to look more closely and in a more informed way at their beauty and their ugliness, their joys and their sorrows, their tender and violent impulses, and the physicality of these domains of experience. Like writers of autobiographies and confessional poetry, therapists have experience-based knowledge of how difficult it is to give voice to disagreeable truths about oneself. Bold therapists and artists appreciate that if they are to achieve their goals, they will have to muster the "courage" (Geller, 2013) to confront fear and disgust-inducing taboos that are avoided in other interpersonal contexts.

All of the authors practice a version of the talking cure, but they do not have a language-centric view of psychotherapy. They all recognize that face-to-face conversations are more than the mere exchange of words. Their educations have sensitized them to the importance of paying nuanced attention to the nonlinguistic aspects of the therapeutic dialogue. They are all committed to the view that listening for therapeutic purposes requires the capacity to receive and interpret the collateral sensory and perceptual experiences that precede, accompany, and follow the exchange of words.

In tandem, their training has sensitized them to the importance of giving thoughtful attention to the "forms" in which they express the "content" of their therapeutic intentions. By contrast, for patients it is the content of their experiences and communications that is of first importance, and the formal or structural properties of their experiences and communications are unlikely to be brought into focal awareness unless patients are encouraged by their therapists to focus their attention on them.

Like philosophers of art, I rely on the time-honored concept of "style" (Geller, 2005) as a shorthand way of referring to the complex interplay between the content or subject matter of a representation and the form or manner in which it is experienced and expressed. Clinical and research findings indicate that there are substantial differences in the styles in which therapists who practice the same type of therapy verbally and nonverbally communicate with their patients and strongly suggest that these stylistic differences have a significant effect in determining whether the use of a particular technique will be helpful to a patient, prove ineffective, or in the worst cases intensify a patient's suffering (Norcross, 2011).

I presume that well-educated therapists understand that, to be effective, therapeutic techniques need to be implemented in a style that is congruent with a particular patient's aesthetic preferences. For example, I believe they take into account the possibility that the declarative statement "You look sad today" might be experienced as an empathic failure by a patient who would have felt deeply understood if asked the question, "Are you feeling sad today?"

WHAT DOES IT MEAN TO CONDUCT PSYCHOTHERAPY CREATIVELY?

Cognitive-behavioral, psychoanalytic, and existential theorists have all described doing psychotherapy as a creative activity. There is no universally agreed-upon operational definition of creativity. The dominant approach has been to conceptualize creativity as a talent that supports the ability to flexibly consider original or unique and diverse solutions to problems, be they artistic, scientific, or practical. According to this definition, therapists are worthy of being thought of as creative if their technical choices honor the specificity of each new patient and if they are able to construct highly individualized case conceptualizations and treatment plans. Multiple readings of the essays to follow have strengthened my conviction that adopting an aesthetic perspective on therapy can enhance the creativity with which therapists do their work and that creativity is worthy of being regarded as one of the "facilitating human qualities" (Rogers, 1975) that render therapists capable of serving as agents of change.

To strengthen their own creative powers as therapists, each of the authors who contributed essays to this issue has seriously studied or practiced one or more of the traditional genres of art.

DANCE, PAINTING, AND PSYCHOTHERAPY

Dance is the creative art form that uses movement to express and communicate what a dancer knows or feels is meaningful, personal, and important to him or her (Geller, 1978). Wexler's memoir-like paper courageously narrates how first witnessing and then studying dance has contributed to her own healing and informs her efforts to honor the uniqueness of each patient. She candidly tells us that these experiences taught her that giving self-expression through movement to one's deepest fears and sadness can transform these painful experiential states into a source of power that mitigates against their wreaking havoc by remaining hidden.

Schwartz's narrative vividly takes a reader into her studio and describes the step-by-step process of creating and then naming her paintings to bring to life the parallels between the creative process and the challenges patients face when they try to identify, distinguish, and put into words ambiguous and unfamiliar subjective experiences.

Like evocative works of art, Schwartz's and Wexler's ideas about seeing and being seen stimulated me to think about the technical implications of the following questions: What do I visually convey to patients when I am listening and speaking? In what ways is my listening influenced by what I am seeing or not seeing? When is showing (e.g., gesturing or demonstrating) preferable to saying as a means of communicating my therapeutic intentions? How do visual images of having been seen by caregivers and authority figures from the past influence the ways in which my patients form visual percepts of my physical presence? What are the similarities and differences between "insights" that are the product of verbal thought and those that are discovered by sight? When is it advisable to choose facial expressions and expressive movements rather than words to communicate with my patients? Do my observational skills lag behind the development of my listening skills? Are there visual cues that reliably distinguish between silences that serve as resistances and those that are perhaps reflective of a newfound ability "to be alone in the presence of another" (Winnicott, 1958)? How much of what is potentially available for seeing in the therapeutic situation is "actually" seen and stored in long-term memory? In what ways can I train myself to realize the ideal of seeing with fresh and unbiased eyes? On what occasions do the visual and auditory aspects of the therapeutic dialogue compete for attention? What are the consequences of "the always present gap between words and seeing" (Berger, 1972, p. 7) for patients and therapists? I anticipate that systematic empirical studies of these questions will reveal that psychotherapy is as much a "looking cure" as it is a "talking cure," at least for some subtypes of patients.

ARCHITECTURE, INTERIOR DECORATION, AND PSYCHOTHERAPY

Provocative ideas about the vision-based questions listed above can be found in papers written by Pivnick and Jackson. At the center of Pivnick's emotion-charged essay are multiple stories that explore the ways in which her efforts to heal her own, her son's, and her patient's experiences of traumatic levels of grief have drawn inspiration from what she has learned about people's responses to architecture, music, painting, and literature. The conceptual starting point of Pivnick's essay is that an aesthetically informed perspective on therapy strengthens one's capacity to "find beauty amidst ugliness and pain." I would add the hypothesis that the positive sensory experiences that are aroused when one stands in the presence of and gazes upon beauty are similar to the sensory experiences that are aroused when one sees that one is being seen by an empathic therapist.

A central premise of Pivnick's and Jackson's chapters is that patients' pleasurable and unpleasurable sensory and perceptual reactions to the aesthetic qualities of the neighborhoods, buildings, and offices in which their therapies take place can either enhance or detract from the credibility and healing authority that they attribute to their therapists.

Two related lines of inquiry lend support to the hypothesis that the spaces therapists inhabit are pregnant with meanings that can potentially heighten or diminish their patients' confidence in their therapists' ability to be of help to them. First, there is increasing evidence that creating physical environments that are "psychologically supportive" (Ruga, 1989) facilitates the recovery of patients who are medically ill. Second, our research indicates that during the early stages of therapy patients create enduring internalized images of their therapists' offices and that these images have a decided effect on the outcome of therapy (Geller & Freedman, 2011).

Jackson's paper distinguishes between the challenges faced by therapists who are provided furnished offices by the organizations that employ them or are responsible for educating them and those faced by therapists who deliberately choose the neighborhoods, buildings, and offices in which to practice therapy. The former group must accommodate themselves to environments ranging from those that are inspiring, attractive, and original to those that are boring, hideous, and physically or psychologically uncomfortable.

Therapists of all persuasions are educated to offer their patients a "safe place" (Havens, 1989) that protects their privacy. But my inquiries suggest that very few are taught how to choose or create physical environments that support and reinforce their efforts to serve as agents of therapeutic change. Jackson's chapter can be read as a primer that instructs therapists on how to transform empty rooms into therapeutic environments. Visually imagine the architectural qualities and décor of the office in which you would ideally like to practice psychotherapy. Did your thought experiment take into account the color, textures, shapes, sizes, and placement of the furniture in this office? My patients and I both sit in matching Eames chairs. The Eames chair is both an iconic work of art and a multifunctional piece of furniture. Its construction accommodates a wide variety of sitting possibilities. You can recline in it, especially if you use the hassock that is positioned between the two chairs to rest your legs. You can crawl up in it, or you can sit upright. Eames lounge chairs also rotate, so that therapists and patients can exert greater control over where they look.

My patients' verbalized reactions to the Eames chairs in which they and I sit have ranged from seeming obliviousness to "it's a little too feng shui" to "I am reassured by seeing you have good taste and that you take sensual pleasure seriously." I welcome these comments as an opportunity to explore what patients find helpful or nonhelpful about my offerings. I similarly welcome the moments when patients see for the first time what has always been there to be seen in my office. I take these often surprise-filled moments as a sign that a patient is becoming more open to receiving the sensuous fullness of the therapeutic situation and as an opportunity to express curiosity about what else a patient does not see when it comes to the visible aspects of his or her daily life and interpersonal world.

PSYCHOTHERAPY AND THE LITERARY ARTS

For centuries, the art of storytelling has been used by shamans, clergymen, bards, novelists, and playwrights as an instrument of teaching and healing. Orlinsky's beautifully written paper contains many wise observations about the therapeutic value of well-told stories that were inspired by his rereading in his 80s a set of novels written by Lawrence Durrell (collectively known as *The Alexandria Quartet*) that had inspired him in his 20s. His paper reads like a prose poem that argues on behalf of empirically testable hypotheses that are echoed in several of the other papers included in this issue. The first is that cocreating coherent and meaningful narratives out of patients' autobiographical memories can serve multiple therapeutic functions. Theoretically, at one and the same time, therapists who strengthen their patients' ability to use the narrative format to tell the stories of their lives can support their sense of personal continuity, help them to understand how their past influences their current functioning, facilitate the activation of corrective emotional experiences, and set in motion the internalization processes that store in long-term memory functionally useful representations of these benignly influential experiences (Geller, 1987).

The second is that well-chosen metaphors that appeal to the senses and that convey multiple meanings simultaneously can serve therapeutic functions comparable to well-told stories. Most broadly stated, metaphors are figures of speech that describe one thing in terms of another. Therefore, metaphors, which themselves are products of the imagination, can be used to translate difficult-to-describe, amorphous, and/or transitory pleasurable and unpleasurable bodily sensations into distinctive, intelligible, and communicable subjective experiences (Geller, 1984).

Therapists have no objective way of gaining knowledge about the historical accuracy of the stories that patients tell about their lives. Therapists who subscribe to the view that therapy is a hermeneutic enterprise have given up the quest to gauge the accuracy of patients' stories about their past experiences or adjudicate among different interpretations for any particular event. Rather, they are concerned with cocreating with their patients "narrative truths" as opposed to unearthing "historical truths" (Spence, 1982). They are also committed to the view that narratives that are not historically accurate may, nevertheless, serve the therapeutic functions if they are self-consistent, coherent, and comprehensive. Orlinsky concludes his paper by recommending that therapists would be well advised to remember that narrative perspectives on the "same" event can vary widely.

MUSIC AND THERAPY

The psychological benefits of making and listening to music have been amply documented in a wide variety of cultures. There is also a considerable amount of literature on the salutary effects of various forms of music therapy (e.g., Clarkson & Geller, 1996) and the healing powers of music-based shamanic remedies (Assagioli, 1971). Steinfeld's and Johnson's essays are pioneering attempts to demonstrate the therapeutic value of thinking about the interactions that take place in mainstream forms of therapy through the lens of listening to and making music (see also Farber, 2017).

Steinfeld's paper focuses on the reasons why the sensuous pleasure of hearing the tonal qualities of a therapist's comforting voice can serve as an "instrument of healing." He and I are inclined to think that the sensorial effects of listening to a therapist whose vocal qualities are infused with compassion are similar to those that are evoked by listening to the deep notes laid down by an upright bassist. Both experiences are multisensory in nature. They are simultaneously heard and resonate or reverberate kinesthetically throughout the body. Perhaps because we listen with our muscles as well as with our ears, many patients report that they feel as if they are in the felt presence of their therapists when they recall internalized representations of the tonal qualities of their therapist's voice in between sessions and after termination (Geller & Farber, 1993).

Many aesthetic concepts are used as interpretive tools throughout this issue, none more so than the concept of rhythm. Viewing psychotherapy, as does Johnson, from the perspective of jazz brings into center stage the salutary consequences of rhythmizing the therapeutic dialogue and the improvisational skills that are required to accommodate to the communicative requirements of each patient. Most abstractly stated, musical rhythms refer to the regular recurrence or natural flow of related sounds through time. They are the plans or designs that embody or convey the principles of continuity, direction, unity, and order. So understood, the concept of rhythm offers an illuminating perspective on the reasons why the stability and reliability of weekly sessions of more or less fixed duration function like a scaffolding that invisibly supports the development and maintenance of a positive therapeutic alliance. For example, as sessions accumulate, their sequencing takes on a pattern that resembles rhythms that pulse with a regular beat; consequently, they can have an organizing influence on patients whose lives are otherwise chaotic or directionless.

A major theme that reverberates through Johnson's chapter is that therapists can bring more vitality, surprises, and individuality into their back-and-forth conversations with their patients if they develop improvisational skills comparable to those that guide the interactions between jazz musicians. I found his exploration of the linkages between the improvisational nature of playing jazz and therapists' responses to the unscripted and nonmanualized aspects of therapy, of which there are many, particularly instructive. For example, prescriptive therapy manuals provide therapists with very little guidance when it comes to deciding how to greet patients, how to interact with them in the waiting room, when to make and break eye contact (especially during silences of varying durations), when and how to initiate conversations about topics they would prefer to avoid, and how to bring a session to a natural conclusion. Like jazz musicians who play the same song in different styles, therapists have the responsibility of choosing between alternative styles of performing these unscripted tasks. Years of dedication and discipline may be required before a therapist acquires the improvisational skills to perform these tasks effortlessly.

Each patient brings to therapy interaction rhythms that manifest themselves in the ways in which they exchange the roles of listener and speaker (Geller, 1994). Consequently, technical expertise requires the capacity to flexibly adjust the intervals between listening and speaking to meet the needs of patients who are unable to synchronize their interaction rhythms with others.

A dialogue that is rhythmically synchronized with respect to the exchanging of the roles of listener and speaker has the effects of softening the bodily boundaries that separate the participants and stimulates a sense of bodily closeness. The interweaving of interaction rhythms can be deeply pleasurable or extremely threatening. Patients who are suffering from severe and characterologically based difficulties with intimacy are frightened by the bodily sensations that are aroused when the "distance" between them and their therapists is reduced by interaction rhythms that are tightly synchronized. Similarly, making sustained eye contact with a therapist whose gaze is infused with respect and compassion can stimulate a gratifying or frightening sense of bodily closeness whether or not patient and therapist ever touch in actuality.

Editing this volume has reinforced my belief that bringing an aesthetic perspective to bear on what we do as psychotherapists can contribute new and useable knowledge about the experiential learning that is mediated by the sensory and perceptual aspects of the therapeutic dialogue. For example, read in its entirety, this issue supports the hypothesis that comfortably making "eye contact" and establishing rhythmic synchronization of the therapeutic dialogue singly and in combination increase the likelihood that patients will benefit from the transformative powers of emotional contagion, imitative learning, and the processes of internalization.

It is my hope that the knowledge you gain from reading the essays that follow will prepare you to more creatively fulfill your responsibilities as a therapist.

REFERENCES

Ackerman, D. (1990). *A Natural History of the Senses*. New York, NY: Random House.

Assagioli, R. (1971). *Psychosynthesis: A Collection of Basic Writings*. New York, NY: Viking Press.

Berger, J. (1972). *Ways of Seeing*. London, UK: Penguin Books.

Farber, B.A. (2017). Becoming a more effective psychotherapist: Gaining wisdom and skills from creative others (writers, actors, musicians, and dancers). In L. Castonguay & C.E. Hill (Eds.), *How and Why Are Some Therapists Better Than Others: Understanding Therapist Effects* (pp. 215–231). Washington, DC: APA Books.

Clarkson, G., & Geller, J.D. (1996). The Bonny method from a psychoanalytic perspective: Insights from working with a psychoanalytic psychotherapist in a guided imagery and music series. *Arts in Psychotherapy* 23(4):311–319.

Geller, J.D. (1978). The body, expressive movement, and physical contact in psychotherapy. In J.L. Singer & K.S. Pope (Eds.), *The Power of Human Imagination* (pp. 347–378). New York, NY: Plenum Press.

————— (1984). Moods, feelings, and the process of affect formation. In L. Temoshok, C. Van Dyke, & L.S. Zegans (Eds.), *Emotions in Health and Illness: Applications to Clinical Practice* (pp. 171–186). Orlando, FL: Grune & Stratton.

————— (1987). The process of psychotherapy: Separation and the complex interplay among empathy, insight, and internalization. In J. Bloom-Feshbach & S. Bloom-Feshbach (Eds.), *The Psychology of Separation and Loss: Perspectives on Development, Life Transitions, and Clinical Practice* (pp. 459–514). San Francisco, CA: Jossey-Bass.

————— (1994). The psychotherapist's experience of interest and boredom. *Psychotherapy* 31(1):3–16.

————— (1998). What does it mean to practice psychotherapy scientifically? *Psychoanalysis and Psychotherapy* 15:187–215.

————— (2005). Style and its contribution to a patient-specific model of therapeutic technique. *Psychotherapy: Theory, Research, Practice, Training* 42:469–482. https://doi.org/10.1037/0033-3204.42.4.469

————— (2013). Courage and the Effective Practice of Psychotherapy. Unpublished manuscript.

————— & Farber, B.A. (1993). Factors influencing the process of internalization in psychotherapy. *Psychotherapy Research* 3(3):166–180. https://doi.org/10.1080/10503309312331333769

————— & Freedman, N. (2011). Representations of the therapeutic dialogue and the post-termination phase of psychotherapy. In N. Freedman, M. Hurvich, R. Ward (Eds.), J.D. Geller, & J. Hoffenberg (Collaborators), *Another Kind of Evidence* (pp. 55–66). London, UK: Karnac Books.

Havens, L. (1989). *A Safe Place: Laying the Groundwork of Psychotherapy*. Cambridge, MA: Harvard University Press.

Jackson, D. (2018). Aesthetics and the psychotherapist's office. *Journal of Clinical Psychology* 74:249–260.

Johnson, D.R. (2018). Playing off the beat: Applying the jazz paradigm to psychotherapy. *Journal of Clinical Psychology* 74:233–238.

Kandel, E.R. (2012). *The Age of Insight*. New York, NY: Random House.

Kant, I. (1966). *Critique of Judgment* (J.H. Bernard, Trans.). New York, NY: Hafner. (Original work published 1790.)

Kohut, H. (1957). Observations on the psychological functions of music. *Journal of the American Psychoanalytic Association* 5:389–407.

Norcross, J.C. (Ed.). (2011). *Psychotherapy Relationships That Work* (2nd ed.). New York, NY: Oxford University Press.

Orlinksy, D.E. (2018). Lessons from literature for psychotherapy practice and research. *Journal of Clinical Psychology* 74:213–217.

Pivnick, B.A. (2018). Behind the lines: Toward an aesthetic framework for psychoanalytic psychotherapy. *Journal of Clinical Psychology* 74:218–232.

Rogers, C. (1975). Empathic: An unappreciated way of being. *The Counseling Psychologist* 5:2–10.

Ruga, W. (1989). Designing for the six senses. *Journal of Health Care Interior Design* 1:29–34.

Schwartz, K.M. (2018). Making unformulated experience real through painting: Painting and psychoanalytic psychotherapy practice as two ways of making sense. *Journal of Clinical Psychology* 74:239–248.

Spence, D.P. (1982). *Narrative Truth and Historical Truth: Meaning and Interpretation in Psychoanalysis*. New York, NY: Norton.

Steinfeld, M. (2018). The acoustics of therapeutic subjectivity and their impact on the resonance of mutual recognition. *Journal of Clinical Psychology* 74:261–268.

Stern, D.N. (2010). *Forms of Vitality: Exploring Dynamic Experience in Psychology and the Arts*. New York, NY: Oxford University Press.

Wexler, J. (2018). Therapeutic action and aesthetic experience: Resonance and reorganization. *Journal of Clinical Psychology* 74:208–212.

Winnicott, D.W. (1958). The capacity to be alone. *International Journal of Psychoanalysis* 39:416–420.

CHAPTER 20

Psychotherapy Through the Lens of Cinema

[J.D. Geller (2020). *Journal of Clinical Psychology* 76:1423–1437.]

ABSTRACT: The primary aim of this issue of the *Journal of Clinical Psychology: In Session* is to demonstrate the myriad ways in which the viewing and discussion of movies can be used to serve therapeutic and educational purposes. It collects together eight essays, an empirical study, and a film script that offer shifting perspectives on questions that are of interest to all therapists, irrespective of their theoretical persuasions: What can be learned about the transformative powers of psychotherapy by studying how filmmakers inspire deeply felt and memorable experiences in their audiences? What are the beneficial and detrimental effects of the ways in which psychotherapists and their patients have been portrayed in films and TV programs? What psychological functions can be served by recommending that a patient watch a particular film? When is it advisable to inquire about the characters in films who have served as the role models that played an important role in the formation of a patient's sense of self? Can films that portray what is best about human beings inspire life-changing forms of imitative learning? What roles can the viewing and discussion of films play in the education of therapists?

> *The cinema is the truth*
> *twenty-four times per second.*
> —Jean-Luc Godard

INTRODUCTION

During the 20th century, psychotherapy and film both exerted a deep and pervasive influence on the way we perceive reality and ourselves. It may be more than a coincidence that Freud's ushering in of the modern era of psychotherapy and Edison's invention of "motion pictures" took place in the last years of the 19th century. The primary aim of this issue of the *Journal of Clinical Psychology: In Session* is to encourage readers to think systematically about the therapeutic and educational benefits of the making and the witnessing of films. This focus was inspired by the following question: Can scholarly studies of the making and "seeing" of films contribute new and usable knowledge about the potentially transformative powers of psychotherapy? In many respects, it is intended to complement and expand upon the knowledge contained in a previous volume of *In Session* that I guest-edited in 2018 (Geller, 2018), one that was devoted to the exploration of the transformative powers of the aesthetic experiences stimulated by dance, painting, music, literature, and poetry. In contrast, cinema is a kind of "pan" art. "It can use, incorporate, engulf virtually any other art: the novel, poetry, theater, painting, sculpture, dance, music, architecture" (Sontag, 1966, p. 245).

To produce this volume, I solicited essays from three psychoanalysts (William Fried, Danielle Knafo, and Sidney Philips) who had previously published works that integrated aesthetic concepts into their theorizing about psychotherapy. I also solicited contributions from David Johnson, the founder of an international network of drama therapists, and from pioneering "cinematherapists" (Christine Eppler and Jen Hutchings, Shea M. Dunham and Shannon M. Dermer, Ryan Niemiec and David Roe). Most broadly stated, "cinematherapy" refers to the strategic selection of films that therapists ask their patients to view and discuss with them based on the belief that this clinical strategy holds the promise of providing patients with enduringly beneficial therapeutic experiences. I was deeply gratified when they all agreed to participate in this project.

The volume also includes the script of a film that Barry Farber and I made along with several clinical psychology graduate students. It portrays an imaginary conversation between three patients who by chance meet in their therapists' waiting room. They discuss the typical dilemmas and confusion encountered by first-time therapy patients. Finally, a last-minute contribution was offered by Barry Farber and two of his current graduate students—a report on their survey of which television series and movies a diverse group of therapists were watching during the early weeks of the coronavirus pandemic.

The articles gathered in this volume vary in their substance and style, but they are all premised on the conviction that cinema can achieve a seemingly inexhaustible number of goals. This art form can do so because there are no limits on what filmmakers can do creatively given the myriad combined effects of visual images, dialogue, music, sound, lighting, special effects, and editing techniques.

Although movies are designed to appeal to the ears and to arouse bodily sensations as well as visual images, in everyday conversations people generally restrict themselves to using the verbs "seeing" and "watching" as a shorthand way of referring to the multisensory nature of experiencing films. We have been linguistically conditioned to speak about movies as if they were a purely visual medium of communication. In keeping with contemporary usage and risking oversimplification, I will limit myself to the vocabulary of vision in my efforts to provide a context for the papers that follow this introduction.

The articles need not be read in the sequence they are presented. Like a film editor, I experimented with arranging and rearranging the placement of each piece with different goals in mind. Because the script of the film *Ready When You Are: Answering Your Questions About Psychotherapy* addresses the basic question, What is therapy and how does it work? I finally settled on making it the opening paper in this issue.

Before presenting the articles, I will first describe the developmental origins of my scholarly interest in forging connections between cinema and psychotherapy and then offer a series of combined autobiographical and science-based responses to the different themes addressed in each of the articles. They can be read before or after you have read the articles themselves: You may not wish to be influenced beforehand by my take on them. According to my brother Mark (personal communication, 2019), when Jean Luc Goddard was asked whether a film should always have a beginning, middle, and end, he supposedly said "Yes, but not necessarily in that order."

A PERSONAL FILM HISTORY

Movies play a variably important, shaping influence on people's lives. For some, like myself, movies matter a great deal. I am what Sontag (1966) called a "cinephile"—a lover of films.

In seminars and in supervision when appropriate, I invite student therapists to think about their own development from the perspective of the films that were personally important to them at different stages of their lives. To model for them what can be learned by remembering and sharing remembrances of the film characters that played a formative role in their lives during childhood, adolescence, and young adulthood, I tell them my history of "going to the movies." An abbreviated version follows:

I have been going to the movies, as often as I could, ever since I was a boy. When I was 9, in 1948, and none of us had a television set, every chance I got on Saturdays I walked from my basement apartment (with a bag filled with salami sandwiches and Devil Dogs) to the RKO movie theater on Tremont Avenue in the Bronx. The theater was the most beautiful and safest place in my life. It provided me with a sanctuary, carrying me away from the urban decay of my ghetto neighborhood to places I never before imagined. The darkness and anonymity of the theater provided me with the last remaining place in which I could soothe my anxiety-ridden body by sucking my thumb without being punished or humiliated. The comfort I felt sitting in soft and supportive chairs that felt just right for the size of my body, eight to 10 rows in front of the vast screen, in nonthreatening darkness, allowed me to pay sensuously receptive attention to the films I loved. Watching films in that safe, evocative environment opened me up to being moved emotionally and aesthetically by the people, places, and things that were being projected onto my eyes and ears.

For 25 cents, the weekend show at the RKO theater offered two feature-length films, a newsreel, cartoons, coming attractions, and a serial that always ended with a suspense-filled "cliff-hanger"—would the explorer be swallowed up by the quicksand? For several hours each time I went to the Saturday matinees as a very frightened boy, I experienced the bliss of self-forgetfulness. Like dreaming, watching movies freed me from the forms of instrumental modes of knowing that are required to cope with the practical realities of daily life. The safety I felt enabled me to step outside of myself to give the fullness of my attention to the 50-times-larger-than-life images of heroes and villains on the silver screen. Their stories and preoccupations, not my own, filled my field of attention.

When I was deeply absorbed in a film, I had the unique experiences of temporarily forgetting that I was watching a pretend reality. Words like "transfixed" and "enthralled" (Geller, 1994) come close to capturing the essential quality of my emotional involvement with films such as *Bambi* (1942), *Pinocchio* (1940), and *The Boy with Green Hair* (1948) that I saw as a boy. I am told that I jumped out of my seat and shouted at the screen "Don't hurt him" when the boy whose hair had suddenly turned green—an orphan whose parents had died in World War II—was being bullied by the malicious kids in his neighborhood. I offer this anecdote as evidence of the power of films to evoke what Coleridge (1967) called "willing suspension of disbelief" and what we now call an "immersive experience." In other words, in childhood, as in a dream, I experienced these films more as a participant in the action than as a detached observer.

The movies of my youth provided me with much more than temporary relief from my dysfunctional fears. Some of my earliest role models were first encountered as the fictional characters that I saw and listened to on Saturday afternoons sitting in the RKO theater. I wanted to grow up to become like the athletes depicted in biographical films (e.g., *The Babe Ruth Story*, 1948), the "good guys" in Westerns (e.g., *High Noon*, 1952), and the heroic soldiers in films about World War II (e.g., *The Wild Blue Yonder*, 1951). On the other hand, I dreaded becoming a liar like *Pinocchio* (1940) or a coward like Henry Fielding in the film *The Red Badge of Courage* (1951). Most of all, I wanted to dance with the athleticism, grace, and rhythm Gene Kelly displayed in MGM musicals (e.g., *On the Town*, 1949; *An American in Paris*, 1951; *Singin' in the Rain*, 1952).

I am inclined to think that treating imaginary characters portrayed in films as if they were real people whose actions could be described and explained might be one of the processes that facilitate observational and imitative learning. I have wondered if functional magnetic resonance imaging studies would show that the brain activity that occurs when we view characters in films with whom we feel connected is similar to the activation of the motor neurons that take place when we are empathetically engaged in in vivo interactions.

As a highly impressionable adolescent, I came under the influence of James Dean's iconic embodiment of virility, alienation, and "being cool" in the film *Rebel Without a Cause* (1955). I self-consciously emulated the way he smoked cigarettes, dressed, and expressed his emotions. In my teens, I also had my first kiss on the balcony of the Liberty Movie Theater. Seeing the lovers kiss in a movie theater in the Academy Award–winning film *Roma* (2018) reminded me that teenagers of my generation went to the movies to "make out" because we had no other place that ensured our privacy.

My peers and I, whether queer or nonqueer, grew up during an era when Hollywood films did not include gay and lesbian characters whom one, whether straight or gay, might want to emulate and identify with. These absences are of more than academic interest because, whether we were heterosexual, homosexual, or not describable by such categorical labels, our views about romantic love and sexuality were probably heavily influenced by the ways these universal themes were portrayed in the movies we saw as adolescents.

The Hollywood film depictions of sexuality that I saw as a lust-filled adolescent were censored by a rigidly enforced set of moral guidelines about what was acceptable and unacceptable content—colloquially known as the Hays Code (1934–1968). Until it was replaced by a less restrictive censorship system in

1968, kisses were not supposed to last more than 3 seconds, and even husbands and wives had to sleep in separate beds. It was not until the Holocaust film *The Pawnbroker* (Lumet, 1964) that fully exposed breasts were to be seen on the silver screen. Thankfully, the European films that I began seeing as a college freshman provided me with more accurate images of "making love," the naked body, and what it means to grapple with the developmental tasks of late adolescence and early adulthood.

Mine is the first generation of college-educated American filmgoers to regularly see what we called in the late 1950s "foreign films." As a college student in New York City (1956–1960), my friends and I eagerly anticipated the arrival of the steady flow of "serious" European films that were weekly presented in the "art houses" of Manhattan. The directors Bergman, Bresson, Fellini, Godard, Rosselini, and Truffaut were our intellectual heroes. They provided us with our "sacred texts." We loved intellectually debating about the meanings of their complex and elusive films.

During the tumultuous period remembered as the 60s (although it extended well into the 70s), my friends and I eagerly anticipated the next film you had to watch from an extraordinary group of American film directors. Within the confines of Hollywood film industry, such directors as Robert Altman, John Cassavetes, Francis Ford Coppola, Sidney Lumet, Stanley Kubrick, Alan Pakula, and Martin Scorsese produced films that were as personal, realistic, and brilliantly realized as the non-American films of the 50s and 60s that inspired them.

Although we admired their work, I do not include references to their films or those that I saw in the years that followed in my history of going to the movies because I believe that in adulthood, once one has achieved a fairly cohesive and continuous sense of self, films may no longer have the power to inspire deep levels of imitative learning. Therefore, I conclude my autobiographical sketch by telling students about my reactions to rewatching the film *David and Lisa* (1962). I saw it for the first time when I was a 2nd-year clinical psychology graduate student and trying to decide whether to pursue a career as a psychotherapist. During the final scenes of the film, David, a hospitalized adolescent, overcomes his dreaded fear that being touched could kill him by holding hands with another patient—a psychotic girl. The first time I saw the film, I found it inspiring, and it reinforced my interest in becoming a psychotherapist. Rewatching it as an elder, I found it disappointing. I found its portrayal of the curative powers of psychotherapy naive, sentimental, inauthentic, and pollyannaish.

I conclude my narrative by describing this change of opinion for two reasons: First, I want to impress upon my students the developmental implications of the fact that they probably saw many more "realistic" images of different types of cinematic depictions of therapeutic "cures" before choosing to become psychotherapists than I did. The cures that I witnessed growing up were almost always brought about by the recovery of repressed traumatic experiences and the accompanying release of a flood of emotions. Alfred Hitchcock's film *Spellbound* (1945) is perhaps the classic Hollywood portrayal of the early Freudian cathartic method of therapy. By contrast, the mass media have provided my students, beginning in the 1990s, with a proliferating number of films that present less theatrical or melodramatic versions of what is healing about psychotherapy.

My second intent is to challenge students to ask themselves, What was the first film I saw that portrayed what happens in psychotherapy? How old was I when I saw this film? How was the character of the patient portrayed? How was the therapist depicted? What type of therapy did he or she practice and in what context (an office, a hospital)? What actors and actresses played the roles of patient and therapist?

PATIENT-INITIATED CONVERSATIONS ABOUT FILMS

Most films are quickly forgotten. But I believe that each of us can bring to mind a movie or a character or scene in a movie that we cannot forget and want to remember.

How often have your patients spontaneously recalled the thoughts, feelings, memories, and fantasies aroused in them by watching a film that they saw during different eras in their lives?

When I am trying to advance a patient's understanding of the cultural influences that have shaped his or her sense of self and values, I am apt to ask the following types of questions: Who were your childhood heroes and heroines? What characteristics did they share? What about them did you wish to emulate and identify with?

Like me, many have discovered that some of their earliest idealized role models were first encountered as fictional characters in films. This finding has reinforced my inclination to ask patients, "Which movies and movie characters provided you with images of who you hoped to become or dreaded becoming?" and, "Were your initial expectations about how therapy works influenced by a movie or a TV program?"

I welcome the times when patients lead us into discussions about remembrances of the films that have personal importance to them. I listen to their descriptions and explanations of a character's actions as if he or she were a real person. I especially value the times when patients' remembrances of a movie or television portrayal of a psychotherapist or of psychotherapy serve as a point of departure for opening up conversations about their uncertainties about therapy, their fears about who I am, and

their satisfactions and disappointments in therapy. The following are some examples that have proven productive: "Are you
going to talk more than Woody Allen's psychoanalyst in *Annie
Hall*?" "My last therapist was a woman. Like Barbara Streisand
in *Prince of Tides*, I found her too sexy and seductive—so I
quit." "I wish you were more like the therapist Robin Williams
played in *Good Will Hunting*." "Your office looks a lot like that
of the therapist in *Ordinary People*, maybe a little neater, but
not too much." "Thank God you are not as narcissistic as the
asshole therapist in *What about Bob?*" "*Do* you talk about me
with a supervisor like Dr. Melfi does in *The Sopranos?*" "I think
you used to look like the therapist Gabriel Byrne portrayed in
In Treatment." The moments when patients voluntarily make
such comparisons obviously lend themselves to advancing the
goals of exploratory psychotherapy. As the next section reveals,
cinematherapists do not wait for their patients to speak about
watching a particular film but rather recommend that they see
specific films for therapeutic purposes.

CINEMATHERAPY AND THE PROMOTION OF CHARACTER STRENGTHS

There is accumulating evidence that, across the life span, reading literary fiction promotes the development of the psychological capabilities that underlie the ability to infer and understand
others' thoughts and feelings (i.e., "theory of mind"; Premack &
Woodruff, 1978). In a similar vein, since the 1920s, "bibliother-
apists" have been exploring the hypothesis that having patients
read serious novels can strengthen their capacity to empathize
with the thoughts and feelings of others. Still more recently,
so-called "cinema therapists" (Berg-Cross et al., 1990) have
explored the therapeutic possibilities of strategically selecting

films for patients to view and discuss in therapy as a means to realize specific therapeutic goals. I invited pioneering practitioners of cinematherapy to contribute essays to this volume.

The promotion of "character strengths" and "virtues" is a primary goal of therapists who align themselves with the aspirations of the positive psychology movement (e.g., Seligman, 2002). To this end, as his paper ("Character strengths cinematherapy: Using movies to inspire change, meaning, and cinematic elevation") illustrates, Niemiec has been developing a rigorous approach to selecting films for patients that inspire identifications with heroic protagonists who personify the best of human beings. Like mine, Niemiec's theorizing about the transformative powers of movies draws heavily on the fundamental precept of Bandura's (1977) social learning theory, according to which "most human behavior is learned observationally through modeling. From observing others one forms an idea of how new behaviors are performed, and on later occasions, this information serves as a guide to action" (p. 22). There is compelling evidence that, long after termination, many former patients continue to benefit from therapy by recalling and engaging in "deferred imitation" (Piaget, 1954) of how their therapist listened to and spoke to them (Geller, 2006a; Geller & Freedman, 2011).

A primary aim of Niemiec's approach to cinematherapy is to offer guidance to therapists who wish to use movie portrayals of character strengths and virtuous actions to engender "cinematic elevation" (the inspiration to do good) and "cinematic admiration" (the motivation to improve oneself) in their patients. Stirring images of the character strength of courage, in all its guises, have appeared in hundreds of mainstream Hollywood films and TV programs. The following scene from *The Wizard of Oz* (1939) may be the most iconic and well-remembered dialogue about courage in Hollywood history:

COWARDLY LION:	Courage! What makes a king out of a slave? Courage! What makes the flag on the mast to wave? Courage! What makes the elephant charge his tusk in the misty mist, or the dusky dusk? What makes the musk-rat guard his musk? Courage! *What have they got that I ain't got?*

DOROTHY, SCARECROW, TIN WOODSMAN: Courage!

COWARDLY LION:	You can say that again! Huh?

Because there is an abundance of film portrayals of courage, one can take the particularities of a patient's life history into account when selecting films that tell the stories of protagonists who courageously overcame the fears, obstacles, and hardships that might have prevented them from realizing their goals. For example, I encourage closeted gay young men who are bereft of positive role models to watch *Moonlight* (2016) because it offers an inspiring example of the courage it takes to face and deal with the vulnerabilities that must be overcome to accept tenderness, sensuality, and one's sexual preferences. Encouraging patients to see R-rated, explicit depictions of sexuality also sends the message that the therapist is prepared to candidly talk about their sexual experiences and their erotic fantasies and strivings.

Eppler and Hutching's paper ("The use of cinematherapy to illustrate systemic resilience") focuses primarily on the use of cinematherapy to promote a character strength valued by therapists of all persuasions—resilience. Like the "fortitude" aspect of the overall concept of courage (Geller, 2014), resilience is a character strength that enhances one's capacity to face and deal with physical and psychological events that undermine one's sense of safety and security. An essential quality of resilience is the capacity to bounce back at least as strong as before after being knocked down by adversity and significant sources of stress.

The fundamental premise of Eppler and Hutching's paper is that the development of resilience plays an especially salient role in the psychotherapy of families whose members are dealing with financial crises, failures, disappointments, and serious illness and that this goal can be realized by integrating the viewing and discussion of films such as *Little Miss Sunshine* (2006) into the practice of systemic family therapy. I share their view that this film recommends itself for this purpose because it portrays, with a sense of humor, a family that remains calm and perseveres during multiple crises and setbacks. I believe that laughter is healing and that films that are lighthearted, playful, witty, and sometimes just silly can reduce unwanted and painful emotions such as depression and anxiety and/or encourage patients to pay more attention to and enjoy previously avoided positive emotions. In his book *Anatomy of an Illness*, literary editor and critic Norman Cousins (1979) reported that he laughed his way back to health by viewing the silent comedies of his youth while he was recuperating from a serious and poorly understood illness.

For purposes of classification and generalization, movies are viewed as examples of different genres. The most familiar genres are action films, comedies, dramas, horror movies, mysteries, romances, and thrillers. Most adult filmgoers are likely to be familiar with these genres and with subgenres such as science fiction/horror films, of which *Jurassic Park* is a prime example. A new subgenre has been added to the list—dramedies, which integrate comedy and drama. *Fleabag* (2016–2019) is a critically acclaimed dramedy. I anticipate that sometime in the future I will recommend seeing it to a patient who has yet to achieve the capacity to experience ambivalence and tends to alternate discontinuously between experiencing pleasurable and painful feelings. The message I will want them to take away from watching this serious and hilarious series is that it is possible to love and to hate a person with whom one can make a lasting commitment to being with.

CINEMATHERAPY AS AN ADJUNCTIVE TREATMENT FOR AFRICAN AMERICAN COUPLES

Failures of love rank near the top of the list of reasons people seek the help of therapists. Much of our work is devoted to helping patients who feel they are not capable of highly loving, sexually satisfying, and intimate relationships. There is an emerging consensus that therapeutic interventions are more likely to be effective in helping patients overcome these problems-in-living if they are framed in ways that honor the specificity of each patient's needs and resources.

In keeping with this conviction, the central thesis of Dunham and Dermer's paper ("Cinematherapy with African American couples") is that therapists would be well advised to take into account such contextual factors as race, ethnicity, gender, socioeconomic status, and religion when selecting films for their patients to see. They illustrate how they apply this methodological ideal by integrating movies featuring African American storylines, actors, and characters into the psychotherapy of African American couples.

Their search of APA PsycInfo revealed that there were no other cinematherapy articles that focused on meeting the culture-specific needs of African American clients. Equally noteworthy is the fact that very few films have given center stage to Black men and women loving each other in emotionally mature and intimate ways. There are still fewer portrayals of loving, intimate, and mature relationships between biracial heterosexual couples or the loves shared by Black homosexual men or women. The paucity of films depicting loving relationships between African American couples is of importance because, more than any other art form, movies provide us with role models of the person we hope to become or dread becoming.

I have asked my middle-aged gay and lesbian clients some version of the question, What was it like growing up and never seeing the realities you were confronting on a daily basis in the movies or in TV programs? Their first response has invariably been some version of "it was awful" or "it sucked." A closeted male psychotherapist-patient of mine went on to say, "Because I didn't see any realistic portrayals of who I was or hoped to become, I had to invent myself. I'm sure the stereotypical ways in which gay men were portrayed in movies like *Boys in the Band* had a detrimental effect on my self-image. I'm a poster boy for internalized homophobia." A serious and very ironically funny man, he paraphrased what Alvy Singer, Woody Allen's alter ego in *Annie Hall,* tells his psychoanalyst: "I'm going to give you a year, and if you don't help me come out, I'm going to Lourdes to begin our first of many discussions about the limitations of psychotherapy."

CINEMA AND A PSYCHOANALYTICALLY INFORMED FRAME

Two years ago, I encouraged a 30-something visual artist who had been raped as a teenager to watch the film *Frida* (2002). *Frida* is a critically acclaimed film biography of the life of Frida Kahlo. Like my patient, Kahlo was a painter. Like my patient, Kahlo was married to an older and professionally successful man. Like my patient, Kahlo turned to creativity to cope with the agony of chronic pain. I was therefore not surprised when my patient deeply identified with Kahlo and told me that viewing the film empowered her to take her career as an artist more seriously.

I was, therefore, delighted when William Fried chose this film to demonstrate his psychoanalytically informed approach to close reading and interpreting the themes that can be discovered in films. Fried's essay (*"Frida*: Portrait of a self") is rooted in a tradition that dates back to the early 1960s, when psychoanalysts began to explore how close readings of films could deepen their understanding of what it means to be a human being. In it, he builds upon the interpretative skills and insights he brought to bear on analyzing 13 different films in his 2017 book, *Critical Flicker Fusion: Psychoanalysis at the Movies*. Fried's approach to discovering the underlying meanings that could be discovered in these films, like the analysis of the filmed representation of Frida Kahlo's trauma-filled life, is based on two fundamental premises and departs from the psychoanalytic tradition of regarding films as autobiographical documents that can be used to analyze the unconscious sources of their authors' personalities.

The first premise is that there are clinically important similarities between close readings of literary texts and films and the form and content of the verbal and nonverbal aspects of the conversations that take place during therapeutic sessions. The second is that creativity can play an important role in healing the ravages of traumatic experiences.

My students and I are still learning from and debating about our idiosyncratic interpretations of Bergman's masterpiece, *Persona* (1966). The principal characters in *Persona* are two women bound together in a passionate, agonized relationship. Elizabeth is a famous actress who voluntarily renounced her career by choosing to remain mute. Alma is a nurse who has been assigned to care for Elizabeth at an isolated house by Elizabeth's psychiatrist. During the course of the film, Alma, who longs to identify with Elizabeth, involuntarily and painfully grows progressively more insecure and vulnerable while Elizabeth mysteriously becomes stronger, though still refusing to speak.

Bergman's film makes visible and audible the ways in which thoughts, feelings, and memories flow through the privacy of consciousness from moment to moment. Therefore, it is one of the tools I can use to teach students how to think about the connections between conscious, preconscious, and unconscious modes of symbolizing experience. What makes the film so difficult to decipher is that Bergman provides few clues as to whether he is showing us what Elizabeth is experiencing or what Alma is experiencing. *Persona* has proven to be an excellent investigatory tool when it comes to exploring such questions as these: What cues enable us to determine whether what we are seeing is actually taking place or is a hallucination, fantasy, or vision? And what are the challenges of deeply empathizing with another's suffering and the dangers of "vicarious traumatization?" In some cases, *Persona* has stimulated discussions about the dynamic tension between striving for intimacy and striving for autonomy. In others, its viewing has led to a discussion about the challenges of differentiating objective reality and fantasy. In still others, it has challenged students who identify with different theoretical perspectives on therapy to come to terms with the realization that there are multiple plausible explanations of what is really happening on the screen.

Based on previous experience, I was not surprised when none of the well-educated clinical psychology doctoral students in this year's seminar (a practicum in psychodynamic psychotherapy) knew who Ingmar Bergman was or had seen any of his films. This fact reconfirmed for me the validity of Paul Simon's (2011) prophetic lyric, "Every generation throws a hero up the pop charts," and inspired me to search for exceptions to this generalization.

FILMS AND THE EDUCATION OF PSYCHOTHERAPISTS

For many generations, educators from diverse fields have exploited the pedagogical uses of films to teach their students a wide variety of skills.

There currently exists a treasure trove of films that can make valuable contributions to the education of psychotherapists. Gabbard and Gabbard (1999) reported that, as of the end of the 20th century, there already existed more than 400 theatrically released American films that included scenes depicting mental health professionals at work.

Snake Pit (1948) was the first film I saw that influenced my understanding of what it means to "go crazy" or to be a psychotherapist. Although I was only 10, I can still vaguely recall black-and-white images of the kind doctor Leo Genn portrayed in an otherwise very disturbing film. Its central character is a psychotically delusional woman who is hospitalized in an "insane asylum" that treats only female patients. It wasn't until 1957 that I saw a second film that portrayed a psychotherapy relationship, *The Three Faces of Eve*. Joanne Woodward won an Academy Award for her portrayal of Eve, a woman who suffered from severe headaches, blackouts, and a multiple personality disorder. Her psychiatrist, Dr. Luther, is portrayed by Lee J. Cobb. He uses hypnosis to help her recall a traumatic event in her childhood—being forced to kiss the dead corpse of her beloved grandmother—which leads to her eventual cure. I did not like him. And it was not until I saw the film *David and Lisa* in 1962 that I once again encountered a film portrayal of a therapist I admired and would want to be my therapist.

During the era when I was learning to be a therapist, Hollywood films tended to portray therapists in either misleading or unflattering ways. For example, in Mel Brooks's widely seen film *High Anxiety* (1977), they were portrayed as farcically inept buffoons, and in Woody Allen's Academy Award–winning film *Annie Hall* (1977), they were portrayed as caricatures of the silent psychoanalyst. The consensus among the midcareer therapists that I have interviewed is that the first Hollywood film that came close to accurately representing what happens in therapy was *Ordinary People* (1980).

Although made more than 40 years ago, the scenes depicting Dr. Berger, portrayed by Judd Hirsch, are still widely considered to be a fairly accurate portrayal of what type of therapeutic "presence" (Johnson, 2020) is required to be of help to adolescent patients suffering from a posttraumatic stress disorder and survivor guilt. In it, Dr. Berger works with Conrad, who has recently been discharged from a 4-month stay in a hospital following a suicide attempt.

During the past 20 years, Hollywood film portrayals of psychotherapy have become more numerous and more realistic. In tandem, the once vilified and "vulgar" medium of television has been transformed into a serious art form by the production of serialized, hour-long dramas about flawed and morally compromised characters. One much-discussed example is *The Sopranos* (1999–2007), which, over the course of 6 seasons and 86 episodes—the equivalent of 25 movies—tells open-ended stories about the development of its characters over time and includes many scenes in which Dr. Laura Melfi does psychotherapy with the Mafia boss Tony Soprano or consults with her supervisor about the emotional, technical, and ethical challenges that arise when treating a dangerous and criminal man. It is widely credited as ushering in the "golden age of TV." Equally groundbreaking is the series *In Treatment* (2008–2010), which portray the beginning, middle, and endings of actual therapy sessions. Both these shows are particularly suitable vehicles for teaching students about so-called countertransference reactions and how difficult it is to do the work of therapy competently and ethically.

DOCUMENTARY FILMS AS EDUCATIONAL TOOLS

Because documentary films represent reality with seemingly greater verisimilitude than any other medium, they lend themselves to being used explicitly for instructional purposes. Since the film series was made available in 1965, successive generations of therapists have benefitted from watching and discussing the "Gloria film" (*Three Approaches to Psychotherapy,* Shostrom, 1965), in which Albert Ellis, Carl Rogers, and Fritz Perls treated the same woman. Furthermore, thanks to digital technology, today's student therapists can watch videos depicting such highly influential therapists as Aaron T. Beck, Milton Erikson, Otto Kernberg, Marsha Linehan, Martin Seligman, Derald Wing Sue, Virginia Satir, and Irvin Yalom dealing with a wide variety of patient populations and therapeutic issues.

In parallel, because of advances in digital technology, student therapists can now unobtrusively film their sessions with their patients and present their work to the supervisors in this medium of communication. I dreaded presenting my work to supervisors who demanded that I reproduce verbatim accounts of my therapy sessions. Many of my students have told me that once they get over the discomfort of being so exposed and unmediated, being freed of the responsibility of having to remember what was said and heard deepens their ability to give their patients their undivided attention.

I invite my students to watch the Gloria film with the following question in mind: Do my feelings about the "styles" (Geller, 2005) in which Ellis, Perls, and Rogers conduct therapy influence my judgment about their competence and the validity of their theories of therapy? What students discover is that their judgment about the expertise of each of these therapists is heavily influenced by their stylistic and aesthetic preferences. For example, those that admire Ellis' irreverence and the vulgarity of his communicative style tend to be attracted to his cognitive-behavioral theory of therapy, whereas those that find him repugnant tend to be highly critical about his theorizing.

Comparing the conversations that take place in the Gloria film with and without sound lends itself to studying the complex interplay between the verbal and nonverbal aspects of the therapeutic dialogue. Watching the Gloria sessions as if they were silent films makes salient the visual appearance of the participants' facial expressions, gestures, and postures. This strategy is ideally suited to expanding and refining student therapists' observational skills, which, in my experience, tend to lag behind the development of their listening skills.

Like films, dreams primarily express emotional experiences in the language of visual images and have frequently been analogized to "the movies in our minds." To promote the visual literacy of my students, I use this comparison as a rationale for encouraging students to watch films, such as Buñuel's *That Obscure Object of Desire* (1977), as if they were dreaming them. Buñuel's film has served me well in my efforts in psychotherapy seminars to promote the development of the observational skills required to maximize conscious awareness of the information presented to the eyes. In his autobiography, Buñuel (2013) tells us that halfway through creating the film, he fired the actress who was portraying the lead actor's object of desire and, rather than abandon the project, substituted a new actress who looked very similar. He then instructed the actor who was portraying her lover to act as if he did not know that two different women were playing the same role in his life. Strikingly, 70% of the students with whom I have viewed this film have failed to perceive that Buñuel used two different women to play the same role. The fact that they did not see what could be seen has proven to be a useful way of teaching student therapists about the importance of paying nuanced attention to the nonlinguistic aspects of the therapeutic dialogue and the blinding influence of transference-based perceptions. In other words, I have used Bunuel's film to illustrate the phenomenon social scientists call "inattentional blindness" (Chabris & Simons, 2009). This often-replicated phenomenon takes place when visually distinctive or unusual and unexpected events appear right where one is looking but are not seen. The well-educated therapist knows that he or she is not immune to the errors of perception that take place when unexpected events appear right where the eyes are looking but go unnoticed.

FILM AND PSYCHOTHERAPY TRAINING PROGRAMS

Recommending that student therapists watch a film for educational purposes within the context of supervision is one thing. Of a very different order of things is creating an academically based psychotherapy program in which films are accorded the same degree of respect that is attributed to textbooks.

David Roe's essay ("Film as an educational tool to train psychotherapists") is an excellent introduction to learning how to design seminars that teach student therapists how to view films for educational purposes within the context of academically based programs that train mental health professionals. In it, you will find a list of films that can serve different educational purposes and teaching strategies that can be used with groups of student therapists to generate clinically relevant discussions about diagnostic and therapeutic issues as well as the intersubjectivity of perception.

To Roe's list of films I would add our film, *Ready When You Are*, because the script is based on what the research literature has revealed about patients' fears and misconceptions about therapy. We have been using the film, or its script, as an aid to teaching therapists about the questions and uncertainties about psychotherapy that patients tend to conceal from their therapist (Farber & Hall, 2002) and that heighten their risk of ending therapy before they get a chance to benefit from it.

FILM AND THE ELUSIVE QUALITY—BEING COOL

As therapists, we know how important are the words we choose to name things. The drug dealer in *Moonlight*, like an empathetic therapist, answers the question, "What is a faggot?" posed by a preadolescent boy who has been accused of being a fagot by his peers by telling him, "It's the name mean people use to make gay people feel bad about themselves."

By contrast, being told that you are cool is a natural reinforcer of self-esteem. Slang words come in and out of fashion. Not so for "cool." Generation after generation has appropriated "cool" as a favored way of offering praise to people whose appearance, style, sensibility, and intentions we admire. Coolness, like courage and humility, cannot be claimed for oneself. Only other people can render that judgment. In the eyes of others, if you can call yourself cool, you most certainly are not. Therefore, I welcome opportunities to tell my patients, especially adolescents, that they are "cool."

In my adolescent, coolness-valuing subculture of the mid-1950s, "that's cool" was our preferred signifier of admiration, and what we valued most were a muted expressive style, risk-taking, and the qualities James Dean embodied in his celebrated performance of Jim Stark—a sensitive and vulnerable but still manly adolescent—in the 1955 CinemaScope film *Rebel Without a Cause*. In 1990, the National Film Registry added *Rebel Without a Cause* to its catalog of films that are worthy of

being deemed "culturally, historically, and aesthetically significant" (National Film Registry, 1990).

It is for these reasons that I invited Dr. Sidney Phillips to
write an essay that explicates the ways in which Dean's portrayal
of being cool changed the way men sought to understand and
embody masculinity or manliness.

James Dean's best male friend in the film was a closeted
gay boy who "betrays" his unspoken lustful love for his only
friend in his gaze, gestures, and postures—according to those
whose "gaydar" is highly refined. A compelling hypothesis that
runs through Phillips's essay ("On being 'cool'") is that a close
reading of their relationship would reveal important connections
between "homophobia" and the cool version of being a man.

In a related vein, many of the fathers of my generation
taught their sons that "real men don't cry, especially in public."
In my clinical experience, even the most stoic men who paid
obeisance to this prohibition can remember weeping, silently,
while watching a film in a darkened theater. The film *Field of
Dreams* (1989) had the power to release the pent-up sorrow of
my patient X (Geller, 2006b). He had paid rigid obedience to
the prohibition against crying and, like the main character in
Field of Dreams, was unable to grieve the death of his father.
My understanding of the therapeutic benefits he derived from
crying while watching Kevin Costner portray a son reuniting
with his deceased father on a baseball field he had sculpted
out of an Iowa cornfield draws on a tradition that dates back
to Aristotle—the hypothesis that audiences derive benefit from
viewing tragic dramas because they are afforded the opportunity
to vicariously experience their primal fears and anxieties and
then to cathartically release these negative emotions in a safe
and controlled fashion (Butcher & Fergusson, 1961). In the next
section, I will call upon this hypothesis again when offering an

explanation of the power and appeal of Hollywood depictions of violence and aggression.

ON HOLLYWOOD DEPICTIONS OF VIOLENCE AND HORROR

Whoever has given serious thought to the ways in which movies influence people's behavior has grappled with the question, Do Hollywood depictions of violence and aggression promote or cause violence in our culture? An alternative question serves as one of the points of departure of Danielle Knafo's essay ("Film, psychotherapy, and the taming of rage at the mother"): Can viewing film portrayals of violence reduce the risk that a spectator who is filled with raw and intense hatred would destructively attack others?

I invited Dr. Knafo to contribute an essay to this volume after reading her wisely written paper on the psychotherapy of psychotic patients (Knafo & Selzer, 2015) and her analysis of the appeal and power of David Lynch's kinky, disturbing film *Blue Velvet* (1986). It appears in her 2012 book, *Dancing with the Unconscious: The Art of Psychoanalysis and the Psychoanalysis of Art*. Woven throughout the chapters is Knafo's conviction that there is something healing about making or witnessing artistic creations that simultaneously arouse and safely release the expression of powerful and pent-up, dangerous emotions.

For the purpose of this volume, Knafo chose to write about the therapeutic benefits three of her deeply disturbed patients derived from viewing and then discussing within the context of her psychoanalytically informed approach to therapy the films *Joker* (2019) and *Jurassic Park* (1993), a highly controversial, violence-filled thriller and a science fiction/horror movie.

Jurassic Park and *Joker* are films that are capable of tapping into the deepest sources of anxiety in their audiences. *Jurassic Park* was a "blockbuster" 35 years ago and continues to attract huge audiences on TV. At the core of Knafo's essay is an exploration of the reasons why her patient, Mr. P, has watched it 50 times. My understanding of Mr. P's obsession with it again draws on Aristotle's hypothesis that viewing horrifying images allows individuals to cathartically release negative emotions in a safe and controlled situation. I am also inclined to believe that slapstick comedies serve a similar cathartic function. The boy in me still laughs, out loud, when the Three Stooges—Curly, Moe, and Larry—beat up and humiliate one another.

With this interpretive framework in mind, I am apt to ask patients who are suffering from phobias and irrational fears the following types of questions: When you were a child, did you enjoy being scared by horror movies? What films scared you most when you were a child? Can you remember saying to yourself, "It's only a movie, it's only a movie"? Did you, like me, scream the first time you saw the murder scene in *Psycho?* When it flashed on the screen, did you close your eyes when you saw the monster bursting out of a man's chest in *Alien?* If well-timed, these questions can deepen patients' understanding of their fears and the ways in which they cope with them.

In 2019, Joaquin Phoenix won an Oscar for his portrayal of Joker—a mentally ill and failed stand-up comedian who was tormented by violent emotions and violent fantasies and ultimately unable to tame his rage. Like the patients Knafo discusses, I was fascinated and repulsed by the clown's makeup, which garishly decorated his face, and the grotesque yet graceful ways that he moved his emaciated body, but unlike them, I did not identify with his madness, rage, and humiliation. Watching Phoenix's portrayal of ugliness and degradation instead invoked in me what Aristotle called "the tragic pleasure of pity and fear"

(Butcher & Fergusson, 1961; see also Geller, 2006a. But un-like the ancient Greek audiences, who reportedly experienced cathartic relief at the conclusion of tragic plays, I continued to feel disturbed and disoriented by these emotions for hours after the film ended, which in turn led to a lively discussion of the question, Why are horror movies about zombies, man-made monsters, and dinosaurs brought back to life by mad scientists one of Hollywood's highest-grossing genres? Sublimation cre-atively transforms suffering, whatever its source, into subjective experiences that inspire tough-minded curiosity.

FILMS, NOVELS, PSYCHOTHERAPY, AND "PRESENCE"

The discovery that marginally different photographs (still imag-es) could be transformed into one single moving image if viewed in sufficiently rapid succession paved the way for the creation of a new way of telling stories. Anthropologists have discovered that the ability to recognize that a sequence of visual images, with or without words, has been arranged for the purpose of telling a story is both learned and culture-bound (Boyd, 2009).

In our culture, filmmakers, like novelists, have used their craft predominantly to tell stories. In turn, audiences tend to pay most, if not all, of their attention to a film's plot and the fate of its characters; that is, they tend to be exclusively interested in its content. In my experience (2005), neophyte therapists who are exclusively interested in the thematic content of the films they have seen tend to be the same ones who focus all of their attention on the verbal content of their conversations with their patients.

If you are looking for a teaching tool that is a persuasive an-tidote to these consciousness-narrowing biases, Johnson's essay would be a natural place to start. The uniqueness of David Johnson's essay ("Achieving presence in film and psychotherapy") lies in his emphasis on articulating what therapists can learn by studying how films are made, as distinct from interpreting what they mean or are about.

Johnson has been educated by filmmakers such as Jean-Luc Godard, who makes films in which the "artifice" of film-making is made visible and that are meant to be "read" analytically, like philosophical essays. Along the way, Johnson has acquired detailed knowledge about the means cinematographers, film editors, and directors use to tell stories that differ in important respects from the ways in which they are told in written books, especially when created by surrealist filmmakers such as Cocteau (1956), who said of himself, "I write in pictures.... I show what others tell" (p. 23).

Johnson's essay may also be of particular interest to therapists who are seeking a deeper understanding of how to promote the highly valued ability to "be entirely present" to oneself and/or others. As Johnson's essay makes clear, filmmakers have an arsenal of tools with which to shuffle their audiences back and forth between intensified emotional involvement in the story being told in the present moment and reflectively thinking about abstract ideas. One of the most important skills possessed by competent therapists is the capacity to alternate gracefully between listening and thinking about what they have already heard (Geller, 2005). After reading Johnson's chapter, you will come away with new and useable knowledge about how to cultivate this all-important skill.

THE DIGITAL REVOLUTION

In the 21st century, a revolution is taking place in how movies are made and how and where they are watched. Although some filmmakers remain loyal to celluloid, most films are now the products of digital technology.

In parallel, recent estimates indicate that before the arrival of COVID-19, people in the United States who once went to movie theaters regularly were only going to the movies, on average, four times a year (Statista, 2019) and instead were more likely to view films on television sets, computers, and smartphones. To accommodate to the shrinking size of the screens that carry images into view, cinematographers are offering audiences more and more close-ups of actors' facial expressions. Like the microscope, close-ups of micromovements of the facial muscles can make visible subtle shifts in emotion that are not readily apparent to even visually literate individuals. I have wondered whether research would reveal that the visual literacy of individuals who are suffering from face blindness or agnosia would be strengthened by viewing the minute muscular contractions around the eyes and mouths of the actors who are portraying universally identifiable expressions of different emotions. And I would welcome research on the sensorial and cognitive consequences of watching the "same" film on a TV screen, computer, or smartphone at home or while traveling on a plane rather than in a movie theater seated in the dark among strangers.

FILM AND THE CORONAVIRUS

The lockdown brought about by the coronavirus pandemic is accelerating the pace with which digital technology is revolutionizing the ways in which films are experienced. COVID-19 has emptied movie theaters and hastened the arrival of what Lane (2020) calls the "streaming age." With people trapped inside their homes, movies may once again become America's preeminent mode of entertainment.

During the lockdown, many people could only communicate with important people in their lives—family members, coworkers, friends, their doctors—via electronic media. This grim existential reality, as was predicted by McLuhan and Fiore (1967), is dramatically changing patterns of social interaction once taken for granted. For example, working parents have been forced to spend much more time with their children. To make the best of life in the lockdown, parents and their children have had to find new ways of being with one another. Some will be taught how to play video games by their children. Others will discover that video games have come a long way since they played Pacman. Still others will turn to watching more movies and TV programs with their children.

With this shift in mind, Farber, Ort, and Mayopoulos conducted a survey of the ways therapists' viewing habits have changed since the pandemic arrived ("Psychotherapists' preferences for television and movies during the early stages of the COVID-19 pandemic"). It seems fitting to conclude the volume with their up-to-the-minute study.

ONE FINAL NOTE

The words "The End," written in large letters, appeared on the screen in the last seconds of most of the films I saw in my childhood. I still long for the clarity and finality of the happy endings that brought the films of my youth to a seemingly natural conclusion. I felt this yearning even more so when I ushered in the final stages of this "work in progress."

Along the way, I have attempted to demonstrate why I believe that films are an extraordinarily flexible medium of communication that can serve a wide variety of serious and ambitious purposes, including therapists' efforts to "cure" mental illness and educators' attempts to train future generations of competent and ethical therapists. Let me end on a lighter note. I promise you will experience temporary relief from the oppressive and depressive influence of being embedded in a world in which the coronavirus reigns supreme if you watch skillfully produced comedies and dramedies, whether or not you are still quarantined or socially isolated. To repeat myself, laughter is healing, and shared laughter is contagious. Because of my taste and sensibility, I have had fun and laughed a lot when I recently binge-watched the dramedy *Fleabag* (2016–2019) and rewatched *Groundhog Day* (1993), *Bridesmaids* (2011), *Harold & Kumar Go to White Castle* (2004), *Borat* (2006), *Annie Hall* (1977), *Airplane!* (1980), *Napoleon Dynamite* (2004), *Best in Show* (2000), *Knocked Up* (2007), *Dumb and Dumber* (1994), and *Zoolander* (2001).

REFERENCES

Abrahams, J., Zucker, D., & Zucker, J. (Directors). (1980). *Airplane!* [Film]. Paramount Pictures.

Allen, W. (Director). (1977). *Annie Hall* [Film]. United Artists.

Apatow, J. (Director). (2007). *Knocked up* [Film]. Universal Pictures; Apatow Productions.

Bandura, A. (1977). *Social Learning Theory*. New York, NY: General Learning Press.

Berg-Cross, L., Jennings, P., & Baruch, R. (1990). Cinema therapy: Theory and application. *Psychotherapy in Private Practice* 8:135–156.

Bergman, I. (Director). (1966). *Persona* [Film]. AB Svensk Filmindustri.

Boyd, B. (2009). *On the Origin of Stories: Evolution, Cognition and Fiction*. Cambridge, MA: Harvard University Press.

Bradbeer, H.C. (Director). (2016–2019). *Fleabag* [TV series]. Two Brothers Pictures.

Brooks, M. (Director). (1977). *High anxiety* [Film]. 20th Century Fox.

Buñuel, L.C. (Director). (1977). *That obscure object of desire* [Film]. InCine.

——— (2013). *My Last Sigh*. London, UK: Vintage Books.

Butcher, S.H., & Fergusson, F. (1961). *Aristotle's Poetics*. New York, NY: Hill and Wang.

Chabris, C., & Simons, D. (2009). *The Invisible Gorilla*. New York, NY: Broadway Books.

Charles, L. (Director). (2006). *Borat: Cultural learnings of America for make benefit glorious nation of Kazakhstan* [Film]. Everyman Pictures; Dune Entertainment; Major Studio Partners; One America; Four by Two Films.

Chase, D., Grey, B., Landress, I.S., Bronchtein, H., Winter, T., Burgess, M., Green, R. (Executive Producers). (1999–2007). *The Sopranos* [TV series]. HBO; Brillstein Entertainment Partners.

Cocteau, J. (1956). *Journals of Jean Cocteau*. New York, NY: Criterion Books.

Coleridge, S.T. (1967). *Biographia literaria*. In D. Perkins (Ed.), *English Romantic Writers* (pp. 448–491). New York, NY: Harcourt, Brace & World.

Cousins, N.C. (1979). *Anatomy of an Illness as Perceived by a Patient*. New York, NY: Norton.

Cuaron, A. (Director). (2018). *Roma* [Film]. Netflix.

Dayton, J., & Faris, V. (Directors). (2006). *Little Miss Sunshine* [Film]. Searchlight Pictures; Big Beach Films; Bona Fide

Productions; Deep River Productions; Third Gear Productions; Major Studio Partners.

DelRuth, R. (Director). (1948). *The Babe Ruth story* [Film]. Allied Artists.

Donen, S., & Kelly, G. (Directors). (1949). *On the town* [Film]. Metro-Goldwyn-Mayer.

———— & ———— (Directors). (1952). *Singin' in the rain* [Film]. Metro-Goldwyn-Mayer.

Dunham, S.M., & Dermer, S.M. (2020). Cinematherapy with African American couples. *Journal of Clinical Psychology* 76:1472–1482.

Dwan, A. (Director). (1951). *The wild blue yonder* [Film]. Republic Pictures.

Eppler, C., & Hutchings, J. (2020). The use of cinematherapy to illustrate systemic resilience. *Journal of Clinical Psychology* 76:1463–1471.

Farber, B.A., & Hall, D. (2002). Disclosure to therapists: What is and is not discussed in psychotherapy. *Journal of Clinical Psychology* 58:359–370.

————, Ort, D., & Mayopoulos, G. (2020). Psychotherapists' preferences for television and movies during the early stages of the COVID-19 pandemic. *Journal of Clinical Psychology* 76:1532–1536.

Farrelly, P. (Director). (1994). *Dumb and dumber* [Film]. New Line Cinema; Motion Picture Corporation of America.

Feig, P. (Director). (2011). *Bridesmaids* [Film]. Universal Pictures; Relativity Media; Apatow Productions.

Fleming, V. (Director). (1939). *The wizard of Oz* [Film]. Metro-Goldwyn-Mayer.

Fried, W. (2017). *Critical Flicker Fusion-Psychoanalysis at the Movies*. London, UK: Karnac Books.

———— (2020). *Frida*: Portrait of a self. *Journal of Clinical Psychology* 76:1483–1491.

Friedkin, W. (Director). (1970). *Boys in the band* [Film]. Cinema Center Films; Leo Films.

Gabbard, G., & Gabbard, K. (1999). *Psychiatry and the Cinema.* Washington, DC: American Psychiatric Press.

García, R. (Executive Producer). (2008–2010). *In treatment* [TV series]. Sheleg; Closest to the Hole Productions; Leverage Management; HBO Entertainment.

Geller, J.D. (1994). The psychotherapist's experience of interest and boredom. *Psychotherapy* 31(1):3–16.

——— (2005). Style and its contribution to a patient-specific model of therapeutic technique. *Psychotherapy: Theory, Research, Practice, Training* 42:469–482. https://doi.org/10.1037/0033-3204.42.4.469

——— (2006a). Pity, suffering, and psychotherapy. *American Journal of Psychotherapy* 60(2):187–205.

——— (2006b). Research-informed reflections on the processes of introjection and identification: Commentary on Olds. *Journal of the American Psychoanalytic Association* 54:59–66.

——— (2014, April). *Courage and the Effective Practice of Psychotherapy: A Tripartite Model of the Concept of Courage.* Paper presented at the 31st annual spring meeting of the American Psychological Association, Division 39, New York, NY.

——— (2018). Introduction: The transformative powers of aesthetic experiences in psychotherapy. *Journal of Clinical Psychology* 74:200–207.

——— & Farber, B.A. (2020). Ready when you are: Answering your questions about psychotherapy. *Journal of Clinical Psychology* 76:1438–1446.

——— & Freedman, N. (2011). Representations of the therapeutic dialogue and the post-termination phase of psychotherapy. In N. Freedman, M. Hurvich, R. Ward (Eds.), J.D. Geller, &

J. Hoffenberg (Collaborators), *Another Kind of Evidence* (pp. 55–66). London, UK: Karnac Books.

Guest, C. (Director). (2000). *Best in show* [Film]. Castle Rock Entertainment.

Hand, D. (Director). (1942). *Bambi* [Film]. RKO Pictures.

Hess, J. (Director). (2004). *Napoleon Dynamite* [Film]. Searchlight Pictures; Paramount Pictures; MTV Films; Access Films; Napoleon Pictures.

Hitchcock, A. (Director). (1945). *Spellbound* [Film]. Selznick International Pictures; Vanguard Films.

———— (Director). (1960). *Psycho* [Film]. Shamley Productions.

Huston, J. (Director). (1951). *The Red Badge of Courage* [Film]. Metro-Goldwyn-Mayer.

Jenkins, B. (Director). (2016). *Moonlight* [Film]. A24 Films.

Johnson, D.R. (2020). Achieving presence in films and psychotherapy. *Journal of Clinical Psychology* 76:1520–1531.

Johnson, N. (Director). (1957). *The three faces of Eve* [Film]. 20th Century Fox.

Knafo, D. (2012). *Dancing with the Unconscious: The Art of Psychoanalysis and the Psychoanalysis of Art*. London, UK: Routledge.

———— (2020). Film, psychotherapy, and the taming of rage at the mother. *Journal of Clinical Psychology* 76:1514–1519.

———— & Selzer, M. (2015). "Don't skip on Tony!" The importance of symptoms when working with psychosis. *Psychoanalytic Psychology* 32:159–172.

Lane, A. (2020, May 11). Perchance to stream. *The New Yorker*, pp. 68–69.

Leiner, D. (Director). (2004). *Harold & Kumar go to White Castle* [Film]. Endgame Entertainment; Kingsgate Films; New Line Cinema; Senator International.

Litvak, A. (Director). (1948). *Snake pit* [Film]. 20th Century Fox.

Losey, J. (Director). (1948). *The boy with green hair* [Film]. RKO Radio Pictures.

Lumet, S. (Director). (1964). *The pawnbroker* [Film]. Paramount Pictures.

Lynch, D. (Director). (1986). *Blue velvet* [Film]. De Laurentiis Entertainment Group.

McLuhan, M., & Fiore, Q. (1967). *The Medium is the Massage*. New York, NY: Bantam Books.

Minnelli, V. (Director). (1951). *An American in Paris* [Film]. Metro-Goldwyn-Mayer.

Niemiec, R.M. (2020). Character strengths cinematherapy: Using movies to inspire change, meaning, and cinematic elevation). *Journal of Clinical Psychology* 76:1447–1462.

Oz, F. (Director). (1991). *What about Bob?* [Film]. Touchstone Pictures; Touchwood Pacific Partners 1.

Perry, F. (Director). (1962). *David and Lisa* [Film]. Vision Associates Productions.

Phillips, S.H. (2020). On being "cool." *Journal of Clinical Psychology* 76:1504–1513.

Phillips, T. (Director). (2019). *Joker* [Film]. Warner Bros.; Village Roadshow Pictures; BRON Studios; Joint Effort; DC Comics.

Piaget, J. (1954). *The Construction of Reality in the Child*. New York, NY: Basic Books.

Premack, D., & Woodruff, G. (1978). Does the chimpanzee have a theory of mind? *Behavioral and Brain Sciences* 1:515–526. https://doi.org/10.1017/S0140525X00076512

Ramis, H. (Director). (1993). *Groundhog Day* [Film]. Columbia Pictures.

Ray, N. (Director). (1955). *Rebel without a cause* [Film]. Warner Bros.

Redford, R. (Director). (1980). *Ordinary people* [Film]. Wildwood Enterprises.

Robinson, P.A. (Director). (1989). *Field of dreams* [Film]. Universal Pictures.

Roe, D. (2020). Film as an educational tool to train psychotherapists. *Journal of Clinical Psychology* 76:1492–1503.

Scott, R. (Director). (1979). *Alien* [Film]. Brandywine Productions.

Seligman, M.E.P. (2002). *Authentic Happiness: Using the New Positive Psychology to Realize Your Potential for Lasting Fulfillment*. New York, NY: Free Press.

Sharpsteen, B., & Luske, H. (Supervising Directors). (1940). *Pinocchio* [Film]. RKO Pictures.

Shostrom, E.L. (Producer). (1965). *Three approaches to psychotherapy* [Film]. Psychological Films.

Simon, P. (2011). The boy in the bubble [Song]. On *Graceland*. Music Entertainment.

Sontag, S. (1966). *Against Interpretation*. New York, NY: Farrar, Straus, and Giroux.

Spielberg, S. (Director). (1993). *Jurassic Park* [Film]. Universal Pictures; Amblin Entertainment.

Statista, A. (2019). Frequency of going to movie theaters to see a movie among adults in the United States as of June 2019. https://www.statista.com/statistics/264396/frequency-of-going-to-the-movies-in-the-us/

Stiller, B. (Director). (2001). *Zoolander* [Film]. Paramount Pictures; Village Roadshow Pictures; VH1 Television; NPV Entertainment; Scott Rudin Productions; Red Hour Productions; Adam Schroeder Entertainment; MFP Munich Film Partners GmbH & Company I. Produktions KG; Tenth Planet Productions.

Streisand, B. (Director). (1991). *Prince of tides* [Film]. Columbia Pictures; Barwood Films; Longfellow Pictures.

Taymor, J. (Director). (2002). *Frida* [Film]. Handprint Entertainment; Lions Gate Films; Miramax.

van Sant, G. (Director). (1997). *Good Will Hunting* [Film]. Miramax; Be Gentlemen Limited Partnership; Lawrence Bender Productions.

Zimmerman, F. (Director). (1952). *High noon* [Film]. United Artists.

www.ingramcontent.com/pod-product-compliance
Lightning Source LLC
Chambersburg PA
CBHW062107020426
42335CB00013B/881